THE GROWTH OF CHICAGO BANKS

THE CONFLAGRATION OF 1871
Reproduced by courtesy of The First National Bank of Chicago

THE GROWTH OF CHICAGO BANKS

By

F. CYRIL JAMES

PROFESSOR OF FINANCE IN THE
UNIVERSITY OF PENNSYLVANIA

VOLUME I
THE FORMATIVE YEARS
1816-1896

HARPER & BROTHERS PUBLISHERS

NEW YORK AND LONDON

1938

TO

THE OFFICERS AND EMPLOYEES

OF

THE FIRST NATIONAL BANK OF CHICAGO

who,
by their unstinted help and
cordial friendship, have lightened
the travail and enhanced the joy
of my sojourn in Chicago

CONTENTS

VOLUME I

APPENDIX

TABLES

VOLUME I

ILLUSTRATIONS AND CHARTS

VOLUME I

INTRODUCTION

THE story of Chicago banks is interesting for many reasons. Through its pages walk Forgan, Coolbaugh, George Smith and others who, though they may remain unsung by the chronicler of national destinies, are magnificent examples of the men who laid the foundations of the modern American economy. Among the institutions of Chicago are to be found splendid records of success, and dramatic instances of failure. Indeed, it is not too much to say that the story of Chicago banks contains striking examples of every development, both good and bad, that characterized the financial system of the United States during a period of more than a century.

Yet the story is more than a collection of institutional and human biographies. Any large financial center can offer a plentitude of anecdotes, and too much financial history has been written on an anecdotal or, worse still, statistical basis. Chicago banks did not exist in a vacuum: they were an integral part of a thriving community, which grew, within a century, from poverty-stricken desolation to metropolitan grandeur. In that development, the banks played an important part. They influenced political decisions and facilitated economic developments, while their own destinies, in turn, were shaped by the forces in operation around them. Banking history is meaningless unless it is considered in intimate relation to the changing structure of the community which the banks exist to serve.

Even that canvas is too small, however, for a comprehensive picture. Chicago was not an isolated community. It was a part of the United States, rising steadily in importance with the passage of the years. The economic life of the city and its political philosophies were influenced by national events, and banks were no more immune from those influences than any other type of urban institution.

This book, therefore, attempts to weave into the story of Chicago banks enough of local and national history to give that story its full meaning. Because financial institutions were of preeminent importance in the development of the western regions of the United States, the account may help to illuminate some of the more obscure pages in the chronicle of America's growth, and there can be no doubt that it sheds an interesting, if sardonic, light on many contemporary problems. These possibilities do not, however, constitute the primary purpose of the narrative. The story of Chicago banks is complete in itself.

From 1816 to 1845, Chicago was engulfed in the fabulous attempts of the State of Illinois to achieve prosperity by a governmental program of inflation and public works. Banks were the tools of politicians, and they were destroyed completely in the collapse of the fiscal economy of the state. After 1845, there followed a long and painful period in which an attempt was made to build up financial institutions of a more permanent kind. Private bankers attempted the task, with varying success; state-chartered banks flowered and withered. With the single exception of the Merchants Loan and Trust Company,

it was not until the creation of the national banking sys·
tem, in 1863, that the city acquired banking institutions,
that were soundly managed, and equipped with large
resources, but from that moment the influence of state
factors upon the growth of Chicago banks diminished
steadily.

By 1871, the banking structure of the city had acquired
stability and, during the two decades that separate the
conflagration from the panic of 1893, Chicago became the
outstanding money market of the west. In its own region,
its hegemony was complete, and sound banking policies
had earned it high prestige. So high, in fact, was the prestige of Chicago that, during the years from 1893 to 1913,
the bankers of the city began to extend their influence to
all parts of the United States. Even in regard to the policies of the national government, their opinions were important.

Yet that phase of development merges imperceptibly
into the subsequent period. Owing to the continuous increase in the volume of its resources, Chicago developed
to a point where it has become one of the great money
markets of the world, smaller than London or New York,
but approximately equal to Paris. Yet, at the same time,
the banks of the city became so intimately woven into the
structure of the national money market that the financial
independence of Chicago tended to decline. From their
earliest beginnings, fettered to the political policies of
Illinois, the story of Chicago banks, therefore, runs in
a splendid parabola. From 1893 to 1913, the curve reaches
a peak of prestige and independence; after the latter date,

the influence of governmental policies, this time on a national scale, once more shows itself.

To facilitate the use of these volumes by the reader, it may be worth while to call attention to two matters of detail. To many readers, footnotes are an annoyance, while to others the absence of precise references is equally irritating. In order to meet the tastes of both groups, as far as that is possible, all references have been placed at the end of the chapter to which they refer; they may be easily found by those who wish to consult them, but can be ignored by others. Similarly, for those who desire precise chronological details regarding individual institutions, a concise "biography" of each commercial bank that has operated in Chicago at any time since the Civil War is to be found in Appendix VIII at the end of the second volume. All banks are arranged by name, in alphabetical order.

In writing such a book as this, the author must necessarily incur many pleasant debts of gratitude. Above all others, I wish to express my appreciation to the officers and directors of The First National Bank of Chicago for sponsoring the study. In addition to financial appropriations, they have given freely of their time and advice, making available all the records of the institution and obtaining access to other unpublished material that would not otherwise have been available. To my predecessors in the field of local and national history, the bibliography and references indicate the extent of a debt that could not easily be expressed in a few sentences, while to the officers of the Chicago Clearing House Association, the Federal Reserve Bank of Chicago and other Chicago banks I want to offer my thanks for the assistance they have rendered on every part of the study.

In regard to Dr. Donald Masters, who has assisted me throughout my work, any formal phrases must do less than justice to the extent of his contribution. His knowledge of historical source material and his indefatigable energy in the search for information have been invaluable. Individual mention is also necessary in the case of Messrs. Edward E. Brown, Walter Lichtenstein and Roy Nicholls, who have patiently read the manuscript, and aided me by criticisms and suggestions. To them, and particularly to Mr. Brown, must be attributed a large part of any merit that these volumes may have, although the defects that may be found by the reader, and the opinions expressed, are entirely my own.

To Miss Anna B. Rice, who has facilitated my work tremendously by taking charge of all the details connected with the preparation of the manuscript, and to Mrs. Katherine Byrne, who has been responsible for the details connected with Appendix VIII, I am deeply grateful.

Finally I acknowledge with particular pleasure the charming cooperation of my wife who, instead of resenting the fact that these chapters have stolen an inordinate amount of my time, has made my task easier by her sympathetic understanding and spontaneous gaiety.

F. CYRIL JAMES

Chicago
July 1, 1938

THE GROWTH OF CHICAGO BANKS

CHAPTER I

FRONTIER FINANCE

1816–1821

CHICAGO was no more than a few huts around the ruins of a fort when the Bank of Illinois, which laid the foundations for the first epoch of the city's financial development, came into existence in 1816. Two companies of infantry, at that very moment, were marching around the southern end of Lake Michigan to build another Fort Dearborn on the site of the one that had been destroyed by the Indians four years earlier, but more than a year was to pass before a military garrison would be completely reestablished. Apart from the military officers charged with the defense of the frontier settlements from the Indians, and the fur traders, to whom Chicago marked the beginning of a backbreaking portage from Lake Michigan across the swamps to the Illinois River, there were few people to whom the name of the village was known. Indeed, a full decade later, there were to be found in Chicago no more than thirty-five voters, of whom only fourteen were wealthy enough to pay taxes, while the aggregate taxable property was estimated at no more than eight thousand dollars.[1]

Illinois at that time was on the very frontier of civilization, and the extent of her development was rigorously

governed by the slow improvement of facilities for trans-
porting men and carrying goods. Of rivers and creeks
there were plenty and, after steamboats began to plow
her waters, the Mississippi and her tributary streams became the highways connecting the territory with the outside world. From Europe, or from New York, the traveler
made his way to Illinois by voyaging to New Orleans and
then up the river, a journey of unpredictable length since
the speed of the river boats depended less upon the
strength of their engines than upon the amount of water
in the channel. A dry season might mean months of delay.

And when the traveler disembarked, probably at Shawneetown, there was little to encourage him to wander
farther unless he was hardy enough to travel across the
country on horseback or in a springless wagon. Of roads
there were none, until the federal government constructed one from Shawneetown to Kaskaskia in 1817[2]
while the great highway from Vincennes to St. Louis
(which was destined to play a significant part in the subsequent history of western migration) was at this time
just coming into use. It marked, in fact, the extreme limit
of settlement.[3] Not until the spring of 1818 was the
Western Intelligencer able to announce that there would
be two mails a week from Shawneetown to St. Louis, by
way of Kaskaskia,[4] and eight months more passed before
the first announcement[5] inviting passengers to travel by
stagecoach (a conveyance, it may be remarked in parenthesis, that does not seem to have been conducive to
either bodily comfort or mental peace).[6]

In the light of these facts, it is not surprising that Illinois was a new and sparsely settled country. Less than

half of the inhabitants had lived there for three years, and not quite a third had been in the region a full decade.[7] Most of the area comprised within the present boundaries of the state was a wilderness shared, without a great deal of friendship, between the Indians and the hunters, for the valley of the Illinois River at this time constituted one of the most important fur-bearing areas of the northwest.[8] Of these plainsmen and trappers the fiction of the last fifty years has told us much, but they were not the stuff of which great agricultural and trading areas are built. Dressed in "a raccoon-skin cap, linsey hunting-shirt, buckskin breeches and moccasins, with a belt around the waist, to which the butcher-knife and tomahawk . . . were appended,"[9] they were more familiar with the rifle than the plow. Although in many cases they would cultivate a small patch of corn or barley outside their rude log cabins, they had no desire to extend the area of cultivation. When a neighbor moved within gunshot they would gladly sell out their holding and move on westward to new and unsullied hunting grounds.

Moreover, it is well to remember that these men who lived beyond the frontier were not always the chivalrous heroes of freedom that the Victorian novel and the modern screen portray. Such an environment was ideal for criminals who wished to evade the law, and the numbers of early travelers who did not return, reinforced by the hair-raising tales of some of those who did, bear ample testimony to the lawlessness and violence that characterized central Illinois.[10] Even the more civilized branches of crime were not overlooked by these disciples of freedom, for we are told that, when they were "not engaged in robbing or murdering, they were industriously employed in manufacturing bank notes, which they imposed on travellers at every opportunity."[11] So courteous a fashion in robbery comes as a surprise to our preconceptions of frontier life, but we have collateral evidence of its existence in an enactment of the Territorial Legislature, early in 1816, which decreed that any person found guilty of counterfeiting "the notes of any bank within the United States" should be punished with "death by hanging without benefit of clergy."[12]

But, if the inadequacy of transportation permitted such conditions to exist throughout the central and northern parts of the Territory, it permitted a gradual but continuous immigration into the southern triangle. At the time of which we are speaking, the settled part of Illinois "extended a little north of Edwardsville and Alton; south along the Mississippi to the mouth of the Ohio; east, in the direction of Carlysle to the Wabash; and down the Wabash and the Ohio, to the mouth of the last-named river"[13]—a little fringe of farms and villages along the banks of the great rivers that bounded the area. Of towns there were none worthy of the name, unless we except Kaskaskia, the capital, and Shawneetown, the port of entry,[14] but there was already developing a settled agrarian population. By reason of the excellence of its soil, and the favoring factors of its climate and situation,[15] Illinois was attracting large numbers of immigrants from the southern states and even from Europe, so that the manorial common-field agriculture of the earlier French *habitants*[16] was giving way to the independent farms of the southerners and the scientific agriculture introduced

by Birkbeck and Flower in their famous English settlement at Albion.[17] The northward march of economic
exploration had begun.

Even in these settled communities, however, the state
of society was largely nonmonetary—a fact of considerable
importance in any consideration of the financial developments of the following years. "The pursuits of the people
were agricultural. A very few merchants supplied them
with the few necessaries that could not be produced or
manufactured at home. The farmer raised his own provisions; tea and coffee were scarcely used, except on some
grand occasions. The farmer's sheep furnished wool for
his winter clothing; he raised cotton and flax for his summer clothing. His wife and daughters spun, wove, and
made it into garments. A little copperas and indigo, with
the bark of trees, furnished dye-stuffs for coloring. The
fur of the raccoon made him a hat or cap. The skins of
deer or of his cattle, tanned at a neighboring tan-yard,
or dressed by himself, made him shoes or moccasins.
Boots were rarely seen, even in the towns. And a log-
cabin, made entirely of wood, without glass, nails, hinges
or locks, furnished the residence of many a contented and
happy family. The people were quick and ingenious to
supply by invention, and with their own hands, the lack
of mechanics and artificers. Each farmer, as a general
thing, built his own house, made his own plows and
harness, bedsteads, chairs, stools, cupboards and tables.
The carts and wagons for hauling were generally made
without iron, without tires, or boxes, and were run without tar, and might be heard creaking as they lumbered
along the roads, for the distance of a mile or more."[18]

Moreover, as a converse to this practice of satisfying all their needs by their own labors, the early inhabitants of Illinois, until the end of the second decade of the nineteenth century, produced little or no surplus for sale. When an influx of immigrants pressed heavily upon the food supplies of the Territory, the local miller (who received his payment in kind) was often the only person in the community who had grain or flour to sell.[19] Of ready money there was little to be found, because there was small need of it. "Many a family lived a whole year without the possession or use of fifty dollars in cash"[20] and, even as late as 1820, most of the advertisements in the local journals indicated a willingness on the part of the merchants to accept produce in exchange for the articles they had to sell. One publisher, in the period just before the creation of the Bank of Illinois, shipped to his eastern creditor nine and a half dozen deerskins, valued at six dollars each, in settlement of his bill for paper, since he was unable to obtain a more conventional medium of payments in which to discharge his debt.[21]

After the War of 1812, however, a slow but momentous social revolution began. Illinois was changing gradually from a self-sufficient society, performing its few inescapable exchanges by methods of barter, to a fully fledged pecuniary economy. The change was not sudden: fifty years later it would still have been possible to find isolated farmers operating their households on the older principles. But, year by year, the use of money tended to become more important and, as a result, the operations of the financial system began to exercise an increasing influence on the welfare of the people. Profits and prices gradually replaced Indians and the supply of food as the focal points around which the life of the community revolved.

In part, this infiltration of money was due to the fact that immigrants were coming in larger numbers to the territories of the northwest, often bringing a small store of money in the expectation that it would enable them to purchase land and acquire the implements and food necessary to set up as farmers. But, to a greater extent, it must be attributed to the inflationary orgy which was spreading over the whole country and, in some degree, over Europe as well. After the first Bank of the United States passed out of existence, in 1811, a host of mushroom banks had sprung up in every developed section of the United States,[22] and each of them had used every effort to push out into circulation as large an issue of notes as possible. Speculation was rampant, money was plentiful, and in an age when bonds were few and stocks even less familiar, land was the basis of most speculative operations. In Illinois there was plenty of good land. Much of the territory had been surveyed by the federal government, which had held the first public sale of land in Illinois during October, 1814. Three years later the supply of land on the market was still further increased by the distribution of military bounty lands—and between these dates the people of Illinois, as well as the eastern speculators with pockets full of variegated bank notes, had realized that fortunes could be made more easily by the purchase and sale of land than by the cultivation of it.

This enthusiasm for land speculation, which was to exercise a profound influence upon the development of banking in Chicago and other parts of Illinois for more than half a century, was not new. The Territory of Illinois had been one of the pawns in the hands of John Law at the time of the Mississippi Bubble (although few of those who speculated in the Rue Quincampaux could have had very much knowledge of that fact), and it had been the basis of a significant local bubble, at the time of the War of Independence, when the Wabash Land Company and other comparable organizations had taken advantage of the fact that English law vested in the individual, and not in the Crown, the title to any lands obtained by private treaty from the Indians.*

But these early experiences were only pale foreshadowings of the local excitement that Illinois was to experience when government land sales began on a considerable scale in 1817 and, in the light of retrospect, it must be admitted that the practices of the federal government itself did much to encourage the speculative mania. Under the law of 1800 public lands, after they had been surveyed, were offered for sale at public auction. If they were not sold at the auction (and most of the lands, in fact, were not) they might be bought at private sale for the minimum price of $2.00 an acre in units of 320, 160 or 80 acres.† Moreover, at these sales, the buyer was re-

---

* A letter signed by Lord Camden and Charles Yorke, and dated November 4, 1772, pointed out that "in respect to such places as have been or shall be acquired by Treaty or Grant from any of the Indian Princes or Governments, your Majesties Letters Patents are not necessary, the property of the Soil, Vesting in the Grantee by the Indian Grants, Subject only to your Majesties Right of Sovereignty over the Settlements." Cf. Huston: *Financing an Empire*, I, 45. Search in the Record Office has not, however, revealed the original of this document.

† Under the amending acts of 1804 and 1817. Originally the smallest unit was 320 acres.

quired to pay down in cash an amount equal to only 5 per cent of the aggregate price of the land; 20 per cent more was due in forty days and the remainder had to be paid in equal installments at the end of two, three, and four years!

Anybody who had sixteen dollars in his pocket, and could raise another sixty-four dollars within the stipulated forty days, was able to acquire a quarter section of land, and many of those who did so confidently expected either that the land would prove sufficiently productive to provide the remaining installments when they fell due or that they would be able, before that time, to sell it to somebody else at a profit.[23]

Even the military bounty land was, in many cases, promptly resold to eastern speculators[24] and, "when the government land-sales began, speculators were always on hand to pick up the choice tracts which, because of their supposedly favourable location, were expected to rise in value rapidly."[25] Nor were such speculators drawn entirely from the east. Most of the leading men in Illinois, with Ninian Edwards preeminent among them,[26] were actively engaged in the purchase and sale of land, but they felt themselves handicapped in their operations by the fact that there were as yet no banks in Illinois to assist them except one small unincorporated institution at Shawneetown. In Ohio, in Kentucky, in Missouri and Indiana, banks were already in operation, offering generous assistance in the financing of speculation and, since the largest speculators in Illinois were also the outstanding politicians, it was natural that the example should not pass unheeded.

On the twenty-eighth of December, 1816, the Territorial Legislature passed an act incorporating "The President, Directors and Company of the Bank of Illinois" at Shawneetown, "an inconsiderable place" which is vividly described by a traveler who visited it a year later. "The chief occupation of the inhabitants is the salt trade. There is here a 'United States' land office,' and a *log* bank is just established. The *chief cashier* of this establishment was engaged in cutting logs at the moment of my arrival."[27] The Bank of Illinois, however, started its career under the management of some of the most substantial men in the state, among them John Marshall, Leonard White, Samuel and John Caldwell, John McLean and Michael Jones.[28]

This Bank was the first to receive a charter in what is today the State of Illinois and, after its absorption of the earlier private bank, it was for some time the only financial institution. It is, therefore, interesting to glance briefly at the outstanding provisions of its charter,[29] since they reveal clearly the ideals of banking in the minds of western legislators at a time when they were not hampered by considerations of depression and fiscal deficits.

The capital stock was fixed at $300,000, divided into $100 shares, but one-third of the total was to be withheld from the public offering in case the legislature of the Territory (or subsequent State) of Illinois should wish to acquire such stock at any time. Subscribers to the stock were required to pay $10 per share in gold or silver coin at the time of subscription, and the rest in current paper money when called upon by the directors, but the sponsors do not seem to have anticipated a very heavy initial subscription because the charter provided that the Bank might begin business as soon as $50,000 had been subscribed toward the capital, and $10,000 paid in.

The corporation was granted a life of twenty years, and empowered to acquire property to the extent of $500,000, but such property could not include real estate in excess of what was necessary for the transaction of its business unless the land had been mortgaged to it as security, or transferred by a debtor who had previously received a loan. Its debts, exclusive of deposits, might not amount to more than twice its capital, and its operations were restricted to making loans, trading in bills of exchange, and dealing in gold and silver (except that it might sell goods pledged with it and not redeemed, or "goods produced on the bank's land"). The maximum rate of discount on loans was 6 per cent and, as a penalty, it was provided that holders of the bank's notes should collect from the institution at double this rate if it ever suspended specie payments.

The minimum capital of $10,000 was soon paid in, and the twelve directors (all of whom were required to be resident citizens of Illinois) elected, so that the Bank was able to open for business on January 1, 1817. Once in operation, it ceased for a time to be a subject of interest to legislators or to the public press, but the scant evidence available seems to indicate that its early operations were more than usually sound when measured by contemporary banking standards.

Those standards, however, were vastly different from the accepted banking principles of today and it is necessary to appreciate the difference clearly if we are to follow the subsequent march of events. Today it is generally understood that the functions of the banking system are twofold: in the first place it provides an efficient and convenient mechanism of exchange; in the second, it distributes the available supply of capital funds among the many potential borrowers. But the situation during the early years of the nineteenth century was vastly different.

Banks were organized "not because there was capital seeking investment; not because the places where they were established had commerce and manufactures which required their fostering aid; but because men without active capital wanted the means of obtaining loans, which their standing in the community would not command from banks or individuals having real capital and established credit."[30] Throughout the United States, and particularly in frontier communities like Illinois, banks were regarded as powerful engines for the painless provision of capital. In a pioneer community, capital of all kinds was scarce, because there was seldom much surplus product. Feeding and clothing a family tended to consume all the time and resources of each household. Moreover, such capital accumulation as occurred usually took the form of fixed capital, of houses and barns, of fences and herds of livestock, which the farmer was able to build up gradually over the years without the intervention of any monetary transactions whatever. Of moneyed capital, there was very little, and banks were looked upon as a mechanism for increasing the supply without any painful saving on the part of the community.

Moreover, the method by which the banks extended accommodation bore little resemblance to modern practices. Checks were almost unknown, outside the large eastern cities, and few people except the wealthier merchants were familiar with bank accounts. Coin and paper money, throughout the greater part of the United States, constituted the only media of exchange that circulated readily and, in many communities, coin was chiefly noticeable by its absence. If banks were to supply the community with either currency or capital funds, it had to be in the form of bank notes: if banks were to exercise any influence upon the general level of prices, it would have to be through the policies that they adopted in regard to the issue and retirement of such notes.

Both the emphasis upon notes as a medium of exchange, and the desire to use the note-issue power as an easy means of raising capital funds, are clearly apparent in many of the charters that were granted during the first quarter of the nineteenth century. Over and over again, state legislatures would charter corporations for the purpose of constructing canals or railroads, and attempt to free them from the handicap of inadequacy of capital by a grant of banking privileges that would permit issue of circulating notes.[31] Seldom has bootstrap levitation been more obvious in the history of banking. Nor was the position of the independent bank much stronger, even though it had no such morganatic affiliation. In many cases, its operating capital was a phantom of the accountant's imagination, since it received few, if any, deposits from the general public, and was often called upon to lend the shareholders the money that they subscribed to its stock.[32] From the second Bank of the United States down to the most insignificant institutions in the backwoods, it was customary for a bank to make loans against its own stock to enable the stockholders to pay all but the first of their purchase installments, so that in 1820 the Secretary of the Treasury estimated that, out of a nominal banking capital in the United States of $125,000,000, the actual capital did not exceed $75,000,000.[33] In the conservative State of Maine, a few years earlier, the bank returns showed that four-ninths of the banking capital was represented by stockholders' promises to pay.[34]

In the light of this practice, it is apparent that the banks had very little in the way of actual capital funds to lend to the many eager borrowers who came seeking accommodation. To fulfill the tasks that were demanded of them, they resorted to their powers of note issue, and it has been well said that "the chief function of a western bank seems to have been to manufacture paper money and issue it on easy terms to the ambitious but impecunious inhabitants."[35]

The whole ingenious process would, however, have fallen to the ground in a moment if any substantial portion of these notes had been presented for redemption, since the issuing banks held little or no specie for the purpose of meeting the demands of noteholders. By hook or by crook, redemption had to be effectively prevented, and many and various were the devices by which this was accomplished. At one end of the scale were the "Saddle-Bag Banks," which located in an out-of-the-way village and employed traveling agents to put their notes into circulation by making loans in other parts of the country;[36] slightly (but not much) more respectable were the banks that made their notes payable at a town far away from the point of origin,[37] or at a date some time after the time of issue.[38] In still other cases, banks made loans at a reduced rate of interest to borrowers who would undertake to keep the notes in circulation for a stipulated minimum period of time.[39] All these devices, to be sure, were recognized as somewhat unsatisfactory by the leading bankers of the day, although they resorted to them occasionally. Even the leaders, however, were just as anxious to prevent note redemption by other methods and, during the years that followed the War of 1812, they strenuously opposed the efforts of the government to return to a specie standard.[40] Bank notes, to the contemporary mind, were not a device to supplement the circulation of coins, into which they were readily exchangeable. Notes were intended to take the place of a specie circulation and to form the basis of the monetary system.

A less satisfactory monetary system is hard to conceive. Writing after years of painful experience, Secretary Crawford complained that "it is impossible to imagine a currency more vicious than that which depends upon the will of nearly four hundred banks, entirely independent of each other, when released from all restraint against excessive issues,"[41] while Niles was fully as indignant. "It cuts me to the quick," he writes, "that I still suffer . . . at the rate of three or four hundred dollars *per annum* of my hard-gathered earnings, in discounts on bank paper, received at par."[42]

Unquestionably, the banks aided the process of capital formation, and accelerated the pace of the country's development, but they did so by inflationary means. By steadily expanding the volume of currency, they raised the general level of commodity prices and compelled each member of the community to restrict the volume of his consumption. Wealth was not created by their operations, but the distribution of the available wealth was changed without reference to the wishes of any except the most enterprising members of the community. In place of voluntary saving, people suffered involuntary abstinence, in order that the supply of capital goods might be enlarged, and the extent of their suffering was increased by the fact that the divergent policies of innumerable banks gave rise, not to a uniform depreciation of the currency, but to a heterogeneous mass of different bank notes that depreciated at varying rates. Banking, in its first efflorescence, not only taxed the community for the benefit of those to whom it granted loans: it destroyed the nation's monetary system.

The frontier Territory of Illinois offered admirable examples of this process. On the very day on which the charter of the Bank of Illinois passed the Territorial Legislature, it was enacted that creditors could levy execution upon the property of delinquent debtors only if they had previously notified the sheriff in writing of their willingness to receive, in settlement of the claim, "notes of any of the chartered banks of Cincinnati and Chillicothe, in the state of Ohio, and of any of the banks of the states of Tennessee and Kentucky, and of the banks of Vincennes, of Missouri, of St. Louis, and of Illinois."[43] As a preamble to the act points out, it would be disastrous to require the payment of debts in gold and silver!

Moreover, even without this legal endorsement, there would have been a strong demand for the notes of the new Bank of Illinois on the part of any who were fortunate enough to be able to borrow them. As the following table clearly shows, the total sales of land in Illinois during 1817 were five times as great as they had been during the previous year, and in 1818 they increased by more than one hundred per cent.

TABLE I

ACREAGE OF LAND SOLD IN ILLINOIS, 1814–1819[44]

Year Ending September 30	Total Number of Acres Sold
1814	8,837
1815	82,740
1816	46,720
1817	249,665
1818	593,316
1819	383,355

With the profitable example of the Bank of Illinois before them, and the obvious opportunities for increased land speculation, it was natural that the politicians should wish to create more banks. Although Edwardsville at the time was a village of no more than eighteen households, comprising a total of one hundred and sixty-six people, Ninian Edwards succeeded in obtaining a charter for the Bank of Edwardsville on January 9, 1818, and the institution was organized as rapidly as possible in order that it might lose no time in commencing business. It is interesting to notice, however, that, of the $30,000 paid in as the first installment of the capital, $22,625 came from Kentucky (of which $10,000 came from one subscriber), $1,800 came from St. Louis, $100 from New York, and only $5,475 from Illinois.[45] Few of the subscribers from Illinois contributed more than $50. Moreover, although the name of Ninian Edwards was one to conjure with, we have already seen that he was deeply interested in the land speculation that was sweeping the state, and his associates included several men whose financial stability was open to serious question.[46]

The charter[47] of the Bank of Edwardsville was identical in its broad outlines with that of the Bank at Shawneetown, granted a year earlier, although some changes were made in the voting rights of the stock which, in this case, was divided into $50 shares instead of the $100 shares adopted in the previous case. In this case, moreover, there was no specification of a maximum interest rate of 6 per cent: the Bank might charge any rate not in excess of the legal maximum established by the legislature from time to time.

The Bank of Kaskaskia, which also received a charter on January 9, 1818,[48] did not get under way as promptly as its rival at Edwardsville. Perhaps there was a certain lack of commercial energy in the capital city, where a contemporary traveler tells us that the inhabitants were "all generals, colonels, majors, land speculators or adventurers, with now and then a robber and a cutthroat."[49] By the time the organizers were ready to receive subscriptions to the capital stock of this institution, there were no subscribers with enough ready money to pay the $10 per share required by the law, so that the Bank never opened for business.

Much the same thing must be said of the City and Bank of Cairo, which received its charter on the same day,[50] but the idea behind this interesting scheme deserves mention as an outstanding example of the kind of financial operation referred to earlier in the chapter.

Some time previously, an enterprising promoter named Comegys had acquired title to several hundred acres of land on the peninsula between the Ohio and Mississippi rivers, with the expectation that a great commercial city would be built on that site in the near future. This land was transferred to the newly organized company, which promptly surveyed it and marked it out into town lots that were offered for sale at $150 each, on the understanding that $50 of the purchase price was to be expended for levees and other public improvements. The remaining $100, which constituted the capital of the Bank, was to be represented by two shares of stock, one going to the purchaser of the land and the other to Comegys and his associates. In some ways, this was the most delightful of the many mésalliances between banking and land speculation, but the financial crisis in 1819 and the death of Comegys, at the same time, brought the venture to a sad end before a single lot had been sold. Indeed, Ford insists that the company never even accepted its charter.[51]

Both of the banks that were in operation faced a difficult situation when financial contraction spread throughout the south and west during the summer of 1818, but the Bank of Edwardsville, being a younger institution, faced the more serious problem. When the directors called for payment of the second installment on the capital stock, within a few months of the Bank's opening, more than five thousand shares were forfeited for nonpayment.[52] It was suggested, moreover, that many of the payments actually made were only possible because shareholders were accorded the doubtful privilege of borrowing from the Bank against the pledge of the very stock for which they were paying.[53]

Nevertheless, both banks succeeded in weathering the storm and, early in 1819, both of them were designated by the federal government as depositories. The distinction, although sought after, was of doubtful advantage. In return for a fixed government deposit of $50,000 and $40,000, respectively, the Bank of Illinois and the Bank of Edwardsville were to receive from the land offices all the heterogeneous mass of notes paid in by the purchasers, transmitting the proceeds, without any depreciation from parity, to the nearest branch of the second Bank of the United States.[54] Moreover, since the government, when it made payments in the neighborhood of the bank, might draw upon the fixed deposit, there was no certainty that the depository banks would have even that much compensation for their risk in assuming responsibility for the payment at par of all the notes received by the land office, to say nothing of the expense and labor of transmitting the funds.

Local pride, however, was satisfied by the use of local banks, in place of the Bank of Missouri, as depositories for the funds received in Illinois, and there was undoubtedly some advantage to the community in the fact that the large fixed deposits remained within the state. Moreover, since the government at this time paid reasonably close attention to the condition of depository banks, the designation served as a kind of endorsement of the soundness of the newly created institutions in Illinois. The action of the Secretary of the Treasury did not, however, rouse any enthusiasm among the directors of the older

Bank of Missouri, which appears to have gone out of its way to make things uncomfortable for its upstart competitors. On one occasion, a representative of the Bank of Missouri appeared in Shawneetown with $12,000 in notes of the Bank of Illinois (an amount equal to almost a quarter of the outstanding circulation), in return for which he demanded specie at the counter of the Bank.[55] On other occasions, the receiver of public moneys at Kaskaskia, who (for reasons of tradition and civic pride perhaps) had less love for the Bank at Shawneetown than for the Bank of Missouri, with which he had previously dealt, would seek to embarrass the new Bank by refusing to accept its notes in payment of sums due to the government.

At first, the Bank of Edwardsville and the Bank of Illinois appear to have competed with each other almost as fiercely as they both competed with the Bank of Missouri, and early in 1819 the Bank of Illinois refused to accept the notes of the Bank of Edwardsville at its counters. Such an attitude of mind could not persist, however, since it quickly became apparent to the officers of both banks that, unless they worked together, neither of them could expect to survive the competition of the more powerful institutions in neighboring states. Indeed, it was suggested to Ninian Edwards by the Bank of Illinois that neither bank should present the notes of the other for redemption, if such a step could possibly be avoided, and that, in addition, each bank when it received notes issued by the other should send those notes as far from the point of issue as possible, in order to make redemption by other parties more difficult.[56] Cooperation could scarcely go much further.

As a result, by the summer of 1819, the two Illinois banks were effectively established, and appeared to be operating efficiently in harmony with each other. The following statement of their joint condition,[57] the only one that has come down to us, is therefore an interesting revelation of their situation at its best.

TABLE II

Aggregate Statement of Condition of Illinois Banks, 1819

Liabilities

Note circulation outstanding...........	$ 52,021.00
United States deposits.................	119,036.92
Individual deposits...................	32,568.60
Capital paid in......................	140,910.00
Undivided profits....................	2,994.49
	$347,531.01

Assets

Specie on hand......................	$ 74,715.51
Due from other banks.................	59,332.18
Loans and discounts..................	206,694.32
Securities..........................	6,614.00
Real estate owned....................	175.00
	$347,531.01

From the angle of contemporary banking practice, their condition at this time appears to have been extraordinarily strong. To be sure, the large specie reserve and the equally large sum held in the form of notes of other banks were a direct result of the sums received from the government land office, but it will be noticed that, taken together, these items more than offset the large deposit of the United States government, which is another indication of land-office activity. Although the banks might be called upon at a moment's notice to transfer large sums to the east, for the account of the government, they were in a comfortable position to do so. More-over, the total note issue outstanding amounted to less than half of the paid-in capital, an unusually conservative relationship at that time, while the high proportion of deposit liabilities is interesting in a period when deposit banking was not common throughout the west. The out-standing weakness of the whole picture lies in the fact that much of the "capital paid in" obviously represents the result of loans made by the banks to their stockhold-ers. Like most of the institutions in the country at that time, the Illinois banks were piling Ossa on Pelion in their effort to provide the community with capital funds by the legerdemain of bookkeeping entries. To have built an enduring institution on such uncertain founda-tions of sand would only have been possible if the build-ers were certain that no storms would occur, but a finan-cial storm of extreme severity was already sweeping across the world at that very moment.

In Europe the Napoleonic wars had been financed by inflation, moderate in England but quite severe in several of the continental countries. In the United States, the War of 1812, much less important to world history but sig-nificant because of the financial problem it created for the young Republic, had been financed in a similar fashion. Moreover, on both sides of the Atlantic, the sus-pension of specie payments, resulting from inflation, had given rise to a situation in which the commercial banks had expanded their note issues inordinately, under the encouragement of a supine central banking policy in the one case, and of the failure to recharter the first Bank of the United States in the other.

At last, the day of reckoning had come. In 1818, and even more in 1819, the world was struggling manfully to return to a specie standard. Every country was trying to build up its reserves of gold and silver, international stabilization loans were the order of the day, and the precious metals were moving across national frontiers in unusually large amounts. All over the world banks were adopting policies of credit contraction and the general level of prices was tumbling rapidly, while, in this country, the second Bank of the United States found its easy money policies brought to an abrupt halt by a Congressional investigation. Its President "fled in affright from the institution," and left Langdon Cheves to assume the thankless task of restoring soundness and solvency.[58]

Illinois could not have hoped to escape from the effects of this storm, as it moved steadily westward, particularly in view of the fact that her domestic financial strength was already impaired by the previous speculative mania and the resultant financial stringency in the summer of 1818. For the United States, as a whole, the total bank-note circulation declined from more than $110,000,000, in 1815, to $45,000,000, in 1819,[59] but the extent of the contraction had differed greatly from one state to another. In Pennsylvania, the circulation in 1819 amounted to only $1,300,000, as compared with $4,700,000 in 1816, while in Ohio very little contraction had occurred and not more than six or seven out of the twenty-five banks in operation were redeeming their notes in specie.[60]

In the spring of 1819, however, Ohio began to put pressure on its banks, reinforcing the influences already exerted by the policies of the Bank of the United States, so that contraction progressed rapidly. This tendency spread to Missouri, and (to a lesser extent) Indiana, so that bank failures became increasingly common and "the prices of all articles produced in the western states fell so low as scarcely to defray the expenses of transportation to the ports from whence they were usually exported to foreign markets. This condition of things, which had not been anticipated when the debt for the public lands was contracted, produced the most serious distress . . . and excited alarming apprehensions for the future."[61]

Most of the banks of Kentucky and Tennessee, and many of those in Ohio, had failed before the end of 1819, and in several states legislation had been written upon the statute books for the relief of debtors. Illinois joined promptly in the latter movement, providing that no debtor should, in any circumstances, be imprisoned for his debt if he expressed willingness to transfer to his creditor what property he had,[62] while in the case of debtors with families it was further provided that they might retain "one bed and reasonable furniture, one milch cow and one spinning wheel."[63] Moreover, a new law was passed, reiterating the earlier provision that no execution might be levied on the property of a defaulting debtor for a period of twelve months, unless the creditor had authorized the sheriff to receive in discharge of the obligation "such bank notes, as may be then receivable in payment for public lands, in the office of the land district" in which the real estate was situated.[64]

In spite of the widespread business depression, and of the handicaps imposed by this legislation for the protection of its debtors, the Bank of Illinois continued to operate efficiently and profitably. Late in 1819, the directors decided, for the future, to confine the operations of the Bank to the discounting of bills, which necessarily contracted the scope of its operations but also saved it from many losses that might otherwise have been incurred.[65] Its notes continued to circulate at par in Illinois[66] even after it was compelled to suspend specie payments, toward the end of August, 1821.[67] At no time prior to that had it ever refused to redeem a note when it was presented.

In spite of its excellent reputation, the business of the Bank declined so rapidly that the directors finally decided to suspend operations in 1823, although they succeeded in doing so without surrendering the charter. All the noteholders appear to have been paid in full, but the remaining liabilities, among which was a balance of $28,367 due to the United States government, could not be met.[68]

The Bank of Edwardsville, being a newer institution with less efficient management, fared even worse in this crisis than the Bank of Illinois.[69] As early as 1819, Ninian Edwards became dissatisfied with the way in which his associates were running the Bank and decided, in view of its condition, to escape from responsibility by resigning from the directorate. He did so in an exceedingly cautious manner and, although himself a Senator in Washington at the time, he failed to acquaint the Secretary of the Treasury with his decision. Instead, he suggested that Stephenson, the President of the Bank, should inform the Secretary about the resignation and insist that no more public moneys be deposited in the Bank until the Treasury had investigated its condition. These fears, however, were not revealed to the community; when he announced his resignation to the public, a little later, Edwards insisted that the Bank was in excellent condition.

There is no evidence that the President of the Bank accepted the advice that Edwards gave him; nor would his failure to do so be surprising in view of the fact that he was himself the receiver of public moneys at Edwardsville! Moreover, in addition to this complicating factor, the Bank of Edwardsville was intimately associated with the Bank of St. Louis, a rival of the Bank of Missouri. The Bank at Edwardsville continued to act as a public depository long after Ninian Edwards' resignation, but its record in that capacity was far from satisfactory. It was in continual difficulty with the Treasury, as a result of its failure to make remittances when called upon to do so, and its excuse that eastern exchange and specie could not be procured in Illinois sounds inadequate in view of the demonstrated ability of the Bank at Shawneetown to make prompt remittance. Obviously, political pressure was exercised to strengthen the Bank's position by means of federal deposits but, even so, it was tottering.

Early in the autumn of 1821, the failure of the Bank of Missouri caused a panic at Edwardsville that precipitated a run which the Bank tried valiantly to meet. In order to restore confidence, it opened its doors at seven o'clock in the morning, and kept them open long after normal banking hours.[70] Within a few days, however, the Bank of Edwardsville was compelled to close its doors permanently, although even then the President was so optimistic that, in informing the Secretary of the Treasury of the decision, he assured him that the government deposits were perfectly safe and adequately secured. The optimism was not justified by events. Although Coles, afterward Governor of Illinois, was immediately appointed by Secretary Crawford to adjust the claim, and succeeded in getting the Bank to set aside, in trust, assets presumed to be adequate to cover the deposit liability to the government, the sum finally realized was totally inadequate. To be sure, Ninian Edwards (whose fortune was almost wiped out by the failure of the Bank, and the slump in the price of land) insisted that these assets, at the time when they were set aside, were worth more than enough to pay the debt, and that Crawford allowed them to depreciate by failing to act promptly. This statement, however, like others that were made by Edwards, who had resigned the Embassy to Mexico in order to carry on a political controversy with Crawford on the subject of the Bank, would not convince an impartial jury. He only proves the extent to which the Bank was mixed up in the political activities and controversies of the day.[71]

In the end, the government obtained a judgment against the Bank for $54,000,[72] but several years later it was reported that the sum had never been recovered from the liquidators.[73] The Bank of Edwardsville had failed utterly and completely, and Illinois' first effort to develop a financial system ended by leaving the state without a single bank of any kind. The attempt to create wealth by financial manipulation, born of the marriage of banking and politics, had produced chaos instead of prosperity. As a contemporary satirist suggests, the legislature "was swallowing, and thereby exterminating, the several banks of the Illinois Territory. . . . This extermination of banks was not a difficult matter, as the people of Illinois had learned by experience that banks without any capital, created for private speculation, were injurious to the public."[74]

REFERENCES FOR CHAPTER I

[1] Pierce: *A History of Chicago,* I, 31.
[2] Buck: *Illinois in 1818,* p. 117.
[3] *Ibid.,* p. 119.
[4] *Western Intelligencer,* April 22, 1818.
[5] *Illinois Intelligencer,* January 2, 1819.
[6] Quaife: *Chicago's Highways Old and New,* pp. 154-167.
[7] Buck: *op. cit.,* p. 93.
[8] *Ibid.,* p. 22.
[9] Ford: *History of Illinois,* p. 94.
[10] Cf. Quaife: *op. cit.,* pp. 188-204; Buck: *op. cit.,* pp. 119-123.
[11] Buck: *op. cit.,* p. 120; also Pease: *The Frontier State,* pp. 46-47.
[12] *Laws of Illinois,* 1815-16, p. 77.
[13] Ford: *op. cit.,* p. 38.
[14] Buck: *op. cit.,* p. 58.
[15] *Western Intelligencer,* March 25, 1818.
[16] Buck: *op. cit.,* p. 91; Ford, *op. cit.,* p. 35.
[17] Cf. Buck: *op. cit.,* pp. 53, 103-112, 168-170; Pease: *op. cit.,* pp. 12-16.
[18] Ford: *op. cit.,* pp. 41-42.
[19] Buck: *op. cit.,* p. 130.
[20] *Ibid.,* p. 132.
[21] Huston: *Financing an Empire,* I, 47.
[22] This development is discussed at greater length on pp. 79 to 81.
[23] Buck: *op. cit.,* pp. 45-46; Birbeck: *Letters from Illinois,* p. 97; *Niles' Weekly Register,* XII, 99.
[24] Buck: *op. cit.,* p. 44.
[25] *Ibid.,* pp. 52-53.
[26] *Ibid.,* pp. 152-156.
[27] Thwaites: *Early Western Travels,* VIII, 291; XIII, 70; and Buck: *op. cit.,* pp. 69-70; Fearon: *Sketches of America,* p. 258.
[28] Cf. Pease: *op. cit.,* p. 55.

[29] *Laws of Illinois*, 1816-17, pp. 11-19. Approved December 28, 1816.

[30] *Report of the Secretary of the Treasury*, February 24, 1820.

[31] Cf. Dewey: *State Banking before the Civil War*, pp. 49-52.

[32] Dewey: *op. cit.*, pp. 5-22.

[33] *Report of the Secretary of the Treasury*, February 24, 1820.

[34] Dewey: *op. cit.*, p. 14.

[35] Dowrie: *The Development of Banking in Illinois*, p. 8.

[36] Dewey: *op. cit.*, p. 103.

[37] Dewey: *op. cit.*, p. 101; *History of Banking*, I, 82, 91.

[38] Dewey: *op. cit.*, pp. 104-107.

[39] *Idem*, p. 102.

[40] *History of Banking*, I, 76-81.

[41] *Report of the Secretary of the Treasury*, February 24, 1820; *History of Banking*, I, 64.

[42] *Niles'*, XII, 262.

[43] *Laws of Illinois*, 1816-17, p. 19. Approved December 28, 1816.

[44] Cf. Buck: *op. cit.*, 50n.

[45] *Idem*, p. 148.

[46] Pease: *op. cit.*, p. 55.

[47] *Laws of Illinois*, 1817-18, pp. 65-72. Approved January 9, 1818.

[48] *Laws of Illinois*, 1817-18, pp. 82-90. Approved January 9, 1818.

[49] Buck: *op. cit.*, p. 76.

[50] *Laws of Illinois*, 1817-19, pp. 72-82. Approved January 9, 1818.

[51] Greene and Thompson: *Governor's Letter Books*, II, 60.

[52] *Niles'*, XVII, 186.

[53] Dowrie: *op. cit.*, p. 15.

[54] *U. S. H. of R., 17 Congress, 1 Session, Document No. 66.*

[55] *Edwards' Papers*, p. 155.

[56] *Ibid*, p. 156.

[57] *U. S. H. of R., 16 Congress, 1 Session, Document No. 86*, facing p. 40.

[58] *History of Banking*, I, 97-98.

[59] *Idem*, 116.

[60] *Idem*, 105 and 152.

[61] *U. S. H. of R., 17 Congress, 1 Session, Document No. 66; History of Banking*, I, 111.

[62] *Laws of Illinois*, 1819, p. 301. Approved March 27, 1819.

[63] *Laws of Illinois*, 1819, p. 160. Approved March 22, 1819.

[64] *Laws of Illinois*, 1819, p. 158. Approved March 22, 1819.

[65] *Illinois Gazette*, December 11, 1819; Pease: *op. cit.*, p. 56.

[66] *Illinois Intelligencer*, June 15, 1822.

[67] *Edwardsville Spectator*, August 28, 1821; Hunt's *Merchants' Magazine*, XI, 241.

[68] *Letter of the Secretary of the Treasury, 1838, U. S. H. of R., Documents Nos. 79 and 780;* Andreas: *History of Chicago,* I, 526; Dowrie: *op. cit.,* p. 14. It may be mentioned here that when the Bank of Illinois reopened, ten years later, a settlement of these outstanding liabilities was negotiated.

[69] Since the controversy between Ninian Edwards and the Secretary of the Treasury, together with certain other matters connected with the failure of the Bank of Edwardsville, was later investigated by Congress, a full account can be found in *U. S. H. of R., 18 Congress, 1 Session, Documents Nos. 128 and 133.*

[70] *Edwardsville Spectator,* August 21 and September 11, 1821.

[71] *Report of the Secretary of the Treasury, U. S. H. of R., 18 Congress, 1 Session,* pp. 560-566; Dowrie: *op. cit.,* pp. 17-18.

[72] Andreas: *op. cit.,* I, 526.

[73] *U. S. Reports on Finances,* 1829-36, p. 605.

[74] *Illinois Intelligencer,* September 9, 1818.

CHAPTER II

BANKING AS AN INSTRUMENT OF SOCIAL WELFARE

1821–1830

THE postwar boom was already waning when Illinois became a state. While the Constitutional Convention was meeting at Kaskaskia, in August, 1818, speculative enthusiasm still persisted in certain quarters; several people (among them Edwards and Stephenson, of the Edwardsville Bank) hoped that, by locating the capital of the new state on one of their colorfully platted town sites, a good deal of money could be made.[1] But when Congress formally admitted Illinois to the Union, in December of that year, these hopes, even among the hardiest and most optimistic, were growing dim. Black depression was fast approaching.

Of the *opéra bouffe* characteristics of the monetary system, little need be said in addition to the account offered in the previous chapter. "Nor did the notes composing it merely pass at a discount; they passed at forty different discounts, varying with the reputation of the banks from which they issued or purported to issue. Some were issued by solvent banks, some by specie paying banks, some were issued by banks that had failed, some were counterfeit notes of existing banks and others of purely fictitious ones. Of the notes in circulation [in Illinois], a few were issued by New England banks, a few came from western New York, more came from Pennsylvania and the District of Columbia, still more from the banks of Ohio and of the south, in particular Tennessee and Kentucky. Local notes composed but a small fraction of the total."[2]

Moreover, the burden of debt that rested upon the people of the new state was considerable. Everybody had speculated during the boom, and almost everybody had speculated on credit. Men had bought land from the government when their total resources barely sufficed to cover the amount of the first installment, and some had borrowed even that initial sum from the banks or from eastern capitalists. Nearly the whole people were "irrecoverably involved in debt," as Ford points out, and much of this debt had been incurred in the confident expectation that the prices of land, and of the things that land produced, would continue to rise. During 1819, however, the prices of agricultural produce tumbled rapidly and Congress became alarmed at the amount of land speculation that was going on. The extent to which land had been bought on credit only served to make the problem more serious in the eyes of the legislators. In 1820, therefore, the Congress decided to reduce the price of the public lands from $2.00 to $1.25 an acre, and to insist upon full payment in cash at all future sales.[3]

The idea underlying this change in governmental policies regarding land sales was probably sound, but the effect of the Act was to accentuate the depression. In the first place, the new policy made it more difficult for an immigrant to buy lands in the western territories, and so accentuated the influence of the depression in discouraging migration; in the second, it tended to reduce the value of the lands already held by speculators, thus augmenting the discrepancy between the volume of their debts and the amount of their resources. On both counts, the Act tended to aggravate a situation that was already unpleasant enough.

The depression was not, however, confined to Illinois: it covered the whole United States. Indeed, bank and business failures were more serious in the east than they were in the newer territories of the west, where the economic organism was still so primitive that it was less likely to be deranged by financial shocks.[4] It soon became apparent, however, that the policies of the several states differed widely in their treatment of the situation. A few of the older states in the east, which had already tasted the flavor of inflation on earlier occasions, adopted policies of stringent liquidation as the best method of strengthening the banking system and reducing the top-heavy credit structure. In New York, it became much harder to obtain banking charters;[5] in New England, the Suffolk System for the redemption of bank notes at par was developed and such states as Massachusetts and Rhode Island took steps to strengthen the condition of the issuing banks.[6] Moreover the second Bank of the United States, under the administration of Langdon Cheves, was making great strides in the improvement of its own condition and had begun to undertake its function of restoring the paper circulation to parity with specie.[7]

In the long run, however, this policy of the Bank of the United States proved to be the point of conflict between the divergent policies of the eastern states, on the one hand, and the southern and western states, on the other. The latter did not wish to return to specie payments and had no enthusiasm for policies of liquidation.[8] There arose among them, as has often occurred before and since that period, men who demonstrated oratorically and emphatically that the depression was due to an inadequacy of money. The farmer could not pay his debts because he was unable to sell his goods: to enforce policies of liquidation would only drive him from his farm. What was needed, they insisted, was relief and sustenance: relief in the form of legislation that permitted the debtor to postpone payment of his obligations until some more comfortable time, and sustenance in the form of additional loans that would give him money to spend meanwhile.

It was a magnificent scheme, well calculated to appeal to legislators who were themselves heavily in debt and who represented debtor constituencies in many cases. Laws for the relief of debtors, of which we have already seen examples in the territorial history of Illinois, blossomed out in Missouri, Kentucky, Tennessee and half a dozen other states. As a corollary, there were set up the great Banks of the States, to the study of which it might be profitable to give more attention in the light of some of the economic tendencies of the twentieth century.

Much of the antagonism to banks which existed in Illinois and other western states at this period was really an objection to *private* banking. With the exception of a few unheeded voices, crying in the wilderness, all men believed that banks were profitable engines for the production of wealth, but the very recognition of this idea led many people to object to the use of such engines to promote the private profits of a few individuals. Most people in the west wanted banks that would be operated by the government in the interests of that elusive soul, the common man, and the great Banks of the State were created under this impulse in Alabama, Georgia, Indiana, Kentucky,* Louisiana and Mississippi.

All these institutions had but two purposes. They were expected to provide money to meet the expenses of state government, thus permitting a reduction of taxes, and to provide more money for the purpose of lending it to the citizens of the states. Both of these laudable aims, it was realized, would alleviate the burdens of economic depression and, since the states had no money of their own, what could be wiser than the creation of a bank which would supply all that was needed?

Such a comfortable philosophy was very attractive to many people in Illinois, burdened by land for which they had not yet paid and realizing that a policy of liquidation would force them to bear the full burden of their own mistakes. As a result of this attitude of mind, and of the fact that Indiana had taken a similar step two years earlier, the Constitution of Illinois, in 1818, provided that

* The Bank of the Commonwealth of Kentucky is interesting as the most villainous of a series of unsound financial experiments. As W. G. Sumner so aptly states, "The great Banks of the States were financially unsound and mistaken, but this is the only one which deserved to be characterized as a shameless fraud. It was devised only to wipe out debts. Its pretenses were all transparently false" (History of Banking, I, 144). The State Bank of Indiana, by contrast, proved to be one of the soundest banks in the whole country when it was reestablished subsequently.

"there shall be no other banks or monied institutions in this state than those already provided by law, except a state bank and its branches, which may be established and regulated by the general assembly of the state as they may think proper."[9] To be sure, there was some uncertainty as to the precise meaning of the phrase "state bank," particularly in view of the fact that the records of the convention do not show clearly what was in the minds of the members. A subsequent investigation led the editor of one of the leading newspapers to the conclusion that the Constitution envisaged an institution under state control, although not necessarily owned by the state,[10] but it is highly probable that most people at the time regarded state ownership as a condition necessary to the policies of relief and social amelioration that were envisaged.

At the very first session of the legislature, action was taken under this provision of the Constitution to charter a State Bank of Illinois.[11] It was to be a Gargantuan institution, when contrasted with the general economic life of the state, since the capital was fixed at $4,000,000. One-half of this was to be provided immediately by the subscriptions of private capitalists: the remainder might be provided by the state whenever the legislature saw fit to authorize a subscription to the stock. In spite of these grandiose ideas, the promoters were realists. The charter goes on to provide that the Bank might start business as soon as it had received "in gold or silver, or in notes of banks of the western country paying specie," an initial payment of 10 per cent on not less than $150,000 of the capital stock. Only $15,000 was required to bring the institution into effective existence, but even this amount could not be collected from the people of Illinois, so that the legislature was compelled to pass an amending act permitting the subscribers to pay the initial installment in State Auditor's warrants.[12] Notwithstanding this further aid, the promoters were still unable to find enough people who were willing, and able, to subscribe the minimum amount of capital that was needed. The Bank never came into existence as an operating institution.

The charter had, however, served to crystallize opinion in the state, and there was already apparent that conflict of opinion which was to mark the political treatment of banking problems for almost three decades. All the people who wished to accelerate the economic development of the state, most of the politicians and all the speculators, were enthusiastically in favor of setting up the Bank, although they were not able, among them all, to raise the $15,000 necessary to start it! On the other side was a small minority, destined to grow in strength with the passing years, that was bitterly opposed to the whole scheme. "What business have we . . . with banks? . . . The people never desired it (it is a gross insult to the good sense of the community). The people know that some citizens of Kaskaskia, and none else desired it, and that there was not enough virtue in their representatives to preserve the state from disgrace, and themselves from the imputation of trifling with their powers and the wishes of the people. . . . So fraught is banking with every evil consequence, so truly is it 'the offspring of ignorance, chicanery, and a spirit of speculation.' "[13]

The indignation of the opposition did not, however, discourage the proponents of banking legislation, nor were they much perturbed by the difficulty of raising capital. At the next session of the legislature, in 1821, a bill was introduced for the purpose of creating a Bank that should rest wholly upon the faith and credit of the state, a Bank that could perform its beneficent work without worrying about such difficulties as the sale of stock to the general public.

The measure seems to have aroused considerable interest, and several meetings were held in various parts of the state to endorse or oppose it.[14] Even in the legislature itself the bill had bitter opponents. In the Senate, the Bank was denounced because it would not have a dollar of specie with which to redeem its notes, while a group of members of the House protested against the measure on the grounds that it was a transparent violation of the constitutional prohibition of bills of credit and would only serve to encourage speculation.[15] At long last, however, the bill passed both houses by a small majority.

Governor Bond had already expressed his strong objection to the scheme, but in Illinois at that period the Governor had no individual veto power.[16] The bill went from the legislature to the Council of Revision, composed of the Governor and the justices of the Supreme Court sitting together, and the Council emphatically rejected it, on the ground that the notes of such a Bank were nothing but bills of credit and, therefore, unconstitutional. They pointed out, moreover, that such a remedy might be worse than the disease; that inflation would not solve the problems confronting the state; and that the notes of the Bank would not be generally accepted by the people.[17]

Under the Constitution of 1818, bills might still become law if they were passed, over the objection of the Council of Revision, "by a majority of all the members elected," so that the Bank charter again became the subject of bitter debate in the legislature.[18] The constitutionality of the proposed notes was hotly argued and the Council of Revision was reminded that this point had not been raised when it approved the 1819 charter. Some of the more enthusiastic Bank proponents made light of the suggestion that these bank notes would not be acceptable in other states by remarking that, if this should prove to be the case, there would be a more plentiful supply of money in Illinois. Finally, the bill passed the House by 17 votes to 10, and was sent to the Senate where it was promptly passed by a small majority.*

As finally passed,[19] the Act provided for the creation of The State Bank of Illinois, with its principal office at Vandalia and branches at Shawneetown, Edwardsville, Brownsville and Palmyra. Two of these towns, although important then, are no longer in existence. The entire capital, which was not to exceed $500,000 (and was actually fixed at $300,000), was subscribed by the state. Provision was made for a President, a Cashier[20] and six directors of the principal bank, as well as for five local directors at each of the branches. All these offices were to be filled by the legislature biennially, in joint session, but the local directors of the branches were allowed to elect their own President and Cashier (being to that extent better off than the principal bank itself). As remuneration for his services the President of the principal bank was

* There may be evidence of the persuasive powers of the Bank proponents in the fact that a Senator who voted for it was immediately appointed Cashier of one of the branches of the Bank. Cf. *Alton Spectator*, January 25, 1834.

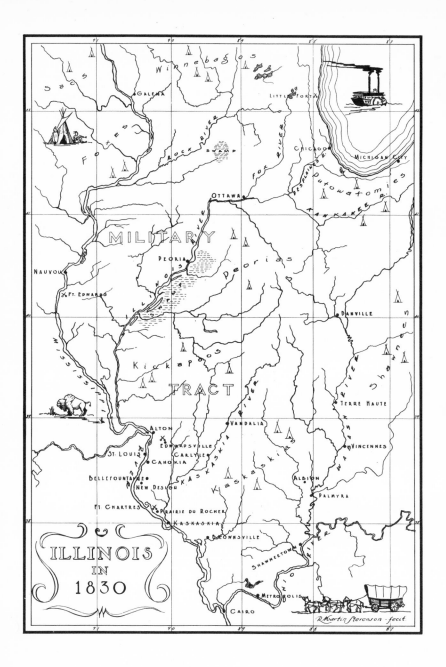

ILLINOIS
IN
1830

R. Martin Stevenson - fecit

given a salary of $800 a year,[21] and the Cashiers were to re-
ceive salaries not in excess of this amount, while the other
officials, who received no salary, were compensated by
loans at low rates of interest. The branch Presidents were
entitled to borrow $1,000 at 2 per cent per annum and
the directors were each awarded accommodations of $750
at the same rate.

The principal bank, after its organization had been
completed, was authorized to prepare $300,000 of notes,
in denominations ranging from $1 to $20, and to distribute these notes among the branches in proportion to the
population contained in the area served by each.* These
notes, which were all to be retired at the end of ten years,
were unconditionally guaranteed by the State of Illinois,
which pledged all of its property and revenues for their
redemption at the end of the period specified. Meanwhile,
they bore interest at the rate of 2 per cent per annum and
were receivable by the State Treasurer in payment of
all dues and taxes owing to the state, which was as near to
a grant of full legal tender as any state could go under
the terms of the federal Constitution. Moreover, the Bank
was required to retire one-tenth of the original note issue
each year, and not to reissue any of the currency thus
retired.

Upon receiving these bank notes, the officers of the
Bank were to lend them, at a rate of 6 per cent, in return
for obligations of the borrower secured by a mortgage on
unencumbered real estate worth twice the amount of the
loan, although provision was made for loans on personal

* As a result, $83,517 went to Edwardsville; $48,834 to Brownsville; $84,685
to Shawneetown; $47,265 to Palmyra; and $35,699 to the principal office at
Vandalia.

security in cases where the amount was $100 or less, and two-thirds of the board of directors approved the transaction. No individual was to borrow more than $1000, nor could anyone borrow from any office of the Bank except the branch in whose territory he resided, since the Bank was charged by the Act with distributing the aggregate amount of its loans among the several counties of the state in proportion to the distribution of population. All notes were to be payable twelve months after date but, as an indication of the attitude of the legislature toward debtors, the Bank was required to renew the note of any debtor who could not pay the whole amount, provided that he was willing and able to reduce the principal by 10 per cent.

The issue of these notes, and their prompt distribution among the many eager borrowers, was, of course, the primary purpose of the Bank. In addition, however, it was required to act as fiscal agent and depository for the state, receiving all state revenues from the Treasurer and paying them out on his warrant. It was also authorized to receive deposits and do a general banking business, but was prohibited from charging its depositors for the service and required to conduct all its exchanges at par. Provision was also made for periodic reports to the state, and the legislature reserved to itself the right to investigate the Bank at any time.

Such was the first State Bank of Illinois, in the pristine splendor of its sponsors' dream. Steps were immediately taken to organize it so that it might start operations under the most favorable auspices. Although the subscription of the capital stock on the part of the State of Illinois was nothing but a bookkeeping transaction, since the state never had $300,000 to invest and the Bank did not expect to receive any such sum, the legislature did appropriate $2,000 in actual money for the purpose of paying for the manufacture of plates from which the notes were printed.[22] Moreover, in order to give these notes as wide a field of circulation as possible, the laws making them acceptable in payment of all dues and taxes by the state were reinforced by legislation designed to prohibit the issuance of any paper currency on the part of private bankers or corporations not legally invested with banking powers.[23]

Further than this the state could not go in forcing the circulation of the notes by its own authority, but it attempted to supplement that authority by resolution of the legislature requiring the Representatives and Senators of Illinois in Washington "to use their utmost exertions, at the next session of Congress, to procure the notes and bills of the State Bank of Illinois to be made receivable in the different land offices in this state."[24] Some members of the legislature, however, were still highly skeptical regarding the prospects of the Bank, despite this enthusiasm on the part of its promoters, as is amply demonstrated by the story that Ford tells so well. When the above resolution was put to a vote in the Senate, "the old French lieutenant-governor, Col. Menard, presiding over that body, did up the business as follows: 'Gentlemen of *de* Senate, it is moved and seconded *dat de* notes of *dis* Bank be made land office money. All in favour of *dat* motion, say aye; all against it, say no. It is decided in *de* affirmative. And now, gentlemen, *I bet you one hundred dollar he never be made land office money.' "*[25] It is not recorded that anybody covered the bet, but if they did Menard must have won his money.

Having set up the State Bank, and done all that seemed possible to encourage the circulation of the notes, the legislature turned its attention to the problem of insuring to the overburdened debtors of the state the relief that the Bank was intended to provide. To give it sufficient time to get started, the legislature (while the Bank charter was still under debate at the beginning of 1821) provided that no execution should issue on any judgment or replevin bond until November 20 of that year, and that property previously seized should be restored to the debtor until that date if he was willing to give bond for twice the amount of the debt.[26] Moreover, in case creditors should prove reluctant to accept bank notes in payment of the sums due to them, thus preventing the debtor from deriving any benefit from the institution, the act of incorporation provided that seizure of property under execution should be postponed for three years in all cases where the plaintiff had not stated in writing that "the notes or bills of the State Bank of Illinois, or of either of its branches, will be received in discharge of this execution."[27] In effect, the debtor need not pay his debts for three years, unless the creditor permitted him to pay in notes of the Bank.

In July, 1821, at the moment when thousands of Indians were gathering in the still primitive village of Chicago to sign a treaty ceding their lands to the United States,[28] the State Bank of Illinois opened its doors for business. "Every man who could get an endorser borrowed his hundred dollars,"[29] and the few who had unencumbered real estate to mortgage obtained larger amounts. Within a few days, the whole sum of $300,000 had been disbursed in loans throughout the state, and before the end of the month complaints were heard from dissatisfied would-be borrowers, who insisted that nobody had a chance to get a loan unless he was a friend of one of the directors.[30] Very little, if any, attention was given to the credit standing of either borrowers or endorsers in this wholesale process of lending. In the first place, several of the officials of the Bank were politicians with little financial experience, since the legislators could scarcely be expected to overlook political friends when making appointments to lucrative jobs. Such officials wished to please everybody while offending nobody and it was not to their interest to refuse any applicant for a loan. Even if the Bank had been administered by trained financiers, however, the result would not, in all probability, have been much different. Sitting on the Council of Revision, the judges of the Supreme Court had, extralegally, insisted that the whole plan was unconstitutional. Before long, they might reiterate that opinion from the bench and wipe out the institution. What, therefore, could be gained by scrupulous care in the granting of loans, except political odium? The state had decided to aid indigent debtors, and the officers of the Bank gaily carried out the policy. After all, a man's indigence was greatest when his credit standing was least.

Momentarily the whole state enjoyed the pleasant intoxication of its inflationary spree, but what of the morning after? By the beginning of 1823, the policies of liquidation in the eastern states had brought their paper currencies back to par; business was already reviving and moving slowly onward to the prosperity that was to last until the end of 1825. Of the west, however, there is a different story to tell, and Illinois was far from being the only state to which that story referred. "A currency, composed entirely of irredeemable paper, flooded the country, and expelled the precious metals. The destruction of public and private credit, national torpor, individual ruin, disgraceful legislation and the prostration of morals, followed of course. . . . Nothing was seen but a boundless expanse of desolation. Wealth impoverished, enterprise checked, the currency depreciated, and all that was indicative of public and private prosperity plunged, apparently, into the vortex of ruin. The farmer had no incentive to industry or exertion. The efforts of the merchant were fruitless, and the energies of the state, to all appearance, temporarily annihilated. The guilty authors, however, of the mischief, escaped with impunity;* while the innocent, the unsuspecting and uncorrupted, were plundered without necessity and without mercy."[31]

The notes issued by the first State Bank of Illinois were intended to circulate at a parity with gold and silver coin. Within a few weeks of the opening of the Bank, however, they were worth only seventy-five cents on the dollar and, by the end of the year, they could not be exchanged at more than half their face value in terms of the standard money of the country.[32] By 1825, they were worth only

* Ford points out that Richard Young, who was one of the leading sponsors of the first State Bank of Illinois, did not suffer by its collapse. He was for many years afterward one of the most prominent politicians of Illinois and a judge of the Supreme Court. Cf. Ford: *op. cit.,* p. 46.

thirty cents on the dollar.[33] Naturally, the forced circulation of such depreciated currency within the state led to
the rapid disappearance of all gold and silver coins; even
the ancient pieces that had been clipped and sweated
until they were far below the legal weight were exported
or went into hiding. The subsidiary coinage disappeared
just as rapidly as standard money, so that it became necessary, in making change for less than a dollar, to tear the
bank notes into smaller pieces whose size approximately
indicated their value. "For about four years there was no
other kind of money but this uncurrent State Bank
paper."[34]

Nor is it hard to find reasons for the rapid depreciation
of the bank notes that had been issued on the enthusiastic
assumption that they would make the state prosperous.[35]
In the first place, no provision was made for the redemption of the notes on demand.* The whole tenor of the
Act, with its provision of 2 per cent interest to the noteholder and its elaborate insistence on the fact that the
state assumed full responsibility for the redemption of
the notes at the end of ten years, indicates a belief that no
notes would be presented for redemption during the
decade, except in so far as they were handed over to the
Bank in repayment of the loans that it had made. The
underlying theory, so often stated, and even more often
disproved by experience, was that the notes would stay
in circulation until the debtor repaid his loan, and that,

* Except in the case of the unimportant supplementary issue of notes based
upon the deposit of school funds and other cash resources. The amount of
notes issued under this provision was never large, and they can conveniently
be omitted from this discussion.

out of these repayments, the Bank would annually retire
10 per cent of the original issue.

But even if the legislators had envisaged the presentation of notes for redemption, the Bank had no specie with
which to redeem them. No specie had been paid in connection with the capital subscription by the state and,
apart from a few special funds, the Bank did not receive
any deposits in specie, so that its aggregate holdings of
coin can never have been large at any time. In March,
1823, when robbers broke into the principal office of the
Bank and made off with $4,200, the *Illinois Intelligencer*
stated that this constituted "a large part of its specie,"[36]
while it is reported that one of the branches was so surprised and delighted to receive two silver dollars that it
was immediately decided to put them on exhibition as a
curiosity![37] Certainly there is no evidence here of any
ability on the part of the Bank to redeem its notes, and
the report of the examination made in 1825 confirms that
conclusion.[38]

Apart from the technical question of redemption, however, the value of the notes must have been seriously
affected by the general opinion of the public regarding
the soundness of the Bank, and there is plenty of evidence
that the opinion was not very high. Loans had been made
with little scrutiny of the borrowers and, in many cases,
the funds were squandered almost as soon as they were received.[39] Few of the debtors had any intention of repaying
the loans, which they regarded as a benevolent gift from
the state,[40] and the state did its best to encourage this idea
by the steady stream of relief laws that were passed to
legalize successive postponements of repayment. The

Bank suffered seriously from the fact that, in Illinois, there existed little conscious integrity among the debtors and even less possibility of legally enforcing payment. As Ford points out, "A kind of inefficient remedy has been held out to the creditor, which might succeed in making a debt from an honest man, but never from a rogue. The ease with which it could be evaded, put the debtor part of the community under strong temptation to dishonesty. If a creditor, no longer to be put off by fair promises, sued for his debt at law, the debtor leaves him to his remedy thus chosen. He satisfies his conscience by a train of reasoning of this sort: 'If I had not been sued I would have paid as soon as I possibly could. My creditor is not disposed to rely upon my honor, he has sued me at law, and thereby chosen mere legal means to recover his debt. He does not rely upon me any longer. Now let him get his money as soon as the law will give it to him. I feel absolved in conscience from making any further efforts to pay, and will be justified in throwing all the obstacles in his way which the forms and delays of the law can furnish.' "[41]

Finally, and most damaging of all to the value of its notes, it would seem that the directors and officers of the Bank were anxious to see them depreciate. Under the charter, these men had been permitted to borrow unusually large amounts from the Bank at a rate of interest of 2 per cent, and they had taken full advantage of this privilege.[42] Any depreciation in the value of the notes made it that much easier for them to repay their loans, which in the aggregate amounted to one-sixth of the total amount lent by the institution, whereas they had nothing whatever to gain from an appreciation in the value of the paper. It is, therefore, highly improbable that they took any action to prevent the notes from falling to a discount.

State officials generally, on the other hand, looked upon the depreciation of the bank notes with much less enthusiasm, because all salaries and fees were paid in this currency. In his annual report for 1822,[43] the Auditor of the state drew attention to this fact. Although he diplomatically suggests that the chartering of the Bank may, at the time, have been a wise measure to save many citizens of the state from the ruin that was staring them in the face, he insists that the proponents of the scheme could not have intended that it should deprive state officials, and others with claims on the state, of half the amount that was due to them. In the best interests of the state, he suggests, the Bank should be immediately wound up or, failing that, the charter should be amended in a fashion that will bring about a rise in the value of the currency.*

The legislature did nothing at all regarding the fundamental problem of reorganizing or liquidating the Bank, but the question of salaries received prompt attention. Early in February, 1823, an act[44] was passed authorizing an increase of 50 per cent in the salaries fixed by the Constitution for the justices of the Supreme Court, the Governor and the Secretary of State. The Speakers of the House and Senate were to receive $9 a day, in place of the $5 they had received before, while each Representative and Senator (who had previously received an allowance

---

* Short of winding up the Bank, the Auditor, unfortunately, does not suggest the precise way in which an amendment to the charter would raise the value of the currency.

of $3.50 a day) was asked to write on a slip of paper the amount, not in excess of $7.00 a day, that he was willing to accept.*

This eagerness to protect the standard of living of state officials and of the legislators themselves, admirable though it was, necessarily increased by a substantial amount the payments that the state was called upon to make during the course of the fiscal year. But the legislators, who were not anxious to impose burdens that the voter would remember at the next election, did not consider it advisable to provide for any taxation, so that the immediate effect of the act was to increase the fiscal deficit of the state. As a painless solution to the problem, the Auditor was authorized to pay his bills by means of state warrants, bearing interest at 6 per cent, when he had no other funds on hand with which to pay them and, despite the recent experience with the notes issued by the Bank, it was assumed that these warrants would constitute a satisfactory medium of exchange for general circulation.[45]

The general public, being unable to compensate itself for the depreciation of the paper currency as easily as the legislators had done, experienced a strong revulsion of feeling. The State Bank of Illinois had not fulfilled the hopes of many of its original supporters and, in January, 1823, a bill authorizing the institution to issue another $200,000 in the form of bank notes was emphatically beaten in the House by 24 to 9. Moreover, a resolution was adopted appointing a legislative committee to make an investigation of the Bank.[46] This committee reported

* It may be noted, parenthetically, that to nobody but themselves did the legislature offer an increase in salary that was anything like sufficient to counterbalance the depreciation of the paper.

that the annual report, presented to the legislature at the end of the previous year, appeared to tally with the books of the Bank, but that these books, particularly in the case of the branches, were in such poor condition that it was impossible to obtain any accurate information from them. It was, therefore, recommended that a responsible committee be appointed to supervise the operations of the Bank, and see that it operated according to the terms of the laws creating it, particularly in the matter of retiring and destroying one-tenth of the original note issue each year.

Once again, the legislature did nothing to solve the fundamental problems raised by the report. To make a show of interest, they passed an act[47] raising the salary of the principal bank's Cashier to $1,000 a year and lowering that of the President to $200 a year, at the same time requiring the Cashiers of the branch banks to transmit to the principal bank at the end of each calendar year a complete abstract of their discount books. The provision of the original act that the Bank could issue additional notes to the extent of twice the deposits received from the federal government on account of school funds, a provision that never appears to have had much importance, was repealed.

In theory, these evasions offered a breathing spell in which the problem could be carefully considered but, since no action was taken, the situation grew progressively worse and the currency continued to depreciate. When the next legislature met, at the end of 1824, the Governor's message was highly critical of the whole situation. He condemned the criminal folly of those who had created the Bank in the first place, pointing out that the depression of 1819 and 1820 was itself the result of earlier inflation, and recommended the passage of legislation leading to the orderly liquidation of the institution in a manner that would protect the state from loss.[48] Even so, the reaction to the message was not startling. The legislature contented itself by passing an act[49] appointing three commissioners to make a thorough examination of the Shawneetown branch, which appears to have had the reputation of being the worst of all the offices of the Bank.

This investigation may be said to mark the beginning of the long and painful process of liquidating the first State Bank of Illinois since, although that process was to continue for six more years, the Bank was never again to operate as an active financial institution. Before the first examination was completed, a joint committee of the legislature was appointed to investigate, once again, the whole institution, and the results were far from pleasant. The net loss of the whole Bank amounted to $2,403, and the only offices that showed any profit at all were those at Edwardsville and Palmyra. At Shawneetown the condition of the books made it impossible to form any clear picture of the situation and the Cashier, who admitted making an illegal loan of $3,750 without security, was unable to account for a sum of $4,800 which appeared to be omitted from the books altogether.[50]

No criminal proceedings were instituted as a result of these disclosures, but definite steps were taken to liquidate the Bank. Early in January, 1825, an act[51] was passed ordering the Cashier to burn all notes in the possession of the Bank, both those that had never been issued and those that had come back from circulation. The bonfire was to be held in the public square of Vandalia, in the presence of the Governor and the judges of the Supreme Court. The offices of President of each of the branch banks were abolished, and the task of winding up the business of these offices entrusted to the Cashiers, but these officials were prohibited from accepting any more deposits and were required to take all steps necessary for the collection of the amounts due from the Bank's debtors. At intervals of six months, they were to send in to the Cashier of the principal bank all the bank notes received in repayment of loans, in order that these could be officially burned. Auditor's warrants, moreover, were to be received in payment of any debts due to the Bank and, when received, were to be exchanged at the Auditor's office for bank notes, which were to be burned along with those received by the Bank from its debtors. In addition, the Governor was authorized to appoint a competent accountant to make a thorough survey of the condition of the Bank.[52]

Five days after the act was approved, the first public holocaust occurred amid great rejoicing.[53] Notes with a face value of $75,000 were destroyed on this occasion, and smaller sums followed them into the flames at similar ceremonies held in June and December. By the end of the year, one-third of the original note issue had been retired from circulation, and the value of the notes in terms of specie had risen substantially.[54] The liquidation had commenced, and Governor Coles, who had a realistic knowledge of the problems involved as a result of his experiences in winding up the Bank of Edwardsville,

pressed it steadily forward during the rest of his administration.

At this singularly inappropriate moment, Ninian Edwards reappeared on the stage! Having lost most of his
political prestige through his irascibility and lack of common sense,[55] and a good deal of his money through the depression and the failure of the Bank at Edwardsville, he
decided, in the summer of 1826, to run for the office of
Governor of Illinois in order to vindicate himself before
posterity. It was an odd campaign of vituperation, in
which Edwards indicted the motives, and belittled the
ability, of everybody who had been prominent in Illinois
politics except himself! He criticized governors and legislators, and insisted that the State Bank had been deliberately mismanaged in the interests of the politicians who
had promoted and administered it. He was elected, by a
singularly narrow margin, over a very insignificant opponent, and the battle ground was transferred from the
hustings to the legislature, where Edwards appeared in
his gold-laced cloak,[56] with great pomp, to berate the officials of the Bank both individually and as a group.

Many of the things that Edwards said were true. The
most cursory examination of the Bank's history indicates
mismanagement so gross that it borders upon, and perhaps constitutes, criminal negligence. It is more than
probable, too, that some of the politicians associated with
the institution had not hesitated to do things that advanced their own fortunes at the expense of the general
welfare. But, once again, he repeated his mistakes of the
Crawford controversy, and defeated his own interests by
an excess of choler and a mass of pettifogging detail. He

had attacked so many prominent people that they combined in the pleasant task of vindicating one another and, out of all the legislative investigations[57] that Edwards instigated, there developed no more than a provision that no money should be paid out of the treasury to any officer of the state, in debt to the State Bank, who had not yet discharged his obligation.[58] For the rest, it was concluded that the records of the Bank officials did not justify "the belief that they acted corruptly and with bad faith in the management of said bank."

All this political recrimination retarded considerably the quiet process of liquidation that Governor Coles had so ably begun, and the antagonism between the Executive and the legislature during Edwards' administration further complicated matters. Nevertheless, a further step was taken in 1827[59] when the receipt of further deposits from the general public was prohibited, and the Bank was ordered to repay the small amount of private deposits then standing on its books. All promissory notes for amounts of less than $100 were to be placed in the hands of a justice of the peace for collection, and no expenses were to be paid by the Cashier during the period of liquidation without the specific authorization of the legislature. Moreover, it was provided by the same act that no more compensation should be paid to the President of the principal bank, while the annual salaries of the Cashiers were reduced to "five hundred state paper dollars" in the principal bank and "four hundred state paper dollars" in the case of the branches.

By the beginning of 1828, therefore, Illinois (like Indiana, Kentucky and Missouri) had no banks whatever in operation, while the process of liquidating the State Bank was retarded by the continuous agitation for the relief of debtors. In 1829, an act[60] was passed to facilitate the destruction of the notes; another act[61] abolished the office of Cashier of the principal bank, and required the incumbent of that office to turn over all his assets and records to the State Auditor and Treasurer, who were charged with the task of completing the liquidation. But James Duncan, the Cashier, who was thus discharged from office, seems to have disapproved of this law. He retained the books and assets of the Bank for more than two years, on the ground that the law abolishing his office did not provide for an audit to clear him of liability, so that a long course of legal and extralegal negotiation, culminating in three special acts of the legislature,[62] was necessary in order to persuade him to surrender them. Even when the legislature met in December, 1832, the auditors appointed to settle the matter had not completed their examination of his accounts.

Before we turn to the final act of the drama, however, it is important to consider briefly two collateral developments that are inextricably interwoven with the story of the liquidation: the fiscal policies of the state and the perennial problem of relief.

In some respects the public finance of Illinois was as fantastic as its banking policy. During the fiscal year 1821-22, before the State Bank had begun to complicate the problem, the state raised only $7,121, out of a total revenue of $60,000, from levies on resident taxpayers. Some $38,000 was received from taxes imposed on non-residents who owned land in the state, but the remainder,

comprising more than a quarter of the total revenue, represented the proceeds of the sale of land in Vandalia and
the rents received for the salines near Shawneetown.[63]
Such a program could scarcely be expected to provide the
increased revenue required to meet the additional disbursements called for by the increased salaries and growing extravagance that the inflationary policy had encouraged. To increase the taxes on residents was deemed
unwise, while it was difficult, if not impossible, to tax
nonresidents more heavily. The number of lots which
the state could sell at Vandalia was limited, and the profits
derived from the salines were being sharply reduced by
the import into Illinois of a higher grade of salt, so that
there was little chance of increasing the revenue derived
by the state from leasing them. In such circumstances, the
deficit was bound to grow continuously, and the Auditor's warrants, which were issued to finance it, augmented
the influence of the note issue in depreciating the value
of the currency. In view, however, of the fact that the state
government was primarily liable on both types of currency, it was bound to receive them at par in payment
of all obligations due to it, even when their value in the
market was as low as thirty cents on the dollar.[64]

The rest of the community showed no willingness to
receive the paper at par, even from the state. We have
already noticed the action of the legislators in raising salaries to offset the depreciation and, as early as 1824, in a
special act for the relief of John Kain, the legislature
provided that, if gold or silver were not available, payment should be made in notes of the Bank *"at their specie
value."*[65] Six weeks later, an even more significant step

was taken. It was decided that the state should pay out the paper money, under all appropriations, at its current market value, and the Auditor, Treasurer, Secretary of State and Cashier of the principal bank were constituted a committee for the purpose of deciding, on the first Monday of each month, the official rate at which such payments were to be made. Until they met, the rate was legally fixed at three dollars in bank notes or warrants for each dollar of specie.[66]

Such a policy was ruinous. The state was, in effect, paying for its banking folly by having to borrow money at an interest rate of 200 per cent, so that it was vitally interested in raising the value of the notes. The retirement and official incineration of a part of the issue was a step in the right direction; but the state was really on the horns of a dilemma, because its fiscal obligations compelled it to issue Auditor's warrants to an amount even greater than that of the notes destroyed. Short of increased taxation, on the one hand, or avowed bankruptcy and repudiation, on the other, there was no solution that would immediately solve the problem.

Slow improvement did, however, take place. Never again did the value of the paper sink to the low level of 1825 and, by the end of the following year, it had risen to more than 60 per cent of par. In February, 1827, therefore, the legislature provided that the official committee need only meet once a quarter. Moreover, the range of the committee's decision was greatly circumscribed. After June, 1827, the discount officially stated might not be more than $27\frac{1}{2}$ per cent, and this was to be reduced by at least $2\frac{1}{2}$ per cent each quarter, so that paper money would be paid out of the Treasury at par by March, 1830, at the latest.[67] Contrary to the usual experience with legislation of this kind, the mandate was actually enforced, largely because the work of liquidating the Bank was steadily continued during the period.

Both the fiscal problem and the liquidation of the Bank were, however, made more difficult by the pusillanimous attitude of the legislature regarding the payment of debts. The attitude of the state toward the relief of debtors has already been mentioned, and will crop up again on several subsequent pages, because it exercised a turbulent effect upon every financial problem that arose during the early history of the state. A complete history of the developments involved might well constitute a handbook of the way to discourage the payment of debts!*

Beginning as early as 1823, with a perfectly reasonable act for the relief of insolvent debtors,† the policy steadily went from bad to worse. In 1827, it was enacted[68] that property could not be seized without the consent of the debtor, if he was willing to give his bond for double the amount of the debt, while all debtors to the State Bank were confirmed in their right to renew their notes when due, provided that they were willing to pay back interest

* During these years the effect of legislation was aggravated, as far as enforcement of debts was concerned, by the fact that the State Bank, being in doubt as to the constitutionality of its existence, was reluctant to resort to legal action.

† *Laws of Illinois,* 1822-23, p. 169. Approved February 17, 1823. This act constitutes an interesting commentary on the economy of the period since it provides that, when the debtor's goods are seized under execution, he must be allowed to retain "a sufficiency of beds and bedding, wearing apparel . . . reasonable furniture . . . one spinning wheel, one milch cow and calf, one axe, four hogs, three sheep, one horse, harness and plough"—enough, in fact, to set up as a farmer and rehabilitate himself.

and the appropriate annual installments of 10 per cent of the principal.[69] Even if judgment had already been rendered, they might still recover their property on these terms.

In 1829, more relief was necessary. Everyone indebted to the Bank was allowed to pay his debt in three equal annual installments, the last of which was due on or before May 1, 1832; if the installments were paid before they were due, the debtor was not to be charged any interest whatever.[70] As a further inducement, any debtor who paid in full before September 1, 1829, was to have one-tenth of the principal, as well as all the interest, remitted. Two years later these privileges were again extended to the recalcitrant debtors. Anyone who paid the debt by May 1, 1832, even if he had not paid any previous installments, was not to be charged interest, and an additional rebate of 6 per cent of the principal was allowed if payment was received prior to December 1, 1831.[71] In 1833, it was provided that, if the debtor settled his account with the Bank on or before January 1, 1834, he should still be entitled to a rebate of all the interest and 10 per cent of the principal.[72] Moreover, if the debtor had died meanwhile and the courts considered that payment of the obligation would unduly distress his widow and family, it was provided that the debt might be entirely canceled. Finally, in 1835, the legislature tried to coax the remaining debtors to pay by remitting all interest and one-quarter of the principal, provided that they would undertake to pay the remainder in three equal annual installments![73]

The courts had, however, entered the picture long before this stage was reached.* At the very inception of the Bank, the judges of the Supreme Court of Illinois (sitting as members of the Council of Revision) had declared against the constitutionality of the charter, but in 1826, in the case of a debtor who wished to escape on that same plea of unconstitutionality, they evaded the issue. "Debtors of the bank can not raise the objection that the charter of the bank is a violation of the constitution. After having borrowed the paper of that institution, both public policy and common honesty require that the borrowers should repay it. *It is, therefore, unnecessary to decide whether the incorporation of the bank was a violation of the constitution or not.*"[74] Such evasion seems to have been deliberate in the light of subsequent events.

Three years later this position was modified somewhat, when the court decided that a debt due to the Bank was, in reality, a debt to the state, so that the state might release the debtor if it chose to do so,[75] but it was not until 1833, two years after the charter of the Bank had expired, that the court really faced the basic issue. In the interim, the Supreme Court of the United States had decided, in a masterly opinion by Marshall, that the notes issued by the Missouri Loan Office were bills of credit, and that any promissory note given for such bills as consideration was repugnant to the law and void.[76] The Illinois court felt bound (dare we say, reluctantly?) to follow the rule laid down in that case. It, therefore, reversed the earlier deci-

---

* This was true of many western states, and it should be pointed out that conditions in Illinois must have seemed almost ideal when compared with the chaos in Kentucky, where an insoluble financial problem led to a situation where two Supreme Courts were sitting at one time, each refusing to recognize the existence of the other. Cf. *History of Banking*, I, 128-137.

sion noticed above, and decided that the charter of the first State Bank of Illinois was in contravention of the Constitution of the United States, that the bank notes were nothing but bills of credit, and that promissory notes given in consideration of such bills were void, and could not be collected at law.[77] The most recalcitrant debtors, who had resisted the lure of rebates, did not have to pay anything at all in the end!

The unconstitutionality of the charter did not, however, absolve the state from its guarantee that the notes of the Bank would be redeemed in full during 1831. Each administration and legislature had carefully avoided this question but, for the session which met early in December, 1830, postponement was no longer possible. The notes had to be paid, or else repudiated by nonpayment.

The Bank itself was certainly in no position to pay off the notes. At the end of 1830, it still had on its books almost $100,000 of unpaid loans, and some $150,000 of its notes were still in circulation. To meet this liability the bank had on hand about $35,000 in cash, $20,000 of which stood to the credit of the state, but even if this was included it would still be necessary for the state to raise another $100,000 in order to pay off the outstanding notes.[78] The raising of such a sum was a perplexing problem. "The popularity-loving members of this legislature came up to the work with fear and trembling. They feared to be denounced as a band of perjured and faithless men if they neglected their duty, and they dreaded to meet the deep roar of indignant disapprobation from their angry constituents, by performing it."[79]

Under the strong leadership of Governor Reynolds,

however, the problem was squarely faced and, since it was obvious that the money could not be raised by taxation or conjured out of an empty treasury, an act was passed authorizing the Governor to borrow $100,000 by means of a sale of 6 per cent state stock.[80] In view of the urgency of the situation, the act further provided that the lender should be required to pay $20,000 "in specie or paper of the Bank of the United States and its branches" on or before February 10, 1831, and another $30,000 in similar funds prior to October 1. The remaining $50,000 which was also due on October 1, might be paid in "specie funds, state paper and Auditor's warrants." Repayment was to be made in specie, or notes of the Bank of the United States, after 1850.

Under the authority of this act, the Governor entered into negotiations with Samuel Wiggins, of Cincinnati, who appears to have been very much interested in the development of transportation facilities in Illinois and may, perhaps, have expected to improve his position as a result of the loan.[81] The funds were thus made available and the legislature promptly passed an act[82] "for finally closing the affairs of the State Bank of Illinois and branches." Cashiers of the branch banks were to vacate their offices and turn over all records to the State Treasurer, who would combine them with those of the principal office and conclude the liquidation. At the same time, lest bank notes should be presented for redemption more rapidly than funds became available from the Wiggins loan, it was provided that the Treasurer might issue 6 per cent state stock in exchange for the notes.[83] Such stock was to be redeemed at the discretion of the Treasurer whenever he had a surplus of funds on hand.

This courageous policy saved the reputation of the state. By the beginning of 1832, $289,000 of the notes had been redeemed and destroyed[84] and, by 1835, only $6,554.50 of the notes were still outstanding[85]—an amount that must have represented, in large part, the losses by destruction during the decade for which the notes had been in circulation.[86] "But the legislature was damned for all time to come. The members who voted for the law were struck with consternation and fear at the first sign of the public indignation. Instead of boldly defending their act and denouncing the unprincipled demagogues who were inflaming the minds of the people, these members, when they returned to their constituents, went meanly sneaking about like guilty things, making the most humble excuses and apologies. A bolder course by enlightening the public mind might have preserved the standing of the legislature and wrought a wholesome revolution of public opinion. . . . But as it was, the destruction of great men was noticeable for a great number of years."*

Thus ended the first State Bank of Illinois, even more dramatically than it had come into existence, and it is impossible to compute the aggregate loss imposed on the people by its miasmic influence. The loss of the State Treasury alone must have exceeded the $300,000 that the Bank originally supplied,[87] without allowing anything for

---

* Ford: op. cit., p. 107. Ford points out that the only other law in the history of Illinois which caused so much popular indignation was one which prohibited small bulls from running at large, in order to improve the breed of cattle. The populace sided with the small bulls!

the economic and social losses imposed on every member of the community by the debacle. William Kenney and others had suggested in response to Governor Edwards' allegations that the Bank was a "measure of relief" and should not be judged by ordinary financial standards,[88] but even by that criterion it cannot be regarded as anything but a blighting influence upon the economic development of the state.

REFERENCES FOR CHAPTER II

[1] Buck: *op. cit.,* pp. 286-291; Pease: *op. cit.,* p. 92.

[2] Pease: *op. cit.,* p. 52.

[3] *Idem,* pp. 4-5.

[4] Cf. *Niles',* XVI, 114-115, 390, and various other contemporary issues.

[5] *History of Banking,* I, 171.

[6] Dewey: *op. cit.,* pp. 10 and 55.

[7] *History of Banking,* I, pp. 95-108.

[8] *Ibid.,* I, 113-116.

[9] *Constitution of 1818,* Article VIII, Section 21; Buck: *op. cit.,* p. 283.

[10] *Sangamo Journal,* January 25, 1834; Dowrie: *op. cit.,* pp. 22-23.

[11] *Laws of Illinois,* 1819, pp. 151-157. Approved March 22, 1819.

[12] *Laws of Illinois,* 1819, p. 299. Approved March 27, 1819.

[13] *Illinois Emigrant,* March 20, 1819; Buck: *op. cit.,* pp. 151-152.

[14] *House Journal,* 1820-21, p. 227; *Edwardsville Spectator,* February 13 and March 20, 1821; Dowrie: *op. cit.,* pp. 24-25.

[15] *House Journal,* 1820-21, pp. 145-227.

[16] Cf. Pease: *op. cit.,* pp. 34-35; Buck: *op. cit.,* pp. 274-275.

[17] *House Journal,* 1820-21, p. 236; *Edwardsville Spectator,* February 13, 1821.

[18] *House Journal,* 1820-21, pp. 261 ff.

[19] *Laws of Illinois,* 1820-21, pp. 80-93; all the following details are taken from this Act unless other sources are stated.

[20] *Amending Act, Laws of Illinois,* 1820-21, p. 144. Approved February 12, 1821.

[21] *Amending Act, Laws of Illinois,* 1820-21, p. 144. Approved February 12, 1821.

[22] *Laws of Illinois,* 1820-21, p. 83, Section 8. This sum represented all the money that was actually paid by the state to start the bank.

[23] *Laws of Illinois,* 1820-21, p. 115. Approved February 8, 1821.

[24] *Laws of Illinois,* 1820-21, Appendix p. 188.

[25] Ford: *op. cit.,* p. 45.

[26] *Laws of Illinois,* 1820-21, p. 17. Approved January 16, 1821. This was reenacted in February as Section 27 of the Act incorporating the Bank, when the date was moved up to November 1, 1821.

[27] *Laws of Illinois,* 1820-21, pp. 90-91, Section 27.

[28] Pierce: *op. cit.,* p. 29.

[29] Ford: *op. cit.,* p. 47.

[30] *Edwardsville Spectator,* July 3, 1821 and August 14, 1821; Dowrie: *op. cit.,* p. 30; Pease: *op. cit.,* p. 59.

[31] *Hunt's Merchants' Magazine,* XI, 244.

[32] *Bankers Magazine,* IX, 12; Dowrie: *op. cit.,* p. 31.

[33] *Chicago American,* December 25, 1840 (Lecture by W. H. Brown before the Chicago Lyceum); Dowrie: *op. cit.,* p. 31; Ford: *op. cit.,* p. 46.

[34] Ford: *op. cit.,* p. 47.

[35] An excellent discussion of this problem by Dowrie (*op. cit.,* pp. 32-34) has been drawn on in this and the following paragraphs.

[36] *Illinois Intelligencer,* March 29, 1823.

[37] *Bankers Magazine,* IX, 12.

[38] *Illinois Intelligencer,* June 17, 1825.

[39] *Edwardsville Spectator,* December 11, 1821.

[40] Ford: *op. cit.,* p. 47.

[41] *Idem,* pp. 311-312.

[42] *Senate Journal,* 1826-27, p. 54; Pease: *op. cit.,* p. 61.

[43] *Laws of Illinois,* 1822-23, Appendix pp. 222-228.

[44] *Laws of Illinois,* 1822-23, pp. 163-167. Approved February 17, 1823.

[45] *Illinois Intelligencer,* January 4, 1823; Dowrie: *op. cit.,* pp. 34-35; Pease: *op. cit.,* p. 58.

[46] *House Journal,* 1822-23, p. 108; *Illinois Intelligencer,* January 11, 1823.

[47] *Laws of Illinois,* 1822-23, pp. 180-181. Approved February 18, 1923.

[48] *Governor's Message, 1824, House Journal,* 1824-25.

[49] *Laws of Illinois,* 1824-25, p. 16. Approved December 16, 1824. See also the Act approved on January 15, 1825, p. 120.

[50] *House Journal,* 1824-25, p. 203; *Senate Journal,* 1824-25; Knox: *History of Banking,* pp. 716-717.

[51] *Laws of Illinois,* 1824-25, pp. 82-85. Approved January 10, 1825.

[52] *Laws of Illinois,* 1824-25. Appendix p. 185.

[53] *Illinois Intelligencer,* January 21, 1825.

[54] *Illinois Intelligencer,* June 24, 1825; *Chicago American,* December 25, 1840 (Lecture by W. H. Brown); *Niles,* XXIX, 326, 369; Dowrie: *op. cit.,* p. 39.

[55] Cf. Pease: *op. cit.,* pp. 92-113.

[56] Ford: *op. cit.,* p. 64.

[57] Cf. *House Journal* 1826-27, pp. 409-595, *passim.*

[58] *Laws of Illinois,* 1826, p. 72. Approved January 25, 1826.

[59] *Laws of Illinois,* 1826-27, pp. 377-378. Approved February 13, 1827.

[60] *Revised Code of Laws of Illinois,* 1828-29, p. 165. Approved January 2, 1829.

[61] *Idem,* p. 166. Approved January 23, 1829.

[62] *Laws of Illinois,* 1830-31, pp. 178-79. (Approved February 1, 1831); p. 180 (Approved February 16, 1831).

[63] Cf. Pease: *op. cit.,* p. 62.

[64] Cf. *Laws of Illinois,* 1826-27, section 30 (Approved February 19, 1827) where this fact is reiterated.

[65] *Laws of Illinois,* 1824-25, p. 4. Approved December 7, 1824.

[66] *Laws of Illinois,* 1824-25, pp. 179-182. Approved January 18, 1825.

[67] *Laws of Illinois,* 1826-27, p. 81. Approved February 19, 1827.

[68] *Laws of Illinois,* 1826-27, p. 349. Approved January 29, 1827.

[69] *Laws of Illinois,* 1826-27, p. 376. Approved February 15, 1827.

[70] *Revised Code, Laws of Illinois,* 1828, pp. 166-169. Approved January 23, 1829.

[71] *Laws of Illinois,* 1830, pp. 182-185. Approved February 15, 1831.

[72] *Laws of Illinois,* 1832-33, p. 584. Approved February 25, 1833.

[73] *Laws of Illinois,* 1834-35, p. 67. Approved February 14, 1835. It should be pointed out that these debts were no longer collectible at law—so that there was no reason why the debtor should even pay 75 per cent of the principal.

[74] *Snyder v. President and Directors of the State Bank,* I Breese 161.

[75] *Administrators of Ferdinand Ernst, deceased v. Mary Ann Ernst,* I Breese 316.

[76] *Craig, et alia v. The State of Missouri,* 4 Peters 410. This opinion was handed down by a bare majority. When Banks of the State were subsequently held to be constitutional in *Briscoe v. The Bank of the Commonwealth of Kentucky* (8 Peters 118) an elaborate effort was made to distinguish between two situations that were almost identical from a financial viewpoint, and if they differed at all the Illinois situation was more closely allied to the problem dealt with in the Briscoe case than to that in the Craig decision.

[77] *Linn v. President and Directors of the State Bank,* I Scammon 87.

[78] Cf. *Report of the State Treasurer, January 1, 1831, Senate Journal,* 1830-31, pp. 181-183.

[79] Ford: *op. cit.,* p. 107.

[80] *Laws of Illinois*, 1830-31, p. 92-94. Approved January 27, 1831.

[81] Cf. *Laws of Illinois*, 1830-31, p. 22 (*An Act to authorise Samuel Wiggins to build a toll bridge across the Kaskaskia River*) and *Laws of Illinois*, 1830-31, p. 78 (*An Act relating to Wiggin's Ferry on the Mississippi*).

[82] *Laws of Illinois*, 1830-31, pp. 182-185. Approved February 15, 1831.

[83] *Laws of Illinois*, 1830-31, p. 181. Approved February 15, 1831.

[84] *Senate Journal*, 1832-33, p. 240.

[85] *Idem*, 1834-35, p. 295.

[86] The liquidation of the bank's "assets" was not so successful. In 1835 there were still outstanding more than $100,000 of unpaid loans, but the Treasurer of the State estimated that only seven or eight thousand dollars would be realized. Cf. Dowrie: *op. cit.*, pp. 56-58 for an account of the final collections, which were not far from this estimate.

[87] Cf. Ford: *op. cit.*, p. 48.

[88] *Illinois Intelligencer*, February 3, 1827; Pease: *op. cit.*, p. 58.

CHAPTER III

CHICAGO EMERGES

1831–1837

CHICAGO played no part in the activities by means of which the first State Bank of Illinois was setting the stage for the city's debut. The community nestling around the new Fort Dearborn was far from stagnant, however, and, to anyone who studied it closely, there was already apparent that upward thrust of economic forces which, in a few years, was to make the name of Chicago familiar to millions who had never been within a thousand miles of Lake Michigan. Out of the frontier settlement of 1821, where a few factors of the American Fur Company traded with the Winnebagos and Potawatomis, there was to emerge the incorporated city of 1837 which, in many ways, served as the focal point of a nationwide fever of land speculation.

During the earlier years of that short period, there was little perceptible expansion. In 1830, when Chicago first attained specific geographical existence through the town plat prepared by John Thompson,[1] the area of the town was only three-eighths of a square mile and its population numbered no more than fifty souls. Nor did the land sale that was held to defray the costs of the survey offer any foreshadowing of the events that were to march so swiftly across the page of history during the next ten years. Choice lots, in what is now the heart of the business district, sold for between five and twenty dollars each.[2]

If further proof were needed that Chicago in these years was nothing but a frontier village, the Black Hawk War provided it. The modest size of the population and the simplicity of domestic life are both evidenced by the haste with which the panic-stricken folk from Chicago and all the surrounding country took refuge in the abandoned fort at the first sign of Indian hostilities, and by the even greater haste with which these same people took to the woods when General Scott arrived with his cholera-infected troops.[3] Yet, in a sense, that last Indian foray may be said to mark the final emergence of the city into the economic life of the modern world. For the first time, Chicago found effective advertisement. As the soldiers returned home from the campaign, which had taken them across the open prairies of Illinois and Wisconsin, their tales fired the imagination of many an easterner and persuaded him to seek his fortune in the bounteous west. Moreover, when he decided to do so, he found that the difficulties of transportation were much less than they had been a decade earlier. No longer was it necessary for him to travel laboriously by wagon train, or to take the interminable route by way of New Orleans and the Mississippi. The opening of the Erie Canal, in 1825, and of the Oswego Canal four years later, had provided a continuous water route from New York, through the Great Lakes, to the west, and Chicago was the logical terminus of that route for all who wished to settle in Illinois. As a further facility, and a protection against the ever-present danger of transportation monopoly, the Welland Canal was also developed in 1829.

In August, 1833, less than a year after the close of the Black Hawk War, Chicago became an incorporated village with a population that had already increased to three hundred and fifty. A month later, when it acted as host to the vast council of Indians, who gathered to negotiate a treaty ceding to the United States all of the lands east of the Mississippi, Chicago was celebrating the end of its existence as a frontier village of Indian barter.[4] Henceforth it was to take its place as an outpost of the steadily advancing machine civilization of the nineteenth century and, within two years, the *Chicago American* was proudly advertising the growth of the business district. "There are now upward of 50 business houses, 4 large forwarding houses, 8 taverns, 2 printing offices, 2 book stores, 1 steam sawmill, 1 brewery, 1 furnace, and 25 mechanics' shops of all kinds"—a goodly evidence of infant industries as well as of the steady commercial development.[5]

Such changes in the status of the city were bound to raise serious economic problems, particularly in matters of transportation, and among the most important of these was the Illinois and Michigan Canal. Perhaps no other single factor played so significant a part in the first decade of the city's development, yet the Canal itself was not new. The very site of Chicago had been chosen for settlement because of the portage from the Chicago River to the headwaters of the Illinois River, which had opened up the whole Mississippi valley to the French fur traders coming down from Canada. As early as 1673, Joliet had pointed out the tremendous saving of time and labor that would be achieved by a canal uniting the waters of the two rivers.[6]

For reasons of strategy as well as of commerce, Gallatin included the Canal in his program of internal improvements drawn up in 1808, and six years later Madison recommended the project to Congress.[7] In 1816, the United States purchased from the Indians the land along the proposed route of the Canal, and conducted a survey the following year, so that there is nothing surprising in the fact that Governor Bond, in his first inaugural message to the newly created State of Illinois, should have recommended immediate consideration of the project.[8] In 1821, the legislature followed his advice by appropriating $10,-000 for a survey of the Canal route and when, in the following year, Congress authorized the state to take possession of a strip of land, ninety feet wide, between the two rivers, a Board of Canal Commissioners was appointed to undertake the preliminary study that was necessary.

In 1825, the legislature apparently decided to permit the construction and operation of the Canal by a private corporation, granting a charter to the Illinois and Michigan Canal Company for that purpose,[9] but public fears of monopoly, and political hopes that federal aid would be obtained if the Canal were constructed by the state, led to a prompt reversal of this policy. The charter was repealed[10] at the special session in 1826, and the legislature brazenly appealed to Congress for federal assistance. Despite the opposition of New Orleans and other southern Mississippi interests, Congress acted favorably on this request.[11] Illinois received alternate sections of land, five

miles deep, on each side of the Canal, subject to the condition that work should be commenced within five years
and completed within twenty years of the passage of the
act and, in 1829, the legislature authorized the Governor
to appoint three Canal Commissioners to undertake the
work[12] on the basis of funds received from the sale of
these lands. The emergence of Chicago as an economic
center was, therefore, closely related to the final effort to
realize the ancient dream of the Canal. "The Canal made
Chicago. . . . The first plat of Chicago was made by the
Canal Commissioners; the first sale of lots in Chicago was
made by the Canal Commissioners. Chicago was made by
the Canal as clearly and positively as western towns have
been made . . . by the advent of railroads."[13]

The repeated delays which the construction of the
Canal encountered during the first quarter of the nineteenth century, in spite of the manifest enthusiasm, calls
attention vividly to the problems raised by the scarcity of
capital. Chicago, like most other rapidly growing communities, did not possess the capital necessary to finance
its own development and was eager to obtain funds from
any source that offered them.[14] Money was borrowed from
eastern capitalists on the security of real-estate mortgages,
trade was financed on long credits by embryo bankers like
Gurdon Hubbard, loans were obtained from eastern
banks that wished to circulate their notes at a distance—
but all these sources together did not provide capital
funds adequate to finance the many ambitious schemes
that were afoot in the new community. Finance was the
factor that governed the rate, if not the direction, of the
community's growth, and it offers the only helpful clue

by which to unravel the tangled skein of Chicago's early
story.

If the thirties of the last century had been a period of
economic stability and monetary soundness in the United
States, the early history of Chicago would have been very
different. The development of the city would unquestionably have been slower, and its economic importance
would not have impressed the world so quickly, but the
process would have been much less painful for those who
were most intimately associated with it. Such ideas are
purely speculative, however, for the whole nation was on
the verge of financial controversy, sometimes bordering
on chaos, at the very moment when Chicago came upon
the stage. The inflationary traditions of Illinois, and the
impact of Jacksonian democracy on the financial system
of the nation, were destined to combine in producing all
the phantasmagoria of feverish boom and black depression before the city was ten years old.

By 1830, the financial position of the United States was
unusually good. The Bank of the United States had recovered from its first frenzy of speculative intoxication
and was operating efficiently and profitably.* Many of
the weaker and less desirable state banks had been eliminated by the painful process of failure, during the panic
of 1825, and the policies of the national bank (reinforced
by local developments in such areas as New England and
New York) had succeeded in restoring parity among the
notes of those that were still in operation. Business was

* In qualification of this statement, it should be pointed out that the Bank
had begun the use of branch drafts which, although sound at this time, were
later to degenerate into the "race-horse bills" that caused so much of the subsequent trouble. Cf. *History of Banking*, I, 186-187.

becoming prosperous, employment was plentiful and trade was increasing.

Jacksonian democracy had, however, already taken its place on the stage of American politics. The extension of the franchise in one state after another, whether wise or unwise from the political angle, placed a vote in the hands of many people who were even less familiar with financial problems than the older group of propertied electors. The direct election of the President gave him a mandate from these voters which was not refined and emasculated in the political maneuvering of a Congressional caucus, and Jackson was preeminently the kind of man who was willing to accept, and eager to exploit, such a mandate. Moreover, the Democratic party had not yet come under the domination of the wealthy slaveowners of the southern states. It was the party of the worker and the western farmer, fundamentally opposed to "monopolistic privileges of exploitation" and firm in the belief that Blair set at the head of his Democratic *Washington Globe*: "The world is too much governed."

The Bank of the United States, as the largest corporation in the country and the obvious possessor of semi-monopolistic privileges, could scarcely have expected to be looked upon with favor by Jackson, whose first annual message contained veiled threats against its continued existence.[15] But those threats might not have become actualities had it not been for two coincidental developments. In the first place, many of the state bankers hated the Bank of the United States quite as much as Jackson did and, as "bank democrats," eagerly supported every move of the Administration to cripple, and finally de-

stroy, that institution. In the second place, the Bank itself, under the brilliant, but unreliable, management of
Nicholas Biddle, played into the hands of its enemies by
unsound financial policies and unwise political operations.[16]

Before public discussion of the inaugural address had
died down, the first skirmishes of the battle were fought.
Senator Woodbury alleged that the manager of the branch
at Portsmouth was a brusque man and a Whig, both important defects of character from the viewpoint of a
somewhat pompous Democratic Senator.[17] In August,
1829, the Secretary of War tried, unsuccessfully, to deprive the Bank of its work in handling pensions while, in
October, during the exchange of argumentative letters
that Biddle's literary enthusiasm encouraged, the Secretary of the Treasury referred for the first time to his
power to discipline the Bank by removing from it all
government deposits.[18]

Up to this point, the controversy was not really serious.
Biddle, to be sure, had written too many letters, but no
great harm had been done. But, in the light of the situation revealed by these preliminary encounters, it is obvious that the policy of the Bank during the next few years
was suicidal. When Clay was nominated, as the Whig
candidate, for the Presidency of the United States, in
December, 1831, he insisted on making the renewal of
the Bank charter a central part of his platform, and the
Bank frankly and fully allied itself with his cause. Jackson, in his annual message to Congress during the following month, retaliated by questioning the solvency of the
Bank, and suggested that the government deposits might

be in danger. Unfortunately, the allegation, although exaggerated, was not without some foundation of truth. The inflationary policies of the Bank at this period, as Gallatin points out, had placed it in a position where it could not control the currency[19] and "a mass of accommodation bills were chasing each other from branch to branch."[20] Although Congressional committees reported that the public deposits were in no danger, it is apparent that serious questions could be raised regarding the management of the Bank. Yet the Bank gave no consideration to that problem: it retorted politically by memorializing Congress for a renewal of its charter, and Biddle foolishly went down to Washington to set up offices from which he directed the Congressional campaign to that end.

Such action would have been unwise in any circumstances but it was sheer madness at that moment, in view of both Jackson's temperament and the condition of the Bank. Although both houses reported favorably on the petition of the Bank, the Committee of Investigation appointed by the House of Representatives, in February, 1832, brought in no less than three separate reports, and the most impartial of them (signed by John Quincy Adams alone) was highly critical of the Bank's financial policies in several respects.[21] The Bank did not have clean hands, and although both houses of Congress, in pursuance of Clay's political strategy, were persuaded to pass, during the summer of 1832, a bill rechartering the institution, Jackson showed no hesitation in vetoing the measure.

Since the Whigs were not strong enough to pass it over the veto, the question of the charter became one of the central points at issue in the campaign between Clay and Jackson, with the Bank eagerly supporting its defender. The tremendous victory of Jackson might, therefore, be regarded as a mandate for the destruction of the Bank and, in the cold retrospect of history, the Bank was as much responsible for that event as were the antibank demagogues. Moreover, Biddle showed no signs of learning anything from experience. Although Jackson ordered the public deposits to be withdrawn from the Bank in September, 1833, it is possible that a well-managed and conservative institution might have won sufficient public support to obtain a new charter at a later date. Already there were evidences that Jackson was losing his hold on the more conservative members of his party. But Biddle chose, first, to exacerbate public feeling by adopting policies of credit contraction, which caused undue stringency throughout the money market in 1833, and then, equally unreasonably, to indulge in flights of inflationary frenzy that went even further in the opposite direction. If he had wished to convince the public that the Bank was an unreliable institution, operated with no thought of the public welfare, he could not have selected a course of action more appropriate to that end.

In spite of the spasmodic unwisdom of its policies, the second Bank of the United States had, however, been national in its scope. At its best, it had coordinated the various regions of the country into one financial system, facilitating the movement of funds and providing a currency that circulated everywhere at, or near, a parity with specie. As it declined, there grew up a host of state banks, eagerly competing with one another for the gov-

ernment deposits that were withdrawn from the Bank of
the United States. Between 1829 and 1836, the number of
banks in the country doubled, the total quantity of notes
in circulation increased by 150 per cent and the total
volume of loans made by the banks almost quadrupled.[22]
Moreover the rate of increase was as great in the conservative east as in the supposedly radical west. In New
England, 90 new banks were chartered between 1831 and
1833, of which 45 were in Massachusetts alone, while, in
1835 and 1836, the latter state created 32 additional
banks! A banking mania gripped the whole country.

These new banks, when they received government
funds, were informed by the Secretary of the Treasury
that "the deposits of public money will enable you to afford increased facilities to commerce, and to extend your
accommodations to individuals," a frank invitation to
adopt a generous policy of credit expansion that the banks
were only too delighted to accept. "The Executive had
resumed the control of the public money which belonged
to him before the national bank was chartered."[23] To the
uninitiated layman, however, the evidences of control
were not very obvious, save in the case of a few states in
which the authorities enacted measures of restraint.[24]
Banking operations all over the country expanded at a
phenomenal rate. In the case of a Philadelphia bank "a
system of prodigality in loaning . . . was commenced,
which baffles the conception of sober and reflecting
minds";[25] in New York four persons who were found
manufacturing notes in a small room insisted indignantly
(and truthfully!) that they were not counterfeiters but
officers of a properly incorporated bank;[26] while, in

Michigan the currency was said to consist of three kinds, red dog, wildcat and catamount.* "Of the best quality it is said that it takes five pecks to make a bushel."[27] Money, of a kind, was more plentiful than it had been at any time since the days of the continental currency.

To expect that Illinois would escape from the epidemic that was sweeping the country would be unreasonable, particularly in view of the fact that capital was scarce in the growing state and that the citizens customarily regarded money and capital as synonymous terms. In view of the painful experience with the first State Bank of Illinois, and of the storm of indignation aroused by the Wiggins loan that permitted its liquidation, the Jacksonian Democrats of the state hated all banks as enthusiastically as their colleagues in the east hated the Bank of the United States. The Whigs, to be sure, introduced bills for the creation of new banks, both in the session of 1830-31 and in that of 1832-33,[28] but they were defeated on both occasions. It is significant, however, that the measure presented in 1833 was lost by only one vote,[29] and during that year the newspapers were taking up the discussion of banking with increasing frequency.[30]

Reasons for such a gradual change of public opinion are not hard to find. By 1834, Illinois had recovered from the depression precipitated by the breakdown of the first State Bank, and was already sharing in the general business recovery that characterized the country as a whole.

* These terms, which are admirably expressive of the familiar disdain with which the public regarded the bank notes, all indicate the rural character of the place of redemption. Banking offices were set up so far away from civilization that wildcats were their only neighbors. In some cases, of which "red dog" is one, the nickname arose from some striking aspect of the printing that covered the face of the note.

Indeed, her share of prosperity was unusually large, in proportion to the size of the state, since the heavy surge of westward immigration, which was destined to settle the northern and central sections of Illinois during the decade, had already begun. But this resurgence of economic activity emphasized anew the financial problems to which attention has already been called. There was an inadequacy of real capital, and there was also a scarcity of hand-to-hand currency for the purpose of facilitating the exchange of goods and services. "Aside from a few notes of the Bank of the United States and still fewer United States silver coins, Spanish, French and Mexican pieces constituted the only generally acceptable medium of exchange"[31] within the State of Illinois prior to the deluge of paper money that poured out of the newly created banks.

If Illinois should charter a new bank, it would certainly provide a domestic currency, and it might even do something to augment the supply of capital. Moreover, theoretical arguments were reinforced by the enthusiastic examples furnished by other states. Even Kentucky appeared to have forgotten, by 1831, the political and economic chaos precipitated by the failure of the old Bank of the Commonwealth and was engaged in the creation of a new, and greater, institution on the same model. If Illinois did not establish banks of her own, the state would be flooded with the notes of banks chartered elsewhere, notes that differed vastly from one another in quality yet tended, in almost every case, to inflict loss upon anyone who received and held them. Moreover, even in Washington, it was feared that, unless banks were

chartered by the states, the country might suffer from a
credit stringency when the charter of the second Bank of
the United States expired, and "from this, very many
Democrats inferred it to be the wish of Gen. Jackson's
administration, that State banks should be created where
they did not exist."[32]

The political significance of the banking question in
Illinois, by the end of 1834, is amply apparent from the
fact that both the outgoing and the incoming Governor referred to it in their messages to the legislature. Reynolds,
in his valedictory, suggested that a bank should be set up
that was based solidly upon gold and silver specie, in
order to avoid the fiasco of the earlier experiment,[33] but
Duncan was even more cautious on the following day, and
attempted to inspire the legislature with his own caution.
Admitting the usefulness of banks when their policies
were appropriate to the economic structure of the society
in which they operated, he suggested that careful study
and consideration were essential if a bank were to be developed capable of functioning soundly in the peculiar
frontier conditions of a state like Illinois.[34]

Gubernatorial suggestions, however, have seldom received much consideration from the Illinois legislature,
and this occasion was no exception to the rule. A banking
bill was immediately taken up for discussion, and passed
by both houses in a very short space of time, without any
of the careful study that Governor Duncan had recommended. There is evidence, however, that its passage was
more of a tribute to the political ability of its sponsors
than to a genuine change of sentiment on the part of the
legislators. One member of the Senate, who was bitterly

hostile to all banks, as he declared from his place in the Senate, gave the bank charter his hearty support on condition that his colleagues would pass a law imposing a tax on lands in the military tract* to finance the construction of roads; and a member of the House supported it because the bank sponsors made him a State's Attorney.[35] Perhaps, too, there is unconscious irony in the fact that, two days after the passage of the new bank bill, the legislature passed the act remitting all interest and 25 per cent of the principal to the recalcitrant debtors of the first State Bank.[36]

In the Council of Revision the new law received better treatment than its predecessor. Governor Duncan opposed it strongly, but the judges of the Supreme Court gave it their benediction and it was approved February 12, 1835. To understand this decision it must be remembered that the act[37] by which "the President, Directors and Company of the Bank of the State of Illinois" were incorporated differs in several important respects from the legislation of 1821. The Bank was to last until January 1, 1860, with its head office at Springfield and six† branches at such places as the directors should select. The capital of $1,500,000 was all to be subscribed by the general public, with the exception of $100,000 which was reserved for the state if the legislature at any time should wish to subscribe, and there was the usual provision that $10 on each $100 share should be paid in specie at the time of subscription, while the rest was subject to call by

* This was largely owned by nonresidents, while the roads benefited the residents!

† The number of branches was raised to nine a year later. One branch had to be at Vandalia, the state capital until 1839.

the directors. The Bank might legally commence business when $250,000 had been received in specie and, in the event that the business of the Bank developed to a point where additional capital was necessary, the directors were authorized to issue another $1,000,000 of stock to the public whenever they saw fit.

In view of the contemporary enthusiasm for banks, the charter made elaborate provisions for the allotment of stock in the case of a possible oversubscription on the part of the public. Subscriptions received from nonresidents were to be eliminated first, then those received from corporations, and, if these steps did not reduce the aggregate amount of the subscriptions to $1,400,000, all subscriptions for amounts of more than $1,000 were to be reduced to that figure. If there was still an excess after these steps had been taken, all subscriptions were to be reduced proportionately by an amount sufficient to bring the total down to the amount of stock available. Obviously the act was intended to provide for a wide distribution of ownership among residents in the state, so that no small group could obtain control of the institution.

The same ideal is apparent in the provisions governing the voting rights of stock. The shareholder was to have, "for each and every share, not exceeding four shares, one vote; for every two shares above four and not exceeding thirty, one vote; for every four shares above thirty and not exceeding ninety, one vote; for every six shares above ninety and not exceeding one hundred and fifty, one vote; and for every ten shares above one hundred and fifty, one vote."[38] In no case could any person, partnership or corporation cast more than 100 votes as a stockholder.

The management of the Bank was entrusted to nine directors, all of whom were required to be citizens of Illinois, elected annually in the above manner, provided that, if the state should at any time see fit to subscribe to the $100,000 of stock reserved for it, the Governor should have the right to enlarge the board by appointing two additional directors to represent the interests of the state. The directors, in their turn, were to elect the President and Cashier, and to decide upon the duties and remuneration of all subordinate officers of the Bank.

In regard to the operations of the institution, the charter indicates a considerable development of legislative thought on the subject of banking and the relevant provisions have an almost modern sound. The Bank was empowered "to carry on the business of banking, by discounting bills, notes and other evidences of debt, by receiving deposites, and making all other contracts involving the interest or uses of money; by buying or selling gold and silver bullion, foreign coins and bills of exchange, by issuing bills, notes or other evidences of debt, and by exercising such other incidental powers as shall be necessary to carry on all such business."[39] It was prohibited from holding real estate, except that which was necessary for its business or had been taken as security for loans, and the latter was to be put up for sale at least once a year and disposed of as soon as a price was offered that covered the principal and interest of the loan due to the bank. In no case was the Bank to trade, "directly or indirectly," in any goods or merchandise.

Similarly, in regard to the notes to be issued by the Bank, Illinois had learned much from experience. This time there was no guarantee by the state, but there were important restrictions designed to maintain both the convertibility of the notes and their value. The total amount of notes in circulation was never to exceed two and a half times the paid-in capital, and the maximum set for loans was three times the paid-in capital. Each director was personally liable to the noteholder if these limits were transgressed. Moreover, the notes were to be redeemable in specie at all times and, if the Bank failed to redeem any note within ten days of presentation, it was to forfeit its charter and go into liquidation. Even beyond all this, the legislators showed a degree of wisdom that, in the light of the experience with the first State Bank of Illinois, is as unexpected as it is commendable. Section 31 of the act provided that "The Legislature of this State shall never pass any law retarding, obstructing, staying, protracting, or in any wise suspending the collection of any debt or debts due the said Bank." The laws for the relief of debtors which had made a fantastic mockery of the first State Bank were not to be repeated!

In the light of contemporary standards, this was a good charter and, when the books were opened for subscription to the capital stock on April 10, 1835,[40] the auguries for the future of the Bank were bright. The response of the public was immediate and enthusiastic. Within a few weeks subscriptions aggregating more than $8,000,000[41] had poured into the office at Springfield, and commissioners were confronted with the task of allotting the stock in accordance with the elaborate provisions of the act. But, at this point, trouble began. Early in the spring of 1835, a group of prominent citizens of Illinois, together with Samuel Wiggins of Cincinnati, had arranged to secure control of the Bank by the simple process of borrowing large sums of money in New York and Connecticut to finance the purchase of substantial blocks of stock. In order to get around the allotment provisions of the charter, they had employed large numbers of people in Illinois to subscribe for stock, in their own names, transferring the stock to the financial group after it had been allotted. "Many thousands of such subscriptions were made, in the names of as many thousands who never dreamed of being bankers, and who do not know to this day that they were ever, apparently, the owners of bank stock."[42]

All this could not go on without the knowledge of the commissioners who were appointed to receive the subscriptions, particularly in view of the fact that a battle for the control of the Bank broke out, even before the stock had been allotted, between two factions of the financial coterie. Arrayed against the group headed by Judge Smith, who had been bitterly criticized by Ninian Edwards a few years before in connection with the mismanagement of the first Bank of the State, were the combined forces of Samuel Wiggins, Thomas Mather, and Godfrey, Gilmore & Co.,* and it became evident at an early stage that the latter group was the more powerful. A motion to go behind the subscription blanks, in order to facilitate allotment to persons subscribing on their own account,

* An Alton firm of commission merchants which will appear again in connection with the subsequent wrecking of the Bank.

was supported by Judge Smith, but effectively defeated
by the opposing interests.

As a result, the Bank was not owned in Illinois, nor
was its stock widely scattered in small holdings. Of the
14,000 shares offered, sixteen persons controlled a total
of 11,487 shares. While the largest individual shareholder,
controlling 2,567 shares, did live in Illinois, the Cincinnati group headed by Samuel Wiggins controlled 3,421.[43]
The first breach had been made in the ideals set forth by
the charter.

As soon as the stock was allotted, the directors were
elected, and even Ford, who had no love for the Bank,
admits that these were thoroughly competent men.[44] The
directors, in turn, elected Thomas Mather as President
of the Bank, and N. J. Ridgeley, from the Bank of the
United States, as Cashier. In July, 1835, having received
the necessary $250,000 in specie, the institution opened
the doors of its head office at Springfield and, during the
next eight months, branches were established at Alton,
Belleville, Chicago, Danville, Galena, Jacksonville,
Mount Carmel, Quincy and Vandalia. For the administration of these establishments the directors found it necessary to appoint thirty-five officers with annual salaries
amounting to $30,600,[45] a substantial overhead for a bank
at that time. In addition, local inspectors were appointed
in various parts of the state for the purpose of appraising
real estate offered as security for loans and generally
supervising the use of the property after the loan had
been granted.[46]

Almost as soon as operations began, the stock went to
a premium, rising gradually to a high point of 113 in

December, and this rise was quite as much due to the sound management of the Bank as to the general enthusiasm for banks that Illinois was beginning to share with the rest of the country.[47] An exchange committee was established, consisting of the President and Cashier, as permanent members, with two of the directors elected for periods of one month at a time, and this committee met daily for the purpose of considering loans and discounts. As a general practice, the decisions of the committee were laid before the fortnightly meetings of the full board for confirmation.

As to the type of operations, real-estate loans naturally played a substantial part, in view of the general economic condition of the state at that time, but the statements of the Bank indicate that it also granted a substantial number of loans to finance current business activity which were either secured by merchandise or based on the general credit standing of the borrower. Such mercantile loans, however, often remained outstanding as long as those based on real property, since the delays that were imposed by imperfect transport tended to retard the rate of business turnover considerably.[48] As a result, particularly during the initial period of the Bank's operation, there was a distinct preference on the part of the exchange committee for bills of exchange arising out of actual trade, which was defended on the ground that an efficient domestic exchange market was of considerable importance to Illinois in the light of the fact that most of its exports moved southward down the Mississippi while most of its imports came from the eastern seaboard. In addition, it was clearly recognized that first-class bills of exchange were more liquid and certain of payment than local accommodation paper. "Payment of a bill of exchange was thrown to a distant point, and aid was thus given by banks other than that to which the bills belonged or at which they originated, while in the payment of ordinary notes custom had come to require whatever indulgence the bank could give."[49]

Such a philosophy of banking accorded well with the best ideas that were being brought to the surface at that time by the controversy between the Banking and Currency Schools, in both England and the United States, but the directors of the second State Bank of Illinois appear to have pushed the doctrine a little too far in one direction. They were right in the assumption that a portfolio of bills would enable them to obtain specie much more readily than would be possible if they held nothing but accommodation notes, but at times they appear to have thought that bills and specie were *instantaneously* interchangeable. On many occasions, their specie reserves were unpleasantly low in periods of emergency. Since they were determined, at all costs, to prevent any depreciation of the Bank's notes, this dearth of specie reserves forced them at times to take rather unusual steps to discourage redemption. On two occasions, funds were sent to distant points to purchase notes of the Bank that had fallen to a discount, and on one occasion the Bank suspended operations for several days while waiting for the arrival of a consignment of specie from New Orleans. At all times, moreover, the presentation of notes for redemption was somewhat discouraged by the provision that notes could be redeemed only at the branch from

which they had been issued, and not at any other branches
of the Bank.

In one respect, however, the Bank was less happy during its early months of operation. At the time at which it
was chartered, there was general expectation that it
would become a depository of the federal government,
bringing substantial quantities of funds into the state,
and Mather took the matter up with the Treasury on the
very day on which the bank act was passed.[50] The request was endorsed by Senator Kane, Judge Smith and
other men prominent in Illinois politics, but Secretary
of the Treasury Woodbury showed no enthusiasm in
response.

At first, he suggested that the matter could wait until
the Bank was in operation; then he professed ignorance
of the financial standing of the men behind the Bank;
still later he excused himself on the ground that there
was little need for a government depository in an unde-
veloped territory such as Illinois then was. Through all
these delays, Mather refused to be discouraged. He continued an interminable correspondence with Woodbury,
and dealt specifically with each of the points raised by the
latter, but the task was hopeless in view of the fact that
the Jacksonian Democrats of Illinois were using every
effort they could exert in Washington to discourage the
administration from putting money into a bank which,
they insisted, was entirely in the hands of Whigs. It was
the story of the second Bank of the United States repeating itself.

In a last, almost desperate, effort to persuade the federal government, the directors of the Bank sent John

Tillson, one of the original sponsors of the Bank, to Washington; and Tillson, with more political shrewdness than wisdom, sought to achieve his end by bribing Reuben Whitney, the special examiner of government depositories. Naturally, the whole matter was handled politely, as such things should be among gentlemen, but the results were far from satisfactory. As far as Whitney was concerned, the immediate result was a Congressional investigation of his activities, while the only reply that the Bank received in answer to its formal request was a letter from Woodbury reiterating the reasons why he did not choose to deposit government funds with it.

To most people, these developments would have constituted a sufficient discouragement, but the directors of the Bank were pertinacious. Woodbury had inclosed a printed application form, which prospective depositories were required to fill in, and a blank bond, so that Mather girded himself for the fray once more. Returning these documents to the Secretary, duly filled in, he sent a covering letter in which he attempted to dispose of Woodbury's charges by evasion.

Woodbury was not convinced. In order to terminate a correspondence that showed signs of going on forever, he submitted to the Attorney-General the question of the legal status of the second Bank of the State of Illinois, maintaining that it was contrary to the Constitution of 1818 because it was not "a State Bank" and there was not a penny of state money invested in it. Attorney-General Butler agreed that the Bank was unconstitutional, on which point, strangely enough, he was supported by Judge Smith who, although he had drawn up the original charter and fought for its passage through the legislature, was now in bitter opposition to it because he had been forced out of control.[51] Obviously, further efforts on the part of the directors would be futile, and they formally requested the Secretary of the Treasury to hold their application in abeyance for the time being.

Other significant developments had taken place in Illinois before this controversy was over. When the legislature convened for a special session, on December 7, 1835, Governor Duncan suggested in his message that they should pass a bill permitting the state to take up and sell the Bank stock reserved for it under the charter, thereby giving the state the benefit of the premium at which the stock was then selling in the market. The supporters of the Bank were numerous enough to defeat any such proposal, but the alternative bills that they introduced and passed were scarcely more beneficial to that institution than Duncan's proposal would have been.

In the first[52] of the two acts that were finally passed, the Bank of the State was invited to take over the full responsibility for the payment of both interest and principal of "the Wiggins loan." If it did so, it was to receive, as a *quid pro quo*, the right to open three more branches and the right to retain for its own use any profits derived from the sale at a premium of the additional million dollars of capital stock which the charter authorized the directors to sell. It was also to have a period of sixty days after presentation within which to redeem its notes, instead of the ten days provided in the original charter. On these terms, the Bank willingly took over the Wiggins loan, so that the State Treasury was able, it was hoped permanently, to rid itself of an incubus that had proved distinctly unpleasant.

The second act[53] increased the general acceptability of the bank's notes somewhat by providing that they should be received in payment of all monies due to the state. But, even in this provision, the state had learned caution, for the act went on to confer on the Governor, the Auditor and the Treasurer the power to prohibit the further acceptance of bank notes if, at any future time, they should become convinced that there was danger of loss from receiving them.

Certainly the state could not be accused of undue generosity to the Bank in either of these acts, and there was evidence that its standing was not much higher with the public at large. The premium on its stock had almost disappeared, despite the fact that it paid a dividend equivalent to 9 per cent on the paid-up capital[54] and, when the additional million dollars' worth of stock was offered for sale at auction, the interest of the people was so slight that $866,500 of it had to be taken over by Samuel Wiggins, who had agreed to underwrite the issue.[55] As a result the stockholdings of nonresidents, who were interested in using the Bank for their own purposes, were substantially increased, but a secondary result, not generally appreciated at the time, was even more serious. Wiggins was as surprised as everybody else at the lack of public interest, and was in no position to take up so large a block of securities on his own account, so that the Bank was compelled to lend him most of the money that he deposited in payment for its own stock!

Before this time, however, the enthusiasm of the Whigs

for banks had led to the resuscitation of two of the old territorial institutions. Although the Constitution of 1818 had provided that there should be only one state bank chartered by the legislature, it had specifically reserved to the old territorial banks then in existence the right to continue operations. All these institutions had ceased operations in the early twenties,[56] but neither the Bank of Cairo nor the Bank of Illinois at Shawneetown had ever surrendered its charter, and the Supreme Court of the state, in *The People v. Marshall*,[57] had held that these charters were still legal.

In the case of the Bank of Cairo, which had originally been chartered for thirty years, no further legislative action was necessary. It began operations in 1834 and, abandoning entirely the ambitious real-estate promotion envisaged by its charter, concentrated on its function of note issue with singularly little attention from either the state authorities or the public. The scant evidence we have regarding it seems to indicate that it was efficiently managed on behalf of the English stockholders who controlled it, and that its notes constituted a large portion of the circulating medium in the southwestern part of Illinois.[58] The Bank of Illinois at Shawneetown, which also resumed operations in 1834, could not so easily escape the limelight. In the first place, it was a larger institution while, in the second, its original charter expired on January 1, 1837, and would need to be renewed by the legislature if the Bank was to continue in existence. Early in 1835, the necessary act was passed[59] but, in return for a twenty-year extension of the Bank's life, the state exacted certain conditions. One of these was the reiteration of the clause in the original charter which provided a maximum rate of interest;[60] the other was the provision that the $100,000 of stock reserved for the state in the original charter should now be sold at auction, and any premium received from such sale should be paid into the State Treasury. Neither of these conditions could be considered particularly onerous, and the Bank was soon operating efficiently, and profitably, under the same men who had managed it during its first incarnation.

Moreover, despite the failure of the second Bank of the State to obtain the approval of the federal government, the Bank at Shawneetown was appointed a special depository in August, 1836.[61] The appointment provided that the Bank should only be used to hold and transmit the funds received at the Shawneetown land office but, as a result of the prevalent land speculation, this resulted in a federal deposit of more than $80,000 by the end of the year. But, even with this augmentation of its resources, the Bank was not able to meet all the demands for funds and, early in 1837, the legislature authorized it to borrow $250,000 from eastern capitalists in order to relend the funds on "bonds and mortgages of unencumbered real estate within the state."[62]

On the whole, the operations of the Bank appear to have been more than satisfactory.[63] Loans were made, primarily, to merchants of good standing and, like the second Bank of the State, the Bank at Shawneetown preferred exchange operations to the discounting of accommodation notes. Most of the profit seems to have been derived from the purchase of bills on New Orleans at one per cent discount, and the sale of drafts on the east at one per cent premium. In connection with this exchange business, however, the Bank, out of a total issue of $105,-000, had $14,900 of its bank notes payable only in Philadelphia, $2,825 payable at Louisville and $4,660 payable at New Orleans, an arrangement which, although common, was scarcely commendable.*

As we enter 1836, however, it is necessary to survey the national horizon again, since Illinois was soon to be caught up in the wake of the speculative mania that stretched from the Mississippi River to the Atlantic Coast, and then eastward to Europe. As a result of the abolition of land sales on credit, and of Congressional debates on the desirability of reducing the price of government lands below the figure of a dollar and a quarter an acre, set in 1820, there had been a distinct slump in land sales during the third decade of the nineteenth century.[64] But, with the coming of the thirties and the phenomenal expansion of banking activity that occurred during Jackson's administration, the unwillingness of the government to sell on credit was no longer a serious obstacle to the speculator, who was already beginning to feel that the time was ripe for the making of fortunes out of land. As the President sardonically pointed out in his annual message to Congress in 1836, "the banks lent out their notes to speculators; they were paid to the receivers, and immediately returned to the banks, to be lent out again and again, being mere instruments to transfer to speculators the most valuable public land, and pay the Government by a credit on the books of the

* It is not without interest to find that the Bank at Shawneetown provided the investigators who made this report with "plenty of good liquor, and sugar to sweeten it." Ford: *History of Illinois,* p. 197.

banks. Those credits on the books of some of the Western banks, usually called deposites, were already greatly beyond their immediate means of payment and were rapidly increasing."[65]

Moreover, there was already beginning that enthusiasm for railroads which was to cover the whole country, in the course of a few years, with an elaborate network of projected railway lines and, in a large number of railroad charters, the embryonic corporation was given the power to inflate the currency still further by issuing its own circulating notes in payment of the bills that it incurred during the course of construction.[66] Real-estate banks, chartered for the specific purpose of lending money against the security of mortgages on land, operated in a similar fashion.[67] Truly, as Niles suggests, "to make a *bank* is the grand panacea for every ill that can befall the people of the United States,"[68] and wildcat banking of the worst kind was granted standing ground under the Constitution by the new decision of the Supreme Court that notes issued by the inflationary Banks of the State were not bills of credit but legitimate circulating currency.[69]

This wild enthusiasm was shared even by those groups that might have been expected to show a restraining conservatism. European investors were almost as liberal with their funds as the wildcat banks, and the second Bank of the United States, which obtained a state charter from Pennsylvania by unusually pungent bribery early in 1836,[70] became a speculative Credit Mobilier. Indeed, the unwise and unsound operations of the Bank of the United States at this period were more responsible than those of any other single institution for the financial situation that developed.

In spite of the unprecedented plenitude of funds, interest rates often rose as high as one per cent a month, and sometimes as high as three per cent.[71] The rate of speculation was outrunning all resources, so that funds were never plentiful enough. Nor could it be hoped, even by the most optimistic, that funds would be found to finance all of the fantastic schemes that attracted support at the time. "So utterly reckless had the community grown, that they chased every bubble which floated in the speculative atmosphere; madness increased in proportion to the foulness of its aliment; the more absurd the project, the more remote the object, the more madly were they pursued. The prairies of Illinois, the forests of Wisconsin, and the sand-hills of Michigan, presented a chain almost unbroken of supposititious villages and cities. The whole land seemed staked out and peopled on paper. If a man were reputed to be fortunate, his touch, like that of Midas, was supposed to turn everything into gold, and the crowd entered blindly into every project he might originate. These worthies would besiege the land offices and purchase town sites at a dollar and a quarter per acre, which in a few days appeared on paper, laid out in the most approved rectangular fashion, emblazoned in glaring colors, and exhibiting the public spirit of the proprietor in the multitude of their public squares, church lots, and school lot reservations. Often was a fictitious streamlet seen to wind its romantic course through the heart of an ideal city, thus creating water lots and water privileges. But where a *real* stream, however diminutive, did find its way to the shore of the lake—no matter what was the character of the surrounding country—some wary operator would ride night and day until the place was secured at the Government price. Then the miserable waste of sand and fens which lay unconscious of its glory on the shore of the lake, was suddenly elevated into a mighty city, with a projected harbor and light-house, railroads and canals, and in a short time the circumjacent lands were sold in lots fifty by one hundred feet, under the name of 'additions.' Not the puniest brook on the shore of Lake Michigan was suffered to remain without a city at its mouth, and whoever will travel around that lake shall find many a mighty mart staked out in spots suitable only for the habitations of wild beasts."[72]

Chicago, in more than a geographic sense, provided an important focal point for the speculative operations in western lands. To be sure there were other cities, such as Alton, that attracted a good deal of attention, and many speculative operations went on far from any city, but Chicago as the terminus of the westward water route, and a city that was itself growing by leaps and bounds, seemed to crystallize within itself the spirit of that short period. In Chicago, the "bank and speculation went hand in hand, like Adam and Eve as they departed from Paradise."[73]

When the town was first platted in 1830, it had no more than fifty citizens, even when all ages and races are included: at the time of its incorporation as a city, in 1837, there were 4,170 people resident within its boundaries,[74] and almost 4,000 of those people had arrived since the beginning of 1833. This rate of growth astounded even those who saw the changes going on under their eyes, and a correspondent of the *New York Evening Star* gives voice to his amazement during the early part of 1837. "I have just returned from a stroll to the Lake shore, where two years ago I gladly landed after a long and perilous voyage. I can scarcely recognize it as the same spot. Where I then walked over the unbroken prairie, the spacious avenue is now opened, crowded with carts and wagons, and occasionally a showy family rolling and dashing in the hurry of trade or the pomp of a native 'sucker,' stumbling, as I do, over bales and boxes on the sidewalks, or gaping at the big signs and four-story brick houses."[75]

The significance of these developments in terms of land values can be more easily imagined than described. Housing accommodation was at a premium, and buildings were being erected as fast as there was labor to put them up, since it seemed that the influx of new citizens was always greater than the expansion of the facilities for their reception. "The hotels and boarding houses were always full; and full meant three in a bed sometimes, with the floor covered besides. Many of the emigrants coming in their own wagons had only them or a rude camp, hastily built, for home or shelter. All about the outskirts of the settlement was a cordon of prairie schooners, with tethered horses between, interspersed with camp fires, at which the busy housewives were ever preparing meals for the voracious pioneers."[76]

Even in 1833, the slow increase of population had carried land values far above the prices obtained at the sales of 1830. The demand for land increased because of what

Andreas calls the "legitimate" force of men's need for additional land on which to build stores and houses,[77] but the resultant rise in prices tempted the authorities to an outstanding act of financial folly. In 1833, they sold the square mile of school lands denoted by the government, an area that corresponds roughly to the present business district of Chicago, for the sum of $38,700.[78] At the moment, they were gratified by what they considered to be the high prices realized at the sale, but within a few months their joy was turned to regret and consternation. In 1834, the Chicago real-estate boom began in earnest, and the sale of Canal lands on long credits, in 1835,[79] only added fuel to the flames. Land speculation was the one absorbing business of the new town; town lots, its only export. "The streets were crowded with land speculators, hurrying from one sale to another. A negro, dressed up in scarlet, bearing a scarlet flag, and riding a white horse with housings of scarlet, announced the times of sale. At every street corner where he stopped, the crowd flocked round him; and it seemed as if some prevalent mania infected the whole people. . . . As the gentlemen of our party walked the streets, storekeepers hailed them from their doors, with offers of farms, and all manner of land lots, advising them to speculate before the price of land rose higher."[80]

By the summer of 1836, when Jackson's *Specie Circular* called a halt to the speculative mania throughout the west,[81] the total value, at the prices then current, of the land in the present city limits of Chicago had reached a figure of $10,500,000, an amount sixty times as great as its total value in 1830.[82] Moreover, there was already apparent that concentration of settlement which marks the growth of commercial and financial communities. Even though there were millions of acres of unused land in the surrounding prairies, "values rose to the peak along the Chicago River and its branches, where land was worth eight to ten times as much as land half a mile back, twenty-five times as much as land a mile away, fifteen hundred times as much as land seven miles away, and twenty-five hundred times as much as land ten miles away."[83]

Prior to the opening of a branch of the second Bank of the State, Chicago was definitely handicapped by the inadequacy of its financial facilities. Gurdon Hubbard, the leading merchant of the city, had ventured into the field of banking, under the title of Hubbard and Balestier, and was lending money on good mortgages at 12 per cent,[84] while firms like those of Peabody, or Strachan and Scott, were being established for the same purpose. Even a cautious and able Scotsman like George Smith was convinced of the profit to be derived from financing land speculation and, after his brief visit to Chicago in 1834, hastened back to Scotland to form the Scottish Illinois Land Investment Company, by means of which increasing quantities of European capital might be made available in Chicago and some of the speculative profits diverted to Scottish capitalists. All these efforts combined could not, however, satisfy the unsatiable demand for funds, and Chicago was delighted when the Bank opened a branch on December 5, 1835, with John Kinzie as its President and a local board of directors that included most of the leading merchants of the city.

Here was a financial institution, with comparatively large resources, ready to lend to all who had good security and unquestioned credit standing, conditions that any successful speculator can easily meet on a rapidly rising market. On Tuesdays and Fridays the board of directors met to pass upon discounts,[85] and the offices were open from nine until five o'clock on every day of the week, except Sunday, for the transaction of other business. The extent of its services can be judged from the fact that one firm of land auctioneers, Garrett Brown and Brother, deposited with the Bank more than $17,000 in cash during the first two months of 1836, but presumably borrowed even larger amounts because the Bank, early in March, refused to discount any more notes for the firm and warned all its customers that it would no longer grant emergency loans after banking hours.[86]

Another factor of tremendous significance to the Chicago situation was the Canal, which was destined to play a leading role in the city's economic life from 1835 to 1840. The long years of agitation and preliminary discussion were passed, and everyone was eager to start with the actual work of construction.[87] Early in 1835, therefore, the legislature passed an act[88] authorizing the Governor to borrow $500,000 by means of the sale of "Illinois and Michigan Canal Stock" bearing interest at the rate of 5 per cent, the proceeds of which were intended to supplement the funds derived from the sale of lands by the Canal Commissioners. But the experiences of the preceding decade had made the legislature cautious: the bonds carried no state guarantee and were secured solely by the Canal lands and the prospective earnings of the Canal in regard to the payment of both interest and principal.

Eastern investors were not interested in the project on these terms, so that it was necessary, during the following year, to raise the rate of interest to 6 per cent and pledge the credit of the state for the repayment of the bonds.[89] This step roused no tremors in the mind of Governor Duncan, who told the legislature that "it is now no longer to be dreaded that any reasonable sum of money borrowed for the purpose of constructing this canal, will become a charge on the State Treasury."[90] Speculative optimism had already affected political administration.

Funds were easily obtained on these terms, and work was begun, with appropriate celebrations, on July 4, 1836.[91] In the spring of the following year, enthusiasm had become tinged with impatience, and efforts were made to accelerate the work of construction so that the Canal might be finished even more rapidly.[92] But by this time, the rest of the state, and particularly the southern section, had become jealous of the benefit that Chicago was deriving from the Canal, even during the construction period, and there was a widespread and insistent demand for public improvements in other parts of the state. Many such projects had been aired in the legislature during the years from 1830 to 1835,[93] and several charters for stillborn schemes had been passed during the early months of 1836. Public enthusiasm was growing rapidly and every newspaper and every politician had a pet scheme that was intended to confer inestimable benefits upon the people of his constituency. Indeed "inestimable" is the only appropriate word that can be used to describe the results that were to flow from the projected developments since, as Ford pungently points out, "no previous survey or estimate had been made, either of the routes, the cost of the works, or the amount of business to be done on them. The arguments in favour of the system were of a character most difficult to refute, composed, as they were, partly of fact but mostly of prediction."[94]

All this enthusiasm came to a head when the legislature convened in the autumn of 1836. Prior to its meeting, a convention of the sponsors of internal improvements had met at the capital to agree upon plans, and it was these plans, embodied in the Douglas resolutions, that formed the first business of the legislative session. To trace the history of the measure in detail would be wearisome, since it became entangled with the interests of the Illinois and Michigan Canal, and with the efforts of the Sangamon County delegation to move the state capital to Springfield, but Ford's comment is a reasonable description of the legislative wisdom devoted to the consideration of the problem. "By log-rolling on the canal measure, by multiplying railroads, by terminating three railroads at Alton, that Alton might become a great city in opposition to St. Louis, by distributing money to some of the counties, to be wasted by the county commissioners, and by giving the seat of government to Springfield, was the whole State bought up and bribed, to approve the most senseless and disastrous policy which ever crippled the energies of a growing country."[95]

As might be expected from such a session, the Public

Improvements Act[96] is a unique and fascinating document. Since it included everybody's pet scheme, it provided for the dredging and canalizing of every important river in the state, for the improvement of the highway from Vincennes to St. Louis, and for the construction of a network of eight railroads along the routes specified in the following table.[97] All the projects were to be undertaken simultaneously, and prosecuted with the utmost dispatch. Moreover, as an obvious bribe to secure the passage of the act, $200,000 was to be distributed among "the counties through which no railroad or canal is provided," in order that this sum might be spent on such local improvements as highways and bridges.

TABLE III[97]

RAILROAD PROJECTS INCLUDED IN THE PUBLIC IMPROVEMENTS ACT OF 1837

	Miles	Estimated Cost per Mile	Estimated Total Cost
Central Railroad................	457½	$ 8,326	$ 3,809,145
Southern Cross Railroad..........	294	8,200	1,410,800
Northern Cross Railroad..........	234½	8,480	1,976,355
Shelbyville and Paris Branch.......	71½	19,588	757,113
Peoria and Warsaw Railroad.......	116	8,351	966,396
Alton and Shelbyville Railroad.....	71	8,295	754,845
Belleville and Lebanon Railroad....	23½	7,000	164,700
Bloomington, Mackinaw, Peoria and Pekin Railroad................	53¾	11,736	630,810
Total.....................	1,341¾		$11,470,444

To realize these dreams, an elaborate organization was set up, entirely apart from that which already existed for the construction of the Illinois and Michigan Canal. While the individual projects were to be let out under contract, the whole scheme was placed under a Board of Commissioners of Public Works, consisting of seven members (one from each of the judicial districts in the

state) elected for two-year terms by a joint session of both
houses of the legislature. This Board was "to locate,
superintend, direct and construct . . . all works of Internal Improvements which have been or shall be authorized to be undertaken, prosecuted and constructed
by the state," except the Illinois and Michigan Canal.

The total appropriations made by the act, on the
basis of estimates that certainly did not exaggerate the
costs involved, amounted to $10,250,000, an amount ten
times greater than the aggregate expenses of the State
of Illinois from its creation in 1818 to the end of 1835.
But considerations of this kind did not bother anyone
unduly in an age when money was so plentiful. Already
Illinois had received $477,914 from the federal govern-
ment, under the law providing for the distribution of
the surplus revenue,[98] and further amounts would probably be forthcoming from that source. Moreover, all of
the public improvements were regarded as highly profitable self-liquidating projects, which could reasonably be
financed by borrowing eastern, or even European,* capital. The act, therefore, authorized the state to borrow
$8,000,000 immediately, and created a Board of Fund
Commissioners, composed of three "experienced financiers," to undertake the negotiation and subsequent management of the loan. They were to sell certificates of
Illinois Internal Improvement Stock, from time to time,
in such amounts as were necessary to meet current construction costs, the stock bearing an annual interest of

* The relevant acts provided that the bonds might be engraved in any
foreign language and that payment should be provided in a foreign currency,
and at some European financial center, if such a step seemed desirable. *Laws
of Illinois*, 1836-37, p. 152, Section 2.

6 per cent and being secured by the property and revenues of the canals and railroads to be created.

Capitalists did not seem very eager to subscribe to these excellent securities, and the Board of Fund Commissioners was having a difficult time. On March 4, therefore, an act was passed to strengthen their position by making the bonds an unconditional obligation of the state.[99] Even so, it was not easy to dispose of the bonds because 6 per cent was not a particularly high rate of interest for the time, and the law prohibited the sale of the securities for less than par. Why, then, should not the banks be called in to supply the capital funds so urgently needed to advance the public welfare?

Such a suggestion, at that period, could lead to only one result, the socialization of the banks. After all banks and internal improvements were both for the welfare of the state, "the interests of both are alike and rest alike on an enlightened public opinion. One is the hand-maid of the other, and since the internal improvement system is based upon credit it cannot be carried on without the aid of the banks."[100] In this suggestion, the Bank of Cairo was ignored, but the second Bank of the State and the Bank at Shawneetown were encouraged to make loans to finance the program. Moreover, since both of these banks were earning good profits, it seemed possible that the revenue of the state might be augmented, just as much as social control was increased, if the state acquired substantial holdings of bank stock.

Once this decision was reached, events moved quickly. On March 2, 1837, the state decided to subscribe to the $100,000 of stock reserved for it under the charter of the

second Bank of the State,[101] paying for it by warrants
drawn on the State Treasurer. Two days later, a more
comprehensive measure was passed. The capital of the
second Bank of the State was increased by $2,000,000,
all of which was taken by the state, and that of the Bank
at Shawneetown was increased by $1,400,000 on the
understanding that, if the Bank consented to the act,
$1,000,000 would be taken by the state and the remainder
could be sold to the general public.* To pay for the stock,
the overworked Board of Fund Commissioners was authorized to sell another $3,000,000 of bonds, this time
with the title of "Illinois Bank and Internal Improvement Stock," which bore interest at 6 per cent and were
unconditionally guaranteed by the state.

Under the act, the legislature was given the right to
elect five additional directors to the second Bank of the
State, and nine to the Bank at Shawneetown. Both banks
were to be used by the state as depositories for its funds,
on condition that their notes were all redeemable in the
state and that they agreed to remit public funds from
one part of the state to another without charge.[102]

The initial deposit on the bank stocks to which it
had subscribed was made by the state out of the moneys
that it received from the United States government
through the distribution of the federal surplus, $100,000
in cash going to the Bank at Shawneetown and $235,000
to the second State Bank. That, however, was all the
cash that the banks were destined to receive out of the
whole transaction for, once again, the Board of Fund

* This inducement, along with permission to establish five more branches,
persuaded the Bank at Shawneetown to agree to the terms of the act.

Commissioners found it impossible to sell Illinois 6 per cent bonds at par. The state authorities, therefore, offered these bonds in settlement of the remainder of the purchase price, so that the condition of the banks and the financial soundness of the state were both entangled in the internal improvements madness at the very moment when the wave of prosperity was nearing its dizzy summit. Nor was there any wish on the part of the legislature to disentangle the two, since an act[103] was passed providing that the state could not sell any of its holdings of bank stock "before the complete redemption of the bonds or certificates of stock" that were issued for the purpose of subscribing to it, an event that was certainly not imminent in the light of economic conditions at the time. The speculative intoxication had attained its final stage. "The whole State [of Illinois] was excited to the highest pitch of phrenzy and expectation. Money was as plenty as dirt."[104]

REFERENCES FOR CHAPTER III

[1] Pierce: *op. cit.*, I, 3; Andreas: *op. cit.*, I, 111-112.
[2] Pierce: *op. cit.*, I, 56-57; Andreas: *op. cit.*, I, 115; Hoyt: *One Hundred Years of Land Values in Chicago*, pp. 23-24.
[3] Andreas: *op. cit.*, I, 117-122.
[4] Pierce: *op. cit.*, I, 37-42; Quaife: *Chicago Highways Old and New*, p. 23; Andreas: *op. cit.*, I, 122-128.
[5] *Chicago American*, August 15, 1835.
[6] Andreas: *op. cit.*, I, 165. See the whole of pages 166-173 for an account of the early history of the Canal.
[7] Cf. Hoyt: *op. cit.*, pp. 11-13 for a useful summary of the events.
[8] Ford: *op. cit.*, p. 28; Goodspeed and Healy: *History of Cook County*, I, 89.
[9] *Laws of Illinois*, 1824-25, pp. 160-161. Approved January 17, 1825; Pease: *op. cit.*, pp. 196-197.
[10] *Senate Journal*, 1826, 2 Session, p. 58.

[11] *Public Statutes at Large of the U. S.,* II, 234. There is good reason to suspect that the decision to assist Illinois was rather closely related to the desire of the Jackson men in Congress to obtain the political support of Ninian Edwards, who was the Governor of Illinois at the time. Cf. Pease: *op. cit.,* p. 124.

[12] *Laws of Illinois,* 1828-29, p. 14. Approved January 22, 1829. This act was amended two years later to increase the efficiency of the board (*Laws of Illinois,* 1830-31, p. 393. Approved February 15, 1831).

[13] *Chicago Tribune,* May 13, 1900.

[14] Cf. Pierce: *op. cit.,* I, pp. 63-64, 124-127 and 148-152.

[15] *History of Banking,* I, 197-198.

[16] The whole story is admirably told by W. G. Sumner in *The History of Banking,* I, 191-225.

[17] *Idem,* 193.

[18] *Idem,* 196.

[19] Gallatin: *Writings,* III, 394 (1841 ed.).

[20] *History of Banking,* I, 213.

[21] *U. S. H. of R., 22 Congress, 1 Session, Document No. 460;* Catterall: *Second Bank of the United States,* Ch. XI.

[22] During this period a mass of information concerning state banks is available in the letters and reports of the Secretary of the Treasury, Levi Woodbury. See particularly *Executive Documents No. 498, 23 Congress, 1 Session; 190, 23 Congress, 2 Session; 204, 225, 226, 252, 312, 379 and 423, 24 Congress, 1 Session; 65, 24 Congress, 2 Session.*

[23] *History of Banking,* I, 219, citing a statement of Silas Wright on behalf of the administration.

[24] Cf. Dewey: *op. cit.,* pp. 14 and 141; *History of Banking,* I, 219 and 248.

[25] *History of Banking,* I, 236.

[26] *Idem,* 313.

[27] *Idem,* 330. *Niles',* LIV, 224. For a sardonic contemporary description of bank notes in general, see Theophilus Fisk: *The Banking Bubble Burst, being a History of the Enormous Legalised Frauds practised upon the Community by the Present American Banking System* (Charleston, S. C., 1837).

[28] Pease: *op. cit.,* p. 303; Ford: *op. cit.,* p. 170.

[29] *Sangamo Journal,* March 9, 1833.

[30] Cf. *Alton Spectator,* December 7, 1833; *Illinois State Register,* November 30, 1833.

[31] Dowrie: *op. cit.,* p. 60.

[32] Ford: *op. cit.,* p. 170.

[33] *Senate Journal,* 1834-35, p. 12.

[34] *Idem,* p. 13.

[35] Ford: *op. cit.,* pp. 170-171.

[36] *Laws of Illinois,* 1834-35, p. 67. Approved February 13, 1835.

[37] *Laws of Illinois,* 1834-35, pp. 7-14. Approved February 12, 1835.

[38] *Section 14.*

[39] *Section 4.*

[40] *Sangamo Journal,* April 11, 1835.

[41] *Ibid.,* May 2, 1835; May 23, 1835; *Chicago Democrat,* May 20, 1835.

[42] Ford: *op. cit.,* pp. 175-176; Dowrie: *op. cit.,* pp. 65-66.

[43] *Sangamo Journal,* March 5, 1836.

[44] Ford: *op. cit.,* p. 176.

[45] *Reports of Session,* 1839-40, pp. 285-286.

[46] *Sangamo Journal,* August 15, 1835; Dowrie: *op. cit.,* p. 67. The expense of such appraisals was, however, borne by the borrower.

[47] Much information regarding the early operations of the Bank is contained in the *Report of the State Bank Investigating Committee,* Springfield, 1837. See also Dowrie: *op. cit.,* pp. 67-70.

[48] The usury Law distinguished only between six-month loans and loans for longer periods: no provision was made for what we should now call short-term loans. *Laws of Illinois,* 1834-35, p. 21, Section 1. Approved February 12, 1835.

[49] Dewey: *op. cit.,* p. 155.

[50] An elaborate discussion of this controversy appears in the reports of the investigation that Congress subsequently conducted regarding the activities of Reuben M. Whitney. Cf. *U. S. H. of R., 24 Congress, 2 Session (Series 353, Vol. III), Report No. 193* (March 1, 1837); *Report No. 194* (March 3, 1837).

[51] Ford: *op. cit.,* p. 179; *Sangamo Journal,* May 13, 1842.

[52] *Laws of Illinois,* 1835-36, pp. 237-238. Approved January 16, 1836.

[53] *Laws of Illinois,* 1835-36, p. 244. Approved January 16, 1836.

[54] *Report of State Investigating Committee,* p. 36.

[55] *Reports of Session (Senate),* 1840-41, p. 336.

[56] See above pp. 10-29.

[57] 1 Gilmore 672.

[58] *Hunt's:* XI, 241; Dowrie: *op. cit.,* p. 126.

[59] *Laws of Illinois,* 1834-35, pp. 21-22. Approved February 12, 1835.

[60] Ford *(op. cit.,* p. 232) suggests that this reiteration was the first mention of maximum interest rates in Illinois law, which is obviously inaccurate. The provision appears in Section 7 of the original Charter of 1816.

[61] *Sangamo Journal,* August 27, 1836.

[62] *Laws of Illinois,* 1836-37, p. 17. Approved February 28, 1837.

[63] *Senate Journal,* 1836-37, p. 352 ff.

[64] *American State Papers, Public Lands,* V, 556. See also Pease: *op. cit.,* pp. 173-182.

[65] *24 Congress, 2 Session, Message of the President, December 6, 1836,* p. 14.

[66] Dewey: *op. cit.,* pp. 49-51; *History of Banking,* I, 249-250.

[67] Dewey: *op. cit.,* p. 160; *History of Banking,* I, 245, 250, 253 and 332.

[68] *Niles',* XLIX, 298.

[69] *Briscoe v. Bank of the Commonwealth of Kentucky,* 8 Peters 118.

[70] Cf. *History of Banking,* I, 227-228.

[71] *Idem,* 265; Pierce: *op. cit.,* I, 124.

[72] Speech of J. N. Balestier, given in Chicago in 1840, quoted by Andreas: *op. cit.,* I, 135.

[73] *Hunt's,* XI, 245.

[74] Pierce: *op. cit.,* I, 44n.

[75] Andreas: *op. cit.,* I, 138, quoting the *New York Evening Star,* January, 1837.

[76] Andreas: *op. cit.,* I, 134.

[77] *Idem,* 115.

[78] Pierce: *op. cit.,* I, 57.

[79] Andreas: *op. cit.,* I, 135-137; Pierce: *op. cit.,* I, 58-59 and 61.

[80] Harriet Martineau: *Society in America,* I, 159-260.

[81] Cf. *History of Banking,* I, 261; Dowrie: *op. cit.,* p. 77.

[82] Hoyt: *op. cit.,* p. 33.

[83] *Ibid.,* p. 37.

[84] *Pierce:* I, 157.

[85] *Chicago American,* February 13, 1836.

[86] *Chicago American,* March 12, 1836.

[87] Pease: *op. cit.,* pp. 198-199.

[88] *Laws of Illinois,* 1834-35, p. 222. Approved February 10, 1835.

[89] *Laws of Illinois,* 1835-36, pp. 145-154. Approved January 9, 1836.

[90] *House Journal,* 1835-36, 2 Session, p. 9.

[91] Andreas: *op. cit.,* I, 168.

[92] *Laws of Illinois,* 1836-37, p. 39. Approved March 2, 1837.

[93] Ford: *op. cit.,* p. 166; Pease: *op. cit.,* p. 205-206.

[94] Ford: *op. cit.,* p. 185.

[95] *Idem,* p. 187.

[96] *Laws of Illinois,* 1836-37, pp. 121-140. Approved February 27, 1837.

[97] *Hunt's,* XXVII, 662. The manifest inaccuracies of this table, which is copied *verbatim,* amply illustrate Ford's comment regarding the

lack of care which characterized the preliminary stages of the public improvements program.

[98] *Auditor's Report* appended to *Laws of Illinois*, 1836-37, p. 193.

[99] *Laws of Illinois*, 1836-37, p. 152, Section 3.

[100] *Sangamo Journal*, January 27, 1837.

[101] *Laws of Illinois*, 1836-37, p. 18. Approved March 2, 1837.

[102] *Laws of Illinois*, 1836-37, pp. 23-24. Approved March 4, 1837.

[103] *Laws of Illinois*, 1836-37, 2 *Session*, p. 5. Approved July 21, 1837.

[104] Ford: *op. cit.*, p. 196.

CHAPTER IV

THE LEGACY OF PUBLIC IMPROVEMENTS

1837–1843

THE house of cards collapsed in the spring of 1837, and financial panic gripped the nation. Business failures and the closing of banks spread from one community to another, like wildfire, bringing private loss and human misery in their train with a suddenness that was terrifying to those whose hopes had reached the skies a few weeks earlier. The natural human reaction was to seek a scapegoat, somebody who could be held responsible for the collapse of all the dreams that had appeared so wonderful, and the citizens of New York were only expressing the views of many other people when they met in a vast public assembly and passed resolutions to the effect that the whole trouble "was due to presidential meddling with business and currency."[1]

But Condy Raguet was much nearer to the truth when he pointed out that the financial crisis was the natural consequence of banking policies that had encouraged loans for highly illiquid purposes.[2] While Jacksonian democracy had done nothing to moderate the American inflation, it is important to bear in mind the fact that English financial policies, which exercised a predominant influence throughout the world at that period, were hardly more conservative. Indeed, the crisis made its first appearance in England, where commercial banks, under the influence of panic demands from their depositors, had to appeal to the Bank of England for aid in November, 1836.[3] In March, 1837, three English banks were compelled to close their doors in the face of serious runs.

In New York, there were signs of impending trouble in January, 1837, when some of the stronger banks refused to grant immediate credit to depositors for the checks or notes of weaker New York banks, but the general public did not become conscious of the danger for several weeks. On March 4, the storm broke. A sharp fall in the price of cotton led to the immediate bankruptcy of several commission houses in New Orleans, and seriously weakened those New York merchants and bankers who were interested in the cotton trade.[4] During the five weeks from March 4 to April 8, ninety-eight failures occurred in New York with aggregate liabilities in excess of $60,000,000, and by the latter date the whole commercial community of New Orleans was practically bankrupt.

Perhaps it was too late for constructive policies; perhaps the principles of self-defense forbade cooperative action to save the situation. In any case, nothing was done to stop the process of deterioration that was making rapid headway in the nation's financial system. On May 8, the Dry Dock Bank failed in New York, producing such severe runs on several of the other banks that specie payments were suspended two days later.* On the fol-

* The attitude of the populace was so hostile that the militia was called to arms the evening before the suspension of specie payments was made public. Cf. *Niles'*, LII, 162.

lowing day, a similar decision was reached by the Philadelphia banks and, within ten days, financial institutions
in all parts of the country were refusing to pay out coin
when it was demanded, often with the official consent of
the various state governments which hastened to pass
laws authorizing the action already taken by the banks.
The United States woke up to find itself with an inconvertible paper currency.

As on previous occasions, the immediate effect of the
suspension was to paralyze the domestic exchange market,
rendering remittance from one part of the country to
another difficult, or even impossible. There was no standard currency for the country, since the second Bank of
the United States had become a state institution operating under a Pennsylvania charter,' and by the end of
1837, western notes were at 25 per cent discount in New
York (as were those from Mississippi), Tennessee notes
were at 20 per cent discount, and notes of other southern
states were received at amounts varying from 8 per cent
to 17 per cent below par. Moreover, there is ample evidence that banks in many parts of the country made
strenuous efforts to enlarge the disparity between the
several kinds of paper currency, gaining for themselves,
by that operation, a substantial exchange profit which
augmented the earnings derived from loans and discounts.[5] Once again, it became apparent that the interests of the note-issuing banks did not harmonize with
the desire of the general public, and of business, for a
uniform currency.

The federal government, which in the normal course
of its operations had to transfer large sums of money

from one part of the country to another, suffered severely from this situation. But it was even more seriously embarrassed by another aspect of the suspension, since, under the Specie Circular[6] issued in July, 1836, the government could receive payments only in specie and could deposit its funds only in specie-paying banks! To overcome the first of these difficulties, Congress revoked the Specie Circular on May 31, 1838,[7] making all kinds of money equally acceptable to the government and placing the fiscal system, like the finances of private business, upon an inconvertible paper basis. Moreover, to remedy the apparent dearth of currency (as well as to solve its own fiscal problem) the Treasury issued $50,000,000 in the form of circulating Treasury notes, which were intended to serve as a medium of exchange and were receivable by the government in payment of all taxes and other obligations.

The problem of finding good depository banks was less easily solved. In his report for December, 1837, the Secretary of the Treasury pointed out that, of the $34,-000,000 which was nominally in the Treasury, there was only $700,000 actually available to meet the expenses of the government. Under the Act of Congress providing for the distribution of the federal surplus, $28,000,000 had already been transferred to the states and could not be recovered; $3,500,000 was locked up in depository banks that had suspended specie payments; $1,100,000 was in the form of worthless bank notes and the rest, apart from a small quantity of metal in process of being coined, consisted of trust funds that could not be touched. The whole system of "pet banks" had collapsed overnight and, if the second Bank of the United States had been sound enough, and wise enough, to continue to pay out specie,[8] the government, despite Jackson's personal antagonism, would have been compelled to make use of it. But the Bank was neither sound nor wisely administered, so that the government was ultimately driven to a vastly different solution of its problems.

In the light of her domestic policies during the early thirties, it was only natural that Illinois should have felt the full impact of the panic, yet her banks continued to pay out coin for two full weeks after those in the east had suspended. Finally, on May 29, all the Illinois banks decided to suspend specie payments,[9] despite the clause in the charter of the second Bank of the State which imposed liquidation as the penalty for any failure to redeem notes within sixty days of presentation. The relationship of the Bank to the state was so intimate, by this time, that there was little fear of any such unpleasant consequences.

In Chicago, the crash brought business to a standstill, and the local real-estate boom collapsed along with all the other bubbles. Capital funds, which had seemed so plentiful a few weeks earlier, were now unobtainable, save in small amounts from eastern sources and, even on those loans, the borrowers had to pay extremely high rates of interest. So great was the stringency that the newly organized city council of Chicago was utterly unable to obtain a loan of $25,000 from the local branch of the second Bank of the State,[10] so that, in order to meet its financial obligations it was compelled to issue $5,000 of circulating scrip in denominations ranging from one to three dollars.[11] Shortly afterward, the Canal Commissioners, confronted with similar difficulties in raising the funds needed to pay contractors, resorted to the same expedient and issued more than $150,000 in the form of circulating scrip. The Chicago Marine and Fire Insurance Company, "being desirous of rendering to the community . . . every legitimate aid sanctioned by prudence," issued certificates of deposit that were intended to circulate as a medium of exchange.[12]

The effect upon the local monetary situation of such issues of irredeemable paper can well be imagined. The expansion in the note issues of the Illinois banks had already displaced most of the gold and silver coin in circulation, and the new flood of scrip quickly drove the remainder into hoards. Moreover, as private individuals began to follow the example of the city council, the currency in circulation came to consist of an extraordinary congeries of all sorts of paper. "The small tradesman issued tickets of credit for change from 5 cents to 50 cents, 'good for groceries,' 'payable in goods,' 'good for tobacco,' 'good for a drink,' or good for anything else which the issuer might happen to deal in. In addition to this there was county scrip, State Auditor's scrip, St. Louis scrip, and . . . a flood of bills issued by Michigan banks under the Land Loan banking law of the State."[13] It is not surprising that many people earnestly desired the creation of a new Bank of the United States to undertake the task of supplying a satisfactory currency in adequate quantities.[14]

In July, the Governor called a special session of the legislature to consider the situation, and prompt action was taken to legalize the suspension of specie payments by the banks "until the end of the next general or special session of the General Assembly."[15] But the demands of the debtor classes for relief were even more urgent than those for legalizing a policy that was already in practical effect, and the legislature could not ignore the clamor. The continued suspension of specie payments was declared to be legal only if the banks agreed to certain conditions, a polite way of forcing them to accede to the demands of the legislature, since their condition at that moment made immediate resumption impossible.

No dividends were to be paid to stockholders, no specie was to be paid out or sold, and no increase in the amount of notes outstanding was to be permitted; all these were reasonable conditions designed to protect the community. In addition, however, the law provided that the banks must allow the debts owing to them to be repaid in ten annual installments, renewing the note, as a matter of course, if the debtor was willing to pay the accumulated interest and 10 per cent of the principal. A first breach was thus made in the law, passed two years earlier, which prohibited relief measures that interfered with the efforts of the banks to collect the amounts owing to them, and the breach was a matter of considerable significance in the light of the events that were soon to follow. Moreover, a few days later, a similar law was passed for the relief of debtors who had not yet paid for the lands they had purchased from the state. Lands were not to be forfeited for nonpayment of the amounts due if the debtor would agree to pay the interest and 10 per cent of the principal on October 1, 1838, and October 1,

1839, with annual payments of 20 per cent of the principal thereafter.[16]

The effect of the slump in land values, which gave rise to these demands for relief, was accentuated by the immediate collapse of the grandiose scheme of internal improvements. For political purposes, the law had provided that all the public works should be commenced simultaneously, so that contracts had been let for 105 miles on the Northern Cross Railroad, 69½ miles on the Illinois Central, 24 on the Peoria and Warsaw, 15 on the Alton and Shawneetown, 38 on the Alton and Mount Carmel, 33 on the Alton and Shelbyville and 9¼ on the Bloomington and Pekin.[17] Similar contracts had been let for the improvement of all the rivers specified in the act and, to make matters worse, several private companies had started operations on the construction of transportation systems designed to supplement those of the state.

The country was dotted with construction camps but, owing to the chaotic planning of operations, frequently made even worse by inefficiency of management,[18] there was no prospect that any of the projects would be completed, and put into operation, within a reasonably short period of time. To an increasing number of people, the scheme of public improvements seemed as dangerous as the banks, to which they had been closely tied by the state, and insistent demands arose that both should be scrapped.[19]

One exception must, however, be made to the general condemnation. Work on the Illinois and Michigan Canal was pushed forward, since the rapid completion of the work was required by the agreement under which the federal government had donated the Canal lands to the state, and legislation was passed authorizing the commis-sioners to sell additional lands to the aggregate value of $400,000 to meet immediate expenses. Moreover, if ex-isting funds, even with this addition, should prove in-adequate, the Governor was authorized to negotiate a loan for $300,000 on the credit of the state.[20] Indeed, during the darkest days of the depression the Canal offered the chief support of Chicago. Psychologically, it maintained the hopes of those who believed that the city would grow into a great trading center; financially, the $75,000 paid out to contractors each month "furnished a substantial though temporary basis for commercial de-velopment, bolstering up rents and prices and preventing a complete collapse of real estate values."[21] The Canal alone, out of all the halcyon projects that had dazzled the expectations of the people of Illinois, was able to give aid and succor: for the rest, conditions were so bad that Governor Duncan suggested the issue of circulating state scrip, based on farm mortgages, which should be lent, free of all interest, to those impoverished landowners who were willing to mortgage their farms.[22]

By October, 1837, the panic was over, and the slow process of liquidation began. In some parts of the east, the contraction of credit rapidly attained staggering pro-portions, New York alone reducing the amount of bank notes in circulation from $24,198,000 to $12,460,000 in the course of a single year. To make matters worse, the total demand deposits were also cut in two.[23] The process was, however, much slower in other parts of the country and, in Illinois, although the banks undoubtedly made efforts to collect the loans that were due and reduce the volume of credit outstanding,[24] the policy had no appreciable effect whatever, apart from the popular indignation that it aroused. The poverty of the debtors made settlement difficult, and the renewed enthusiasm for relief laws made it unpopular. Honest and solvent debtors were discouraged from paying their obligations lest they should, by so doing, deprive themselves of benefits later conferred upon their less honest companions in debt.

But the New York policy, painful though it must have been, was eminently successful. A convention of bankers from the eastern states met in New York City on May 11, 1838, and agreed to resume specie payments on the first of January, 1839.[25] Specie was imported from England to implement this decision and, in the face of violent opposition from the inflationist bankers of Philadelphia, the banks of New York City actually resumed specie payments on April 23,[26] seven months before the time agreed upon.

Such single-handed action was uncomfortable for a few months, since the rest of the country did not immediately follow suit, but New York withstood the drain of specie resulting from its action and, on August 13, after a series of meetings in Philadelphia, the bankers of some ten states all resumed specie payments simultaneously. Illinois was included in this group,[27] and most of the other states soon followed the joint example. By the end of the year, 730 banks, in twenty-two states, had resumed specie payments, while 70 more were in a position to resume during the early days of 1839.[28] Once more, the country was on a metallic standard.

Illinois, to rid herself of the mass of paper currency that had come into existence during the depression, prohibited the issue of circulating notes by individuals and corporations that had not been chartered as banks.[29] Notes issued by the incorporated banks once again had a clear field, but this action did not denote any revival of enthusiasm for these institutions on the part of the general public. Although Governor Duncan, in his valedictory, had commended the banks for their voluntary resumption of specie payments,[30] the incoming Governor began his administration by a stinging condemnation of their whole policy.[31] He insisted that they existed primarily for the purpose of financing large speculators, and meddled in politics to make their speculations more profitable; he blamed the legislature, on both counts, because no adequate machinery had been provided, when the banks were created, to regulate and supervise their operations.

Little immediate attention was paid to Governor Carlin's indictment, since the resumption of work on the internal-improvement projects was an ideal that was much closer to the hearts of the legislators. On this question, Carlin had suggested that, whatever may have been the original wisdom or unwisdom inspiring the plans, the state had already gone too far to withdraw from her commitments. He, therefore, recommended that the legislature consider the methods by which the completion of the proposed public works might be financed.

The legislature displayed even more enthusiasm than the Governor. Far from curtailing the scope of the original plans, it approved additional schemes that involved a further expenditure of $800,000.[32] A general taxation law was also passed, which imposed a tax of twenty cents on every hundred dollars' worth of real estate and attempted to increase the efficiency of collection,[33] but the measure proved to be very unsatisfactory. While the new taxes were utterly inadequate to meet the obligations of the state, they caused a considerable amount of opposition and indignation among the people. As a result, the public works became more unpopular than they had previously been, and the politicians were discouraged from further attempts to rehabilitate the finances of the state.[34]

Even in the case of the Illinois and Michigan Canal, which was again in need of funds, there was no attempt to work out a complete financial program. First of all, the authorization for a loan of $300,000, to be floated on the credit of the state, was renewed and,[35] when the Canal Commissioners failed to find a purchaser for these bonds, they were authorized to borrow the $300,000 from the Fund Commissioners of the state, who still had some of the internal improvement funds on hand.[36] A month later, the Canal Commissioners were authorized to raise money by the sale of water rights,[37] while an attempt was made to facilitate the sale of Canal lands to individuals who had "squatted" on them extralegally by making a generous allowance for past improvements.[38]

None of these measures was of more than temporary assistance, and the annual expenses of the Canal Commissioners were increasing as the work progressed. An act was, therefore, passed to authorize them to borrow an additional $4,000,000 by the sale of Illinois and Michigan

Canal Stock, which carried an interest rate of 6 per cent and was unconditionally guaranteed by the state as to both interest and principal.[39] Since the stock was to be sold by agents, either in the east or in Europe, the funds could not become immediately available, so that further temporary financing had to be arranged. Four days after authorizing this loan, the legislature permitted the Canal Commissioners to pay their bills by "checks" drawn upon the second Bank of the State,[40] but these checks, which were issued in even denominations and intended to circulate as money, could be drawn in large amounts even if the Commissioners had no funds standing to their credit at the Bank. The act merely provided that settlements of accounts between the Canal Commissioners and the Bank should be made four times a year. In reality, the checks provided a method by which the Canal could, for the time being, be financed through short-term loans, free of interest, and to supplement the funds obtained in this way, the act also provided that Canal lands could be sold on twenty-year credit, with an initial deposit of 10 per cent and interest on the remainder at 6 per cent per annum.

Obviously the State of Illinois was not making any serious attempt to put its financial affairs in order: instead it was building the house of cards still higher, on the assumption that the panic of 1837 had been no more than an unpleasant flash in the pan. Nor was Illinois alone in this assumption. A commercial convention, meeting at Richmond in the summer of 1838, resolved that the shortest road to prosperity was by means of an increase of banking facilities and a further expansion of railroads,[41] while the state-owned banks in Arkansas suspended specie payments, early in 1839, with the deliberate intention of bringing about an expansion of the currency that was impossible as long as they adhered to a specie standard.[42] For the first time in its history, the United States set out to cure the depression by increased spending and monetary expansion was encouraged to facilitate the expenditure. Inflation of the currency went hand in hand with the revival of business hopes, and the Bank of the United States, which was still the largest financial institution in the country, led the van. Industry and trade were gripped by what Niles aptly called "one of the most rash and insane speculations of modern times."[43]

In such a nationwide atmosphere, and with the unsatisfactory example of the Illinois legislature before them, it is not surprising that the banks of Illinois responded warmly to the speculative enthusiasm that surrounded them. Since the slump in land values had diminished the possibility of profitable speculation in that field, and there was as yet very little industrial development within the state, the interest of the second Bank of the State was diverted toward the lead mines of Galena. The exploitation of these mines, and the development of Alton into a commercial center that would rival St. Louis, were closely interwoven dreams of the firm of Godfrey, Gilman and Company, which did a commission business in Alton. Since these gentlemen were directors of the second Bank of the State, and among its largest stockholders, what could be more natural than to use the resources of the Bank to realize their dreams?[44]

If all their loans be added together, this firm is found to have borrowed more than $800,000 from the second Bank of the State, for the purpose of financing speculative operations, so that it was able, with the assistance of other Alton merchants who also received generous bank loans, to raise the price of lead from $2.75 to $4.25 a hundredweight. In doing this, however, the agent who operated at Galena, on behalf of Godfrey, Gilmore and Company, was "wild and reckless in the extreme. He bought all the mines and smelting establishments he could get . . . and . . . scattered money with a profuse and princely hand."[45]

During this period of expanding operations, the directors of the second Bank of the State made another effort to attract the deposits of the federal government, and the Illinois legislature passed a joint resolution requesting the Secretary of the Treasury to appoint the Bank a federal depository. In a sense, this application was successful since, for reasons of convenience, the government did make use of the Chicago branch as a depository, sometimes carrying a balance as large as $150,000 with that office,[46] but the Treasury was still adamant with regard to the principal bank. While an official excuse was found in the fact that the Bank did not operate in strict accordance with the principles that were supposed to govern the activities of the United States depositories,[47] it is apparent that the Whig politics of the institution still constituted the main stumbling block to the ambitions of its directors. This was the largest fly in the ointment of inflationary prosperity, since the receipt of large federal deposits would have enabled the Bank to expand its operations still further!

The Bank of Illinois, at Shawneetown, took no part in the Alton speculations, since Alton was, in many respects, a commercial rival of the city in which it operated, but it engaged in financial relations with the state that were no less dangerous to its stability. First of all, it lent $80,-000 for the purpose of completing the new State House and later, in September, 1839, "upon the recommendation and urgent request of Governor Carlin, and upon his promise to deposit $500,000 in internal improvement bonds as collateral security, which promise was never performed, the bank was induced to lend the Commissioners of Public Works the further sum of $200,000."[48]

Both the banks of Illinois and the public finances of the state were in thoroughly unsound condition by the summer of 1839, as a result of these developments, while a similar situation existed in many other parts of the country. In spite, however, of the fact that it is always easy to be wise after the event, to look backwards, with Olympian detachment, and point out the errors that were made by people who were so close to their problems that they could not see them clearly, an analysis of the developments that occurred from 1836 to 1839 will amply repay the student for the trouble that it involves. When all the unwisdom and political knavery is stripped away, to lay bare the monetary and banking policies that were followed at the time, it is apparent that two opposing ideals were in conflict. In New York, and throughout New England, banking sentiment leaned strongly toward the gold standard, under which England was rapidly attaining wealth and prestige. Perhaps it was a mistake to attribute England's economic progress to that factor alone but, whether the ideal was true or false, it implied that recovery from the crisis of 1837 could be attained only by the hard road of deflation. The volume of bank credit had to be reduced, and the amount of banking reserves increased, until it became possible to resume, and maintain, specie payments. By means of Herculean efforts, the bankers of New York had attained this goal in the spring of 1839 and, from that point onward, they stood solidly by their guns.

The opposing school of thought was led by the great Bank of the United States, now a Pennsylvania corporation, and followed by the majority of bankers outside New York and New England. To the conservatives this inflationary ideal was childish, and Niles suggested pungently that "The Philadelphians are a peculiar people in the matter of currency. They have a strange fondness for inconvertible paper."[49] Yet this fondness was not entirely strange, in view of the fact that the general price level was falling steadily from 1814 to 1843, with the exception of a sharp cyclical increase from 1835 to 1837, and that the recession after the panic had carried commodity prices down to the lowest point recorded since the United States came into existence.[50] In the light of these circumstances, it is not surprising that many bankers, under the brilliant, but unreliable, leadership of Biddle, should have thought that a policy of currency inflation, made possible by inconvertible paper, would facilitate industrial activity and encourage business revival.

Unfortunately, the events of these years did not lead to

any clear settlement of the dispute, which is as bitter to-day as it was then, but a close study of the facts indicates that the failure of the inflationists was due more to unsound policies, and inefficient operations, than to any defects that were apparent in their ideals. Indeed, the basic conflict of theory is hard to isolate, since the inflationists were guilty of so much knavery, in their efforts to bring about currency expansion, that appreciation of their ideals becomes clouded by a general condemnation of their practices. The gold-standard school, by contrast, showed a perfect, if rather wooden, rectitude which invariably commanded the respect of the critical observer. And the gold standard triumphed in the conflict. The Bank of the United States, although it spent a fortune shamelessly, at Harrisburg, to prevent any legislative demand for the resumption of specie payments,[51] and made determined efforts to produce a run in New York serious enough to lead to a new suspension,[52] was unable to accomplish its aims. Weakened by its inflationary policies, particularly in regard to the financing of cotton and of public improvements, it failed on October 9, 1839, and ironically enough, the failure produced the results that policy could not attain. Specie payments were suspended once more, in all parts of the country, except New York and New England, during the following weeks.

On October 20, the news of the failure reached Springfield, and the directors of the second Bank of the State of Illinois hastily decided to follow the example set by other financial institutions. Specie payments were suspended once more and special messengers were sent to carry the order to each branch, in order that there should be no delay.[53] The Bank at Shawneetown did not, at once, take similar steps, being in stronger condition, but the large demands for specie with which it was confronted led to the decision to suspend before a fortnight had passed.[54]

Once again, Illinois was forced to operate on an inconvertible paper currency and, once again, the legislature hastened to legalize the action of the second Bank of the State in order to protect its charter.[55] Conditions were imposed similar to those prescribed in the Act of 1837, including the provision that debtors might pay in ten installments, but two additional clauses were added. In the first place, it was provided that no individual or firm might owe the Bank more than $10,000 on promissory notes, either as maker or endorser, although a maximum accommodation of $25,000 was allowed when the debtor discounted bills of exchange arising out of actual commercial operations. In the second place, in order to bring about a change in the management of the Bank, the stockholders were required to replace three of the directors by new men at the next annual meeting, and to elect at least two new directors to the board during the following year. Moreover, the act specifically required the Bank to accept its own notes in payment of any debts due to it, which seems to indicate that it was trying to make its debtors pay in specie at a time when it met its own obligations by paying out paper.

These rather stringent terms were due to a growing recognition of the fact that the activities of the Bank were far from satisfactory, when viewed from the angle of the state's welfare. Governor Carlin, in opening the session, had criticized the Bank very severely, calling attention to its speculative operations and suggesting that the suspension of specie payments, if it was necessary at all, was entirely due to these activities. Further, he insisted that the incorporation of large banks was undemocratic, since they controlled the supply of money in their own interests, rather than in the interests of the community as a whole, and suggested that the legislature should conduct a searching investigation of the operations of the second State Bank in order to find out whether it was of any value to the community at large.[56]

The report of the investigating committee[57] did nothing to raise the prestige of the second Bank of the State. Although the committee seemed, on the whole, rather friendly to the institution, it was forced to record the speculative operations in lead, to which attention has already been drawn, as well as considerable speculation in pork at the Chicago branch.[58] The relationship of the Bank to Samuel Wiggins was also described, in all its unsatisfactory aspects, and on both counts it was clear that the directors of the Bank had violated both the spirit and the letter of the law. Even worse, the report showed that the policies of the management had been utterly unsound. A minority report, which analyzed the assets of the institution more critically than did that of the whole committee, insisted that many of these assets were carried on the books of the Bank at a figure considerably in excess of their market value, while the portfolio contained an excessively large amount of Illinois state obligations,[59] which were then selling at a discount of approximately 40 per cent on the New York market.[60] Obviously, if the

Bank were compelled to liquidate, the creditors and stockholders would incur substantial losses.

Although business conditions throughout the state showed some improvement, during 1840, the publication of such a report as this was bound to have an adverse effect upon the reputation of the Bank, particularly during a period when it was not redeeming its obligations in specie. The notes fell rapidly to a discount of 10 per cent, and were scurrilously referred to as "bank rags" by the press.[61] Opposition to all financial institutions grew apace; it was estimated that depreciated paper currency was costing the people of Illinois $160,000 a year, as a result of the higher prices that were paid for goods purchased in the east and the lower prices received for produce sold there.[62]

For reasons connected with the fiscal problems confronting the state, the legislators were convened two weeks before the normal time, and the events of the preceding months had not induced them to feel any particular kindness toward the banks. Moreover, there was before them the example of the Pennsylvania legislature which, tired of the evasiveness of the financial community, had passed an act peremptorily ordering the banks to resume specie payments on January 15, 1841.[63] As a result of that action, the Philadelphia banks had entered into negotiations with banks throughout most sections of the country and arrived at a general agreement, which included Illinois, that general resumption should take place on the date fixed by the legislators at Harrisburg.

Why should not the Illinois legislature take action to bring about a local resumption even earlier, and put an end to the evils of depreciated paper from which the state was suffering? The law under which the suspension had been legalized was effective only "until the close of the next session of the Assembly,"[64] and this provision offered a brilliant opportunity to Democratic opponents of the Bank. By insisting that the regular session of the legislature could not constitutionally be called before December 7, 1840, it was possible to turn the preceding two weeks into a special session. To make this thesis effective, they proposed in both houses, on December 5, a resolution to adjourn *sine die* and, although Abraham Lincoln and several other Whigs hurriedly left the chamber (even by jumping out of windows) in order to kill the resolution by the absence of a quorum, it was carried by a substantial majority.[65]

Since this resolution would have deprived the Bank of its charter, if it did not immediately redeem its notes in specie, the directors of the second Bank of the State took action at once to authorize the resumption.[66] Such a step was fraught with considerable danger to the institution. Since the surrounding banks would not begin to pay out specie for another six weeks, under the terms of the general agreement negotiated by Philadelphia, all demands for coin throughout the west would concentrate upon the second Bank of the State of Illinois. Moreover, even though the Bank was willing to pay a premium for specie, it was doubtful whether much assistance could be expected from the New York banks, which were not finding it easy to maintain their own position in the face of the general suspension.

To strengthen the Bank for its ordeal, the directors

decided to make no more loans or discounts, so that no new notes would be paid out, and (with poetic irony) they extended this ruling to cover the account with the state. The embarrassment of the Treasurer was thus increased by his inability to obtain further short-term accommodation.[67] Moreover, the Bank, for the same reason, refused to continue its practice of cashing salary warrants at par for the legislators, who were thus compelled to sell them on the market at a discount of 50 per cent, and the directors must have enjoyed the use of this means of bringing home to their enemies, in unpleasant fashion, the seriousness of the situation.[68]

Unfortunately for the Bank, the long-awaited fifteenth of January proved to be a day of disappointment. Although the banks in Philadelphia resumed specie payments, as did those in Virginia and Maryland,[69] the bankers of the south and west made no effort to live up to their agreement. Instead, they called a convention, which met at Louisville on January 25, to discuss the question of resumption, but were totally unable to arrive at any definite conclusion and adjourned without taking action.[70]

The quandary of the second Bank of the State of Illinois was then worse than ever, since the experience of two months had definitely convinced the directors that they could not much longer continue to pay out specie when none of the neighboring banks were doing so. Already, they had paid out $455,000 in coin, and the reserves of specie had fallen to a dangerously low point.[71] The Bank, therefore, appealed to the legislature, setting forth these facts in their argument and praying that a law might be passed permitting the suspension of specie payments until such time as a general resumption actually occurred. The force of the Bank's arguments, coupled with the matter of the salary warrants, led the legislature to accede to the petition. Suspension was authorized until such time as the banks of the south and west should resume.[72] Moreover, since there was a growing scarcity of coins, as a result of the operation of Gresham's Law, the Bank was authorized to issue notes in denominations of one, two and three dollars until January 1, 1843.

In return for these favors, the legislature imposed hard conditions. The previous limits on the amount of the note issue, and the prohibition on all payments of specie were repeated, as was the requirement that the Bank should allow its debtors to pay in ten installments. In addition, it was provided that loans to directors should in no case exceed $5,000 at any one time. To assist the state in solving its fiscal problems, the Bank was required to purchase $50,000 of state bonds each year, for the next four years, thus increasing the excessive quantity of these obligations that the Bank already owned. Moreover, while the payment of dividends to private stockholders was forbidden during the period of the suspension, the Bank was obliged to pay "just and proper dividends" to the state on all the stock owned by the latter. More unconscionable provisions, from the viewpoint of banking soundness, can scarcely be imagined but, by this time, the Bank had become an integral part of the fiscal machinery of Illinois, and was bound to suffer the consequences of the chaotic financial policy.

At the same session of the legislature, for reasons that are not apparent, unless we assume that it was part of the political bargain relating to the authority for renewed suspension, the State Treasury resumed responsibility for the Wiggins loan of 1831, allowing the second Bank of the State to turn over to the Treasurer $100,000 of state bonds in full settlement of its obligation in that matter. With a return to the melodramatic holocausts that accompanied the extinction of the first State Bank of Illinois, it was provided that these bonds should be publicly burned by the Governor,[73] although it is scarcely probable that the extinction of so small a part of the total outstanding obligation could have had any appreciable effect on their value.

The Bank of Illinois at Shawneetown was no more able than the second Bank of the State to escape from the attentions of the politicians. Although the suspension of specie payments did not legally entail any forfeiture of the charter in this case, the Bank was persuaded to accept the conditions imposed upon the second Bank of the State by a provision allowing it to charge higher rates of interest on its loans if it did so.[74] Moreover, as a condition imposed by the state in regard to the settlement of the loans that the Shawneetown Bank had made for the building of the new State House, it was required to accept Auditor's warrants in payment of the amounts due,[75] so that its relationship to the finances of the state became almost as close as that of the second Bank of the State.

The perilous position in which the banks were placed by this legislation did not, however, exercise a sobering effect upon their officers and directors. If anything, the result was the exact reverse; both institutions gave up the policies of credit contraction that they had espoused dur-

ing the preceding months, and began to make loans freely
once again. The second Bank of the State, although it was
practically insolvent, and saw its stock selling in New
York for thirty-seven cents on the dollar, began to build
new and expensive banking premises,[76] while the directors, as further evidence of their frenzied optimism,
worked out a plan by which they could use the funds of
the Bank for the purpose of taking over from the state
the unfinished Northern Cross Railroad, and completing
it for their own profit.[77] Moreover, as an indication of the
lax attitude of the management, it is interesting to note
that in July, 1841, a teller of the Jacksonville branch of
the Bank, who had been systematically robbing it for
years, was able to destroy all the accounts and records in
the branch before making his escape.[78]

Under a new agreement, negotiated among the western
banks, specie payments were to be resumed on June 15,
1842, and the Bank of Illinois at Shawneetown (in common with the banks of Kentucky and Missouri) appears
to have anticipated this date by redeeming its notes in
coin as early as February of that year.[79] The second Bank
of the State suffered by comparison, since it was in no position to take such a step, but the triumph of the Bank at
Shawneetown was short-lived.

In the spring of 1842, a minor panic destroyed more
than one hundred and fifty banks in various parts of the
United States. Almost all the financial institutions that
had been heavily interested in real-estate mortgages or
public improvements succumbed, and both of the Illinois banks were among the casualties. At the end of February, 1842, the directors of the second Bank of the State

announced that the Bank was compelled to suspend further operations and, in the course of a few weeks, the value of its notes had fallen to forty-four cents on the dollar.[80] The Bank at Shawneetown was able to hold out a little longer but, in June, "it followed in the footsteps of its illustrious predecessor" and closed its doors.[81]

Before the end of 1842, specie payments were resumed in most parts of the United States, but in Illinois there was monetary chaos. The steady depreciation of the bank notes, and the issue of these notes in small denominations, had effectively driven all other kinds of money out of circulation, so that the business of the state had to be conducted by means of an ephemeral currency of uncertain value. Farmers refused to sell their crops unless specie were offered in payment,[82] business came to a standstill, and the neighboring states began to complain bitterly about the inconvenience they suffered from the influx of Illinois paper money.[83] Even the banks themselves were so reluctant to accept their own notes that a law was passed for the specific purpose of compelling them to do so.[84]

Yet, serious as the banking collapse was, it constituted only a part of the whole picture. Banks were intimately related to the fiscal policies of the state, and both were involved in the public-improvements nightmare, so that the final breakdown of the banks can be appreciated only when it is considered in conjunction with the collapse of public credit. The bonds of the State of Illinois, which had sold around fifty-five on the New York market, during the late summer of 1841, were quoted at nineteen on March 1, 1842, and had fallen to fifteen by April 15.[85]

By that time Illinois was listed, along with Mississippi and Pennsylvania, as a defaulting state. It is necessary, therefore, to retrace the sequence of events in order to watch the development of the fiscal situation during the period of banking disintegration.

As a result of the second suspension of specie payments, in 1839, the whole scheme of internal improvements was finally abandoned by the legislature.[86] The Board of Commissioners of Public Works was abolished, and the number of Fund Commissioners was reduced from three to one, while provision was made for the sale of all the uncompleted public works to any purchasers that could be found. But this decision, significant as it was, did not solve the fiscal problems of Illinois. Work on the Canal had to be continued, since the state was under obligation to the federal government to complete the project, and an annual interest bill of $637,800 had to be paid on the $11,000,000 which had already been borrowed to finance the program,[87] both of these expenditures being in addition to the normal expenses of state government.

Logically, the sanest method of approaching the problem would have been to increase taxation to a point where the revenue would meet all the financial obligations of the state, but to the Governor and the legislature this must have seemed a counsel of impossible perfection. The people were already impoverished by the depression, and had violently resented the increase in taxation two years before—so violently indeed that it had been impossible to collect the levies in some parts of the state. To meet the demands of the Governor, the legislature did impose an additional tax of ten cents on every hundred

dollars' worth of property, and an effort was made to increase the yield of all taxes by fixing three dollars an acre
as the minimum valuation of farm lands,[88] but these
amendments were not expected to provide more than a
small portion of the revenue needed. In order to supplement them, an effort was made to find some painless
method by which the financial reputation of the state
could be saved, and one of the first suggestions was that
the state should buy $3,000,000 more bank stock for the
purpose of augmenting its revenue by the dividends
which it would receive.[89]

This was too much, even for legislative optimism, and
the report of the committee to which the matter was referred is withering in its scorn. "Up to the period of 1836
and '37, when that capital [of the banks] was increased,
our whole debt was only one hundred thousand dollars.
Three years have since elapsed, and what is the history of
that short period? Paper money multiplied—foreign debts
created—visionary schemes of internal improvements
commenced and abandoned—prodigality abounding in
every department, till we now find ourselves burthened
with a debt of thirteen millions. . . . The baseless fabric
has vanished and left nothing but the debt behind. Can
we expect a different result should we add three millions
to our present capital? . . . As these institutions, therefore, have been unable to manage a State investment of
three millions of dollars, for a period of three years, but
by expansions, contractions, and consequent suspensions . . . your committee would submit whether it be
the part of wisdom to entrust such agents with the control
of an additional sum of three millions."[90]

But the same scorn might equally well have been applied to other schemes that the legislature saw fit to adopt. Canal lands were sold, on long-term credit, to pay the current interest on outstanding bonds,[91] and authority was given to the Canal Commissioners to sell additional bonds, from time to time, for the same purpose.[92] Moreover, when the bonds could not be sold for par, the Governor was authorized to hypothecate them as security for loans of lesser amounts.[93] The state was disposing of its capital, often at ruinous prices, and pledging its future income up to the hilt, for the purpose of meeting current obligations, apparently on the assumption that the federal government would sooner or later step into the breach and save it from the consequences of its own folly.[94]

Such a policy could not have been other than ruinous, but its effects were exaggerated by the extraordinarily loose fashion in which the raising of loans was handled. When a loan was authorized by the legislature, the bonds were signed by the appropriate officials and, sometimes without any precise record of the transaction, turned over to agents "who undertook costly journeys at the expense of the State, exacted and gave extravagant commissions, hypothecated the bonds for a fraction of their value with bankers who failed and involved the collateral in their bankruptcy; or sold them to be paid for in installments, delivering the whole in advance, so that when the bankers failed, as a great many of them did, the bonds had passed out, by sale or as collateral, into the hands of innocent holders. . . . What wonder that the whole system was a carnival of waste, extravagance and peculation?"[95] Nor were adequate records kept, even after the bonds had been finally sold, since the preamble to the funding act of 1847 suggests, rather lamentably, that "from the want of a full and perfect record of the classes, numbers and description of the bonds so issued, it is impossible at the present time to determine the precise amount of the indebtedness of the State, its character, and when payable."[96]

By such loose methods, with different agents of the state often in competition with one another, every conceivable source of accommodation was tapped during these years of frenzied finance. Whenever other lenders refused to supply the necessary funds, the Illinois banks were called upon to lend additional sums to the state, while the financial institutions of other states were warmly invited to extend similar assistance. Large blocks of bonds were sold to the Bank of the United States, under an arrangement by which the notes of that Bank would be taken in payment and disbursed to the workers along the line of the Canal.[97] When the free banking system[98] was adopted by New York, the Fund Commissioners supplied New York bank promoters with Illinois bonds that could be deposited as collateral to secure the circulation of notes. Payment was supposed to be made in the notes of the projected bank, after it was organized, but many of the "swindling banks" failed utterly, so that Illinois received nothing at all. Even at the end of 1842, there were outstanding some $327,000 of Illinois bonds supplied to New York banks, on which no payment had been received.[99]

Funds obtained from banks were, however, less important, in the aggregate, than the loans negotiated by agents who sold, or pledged, securities in the capital markets of New York and London. Sometimes there were two or more agents operating at cross purposes, frequently an agent would exceed his authority when arranging a contract, while inefficiency was aggravated by dishonesty in some cases, so that innumerable problems arose for which no single individual could be held definitely responsible. In May, 1839, for example, $283,000 of Illinois bonds were sold by an agent to John Delafield, of New York, on very liberal terms. The purchaser was to pay for them in five installments spread over a period of fourteen months, and he was assured that no other bonds of the state would be sold during that period. But another agent, a few weeks later, arranged for the public offering of a large block of bonds in London, which depressed the New York price by 20 per cent, so that Delafield repudiated the contract on the ground that the state had violated it.[100] At the time, he had already paid $170,000, but he refused to pay any more, and the state was compelled to declare the transaction illegal on the ground that the agents had sold the bonds below par and on credit. The New York courts, however, while admitting this contention as between Delafield and the state, insisted that the securities were perfectly valid in the hands of innocent holders, and would have to be paid in full by the state when presented by such third parties.[101]

Much the same story has to be told in the case of the negotiations with John Wright and Company, of London.[102] The agents of the Fund Commissioners agreed to turn over to Wright $1,500,000 in Illinois bonds, in return for two advances and, at the same time, the agents of the Canal Commissioners also signed an independent contract with him for the sale of $1,000,000 Canal bonds. As in the case of all Illinois securities, the law prohibited the sale of either of these blocks of bonds at less than par, but the parties to the contract seem to have interpreted this provision of the statutes in very strange fashion. In the case of the Internal Improvement securities, it was arbitrarily decided that the State of Illinois should receive $1,000 for each £225 sterling bond, a decision that allowed a liberal margin, at current foreign-exchange rates, for the compensation of the London bankers and the agents of the Fund Commissioners. The scheme for the sale of Canal bonds was even more blatantly illegal. Wright agreed to pay ninety-one for the securities, and to sell them on the London market at not less than that figure. If he received a higher price than that, but not in excess of ninety-five, he could pocket the difference but, if the price went above the latter figure, he was to pay the Canal Commissioners half of the amount received in excess of ninety-five.

In all probability, these arrangements were the best that Illinois could expect, in the light of its financial condition, but the contract was held to be illegal by the legislature and Wright was denounced as a shark and a leech.[103] The contract was not repudiated, however. Instead, a plan was resorted to whereby the Canal contractors received the bonds at par and reimbursed themselves by marketing the securities at a discount, under the state's contract with Wright, accepting the resultant loss as a lesser injury than they would sustain if work on the Canal were entirely stopped by lack of funds. Matters became complicated, however, by the fact that the discussion of the contract, and the uncertainty regarding the fiscal policies of Illinois, made Wright's position impossible. He failed in November, 1840, after selling more than $500,-000 of the bonds, and the state was compelled to participate as a creditor in the liquidation in order to get its money.

Finally, as a last resort, $804,000 of bonds were pledged with McAllister and Stebbins, of Philadelphia, on June 17, 1841, to secure a loan of $261,500 and, since these bankers sold several of the bonds to innocent third parties, Illinois once again found itself in a position where it was called upon to assume full responsibility for securities that it had disposed of at a few cents on the dollar. Years of legislation and litigation were necessary to determine precisely the amount of the obligation thus incurred.[104]

All these transactions left a permanent record in the elaborate compilation of the public debts of Illinois which is reproduced in Appendix I. Yet these figures, fascinating as they are, do not reveal the whole situation. By the end of 1842, the whole fiscal system had collapsed as completely as the banks. The public debt, exclusive of the obligation to the School Fund, amounted to $14,-237,348, and the School Fund itself held $472,493 in state bonds.[105] No provision had been made for the payment of interest and the Treasury was empty, so that the securities of the state were selling as low as fifteen in New York and the bank notes in circulation were worth only a third of their face value. "The whole people were indebted to the merchants; nearly all of whom were indebted to the banks, or to foreign merchants; and the banks owed everybody; and none were able to pay."[106] So low had the credit of the state sunk that the postmaster would not deliver documents to the State House unless one of the officials became personally responsible for the postage.[107]

In such circumstances, it was only natural that the people of Illinois should turn to the idea of repudiation. "All their grand schemes were frustrated, their visions of wealth were dissipated, and their present and future resources pledged for the payment of debts" to an extent that appeared unconscionably burdensome.[108] Moreover, repudiation was in the air. Even New York had only scotched the idea by completely abandoning her program of public works, in which even the banking Safety Fund had been invested, and imposing upon her citizens an enormous burden of taxation,[109] while states like Florida and Mississippi had not only repudiated openly, but had boasted of the action as a humanitarian measure.[110] "So far from there being bad faith or a want of honor or honesty in repudiating these bonds," the Governor of Florida insisted that "it is entirely consistent with good faith thus to deal with them. They were obtained through a legislation partial and unjust. What right had a few hundred stockholders to make the whole people tributary to their schemes of moneyed aggrandizement? Why should the holders of these instruments be longer deceived?"

Illinois, under the able administration of Governor Ford, did not resort to either of these extremes. While the legislators were unwilling to go to the lengths to which New York had gone in the matter of taxation, they stated their determination to avoid open repudiation at all costs.[111] The previous failure to meet the State's obligations was due, they insisted, to a lack of means and not to any lack of desire, and temporary default could not be regarded as dishonorable "when such failure proceeds from inability and inevitable circumstances." Since the total debts of Illinois were small when compared with the natural resources, they resolved that "we must only await with patience that period, which cannot be remote, when a sufficient amount of sound currency will be in circulation to secure to our agricultural population a fair price for their productions, and will enable them to pay all necessary taxes to meet the wants of the government at home and discharge with integrity all our obligations to our creditors abroad."

The phraseology may not sound strong to a modern reader, who is used to more definitive promises, but to those men gathered in Springfield, in 1843, the passing of such a resolution required a degree of courage that cannot be too highly admired. Only twelve years before, the legislators had committed political suicide when they undertook to honor an obligation of $100,000, and repudiation sentiment among the populace had not diminished during the intervening years. Moreover, the promise, for all its cautious phrasing was sincere enough, and action was promptly taken to implement it.

Legislation was passed imposing a tax of twenty cents on every hundred dollars' worth of property, with provision that the tax should be collected annually "until otherwise provided by law."[112] All payments on account of this tax were to be made "in gold and silver coin or Auditor's warrants, and in no other currency," while severe penalties were imposed upon all who were delinquent in regard to this, or to previous, taxes. Moreover, serious efforts, were made to improve the machinery for the collection of all taxes, in order to eliminate the heavy losses that had regularly occurred, in the past, as a result of the inefficiency and dishonesty of public officials.[113] To prevent any continuance of the haphazard practices by which the public debt had grown so rapidly, the office of Fund Commissioner was abolished, his duties being taken over by the Governor *ex officio*,[114] while all agents or bankers who had unsold bonds of the state in their possession were ordered to return them immediately for destruction. Any refusal to obey these orders, or any attempt to sell bonds after the acts were passed, was to constitute a felony punishable with from one to ten years' imprisonment.[115]

To bring order out of the monetary chaos, all cities and towns throughout the state were forbidden to issue circulating warrants of any kind,[116] and any local officers who had such warrants, or other "uncurrent money," in their treasuries were ordered to dispose of it at once to the best advantage.[117] No more notes of the Illinois banks were to be received in payment of amounts due to the state,[118] and the State Treasurer was to pay out, in settlement of any warrants drawn upon him, the bank notes that he already had on hand. Such notes were to pass at 50 per cent of their face value. When all paper money had been disposed of, however, warrants were to be paid in specie, at par, and the Treasurer was ordered to retire all of them as rapidly as possible.[119]

These measures did much to put the fiscal affairs of the state in better condition, but there remained two inescapable problems: public works and the banks. All the internal improvements, except the Canal, were to be offered for sale to the highest bidder, at public auction, the buyer being required to make payment in gold, in silver or in internal-improvement bonds at par,[120] but the Canal could not be disposed of in this fashion. Illinois was under obligation to the federal government to complete this project, and completion would involve additional expenditures of some $1,600,000. The legislature, therefore, proposed that, if the creditors would advance this sum, the whole enterprise should be turned over to a Board of Trustees on which the bondholders would have a majority representation. These trustees would be required to finish the construction of the waterway in a period of not more than two years but, in return, they would receive title to all the assets of the Canal, and all its revenues after completion. Only when all the new loan had been repaid should the Canal revert to the ownership of the state.[121]

It was a thoroughly reasonable proposition. Even though many obstacles were to be encountered before it passed from the realm of suggestion to that of formal agreement, the mere proposal was a constructive step. Taken in conjunction with the other measures passed at the session, it raised the credit of Illinois substantially, both in London and in New York. By September, 1843, Illinois bonds were selling at forty in the latter market.[122]

The solution of the banking problem was even more difficult, since nobody wanted to buy the banks, or put more money into them, while their immediate liquidation promised to impose serious losses upon the State Treasury, which was already in dire straits, and upon the whole population of Illinois. In spite of this unpleasant prospect, liquidation was strongly recommended by Governor Carlin, in his valedictory message to the legislature. "It is folly," he insisted, "to hope for better times while the channels of trade are choked up with depreciated paper. So long as the banks are continued in existence, so long will the prosperity of our people be retarded. They have almost sucked the life-blood out of the State already. Instead of bringing in foreign capital and disseminating it amongst the people, they have been effective engines in the hands of foreign speculators to drain the State of all its substantial wealth. Since the establishment of these institutions, there have been $10 millions of money borrowed and expended amongst the citizens of Illinois. Wealth has also been obtained from immigration, and the exportation of domestic products, and yet all this has disappeared as if by enchantment, and the State, in 1842, finds itself steeped in poverty and depending for a currency upon depreciated paper."[123]

This philippic oration was rather surprising, and it did not accord with the plans of the incoming Governor. Ford recognized as clearly as Carlin that the banks would have to be wound up; he was equally aware that their operations had not been in the best interests of the community, as a whole. But Ford's ambition was to restore the finances of Illinois to a sound basis, and he was anxious to avoid the losses that such peremptory liquidation would impose upon the Treasury. Even though they were on their last legs, the banks might be milked once more for the benefit of the state.

With that end in view, the legislature was persuaded to pass a resolution, authorizing the Governor to open negotiations with the banks, for the purpose of deciding "upon what terms an amicable dissolution between the State and said Banks can be effected."[124] This was a more subtle procedure than Carlin's; and the report[125] of the negotiations is Machiavellian in its simplicity. The state owned $2,100,000 of stock in the second Bank of the State, while the Bank held Illinois bonds and short-term obligations to an aggregate amount of $2,152,404. What could be more reasonable than an exchange of bank stock for state bonds, thereby dissolving the relationship between the two without any loss to the state? Moreover, why should not a similar policy be applied in the case of the Bank of Illinois at Shawneetown? Obviously, such a plan would be of tremendous benefit to the state, since it would diminish the outstanding debt by more than $3,-000,000, and nobody appears to have worried very much about the fact that it would seriously increase the loss of private individuals who held notes of the banks, and of private capitalists who had invested in their stock.

The bill drawn up, on this basis, for the liquidation of the second Bank of the State[126] was promptly passed by the legislature. Despite the heated opposition of such men as Peck and Trumbull, the final vote in the House was 107 to 4. The Bank was to undertake no new operations, and the directors were required to wind up its affairs during the course of the next four years. Branch offices were to be closed immediately, and all records transferred to the principal office, where debtors might settle their obligations in five equal annual installments. Within five days after the passage of the act, the directors of the Bank were required to give the Governor $2,050,000 in the form of state obligations in exchange for $2,050,000 of bank stock, which they were required to cancel immediately, while, even in the case of the remaining $50,000 of stock, which the state retained during the liquidation to avoid any arguments regarding the constitutionality of the Bank, it was provided that, at the expiration of the time allowed for winding up, the Bank should redeem this stock "by bonds or other state indebtedness, or gold and silver." The Governor was also impowered to appoint a Bank Commissioner to supervise the liquidation and see that the terms of the act were properly carried out.

The Bank of Illinois at Shawneetown was not so easy to handle. Although the directors had no objection to an exchange of bank stock for state bonds, they were strongly opposed to any liquidation of the Bank, which had the right, under its charter, to continue operations for another fifteen years. Governor Ford and the legislature were both determined, however, that it should go into liquidation, and equally anxious to achieve that end without such formal bankruptcy proceedings as would involve the state in loss.

Skillful legislative blackmail was resorted to by passing two separate and independent acts in regard to the Bank. The first of these[127] repealed the charter of the Bank and placed the assets in the hands of three Commissioners, appointed by the Governor, who were required to liquidate the institution as rapidly as possible. Even in this act, it was provided that the Commissioners should not sell any Illinois bonds until all the other assets had been realized and, even then, they might not sell them at less than par value! The other act[128] allowed the Bank at Shawneetown to go into voluntary liquidation, under the continuing control of its existing management, subject to conditions similar to those imposed on the second Bank of the State, provided that the directors surrendered to the Governor an amount of Illinois bonds equal in par value to the $1,000,000 of bank stock held by the state. If the terms of the second act were voluntarily accepted by the management of the Bank, the first act was to be suspended for a period of four years, in order to allow ample time for voluntary liquidation.

Few legislative acts, at any time or in any country, have more deliberately and cold-bloodedly served the interests of the government at the expense of a substantial minority of the population, but in both cases the terms of the law were duly carried out. As Ford himself says of the banks, "in the day of their power they had friends, many of whom were the first to desert them in their troubles and weakness. They were shorn of their strength. There were none so poor now as to do them reverence."[129] The Bank at Shawneetown willingly accepted the terms of the second act, in order to avoid the open bankruptcy threatened by the first, and the state bonds surrendered by the two banks were publicly destroyed in a great bonfire before the members of the General Assembly. Moreover, when an effort was made by some of the private creditors of the banks to improve their own position in the liquidation, the legislature promptly emphasized the difference between governments and private individuals. A law was passed making the specie of the banks immune from seizure by execution.[130]

The little Bank of Cairo was not able to escape the general enthusiasm for bank destruction. Although it had been operating soundly, and inconspicuously, for several years and, as late as 1840, was furnishing two-thirds of the small notes used in the southwestern portion of Illinois, its directors grew too optimistic soon after that and used a substantial portion of the Bank's funds to finance the Cairo City and Canal Company.[131] As a result, the institution was forced into bankruptcy during the general collapse of February, 1842, and suspended all operations.[132]

Since the Bank was small, and the state had no money invested in it, the legislature was merciless. Instead of any polite bargaining, comparable to that used in the case of the Bank of Illinois, the charter of the Bank of Cairo was peremptorily repealed[133] and a Commissioner was appointed by the Governor to take over the assets and liquidate the institution as rapidly as possible. Moreover, to add insult to injury, the Commissioner was also instructed to conduct an investigation of the past management of the Bank, at the expense of the shareholders and creditors.

Although the sad story of these bank liquidations was to drag on for many years, it is perhaps worth while to pause a moment in order to consider their history. Twice, in as many decades, Illinois had experimented with a Bank of the State, and on both occasions the experiment had come very near to destroying the economy that it was intended to serve. That the fault did not lie in the nature of the banks is obvious from the admirable record of the State Bank of Indiana, a few miles away across the border, a record that was to continue until that Bank was voluntarily wound up in 1865. In part, the responsibility for the failure of the Banks of the State of Illinois rests upon the shoulders of their directors and officers, who were responsible for the adoption of policies that were both unwise and unsound; in even larger proportion, it rests upon the shoulders of the legislators who had attempted continuously to use the banks for political ends. Banking as a relief measure had proved painful; banking as an instrument for the promotion of internal improvements and public works was disastrous. In both cases, a lack of wisdom on the part of the politicians had combined with the inefficiency of politically appointed bankers to bring about conditions of financial chaos and economic depression.

REFERENCES FOR CHAPTER IV

[1] *History of Banking*, I, 270.
[2] Raguet: *Currency and Banking*, p. 96; *Financial Register*, 1838, p. 9.
[3] *History of Banking*, I, 266.
[4] For a detailed account of the financial revulsion, cf. *History of Banking*, I, 266-285, from which much of the material for these paragraphs is drawn.
[5] Cf. Dewey: *op. cit.*, pp. 170-172 and 179-180.
[6] See above p. 103.
[7] *History of Banking*, I, 294.
[8] Six banks, including the Bank of Missouri, did refuse to suspend specie payments. Cf. *History of Banking*, I, 280.

[9] *Sangamo Journal,* June 3, 1837.

[10] Andreas: *op. cit.,* I, 181.

[11] *Idem,* 150; Pierce: *op. cit.,* I, 67. The scrip bore interest at 1 per cent per annum until paid.

[12] *Chicago American,* May 16, 1837.

[13] Andreas: *op. cit.,* I, 531.

[14] Memorials on a National Bank of the Citizens of Illinois, *Executive Documents Nos. 8 and 23; 25 Congress, 1 Session.*

[15] *Laws of Illinois,* 1837, *Special Session,* pp. 6-7. Approved July 21, 1837.

[16] *Laws of Illinois,* 1836-37, 2 *Session,* p. 9. Approved July 21, 1837.

[17] Cf. Pease: *op. cit.,* pp. 216-218.

[18] Ford: *op. cit.,* p. 184.

[19] *Sangamo Journal,* July 29, 1837, August 19, 1837; Pease: *op. cit.,* pp. 219 ff.

[20] *Laws of Illinois,* 1836-37, 2 *Session,* pp. 10-13. Approved July 21, 1837.

[21] Pierce: *op. cit.,* I, 70.

[22] *House Journal,* 1838-39, p. 14.

[23] *Hunt's,* IX, 279; See also *Report of a Committee of New York Banks on Resumption,* February 28, 1838.

[24] Dowrie: *op. cit.,* p. 85; *Report of the Comptroller of the Currency,* 1876, pp. cxviii-cxix.

[25] *History of Banking,* I, 291.

[26] *Journal of Commerce,* New York, April 23, 1838.

[27] *Sangamo Journal,* August 18, 1838.

[28] *Annual Report of the Secretary of the Treasury,* 1838; *History of Banking,* I, 292-293.

[29] *Laws of Illinois,* 1838-39, pp. 7-8. Approved December 4, 1838.

[30] *House Journal,* 1838-39, p. 14.

[31] *Senate Journal,* 1838-39, p. 18.

[32] *Reports of the Session (Senate),* 1839-40, p. 5.

[33] *Laws of Illinois,* 1838-39, pp. 3-17. Approved February 26, 1839.

[34] Cf. Pease: *op. cit.,* pp. 211-222.

[35] *Laws of Illinois,* 1838-39, p. 41. Approved January 5, 1839.

[36] *Laws of Illinois,* 1838-39, p. 41. Approved January 21, 1839.

[37] *Laws of Illinois,* 1838-39, pp. 150-152. Approved February 22, 1839.

[38] *Laws of Illinois,* 1838-39, p. 157. Approved February 22, 1839.

[39] *Laws of Illinois,* 1838-49, pp. 168-169. Approved February 23, 1839.

[40] *Laws of Illinois,* 1838-39, pp. 177-182. Approved February 26, 1839.

[41] *History of Banking,* I, 298.

[42] *Niles',* LXIV, 5; *History of Banking,* I, 334.

[43] *Niles',* LVI, 351, quoting *Manchester Guardian,* July 3, 1839.

[44] Details of this operation, and of the other activities of the Bank are presented fully in the report of the legislative committee that investigated the institution in 1839. *Reports of the Session (Senate),* 1839-40, pp. 241 ff. See also Dowrie: *op. cit.,* pp. 176-178.

[45] Ford: *op. cit.,* p. 177.

[46] *Reports of the Session (Senate),* 1839-40, p. 310.

[47] *Letters of the Secretary of the Treasury Relative to certain Illinois Banks, Feb. 13, 1839. Senate Document 219, 25 Congress, 3 Session.*

[48] Ford: *op. cit.,* p. 224; *Reports of the Session (House),* 1842-43, pp. 203-205.

[49] *Niles',* LIX, 227.

[50] Benzanson, Gray and Hussey: *Wholesale Prices in Philadelphia,* 1784-1861. See chart opposite p. 300 for summary picture.

[51] *Report of the Committee on Bribery and Corruption by the Banks,* Harrisburg, 1840.

[52] *Niles',* LX, 121; *History of Banking,* I, 304-305.

[53] *Niles',* LVII, 167.

[54] *Reports of the Session (Senate),* 1839-40, p. 46.

[55] *Laws of Illinois,* 1839-40, *Special Session,* pp. 15-17. Approved January 31, 1840.

[56] *Senate Journal,* 1839-40, *Special Session,* pp. 9-19. No investigation of the Bank at Shawneetown was demanded.

[57] *Reports of the Session (Senate),* 1839-40, p. 241 ff.

[58] See below pp. 130-131.

[59] *Reports of Session (Senate),* 1839-40, p. 308.

[60] *Hunt's,* VIII, 78.

[61] *Chicago American,* October 9, 1840; Ford: *op. cit.,* p. 227.

[62] Congressman Stuart, quoted in Dowrie: *op. cit.,* p. 96.

[63] *History of Banking,* I, 340.

[64] *Laws of Illinois,* 1839-40, *Special Session, Section 1,* p. 15.

[65] Pease: *op. cit.,* pp. 310-311; Dowrie: *op. cit.,* pp. 97-98; Ford: *op. cit.,* pp. 225-226; *Chicago American,* December 10, 1840.

[66] *Sangamo Journal,* December 18, 1840.

[67] *Reports of Session (Senate),* 1840-41, p. 14.

[68] *Chicago American,* December 18, 1840; Ford: *op. cit.,* p. 225.

[69] *History of Banking,* I, 342 and 364.

[70] *Idem,* 398-399; Dowrie: *op. cit.,* p. 99.

[71] *Reports of Session (Senate),* 1840-41, p. 416 ff.

[72] *Laws of Illinois,* 1840-41, pp. 40-42. Approved February 27, 1841.

[73] *Laws of Illinois,* 1840-41, p. 246. Approved February 27, 1841.

[74] *Laws of Illinois,* 1840-41, *Section 2,* p. 40; *Section 6,* p. 41.

[75] *Laws of Illinois,* 1840-41, p. 39. Approved February 26, 1841.

[76] *Chicago Democrat,* September 14, 1841.

[77] Ford: *op. cit.,* pp. 223-224.

[78] *Report of the State Auditor,* 1842.

[79] *Hunt's,* VII, 78-79.

[80] *Sangamo Journal,* March 25, 1842; April 8, 1842.

[81] Ford: *op. cit.,* p. 223.

[82] Pierce: *op. cit.,* I, 129-130.

[83] *History of Banking,* I, 412.

[84] *Laws of Illinois,* 1842-43, p. 21. Approved December 22, 1842.

[85] *Hunt's,* VIII, 78-79.

[86] *Laws of Illinois,* 1839-40, *Special Session,* p. 93. Approved February 1, 1840; *Laws of Illinois,* 1840-41, p. 166. Approved December 14, 1840.

[87] *Reports of the Session (Senate),* 1839-40, p. 3.

[88] *Laws of Illinois,* 1840-41, p. 165. Approved February 27, 1841.

[89] *Reports of the Session (House),* 1840-41, pp. 13-14.

[90] *Idem,* pp. 14-16.

[91] *Laws of Illinois,* 1839-40, pp. 79-80. Approved February 1, 1840.

[92] *Laws of Illinois,* 1840-41, p. 165, *Section 4.* Approved February 27, 1841.

[93] *Laws of Illinois,* 1840-41, p. 167. Approved December 16, 1840.

[94] Pease: *op. cit.,* p. 235.

[95] *History of Banking,* I, 384.

[96] *Laws of Illinois,* 1846-47, p. 161. Approved February 28, 1847.

[97] *Hunt's,* XXVII, 662; XXXVIII, 278. This naturally reduced the chances of such notes being presented in Philadelphia for redemption.

[98] See below p. 184.

[99] *Hunt's,* XXVII, 664; Ford: *op. cit.,* p. 193.

[100] *Reports of the Session (House),* 1839-40, p. 393; *Hunt's,* XXVII, 664; *History of Banking,* I, 411; Pease: *op. cit.,* p. 225.

[101] *Delafield v. The State of Illinois,* 26 Wendell 192-228.

[102] *Reports of the Session (House),* 1839-40, p. 393; *Reports of the Session (Senate),* 1840-41, pp. 360-374; Pease: *op. cit.,* pp. 225-227; Ford: *op. cit.,* p. 193.

[103] *Senate Journal,* 1839-40, *Special Session,* p. 140.

[104] *Laws of Illinois,* 1842-43, p. 287. Approved March 4, 1843.

[105] Ford: *op. cit.,* pp. 79 and 198; *Hunt's,* VIII, 561, gives the total debt of the State as $13,836,379, but Ford's figures are presumably more accurate.

[106] Ford: *op. cit.,* p. 278.

[107] *History of Banking,* I, 407.

[108] *Hunt's,* VIII, 153-156.

[109] *History of Banking,* I, 336 and 359.

[110] *Idem,* 319 and 381 ff.

[111] *Resolutions in Relation to the State Debt* (Passed February 21, 1843); *Laws of Illinois,* 1842-43, pp. 335-337.

[112] *Laws of Illinois,* 1842-43, pp. 228-229. Approved February 20, 1843; pp. 231-237. Approved March 6, 1843.

[113] *Report of the State Auditor,* December 1, 1850, *Laws of Illinois,* 1851, p. 23.

[114] *Laws of Illinois,* 1842-43, pp. 147, 148 and 339. Approved March 4, 1843.

[115] *Laws of Illinois,* 1842-43, pp. 42 and 43. Approved March 3, 1843.

[116] *Laws of Illinois,* 1842-43, p. 67. Approved March 4, 1843.

[117] *Laws of Illinois,* 1842-43, p. 239. Approved March 6, 1843.

[118] *Laws of Illinois,* 1842-43, p. 39. Approved February 23, 1843.

[119] *Laws of Illinois,* 1842-43, p. 288. Approved March 4, 1843; p. 231. Approved February 25, 1843.

[120] *Laws of Illinois,* 1842-43, pp. 191-193. Approved March 4, 1843.

[121] *Laws of Illinois,* 1842-43, pp. 54-61. Approved February 21, 1843.

[122] *Hunt's,* IX, 562.

[123] See *History of Banking,* I, 409 for a pungent yet justifiable comment on this indictment.

[124] *Joint Resolution.* (Passed December 12, 1842.) *Laws of Illinois,* 1842-43, p. 321.

[125] *Reports of the Session (Senate),* 1842-43, p. 94.

[126] *Laws of Illinois,* 1842-43, pp. 21-26. Approved January 24, 1843.

[127] *Laws of Illinois,* 1842-43, pp. 27-30. Approved December 5, 1842.

[128] *Laws of Illinois,* 1842-43, pp. 30-36. Approved December 5, 1842.

[129] Ford: *op. cit.,* p. 300.

[130] *Laws of Illinois,* 1842-43, p. 27. Approved January 27, 1843; p. 36. Approved March 4, 1843.

[131] *Chicago American,* December 18, 1840; January 15 and 21, 1841.

[132] *Chicago Democrat,* March 21, 1843.

[133] *Laws of Illinois,* 1842-43, pp. 36-38. Approved March 4, 1843.

CHAPTER V

CONVALESCENCE

1843–1850

FIFTEEN years is not a long period, even in terms of human life, but during the years from 1835 to 1850 Illinois grew from reckless youth to sober maturity. In 1835, the enthusiasm for internal improvements, and economic panaceas of all kinds, overrode any pessimistic consideration of the probable consequences of such policies. Even when those consequences could no longer be ignored, there was still a lighthearted feeling that escape was still possible by means of repudiation, or through the assumption of state debts by the federal government. By 1850, the state had assumed the full burden of its responsibilities, and learned to husband its resources so that they might be used more wisely and effectively. Its credit was fully restored, and it carried its head high among its sister states of the Union.

Such a change was not achieved miraculously in the twinkling of an eye. Although the events of the years from 1837 to 1842 gave rise to an increasing disgust, on the part of most of the people of the state, there was little indication of any enthusiasm for reform. Perhaps the story of the years that followed might have been different if the unexpected death of the Democratic nominee for

Governor had not, at the last minute, led to the selection of Thomas Ford, but even Ford, with his high wisdom and magnificent courage, could not cure the patient by a laying on of hands. He could prescribe the method of treatment, and insistently demand, during the early, restless years, when the cure sometimes appeared more painful than the disease itself, that the prescription be consistently adhered to, but several years of painful convalescence were necessary to effect a complete recovery.

In regard to the Illinois and Michigan Canal, the only project saved from the general disaster, the legislation referred to in the previous chapter marked the initial step in a long process of rehabilitation.[1] In persuading the legislature to turn the Canal over to the bondholders, and allow it to be operated by a committee of trustees, Ford had accomplished much. The reputation of Illinois was raised considerably even by the prospect of such action. But it was a long road from the initial legislation to the final execution of the plan. The law provided that the trustees should assume control on condition that the bondholders advanced another $1,600,000, but the bondholders were extremely reluctant to pour good money after bad. When the Illinois commissioners arrived in London to negotiate the formal agreement with Barings, Rothschilds, Hope and Jardine, the four bankers representing the bondholders, they were not met with enthusiasm. Indeed, the bankers flatly refused to raise the sum demanded by Governor Ford's measure. Illinois, they pointed out, was in default, and an important matter of principle was involved. The state was making no effort to pay interest on the obligations already outstanding, so that it was unreasonable to expect investors to purchase more bonds. No formal agreement was possible until the government of Illinois had demonstrated its good intentions.

To tide over the immediate situation and to show that they were eager to cooperate, if the state would do its part, the bankers agreed to subscribe to new Canal bonds to the extent of one-eighth of the par value of the securities they already held, on condition that other bondholders would do the same. Such an arrangement would provide about $600,000, enough to finance the resumption of construction, but it was made perfectly clear that no further funds would be forthcoming unless Illinois took steps to increase its current revenue to a point where some payment of interest on its obligations became possible. Even if the state was unable, immediately, to shoulder the full burden, a regular partial payment of interest would dispel, to some extent, the fear of repudiation, which overhung the international capital market like a cloud. In that event, the bankers undertook to subscribe to a further issue of $1,000,000 of Canal bonds whenever the funds were needed to complete the project,[2] and would formally agree to set up the Board of Trustees, and assume the responsibilities, envisaged by the Illinois law.

Fair as this temporary arrangement was, funds came in very slowly from the creditors. Although work was resumed on the Canal in September, 1843, it was soon suspended again when an epidemic of fever aggravated the difficulties of the commissioners. Serious operations did not commence until much later, and even in June, 1845, the subscriptions to the new loan amounted to no more than $308,000.[3]

This delay was due, in large measure, to the back-sliding and bickering of the state legislature during the session that began in December, 1844. The moral enthusiasm of the previous session had ebbed away, and several members were opposed to the plan on the ground that the trustees of the Canal would constitute a dangerous monopoly.[4] At the other extreme, but equally strong in opposition, were members who thought the plan unnecessary. The state itself, they insisted, could complete the Canal by obtaining a further land grant from the federal government;[5] meanwhile, additional issues of state scrip could be made to finance the work.

Governor Ford, however, stuck to his policies in the face of all opposition, and succeeded in carrying them through the legislature. On March 1, 1845, an act was passed[6] reiterating the provisions of the Canal Act of 1843. All of the lands and other assets of the Canal Commissioners were transferred to the Board of Trustees for the bondholders, and the latter were given the right to register one thousand-dollar bond for every three-hundred and twenty dollars subscribed to the new loan.* Out of the proceeds of the sale of lands, and the revenue derived from the Canal, holders of the new securities were to be repaid first, registered bondholders second, and unregistered bondholders last of all—so that existing holders of Canal bonds had a strong inducement to subscribe to

* Actually this act provided for the registration of one bond for every $400 subscribed, but the English bondholders were operating on the basis of $320 and, in 1847, American bondholders were placed on the same footing. *Laws of Illinois*, 1846-47, p. 22.

the new loan.[7] Moreover, on the same day, the legislature imposed the taxation demanded by the London bankers as evidence of their good intention.[8] During 1845, a supplementary tax of one mill was levied upon all property, while, in 1846 and subsequent years, the rate was to be one and a half mills, with the express provision that the proceeds of this tax should constitute an "Interest Fund . . . pledged for the payment of interest on the State debt."

These measures, at last, justified the claim of Governor Ford that Illinois would not repudiate her obligations. As soon as they were passed, he sent out a circular to all bondholders announcing the joyful news.[9] From that point onwards, the affairs of the Canal progressed smoothly. The London bankers were fully satisfied with the gestures that the state had made and agreed to the plan that Ford had originally suggested. In June, 1845, the Board of Trustees was finally appointed, two members by the bondholders and one by the Governor. By November of the following year, considerably more than $1,000,000 of the new loan had been subscribed, $721,000 coming from Europe (chiefly London), $273,841 from New York, and $94,810 from Illinois.

Apart from personal quarrels among the trustees, and some political controversies centering around the gubernatorial appointee, the story of the construction of the Canal presents no more problems. Funds became available in ample quantities long before they were needed, and operations were pushed forward by the trustees in a manner that made possible the opening of the Canal for navigation on April 10, 1848.[10] A similar efficiency characterized their handling of the financial problems entrusted to them, so that the Illinois and Michigan Canal was no longer a factor of importance in regard to either the fiscal affairs or the banking development of the state. With its commercial importance, both to Chicago and to other parts of the country, we are not immediately concerned.*

The problems raised by the remainder of the public debt were more difficult to solve, yet the accumulation of unpaid interest, which increased the size of the debt year by year, made speedy settlement of the matter imperative. If the Canal bonds, and the state bonds held by the Illinois banks, are excluded from the calculation, the interest-bearing debt of the State of Illinois amounted to $7,003,000 when Governor Ford came into office in 1842;[11] by the end of 1844 it had grown to $8,550,000,[12] despite the sale of land and other assets during the intervening period.

The supplementary taxation imposed early in 1845, to which reference has already been made, was a step in the right direction. There was, however, no expectation that the revenue derived from these taxes would, during the early years at any rate, be adequate to meet current payments of interest in full, let alone provide for the payment of the arrears. Nor could very much be expected from the various laws passed, in 1845, to increase the efficiency of tax collection,[13] or from the effort to persuade the federal government to cede its lands to the state.[14]

---

* It may be of interest, however, to record that the last bonds of the "new loan" were paid off by the trustees in the autumn of 1853, much earlier than anyone had expected. Cf. Chicago *Daily Democratic Press*, October 14, 1853; *Hunt's*, XXXVIII, 279.

Nevertheless, a beginning had been made and, as an evidence of the financial responsibility of the state, the gesture was reinforced by the passage of a law providing that, in future, no money should be paid out of the Treasury without specific authorization by the legislature.[15] Moreover, all taxes were required to be paid in specie, since the Treasurer of the State had made the profound discovery that, "while taxes and other dues can be paid in a cheaper currency than that provided by the Constitution, neither gold, nor silver, nor their equivalent, will find their way into the Treasury."[16]

By 1848, when the delegates convened at Springfield to prepare a new constitution for the state, the determination of Illinois to assume its financial responsibilities was well recognized in the money markets of the world, although the inability of the state to pay interest in full had prevented the price of its bonds from rising much above the figure of forty-six, which was attained by the end of 1843.[17] But the action of the Constitutional Convention was decisive in reestablishing the public finances. In the first place, the new Constitution provided that Illinois should never contract debts exceeding $50,000, in the aggregate, unless the law authorizing the loan should specifically provide for taxation sufficient to repay it; even in that case, the law was not to take effect until it had been approved by referendum.[18] Secondly, it provided that, in addition to the existing tax of one and a half mills to pay interest on the state debt, another supplementary tax of two mills should be levied annually for the purpose of repaying the principal,[19] both of these being additional to the levies imposed for the purpose of paying current expenses.

While some question may be raised as to the wisdom of beginning repayment of the principal before arrears and current interest were met in full,[20] there can be none regarding the courage of the action taken. The revenue derived from these special taxes grew year by year, as the wealth of the state increased, and the resultant flow of payments to the bondholders caused a steady rise in the price of outstanding securities. By the end of 1850, Illinois bonds were selling at sixty-four, during 1854 they rose to eighty-five, and the following year they were selling well above par.[21] By that time, Illinois had attained a financial prestige greater than that enjoyed at any previous period in her history, and her securities were eagerly purchased by European investors.[22]

One aspect of the process of rehabilitation deserves special mention, however, since it brought to light some strange examples of the earlier financing. Early in 1847, the legislature passed a refunding act,[23] admitting in the preamble that the method of issuing securities in the past, and the similarity of coupons belonging to different issues, had caused great confusion and facilitated fraud. In order "to discover the actual amount and character of the State debt," bondholders were asked to present all securities (except those issued by the Canal Commissioners) to the Governor of the state, so that they might be examined and, if valid, exchanged for an equal amount of "New Internal Improvement Stock of the State of Illinois." At the same time, the bondholders were to receive, for the arrears of interest, state scrip that was to bear "interest after 1856 if it had not been paid before that time." It was hoped, moreover, that it would be possible, by these methods, to determine the precise amount of the unliquidated claims against the state, and to settle these in similar fashion by the transfer of new bonds.[24]

These were not simple tasks. The time allowed for the refunding of the old bonds was utterly inadequate and, in 1849, was extended indefinitely until such date as the Governor might fix.[25] A transfer agent was also appointed in New York to facilitate the exchanges made by eastern investors.[26] As late as 1852, the question of unliquidated claims was far from settled, and a legislative committee (with Abraham Lincoln as one of its members) was appointed to study the contentions of the various claimants.

Nor is the delay surprising, in view of the problems that confronted the Governor in his *ex officio* capacity as Fund Commissioner. In 1839, to take one of the most complex cases, the Canal Commissioners were short of funds and had borrowed from the Fund Commissioners. Canal bonds were given in exchange for the loan. At a later date, these Canal bonds were sold by the Fund Commissioners, to finance the building of the Northern Cross Railroad, and, at the time of sale, a pledge was endorsed on the face of each of them that all profits derived from the railroad would be applied to the payment of the interest coupons. Since that time, the railroad had been sold by the state, and there were no profits, but the securities were still in the hands of investors and the question of liability for their payment had to be settled. Were these bonds an obligation of the Canal, now in the hands of the trustees, or of the Internal Improvement Fund, for which the state was liable? At first the legislature tried to pass the burden on to the Canal trustees, but this action gave rise to a flat refusal, on their part, to assume responsibility for the bonds. After a long controversy, they were acknowledged by the state and exchanged for new bonds under the refunding act.[27]

Even more serious were the activities of ex-Governor Matteson, who had been, and (stranger still) continued to be, one of the leading financiers and politicians of the state. As a contractor on the Canal, Matteson had received large quantities of state scrip, which he later surrendered in exchange for state bonds under the terms of the law passed, in 1847, for the purpose of settling the financial obligations that had arisen in connection with the Canal during the period immediately preceding the appointment of the Board of Trustees.[28] But Matteson, who was a leading stockholder in the Bank at Shawneetown and actively concerned in its management, succeeded in getting possession of the scrip once again when it was sent to the Bank for cancellation by the State Treasurer. He withheld it from cancellation and, after allowing a year or two to elapse, presented it a second time for the purpose of funding it into bonds.[29] Since Matteson had been Chairman of the Senate Finance Committee before he was elected Governor of Illinois in 1852, it is difficult to accept his plea of ignorance that any fraud was involved in the transaction, and it is even harder to understand his apparent confidence that the operations would not be discovered. Analysis of the Auditor's accounts from 1854 to 1856 revealed that ten thousand dollars more than the total amount of Canal scrip outstanding had been funded or taken up by the state,[30] and the resultant legislative investigation brought the whole situation to the public notice. An act was promptly passed requiring Matteson to indemnify the state to the amount of $223,182.66, spreading the payments over a period of five years,[31] and he at once executed a mortgage and indemnity bond for that amount. The Grand Jury of Sangamon County did not, however, indict him for larceny, when it sat on the case three months later.[32]

Most famous of all, however, is the case of McAllister and Stebbins, whose names appear so frequently upon the statute books of Illinois that some future antiquarian may well assume that they were the greatest men in the state at this period. In 1841, the Fund Commissioner had deposited $804,000 of state bonds with this firm of bankers to secure a loan of $261,000,[33] and various smaller amounts in bonds were also deposited at later dates.[34] All these facts are set forth in the preamble of the act of 1843,[35] providing for the settlement of the case by means of an issue of new state bonds equal to the amount of the loan on condition that the old collateral was returned.

McAllister and Stebbins were not at all anxious for such a settlement and had, as will appear later, sold some of the collateral on their own account. The State Auditor presents the case vividly in his annual report: "After a controversy of some duration between us as to the mode of calculating the interest on their claim, and the rate thereof (all of which points were yielded without being convinced) with a view solely to test their sincerity in desiring a settlement, correspondence between us on the subject ceased, and the act stands a dead letter on the statute book. Whether this failure was occasioned by their inability to settle agreeably to the provisions of the act, or by a less worthy cause, I cannot determine."[36]

The legislature promptly responded by passing, and publishing, a law providing that the bonds deposited with McAllister and Stebbins should be honored by the state at no more than twenty-six cents on the dollar, this figure being an approximate proration of the amount of the loan to the par value of the bonds covered.[37] Still no settlement was made, although laws were passed regarding it at each of three following legislative sessions.[38] Meanwhile, every law that had to do with the payment of interest or principal on the obligations of the state contained a clause expressly stating that its terms were not to apply to the "McAllister and Stebbins Bonds," although the banking house that was thus immortalized had failed in 1847, and a final solution of the problem was not reached until the spring of 1881.[39]

Against the background of fiscal rehabilitation, the liquidation of the banks had gone slowly forward. As early as 1844, an observer had written philosophically, "All the banks in Illinois have ceased to be. Their history is brief, their story is instructing,"[40] but the story was not as brief as he imagined even though it continued to be instructing. In view of the fact that the legislature was passing acts concerning the liquidation of the first Bank of the State as late as 1851,[41] the winding up of its successor could not be expected to occur overnight.

During the years immediately following the legislation

of 1843, considerable progress was made with the liquidation of the second Bank of the State.[42] The specie
reserves, amounting to $503,836, had been distributed
pro rata among the creditors, the bills of exchange had
all been paid off, and more than half of the loans on
personal security were collected prior to 1847. But,
when the charter expired in that year, the task of the
liquidators was far from finished. Real estate to the
value of more than a million dollars was still owned
by the Bank, most of which had been acquired by foreclosure, while the uncollected loans and the suspended
debt, together, amounted to another million. Moreover,
the Bank still owed its creditors approximately $1,000,-
000, entirely apart from the item of $1,364,000 repre-
senting the capital contributed by private stockholders.

An extension of the charter was obviously necessary,
and the advocates of bank expansion seized upon this
opportunity to introduce a bill extending the charter
for five years without any restrictions. This bill was not
permitted to pass, although (in the light of the experiences of the state) a surprisingly large number of votes
were found to support it.[43] As a more reasonable measure,
the House Committee on Banks recommended an extension of the charter for a single year, to facilitate the liquidation of the institution, and insisted that the act should
"leave no spark of vitality in the Bank or its charter."[44]
Certainly the act[45] fulfilled those conditions. It extended
the charter to November 1, 1848, but no debtor of the
Bank was required to pay interest to the institution after
the date on which the act was passed, while all creditors
were to receive 6 per cent interest from that time. More-

over, the expenses of the Bank Commissioner were to be paid by the liquidators,[46] and it was further provided that, if they had not completed the winding-up of the institution when the act expired, the Governor should appoint three trustees to take over the assets and finish the task.

Little progress was made during 1848, so that the Governor appointed N. H. Ridgeley (the Cashier of the Bank), U. Manly and John Calhoun, as trustees in liquidation,[47] at an annual salary of one thousand dollars. By 1851, when the remaining $50,000 of the bank stock in the hands of the state was exchanged for state bonds presented by the trustees,[48] it was generally admitted that the capital of the private stockholders was irretrievably lost and that the realization of the remaining assets was extremely difficult,[49] but there was no suggestion regarding a summary completion of the liquidation.

In 1857, the Governor of the state tried, without success, to discharge the trustees, but a legislative investigation revealed that Manly and Calhoun had both ceased to take any interest in the affairs of the Bank, which was entirely in the hands of Ridgeley. In consideration of this arrangement, Ridgeley received $1,500 a year while the other trustees contented themselves with $750 each.[50] Nothing seems to have been done about this situation except to confirm Ridgeley in his position, which he held until his death. Indeed, his son succeeded to a tenuous trusteeship, which he continued to exercise until the end of the century, being called upon occasionally to validate the titles to pieces of real estate in which the Bank had been interested at some time.[51] Meanwhile, the assets of the institution were finally disposed of by auction, in 1862,[52] leaving the creditors with a net loss of $150,000 and wiping out the private stockholders entirely.

The story of the Bank of Cairo is simpler, since the Cashier absconded with all the specie in 1843, and the creditors ultimately received very little,[53] but that of the Bank at Shawneetown has some interesting aspects. At the annual meeting of the shareholders, in January, 1843, Marshall, who had guided the destinies of the Bank since its original creation, resigned from the Presidency, so that the control of the institution passed into the hands of a new group on the eve of the final collapse.

Having formally accepted the alternative of voluntary liquidation,[54] the directors handed over to the state the first installment of $500,000 in state bonds, receiving for cancellation a like amount of stock, and proceeded to wind up the institution. By the end of 1844, the specie had been distributed *pro rata* among the creditors, more than half of the assets had been turned into cash, and the liabilities had been reduced from $1,384,924 to $580,-410.[55] But, during the same period, a much less satisfactory development had occurred. Since the Bank of Illinois did not, in the spring of 1843, own enough state bonds to redeem all its stock held by the state, it had been provided that $500,000 should be redeemed at once and the remaining $500,000 at the end of twelve months.[56] The new directors found in this provision an opportunity for personal profit that was too attractive to miss. State bonds were selling at twenty cents on the dollar when the liquidation act was passed, so that the directors borrowed $100,-000 from the Bank and purchased substantial quantities of the bonds from several sources, including some $330,000 of those hypothecated with McAllister and Stebbins by the state. These bonds were then turned over to the Bank by the directors, in settlement of their loans, at a profit of nearly eighty cents on the dollar, while the Bank, in turn, offered them to the state in exchange for the remainder of the state stock.[57]

Ford was naturally indignant, and the legislature shared his feelings, so that the tender was, at first, flatly refused. But, in view of the fact that McAllister and Stebbins showed no signs of agreeing to a settlement, an act was finally passed authorizing the Governor to accept the bonds (which nominally totalled $421,260) in exchange for $205,000 of bank stock, requiring the Bank to present $295,000 in bonds, "other than the McAllister and Stebbins bonds," in exchange for the remainder of the stock held by the state.[58]

The directors of the Bank at Shawneetown paid heavily for their avarice. By the same act, they were ordered to transfer all the assets of the Bank to four designated assignees, and terminate their connection with the institution. These assignees were to assume the full responsibility for winding up the affairs of the Bank during a period of four years and, having learned from its experience with the second Bank of the State, the legislature provided that the aggregate compensation of the trustees should not exceed 8 per cent of the amounts collected by them. All other payments to officers and directors ceased at the time when the assignees took over the assets.

Liquidation proceeded slowly, on this basis, in a fashion that was far from satisfactory to the state, in view of its impatience to obtain the $295,000 that was still due from the Bank.[59] At the end of four years, another act was passed extending the time allowed for winding up until January 1, 1851,[60] but, before that period had expired, the assignees were ousted through a chancery suit brought by the State Bank of Missouri and several other creditors. Three receivers were appointed[61] to complete the liquidation as speedily as possible, and the remaining assets of the Bank were sold at public auction in 1853. The state and the creditors appear to have been reimbursed in full, and the buildings of the Bank were acquired by Matteson, but the private stockholders received nothing at all.[62]

Despite all these experiences, the Whigs remained loyal to the banking ideals of their party, and reiterated their demands for a general banking law under which banks might be freely chartered.[63] But Illinois was in the control of the Democrats, who carried the state in 1846 as easily as they had four years earlier, and the Democrats were resolutely opposed to banking in any shape or form. To many members of the party, a bank appeared to be an institution by means of which the promoters, without any capital of their own, were able to reap a fortune at the expense of the community[64] and, although Governor French, who succeeded Ford in 1846, was too much of a realist to accept this thesis, he agreed that "the creation of any new bank in Illinois . . . is uncalled for by the people."[65]

Since most of the members attending the Constitutional Convention in 1847 were Democrats, the outlook for any generous provision regarding banks was scarcely to be expected. A motion to include in the new Constitution a prohibition of all incorporated banks was lost by only one vote during the preliminary debates,[66] and the clauses finally adopted were much more rigorous than anything that had previously appeared on the statute books of Illinois.[67] No banks might, in future, be created by special acts of the legislature, and the state was specifically prohibited from owning stock in any bank whatsoever. If, and when, a general free-banking act was passed by the legislature, under which banks could be incorporated, the bill was to provide for double liability of the stockholders and could not, in any case, "go into effect, or in any manner be in force, unless the same shall be submitted to the people at the general election next succeeding the passage of the same, and be approved by a majority of all the votes cast at such election." Only the people themselves should have the right to decide whether they wanted banks, and on what conditions.

Such deep-rooted antagonism to banks was not confined to Illinois: it was heartily shared by other states that had suffered from the banking experiments of the preceding decade. Pennsylvania, which had received back only $369,056 on its investment of $2,533,676 in bank stock,[68] passed stringent laws regulating the activity of banks; Alabama, with a debt of $9,200,000 incurred "by the State in aid of her late banking operations," did likewise.[69] The Louisiana Constitution of 1845 prohibited the creation of corporations with banking or discounting privileges, while Arkansas, in the following year, provided specifically that "no bank or banking institution shall be hereafter incorporated or established in this State."[70]

Ohio and Michigan, among other states, took a less extreme stand, and followed the example of Illinois in requiring that all banking laws be approved by a popular referendum before becoming effective.[71]

In spite, however, of these evidences of antagonism to banks, the forties represented a period of rapid, and even dangerous, banking expansion in the United States. In a sense, they constitute the years in which the idea of Jacksonian democracy was applied to banking, the idea that all men are equally good bankers and that all who wish to do so should have the right to acquire a banking charter on comparatively easy terms. Since that time, we have grown so familiar with the idea of what is generically called "free banking" that we are inclined to overlook its revolutionary aspect, for revolutionary it was in every sense of the word. Up to that time, banking, in every country, had been a privileged profession, requiring a substantial investment of capital and receiving the protection of the law by special acts of the legislature which, in theory at any rate, were passed only after very careful consideration of all the factors involved. America was, therefore, blazing a new trail when she adopted the practice of passing general free banking acts, under which any small group of men, possessing a little capital, could acquire a charter by the simple process of applying to an appropriate official. It is hard to imagine a more appropriate culmination of the Democratic doctrine of antagonism to privileged banks, which had been one of the most advertised planks of the platform on which Jackson reconstructed the party.

The germ of the idea is contained in the *Hints on*

Banking published by McVickar, in 1827, but no attention seems to have been paid to his proposal until 1838, when New York, having wrecked the Safety Fund System,* passed a general banking law providing that any group of individuals could obtain a bank charter by making application to the State Comptroller and depositing with that official a specified amount of the bonds of the United States, New York State or such other states as he was willing to approve.† In return for the bonds, the Comptroller delivered to the applicants an equal quantity of notes, engraved by him on a standard pattern, and these notes could be put into circulation as soon as they had been signed by the officers of the newly chartered bank. The plan was beautifully simple, and was assumed to be perfectly safe, since the Comptroller held sufficient bonds to redeem the notes of any bank that failed by selling them and distributing the proceeds.[72]

The plan was enthusiastically received. From the passage of the act, in April 1838, to the end of 1839, one hundred and thirty-four "free banks" were chartered in New York State and seventy had commenced business by the latter date. Other states adopted similar legislation,[73] but things did not work out as smoothly as had been anticipated. Even in New York, the sudden issue of more than $6,000,000 in the form of additional currency brought about a slight depreciation of the new bank notes in terms of specie and, to make matters worse, during the five years following the passage of the act, the failure of

* Even in 1843 the Safety Fund was $579,000 in arrears in its payments to the creditors of failed banks. *History of Banking*, I, 360.

† Mortgages might also be deposited under the original act, but this provision was repealed in 1840.

twenty-nine of the new banks imposed substantial losses on the holders of the bank notes.

The problems encountered in New York were, however, insignificant compared to those encountered in states where the traditions of bank operation and administration were less well developed. In Indiana, where the currency in circulation was worth anything from a hundred cents on the dollar for notes of the State Bank to less than forty for the "blue pups,"[74] the Governor complained bitterly of the evils of the new system. "The speculator comes to Indianapolis with a bundle of bank-notes in one hand and the [bank] stock in the other; in twenty-four hours he is on the way to some distant part of the Union to circulate what he denominates a legal currency authorised by the legislature of Indiana. He has nominally located his bank in some remote part of the state, difficult of access, where he knows no banking facilities are required, and intends that his notes shall go into the hands of persons who will have no means of demanding their redemption."[75] It was a complaint familiar to any student of American banking history, but the evil was greater than it had ever been before. In Ohio, the circulating currency consisted of yellow dog, red cat, smooth monkey, blue pup and sick Indian notes,[76] while in Michigan the gold and silver, which the bank was supposed to hold as a reserve, was often borrowed from a neighboring institution in anticipation of a visit from the Banking Commissioner. "Gold and silver flew about the country like magic; its sounds were heard in the depths of the forest; yet, like the wind, one knew not whence it came or whither it was going." In one case, indeed, the bank did not even take the trouble to borrow specie. It attempted to satisfy the commissioner by telling him that nine boxes in the vault were full of silver dollars, and the cashier opened one box to prove it. But the commissioner opened the other nine in skepticism, and found only nails and broken glass.[77]

Admittedly, conditions in other parts of the country were not as bad as those in Michigan and Ohio. In 1842, Louisiana had enacted a general banking law that was infinitely better than any comparable legislation passed in the United States, or any part of it, during the nineteenth century, and several of the eastern states had modified their banking laws to require the maintenance of a specie reserve and provide other safeguards for the noteholder.[78] Moreover, the banks in the larger eastern cities, on their own initiative, were adopting sounder banking practices, relying on deposit banking more than on the issue of notes, and confining their operations to the financing of short-term business operations. By 1850, accommodation paper representing unsecured and illiquid local loans was rarely offered to banks in the larger cities, and even more rarely accepted.[79]

Nevertheless, the banking system of the country was far from satisfactory, and the currency consisted of a diversity of notes that made remittance (and even local payments) extraordinarily difficult. In view of the magnitude of its financial operations, the federal government suffered severely from this situation, but the attempts of the Whigs to solve it by creating a third Bank of the United States were resolutely defeated.[80] Instead, the government turned to the idea of an Independent Treasury system, by means of which it would receive all payments in specie, holding the coins in its own vaults until the time came to pay them out in making the regular public disbursements.[81]

This plan, primitive in its simplicity, had been suggested by Jackson, in the summer of 1837, when the "base treachery and perfidy" of the depository banks made him regret his action in leaving the public funds with them.[82] In the autumn of that year, Van Buren recommended the idea to Congress, but it was not until 1840 that the first Independent Treasury Bill was passed,[83] only to be repealed by the Whigs a year later. In 1846, however, the Independent Treasury Bill was again passed, in a more elaborate form,[84] and for more than half a century the United States government was to operate a financial system of its own, independent of the banks yet exercising important influences upon them. In effect, the country was to operate under two distinct monetary systems: on the one side the activities of the government were handled entirely in specie while, on the other, the business of the country was carried on by means of paper bank notes.

REFERENCES FOR CHAPTER V

[1] *Laws of Illinois,* 1842-43, pp. 54-61. Approved February 21, 1843.

[2] *Hunt's,* IX, 563-564.

[3] Andreas: *op. cit.,* I, 170-171.

[4] Pease: *op. cit.,* p. 324.

[5] *Resolution* appended to *Laws of Illinois,* 1844-45, p. 375.

[6] *Laws of Illinois,* 1844-45, pp. 31-33. Approved March 1, 1845.

[7] *Hunt's,* XXXVIII, 279.

[8] *Laws of Illinois,* 1844-45, p. 44. Approved March 1, 1845.

[9] *Bankers Magazine,* I, 45.

[10] Andreas: *op. cit.,* I, 171.

[11] *House Journal,* 1842-43, 1 Session, pp. 39-51; *Hunt's* XXVII, 662-664.

[12] *Ibid.,* XXXVIII, p. 278.

[13] *Laws of Illinois*, 1844-45, pp. 3-21; pp. 37, 47 and 163.

[14] *Resolution* appended to *Laws of Illinois*, 1846-47, p. 176; Pease: *op. cit.*, p. 336.

[15] *Laws of Illinois*, 1844-45, p. 45. Approved February 21, 1845.

[16] *Reports of the Treasurer, Laws of Illinois*, 1844-45, p. 27.

[17] *Hunt's*, X, 74; XIII, 84; XVIII, 412.

[18] *Constitution of 1848*, Article III, *Section 37, Laws of Illinois*, 1849, p. 7; *Hunt's*, XXVII, 671.

[19] *Constitution of 1848*, Article XV, p. 23; *Hunt's*, XXXVIII, 280; *Bankers' Magazine*, III, 335.

[20] *Hunt's*, XXXIV, 209-210.

[21] *Bankers Magazine*, V, 510; IX, 229; *Hunt's*, XXXVI, 220.

[22] *Bankers Magazine*, VII, 252.

[23] *Laws of Illinois*, 1846-47, pp. 161-163. Approved February 28, 1847.

[24] *Laws of Illinois*, 1846-47, p. 32. Approved March 1, 1849.

[25] *Laws of Illinois*, 1849, pp. 70-71. Approved February 12, 1849.

[26] *Laws of Illinois*, 1849, p. 45. Approved February 10, 1849.

[27] *Laws of Illinois*, 1851, p. 88. Approved February 14, 1851.

[28] *Laws of Illinois*, 1846-47, p. 165. Approved February 22, 1847.

[29] Andreas: *op. cit.*, I, 173; *Bankers Magazine*, XIII, 821.

[30] *Hunt's*, XLI, 89.

[31] *Laws of Illinois*, 1859, pp. 190-192. Approved February 19, 1859.

[32] Andreas: *op. cit.*, I, 173.

[33] See above pp. 146-150.

[34] *Hunt's*, XXXVIII, 663.

[35] *Laws of Illinois*, 1842-43, pp. 287-288. Approved March 4, 1843.

[36] *Report of the Auditor of Public Accounts, Laws of Illinois*, 1844-45, p. 25.

[37] *Laws of Illinois*, 1844-45, p. 371. Approved February 27, 1845.

[38] *Laws of Illinois*, 1846-47, pp. 163-164; *Laws of Illinois*, 1849, pp. 43-45; *Laws of Illinois*, 1851, p. 22.

[39] *Laws of Illinois*, 1861, p. 203. Approved February 22, 1861; *Laws of Illinois*, 1881, p. 51. Approved May 30, 1881.

[40] *Hunt's*, XI, 240.

[41] *Laws of Illinois*, 1851, pp. 119-120. Approved February 15, 1851.

[42] *Report of the Secretary of the Treasury*, February 28, 1847, *House Document, No. 120, 29 Congress, 2 Session*, p. 248.

[43] *Chicago Democrat*, February 23, 1847.

[44] *Reports of the Session (House)*, 1846-47, p. 280.

[45] *Laws of Illinois*, 1846-47, pp. 20-21. Approved March 1, 1847.

[46] *Laws of Illinois*, 1844-45, p. 144. Approved March 3, 1845.

[47] *Bankers Magazine*, III, 382.

[48] *Reports of the Session*, 1859, I, 841.

[49] *Reports of the Session (Senate)*, 1851, pp. 137-138.

[50] *Reports of the Session*, 1859, I, 832-839.

[51] Knox: *op. cit.*, p. 722.

[52] *Bankers Magazine*, XVII, 476.

[53] *Illinois State Journal*, February 2, 1862.

[54] See above pp. 157-159.

[55] *Executive Document No. 226, 29 Congress, 1 Session*, pp. 1086-1088.

[56] *Laws of Illinois*, 1842-43, p. 30, *Section 1*.

[57] Ford: *op. cit.*, p. 399; Greene and Thompson: *Governor's Letter Books,*
    II, 106-107; *History of Banking*, I, 410.

[58] *Laws of Illinois*, 1844-45, pp. 246-249. Approved February 28, 1845.

[59] *Reports of the Session (Senate)* 1849, p. 105.

[60] *Laws of Illinois*, 1849, p. 38. Approved February 10, 1849.

[61] *Laws of Illinois*, 1851, pp. 120-121. Approved February 15, 1851.

[62] *Chicago Democrat*, September 10, 1853; Knox: *op. cit.*, p. 714.

[63] *Alton Telegraph*, July 4, 1846.

[64] *Chicago Democrat*, October 28, 1845.

[65] *Ibid.*, March 10, 1846.

[66] *Niles'*, LXXII, 307; *Chicago Democrat*, July 29, 1847.

[67] *Constitution of 1848*, Article X, *Laws of Illinois*, 1849, p. 10.

[68] *History of Banking*, I, 356.

[69] *Idem*, 376.

[70] *Idem*, 391 and 394.

[71] *Idem*, 441 and 443.

[72] *Bankers Magazine*, VII, 300; *De Bow's Review*, XII, 610-613; XIII,
    127-134; XIV, 28-33 and 151-157.

[73] See below p. 211.

[74] *History of Banking*, I, 406.

[75] *Annual Message of the Governor of Indiana*, 1853, quoted in Scroggs:
    Century of Banking Progress, p. 125.

[76] *Niles'*, LXVIII, 272.

[77] *History of Banking*, I, 329-330.

[78] Cf. R. G. Rodkey: *Legal Reserves in American Banking, (Michigan
    Business Studies*, VI,) pp. 369-382.

[79] Dewey: *op. cit.*, p. 157.

[80] *History of Banking*, I, 348-349.

[81] Cf. D. Kinley: *The Independent Treasury of the United States and
    its Relation to the Banks of the Country*, pp. 26-83, for the origin
    and early development.

[82] *Raguet's Register*, II, 58.

[83] *Hunt's*, II, 93-94.

[84] *Ibid.*, XV, 497-502.

CHAPTER VI

THE ROLE OF THE PRIVATE BANKER

1845–1855

THE banking problems that excited the citizens of other states aroused little interest in Illinois, while the discussions attending the creation of the Independent Treasury seemed even less important, in terms of the practical realities of everyday life. Having experienced its own financial crisis, in 1842, and taken stern measures to meet the problems which that crisis left in its wake, Illinois was able to pass through the general panic of 1847 without excitement or injury. The story of conditions within the state, during the period from 1843 to 1856, is one of uninterrupted growth and continually increasing prosperity. In 1840, there were only 473,137 inhabitants to be counted in the entire state but, by 1850, the population had risen to 851,420 and, five years later, it exceeded 1,300,000. Immigrants were pouring into the area from the Atlantic states, as well as from Europe.[1]

During the same period, the taxable property increased at an even greater rate. From a total of $69,000,000, in 1840, it rose to $105,000,000 by the end of the decade, and to $334,000,000 in 1855.[2] Illinois was no longer a frontier state at the end of this period; the last sale of government land occurred, at Danville, in December,

1856, and there were already developing the industries and public services that characterize a settled, yet progressive, community.

All this was true in even greater measure of Chicago. In the early forties, Chicago was little more than an overgrown village "strung along the banks of the river for half a mile from the Lake. It hadn't a paved street or a foot of brick sidewalk. The business part of the town was Lake Street from State to Wells Street, while the residences were scattered along Wabash, Michigan and State as far as Washington Street. What is now Madison Street was out of town. South of where the Grand Pacific stands was an unbroken prairie. There was no business and only a few dwellings north of the River, on account of the uncertainties and delays in getting back and forth. There was no sewerage whatever, and the water and the surface drainage was the only way to get rid of sewage. The mud is described as having been simply horrible. The low marshy land filled with water like a sponge and the streets were well-nigh impassable for eight months in the year."[3]

The limited economic activity of the city is apparent from the fact that more than half of the business that Chicago carried on with the surrounding territory took the form of barter transactions,[4] but even these operations were adversely affected by the general depression that descended upon the state with the collapse of the banks and the internal-improvement program. During the latter half of 1842, more than forty of the city's merchants went into bankruptcy.[5]

From this low point, progress was rapid and continuous throughout the ensuing decade. As early as 1843, Chicago was recognized as the outstanding western market and, by 1847, McCormick was manufacturing, in the city, the agricultural machinery that was to revolutionize the activity of surrounding farms. The wheat trade, in particular, forged ahead rapidly. By 1846, it was recognized as a primary factor in the development of Chicago and, in the following year, the importance of the Chicago market to the rest of the world was demonstrated by the rapid rise of local prices on account of foreign buying to compensate for the anticipated shortage in the European crop. Similarly, in the case of the packing industry, there occurred between 1843 and 1847 a growth that laid the foundations of later expansion, even in regard to the development of important by-products designed to insure profitable use of material that would otherwise have been wasted.[6]

Moreover, the increasing commercial activity of their city made the inhabitants of Chicago exceedingly jealous for the financial reputation of the state in which it was situated. At a time when the whisper of repudiation was on so many lips, and the population of Bond County had openly avowed its unwillingness to pay any part of the vast debts incurred for internal improvements, the citizens of Chicago were convinced that the state should honor its obligations in full, no matter how painful the task might be. In January, 1841, at a meeting in the Saloon Building, they memorialized the legislature to raise sufficient money by direct taxation "to pay the interest on the state debt and thereby restore its impaired credit."[7] That resolution, it should be noticed, was one of the first public protests against repudiation that were

GEORGE SMITH

Reproduced by courtesy of Saint Luke's Hospital, Chicago

heard in Illinois. Four years later they reiterated the request, and strongly endorsed Governor Ford's suggestion that a supplementary tax of one and a half mills be imposed specifically for that purpose.[8]

These developments, in a sense, prepared Chicago for the opportunity presented to it by the opening of the Illinois and Michigan Canal in the spring of 1848.[9] For thirty years the city had worked and waited for the Canal. In 1846, it had persuaded Congress to elevate it to the status of a port of entry and, in the following year, it had attracted delegates from every section of the country to attend the great River and Harbor Congress designed to accelerate the more rapid development of water transportation in the United States.[10] At last, the Canal was opened and the dream realized. Chicago stood at the point where the traffic of the Mississippi valley met that coming from the east by way of the Lakes, and its importance as a great trading center was assured.

Endorsing, in a sense, the promise of future greatness which the Canal gave to the city, was the advent of the first railroad in the autumn of the same year.[11] The secondhand locomotive and the two old freight cars, which constituted the first train running out of a Chicago terminus, were an augury. During the years that were yet to come, the railroads would open up vast areas of rich land that were inaccessible to trade by means of river or canal, and even in 1850 there were people who foresaw that possibility.

Almost immediately, the city began a period of rapid development and growth. In 1845, a hardy traveler had gone from New York to Chicago in five days and five hours, by means of an incredibly rapid combination of railroad, lake steamer and stage coach;[12] in 1852, the first through train from the east reached Chicago in half that time.[13] In 1848, telegraphic communication was established between Chicago and New York,[14] and two years later the city was lit by gas, for the first time, so that "brilliant torches flamed on both sides of Lake Street as far as the eye could see."[15] In 1852, more debatable evidence of the growing importance of the city appeared: Chicago floated its first big loan in New York, without any difficulty.[16]

As a result of this expansion, the businessmen of the city decided, in 1848, to combine for the purpose of facilitating their operations and, in the spring of that year, the Board of Trade came into existence. In 1850, the Board was legally incorporated but, even before that time, it had begun to undertake its basic function of developing a uniform system of grading and standardizing the products in which its members dealt. Official Inspectors of Fish and Provisions were appointed. It must be admitted, however, that the organization of the Board was a little premature. After the first flush of enthusiasm had passed, the members discovered that they could do their business just as easily in the old way, so that, in the summer of 1851, "during nine business days only five members had sufficient interest in the institution to put in an appearance at the place appointed for daily sessions."[17]

These developments were related to the growing size of the city, both as cause and effect. In 1840, there were only 4,479 people in Chicago, but a decade later the population numbered 29,963 and, by 1857, the total was rapidly approaching 100,000.[18] Each event in the progress of the city attracted immigrants, and the process was self-perpetuating. The increasing population enlarged the local market and provided an increased labor supply to aid in the production of the goods that were needed to supply the demands of the city and its growing hinterland. Nowhere is this growth more clearly reflected than in the tax returns, which show that the aggregate taxable property increased from $1,400,000, in 1843, to $3,600,-000, in 1857, while the amount of the taxes collected rose from less than $90,000 to more than $430,000.[19]

Even if Chicago had developed more slowly, difficult problems would have arisen in regard to the financing of its many infant industries, particularly in view of the extent to which available funds were absorbed by the grain and meat trades, but the phenomenal rapidity of the city's growth complicated these problems seriously. Capital was perennially scarce, and rates of interest on private transactions varied between 8 per cent and 100 per cent per annum during the forties, with very few loans negotiated at less than 20 per cent except in the case of those based on bills of exchange drawn against produce shipped to the east.[20] The 6 per cent maximum set by the usury laws of the state had no significance whatever. It was evaded in almost all lending operations and, as late as 1848, a meeting of Chicago merchants resolved that "it is contrary to honour, reason, and the laws of trade to suppose that Illinois can enjoy the use of sufficient capital to transact her business and develop her resources at six per cent interest while New York, Indiana, Wisconsin and a number of other states offer, by their interest and collection laws, from seven to twelve per cent."[21] The complaint carried considerable weight, since merchants are the last people in the world to pay rates of interest higher than the necessary minimum, so that the legislature raised the legal limit to 10 per cent early in the following year.[22] Gradually, the increase in interest rates and the improved financial reputation of the state began to make themselves felt. Foreign investors overcame their reluctance to purchase Illinois securities and the flow of European capital was renewed. Much of this foreign capital, as the years passed, came to Chicago,[23] but the supply was never large enough to finance all the stupendous projects that were conceived by the citizens.

Financial problems of this kind were intimately related to the banking facilities of the city, since an efficient banking organization would have acted as a reservoir of short-term capital funds and provided a sound medium of exchange by means of which financial operations could be conducted in confidence. But Chicago did not possess any financial institutions that were competent to undertake either of these functions; her merchants were compelled to rely upon small private banks for the accommodation that they needed, while the only currency in circulation consisted of the notes issued by banks in other parts of the country and the illegal certificates of deposit circulated by George Smith. In the light of what has already been said regarding the flood of bank notes, many of them worthless, that surged over the country during .

this period, it is not surprising that Chicago preferred the illegal currency which, despite its status in the eyes of the law, was always redeemed in specie on presentation.

But an appreciation of this situation is only possible if the story is told in chronological order. When the second Bank of the State established a branch in Chicago,[24] there became available to the merchants of the city, for the first time, the facilities of a large incorporated bank. The branch was enthusiastically welcomed. During the first four years of its existence, it furnished eastern exchange at a discount of not more than 2 per cent, thereby facilitating tremendously the movement of goods to Chicago, while its discounts amounted to more than $500,000 on an average. But the enthusiasm waned considerably, during 1839, when it was discovered that the Chicago branch was heavily interested in the operations of several pork speculators.[25] If the price of pork had remained high, this might not have been serious, since Chicago was already one of the most important centers from which pork products were shipped to the east, but the price fell catastrophically in 1840.

In view of the fact that the Democrats, who dominated Chicago politics, were already strongly opposed to the second Bank of the State of Illinois, the unsuccessful pork speculation only added fuel to the flames. During December, 1839, a large Democratic meeting, which was held in the city, resolved "that it would be a benefit to this community if the Branch of the State Bank at Chicago should be forthwith removed therefrom, because it has in all respects acted adverse to the interests of the people," and the legislature promptly acceded to the request.[26] The branch was ordered to move to Lockport, some forty miles away.[27]

This Democratic ardor was not, however, shared by the business community of Chicago. In accordance with the law, the branch was moved to Lockport on July 30, 1840,[28] but the removal appears to have been, in large part, a legal formality. Much of the business of the branch was still conducted through an agency in Chicago,[29] and the following session of the legislature rescinded its former action by permitting the Bank "to relocate said branch at Chicago" once more.[30] By this time, however, the change was not important. When the branch was reopened in Chicago the signs of financial crisis were already apparent on the horizon; within a few months, the Chicago office was to go down in the maelstrom that engulfed all the incorporated banks of Illinois.

Once again, Chicago was compelled to depend upon the facilities offered by its private banks, and it was fortunate that the number of these firms had increased rapidly during the years following 1837. By 1845, there were seven private banking firms in Chicago important enough to be listed in the directory[31] and, although no precise figures are given as to the scale of their activities, it is reasonable to assume that, in the aggregate, they handled considerably more than half of the business transacted by the fifteen private banks reported to be operating in Illinois at that time.[32] On that basis the capital investment would have been from $1,500,000 to $2,000,000, the liability to depositors and noteholders around $750,000, and the loans and discounts somewhat less than $2,000,000.

Such estimates cannot give more than a very rough idea of the extent of the local financial facilities at that time, but we are on firmer ground when we attempt to discover the nature of the institutions and the kind of business they did. Alexander Brand and Company, a partnership of Scotsmen that took over the business of Strachan and Scott in 1840, appears to have been very much interested in foreign and domestic exchange: "Collections and re-mittances made on all parts of the United States, Great Britain and Ireland, and the continent of Europe. Money remitted to or from settlers or emigrants in sums as may be required. Deposit accounts kept. Interest paid on spe-cial deposits."[33] Similarly in the case of R. K. Swift, whose office was "over Kohn's Store, No. 111 Lake Street," the development of the business appears to have been closely associated with the domestic exchange market. In 1849, an affiliated organization under the name of the California Loan Office was set up in San Francisco[34] and, at a later date, an office was opened in New York under the title of Swift, Ransom and Co.,[35] so that the firm was peculiarly fitted to handle the remittance of funds to all parts of the United States as well as to foreign countries.[36] Its business was not, however, confined to remittance: all branches of banking were included in its orbit during the period of its greatest development,[37] in the early fifties, and the following advertisement (which appeared in the autumn of 1849) is interesting as an indication not only of the growth of deposit banking but also of the prevailing rates of interest:

The undersigned will receive deposits of money, and allow interest as follows:

On Certificates payable

5 days after demand, 4 per cent per annum
10 days after demand, 5 per cent per annum
15 days after demand, 6 per cent per annum
20 days after demand, 7 per cent per annum
25 days after demand, 8 per cent per annum
30 days after demand, 9 per cent per annum
45 days after demand, 10 per cent per annum

If the sum or sums deposited by one person exceed $1000, the time of demand before payment to be arranged by special contract.

Time being valuable, depositors will be expected to "tell short stories."

A deposits book will be opened from 1 till 2 o'clock P.M. every day (holidays and Sundays excepted) at the residence of the subscriber, No. 48 Michigan avenue for the benefit of Ladies, and one per centum extra will be allowed them over the rates above named.*

The old adage says

"A dollar saved, is a dollar earned."

R. K. Swift

Office over Kohn's Store, 111 Lake Street

Of the important operations of "George Smith and Company, La Salle Street Bankers" more will be said in later paragraphs, but J. Coe Clarke, Newberry and Burch, together with the Chicago agencies of the Farmers and Mechanics Bank of Michigan and of the Mississippi Marine and Fire Insurance Company, appear to have been primarily interested in the financing of local business operations and real-estate speculation.

By the early fifties, the number of private banks had

---

* It may be pointed out that this is the first evidence of a Ladies' Banking Department, although the idea was quite popular among Chicago banks seventy years afterward.

increased still further, and the *Chicago Democrat*, still staunch in its antagonism to all banking operations, was complaining bitterly that "before long we shall be blessed (?) with more home-made money. . . . Glorious times bye and bye, if paper money will make them."[38] Among the new names that are listed, by 1850, are those of G. P. Baker, J. S. Dole, Thomas Parker, and E. G. Hall (all of them classed as moneylenders), together with the fully fledged banking firm of Curtis and Tinkham "who, having command of considerable funds in Ohio and other currency . . . will be able to extend the facilities now afforded for the purchase of the productions of the country."[39]

The most interesting development of the period was, however, the tremendous popularity of the illegal currency issued by the insurance companies. When the legislature granted a charter to the Chicago Marine and Fire Insurance Company,[40] in 1836, it inserted a clause in the law to the effect that "nothing contained in this act shall confer on said corporation banking powers, or authorize it to issue notes in the similitude of bank notes, to be issued as a circulating medium in lieu of money." The intention of the legislature could not have been more clearly stated, but the prohibition proved ineffective. In the fifth section of the charter, the company was permitted "to receive money on deposit and loan it on bottomry and respondentia," and this power to finance shipping ventures became the basis of currency operations. In 1837, the company issued, in exchange for such deposits, certificates of deposits, in round denominations of from one to five hundred dollars, which were intended to circulate as an ordinary medium of exchange.[41] Most of these certificates were withdrawn immediately after the panic, but the illegal issue was never completely stopped and, in 1849, under the Presidency of J. Young Scammon, the deposit business attained a more permanent position in the affairs of the institution. Although the board of directors resolved "that it is not the intention of this institution to exercise any doubtful powers, or to do any act not clearly within the limits of its charter," they decided to divide the operations of the company into two distinct parts in order that the banking activities, which were steadily growing in importance, might not become mixed up with those undertaken in the handling of the insurance business.[42]

Meanwhile, George Smith had become very much interested in the whole idea of issuing circulating certificates of deposit and, after carefully studying the charter of the Chicago Marine and Fire Insurance Company, he obtained from the Wisconsin legislature, in February, 1839, a charter of identical wording for the Wisconsin Marine and Fire Insurance Company.[43] Of the total capitalization, amounting to $225,000, half was taken by George Smith and his associates in Chicago, while the remaining stock was eagerly purchased by Scottish capitalists. An office was immediately opened in Milwaukee, under the control of Alexander Mitchell, the secretary of the company.

From its very inception, the Wisconsin Marine and Fire Insurance Company began to issue certificates of deposit, in round denominations, which were payable to bearer and redeemable in specie, either at the Milwaukee office of the company or at the offices of Strachan and Scott, who acted as agents in Chicago. In 1841, when Strachan and Scott retired from business in Chicago, the business of redemption was transferred to the office of George Smith and Company, and the amount of notes in circulation had attained some $29,000. In spite of the competition of the Illinois banks, George Smith was able to state that "the parties by whom the bills of the institution are redeemed in this city have never been without the means of taking up its whole circulation at a moment's notice, either in Illinois funds or Eastern exchange."[44] Nor was the boast an idle one, since the statement of the company showed that it had $22,000 on hand in the form of cash, and more than $155,000 on deposit with banks in New York, Chicago, Detroit and St. Louis.[45]

This certainty of redemption in specie, at a time when the notes of the Illinois banks were rapidly depreciating to the point of extinction and the currency of banks in other states was of uncertain value, led to a phenomenal increase in the popularity of the certificates issued by the Wisconsin Fire and Marine Insurance Company. Moreover, in the spring of 1846, George Smith had voluntarily pledged his own personal fortune to guarantee the redemption of them whenever presented, an act of unusual personal courage.[46] From a figure of $100,000, in 1843, the circulation, therefore, expanded rapidly to $250,000 in November, 1845; by October, 1849, it had reached $1,000,000 and by the end of 1851 $1,470,000 of the certificates were outstanding.[47] So great was the popularity of "George Smith's Notes" that they were readily accepted in towns hundreds of miles away from the home office of the company and, by the end of the fifties, re-demption agencies were set up in Galena, St. Louis, Cin-cinnati and Detroit, in addition to the original agency in Chicago.[48]

The bankers of Illinois and the surrounding states did not, however, regard the popularity of Smith's bills with any enthusiasm, since they would have preferred to see their own notes in circulation. On several occasions, con-certed attempts were made to organize runs on the Insur-ance Company, notably in 1849, when a group of Mich-igan and Chicago bankers collected $100,000 of the notes and presented them at Milwaukee on the morning after Thanksgiving, having sedulously spread the rumor that Smith was about to fail.[49] Runs began at Milwaukee, and at every redemption agency, but were easily met. Indeed, the volume of new deposits received during the panic was more than equal to the amount of funds withdrawn by the general public, so that the net loss of deposits amounted to slightly less than the $100,000 originally withdrawn by the instigators of the run. Moreover, a group of the leading merchants of Chicago, immediately after the panic, published a circular reaffirming their confidence in Smith's notes and their willingness to accept them at all times.[50] This paper had become the favorite currency of the west and, with a sound currency and a rehabilitated fiscal system, the period of convalescence was at an end.

REFERENCES FOR CHAPTER VI

[1] *Hunt's,* XXXVIII, 285; Cole: *The Era of the Civil War,* pp. 10 and 15-16.
[2] *Hunt's,* XXXVIII, 285.

[3] *Chicago Herald*, September 25, 1882. See also Cole: *op. cit.*, pp. 3-5.

[4] *Hunt's*, XVIII, 169; Pierce: *op. cit.*, p. 132.

[5] Andreas: *op. cit.*, I, 153.

[6] *Hunt's*, XVIII, pp. 168-171; Pierce: *op. cit.*, I, 128-131 and 139-141.

[7] Andreas: *op. cit.*, I, 152.

[8] *Idem*, 154.

[9] *Idem*, 172.

[10] Pease: *op. cit.*, p. 334.

[11] *Chicago Democrat*, October 26, 1848; Pierce: *op. cit.*, I, 118.

[12] Pierce: *op. cit.*, I, 104.

[13] Andreas: *op. cit.*, I, 156.

[14] *Hunt's*, XVIII, 165.

[15] Andreas: *op. cit.*, I, 155.

[16] *Idem*, 183.

[17] *Idem*, 583; also 581-583.

[18] *Idem*, 183; Pierce: *op. cit.*, I, 44n.

[19] Andreas: *op. cit.*, I, 183.

[20] *Chicago Daily American*, January 27, 1842; *Chicago Democrat*, June 11, 1845; Pierce: *op. cit.*, I, 55-56, 124-127 and 148-152.

[21] Andreas: *op. cit.*, I, 155.

[22] *Laws of Illinois*, 1849, p. 98. Approved January 30, 1849.

[23] *Bankers Magazine*, VII, 252.

[24] See above pp. 104-105.

[25] *Chicago Democrat*, May 1, 1839. See also Pierce: *op. cit.*, I, 154-156; Dowrie: *op. cit.*, p. 95.

[26] *Daily Chicago American*, February 7, 1840; Pierce: *op. cit.*, I, 155.

[27] *Laws of Illinois*, 1839-40, p. 15. See above p. 136.

[28] *Daily Chicago American*, July 31, 1840.

[29] Andreas: *op. cit.*, I, 530n.

[30] *Laws of Illinois*, 1840-41, p. 40. Approved February 27, 1841.

[31] Norris: *Business Directory and Statistics of the City of Chicago for 1846; Hunt's*, XVIII, 171; Andreas: *op. cit.*, I, 534; Pierce: *op. cit.*, I, 158-159.

[32] *Annual Report of the Comptroller of the Currency*, 1876, pp. cxviii-cxix.

[33] Norris: *op. cit.*, Andreas: *op. cit.*, I, 534.

[34] *Chicago Democrat*, September 19, 1849; *Chicago Weekly Democrat*, November 13, 1849.

[35] *Chicago Weekly Democrat*, April 25, 1857.

[36] Chicago *Daily Democratic Press*, March 16, 1854.

[37] *Chicago Democrat*, September 19, 1849.

[38] *Chicago Democrat*, December 1, 1849.

[39] *Chicago Democrat,* June 26, 1849; Andreas: *op. cit.,* I, 534-535.

[40] *Laws of Illinois,* 1835-36, 2 *Session,* pp. 30-35. Approved January 13, 1836.

[41] *Chicago American,* May 20, 1837.

[42] *Chicago Democrat,* December 6, 1849.

[43] *Laws of Wisconsin,* 1838-39, pp. 64-67.

[44] *Chicago American,* September 28, 1841.

[45] *Milwaukee Courier,* May 9, 1842; Andreas: *op. cit.,* I, 533.

[46] *Thompson's Bank Note and Commercial Reporter,* December 1, 1849; *Chicago Democrat,* December 7, 1849.

[47] Andreas: *op. cit.,* I, 532.

[48] *Idem,* 533.

[49] *Idem,* 534-535.

[50] *Chicago Democrat,* December 11, 1849.

CHAPTER VII

THE FRUITS OF EXPERIENCE

1851–1856

ILLINOIS had learned her lesson and, painful though the convalescence had been, she had recovered financial prestige and economic prosperity by the end of 1850. Yet there is a vein of sardonic humor, in the history of the years from 1851 to 1860, that would have delighted a Greek tragedian. Illinois was doomed to suffer from the inflationary policies of neighboring states, in a fashion almost identical to that in which her own public-improvement mania had imposed losses on investors throughout the country.

The tragedy was not apparent, however, during the early fifties. In common with Florida, Texas, Arkansas, Wisconsin, Iowa, Minnesota, Oregon and California, Illinois had not a single incorporated bank within her boundaries when the fifth decade of the century drew to a close, and the steady increase in the volume of business activity tended to emphasize more clearly with every passing day the inadequacy of the circulating currency. A few notes of the old Bank of Illinois at Shawneetown were still in use, at 75 per cent discount, and even fewer of the second State Bank at 50 per cent discount,[1] but these relics constituted the only indigenous currency. In addition to Smith's bills, there were some $500,000 notes of St. Louis banks in circulation in Illinois, as well as untold quantities of paper of all kinds from the wildcat banks of other places,[2] and the *Illinois Journal* pointedly suggested that, "since we cannot prevent the bank paper of other States from flooding ours, and since we must pay so enormously for its circulation, does not necessity and self-preservation call upon us to doff our scruples about banking for the present—make our own banks, use our own money, and pay the profit to our own State?"[3]

Such reasoning was cogent, but there was another argument for large incorporated banks that had even greater weight with the merchant and industrialist. The private banks were too small to supply adequate quantities of capital funds, and the unsatisfactory state of the currency discouraged private capitalists who might have made loans to business houses. "The present system has driven capitalists from the State to invest their wealth elsewhere, and domestic enterprise hobbles about on crutches, being forced to pay the unlicensed usurer twenty and twenty-five per cent interest for the poor privilege of moving at a snail's pace."[4]

Chicago, by reason of its economic preeminence in the state, was keenly aware of these problems. As soon as the vote of the people on the new Constitution[5] had been counted, the Board of Trade appointed a committee to draft a free-banking act that would fit the new constitutional requirements[6] and, toward the end of December, the leading merchants of the city petitioned the legislature to enact sound banking legislation as rapidly as possible.

The desired result could not, however, be achieved by petitions alone. In 1848, the Democratic party, in Illinois, had adopted a plank declaring "hostility to a United States Bank and all kindred institutions, whether of a state or national character," so that little aid could be expected from the Democratic legislature then in power. In 1850, therefore, the business community bent all its efforts to the election of Whigs and "bank-democrats," and succeeded in its attempt to oust the Democratic organization. The banking bill was introduced as soon as the new legislature assembled, in 1851, and, despite the open opposition of Governor French and the downstate legislators, it was forced through both houses by "the Chicago money oligarchy." In the upper house, Senator Joel A. Matteson, an upstate Democrat, cast the deciding vote in favor of the measure on the principle that a question of such importance should be decided by the people themselves at the referendum.[7]

Governor French continued his opposition to the bill by making use of the veto power vested in him by the new Constitution, and returned the bill to the legislature with a vigorous and well-reasoned message.[8] If bonds were as good as specie, he demanded, why not require banks to deposit specie instead of bonds? If bonds were not as good as specie then they were an unsatisfactory foundation for the currency. Moreover, he insisted, a good banking system demands adequate specie reserves, in any case, and should be buttressed by the unlimited liability of the stockholders to all creditors of the bank, while the suggested bill was unsatisfactory on both counts. But such arguments, sound as they were, in some respects, had no effect upon the legislature. The forces that had been marshaled to enact the bill originally were reassembled to pass it over the veto[9] a few days later.

Under the Constitution of 1848, however, this banking law could not become effective until it had been approved by a majority of the voters at "the general election next succeeding," and no general election was scheduled until November, 1852. To avoid two long years of waiting for the banks they so eagerly desired, the legislative majority forced a bill through the Assembly ejecting all county treasurers from their offices, and providing that new treasurers should be elected in November, 1851.[10] By this device the referendum on the banking law was brought about a full year earlier than the Democrats had expected.

Verbose and bitter arguments at once began to fill the newspapers. The Whigs exhorted the voters to approve the banking bill, in order to enhance the prosperity of the state and accelerate its development, while the Democrats (and particularly those from the southern counties) pointed to all the tribulation and loss inflicted upon the state by banks during earlier periods. But the conflict was fought out on economic rather than political lines. As one contemporary newspaper points out, "Illinois is flooded with the issues of foreign banks. Our people pay several hundred thousand dollars for a currency, the whole of which goes to enrich private corporations of the Eastern states. The general banking law, on which we are to vote in a week or two provides securities far superior to those of a large majority of the banks whose issues go to make up our present currency. . . . It will furnish us with a home currency to be kept under the control of

laws of our own making, the interest of which will be retained in the State, augmenting the general wealth, instead of being carried off, thereby impoverishing our
people to the tune of hundreds of thousands of dollars
annually. . . . Shall we have this or that?"[11]

The voters were by no means unanimous in their answer to the question. While the law was approved by
37,578 votes to 31,321, the size of the minority is striking
testimony to the deep-rooted hostility that still persisted
in regard to banks, and this fact becomes even more significant when the geographical distribution of the votes
is studied. Only four counties north of Springfield opposed the measure, while the counties around Chicago returned bank majorities of from eighty-five to ninety-five
per cent; southern Illinois, on the other hand, voted overwhelmingly against the law.[12] Economic forces had split
Illinois Democracy in two, and the two segments were to
find more points of conflict than agreement during the
ensuing years.

The law that was finally approved, as a result of this
extended struggle, can conveniently be referred to as the
Free Banking Act,[13] although the phrase free banking
does not appear in any of its clauses. It was modeled upon
the system adopted by New York in 1838,[14] and copied by
Michigan in 1849, New Jersey in 1850, and more than
half the states in the Union between that date and the
outbreak of the Civil War. Even in the abstract, the
underlying philosophy did not command universal approval among contemporary students of banking[15] while,
in its practical application, wide divergences from one

state to another exercised important effects upon the soundness of the banking institutions that were created.

The Illinois law provided that banking charters, running for not more than twenty-five years, should be issued to any individual, or group of individuals, who applied for them. The only conditions imposed were that the capital stock of each bank so chartered should amount to at least $50,000, and that the shareholders (in the event of failure) should be liable for an amount equal to the par value of their stock, neither of which could be considered particularly severe.

A bank created in this fashion could not issue circulating notes on its own account, but could obtain such notes from the State Auditor in exchange for a deposit of state or national bonds "on which interest is normally paid." In the case of securities issued by the United States, or by all states excepting Illinois, bank notes were to be issued to an amount equal to the current value of the bonds, as determined by the average New York price during the six months preceding the transaction. Illinois bonds, however, were treated in unusually self-sacrificing fashion. Notes were not to be issued against such securities in amounts greater than eighty per cent of the average market price.

Such bank notes, once issued were redeemable in specie, on demand, at the office of the bank whose name they bore, and the law provided that each bank should keep on hand an amount of coin sufficient to meet all such demands. It is significant, however, that the decision as to the precise size of the reserve was left to the discretion of the individual banker, since no specific requirement is found in the act.

If any bank failed to redeem its notes when called upon to do so, the penalties were severe. The noteholder was entitled to damages, at the rate of 12½ per cent per annum, for the period between the presentation of the note for redemption and the time at which he received the specie while, if he chose to protest the note for non-payment, he could force the issuing bank into immediate liquidation. In that event, the State Auditor was required, after due notice, to sell the bonds that he had received from the defaulting bank and pay off the noteholders, but past experience dictated an unmistakable provision that "nothing in this act contained shall be considered as implying any pledge on the part of the state for the payment of said bills or notes, beyond the proper application of the securities pledged to the Auditor for their redemption."[16] In cases where the proceeds from the sale of the securities were inadequate to redeem all the notes, the noteholder was, however, given a first lien on the general assets of the bank.

While much of the act is taken up with these provisions regarding the issuance and redemption of notes, the remaining sections also merit attention. The grant of powers, for instance, has a very modern sound, providing that the newly created institutions should have "power to carry on the business of banking, by discounting bills, notes, and other evidences of debt; by receiving deposites; buying and selling gold and silver bullion, foreign coins, and bills of exchange; loaning money on real and personal securities, and by exercising such powers as may be necessary to carry on said business."[17] As a limitation of these operations, it was provided, however, that no bank might hold real estate, except that necessary for its business or plots transferred to it as security for loans, while in no case might it charge more than 7 per cent per annum on any loan or discount.

Three Bank Commissioners were appointed to supervise the banks, and see that their operations were at all times within the framework of the law. For that purpose, they were given the right to examine the banks annually, and to demand from them quarterly reports of condition. Moreover, the commissioners were required, from time to time, to inspect the securities deposited with the Auditor, in order to assure themselves that the aggregate value of the bonds had not fallen below the amount of the circulation outstanding. If any such depreciation was found to have occurred, the Auditor was empowered to call upon the delinquent banks for additional securities, or else to require a reduction in the amount of the note issue sufficient to bring it to an equality with the reduced value of the bonds.

Finally, elaborate provisions were made to facilitate voluntary liquidation. To retire from business, a bank would naturally have to pay off all the outstanding notes but, in order to shorten the period of liquidation, the act provided that, after ninety per cent of the notes had been redeemed by the bank itself, the directors could present these notes to the State Auditor, together with a certificate showing the deposit in an approved bank of sufficient cash to pay off the remainder of the bank's issue, and receive in exchange the bonds that had been deposited. Such action had to be advertised in the newspapers, and anyone who held notes of the institution could present them to the Auditor for redemption at any time within three years from the date of the advertisement. At the end of three years the remaining funds were returned to the stock-holders of the liquidated bank.

Despite the apparent ease with which charters could be obtained, and the large supply of eligible bonds avail-able on the market, there was no sudden rush to establish new banks during the first few months after the passage of the act. The *Chicago Democrat,* which had never liked the new law, insisted that it would soon become a dead letter because nobody would comply with its pro-visions.[18] Members of the legislature began to discuss the advisability of repealing the law entirely and the Auditor, in order to stir up interest, advertised his willingness to issue bank notes to the full value (which was then con-siderably above par) of any six per cent bonds of the United States, Kentucky, Ohio or Virginia. Illinois bonds could not, he regretted, be used at more than eighty per cent of their current market price.[19]

Chicago agreed with other cities that the provisions of the act were too stringent, but the stringency could not entirely quench the enthusiasm for banks. The lead-ing enthusiast was J. Young Scammon who, after a long and renowned career as a lawyer, had acquired the con-trol of the Chicago Marine and Fire Insurance Company and reorganized it into two separate departments in order to facilitate its extralegal banking operations.[20] To Scammon goes the distinction of obtaining the first charter issued under the Illinois free banking law since, on January 13, 1852, the Marine Bank was incorporated to take over the banking operations of the old Chicago Marine and Fire Insurance Company. Scammon himself became President of the institution, while Edward I. Tinkham was appointed Cashier and, after a few months of operation the capital was increased from the initial sum of $50,000 to $500,000.[21] The notes of the Marine Bank made their first appearance in Chicago on Saturday, April 17, and the *Democrat* remarked enthusiastically that "the plate is a very fine one, and will not be an easy one to counterfeit."[22] But it could not let the occasion pass without a satirical lash. The notes were "finely engraved, having for a vignette, the bust of that distinguished philosopher and theologian, Baron Swedenborg,* with rays emanating therefrom, placed between two beautiful women. The only thing we objected to in the bill is the embellishing it with ladies—emblems of innocence—as though there were anything innocent about banking institutions."[23]

On February 18, the private banking house of Boone and Bronson decided to follow Scammon's example, and obtained a charter for the Merchants and Mechanics Bank in Chicago. The institution was capitalized at $100,000, and the two partners in the private firm, whose business was taken over by the Merchants Bank, became respectively the President and Cashier.[24]

These two pioneering institutions did not, however, overcome the general reluctance to apply for charters. After they had been set up, interest in the banking legis-

* Scammon was the first professed Swedenborgian in Illinois. Cf. Andreas: *op. cit.*, I, 550.

THOMPSON'S
BANK NOTE AND COMMERCIAL
REPORTER

BY J. THOMPSON, BANKER, NO. 2 WALL STREET, NEW YORK.

Published at No. 64 Duane St.]   **NEW YORK, DECEMBER 15, 1854.**   [We have no Traveling Agent.

To Correspondents.

ALL letters and communications intended for "THE BANK NOTE & COMMERCIAL REPORTER," must be addressed to the subscriber, Editor and Proprietor—and correspondents are particularly requested to name the State, as well as town or city.
J. THOMPSON,
No. 2 Wall-st., cor. Broadway, N. Y.

Ourselves.

THE Indiana papers have given us a notoriety unmerited and unenvied. We never have been, and never intend to be, "carpet-bag brokers," or Bank runners. Our correspondents in the various sections of the country are generally able to make our exchanges satisfactory. We never have spoken of the Indiana Free Bank Law as the best. Our opinion has been, and so we have expressed it, that it was calculated to induce purely Banks of circulation, better adapted to outside bankers without capital than any other Free Banking Law in the Union. We have ever spoken of the Indiana Law as too liberal in its provisions for security, and liable to be thrown into the same disreputable condition in which we now find it.

It was a matter of compulsion that we sent a member of our house to Indiana. Before doing so, we sent our packages of Indiana money to Lafayette, Indianapolis, and Terre Haute, and received but one reply, which was "We cannot remit for your packages, and hold them subject to your further orders." Our correspondent at Lafayette charged us 5 ₩ cent on the notes of his next door neighbor, and rejecting all except such as he could draw specie for in his own village. Up to this time, we had quoted and bought Indiana money at 1½ ₩ cent discount. The convention which met at Indianapolis proved a failure. For a few weeks we bought at 5 ₩ cent, then at 10 ₩ cent, and then at 15 ₩ cent discount. There was no alternative left but to make an effort to get our money redeemed, or to know that the banks were broken. We had no doubt but that the Auditor would place in liquidation such Banks as did not pay; and it was our determination to draw a wide distinction between good Banks and broken Banks, as soon as the facts could be ascertained. We desired to use our money and our influence in behalf of the specie-paying Banks, and to crush out of existence all irresponsible banking, and in this way save the currency from a general depreciation.

When the merchants of Indiana find that their debts cannot be paid in this city, (owing to the depreciation of the money they receive,) except at a loss of 10 @ 20 ₩ cent, we shall have justice done us for making an honest effort in behalf of the people against the most scheming set of bankers ever known. And those bankers who have sustained specie payments will rue the day that brought discredit upon the whole system of Free Banking in that State. It was an easy matter for them, with our assistance, to have drawn the line between the specie-paying and suspended Banks. And it was the duty of the newspapers, as well also of the State officers, to have proclaimed every Bank broke that did not honorably and promptly discharge its obligations to the community, "carpet-bag brokers" included.

When a Bank so far falls into the path of honesty as to set at defiance any creditor, whether he holds one or a thousand dollars—whether he be farmor, priest, or broker—that Bank is unworthy of confidence. The debtor is always servant to the creditor—a stubborn fact which the new bankers in Indiana will discover when they again attempt to put their " promises to pay" in circulation.

THE Sunbury & Erie Road, from Milton to Williamsport, will be opened on the 26th inst.

☞ FOR TERMS OF THE REPORTER, &c., SEE PAGE 31.

POSTSCRIPT!

THE EMPIRE CITY BANK, of this city, failed to meet its exchanges on Saturday, at the Clearing House, and was consequently thrown out by some of the Banks. Their bills are well secured, wholly by State and United State Stocks, commanding a premium in the market. For the present we would advise holders of the notes not to submit to a loss on them.

The president and cashier, since the fire on Saturday night, have come out with the following card :—

> EMPIRE CITY BANK, Dec. 11, 1854.
> The office of the Bank having been rendered untenantable by the fire of Saturday evening, the directors give notice that they will procure another office for the Bank in the same neighborhood at an early an hour to-day as practicable, of which due notice will be given.
> All the valuable books and papers of the Bank, and the entire contents of its vault are saved.
> A. M. BININGER, President.
> ROBERT I. BLAMER, Cashier.

Broken and Suspended Banks.

PRESENT VALUE.

Canal Bank, Cleveland. Ohio	90 cents.
City Bank of Columbus, Ohio	90 cents.
Bank of Circleville, Ohio	50 cents.
Merchants' Bank, Bridgeton, N. Jersey.	60 cents.
Wheat Growers' Bank, Newton, N. J..	60 cents.
Government Stock Bank, at Ann Arbor, Michigan	60 cents.
Bank of Washtenaw, Michigan	25 cents.
Erie & Kalamazoo R.R. Bank, Michigan.	25 cents.
Farmers' & Mechanics' Bank of Kent County, Maryland	40 cents.
Newport Safety Fund Bank, Kentucky..	20 cents.
Kentucky Trust Company, Kentucky..	30 cents.
Stark Bank, Vermont	50 cents.
Cochituate Bank, Boston, Mass	50 cents.
Knickerbocker Bank, N. Y. City	90 cents.
Eighth Avenue Bank, N. Y. City	85 cents.
Lewis County Bank, Martinsburgh, N.Y.	25 cents.
Union Bank, Chicago, Illinois	75 cents.
City Bank, Chicago, Illinois	75 cents.
Merchants' & Mechanics' Bank, Chicago, Illinois	75 cents.
Farmers' Bank, Chicago, Illinois	75 cents.
Oshkosh City Bank, Wisconsin	75 cents.
Ship-Builders' Bank, Maine	60 cents.
Bank of Milford, Delaware	75 cents.

BELOIT, Nov. 27, 1854.

J. THOMPSON, Esq.:

Dear Sir—I observe that certain papers in your city publish this Bank as having failed—a false report, which originated in Chicago.

I deem it proper to say that the report is utterly false and malicious. The ROCK RIVER BANK has not failed or suspended. It will not, as we are abundantly able as well as willing to meet all demands upon us, on presentation. This we have ever done, and shall continue to do. And I take pleasure in saying to you that this Bank never was in better condition than at present.

Yours truly, J. M. KEEP, President.

The above is not the only Bank thrown or attempted to be thrown into discredit by certain papers, in this city—whether under false information, or from a desire to keep up an excitement, we leave the public to decide. Among the Banks named were the MEDINA BANK, Medina; the MONROE BANK, Rochester; the SOUTH ROYALTON BANK, South Royalton, Vt., &c., &c., all of which have been purchased by us at the usual rates.

INDEX.

☞ FOR BROKEN, CLOSED and WORTHLESS BANKS, see 30th page.

LATEST COUNTERFEITS.

10s, on the Ballston Spa Bank, N. Y., altered from 1s—Vignette female and child, with a marine view—horse, &c., between the signatures.

20s, on the Bank of Kentucky, Ky., altered from 1s—Vignette portrait of Henry Clay—men and women on each end.

5s, on the N. Y. & Va. State Stock Bank, Ind., altered from 1s—Likeness of Mr. Latham on lower right corner, and likeness of his wife on lower left corner.

5s, on the China Bank, Maine, altered from 1s—Vignette Laplander and sledge on the bottom of the bill—a hunter on the left end.

5s, on the New England Pacific Bank, R. I., altered from 1s—Vignette a harvest scene—a female on the right end.

5s, on the Mechanics' Bank, Newburyport, Mass. —Vignette a female feeding an eagle—female on the right end—head of Washington on the left end.

3s, on the Farmers' Bank, Bridgeport, Conn.—Vignette a reaper lying under a tree, with scythe, rake, &c.—figure 3 on each end—medallion head on the lower right corner—female figure on the lower left corner—well done.

Frauds.

HIGH BRIDGE BANK, High Bridge, Maryland—signed by — Harris, Banker.

THERE are one dollar bills, purporting to be of the AMERICAN EXCHANGE BANK, Springfield, Ill., in circulation. It is a fraud—there is no such Bank.

WE hear that two or three of the smaller Banks in this city are considering the policy of winding up. With the contracted line of discounts now kept up, banking in a small way don't pay expenses.

FOR SALE, in lots to suit, Milwaukee City 7 ₩ cent Coupon Bonds, twenty years to run, interest payable semi-annually in New York. Price 80 and accrued interest.

A. W. GREENLEAF, No. 2 Wall-st.

THOMPSON'S BANK NOTE REPORTER
Reproduced by courtesy of the American Antiquarian Society,
Worcester, Mass.

lation faded away once more, and no other banks were created. By the late spring of 1851, repeal of the law once more became a subject of serious discussion. But the sudden realization that the law might be repealed changed the whole situation. Stringent as it seemed to be, the measure was an infinite improvement over the conditions that had preceded its passage, conditions under which it had been absolutely impossible to set up incorporated banks. Several people, who had been waiting in the hope that the law would be liberalized, suddenly decided to take the bull by the horns and, at once, file an application for a charter. The *Democrat*, surprised at this turn of events, suggested acidly that "banks are now getting as thick as groceries in our city."[25] This was more than a slight exaggeration, but it is interesting to note that the banking fever gripped Democratic districts just as much as Whig communities. St. Clair county, which gave the largest vote of any county in the state against the banking bill, was the source of applications for charters for five new banks, with capitalizations ranging from $500,000 to $1,000,000. Had all these schemes come to fruition (which, fortunately, they did not) St. Clair county would have had as large a banking capital as all the rest of the state.[26]

At the beginning of June, there were only three incorporated banks operating in Illinois, Clark's Exchange Bank, at Springfield, having been created soon after the two Chicago banks.[27] By December, seventeen banks were already operating, and had deposited bonds with the Auditor to an aggregate amount of $1,142,544; sixteen others had filed certificates of incorporation, but not completed organization, and seven more applications had been received which were withdrawn before they could become effective.[28]

In Chicago, the process of bank expansion had been particularly rapid during the latter half of the year. Toward the end of May, the Southwestern Plank Road Company, which had handled a good deal of financial business in addition to its transportation activities, filed papers for the incorporation of the Commercial Bank of Chicago,[29] which was designed to take over the banking operations of the company but had little importance. In June, the private banking house of Bradley and Curtis decided to incorporate their business under the title of the City Bank of Chicago, capitalized at $200,000, and obtained a charter on June 26.[30] During July, I. H. Burch and Company incorporated their business under the name of the Chicago Bank, with a subscribed capital of $100,000, half of which was immediately paid in,[31] while George Smith (of whom we shall hear a great deal more in the following paragraphs) obtained a charter for the Bank of America, situated in Chicago and capitalized at $50,000.[32] Davisson and McCalla obtained a charter for the Bank of Commerce early in August, and took over the old Chicago Post Office to house the new institution,[33] while Forrest Brothers and Company, who had "done business both in this and the old country," incorporated the Union Bank of Chicago on August 18.[34]

After this initial spurt, there was a short period of quiescence broken only by the incorporation of Seth Paine's Bank of Chicago early in October,[35] but two more banks came into existence in Chicago around the end of the

ILLINOIS.

Discount.

Alton Bank, *Alton*.................... 3
[*E. Mersh, Pres.—Chas. A. Caldwell, Cash.*]

Bank of America, *Chicago*................(F.) 3
[*O. Smith, Pres.—E. W. Willard, Cash.*]

Bank of Elgin, *Elgin*.................... 3
[*M. C. Town, Pres.—J. J. Town, Cash.*]
10s, altered from 1s—this Bank has no 10s.

Bank of Galena, *Galena*.................... 3
[*Hezro Corwith, Pres.—C. C. P. Hunt, Cash.*]

Bank of Lucas & Simonds, *Springfield*.....(F.) 3
[*A. Campbell, Pres.—Rob. Irwin, Cash.*]

Bank of Naperville, *Naperville*............(F.) 25
[*Willard Scott, Pres.—A. Keith, Cash.*]
5s, altered—vig. country scene, &c.—FIVE in red letters across the bill.

Bank of Northern Illinois, *Waukegan*......... 3
[*C. D. Bickford, Pres.—Charles R. Steele, Cash.*]

Bank of Ottawa, *Ottawa*....................(F.) 3
[*Burton C. Cook, Pres.—Geo. S. Fisher, Cash.*]
5s, altered from 3s—has FIVE in red letters under the title of the Bank—Bank has no red letters on its bills.
10s, altered from 1s—this Bank has no 10s.

Bank of Peru, ...3
[*T. D. Brewster, Pres.—Edwin C. Allen, Cash.*]

Bank of Rockford, *Rockford*................(F.) 25
[*C. J. Horseman, Pres.—C. C. Wilcox, Cash.*]
10s & 20s, altered from 1s—vig. a harvest scene; long bridge in the distance—hold them to the light—the Bank has no 20s

Belvidere Bank, *Belvidere*.................(F.) 3
[*Alex Neely, Pres.—A. C. Root, Cash.*]

Belleville Bank, *Belvidere*.................... 3

Central Bank, *Peoria*.....................(F.) 3
[*G. H. Rupert, Pres.—R. A. Smith, Cash.*]

Chicago Bank, *Chicago*....................(F.) 3
[*Thos. Burch, Pres.—I. H. Burch, Cash.*]
3s, the words "Chicago Bank" are not shaded : in the genuine they are shaded—otherwise it is said to be a good imitation of the genuine.

City Bank, *Chicago*.......................(F.) 25
[*D. O. Bradley, Pres.—C. B. Curtiss, Cash.*]

Clark's Exchange Bank, *Springfield*........(F.) 3
[*N. H. Ridgely, Pres.—Chas. Ridgely, Cash.*]

Commercial Bank, *Chicago*.................(F.) 3
[*J. Cook, Pres.—A. Gilbert, Cash.*]

Darien Stock Bank.........................(F.) 3

Du Page County Bank, *Naperville*............ 25
[*Willard Scott, Pres.—A. Keith, Cash.*]

Exchange B'k of *H. A. Tucker & Co., Chicago*.... 3
[*H. A. Tucker, Pres.—Hamilton B. Dox, Cash.*]

Discount.

Farmers' Bank, *Chicago*.................... 25
[*P. R. Ring, Pres.—C. L. Chase, Cash.*]
☞ Failed November 8, 1854.
5s & 10s, altered from 1s—vig. female reclining on a bale of goods ; ox team, load of hay, &c., on right—female on the lower right corner—on the lower left corner and on the upper right corner is the denomination.

Farmers' & Traders' Bank, *Charleston*....... 3
[*W. H. Murstin, Pres.—Thos. A. Marshall, Cash.*]
5s, altered from 1s—vig. view of a wheat field—head of Washington on the right end.

Marine Bank of Chicago....................(F.) 3
[*J. Y. Scammon, Pres.—E. I. Tinkham, Cash.*]
20s, this Bank never issued any 20s.

McLean County Bank, *Bloomington*..........(F.) 3
[*A. Gridley, Pres.—T. Pardee, Cash.*]

Mech. & Farmers' Bank, *Springfield*......(F.) 25
[*T. Lewis, Pres.—M. Divelbiss, Cash.*]
☞ Suspended A.M., November 27, 1854.
5s, altered from 1s—vig. a mechanic, &c.—a female, &c., on the left end—man, carrying a basket, on right end.

Merchants' & Drovers' Bank, *Joliet*......... 3
[*Wm. Smith, Pres.—R E. Goodell, Cash.*]

Merchants' & Mech. Bank, *Chicago*......(F.) 25
[*L. D. Boone, Pres.—S. Brorson, jr., Cash.*]
5s & 10s, altered from 1s—Bank has no 10s.

People's Bank, *Carmi*...................... 3

Phœnix Bank, *Chicago*...................... 25
[*L. Reynolds, Pres.—N. C. Roe, Cash.*]
5s, vig. a female sitting, with arms extended, viewing a sea scene ; a ship in the distance.

Quincy City Bank, *Quincy*.................(F.) 3
[*N. Flagg, Pres.—J. C. Woodruff, Cash.*]

Railroad Bank, *Decatur*.................... 25
[*P. D. Kline, Pres.—C. H. Fuller, Cash.*]

Rock Island Bank, *Rock Island*.............(F.) 3
[*M. B. Osborn, Pres.—S. H. Mann, Cash.*]
10s & 50s, altered from smaller denominations—Bank has no larger than 5s.

Southern Bank of Illinois, *Belleville*........... 3
[*R. Hinckley, Pres.—F. Hinckley, Cash.*]

State Bank of Illinois, *Shawneetown*.......... 3
[*Joseph Bowles, Pres.—A. B. Safford, Cash.*]
5s, altered from a broken Washington affair—vig. three females, the centre one holding a Liberty cap in left hand—head of Washington, with 5 above, on the right end.

Stock Security Bank, *Danville*..............(F.) 3
[*E. Kingsbury, Pres.—J. C. Short, Cash.*]

Union Bank, *Chicago*.....................(F.) 25
[*A. J. Brown Pres.—H. L. Forrest. Cash.*]

year. The Farmers Bank, organized by Chase Brothers with the minimum capital of $50,000, began operations late in December,[36] while Tucker and Company incorporated their business as the Exchange Bank early in January, 1853.[37] More than a year afterward, the list of Chicago's free banks was completed when N. C. Roe and Company organized the Phoenix Bank.

By the spring of 1854, therefore, Chicago had ten incorporated banks, if we exclude, for the moment, the little Commercial Bank and Seth Paine's strange institution, and it is possible to obtain a fairly clear picture of the scope of their operations from the figures presented in the following table.[38] Since there was no reduction in the number of private bankers, save in the cases where the business of the older house was taken over by the newly incorporated bank, the city was supplied with financial facilities on a much ampler scale than it had been at any previous time. Moreover the citizens demanded a good deal of their bankers. When the new banks decided to open at ten o'clock and close at three, following the practice which was then general in the east, there was an indignant demand that they should revert to the old Chicago practice, and remain open for business from eight in the morning until five in the evening. There was, however, no objection to their closing for an hour or two at lunchtime, since all business houses did that. "There is a smack of aristocracy in their 10 to 3 o'clock idea, entirely incompatible with the old long established New England Puritanic eating and laboring hours, which our practice and business requires, on Water Street."[39]

The indignation of the business community on the sub-

TABLE IV

CONDITION OF CHICAGO BANKS

April 3, 1854

Name of Bank	Paid-in Capital	Note Circulation	Deposits	Bonds Deposited to Secure Notes	Loans and Discounts	Due from Other Banks	Specie Reserves
Bank of Commerce.......... (Davisson & McCalla)	$ 52,000	$ 55,000	$ 10,244	$ 57,431	$100,000	$ 16,209	$ 16,418
Exchange Bank........... (Tucker & Co.)	54,288	48,595	....	54,288	20,377	....	27,300
Marine Bank............. (J. Y. Scammon)	150,000	197,684	33,917	277,933	58,198	13,183	31,450
Merchants & Mechanics Bank... (Boone & Bronson)	120,700	57,621	199,128	63,700	....	237,577	15,616
Bank of America.......... (George Smith)	50,000	50,000	....	50,000	10,000	....	40,000
City Bank............. (Bradley & Curtis)	66,000	59,985	....	65,623	....	54,076	10,548
Chicago Bank............ (I. H. Burch & Co.)	136,209	136,081	....	136,208	....	94,139	25,000
Farmers Bank........... (Chase Brothers)	53,000	50,000	....	53,000	35,633	....	14,810
Phoenix Bank........... (N. C. Roe & Co.)	50,000	*	*	50,000	*	*	*
Union Bank............ (Forrest Brothers)	70,000	73,382	....	82,000	....	45,409	15,183
Total.............	$802,197	$728,348	$243,289	$890,183	$224,208	$460,593	$196,325

* The Phoenix Bank was not yet fully organized.

ject of banking hours fades into insignificance, however, by comparison with the furore that the Bank of the City of Chicago* aroused among the bankers. In terms of resources the institution was insignificant: its actual capital never exceeded $6,000, and its aggregate note issue (which was entirely illegal) was even smaller. But Seth Paine, the President of the Bank, was a personage who had to be reckoned with, since he had outstanding ability as a speaker and writer, and used that ability, with all the fervor of an evangelist, in the dissemination of his ideas. First, as an abolitionist, he had tried to free the slaves; later, as a disciple of Fourier, he had established a communistic phalanstery on his farm in Lake County; still later, he set out to convert people to a belief in spiritualism.

In the light of all this, it is not surprising that, when Paine entered the banking business as the senior partner of the Chicago house of Seth Paine and Company, he should have become imbued with a desire to reform the practice of banking.[40] For that purpose, he created the Bank of the City of Chicago, which began operations in October, 1852, and issued notes "which for artistic skill and beauty of finish are not exceeded by any bills we have seen."[41] But the prospectus of the Bank was even more unusual than the notes. It specified unequivocally that no loans would be made "to aid in making or selling intoxi-

* It is to be regretted that the sponsors of Chicago banks showed so little imaginative variety in the selection of names. The Commercial Bank, of the Plank Road Company, is often confused with the Bank of Commerce, established by Davisson and McCalla, particularly since contemporary journalists sometimes used either title as a literary variation of the other. The City Bank, the Chicago Bank and Seth Paine's Bank of the City of Chicago constitute an even more confusing trinity of completely independent institutions, in regard to which the reader should be on his guard.

cating liquors, or tobacco in any of its forms," nor were "gamblers or usurers who borrow to loan again" to expect any accommodation. Real-estate loans, and loans to finance speculation, were also prohibited, so that the Bank, in summary, could make loans only for "aiding the natural exchange between the producer and consumer, whether of body, soul or spirit, and for the time necessary to produce the exchange."

Even if matters had rested at that point, the Bank of the City of Chicago would have been unique in the annals of nineteenth-century finance, but it was one of Paine's characteristics that he never stopped halfway to his goal. He intended to bring religion into banking, and he proceeded with his campaign. The next step was to establish "Harmony Hall," the meeting place of an ardent group of spiritualists, in the rooms above the Bank, installing a well-known medium named Mrs. Herrick as the High Priestess of the cult. When customers came to the Bank for loans, the High Priestess was installed on a kind of throne in the bank parlor, where she would consult the spirit of Alexander Hamilton and obtain his advice as to whether or not the loan should be granted. To anyone familiar with the opinions and practices of Alexander Hamilton during his life, those post-mortem opinions must come as somewhat of a shock. Through the lips of Mrs. Herrick, Hamilton invariably refused loans to "smokers, drinkers and bankers," and insisted that "women, children and spiritually-minded men" were to have first claim upon the loanable funds of the institution!

Although this unique improvement of current banking practice excited a good deal of comment, it did not breed opposition. The merchants and industrialists of Chicago evinced no desire to withdraw their money from the old-fashioned banks, in order to place it under the protection of Paine and the shade of Hamilton, and financial operations were carried on in traditional fashion throughout the city in spite of Paine's enthusiasm for reform. On January 1, 1853, therefore, he took a further step in his campaign by establishing a periodical entitled *The Christian Banker*. It was an interesting publication, and the articles had a refreshing originality to anyone familiar with the more orthodox financial journals. Perhaps, the latter might command a wider audience if produce market reports began by pointing out that "there has been but little Christianity in the market, and much that is offered is of the scurvy order. This kind, however, bears a much better price than the more perfect, as the tastes of consumers have been destroyed by rum and smoke, until their heads and hams are in a perfect pickle."[42]

In addition to its unique market reports, and its columns of religious exhortation, *The Christian Banker* offered some pungent comments on the leading financiers of the city. R. K. Swift, "who smokes to drown his conscience, which has been violated so long by huge shaves of his fellow men," was scarcely pleased by the advertisement, nor was George Smith enthusiastic when, in writing of the Bank of America at Chicago, Paine shouted: "Don't mistake this kitten of Illinois, for the old cat [i.e. Bank of America] at Washington, lest you get your eyes scratched out by the mother of frauds. Reject this [paper] as you would the small pox." Messrs. Tucker and Company must have been equally indignant when Paine wrote of their Exchange Bank: "This concern exists only in name, and exists only as the nurse of unfledged goslings hatched from rotten eggs. . . . The issues, . . . like Smith's fraud at Washington, are not taken on deposit by us."

The Chicago bankers rose in their wrath, the more readily since there was a grain of truth underlying Paine's acid comments.[43] Every note of the Bank of the City of Chicago which came into their hands was promptly presented for payment; but they achieved nothing by that, since Paine was able to meet every demand promptly. Finally, on February 11, 1852, the Bank was closed by the police, who had obtained a warrant under a commission of lunacy on Paine's partner, Ira B. Eddy. One of the most fascinating, and exotic, of American financial institutions thereby came to a sudden end, and the atmosphere of Chicago grew quiet once again. But it should be recorded, by way of epilogue, that all the creditors of the Bank were paid in full, and that Paine lived comfortably until 1871, pouring his apostolic fervor into the solution of social, rather than financial, questions.

Turning our attention from local conditions in Chicago to the wider picture, we find that, in the entire State of Illinois, thirty-one banks had come into existence by the spring of 1854. One of these, it may be noted in passing, was the State Bank of Illinois at Shawneetown, built upon the ruins of the old bank at Shawneetown by Joel A. Matteson (who had been elected Governor of Illinois in 1852). Despite its high-sounding name and large capitalization, it had no official connection with the state, but it was the largest unit in the chain of banks (which included the Central Bank of Peoria, the Merchants and Drovers Bank of Joliet, the Bank of Bloomington and the Bank of Quincy) that Matteson was rapidly building up.[44]

The thirty-one free banks had a nominal capital of $17,000,000,[45] but only $2,513,790 of this amount had been paid up, and the aggregate circulation of their notes did not exceed $2,300,000.* Even these notes, however, were not available in their entire amount to facilitate business in Illinois, since many of the banks had followed the ancient practice of putting the paper into circulation in other states, by means of agents, in order to make it harder for the noteholders to demand redemption in specie. The Bank Commissioners, in their annual report for 1854, complain that the notes of Illinois banks comprise less than thirty per cent of the paper money in circulation in the state, adding with sardonic optimism, "This disproportion will, however, gradually diminish as our domestic issues find their way into the State, from the distant points where they were originally put into circulation."[46]

Moreover, even at this early stage, two banks, one at Springfield and one at Quincy, had already been closed by the Commissioners[47] because their notes were inadequately secured.

The amount of attention given to the discussion of the

---

* Figures showing the condition of Illinois banks at various dates are to be found in the table on page 260. Since the returns filed by the banks were not always complete, and some banks failed to file any return at all, these figures must be regarded as approximate estimates, and minor discrepancies, though irritating, are unavoidable.

notes issued by the new banks was not unreasonable in view of the fact that one of the avowed purposes of the banking act was to supply a satisfactory currency. In addition to the notes of banks in other states, there was still a tremendous volume of the illegal certificates of deposit in general use and, in his report for 1852, the Auditor had drawn attention to the fact. "Some legislation seems to be necessary," he suggested, "to prevent the further issuing of certificates of deposit . . . in the similitude of bank notes, and for the immediate redemption of those now in circulation."[48]

This was definitely an understatement of the seriousness of the problem, since a "Bank War" of significant proportions was already going on between the incorporated banks and the illegal issuers of currency. On the one side, J. Young Scammon carried the standard for the legal free-bank notes; on the other, George Smith was still the undefeated champion of illegal, yet convertible, certificates of deposit. The early rounds of the fight must unquestionably be awarded to Smith, who appeared to have everything in his favor. Almost $1,500,000 of the certificates of deposit of the Wisconsin Marine and Fire Insurance Company (now owned in its entirety by Smith) were in circulation, and he set out to add to this large sum additional issues of legal notes. In April, 1852, he acquired control of the Bank of America, in Washington, D. C., and was promptly elected President of that institution. A couple of months later, he obtained a charter for the Bank of America, in Chicago, and deposited the necessary $50,000 to secure the legal issues of the latter bank. But, since the notes of both banks were printed in almost identical form, and no securities had to be deposited in Washington to secure notes issued at that point, Smith was able to keep an extraordinarily large circulation afloat between the two banks.[49] Moreover, Smith had purchased a controlling interest in the Atlanta Bank and the International Bank of Griffin, both in Georgia, where unlimited amounts of notes could be issued without the deposit of specific collateral, and the notes of these banks were shipped in large quantities to the offices of George Smith and Company, in Chicago, to be put into circulation there.[50]

No single Chicago bank, nor all the other banks of the city taken together, could boast an issue as large as that which circulated on Smith's reputation and, since the issue of notes was regarded as one of the major sources of banking profits, other Chicago bankers were naturally indignant. But the battle between the two groups cannot be dramatized as a struggle between law and honesty on the one side, and illegal roguery on the other. Smith's notes, which were backed by his personal fortune[51] as well as by the assets of the institutions he controlled, had a long record of soundness. Their universal popularity had been won, despite their illegality, by many years of unfailing promptness in redemption, while the notes of the Illinois free banks were a new and untried currency. Only a confirmed optimist could expect very much of the new notes, in the light of recent experiences in other western states that had adopted the free-banking system. Moreover, the controversy was still further complicated by the fact that many of the incorporated banks resorted to illegal issues of certificates of deposit, in order to supplement the notes that were issued against the bonds deposited with the State Auditor. The business community and the press were equally indignant when this practice came to light. Under the headline "Damn Shinplasters," the *Chicago Democrat*, while invoking the financial prestige of *Thompson's Bank Note Reporter* for support, condemns the whole fraudulent scheme.

" 'Excuse us, dear reader—we are in bad humor. We cannot see deception substituted for fair dealing so long as open honesty is the only sure road to success.

" 'The Merchant's & Mechanic's Bank, of Chicago, has issued a shinplaster exactly like their notes which are secured as the law requires. The Western papers call it a "dangerous counterfeit." 'Tis worse—'tis a devise, a deception, a fraud, and the only way to avoid it is to REFUSE ALL NOTES ON THE MERCHANT'S AND MECHANIC'S BANK OF CHICAGO.'

"The above from *Thompson's Reporter* is plain talk. We insert it not so much to injure this bank in particular, but because others of our city banks are going into the same operation.

"The thing ought to be stopped at once and we caution people upon this subject. Under our new banking law, the billholder is secured, but there is no security at all for the depositor. So people who prefer security to no security will hereafter take the legal countersigned bills instead of the illegal certificates of deposite."[52]

The people as a whole did not, however, take this advice to refuse all certificates of deposit. Smith's financial reputation was too well established to be undermined by spasmodic journalistic attacks, although there was occasional grumbling over the fact that he charged a commission of one per cent when the certificates of deposit were redeemed in specie.[53] This commission, however, served as a valuable argument for those Chicago bankers who were reluctant to redeem their notes at par as the law required. They could not, it was suggested, redeem at par if Smith continued to redeem at a discount of one per cent: if they did, it was inevitable that Smith's notes would continue to circulate while the notes of the other banks would be presented for payment whenever specie was needed. Obviously, Smith held all the cards; until he was forced to retire his notes, or to legalize them under the Illinois act, the other bankers could do nothing.

To open the campaign, the other bankers tried to break Smith's banks by a series of runs. Under the leadership of Scammon and R. K. Swift,[54] the Chicago bankers collected all the notes of Smith's Georgia institutions that they could lay their hands on, and sent Elihu B. Washburn afterward minister to France, down to Georgia to present them for payment. But Smith was prepared for the assault, and paid all the notes in full, adding insult to injury by paying so many of them in small coins that Washburn was compelled to return to Chicago with a heavy burden.[55] Meanwhile, every one of Smith's notes that came into the hands of the Chicago bankers was promptly presented at the Chicago office of George Smith and Company, with a demand for payment, frequently at the most inopportune times. While these runs were going on, Smith happened to meet Scammon, and immediately asked him how many notes the Marine Bank had in circulation. Scammon, with some pride, said that there were

$175,000, whereupon Smith quietly told him that $125,-000 of those notes were in the vaults of George Smith and Company, and that they were liable to be presented for payment some day.[56] The significance of the remark was obvious, particularly since Smith also held a good many notes of other Chicago institutions. The runs stopped as quickly as they had begun.

As Smith's notes could not be eliminated in this fashion, resort was had to the courts, and on December 23, 1852, the Grand Jury of Cook County found bills of indictment against George Smith and various other persons who had been guilty of issuing certificates of deposit.[57] The charges were very carefully drawn, however, and the public was curious to know "why some irregular banks were indicted and some not." The *Democrat* provided the answer. "We have inquired of the jury, and find that whilst their intentions were good they could not get the requisite information against some, whilst certain of the regular bankers were over-anxious to furnish information against others, the complainants being as prompt in withholding information against some as they were to furnish information against others. The fact speaks volumes, that the wild cats who have regular bankers for dormant partners were not indicted."[58]

The suits brought under the indictments appear to have accomplished nothing at all, and court records do not furnish evidence of a single conviction. The regular bankers, as a last resort, therefore decided to resort to legislative action and persuaded the members of the Assembly to take the necessary steps. On February 10, 1853, an act was passed which made it little less than a felony to issue, or to receive on deposit, any form of paper money other than bank notes legally issued under the statutes of Illinois or of other states.[59] Anyone violating the law was liable to a fine of fifty dollars for each illegal bill that he issued or received and, in addition, he made himself liable to imprisonment in the county jail for not more than a year.

The measure was drastic, but successful. By the end of 1854, the Bank Commissioners were able to report that the use of unauthorized certificates of deposit had entirely ceased in Illinois.[60] George Smith, in 1853, sold the Wisconsin Marine and Fire Insurance Company to Alexander Mitchell (who incorporated the institution as a bank under the laws of Wisconsin), and a few years later he disposed of the remainder of his banks and returned to Scotland with a handsome fortune.[61] The remainder of the illegal issues, having been put out by smaller and weaker houses, were easily suppressed, so that Illinois achieved, at last, a legal bond-secured currency issued by incorporated banks.

But the tribulations of the free-banking system in Illinois were by no means over, since many of the new banks, while abiding by the letter of the law, were very far from fulfilling the spirit of it. In the first place, several of the institutions did not have any real capital and, as Sumner so pungently points out, "if the stockholders of a bank are debtors to it and not creditors of it, it is a swindle. . . . They are not lending a surplus of their own; they are using an engine by which they can get possession of other people's capital. They print notes which have no security and make the public use them as money."[62] In one case of this kind, the sponsors of the bank borrowed bonds on Wall Street for sixty days, and deposited them with the State Auditor in return for an equal amount of currency. With this currency they purchased wheat in Chicago and sent it east to be sold for cash, which was then used for the purpose of paying the broker for the bonds.[63] Without investing a penny of their own, the sponsors of the bank had gained the profit on the speculative transaction as well as the right to receive the interest on the bonds during the period for which the notes remained in circulation. Meanwhile, they had neither the funds nor the inclination to carry on a regular banking business.*

Even when the sponsors of the bank actually provided capital funds, there were many cases where the institution did not do a regular banking business. In 1854, only nine banks, out of a total of twenty-nine, reported any loans or discounts to the Bank Commissioners,[64] and only two Chicago institutions, the Commercial Bank and the Merchant's and Mechanic's Bank, were included among the nine. The remaining banks, after receiving their notes from the Auditor, lent them *en bloc* to an agent, who undertook to relend them to borrowers, and a careful examination of the banking statements reveals the persistence of this habit throughout the decade.† Even the Marine Bank of Chicago appears to have made most of its

---

* These practices, it may be recalled, were identical with those which the government of Illinois had encouraged in the case of New York banks, a decade earlier, by supplying bonds to promoters on the understanding that payment should be made in the notes of the new bank after it was organized.

† The large amounts due from banks, and the small volume of loans and discounts, in Table IV indicate this clearly. See also *Report of the Bank Commissioners*, May, 1854; *Bankers Magazine*, IX, 107.

loans through the Chicago Marine and Fire Insurance Company,[65] which could charge borrowers 10 per cent interest in place of the 7 per cent maximum imposed on the banks, while, in the case of less reputable institutions, the lure of high interest was reinforced by the desire to put notes into circulation so far from the home office of the bank that it would be difficult, if not impossible, to present them for redemption.

From the viewpoint of the businessman this evidence indicated the growth of a particularly unsatisfactory form of wildcatting, within the legal structure of the Illinois free-banking system, but the legislature was more immediately interested in the fiscal problem that arose from the fact that banks were taxed on the basis of their loans and discounts. No effort was made to solve the broader economic problem regarding the issue and redemption of notes, but budgetary legislation[66] was enacted promptly. The amending act provided that banks should be taxed on capital stock, rather than on loans and discounts, and the preoccupation of the legislature with the fiscal aspect of the problem is indicated by a subsequent act which allowed the Auditor to withhold the interest received by him on the deposited securities when the bank that owned them was in arrears in its payments on the capital-stock tax.[67]

This initial development of the free-banking system occurred during years of general prosperity, so that the problems that arose could be handled calmly and unhurriedly. It was not necessary to find immediate solutions in the face of financial and psychological pressure while, in several matters, prosperity permitted the postponement of any decision. But, during the early summer of 1854, there occurred a short business recession that gave the Illinois banks their first real test.

All over the United States, there had been an expansion of credit from 1852 to 1854,[68] under the stimulus of the railroad boom. Funds were needed to build the growing network of tracks that linked up different sections of the country, and still more funds were needed to finance the development of the new areas which the railroads opened up to commerce and industry. The demand for funds appeared to be insatiable and, although large quantities of capital were imported from Europe, the banks were called on for substantial contributions. By 1854, there were 1,208 banks operating in the United States, as against 824 two years earlier, while the loans and discounts of these institutions had expanded from $364,000,000 to $557,000,000.

Moreover, to complicate matters for the Illinois banks, much of this expansion occurred in the neighboring states of the northwest and in the Ohio valley. Missouri was going through a public-improvement mania even worse than that which had afflicted Illinois in the thirties. Indiana, in May, 1852, had passed a Free Banking Act that gave rise to some of the worst examples of wildcat banking;[69] Wisconsin followed suit, in 1853, and Ohio was not far behind.[70] In the latter state, matters had reached a degree of complexity that is almost incredible. Five banks, including the Ohio Life Insurance and Trust Company, were operating under special charters; eleven banks were operating under an old law that required the deposit of bonds to secure notes in circulation; forty semi-independent banks were operating as branches of the Bank of the State of Ohio; and, by the end of 1853, twelve banks were in operation under the new free-banking law. Most of the latter "shingled" brazenly, using the notes obtained by the original bond deposit to purchase more bonds which were deposited as security for further circulation, thus pyramiding the circulation to dizzy heights of unsoundness. One man, starting with $10,000 capital, was able in this way to put out $600,000 of bank notes, doing no general banking business and yet living handsomely on the income from the deposited securities.[71]

It is not surprising that prices in Chicago doubled during the period from 1851 to 1854,[72] or that people began to be troubled about the outlook for business. "The question begins to force itself upon the minds of all thinking men, is this state of things to continue? Can the present prices of provisions, of labor, of every comfort and luxury of life be sustained for any considerable time? It is plain that either the value of money has diminished in a corresponding ratio, or the prices of goods and produce must recede."[73]

From the list of the bonds deposited to secure bank notes in Illinois, which is presented in Table V, it is apparent that the state was in a vulnerable position. Although the notes of all local banks were circulating at par in Chicago on January 1, 1854, and were received at no more than one or one and a half per cent discount in New York,[74] conditions deteriorated rapidly. During May an acute banking crisis developed in Ohio. The premium on domestic exchange rose rapidly and "borrowers, as well as finding it difficult to negotiate loans, were com-

TABLE V

SECURITIES DEPOSITED TO SECURE NOTE ISSUE IN ILLINOIS

Bonds Issued by	Dec. 1, 1854	Dec. 1, 1856
Virginia (100%)	$ 836,500	$ 867,500
Georgia (100%)	87,500	85,500
Missouri (100%)	1,013,000	4,590,000
Ohio (100%)	5,000	16,000
California (80%)	98,500	69,000
Kentucky (100%)	16,000	15,000
Tennessee (100%)	36,000	424,000
South Carolina (100%)	1,000,000	100,000
North Carolina (100%)		85,000
Louisiana (100%)		647,500
Illinois: Liquidation bonds (80%)	12,000	12,000
New Internal Improvement bonds (50%)	327,869	120,604
Interest certificates (100%)	268,417	312,640
Illinois and Michigan Canal (100%)	314,216	235,000
Interest certificates (100%)	55,527	65,844
Total at par	$4,070,529	$7,645,588
Total at eligible rate	2,651,210	6,663,389

Note. The figures in parenthesis show the eligible value for note-issue purposes as a percentage of par.

pelled to submit to high rates of interest. At times the best paper was sold in the streets at 10 to 18 per cent per annum."[75] In Indiana, the suspension of banks was so general that, at the end of the year, the banks which were still in solvent condition held a meeting in Indianapolis to advertise that fact to the public.[76]

It was in New York, however, that the panic reached its climax. Ever since the autumn of 1853, the security market had been weak,[77] so that it was quite unable to stand the shock it received in July, 1854, when the public discovered that Robert Schuyler, President of the New Haven Railroad and actively connected with many other lines, had been fraudulently issuing and selling the securities of the corporations with which he was associated.[78] Although the New York Stock Exchange took steps to make such operations impossible in future, and many

states, including Illinois,[79] passed laws that brought them
into the category of criminal offenses, the damage had
been done. A sharp stock-exchange panic was precipitated
and public confidence in the railroads, upon which the
whole economic expansion rested, was seriously weakened.

The New York panic affected Illinois seriously. Very
few loans were made during the middle of the summer at
less than 12 per cent, and even at that figure funds were
scarce. Good railroad loans were granted only at rates from
15 to 18 per cent, and "street paper" was taken at all kinds
of figures above and below 5 per cent a month.[80] Moreover,
the notes of several Illinois banks fell to a discount, and
by the autumn all Illinois paper was "peculiarly subject
to distrust" in St. Louis.[81]

These developments were due, in part, to the business
expansion that had been going on in Chicago during the
preceding years, but the impact of the crisis on the banking system was accentuated by another force. So general
a revulsion seriously depressed the price of bonds. Investors were less willing to purchase securities, and the
failure of internal improvements had undermined the
financial standing of several states. As bond prices fell, the
State Auditor was compelled to demand additional bonds
to secure the circulation of the Illinois banks, and knowledge of this action led to runs on the institutions that
were affected. By November, these runs had attained such
dimensions, in several cases, that eight Illinois banks—
including such Chicago institutions as the City Bank, the
Farmer's Bank, the Merchant's and Mechanic's Bank, the
Phoenix Bank and the Union Bank—were compelled to
close their doors.[82] The notes of these institutions

promptly fell to a discount of 25 per cent, as can be seen from the statement in *Thompson's Bank Note Reporter*,* (reproduced facing p. 216) and, although they were given a liberal opportunity in the following year,[83] most of the banks were unable to resume business.

Fortunately the panic was of short duration. By the beginning of 1855, business had resumed its upward course, and the Bank Commissioners were able to take a dispassionate view of the things that had happened in Illinois.[84] With unerring accuracy of vision, they blamed the crisis on "the small amount of cash capital . . . employed in the [banking] business," and suggested that more capital might be attracted if the banks, like other lenders, were allowed to charge 10 per cent interest. The fact that the law imposed a 7 per cent maximum on the rate of interest charged by banks had led many institutions to lend all, or a large portion, of their notes to other corporations, "composed for the most part of the same individuals as [the bank] stockholders," to be relent at rates as high as 10 per cent, so that the Commissioners unhesitatingly recommended a change in the law that would discourage the practice by permitting the banks themselves to charge the same interest as other lenders.

But such clarity of vision was remarkable for its absence when they came to consider the fundamental question of specie reserves. That the reserves of the banks had diminished steadily through the withdrawal of specie

---

* *Bank Note Reporters*, of which Thompson's was an outstanding example, were studied each month by bankers and merchants in much the same way that stock-market reports are read today. Only by continuous study could a man be sure of the current value of a particular bank note, since quotations changed frequently. The pages reproduced at the beginning of this chapter constitute an interesting example of such literature.

was admitted, but the blame for this was placed upon the shoulders of the brokers who handled domestic exchange and bullion operations! Regarding the work of the luckless brokers, the Banking Commissioners were as scathing as Samuel Johnson had been in his Dictionary: "It is to be regretted that any class of persons should be enabled to gain merely from this occupation the means of subsistence, without in any manner adding to the wealth of the community and without having any abiding interest in its prosperity."

Unfortunately, specie reserves cannot be increased by abusing brokers, and no attention was paid by the legislature to the suggestion that the maximum rate of interest be raised. As a matter of fact, nothing at all was done at the legislative session of 1855, as far as banking is concerned, if we except the passage of two unimportant acts. One of these provided for the voluntary liquidation of free banks by their directors,[85] while the other specified the respective duties of the State Auditor and of the receiver in the case of banks that failed.[86]

In spite of the failures of 1854, however, the expansion of banking facilities throughout the state continued steadily during the period after the panic. By the end of 1856 there were sixty-one banks listed, with a total circulation of $6,480,873.[87] This represented an increase of more than one hundred per cent over the comparable figures for 1854, and the aggregate value of the securities deposited by the banks had increased even more rapidly so that there was a margin of safety of more than a million dollars.[88] In the light of subsequent events, however, it is important to notice that $4,590,000, out of total securities valued at $7,646,000, consisted of bonds of the State of Missouri.

Chicago, however, did not share in this expansion. Of the ten free banks operating before the crisis of 1854, only three remained at the end of 1856, *viz.,* Smith's Bank of America, the Chicago Bank operated by Burch, and Scammon's Marine Bank. The remainder had gone into liquidation, either voluntarily or as a result of inability to pay their notes on demand, and the Chicago bank-note circulation had fallen from $728,000 to $127,000. The aggregate resources of the Chicago banks, while less severely contracted, had declined from $1,793,000 to $575,000,[89] which was sufficiently serious in view of the steadily increasing demands for capital in the growing community.

Moreover, the sudden contraction in the supply of Illinois bank notes available in Chicago had created a monetary vacuum that sucked in all sorts of wildcat paper from other states. The currency in circulation was, if anything, worse than it had been before the suppression of the illegal issues, and Andreas mentions the case of a conductor on the Burlington Railroad in September, 1855, who, collecting a total of $203, received notes from twelve states.[90] Georgia bank notes amounted to a total of $115, while only $20 came from Illinois banks—including one single dollar bill issued in Chicago. To make matters worse, many of the "foreign" wildcat banks, whose notes circulated in Chicago, were owned by Chicago capitalists who were unwilling to operate their institutions under the somewhat stricter laws of Illinois.

Unfortunately, little could be done about this situation. Early in 1856, the larger railroad companies, after months of discussion, refused to accept Georgia and Tennessee bank notes at their Chicago offices,[91] and this action was promptly followed by a similar step on the part of the Marine Bank and R. K. Swift and Company.[92] At a mass meeting of the leading merchants of Chicago, it was strongly urged that the acceptance of these bank notes was "highly injurious to the business interests of the community,"[93] but the movement to suppress them came to nothing. An equally large group of merchants inserted a notice in the papers stating that they would accept any bank notes, "as long as they are redeemed in specie at the banks where issued," and pointing out that it was foolhardy to reduce the currency still further, by voluntary action, when there was already a dearth of money in Chicago.[94] Obviously the city had gained very little from the free-banking system and, as 1856 drew to a close, it was still largely dependent on the private banking houses that had served its merchants for more than fifteen years.

But the panic of 1854 was destined to bear some fruit, even though the harvest was long delayed. During 1855 and 1856, legislation designed to remedy some of the most obvious defects in the banking system was enacted in Ohio, Indiana, Connecticut, New York and the District of Columbia.[95] Illinois followed suit during the early weeks of 1857. In addition to a measure designed to facilitate the winding-up of free banks that had failed,[96] a law was passed that brought about radical changes in the whole banking structure of the state.[97]

To eliminate the worst forms of wildcatting, it was provided that each bank must transact all its operations at the office specified in its certificate of incorporation, and in no case could that office be situated in a community of less than two hundred people. Banks could no longer be established in the inaccessible backwoods. Moreover, it was provided that no bank should be incorporated unless the Auditor was satisfied that it had a *bona fide* cash capital of $50,000, or more, which belonged to the institution and was going to stay in it, while, as an inducement to such investment, the legal rate of interest that banks might charge was raised from 7 to 10 per cent. Even the banks that were already in existence could not escape from these conditions, since it was provided that no more notes should be issued to any bank until it had satisfied the Auditor of its compliance with the terms of this act.

Regarding the redemption of notes, the law was simplified, and made more stringent. All notes were to be redeemed in specie, on demand, at the office of the bank, and bank officials were forbidden to delay the process of redemption by paying each note separately in small coins. The whole amount of notes presented at one time was to be treated as a single obligation and promptly honored. If any note was not paid on demand, the holder could protest it before a notary, or before two householders if there was no notary available. Within ten days of such protest, the bank had the right to pay the note, with 12 per cent interest, but if the note was still unpaid at the end of that period the bank was to be placed in the hands of receivers.

After nearly six years of experience, it seemed that the free-banking system of Illinois had been developed to a point of efficiency and soundness. The notes were circulating at par, the banks appeared to be in flourishing condition, and the outstanding defects of the original law had been admirably remedied. Yet, at that moment, the forces of disintegration were already apparent.

REFERENCES FOR CHAPTER VII

[1] *Thompson's Bank Note and Commercial Reporter,* November 1, 1852.
[2] Cf. Cole: *op. cit.,* p. 95.
[3] *Illinois Journal,* October 12, 1850.
[4] *Ibid.,* January 3, 1850.
[5] *Constitution of 1848,* Article X, *Sections 1-5, Laws of Illinois,* 1849, p. 20.
[6] Andreas: *op. cit.,* I, 582.
[7] Cole: *op. cit.,* pp. 95-96.
[8] *Reports of the Session (House),* 1851, p. 493.
[9] *Chicago Democrat,* February 22, 1851.
[10] *Laws of Illinois,* 1851, p. 144. Approved February 17, 1851.
[11] *Gem of the Prairie,* October 26, 1851, cited in Andreas: *op. cit.,* I, 537.
[12] Cole: *op. cit.,* p. 96.
[13] *Laws of Illinois,* 1851, pp. 163-175. Approved February 15, 1851. The interest which the act aroused in the east is apparent from two long catechisms in explanation of it which appear in *Hunt's,* XXVI, 96-99 and 479.
[14] See above pp. 184-185.
[15] Cf. *Bankers Magazine,* IX, 13.
[16] *Section 14.*
[17] *Section 9.*
[18] *Chicago Democrat,* January 28, 1852.
[19] *Chicago Tribune,* February 13, 1852.
[20] See above pp. 201-202; also Andreas: *op. cit.,* I, 550-551.
[21] Andreas: *op. cit.,* I, 537.
[22] *Chicago Democrat,* April 21, 1852.
[23] *Ibid.,* April 22, 1852; Andreas: *op. cit.,* I, 537-538.
[24] *Chicago Democrat,* February 18, 1852.
[25] *Ibid.,* May 6, 1852.
[26] *Hunt's,* XXVIII, 611.
[27] *Ibid.,* XXVII, 225-226.
[28] *Report of the Auditor,* December, 1852, *Laws of Illinois,* 1853, p. 5.
[29] Andreas: *op. cit.,* I, 538.
[30] *Idem,* 548.
[31] *Chicago Democrat,* July 7, 1852.
[32] Andreas: *op. cit.,* I, 548.

[33] *Chicago Democrat,* August 5, 1852.

[34] *Ibid.,* May 6, 1852; Andreas: *op. cit.,* I, 548.

[35] See below pp. 219-224.

[36] *Chicago Democrat,* December 25, 1852.

[37] Andreas: *op. cit.,* I, 548.

[38] The figures are taken from the *Report of the Illinois Bank Commissioners,* May, 1854, *Bankers Magazine,* IX, 111-112.

[39] Chicago *Daily Democratic Press,* March 31, 1854.

[40] Much of the material here presented has been drawn from the admirable account of Seth Paine's activities in Andreas: *op. cit.,* I, 540-544.

[41] *Chicago Democrat,* October 18, 1852.

[42] Cited by Andreas: *op. cit.,* I, 541-543.

[43] See below pp. 225-234.

[44] Knox: *op. cit.,* 714 and 724; *Hunt's,* XXXVII, 465.

[45] *Bankers Magazine,* IX, 104.

[46] *Report of the Bank Commissioners,* May, 1854, *Bankers Magazine,* IX, 110.

[47] *Ibid.,* p. 104.

[48] *Report of the Auditor,* December 1, 1852, *Laws of Illinois,* 1853, p. 5.

[49] See Seth Paine's comment above, pp. 223-224; also Andreas: *op. cit.,* I, 538.

[50] Andreas: *op. cit.,* I, 546; II, 617.

[51] See above pp. 202-204.

[52] *Chicago Democrat,* September 3, 1852.

[53] *Ibid.,* May 6 and 24, 1852. No commission was charged if they were redeemed in paper money.

[54] *Ibid.,* October 1 and 9, 1857.

[55] Andreas: *op. cit.,* II, 617.

[56] *Idem.*

[57] *Chicago Democrat,* December 25, 1852.

[58] *Ibid.,* January 1, 1853.

[59] *Laws of Illinois,* 1853, pp. 30-33. Approved February 10, 1853.

[60] *Report of the Bank Commissioners,* December 30, 1854, *Reports of the Session,* 1855, p. 4.

[61] Andreas: *op. cit.,* I, 546; II, 617-618.

[62] *History of Banking,* I, 33.

[63] *Chicago Tribune,* January 19, 1861.

[64] *Report of the Bank Commissioners,* May, 1854, *Bankers Magazine,* IX, 107.

[65] Andreas: *op. cit.,* I, 544.

[66] *Laws of Illinois,* 1853, pp. 6-23. Approved February 12, 1853.

[67] *Laws of Illinois,* 1861, p. 38. Approved February 18, 1861.

[68] Cf. Table VI, p. 259.

[69] *History of Banking*, I, 444; Chicago *Daily Democratic Press*, June 13, 1854.

[70] *Hunt's*, XXVIII, 360; *Bankers Magazine*, XII, 165.

[71] *History of Banking*, I, 445; McCulloch: *Men and Measures*, p. 126.

[72] Chicago *Daily Democratic Press*, June 19, 1854.

[73] *Idem.*

[74] Chicago *Daily Democratic Press*, January 14 and 16, 1854; *Thompson's Bank Note and Commercial Reporter*, January 16, 1854.

[75] *Hunt's*, XXXI, 615.

[76] *Ibid.*, XXXII, 109.

[77] Cf. Chicago *Daily Democratic Press*, October 18, 1853; also September 20, 1853.

[78] Chicago *Daily Democratic Press*, July 10, 12 and 13, 1854; James: *Economics of Money, Credit and Banking*, pp. 377-378.

[79] *Laws of Illinois*, 1855, p. 163. Approved February 14, 1855.

[80] Chicago *Daily Democratic Press*, June 26, July 1 and 10, 1854.

[81] *Bankers Magazine*, IX, 466.

[82] *Thompson's Bank Note and Commercial Reporter*, December 15, 1854; Andreas: *op. cit.*, I, 548.

[83] *Bankers Magazine*, IX, 822.

[84] *Report of the Bank Commissioners*, December 30, 1854, *Reports of the Session*, 1855, p. 183ff.

[85] *Laws of Illinois*, 1855, pp. 32-33. Approved January 10, 1855.

[86] *Laws of Illinois*, 1855, pp. 31-32. Approved February 14, 1855. Another act, of no general importance here, was passed to provide that banks might present for payment any Illinois bonds which they had deposited to secure circulation, as long as other eligible bonds were substituted for them. *Laws of Illinois*, 1855, p. 164.

[87] *Report of the Auditor*, December 1, 1856, *Laws of Illinois*, 1857, pp. 114-119.

[88] *Laws of Illinois*, 1857, p. 112.

[89] *Laws of Illinois*, 1857, pp. 114-119.

[90] Andreas: *op. cit.*, I, 546.

[91] *Bankers Magazine*, X, 572.

[92] Andreas: *op. cit.*, I, 547.

[93] *Chicago Democrat*, December 27, 1855; *Bankers Magazine*, X, 572.

[94] Chicago *Daily Democratic Press*, January 6, 1856.

[95] *Hunt's*, XXXI, 617-618; XXXII, 350 and 613; Dewey: *op. cit.*, pp. 14, 54, 131 and 142.

[96] *Laws of Illinois*, 1857, pp. 220-221. Approved February 18, 1857.

[97] *Laws of Illinois*, 1857, pp. 23-25. Approved February 14, 1857; also *Hunt's*, XXXVII, 84-85.

CHAPTER VIII

THE DEBACLE

1857–1861

IF THE march of events brought revolutionary changes into the banking system of Illinois, during the middle decades of the nineteenth century, it did no less for the whole economy of the United States. Nothing was static, "not even the sacred and immutable Constitution."[1] Inventors were altering the face of the earth and the sea: factories were rising everywhere to manufacture goods at costs that would have seemed incredibly low to the craftsmen of an earlier generation,[2] while railroads and steamship lines were traversing the world with seven-league boots to link these factories to new sources of raw material and larger markets. The frontier was moving westward from the Mississippi to the Pacific Coast, as California surged forward on the produce of her mines. Even agriculture was shaken out of the deep-rooted habits that had characterized it for centuries. Railroad expansion encouraged the ruthless mining of the western prairies by farmers who were only too eager to ship wheat to hungry urban communities in the east, while southern fields and slaves began to be exploited with feverish energy in an effort to satisfy the insatiable appetite of the new cotton gin and the power-driven spinning mills.

Even men's opinion of one another was changed. Railroads carried people as well as goods and, as the number of travelers increased, the exclusiveness of the various regions of the country was broken down. Pleasant illusions were replaced by stark realities, and the realities sometimes failed to fit the theories founded on earlier ideas. A distant city or state became a personal experience to the traveler, instead of remaining a fabulous enchantment of the printed word. Moreover, with the advent of the telegraph, men became instantaneously aware of things that were happening hundreds, or even thousands, of miles away. Emotions could be shared by vast masses of people while the temper of the agitator was still at white heat. Such new-found powers of communication might prove dangerous.

England, to be sure, had gone through similar experiences in an earlier generation, experiences so far-reaching that the phrase "Industrial Revolution" cannot adequately describe them. But, in the middle of the nineteenth century the magnetic center of the disturbance was to be found in the United States; forces from all parts of the world seemed to concentrate upon the American situation and to accelerate the rate of change. Capital was drained away from Europe in quantities large enough to excite astonished comment in markets that had centuries of experience in international finance; iron and steel, as well as machinery, were imported in tremendous quantities because American factories could not produce nearly enough to meet the insatiable demand. From every European country, but particularly from Ireland and Germany, there came hundreds of thousands of immigrants, able and eager to play their part in the vast economic re-creation of the United States. Even the ideas of Europe were imported, the dreams of Wilberforce came to life again in American minds, and the gospel of Fourier and Robert Owen was zealously preached by American lips.

To the historian of a later generation, his mind washed clean by time of all the prejudices and hatreds that embittered those years, the middle decades of the nineteenth century will perhaps appear more important than the Civil War period in their effect upon the subsequent destinies of the United States. At a rough estimate, the wealth of the nation increased from some $380,000,000 in 1830 to more than $4,500,000,000 in 1856,[3] and though these contemporary figures can make no claim to statistical accuracy, they tell an astonishing story. Within a quarter of a century the national wealth had increased twelve times over. Even more significant, however, are the following figures derived from a comparison of the Census Returns in 1840 and 1850:

	1840	1850
Agricultural production of U. S., per capita	$33.24	$41.60
Industrial production of U. S., per capita	25.72	45.18
Total per capita production	$58.96	$86.78

In a short decade, the products of American factories had attained an importance proportionately greater than that of the produce of her farms. Agriculture, which to Washington and Jefferson had seemed the only foundation on which an enduring republic could be built, was rapidly losing its importance in the economic firmament, and the United States was becoming a great industrial economy. Even today, we have not fully grasped all the implications

JONATHAN YOUNG SCAMMON

Reproduced by courtesy of the Chicago Historical Society

of the changes that occurred during those turbulent years, so that it is not hard to appreciate the consternation and perplexity of contemporary observers.

Illinois led the vanguard in the development of railroads, which constituted one of the leading factors in the process of economic change during this period. In 1845, there were but 56 miles of railroad within the whole state; ten years later, 2,761 miles of road were in full operation,[4] which was more than could be found in any other state in the Union, with the possible exceptions of New York, Pennsylvania and Ohio.[5] Much of this development was due to the growth of the Illinois Central Railroad, for the construction of which Stephen A. Douglas had obtained a land grant of 2,500,000 acres in 1850. To achieve this, he had placated southern interests by including in the bill a similar grant to Alabama, while he overcame the opposition of the east by the suggestion that New York capitalists might be interested in undertaking the construction of the railroad.[6] But Douglas' suggestion was not necessary. The attraction of the huge land grant was irresistible, and a consortium of New York capitalists was immediately formed to take over the construction and operation of the projected road. In 1851, they received a charter as the Illinois Central Railroad.[7] The 2,500,000 acres of land received by Illinois from the federal government were immediately transferred to the corporation and, in return for a payment of $200,000 in specie, the state also transferred "the lot of ground obtained by the State of Illinois within the city of Cairo, for a depot; also, the right of way, grading, embankments, excavations, survey, work, materials, profiles, plates, and papers, in any wise appertaining to the said railroad and branches."[8] It was no large return for the sums that Illinois had spent on the project during the earlier internal-improvement mania, but it was all that the company would pay.* Moreover, the creation of the railroad was more important than arguments about past mistakes.

By 1855, seven hundred miles of the road were built and in operation: the Illinois Central was the largest railroad in the world. In a few short years, it had transformed whole sections of the state, opening up the coal beds to profitable exploitation[9] and encouraging the cultivation of vast stretches of land that had been unoccupied because of the lack of transportation facilities. During the years from 1853 to 1855, nearly three million acres of Illinois land, which had previously gone begging at a dollar and a quarter an acre, was sold to settlers at prices averaging around ten dollars, and many of the better sections were sold at much higher figures.[10] By 1856, the average price at which land was sold by the railroad had risen to more than thirteen dollars an acre.

Since a large amount of this land was sold on easy terms, settlers were encouraged to migrate to Illinois and take up farms. Under the usual contract, the settler agreed to pay the purchase price in four annual payments, the first of which was due two years after he took possession of the land,[11] so that little initial capital was needed by an immigrant. It is not surprising, therefore, that the population of the state doubled during the ten years following

* Pennsylvania, in 1857, sold to private interests for $20,400,000 canals and other public works that had cost nearly twice that sum. Cf. *History of Banking*, I, 356.

1845, while the aggregate taxable property increased from
$82,000,000 to $334,000,000.[12]

In a sense, however, the trend of events in Illinois differed from that which characterized the United States as
a whole. As the rest of the country became industrialized,
Illinois tended to concentrate more specifically on agriculture, developing her farm resources energetically
under the stimulus of expanding markets in the eastern
states and in foreign countries. This process continued
steadily throughout the fifties, during which the agricultural population of the state doubled although the number of workers engaged in industry grew by no more than
twenty per cent.[13] Agricultural wages in Illinois were
higher, by 1860, than in any other part of the country,[14]
and the state, by that time, was acknowledged to be the
leading producer of corn and wheat. Moreover, despite
this high concentration on grain, much progress had been
made in the development of other products that would
diversify the activities of the farmer. By means of agricultural societies and state fairs, concerted efforts were
being made to improve the quality of the output of
Illinois farms, and the steady increase in the use of agricultural machinery testifies to the effort that was made to
enlarge its quantity.

The expanding wealth of the state had immeasurably
reduced the burden of the debt that had been handed
down from earlier decades. In 1855, there was momen-
tary doubt as to its financial standing when bondholders
failed to receive the interest on their coupons as a result
of the failure of the New York fiscal agent.[15] But funds
from other accounts were promptly appropriated to meet

the resultant deficit in New York and, at the beginning of 1857, the Treasurer was able to report that the state was meeting all its interest obligations in full as they matured.[16] The fiscal struggle which had lasted for fifteen years had been won conclusively and, as an eastern writer could shout triumphantly, "Illinois credit now stands at the head of the list."[17]

Chicago could not escape the repercussions of these economic developments in Illinois and other parts of the country. Immigrants coming to Illinois usually booked their passages to Chicago and caught their first leisured glimpse of America from the city's railway stations; the flow of eastern and foreign capital to Illinois passed through the channels dug by Chicago bankers and, to a growing extent, the produce of the western plains was collected and forwarded eastward by Chicago merchants.[18] Less than thirty years after its incorporation, the city had become famous throughout the world and Richard Cobden, bidding good-by to Goldwin Smith in London, could add, as a parting injunction, "See two things in America, if nothing else—Niagara and Chicago!"

This phenomenal growth was due primarily to the development of transportation. The completion of the Illinois and Michigan Canal had created a metropolitan center of trade out of the little village which before that time was no more than the western terminus of navigation on the Great Lakes, and the development of railroads during the fifties enlarged still further the boundaries of the region that poured its goods into Chicago and relied upon that city to supply its needs.[19] By 1854, six railroad lines were running out of the city; two years later Chicago was the focus of ten trunk lines, with 2,933 miles of track, leading to all parts of the country, and it had fifty-eight passenger and thirty-eight freight trains arriving and departing daily.[20] By the end of 1860, the community of interest among these railroads had led them to fix a common schedule of through freight rates to the east, and their joint power was great enough to enable them to enforce the agreement.[21]

Chicago, in 1855, was recognized as the greatest primary wheat market in the world,[22] while the shipments of beef and pork from the packing houses of the city increased by more than one hundred per cent during the period from 1851 to 1858.[23] The Board of Trade, which in the early fifties had been so straitened in circumstances that it was almost bankrupted by the cost of the free lunches it gave to members,[24] grew rapidly in wealth and importance. As early as 1851, it had prohibited the circulation of untruthful reports by members regarding their transactions and, a few years later, it was taking steps to improve the units, and define the grades of produce, in which transactions were carried on.[25] By 1857, the volume of business had increased to such an extent that the Merchants Grain Forwarding Association was created to assume the task of accelerating the shipment of grain, thus leaving the Board free to concentrate on its market functions.

But to an eastern, or European, observer the city still bore many traces of its recent frontier origin. Although it had attained a population of one hundred thousand souls, among whom the landless workers already constituted a majority,[26] its plank roads and sidewalks were still far from satisfactory, and the omnibuses that rattled over them offered little comfort.[27] In 1854, the new waterworks was constructed, but drainage was still so unsatisfactory that half the roads were quagmires or stagnant puddles during the winter. In 1856, therefore, it was decided to raise the whole level of the city some six feet by jacking up the buildings and putting more soil under them, or —more simply—by raising the roads and letting the old buildings remain partly buried.[28] Only Chicago could have conceived so herculean a solution to the lowly problem of drainage!

In such circumstances an era of real-estate speculation and building activity was inevitable. Municipal improvements increased the value of land, business expansion gave rise to a demand for more stores and offices, while the steadily increasing population required more and more houses in which to live. Within a period of four years, from 1850 to 1854, the value of Chicago's land and buildings tripled under the impact of these forces.[29] Solid four-story brick houses were being constructed in the center of the town, and thousands of frame cottages on the outskirts, but rents were still "enormously high" and the demand for homes increased more rapidly than the supply.[30] Land values rose proportionately, so that plots which were offered at $200 an acre in 1845, sold in 1856 for as much as $20,000 an acre. "The land value of the territory within the present city limits of Chicago had increased from an estimated total of $1,400,000 in 1842 to $126,000,000 in the latter part of 1856, an increase of over eighty-fold in fourteen years. . . . The new peak was twelve times as high as the peak of 1836, which for many years afterward had been regarded as fantastic."[31]

The banking development of Chicago, however, lagged far behind the progress that was made in almost every other field, as the catalogue of financial facilities reproduced in Appendix II clearly shows. Although Andreas[32] tries to make the list more impressive, by including institutions that were in the course of liquidation, there were only three incorporated banks still operating in the autumn of 1856.[33] Scammon's Marine Bank, with total resources of $398,000, was easily the largest of these, since Burch's Chicago Bank had less than $120,000, while the Bank of America (which was to go into voluntary liquidation early in 1857) had only $57,000. Even in the early days of enthusiasm for the free-banking system, none of the Chicago banks (excepting Smith's Bank of America) had issued any large quantity of notes.[34] In some cases, the capital of the banks amounted to six times their note issue even then, so that it is not surprising that the aggregate issues of the Marine Bank and the Chicago Bank together totaled only $96,000 in 1856.

Supplementing, the activities of the incorporated banks were some twenty-five private banking houses,* varying considerably both in size and in the scope of their operations. Some, like R. K. Swift and Company, were as important as the incorporated banks had ever been, and were equipped to do a general banking business of a substantial kind: others were little more than money-lending pawnbrokers.

Two financial innovations occurred during the fifties,

* See Appendix II for names and other details.

however, that are of considerable significance: the creation in Chicago of trust companies and savings banks. In 1853, the Western World Insurance and Trust Company was chartered with a capital of $500,000 and (like the older Chicago Marine and Fire Insurance Company, which was still active under Scammon's management) it did a general banking business comparable to that of any private banker.[35] Similar, in many respects, was the Union Insurance and Trust Company, incorporated on January 5, 1857, with a capital of $50,000. Under the charter, the company had "full power to make insurance against loss by fire and take risks on buildings and all kinds of property . . . and to receive money, bullion, or other valuable commodities upon deposit, and to loan the same and their surplus, or unemployed capital or money, on personal, real or other security at such rates of interest, not exceeding ten per cent, as they may think proper."[36] Although, at first, this company does not appear to have been of great importance in the Chicago money market, its banking operations expanded steadily during the following years until, in 1870, it was decided to abandon the insurance operations. Under the shorter title of Union Trust Company (which it adopted in 1872) the Bank continued to operate until 1929.

The only other financial institution of the fifties which was destined to continue its existence down into the twentieth century was the Merchants Savings, Loan and Trust Company.[37] Like the Union Trust Company, this institution was created by special charter in 1857 but, unlike the former, it was destined from the first day of its existence to exercise a decisive influence upon financial developments in Chicago, partly because of its large capital of $500,000, and partly by reason of the fact that its governing board of nine trustees included some of the wealthiest and most prominent merchants in Chicago.

Under the Presidency of J. H. Dunham, assisted by A. G. Hammond (previously with the Hartford Bank of Connecticut) as Cashier, the new institution opened for business on Wednesday June 10, 1857. Well might the *Democrat* suggest that "the establishment of the new bank created quite a little excitement among the bankers generally."[38] The disturbance of the money market arising from drafts upon older banks, because of the transfer of funds to the newcomer, was but a faint foreshadowing of the influence that the Merchants Loan and Trust Company was destined to exert during the following years. Chicago, at last, had acquired its first modern bank.

Five specialized savings banks were also established in Chicago, at about the same time as these trust companies, but the only one of outstanding importance was the Illinois Savings Institution founded, in 1856, by John H. Kinzie as the first mutual savings bank in the west.[39] Except for the development of specialized investment banking houses, which did not occur until after the Civil War, the structure of the Chicago money market had, therefore, already assumed that complex pattern of interrelated institutions, each concentrating on a particular type of financial activity, which was to continue until the end of the century.

But the elaboration of the financial structure did not solve the perennial problem of the dearth of capital funds. The sweeping economic changes that were reconstructing

American life produced a demand for capital that would have appeared fantastic to earlier generations, and nowhere was that statement truer than in the west. "Chicago needs twice as much banking capital as she now has," the *Democratic Press* insisted. "Were our banks to increase their facilities a hundred per cent within the next month, every dollar could be safely loaned, at ten per cent, to men who could make . . . ten times as much by using it."[40] Even though the 10 per cent interest rate had become customary, as well as legal, in 1857,[41] it was impossible to attract large enough quantities of funds for investment. Many loans were negotiated at rates well above the legal maximum, but there was competition from other states, which also permitted rates of interest that seem extraordinarily high to a modern reader,[42] so that Chicago's hunger for capital was not appeased. "All the capital we can possibly attract to our city, and all the money we can make in legitimate business, will find ready and profitable employment."[43]

The country as a whole, however, did not suffer from any dearth of banks in the peculiar way that Chicago did. As the figures in Table VI clearly indicate, the tremendous demand for capital funds was being supplied, in part at least, by means of an expansion of bank credit. Loans and discounts had increased from $364,000,000, in 1850, to $684,000,000 by the middle of 1857 and, as a result of almost imperceptible changes in banking operations, a large portion of these credit funds were finding their way into channels that did not fit the traditional liquidity theory preached in the textbooks.

THE DEBACLE

TABLE VI

CONDITION OF ALL BANKS IN THE UNITED STATES

1848–1860

(In millions of dollars)

Years	Banks and Branches	Capital	Loans and Discounts	Specie	Circulation	Deposits
1848	751	$205	$344	$ 46	$129	$103
1849	782	207	332	44	115	91
1850	824	217	364	45	131	110
1851	879	228	414	49	155	129
1852	824	217	364	45	131	110
1853	879	228	414	49	155	129
1854	1,208	301	557	59	205	188
1855	1,307	332	576	54	187	190
1856	1,398	344	634	59	196	212
1857	1,416	371	684	58	215	230
1858	1,422	395	683	74	155	186
1859	1,476	402	657	105	193	260
1860	1,562	422	692	84	207	254

Note. The above figures have been taken from Hunt's Merchants' Magazine.

Southern banking operations were based pretty squarely upon the idea of discounting nothing but first-class bills of exchange arising out of shipments of cotton.[44] This was not true, however, of New York, which had already come to occupy a dominant place in the banking policies of the country as a result of the fact that at least a half of the deposits in its banks were composed of funds standing to the credit of correspondent banks in other parts of the United States.[45] An unusually large proportion of the loans and discounts of New York City banks were security loans, frequently on call,[46] and there were already evangelists eager to prove that the new ideal of shiftability was just as sound as the older banking concept of liquidity.[47] All that a modern generation has added to the argument is a longer and more imposing name.

In the field of railroad financing, the banks had been particularly active, advancing substantial loans for initial

TABLE VII

PRINCIPAL RESOURCES AND LIABILITIES OF INCORPORATED BANKS IN ILLINOIS

1853–1863

(In thousands of dollars)

Years	No. of Banks	Loans and Discounts	Stocks	Due from Banks	Real Estate	Notes of Other Banks	Specie Funds	Specie	Other Resources	Capital Stock	Circulation	Deposits	Due to Banks	Other Liabilities
1853	23	$ 586	$ 1,780	$ 880	$ 13	$233	...	$419	....	$1,702	$1,351	$ 522	$315	$ 14
1854	29	316	2,671	878	31	385	$63	565	$1,368	2,513	2,283	1,286	...	294
1856	36	337	3,777	2,354	79	517	37	759	1,108	3,840	3,420	1,267	...	241
1857	61	1,740	6,129	3,952	52	433	19	635	....	5,872	5,534	1,002	210	157
1858	45	1,146	6,164	2,813	59	265	6	233	4	4,679	5,238	658	19	131
1859	48	1,296	6,486	2,627	87	271	9	269	1	4,000	5,707	640	15	525
1860	74	387	9,826	3,201	92	343	39	223	1,679	5,251	8,981	697	26	552
1861	104	546	12,264	3,793	116	287	37	301	2,035	7,530	12,320	807	64	422
1862	19							4		712	1,415			...
1863	25	221	501	110	206	109	55	904	425	894	619	400	110	42

Note. Figures are for the date nearest to January 1 of each year stated, and are derived from the *Annual Report of the Comptroller of the Currency*, December 4, 1876, pp. cxviii–cxix, corrected, where possible, by reference to the Annual Reports of the State Auditor of Illinois and those of the Illinois Bank Commissioners.

expenses and subscribing heavily to the bonds that were issued to finance construction.[48] Moreover, since railroads were recognized to be the salvation of the west, it is not surprising that the marriage of banking and railroad development produced monstrous offspring in states like Illinois where, if we exclude Chicago, a tremendous increase in bank loans took place during 1855 and 1856.[49] As a contemporary observer sardonically describes the process, "A number of men get together. . . . They want to build a railroad; they have no money. . . . They employ John Thompson* to purchase state bonds for them, and pay therefor, trusting them for his pay till the first batch of bank notes, founded on them, is issued. They issue their railroad bonds, hypothecate them in Wall Street, and pay John Thompson for the State stocks. They are then ready with a state-stock secured circulation, to commence the road. The only trouble is to keep the bills afloat. But this is managed very easily. The bank need only be located where it will not pay the brokers to run on it, either in Rhode Island or Maine [where Matteson established some of his banks] . . . the people take the money as long as it goes; while the Chicago and other bankers . . . are afraid to run upon it, for fear of breaking it and thus creating a panic."[50]

To pretend that such fantastic financing was universal would be absurd, but there was enough of it to make the inflated financial structure of the country dangerously vulnerable by the middle of 1857. Moreover, for the first

---

* John Thompson, most famous as the editor and publisher of *Thompson's Bank Note Reporter*, operated a New York bank that was closely associated, on many occasions, with the Chicago house of his son-in-law, F. Granger Adams.

time in the history of crises, the telegraph had linked every section of the country in such a way that the slightest financial tremor in Maine was immediately felt in Chicago and New Orleans. The American money market was becoming a national organism, rather than a series of imperfectly related local arenas, and there were dangers as well as advantages in that development. Much of the severity of the "Western Blizzard" that swept across the country in 1857 was due to the rapidity with which the electric telegraph transmitted its effects.[51]

While the excessive stringency felt throughout the money market in the spring might have served as a portent to any who could read the signs aright, the full force of the blast did not become apparent until the Ohio Life Insurance and Trust Company closed its doors on August 24.[52] This company, like the Chicago insurance companies, engaged in banking operations, and had handled a substantial part of the domestic exchange business between New York and the west. Moreover, it was, at the moment, heavily indebted to several New York banks, so that the seaboard market was thrown into a panic by its sudden collapse. Within a few days, the Mechanics Banking Association, of New York, had also closed its doors, and there were several failures among business houses but, at this stage, the Chicago money market did not feel a single ripple of the disturbance.[53]

Early in September, however, the panic spread over the country. In Boston, and in Buffalo, important produce and commission houses failed suddenly,[54] and all the railroads, upon which so much of the business prosperity had depended during the preceding years, seemed destined to pass into the hands of receivers.* Before the month was over, Philadelphia suffered one of the most severe financial panics in its history. Every bank in the city was besieged by crowds of depositors, eager to withdraw their money, and most of them were compelled to suspend operations. Banks in other parts of Pennsylvania promptly followed this example.[55] Naturally the Chicago bankers were perturbed by such developments but, locally, there was, as yet, nothing more serious than an increased care in the scrutiny of applications for loans and a slight hardening of the rate of interest.

When the panic actually occurred in New York, the specie reserves of the banks in that city amounted to only ten per cent of the combined obligation to depositors and noteholders,[56] so that credit was contracted savagely in order to strengthen their position. Between August 15 and October 17, the deposits of New York City banks declined by $39,500,000 from the initial figure of $92,-400,000, although specie reserves were reduced by less than $4,000,000 and there was no increase whatever in the quantity of their notes in circulation.[57] Moreover, since they found it impossible to collect most of the capital loans that they had made, the heaviest burden of the contraction fell upon the mercantile community. Early in October, the *Chicago Democrat* complained that "this has been an awful hard tightening up of the screw. . . . The New York banks, we predicted some days ago, would ruin the mercantile community and themselves, if they

* During 1857, fourteen railroads in the United States defaulted on the payment of their obligations, while 5,123 commercial failures occurred.

continued their course of contraction. They have already ruined the mercantile community."[58]

The influence of the New York banks on their correspondents, in other cities, extended the pressure of the contraction over the whole country, and for two months the country suffered without protest. On October 10, the reserves of the New York banks were larger than they had been when the contraction began, and the Clearing House Committee was able to boast of its intention to maintain specie payments at all hazards. But, three days later, the business community retaliated by a run on the banks as savage as the bank contraction had been. More than four million dollars in specie was taken from the banks during one day and, by the end of a week their reserves had fallen to less than $8,000,000.[59] Suspension of specie payments was immediate in New York City, and Boston, Baltimore and other leading cities promptly reached a similar decision. Only New Orleans, among the larger financial centers, was able to stand firm and maintain specie payments continuously throughout the panic.

By this time Chicago was fully embroiled in the maelstrom, but it is interesting to notice that the immediate impact of the crisis came from Missouri and Wisconsin rather than from New York. Although the legislation of February, 1857,[60] had remedied several important defects in the Illinois banking system, it had ignored the fundamental question of the quality of the bonds deposited to secure the note circulation. More than half of these securities, in the autumn of 1857, were obligations of the State of Missouri, which had already piled up a debt of nineteen million dollars in its ardor for the public financing of internal improvements. As early as February, the decline in the price of Missouri bonds had forced many Illinois banks to contract their circulation[61] and, by July, further depreciation compelled the Bank Commissioners to demand additional securities from twenty-seven banks. Despite strong protests from the banks concerned, all but three of them met the call, and the delinquents were promptly liquidated.[62] Fortunately, Missouri did not resort to the repudiation that it had threatened, so that the rapid decline in the price of her bonds came to a stop. In the consternation aroused by that threat, however, the newspapers, for the first time, expressed enthusiasm for the policy of the Chicago banks in issuing so few circulating notes.

Meanwhile, other symptoms of trouble had developed in Chicago. Early in July, the private banking house of E. R. Hinckly and Company had been unable to meet its obligations, and was forced to suspend.[63] A month later, the firm of Hoffman and Gelpcke was faced with a severe run that lasted for more than two days and, although the "wealthiest German citizens came out in a card in the *Staats Zeitung*, pledging themselves to support the Bank," it was compelled to suspend payments temporarily.[64] Shortly after that, the standing of F. Granger Adams was seriously jeopardized by the failure of his father-in-law, John Thompson.[65] This "well-known banker of Wall street," who had combined an expert knowledge of bank notes with a dangerous interest in railroad financiering, had failed completely, although hopes were entertained for a few days that he might be able to reopen after the panic, and the bankruptcy had serious repercussions throughout the west. Because of his position as editor of the *Bank Note Reporter*, Thompson had been selected by many western bankers as their New York agent and, for many years, he had been the leading eastern dealer in western bank notes that were not well known in New York.*

Fortunately, this failure did not destroy Granger Adams' bank, which was supported by the other Chicago bankers after careful investigation had shown it to be sound. It was, therefore, enabled to ride the storm without suspending.

These failures, however, were but a prelude to what followed. When the full force of the panic hit Chicago, late in August, the *Democrat* expressed full confidence in all the Chicago banks. "Keep cool today," it advised. "Look over your rags [i.e. bank notes] and then go and pass all you can to pay your honest debts! Then deposite what you have left . . . but be sure where you deposite."[66] The advice was sound and, stranger still, it appears to have been acted upon by the public. There were more debts paid in Chicago on that day than on any other day in the year![67]

But the fact that this advice was good is a demonstration of the outstanding defect in the Illinois banking system. The most perfect portfolio of bonds, deposited as collateral, could not make a currency circulate at parity unless the notes were freely and promptly convertible into any other type of money that the noteholder desired.

* After the panic, Thompson settled down to earn his living by the manufacture of candles; even the editorship of the *Reporter* was lost in the smash. Cf. *American Banker*, June 15, 1936, Section Three.

The obstacle to the redemption of Illinois notes lay in the fact that the bankers did not possess large enough reserves of gold or of eastern exchange, so that, before August was over, the banks were refusing gold to every-body, except a few favored customers who needed it "in the regular course of business,"[68] and eastern exchange was at a premium of 2½ per cent. From that point, the depreciation of the Illinois currency was rapid. Both gold and eastern exchange were selling at 5 per cent pre-mium by September 9;[69] two weeks later, the premium had risen to 6 per cent and both were unobtainable ex-cept in small amounts.[70] By October, the official rates had risen to 10 per cent premium on eastern exchange and from 8 to 10 per cent on gold, but buyers were unable to obtain all that they needed even when they paid as high as 15 per cent for it.[71]

In view of this depreciation, and of the uncertainty regarding the ability of several Illinois banks to put up the additional collateral demanded by the Bank Commis-sioners, the merchants of St. Louis decided to reject all Illinois bank notes. Although one of the Illinois com-missioners traveled to St. Louis to discuss the matter with them, and assure them of the soundness of the banks, they would only agree to receive the notes at the rate of ninety-five cents on the dollar. Even this was regarded as a vic-tory by the Illinois bankers.[72] Canada, by contrast, was infinitely more helpful to the hard-pressed Chicago money market. By purchasing unusually large quantities of wheat, and paying for it with drafts on New York, Canadian importers provided most of the eastern ex-change that was offered on the Chicago market and, at the same time, their operations prevented a catastrophic fall in the price of grain. Moreover, the notes of Canadian banks that seeped into Chicago were so useful, both as currency and for remittance, that the *Democrat* urged Canadian banks to establish branches in the city. Such a branch "with its immense control of capital . . . could compete with our bankers on their own soil, and also prove the nucleus for the establishment of mercantile houses here, rivalling in extent those of Montreal, Toronto, and Hamilton."[73]

Not often does a city invite the competition, within its walls, of large and powerful banks from other countries, but Chicago at that moment was feeling the effects of several important bank failures. Her own banks did not have "immense control of capital." On September 29, Tinkham's bank had been compelled to close its doors in the face of a run[74] and, a few hours afterward, the important house of R. K. Swift and Company was forced to take a similar step. Such a catastrophe had not been expected and the business community was stunned. A full week after the failure, the newspapers reported that "the crowd still continues to hang around what was once Col. Swift's extensive Banking House. . . . At times the sidewalk is completely blocked with people, and the police are called out to clear a passage."[75]

Swift's failure was apparently due, in some degree, to the enmity of the less conservative bankers, which he had incurred through his leadership of the campaign against George Smith and other issuers of illegal currency,[76] but it was caused in larger measure by his association with the chain of banks operated by ex-Governor Matteson.[77] Not without reason does the *Democrat* call Matteson "the Nicholas Biddle of Illinois."[78] In addition to the chain of Illinois banks, to which reference has already been made, he had acquired control of "the wild-cat Rhode Island Central Bank" for the purpose of using its notes to finance his railroad activities in Illinois. When that bank failed,[79] early in August, Swift appears to have aided Matteson in an attempt to keep the notes afloat in Illinois but, ironically enough, the scheme that saved Matteson from trouble, for the time being, supplied the match to blow up Swift's overextended institution.

The failure of Louis Hitz, on October 14,[80] and of the Chicago office of the Cherokee Banking and Insurance Company soon afterward,[81] served to intensify the gloom, and the newspapers reverted again and again to the weakness and inadequacy of the financial facilities available in Chicago. "In our city we have a number of banks, who, no doubt do all they can to sustain their customers. . . . Most of them, however, are small institutions, depending almost wholly on their deposits for the means of accommodating the community. During these hard times they have been engaged mainly in protecting themselves, at the expense of their customers. No one of them appears to have had the capital, the ability, or the boldness . . . to stand up in the midst of the pressure, and stretch out a helping hand to the public."[82]

With supreme, if unconscious, irony, the same writer expressed a wish that George Smith might return again with his illegal currency. "We have no hesitation in saying that, if George Smith were here, and had the privilege of throwing a million, or a million and a half, dollars of

[his] Atlanta or Interior money into circulation, a great deal of distress, and, perhaps, a very severe financial revulsion, would be prevented. . . . It is known that he never dabbled in stocks, that he has always avoided investments in enterprises of a doubtful character, and indeed heavy investments in unproductive projects of any description. He always confined his capital and his circulation . . . to the legitimate objects of banking—the accommodation of the mercantile community. . . . Were he here today, he could do more to restore confidence in the community than any other man."[83] No sharper indictment could be levied at Chicago bankers of that period, no higher compliment paid to the old Scotsman who had done so much to build up Chicago and the northwest.

Throughout the United States, the financial crisis precipitated a wave of failures. During 1857 and 1858, 9,655 business concerns closed their doors, owing to creditors a sum in excess of $400,000,000. Illinois was not immune from the epidemic. In Chicago alone, 204 failures occurred, with liabilities amounting to $10,000,000; while in the remainder of the state the records show 500 bankruptcies with aggregate liabilities in excess of $8,000,-000.[84] It was a severe purge, accentuated, in Illinois, by the fact that the harvests were unusually poor during 1858. For a while, the business community of Chicago was paralyzed, and the destruction of speculative fortunes dampened the enthusiasm of the city for a full two years.

From the national angle, however, the panic was short, and the depression mild. Specie payments were resumed in New York on December 14, 1857,[85] and almost all financial communities took a similar step before the end of the year. Business activity began to improve in January, 1858, continuing steadily upward toward a minor peak in the autumn of 1860, and banking expansion (especially in the west) was as rapid during these years as it had been immediately before the panic.

Although, in the east, business was being conducted to an increasing extent, by means of checks drawn against bank deposits,[86] bank notes were still the standard medium of payments in the west. Wildcat banking attained its widest, and worst, development during the years immediately preceding the Civil War. All the vicious methods of unsound banking that were known in earlier years flourished with renewed vigor at this period, and the ingenuity of man developed further refinements. In 1859, for instance, an Ohio bank set up in business by purchasing an engraving plate for $165, paying one-quarter of a cent per dollar for the manufacture of its notes, and sending a bribe of $1,900 to the publishers of a Bank Note Detector in order to persuade them to give a high rating to the issue.[87] Could a more efficient use of banking capital be imagined, from the angle of a swindling promoter?

"Money at home and moonshine abroad" was an apt contemporary description of most of the currency that was issued. More than sixteen hundred banks were emitting notes; seven thousand varieties of notes were in circulation. Seventeen hundred different issues of fraudulent notes were listed by the Bank Note Detectors, along with more than three thousand kinds of notes that had been altered, so that it is not at all surprising to find that one group of New England merchants was able, during the period from 1858 to 1861, to secure the conviction of two hundred and twenty-eight persons on the charge of counterfeiting bank notes.[88] Moreover, when it is remembered that, among the notes which had been legally issued, there were wide variations in current value resulting from changes in current opinion regarding the soundness of the issuing bank, the fantastic complexity of the monetary picture becomes apparent. Jay Cooke, who had served his banking apprenticeship as a note teller, in Philadelphia, estimated that the people of the United States lost at least $50,000,000 a year from the handling of fraudulent and depreciated bank notes.[89]

Fundamentally, the motive force behind this unsound currency was the desire of bankers for larger profits, without regard for the losses that other members of the community might suffer. In view of the fact that the citizens of Illinois were as anxious for profits as anybody else, the state did not escape from the wave of banking expansion. By the beginning of 1861, the note circulation of Illinois banks was more than twice as large as it had been prior to the panic of 1857, and the number of banks grew from thirty-nine, in 1858, to one hundred and four at the beginning of 1861.[90] Many of these institutions, in out-of-the-way parts of the state were operated by Chicago capitalists,* but no attempt was made to set up additional banks in Chicago. A bank situated in a large city was likely to have too many of its notes presented for redemp-

* In view of the fact that the Illinois banking law was more severe than that of many other states, Chicago promoters set up their banks under Wisconsin charters in most cases. They did, however, create several Illinois institutions. Cf. *Chicago Democrat*, July 13, 1857.

tion. As a result, Chicago found its banking facilities diminishing steadily at a time when financial institutions were springing up like mushrooms everywhere else. In 1858, the Bank of America and the Bank of Chicago both went into liquidation, so that Scammon's Marine Bank was the only commercial bank in the city,[91] incorporated under the Free Banking Act.

The private bankers of Chicago, who could not legally issue notes themselves, became increasingly concerned about the unsatisfactory nature of the currency in which they had to do business. As early as August, 1858, a group of them decided to refuse the notes of twenty-seven Wisconsin banks,[92] on the ground that their value was doubtful, but no action appears to have been taken regarding the notes of Illinois banks.

The same criticism would, however, have applied to every one of the Illinois bank notes in circulation, as the march of events during the following years was to show. Technically, the Illinois law was better than many; statistically it could be shown that only fourteen incorporated banks had gone out of existence between the passage of the Free Banking Act and the middle of 1860, but Governor Bissell, addressing the legislature at the beginning of 1859,[93] put his finger on the defect that was destined to wreck the whole system.

Illinois paper was current only within the state: elsewhere it circulated at a discount. In 1860, the specie reserve of the banks in Illinois was lower than that of any other group of banks in the country, amounting to only four and a quarter per cent of the note liabilities.* The

---

* If the reserve be compared to notes *and deposits* it amounted to little more than 2½ per cent! Cf. *Executive Document No. 3* (36th Congress, 1 Session), p. 368.

value of the notes depended, in actual fact, upon the value of the bonds behind them, particularly in view of the fact that many Illinois banks had no real capital and few assets that would be worth much in an emergency.[94] At the beginning of 1860, another slump in the price of Missouri bonds called attention to this weakness once again.[95] Although the banks concerned were able to meet the demands of the Bank Commissioners, by depositing more bonds or else reducing the amount of their circulation, the need for constructive reform was evident. Even the *Tribune,* so long a friend of banking interests, admitted that fundamental banking reform was an urgent necessity in order that the country might obtain a satisfactory monetary system.[96]

The demand for banking reform, moreover, drew support from the fact that many other states, confronted with similar problems, had already taken steps to correct an intolerable situation. Missouri, just before the panic of 1857, had amended her banking laws to provide that no bank should be chartered with a capitalization of less than $1,000,000.[97] Louisiana, more than a decade earlier, had passed a banking law so admirably drawn, and efficiently administered, that New Orleans was able to pass through the fire of panic unscathed, and the second Bank of the Commonwealth of Kentucky had earned an enviable reputation by its adherence to similar principles. These lessons were not entirely lost.

Soon after the panic, Connecticut, Rhode Island, Kentucky and Massachusetts passed laws restricting the maximum amount of notes that any bank could issue.[98] Pennsylvania and Massachusetts required all banks to keep

specie reserves bearing a specified relationship to deposit
and note liabilities, while the banks of New York City
(although not legally compelled to do so) agreed to hold
specie reserves equal to at least twenty per cent of demand
liabilities.[99] In New York, moreover, the law of 1851 had
required all banks to redeem their notes, either in New
York City or Albany, at a discount of not more than one-
quarter of one per cent, thus putting a final stop to the
ancient device of preventing redemption by making the
notes payable at an inaccessible spot.[100]

While there were many people in Illinois so disgusted
with their experiences of bank notes that they wished to
abolish the whole system and establish banks founded
squarely on coin and bullion,[101] there was never any
chance that such counsels of perfection would prevail.
The state was too fond of its banking system to desire any
such drastic change, and preferred to spend its time
patching and repairing the existing legislation. Unfortunately, it is not always possible to save the ship if the
crew waits for the inrush of water to demonstrate its
unseaworthiness.

The banking reform act of 1861[102] is an excellent example of the tragedy of procrastination. While it was
far from perfect, it might have gone a long way toward
protecting the citizens of Illinois from serious loss if it
had been enacted five years earlier. In 1861, it was too
late to be of any use.

First of all, it provided that the bonds deposited to
secure circulation must consist of obligations of Illinois
or of the federal government. Both types of security were
to be received at full value and no other state securities

were to be eligible in any circumstances. Secondly, it provided that all banks should be required to redeem their notes, either in Springfield or Chicago, at a discount of not more than one-half of one per cent discount. Both of these requirements were admirable. The experience with Missouri bonds had demonstrated the extent to which the use of "foreign" bonds, as collateral, might weaken the banking system through the operation of forces over which neither the legislature nor the bankers of Illinois could exercise any effective control, while the history of the Suffolk banking system in New England had so convinced Chicago bankers of the desirability of note redemption at some central point that they had called a conference of Illinois bankers to discuss the project several weeks before the new banking bill was introduced.[103]

In addition to these major reforms, several minor matters, of no slight importance, were also attended to. The maximum amount of notes that could be issued by any bank was fixed at three times its paid-in capital, and the State Auditor was required to satisfy himself, in each case, that this capital, to the amount of at least twenty-five thousand dollars, had actually been paid in by the shareholders. No bank was to be established in a community with less than one thousand inhabitants, and none was allowed to make loans through agents or brokers. Moreover, by a subsequent act,[104] the powers of the Bank Commissioners were increased, with a view to enabling them to examine banks more thoroughly, so that they might find out whether all state institutions were operating within the provisions of the law. Apart from the question of specie reserves, therefore, all the significant defects of the

Illinois free-banking system were remedied, in part at least, by this reform act, but specie reserves were destined to become the most important element in the whole problem as a result of forces that were already at work when the legislature approved the bill.

Judging from the contemporary comments of the *Tribune,* the new law did not even achieve the aims that had been in the minds of its sponsors.[105] But, nothing daunted by that, a group of enthusiasts, headed by Scammon, wished to pursue the subject of banking reform even further. Inspired by the outstanding success of the Bank of the State of Indiana, they proposed to create a Union Bank of Illinois, consisting of semi-independent branches in all the principal towns of the state, with a central board of directors to exercise control over questions of general policy and supervise the affairs of the branches in matters of banking soundness. Little difficulty was experienced with the legislature, since the need for a better banking system was evident to everyone, and it would have been hard to find a better model than the Indiana Bank. A lengthy bill was passed in February, 1861, chartering the Union Bank,[106] but it was overwhelmingly defeated in the referendum held in November, 1862. Much water had flowed under the bridges during the interval between those two dates.

Thoughtful people may have entertained doubts as to the soundness of Illinois banks at the time when a clamorous Republican National Convention in Chicago was nominating Lincoln as its presidential candidate, since the recent slump in bond prices had not been fully corrected by the deposit of additional securities. But, when

Lincoln was elected in November, 1860, all doubts had disappeared. Even the State Auditor was optimistic. "During the past two years the circulation of the banks of the state had largely increased, owing partially to the advancing business necessities of the state, but principally to the fact that its known character for security has obtained for it a much wider circulation, in the adjoining states, than it has heretofore had. And I am satisfied that a rigid execution of our banking laws, together with a few amendments, is all that is necessary to make it acceptable to our people."[107] At that moment $12,320,-000 of Illinois bank notes were in circulation.

Politics and economics are not, however, separate entities. They are as interdependent as the parts of the human body, and the ability of a thinker to deal with either in abstract isolation does not give it any more of an independent existence than the surgeon's knife gives to a limb that he amputates. Looked at from the angle of economic theory, the banking system of Illinois may have justified the optimism of its defenders, during the closing days of 1860, but the air was full of political forces that were destined to generate sweeping economic changes.

Even in August, the portents of the coming storm cast a pall over the money market. "The low rates for money are the result of doubts which prevent people from engaging in trade,"[108] wrote a contemporary annalist. In a few weeks, his worst fears were realized. By November, there were heavy shipments of gold from New York to the south, and the growing panic caused the prices of southern bonds to fall from ten to sixteen points.[109] All financial confidence between north and south was at an end long before the end of 1860, and the cessation of cotton and tobacco exports so demoralized the international relations of the New York money market that the drain of gold to the south was augmented by large exports of gold to Europe. On November 20, most of the banks in the southern states, with the exception of those in New Orleans, suspended specie payments, and St. Louis, being economically dependent on the lower Mississippi valley, was compelled to do likewise.[110] Even the New York banks, which had made herculean efforts to maintain the convertibility of their notes, were compelled to suspend on December 30, so that 1861 opened with the whole of the United States, operating, once again, on an inconvertible paper standard.* The events that led up to the formation of the Southern Confederacy, in February, 1861, had smashed the economic system of the country long before that step was formally announced, and the ghostly premonitions of the coming cannonade destroyed prosperity six months before the smoke belched from the gun barrels.

To Illinois, the effect of these political influences upon the economy of the nation represented an immeasurable catastrophe. Two-thirds of the bonds behind the notes in circulation were obligations of southern states, the prices of which declined with an unpredictable rapidity. By May of 1861, Kentucky bonds had fallen to seventy-six, Missouri to thirty-five and one-quarter, Tennessee to forty-three and three-quarters, and Virginia to the same level.[111]

As soon as bond prices began to weaken, in the autumn

---

* See below, Chapter IX, for a fuller discussion of these developments.

of 1860, the Bank Commissioners had issued calls for additional collateral to protect the note issue. In November, twenty-two banks (out of one hundred and twelve in the state) were called upon to deposit additional securities prior to December 20, but the seriousness of the situation was such that the period of grace had to be extended to March 20, 1861. Even then, there were seventeen banks, with an aggregate circulation of almost $3,000,000, which could not meet the call and were compelled to go into liquidation. Meanwhile, further declines in security prices had made it necessary to send out similar calls to practically every bank in the state.

By the beginning of 1861, the monetary situation had become so intolerable that businessmen were threatening to leave the state unless something were done to improve the quality of the currency.[112] Thirty-nine of the banks that were still operating could find very few people willing to accept their notes and, of the remaining sixty-nine banks, only twenty-three had note issues that were generally received at par.[113] Moreover, since the good notes were hoarded, the currency in actual circulation was much worse than these figures suggest.

In such a situation, it was natural that the Chicago bankers should have been unanimous in their desire to throw out the discredited note issues. Apart from the incorporated banks in voluntary liquidation, the Marine Bank was the only note-issuing institution in the city, and its notes were among the few that still circulated at par.[114] Under the strong leadership of Dunham, of the Merchants Loan and Trust Company, an effort was, therefore, made to carry on all business in terms of specie, accepting paper money only at its current market value[115] and, during April, the majority of Chicago bankers refused to accept, at any price, the notes of thirty-two down-state banks.[116] The immediate effect of this action was to depress the market value of the rejected notes to about fifty cents on the dollar.

But this policy aroused prompt resentment. Merchants in the southern portion of the state insisted that such an attitude was merely hastening the ruin of country banks, and making a bad situation worse,[117] while, even among Chicago bankers, there was a good deal of controversy. Many of them held large quantities of country-bank notes,[118] and did not wish to see the paper depreciate before they had unloaded it: others were keenly interested because they owned or controlled banks "in the woods of Egypt," which had been a useful source of profit in the days of wildcatting and might again prove useful if they could be saved from failure.[119] Since Chicago capitalists, in 1860, were listed as officers of thirty-eight downstate banks, while other evidences point to stock control of institutions in regard to which no official connection is recorded, this factor tended to be of considerable weight in any decision that might be reached.

Although the Merchants Loan and Trust Company continued to operate entirely on the basis of cash,[120] several of the other Chicago banks tried to develop a modification of its Spartan policies that would protect their own interests. In May, the merchants of Chicago agreed to accept at par all notes of banks which appeared on a selected list drawn up by these Chicago bankers,[121] but it was obvious that the selection was not made on any principles of economics or finance. "We have told the people the difference between the credited and discredited banks," the *Democrat* pointed out. "We said the credited banks were those of whose currency our Wild Cats had the most. We stated that the object in crediting them was to get the community to take them, and then, when they got out all they had, they were going to discredit them."[122]

These comments, although scarcely flattering, contained a large element of truth so that, a few weeks later, a conference of downstate bankers made another effort, on sounder principles, to draw up a list of bank notes that were worthy of general acceptance.[123] Even in their optimism they could list only fourteen banks, with a total circulation of \$1,076,737,* a catastrophic decline from the \$12,000,000 that were accepted, without question, nine months earlier.

This second effort was no more successful than the first, because the situation had become intolerable by the summer of 1861. All but seventeen of the banks were recognized to be insolvent, even by the Bank Commissioners,[124] and in each community lists were issued, day by day, showing the current rate at which the notes of each bank would be accepted. From town to town, and from one day to another, the quotations varied with unpredictable eccentricity, while the premium on eastern exchange rose to twenty-five per cent in terms of the best local currency available.[125] Specie was unobtainable at any price[126] and, as its scarcity accentuated the demand for

---

* All these notes were supported by the deposit of United States bonds, or the securities of northern states.

it, specie had become the all-absorbing cry by the end of May.

When the *Democrat* thundered against the banks, advising its readers "to avoid all Illinois currency now afloat," on the grounds that good notes were already hidden away in hoards,[127] the bankers of Chicago had indignantly declared that the newspaper was worse than the rebels. They charged it with deliberately trying to destroy the banks.[128] Yet the Republican *Tribune*, whose patriotism was above suspicion, was no less vitriolic in its comments. "We wash our hands of the whole business. If the farmer will sell a dollar's worth of his produce for the pictures of any bank whatsoever which does not redeem its issues at some convenient place in this State *at par*, he loses a share of his just earnings. . . . We have endeavored to show that *all* banks of issue are a curse to the community."[129] Chicago railroad offices were already refusing to accept any bank notes, except those issued by a very small group of institutions that had deposited northern securities as collateral and agreed to redeem their notes at par in Chicago,[130] while many business houses had ceased operations rather than accept any of the paper currency then in circulation.

For a single bright moment, in June, the skies cleared. Even the securities of the southern states rose in price, and the pessimistic *Democrat* was moved to roseate prophecy. "We are glad to notice that the apprehensions of a general collapse of our banks have faded away. The utter unlikelihood of a step of that kind has daily become more apparent. . . . There is no more talk of failures.

Everybody concedes that the days for them have gone by."[131]

Events did not, however, justify the optimism. Within a month, the Marine Bank, the last and greatest of Chicago's banks, incorporated under the Free Banking Act, was in difficulties.[132] Unable to repay the funds that had been deposited with it by the Sewerage Commission and the Board of Education (so that the latter, in turn, was unable to pay the salaries of Chicago schoolteachers), the institution closed its doors on July 8. The Chicago Marine and Fire Insurance Company decided to suspend operations at the same time, and both concerns were placed in voluntary liquidation under the control of J. Y. Scammon, who immediately set up as a private banker once again.[133] The newspapers and the public were as furious as the schoolteachers. Scammon was branded as the Republican counterpart of the Democratic Matteson, and his refusal to allow the appointment of an independent receiver was imputed to the worst motives. "Scammon is to be [him]self; all business is to be done in his name, so long as it is lucrative. But the Marine Bank charter is to be preserved as his other self, so that when the next bubble bursts the Marine Bank will go up . . . and Scammon will remain good."[134] Yet Scammon, despite the abuse, continued to redeem all the notes of the Marine Bank at par whenever they were presented at his office.

The Marine Bank was not alone in its suspension, unfortunately. By October, 1861, there were only $3,500,000 of Illinois notes in circulation according to the report of the State Auditor; at the end of 1862, the figure had fallen to $566,163.[135] Of the one hundred and ten banks chartered, only seventeen were still in operation because, even when the Auditor did not close a bank on account of its obvious insolvency, the directors and officers often put it into voluntary liquidation. By this step, they were enabled to make a profit by buying up the notes at a discount, and exchanging them at par for the bonds that had been deposited to secure the circulation.[136] The collapse of the free-banking system in Illinois was, therefore, complete: all that remained was for the State Auditor to redeem the notes at whatever amount on the dollar the bonds would fetch, and then burn them in the public square at Springfield.[137] By the end of 1864, less than $200,000 of Illinois notes remained in circulation,[138] all of which were secured by Illinois bonds, and in the following month the office of Bank Commissioner was abolished and the liquidation of the remaining banks entrusted to the State Auditor and Treasurer.[139]

Any accurate estimate of the loss suffered by Illinois from this last of her independent banking experiments is impossible. To the measurable losses from the depreciation of the notes one would have to add many intangible items resulting from the disorganization of economic life, and the subsequent stagnation of business enterprise throughout the state. As one result of the collapse, Chicago once again was thrown back upon the services of the private bankers, as the records reproduced in Appendix III clearly show.[140] These firms, with Scammon still in the leading position, constituted the only source of funds for the majority of individuals, and the important additions that had been made to the city's financial facilities were in no way due to the Free Banking Act. The foundation of the Merchants Loan and Trust Company had been the result of the far-seeing vision of a group of leading merchants; the establishment, in September, 1861, of a branch of the Bank of Montreal, was brought about by the utter collapse of all incorporated banks.[141] Yet these two were the only local events of the period that were to have an enduring influence upon the growth of the Chicago money market.

Of the popular opinion of the free-banking system in Illinois, there can be no doubt. The proposed Constitution of 1862 which, although defeated at the referendum, received very nearly half the total votes cast,[142] forbade the incorporation of any banks at all, whether they were authorized to issue notes or not, and provided that, after 1866, no bank notes "of any kind, character or denomination whatever" should be allowed to circulate within the state of Illinois.[143] Moreover, when the federal government issued Treasury notes in a form designed to circulate as a medium of exchange, the people of the state were jubilant. "These Treasury notes are just the thing to form both a reliable and national currency," and "the more the principles upon which they are issued are examined, the more popular will they become."[144] Popular enthusiasm for state banks of issue was at an end.

REFERENCES FOR CHAPTER VIII

[1] Cf. Beard: *The Rise of American Civilization,* Chs. XIV and XV, for an admirable short account of economic and political developments during this period.

[2] *Hunt's,* XL, 32.

[3] *Idem,* 30-36.

[4] *Ibid.,* XXXVIII, 285.

[5] *Ibid.,* XL, 249.

[6] *Ibid.*, XXXVIII, 281; XXVII, 665-668; Cole: *op. cit.*, pp. 36-40.

[7] *Laws of Illinois*, 1851, 61-74. Approved February 10, 1851; *Hunt's*, XXVII, 665-667.

[8] *Hunt's*, XXXVIII, 281.

[9] *Ibid.*, XLII, 492-494.

[10] *Ibid.*, XXXVIII, 276-277 and 283; Cole: *op. cit.*, p. 87.

[11] *Hunt's*, XXXVIII, 282-289

[12] *Idem*, 285.

[13] Cole: *op. cit.*, pp. 75-86, from which account much of the material in these paragraphs is drawn.

[14] *Hunt's*, XLI, 759-760. See also pp. 508-510 for production figures.

[15] *Laws of Illinois*, 1855, p. 153. Approved February 15, 1855; *Bankers Magazine*, X, 227; *Reports of the Session (House)*, 1857, p. 5; *Reports of the Session (Senate)*, 1855, pp. 1-3.

[16] *Reports of the Treasurer*, December 1, 1856, *Laws of Illinois*, 1857, p. 4. See also *Laws of Illinois*, 1857, p. 104. Approved February 18, 1857.

[17] *Hunt's*, XL, 473.

[18] Cf. *De Bow's*, XIII, 197-198.

[19] Cf. Chicago *Daily Democratic Press*, May 11, 1854.

[20] *Hunt's*, XXXVIII, 756; XXXIX, 424.

[21] *Ibid.*, XLIII, 500-501.

[22] Cole: *op. cit.*, p. 5; *Hunt's*, LIII, 588.

[23] *Hunt's*, XL, 230.

[24] Andreas: *op. cit.*, I, 585.

[25] *Idem*, 583-584.

[26] Cole: *op. cit.*, 89.

[27] Hoyt: *op. cit.*, p. 64.

[28] *Idem*.

[29] *Hunt's*, XXXIII, 470.

[30] Hoyt: *op. cit.*, p. 65; Chicago *Daily Democratic Press*, March 13, 1854; *Hunt's*, XL, 229.

[31] Hoyt: *op. cit.*, pp. 69-70.

[32] Andreas: *op. cit.*, I, 549-550.

[33] *Report of the Auditor*, December 1, 1856; *Laws of Illinois*, 1856, pp. 124-131. See also Appendix II.

[34] Chicago *Daily Democratic Press*, March 16, 1854. See also Table IV, p. 220.

[35] Andreas: *op. cit.*, I, 549.

[36] These, and subsequent details, regarding the Union Trust Company are taken from the Minute Books and other corporate records of the institution.

[37] Cf. Harper and Ravell: *Fifty Years of Banking in Chicago,* pp. 31-38.
[38] *Chicago Democrat,* June 12, 1857; Harper and Ravell: *op. cit.,* pp. 39-40.
[39] Andreas: *op. cit.,* I, 549.
[40] Chicago *Daily Democratic Press,* March 13, 1854. See also February 6, 1854.
[41] *Laws of Illinois,* 1857, pp. 45-46. Approved January 31, 1857; *Bankers Magazine,* IX, 547.
[42] Cf. *Hunt's,* XXXII, 335; XLI, 196.
[43] Chicago *Daily Democratic Press,* January 16, 1854.
[44] *Hunt's,* XLII, 321.
[45] *Idem,* 313.
[46] Dewey: *op. cit.,* p. 166.
[47] *Hunt's,* XLIII, 317-319.
[48] *Ibid.,* XXXVII, 665.
[49] See Table VII, p. 260.
[50] *Chicago Democrat,* September 7, 1857.
[51] Cf. *Hunt's,* XXXVII, 659-660.
[52] *History of Banking,* I, 426.
[53] *Chicago Democrat,* August 29, 1857.
[54] *Ibid.,* August 17, 1857; Scroggs: *op. cit.,* p. 150.
[55] *Chicago Democrat,* September 26 and 28, 1857.
[56] *Hunt's,* XXXVII, 715.
[57] *Idem,* 714-715; *History of Banking,* I, 426.
[58] *Chicago Democrat,* October 6, 1857.
[59] *Hunt's,* XXXVII, 715. See also pp. 657-668, and Scroggs: *op. cit.,* pp. 152-153.
[60] See above pp. 241-242.
[61] *Illinois State Journal,* March 25, 1857; *Bankers Magazine,* XI, 622 and 827.
[62] *Chicago Democrat,* August 18, 1857; *Reports of the Session,* 1857, p. 193.
[63] Andreas: *op. cit.,* I, 159.
[64] *Chicago Democrat,* August 3, 1857.
[65] *Ibid.,* August 25, 1857; *New York Herald Tribune,* August 26, 1857.
[66] *Chicago Democrat,* August 27, 1857.
[67] *Ibid.,* August 28, 1857.
[68] *Ibid.,* August 31, 1857.
[69] *Ibid.,* September 11, 1857.
[70] *Ibid.,* September 22, 1857.
[71] *Ibid.,* October 5 and 8, 1857.

[72] Dowrie: *op. cit.,* pp. 151-152; *Chicago Democrat,* October 7, 1857; *Illinois State Journal,* October 21, November 9, 1857.

[73] *Chicago Democrat,* September 23, 1857. See also September 12 and 29, 1857.

[74] *Ibid.,* September 30, 1857.

[75] *Ibid.,* October 9, 1857.

[76] *Chicago Democrat,* October 9, 1857.

[77] *Chicago Democrat,* October 1, 1857.

[78] *Ibid.,* December 24, 1857.

[79] *Ibid.,* August 27, 1857.

[80] *Ibid.,* October 15, 1857.

[81] Andreas: *op. cit.,* I, 159.

[82] *Chicago Democrat,* September 18, 1857.

[83] *Ibid.,* September 18, 1857.

[84] *Hunt's,* XL, 204.

[85] *History of Banking,* I, 428.

[86] Dewey: *op. cit.,* p. 215.

[87] *Bankers Magazine,* XIV, 153.

[88] Scroggs: *op. cit.,* p. 161-162.

[89] E. P. Oberholtzer: *Jay Cooke, Financier of the Civil War,* I, 327.

[90] See Table VII, p. 260.

[91] *Report of the Bank Commissioners,* 1858, p. 11.

[92] *History of Banking,* I, 451.

[93] *Senate Journal,* 1859, p. 23.

[94] Andreas: *op. cit.,* II, 618.

[95] *Illinois State Journal,* February 20, 1860.

[96] *Chicago Tribune,* January 5, 1860.

[97] *Hunt's,* XXXVI, 725-726.

[98] Dewey: *op. cit.,* pp. 54-58.

[99] *Ibid.,* pp. 218-223; *History of Banking,* I, 418.

[100] Dewey: *op. cit.,* p. 99.

[101] *Chicago Tribune,* January 5, June 6 and August 17, 1861; *Hunt's,* XLI, 23; XLII, 446.

[102] *Laws of Illinois,* 1861, pp. 39-52. Approved February 14, 1861.

[103] *Bankers Magazine,* XIV, 581; *Chicago Tribune,* January 1, 1861.

[104] *Laws of Illinois,* 1861, p. 52. Approved February 22, 1861.

[105] *Chicago Tribune,* August 12, 1861.

[106] *Laws of Illinois,* 1861, pp. 53-71. Approved February 20, 1861.

[107] *Report of the Auditor,* December 1, 1860, *Laws of Illinois,* 1861, p. 6.

[108] *Hunt's,* XLIII, 209.

[109] *Idem,* 714-715.

[110] *History of Banking,* I, 457.

[111] *Chicago Democrat,* May 13, 14 and 18, 1861.

[112] *Chicago Tribune,* January 19, 1861.

[113] *Ibid.,* April 2, 1861.

[114] *Bankers Magazine,* XVI, 74.

[115] *Chicago Democrat,* May 14 and July 10, 1861.

[116] *Chicago Tribune,* April 17, 1861.

[117] *Illinois State Journal,* April 6, 1861.

[118] *Chicago Democrat,* May 14, 1861.

[119] *Ibid.,* May 30, 1861.

[120] *Ibid.,* July 10, 1861.

[121] *Chicago Tribune,* May 2 and 16, 1861; *Chicago Democrat,* May 14, 1861.

[122] *Chicago Democrat,* April 29, 1861.

[123] *Illinois State Journal,* June 5, 1861.

[124] *Bankers Magazine,* XVI, 74.

[125] *Chicago Democrat,* May 18, 1861.

[126] *Ibid.,* May 22, 1861.

[127] *Ibid.,* May 13, 1861.

[128] *Ibid.,* May 13, 1861.

[129] *Chicago Tribune,* August 8, 1861. Italics in the original.

[130] *Chicago Democrat,* May 22, 1861.

[131] *Ibid.,* June 27, 1861.

[132] *Chicago Democrat,* July 11, 1861. See also June 27, 1861, and Andreas: *op. cit.,* II, 620.

[133] *Chicago Democrat,* July 16, 1861; *Chicago Tribune,* July 30, 1861.

[134] *Chicago Democrat,* June 27 and July 16, 1861.

[135] *Report of the Auditor,* December 1, 1862, *Laws of Illinois,* 1863, p. 6.

[136] *Chicago Democrat,* June 28 and July 10, 1861.

[137] *Ibid.,* June 27, 1861; *Chicago Tribune,* July 27, 1861; *Bankers Magazine,* XVII, 396; Andreas: *op. cit.,* II, 621; *History of Banking,* I, 449.

[138] *Report of the Auditor,* December 1, 1864, *Laws of Illinois,* 1865, p. 79.

[139] *Laws of Illinois,* 1865, p. 20. Approved February 13, 1865.

[140] See also *Chicago Tribune,* July 30 and August 10, 1861.

[141] *Ibid.,* August 10, September 25 and October 2, 1861.

[142] *Ibid.,* July 1, 1862.

[143] *Ibid.,* March 6, 1862.

[144] *Ibid.,* October 9, 12 and 15, 1861.

CHAPTER IX

A NATIONAL MONETARY SYSTEM

1861–1866

THE newly fledged government of the United States, in 1790, had set out to establish a national monetary system as one of the first of its major objectives. Remembering vividly the chaotic currency conditions of the War of Independence, when creditors had fled from their debtors in mortal fear of being repaid in worthless paper, the members of the Constitutional Convention had specifically forbidden the states to issue bills of credit or coins of any kind. Nor could a state government confer legal-tender power on any currency. Into the hands of the government of the United States was conveyed full monetary powers: Congress was given the right to coin money and regulate its value.

Despite the economic and legalistic arguments which changing economic conditions have aroused regarding that clause of the Constitution, its original meaning is perfectly apparent. The United States was to be one economic unit, with a single monetary system and no barrier might be imposed to prevent the economic intercourse of different sections of the Union. The recent experiences of France and England reinforced those of the American colonies in demonstrating the dangers of a paper currency, and the framers of the Constitution, desiring a monetary system based upon gold and silver, conferred upon the central government powers that they regarded as adequate for the establishment and maintenance of such a system.

Nor was this ideal thought to be endangered by the growth of banking institutions in the young republic. Banks might be necessary for the expeditious transfer of funds, and their notes might prove much more convenient than coin in the handling of large transactions, but those notes must at all times be redeemable in the coins that they were supposed to represent. The metallic dollar, defined by Congress, was the standard of value to which all other money had to conform, and there is no doubt that the government recognized its duty in enforcing this conformity. Loundes, in his report on the first Bank of the United States, pointed out that "the great object of the government, in chartering the Bank, was to provide a currency which should have that degree of stability and uniformity in its value which is required by the interests both of our commerce and revenue."[1] Regarding this purpose there was no dispute, no matter how keen the controversy as to the constitutionality of the Bank might be, and Madison, in his message of December, 1816, reverted to the same theme. "For the interests of the community at large, as well as for the purpose of the Treasury, it is essential that the nation should possess a currency of equal value, credit, and use, wherever it may circulate. The constitution has intrusted Congress, exclusively, with the power of creating and regulating a currency of that description."

Earlier chapters have demonstrated adequately that this ideal was never attained during the first half of the nineteenth century. In each state, the legislature had created banks of various kinds, and the Supreme Court of the United States had declared that those banks could issue circulating notes without, in any way, violating the federal Constitution. As a result, paper money in thousands of different forms had come into existence, each note varying from all the others in value even when they were nominally of the same denomination. Many of them had no general acceptability outside the state in which they were issued. Congress, in fact, had so far abrogated its monetary powers that, recognizing the wretched quality of "the heterogeneous rags," it refused to accept them. For the operations of the federal government, it established the Independent Treasury, which operated solely on the basis of metallic currency, but Congress did nothing at all to provide a sound currency for the nation as a whole. During the years immediately preceding the Civil War, "although one nation, bound together by the ties of consanguinity, of a common language and an interstate and international commerce, we have been separated by diverse systems of currency, bounded by the state lines, and as widely variant as those which mark the alien and often hostile principalities and powers of Europe. London and Munich, Paris and St. Petersburg are not more inaccessible to each other, except by the financial bridge of exchange, than are New York, St. Louis, Boston, and Chicago."[2]

During the dark days of the Civil War, a second great effort was, therefore, made to return to the faith of the

Fathers and establish a currency that would be truly American, circulating freely from Maine to California and accepted by every man at its face value in the confidence that it would not depreciate on his hands. That effort, although in no sense peculiar to the local history of Chicago, constitutes an important page in our story: Chicago fought heroically for the ideal, and the partial success of that battle was destined to exercise important effects upon the subsequent financial growth of the city.

Once again, as had been the case during the infant days of the republic, the need for a sound national currency was demonstrated by the fiscal problems to which the existing monetary situation gave rise. After the panic of 1857, the finances of the federal government were none too strong and, despite the improvement that followed the departure of the Buchanan administration, conditions were still deplorable in 1861. The Treasury was empty, and the revenue from taxation utterly inadequate, while the attempt to finance current expenditures by borrowing was neither easy nor encouraging. Six per cent United States bonds moved sluggishly into the hands of purchasers at eighty-five per cent of their face value.

The outbreak of the Civil War accentuated the problems that Salmon P. Chase was already facing in his administration of the Treasury since, as Napoleon once pointed out, the first necessity for successful prosecution of a war is "money, money, and still more money!" During the first year of hostilities, the federal government was spending money at the rate of $2,200,000 a day; the expenses of two months of war, during the summer of 1861, were equal to the entire national debt of the United

States on July 1, 1860,[3] and soon afterward the expenses of a single month exceeded this amount by a considerable margin. Starting out with an empty Treasury, and a fiscal system that was far from strong, the United States was destined to spend money, for four long years, at a rate which was without precedent in the history of the country, so that problems of governmental finance assumed a position of unusual importance in the eyes of every thoughtful citizen. Patriotic enthusiasm for the Union and the thrill of victorious battles were emotional stimuli that helped a man to carry his share of the load while the conflict was in progress, but an unwise financing of the war might leave him with a heavy burden to carry down the long avenue of subsequent years when there would be no such excitements to lighten it.

To a government in the dilemma that confronted Lincoln's administration there are, from the viewpoint of theory, three alternative solutions. The necessary funds can be raised by a rigorous policy of taxation that forces people to dig into their pockets painfully, month by month. If that appears unwise, in the light of all the circumstances, funds can be raised by the sale of bonds that saddle future generations with the problem of paying off the lenders, while (in the event that neither of these policies is adopted) a third alternative presents itself in the form of policies of monetary inflation. The government can print the money that is needed to pay its bills, taxing the community severely, yet secretly, by depressing the value of the notes in the hands of the general public. Other than these three, there is no way in which a government can finance a vast program of expenditure, if we except the idea of conscripting economic resources which is sometimes proposed in the modern world, but the choice among these alternatives demands careful thought. Each of them produces peculiar effects upon the national economy and upon public psychology.

During the last six months of 1861, the government appears to have seriously considered each of these alternatives.[4] Chase was unequivocally opposed to policies of inflation,[5] and although, ironically enough, he was to adopt policies vastly more inflationary than those of any of his predecessors, he wished to avoid this method as long as possible. Taxation also seemed to him unwise, in the light of all the surrounding circumstances, particularly since everybody expected the war to be short. "He was afraid that the patriotism of the country would not remain proof under the burden of taxes; that if he imposed such taxes as were indispensable to the maintenance of the war on a sound basis, the people might shrink from its prosecution."[6] So strong was this conviction that new taxes were not levied until the summer of 1862, when the stern necessities of war had shown that such a measure could not be avoided any longer.[7]

There remained no alternative but to borrow the necessary funds by a sale of bonds and, on July 17, 1861, Congress passed an act authorizing the sale of $250,000,000 United States bonds.[8] In view, however, of the difficulties previously encountered in disposing of bonds, even in times of peace, the act authorized the Secretary of the Treasury to issue $50,000,000 in the form of noninterest-bearing demand notes. Although not legal tender, these notes were intended to circulate as money, and were accepted by the government in all payments due to it. They were designed, however, as a purely temporary measure, to carry the Treasury over the period that must elapse while the bonds were being sold,* and the bonds were expected to supply the bulk of the funds that were needed.

Unfortunately, the public displayed no enthusiasm for government bonds, a security with which they had little previous experience. Moreover, few Americans, at this period, were in the habit of buying any investment securities, except those of local institutions such as banks or railway companies, so that Chase was compelled to appeal to the banks for assistance in disposing of the issue. In response, the bankers of New York, Philadelphia and Boston, on August 15, 1861, signed a contract with the Treasury agreeing to take over and distribute $150,000,-000 of the bonds and pay for them in three installments of equal amount.[9]

As a result of the contraction of financial operations which had begun in 1860, the banks of these three cities were in an unusually strong position when the agreement was made. In New York, the specie reserve, which amounted to six times the total note issue of the banks, was equivalent to almost fifty per cent of the note and deposit liabilities combined,[10] while conditions in the other cities were almost as good. Moreover, the banks assumed little risk in the transaction, since these advances to the government (on August 15, October 1 and November 16) were all secured by government bonds paying high rates of interest. Yet the banks were full of apprehen-

* An act was passed on August 5, 1861, which provided for the funding of the demand notes into twenty-year bonds.

sion, and took elaborate steps to protect their position. Among themselves, they agreed that specie reserves should not be allowed to fall below twenty-five per cent during the period of the transaction, and loan certificates issued by the central committee were to be used for settlements among the banks involved, in order to protect the reserve position. This fear, however, only serves to accentuate the courage that was displayed in undertaking the commitment. Had the banks not stepped into the breach, it is probable that the bonds could not have been sold, so that the comment of the New York Loan Committee, in 1862, even if lacking in modesty, is fully warranted. "To the banks of the three cities of New York, Boston and Philadelphia the people of the United States owe a debt of gratitude, especially to the banks of this city, who in August last took the lead in expressing their confidence in the stability of the government of this country, by placing at risk the capital of their stockholders for its maintenance. But for such support it would have been revolutionized."[11]

In the light of retrospect, the results of this operation appear sardonically humorous. When the Independent Treasury was set up, in 1846, Congress had provided that all payments to the government should be made in gold or silver coin, which was to remain in the Treasury vaults until it was paid out to meet public obligations. On the whole, the plan had worked satisfactorily during the period from 1846 down to 1860:[12] it had saved the government from losses that might have been incurred from the handling of depreciated bank notes and, since governmental reserves were neither large nor violently fluctuating, it had not unduly disturbed the normal operations of the money market. With the commencement of the Civil War, however, both of the latter conditions ceased to be true. Close adherence to an Independent Treasury policy would, in view of the tremendous increase in public receipts and expenditures, have made ordinary banking operations impossible so that, under the legislation of August 5, 1861, the Secretary of the Treasury was authorized to deposit public moneys in such solvent specie-paying banks as he might select.

Had Chase availed himself of this power, the financial story of the Civil War might have been different. The eastern banks, which provided the initial $150,000,000, could have credited that amount to the government on their books, honoring the drafts of the Treasury as they were drawn against the resultant balance. As the government spent the proceeds of the loan, the funds would have found their way back to the banks in the form of deposits, and the process could have been repeated as often as was necessary, provided that the banks were able to dispose of the bonds in a steady stream to members of the general public and prevent any considerable inflation of bank credit.

All this, however, is a hypothetical might-have-been. Chase was a hard-money man, who distrusted banks and desired that all payments should be made in coin. Instead of using the powers conferred upon him, and leaving the funds with the banks, he insisted that the whole amount of $150,000,000 should be handed over to the Treasury in specie, with the inevitable result that the banks, finding their reserves reduced to the vanishing point by this operation, were compelled to suspend specie payments on December 28, 1861.[13] The unwise, though well-intentioned, policy of a man who bitterly hated inconvertible paper reduced the whole country to a paper standard within a few months of the outbreak of war.

Overnight, the financial problems of the federal government became twice as hard to solve. It was easy enough to pass another Loan Act, early in 1862, providing for the sale of $500,000,000 twenty-year bonds, but in terms of what currency were the bonds to be sold? Silver dollars had been out of general circulation since 1834; gold coins went into hoards as soon as specie payments were suspended, and could not be tempted out again until a substantial premium was offered at a later stage of the war. Even subsidiary silver coins began to be hoarded or melted down. Obviously, therefore, if the bonds were sold at all, payment would have to be received in bank notes, and the government would find itself in possession of the "worthless issues of the State of Maine and of other New England States, the shinplasters of Michigan, the wildcats of Georgia, of Canada, and Pennsylvania, the red dogs of Indiana and Nebraska, the miserably engraved rags of North Carolina and Kentucky, Missouri and Virginia, and the not-soon-to-be-forgotten 'stump tail' of Illinois and Wisconsin . . . mixed indiscriminately with the par currency of New York and Boston."[14]

No sound fiscal program could be erected on such a foundation of shifting sands, and the complexity of the problems that it raised must have gone far to strengthen the desire of the administration for a uniform national currency.* Of Chase's own opinions, we are left in no doubt whatever. In 1856, while he was Governor of Ohio, he had insisted that "a sound and sufficient currency is indispensable to the welfare of every civilized community. The best practical currency in my judgment would be a currency of coin, admitting the use of large notes only for the convenience of commerce. Such a currency, however, is only attainable through the legislation of Congress and the action of the General Government."[15] From that position he had not receded an inch during the intervening years, as he made clear in a letter to Thaddeus Stevens, dated January 20, 1862. "It is not unknown . . . that I have felt, nor do I wish to conceal that I now feel, a great aversion to making anything but coin a legal tender in the payment of debts."[16] A national monetary system was essential for the United States; preferably that system should be based on gold and silver but, whatever its basis, it must be national in scope. That faith is the key to almost all of Chase's actions during the ensuing years, even when unwisdom seems to obscure its flickering light almost completely.

It must be remembered, however, that Chase was not alone in his desire for monetary reform. For more than a decade, the United States had experienced a period of intellectual turmoil that bears a close similarity to the years of controversy which gave birth to the Bank Charter Act of 1844, in England. In both countries, the discussion was provoked by banking policies that endangered the monetary stability of the country, the same arguments

* It is of interest to note that, when Chase resigned in 1865, Lincoln first picked as his successor "Pot Metal Tod," who had earned that sobriquet by a life-long enthusiasm for hard money. Cf. *Hunt's*, LI, 1.

were used in both cases, and the solutions adopted, although widely divergent in many ways, both failed of success because of identical defects. But, with all this in mind, it must be remembered that each controversy was staged in an economic and political arena that was peculiar to itself, so that the points of similarity must not be unduly stressed. It was the American discussions of bank reform, with all their local idiosyncrasies, that gave Chase the power to move toward his objective and, disheartening though the thought must be, a close examination of contemporary American writings shows that very few of the American protagonists were familiar with the vast literature that England had produced on the same subject a decade earlier.

By reason of the Constitutional peculiarity of American government, the first point to be decided was who, legally, had the right to regulate the currency. On that point there was no controversy whatever: all the writers and speakers were unanimous in their agreement with Chase's contention that Congress alone possessed the power to establish a national monetary system.[17] Moreover, there was an almost unanimous agreement that Congress had unlawfully abdicated that power, in favor of the state banks, and it is interesting to quote on this point a typical paragraph, written in 1860, as an indication of the strangely modern quality possessed by the controversy. "The vast power of regulating the value of money, and thence the commerce of the United States, is very properly delegated by the States to Congress in the constitution; it is the chief function of sovereignty without which the stipulation for regulating commerce, as well as that for maintaining the inviolability of contracts, is an utter nullity. But, by reason of the neglect of Congress, this great function is given over to the cupidity of the banks; and to suit first their profits and then their necessities, the value of money is first degraded, then enhanced; the import of foreign goods is, by the same process, first stimulated, then checked; the production, as well as the export, of our domestic merchandise is first diminished, then increased, inversely as the increase and diminution of the currency. . . . This mighty power over the public welfare is now practically exercised by a few gentlemen who control the discounts of the leading banks of the city of New York, the creditor city and center of the exchanges of the nation."*

Admittedly there were a few people, like G. S. Ward,[18] who followed the English Banking School in insisting that banks had no power to influence either the amount, or the value, of the currency. Banks, he pointed out, merely supply working capital to business: by discounting nothing but bills of exchange drawn against actually existing values they furnished working capital in the appropriate quantity, at the right time, so that the elasticity of their circulation was necessary to meet changing business conditions. In a statement that is worthy of Tooke or Fullarton, he calls attention to the "common opinion that a bank can, and that it does, at pleasure, increase and diminish its circulation. . . . This is a great mistake. The true interest of the bank lies in having its customers, and the public generally, successful; consequently it acts with

---

Hunt's, XLIII, 582. It is also interesting to notice that some writers at this period were suggesting monetary management of a kind that would do away with a fixed metallic standard. Cf. *Hunt's*, XLIX, 273 and 275.

caution and prudence, doing all it can to promote the public good, consistently with taking care of itself. It never issues bills gratuitously, nor without securing or putting into its vaults their value. Every bill going from the bank is a debt against itself, payable on demand; and it is in the hands of the public, who, as regards the bank, are jealous, unfriendly, and uncharitable."[19] As a result, the public will promptly present for redemption any notes that are not required for the conduct of its business, so that an overissue of bank notes is impossible.

Even in England, where the banking situation (though bad enough at times) had never been one-tenth as unsatisfactory as that which existed in America at the time of the Civil War, the Banking School had been unable to convince the public. Its arguments, though stimulating, were too complex. They depended for their validity upon a high standard of wisdom and honesty among bankers, and upon the permanence of financial practices which were already undergoing change. In the United States, public reaction followed an identical pattern. It avoided the complex explanations that it could not readily understand, and gave hearty adherence to the oversimplified contentions of the Currency School.

Here there was no possibility of misunderstanding. In the first place, bank notes were clearly defined as money. In the second, it was insisted that changes in the quantity of money influenced commodity prices. From these two premises, it logically followed that the quantity of bank notes in circulation must be controlled, either by requiring precise specie reserves against all issues,[20] or else by appropriate governmental regulation. In the American controversy, moreover, the method of governmental regulation most frequently suggested was a provision that all circulating notes should be secured by the deposit of at least an equivalent amount of United States bonds,[21] a scheme that was suggested by the widespread adoption of the free-banking principle during previous years.

It was against this background of public discussion and agitation that Chase, in his annual report of December, 1861, suggested the idea that was subsequently to develop into the national banking system.[22] Following very closely the details of a plan suggested to him by O. B. Potter during the previous summer,[23] Chase recommended the creation by the federal government of national currency associations which, on depositing with the Treasury an appropriate amount of United States bonds, would receive circulating notes engraved after a uniform pattern. In support of the idea, he pointed out that the people "in their ordinary business, would find the advantages of uniformity in currency; of uniformity in security; of effectual safeguard, if effectual safeguard is possible, against depreciation; and of protection from losses in discounts and exchanges; while in the operations of the government the people would find the further advantage of a large demand for government securities, of increased facilities for obtaining the loans required by the war, and of some alleviation of the burdens on industry through a diminution in the rate of interest, or a participation in the profit of circulation, without risking the perils of a great money monopoly. A further and important advantage to the people may be reasonably expected in the increased security to the Union, springing from the common interest in its preservation, created by the distribution of its stocks to associations throughout the country, as the basis of circulation."

These were the basic arguments that were reiterated during the formative years of the national banking system, and it is interesting to notice that they sprang to life fully armed when that system was first proposed in official form. To Chase, the primary objective was the attainment of a national monetary system and there was a large body of public sentiment behind him. But on the monetary issue alone, it is doubtful whether he could have commanded a majority, particularly during the war, since there were many who felt, with Francis Bowen, of Harvard, that "a great war is the very time for making trial of newly-invented cannon and iron-clad ships; but it is no more a proper season for experimenting with a new banking system than with a new religion."[24] One member of Congress aptly suggested that the government needed a new monetary system about as much as a man struggling in the water wanted somebody to throw him dry clothes.[25]

It was for this reason[26] that Chase added other arguments for his proposal, although there can be no doubt that he believed them. As Secretary of the Treasury for the Union, he must have devoutly prayed that they would prove true, even though they were less important, in his eyes, than the basic monetary ideal. As a means of war finance, he urged, the new associations would prove invaluable since they would purchase government bonds in large amounts, while these scattered holdings of Union securities would give many people a material stake in the cause for which it was fighting, and so strengthen the patriotism of the laggards. It was an ingenious mixture of arguments, designed to draw support from all schools of thought.

Congress displayed no great enthusiasm for the plan, however, despite the force of the arguments. On July 11, 1862, Hooper (of Massachusetts) introduced a bill embodying the Secretary's proposals,[27] but the opposition, led by Thaddeus Stevens, was so strong that it was impossible to do more than get the bill printed. To some extent, this antagonism to the bill may have been the result of personal friction between Chase and the leaders in Congress, while some of it arose from a genuine feeling that the moment was inappropriate for such a measure, but there can be no doubt that the opposition of banking interests to the new plan exercised a great influence on the votes of some Congressmen. "The trouble with Congress is, that a majority of the members are personally interested either as stockholders or borrowers, and have not patriotism or integrity enough to rise above such sordid and selfish considerations."[28]

Meanwhile, the delay in preparing the bill, and the further waste of time in Congress, had created a situation where the absence of funds and the lack of a standard currency had seriously embarrassed the government. As a result, a Legal Tender Act had been passed on February 25, authorizing the issue of $150,000,000 in the form of paper currency, which rapidly came to be known by the familiar name of Greenbacks.[29] One-third of this sum was to be used to retire the $50,000,000 of demand notes, which had not been presented for refunding under the earlier act, while the remainder was available to meet the current expenditures of the Treasury. Moreover, since the Greenbacks were legal tender for all payments, except duties on imports and interest on the public debt, they provided the people and the government, for the first time in many years, with a substantial amount of paper currency that was uniform in value throughout the country.

The Greenbacks, like the demand notes, were regarded as a temporary expedient,[30] and Chase renewed his advocacy of the proposed currency associations when he wrote his annual report for 1862. Once again, he elaborated the three arguments that he had used the year before, reiterating that "the central idea of the proposed measure is the establishment of one sound, uniform circulation, of equal value throughout the country, upon the foundation of national credit combined with private capital."[31] Moreover, he tried to gain additional support for the plan by inviting the assistance of New York bankers and enlisting the persuasive tongue of Jay Cooke. The New York bankers, however, were of no help at all, and the *Journal of Commerce*, reporting the bankers' meeting, suggests sarcastically that it "might have been a success as a social gathering, but we fear has not contributed largely towards replenishing the Treasury."[32]

The contribution of Jay Cooke was more important, since he appears to have persuaded Sherman to introduce the bill, and fight for it, in the Senate.[33] With that sponsorship, and the urgent request of Lincoln that the bill be passed,[34] the outlook became brighter but, even so, the legislative sailing of the bill was by no means smooth.[35] Sherman repeated all the arguments that Chase had already offered and, in the House, Hooper prophesied financial calamity if the bill should fail to pass, but the opposition fought doggedly. As Allen, of Illinois, stated their arguments, "This movement for centralisation is but a reinauguration of the old National banking system under the auspices of Nicholas Biddle. . . . We have no Jackson now, but we have a man at the wheel of power whose early education, in a financial point of view, was dreadfully neglected, as I suppose. He knew there was a machine at work making money. How long did it work without some sort of aid? My friend Mr. Mallory suggests greasing. I adopt the term. I am no State bank man. . . . I have been in favor of those commodities called gold and silver. Even though I was a State bank man I could not favor this bill. I want information, I want to be educated financially. I am in the same condition about this that I think the President of the United States is."[36]

After a long battle, the bill finally passed the Senate by a vote of twenty-three to twenty-one, simply because a few members had been convinced by Sherman that it was an emergency measure. In the House, the vote was almost as close, being seventy-seven to sixty-four, with thirty-eight members absent. On February 25, 1863, it became a law.[37]

In broad outline, this National Currency Act, provided for the appointment within the Treasury of an officer, styled the Comptroller of the Currency, who was given authority to incorporate as banking associations any group of five or more persons, with a minimum capital of $50,000,* which made application to him. Each

* One hundred thousand dollars in cities of more than 10,000 people.

association was required to deposit with the Treasurer of the United States, government bonds equivalent at market value to at least thirty per cent of its paid-in capital, in return for which it was to receive circulating "national currency" equal in amount to ninety per cent of the market value of the bonds. In no case might the notes received be in excess of ninety per cent of the par value of the bonds deposited, nor might any association receive an amount larger than its total paid-in capital.

These new bank notes were to constitute the uniform national currency for which Chase had been working so energetically and persistently. The aggregate issue for the whole of the country was not to exceed $300,000,000, apportioned officially among the states in accordance with their population and banking resources,* and the notes themselves were to be receivable "at par in all parts of the United States in payment of taxes, excises, public lands, and all other dues to the United States, except for duties on imports, and also for all salaries and other debts and demands owing by the United States to individuals, corporations, and associations within the United States, except interest on the public debt."[38] Short of conferring full legal-tender powers, it was impossible for Congress to give the notes a wider range of circulation.

Each association was legally bound to redeem its notes on demand at its place of business, and was required to hold, for that purpose, a reserve of lawful money (which in practice, at that time meant Greenbacks) equal to at least twenty-five per cent of its aggregate note and deposit

* This provision is strangely reminiscent of earlier legislation, in Illinois for instance, which compelled a bank to distribute its loans among the counties in proportion to the voting population. See above p. 42.

liabilities. In recognition, however, of the extensive correspondent relationship that had already developed
among banks throughout the United States, it was provided that three-fifths of the required reserve might be
kept by country banks in the form of demand deposits
with banks in Boston, Providence, New York, Philadelphia, Baltimore, Cincinnati, Chicago, St. Louis or New
Orleans.* Moreover, to assure the unquestioned soundness of the currency, even though any individual association might fail, the act provided that the Comptroller
of the Currency should redeem the notes of any bank that
was unwilling, or unable, to meet its obligations, reimbursing himself by the cancellation or sale of the bonds
that had been deposited. If the total proceeds of those
bonds proved inadequate, the Comptroller had a first lien
on the remaining assets of the issuing bank, which he was
authorized to put into the hands of a receiver as soon as it
failed to redeem its notes.

In the light of contemporary theory and practice, these
provisions of the act showed significant progress in the
monetary policy of the United States. But the corporations created under the act were also expected to do a
general banking business, to replace the old state banking
system in all its operations, and here also the provisions
of the law drew upon some of the best aspects of contemporary practice. In addition to their privilege of "obtaining and issuing circulating notes," the new associations were given the power to "carry on the business of
banking by . . . discounting bills, notes, and other evi-

* Section 41. Banks in any of the cities named were required to hold all
their reserves in their own vaults.

dences of debt; by receiving deposits; by buying and selling gold and silver bullion, foreign coins, and bills of exchange; by loaning money on real and personal security . . . and by exercising such incidental powers as shall be necessary to carry on such business."[39] No loans might be made by a bank on its own stock, however, while the aggregate amount of loans to shareholders, and the maximum loan to any single customer, were rigidly limited.

Only in one respect could the new legislation be regarded as falling short of its goal. It did nothing to prevent the old state banks from continuing in operation and, as subsequent events were to prove, very little to persuade them to enter the new system. From the purpose of the act, it followed that the privileges of note issue would be more restricted under the federal law than they had been under most of the state banking statutes, and the only apparent offset to this disadvantage was the provision that the Secretary of the Treasury might select the new national associations as depositories.* When the new measure had first been discussed there were many suggestions that it should contain a section taxing state bank notes out of existence, but banking influence in Congress was strong enough to prevent such action. As a matter of fact, while the original Hooper bill had levied an identical tax on the circulation of both state and national banks, the tax on state notes had been eliminated from the bill before it was finally passed and the new associations were placed under a comparative

* State banks could no longer qualify as depositories under the law of 1861 because they were not, in 1863, on a specie-paying basis.

disadvantage! It was necessary, on March 3, 1863, to insert a provision in the Revenue Act for the purpose of equalizing the burden of federal taxes on both types of institution.[40]

Having secured the necessary legislation, the administration moved swiftly. On May 9, the National Currency Bureau was set up in the Treasury, with Hugh McCulloch as the first Comptroller of the Currency. A few weeks later, he issued an elaborate circular "for the instruction and guidance of those who may wish to form Banking Associations under. . . . An Act to provide a National Currency"[41] and, by the end of July, twenty-six applications for incorporation had been received.[42] On June 29, the first of the new national banks commenced operations at Davenport, Iowa, while those in Chicago and Philadelphia followed in less than a fortnight.

A year earlier, on July 11, 1862, Congress had passed an act authorizing the federal government to set up a Bureau of Engraving and Printing, and it was this organization that assumed the task of preparing, in collaboration with several New York printing houses, the new national bank currency.[43] By the end of the year, notes in five- and ten-dollar denominations had been prepared and issued to the banks, and their appearance seems to have excited marked comment. "These [notes] are very unlike anything that bankers ever saw, and have not much resemblance to anything that has heretofore represented 'money.' The bills have neither face or back, so to speak, but both sides highly pictured, bordered, and wreathed—with very small figures and the beautiful engraving of the paintings in the Capitol Rotunda blurred by lettering. Somebodys 'fancy' had a large scope to experiment itself in when these notes were gotten up."[44]

In spite, however, of the elaborate preparations, and of the pessimistic fears of the *Merchants' Magazine* that new banks were going "into operation as fast as they can file their papers and procure their notes,"[45] the growth of the national banking system was disappointingly slow. By March, 1864, a full year after the passage of the act, there were only 208 national banks that filed the required quarterly report, while the aggregate paid-in capital was only $42,204,000. The total quantity of notes in circulation was but little more than $12,000,000.[46] By the end of June, there were 469 banks, with capital in excess of $74,-000,000 and a note circulation of $44,000,000.[47] The national system still represented a very small part of the total banking resources of the country, and an even smaller portion of the monetary circulation, so that the *Merchants' Magazine* was forced to revise its earlier prophecy.[48]

Even more serious was the fact that the older banks showed little enthusiasm for the new plan, and that most of the early national banks were incorporated by men of small means who, in many cases, had not previously been engaged in commercial banking. Writing to Chase at the end of 1863, Hooper suggested emphatically, "I do not like having only small banks organised under the law,"[49] and a committee of the New York Clearing House Association drew attention, more pungently, to the same weakness.[50] Moreover, it would seem that many of the smaller national banks made no attempt to do a general banking business, being content to take out notes which they immediately relent to the federal government through the purchase of more securities. Since coin no longer circulated, and most of the Greenbacks had been issued in large denominations, there was a scarcity of small notes for the purpose of paying the troops. "To meet this want, there is a constant and urgent demand by the Treasury for all the National Bank notes. There is, therefore, no difficulty on the part of the banks at present in receiving the national notes and turning them into the Treasury. This will be the case as long as the Government continues to borrow $2,000,000 per day, and refuses old bank notes."[51]

Since the sentiment of bankers as a group is, from the very nature of their business, likely to be conservative, some resistance might have been expected in the case of a reform as sweeping as that envisaged by the National Currency Act. That this factor was of considerable significance is, moreover, apparent from the geographical variations in the reception accorded to the new system.

In the west, where the bank-note currency had been so bad that a woodseller, asked if he would accept Illinois currency, had replied, "Yes, cord for cord!"[52] the response was full of enthusiasm. The *Chicago Tribune* was an early protagonist of the new notes, as it had been of the Greenbacks, on the grounds that Illinois, at long last, would have the opportunity to obtain a currency of undoubted value and wide circulation.[53] Indeed, Medill, the editor of the paper, wrote to Chase urging a tax so severe that it would eliminate the state "debt factories" and their "heterogeneous rags," and leave a clear field for the national currency.[54]

But in the east, and particularly in New York and New England, where the state-bank-note circulation had been of high quality and widely accepted, the reaction of the public was much less favorable. During the early stages of the discussion, the liberal *New York Times* had expressed approval,[55] and even the *Merchants' Magazine* had admitted that the plan had substantial merits[56] but, when the act was finally passed, and the system was put into operation, these early ideas underwent considerable change. By October, 1863, the Currency Act was regarded as "a strange piece of legislation"[57] and, in 1864, although willing to accept "any temporary *war* measure . . . if we considered it an assistance to government," the *Merchants' Magazine* had come to the conclusion that "there is no permanency and no uniformity in this currency. It is a mere irredeemable issue of bank notes, petted and fostered by the Government and, therefore, if the system had any permanency it would only become an immense political machine."[58] Meanwhile, the New York Clearing House had condemned the whole scheme, refusing to take any checks drawn on the new banks and accepting their notes or certified checks only when they were payable at a New York bank belonging to the Clearing House.[59] A "leading Bank President of New York" had written anonymously a stringent indictment of all national banking associations.[60]

Nor can it be contended, if the situation be fairly studied, that these strictures were unwarranted. As a matter of fact, many of the defects in the national banking system, to which the National Monetary Commission called attention fifty years later, were foreshadowed in the contemporary criticisms of the act at the time of its original passage. Passing over the obvious contention that it was unreasonable to condemn all state banks because of the shortcomings of particular institutions,[61] and the minor difficulties of detail, such as the unwillingness of established banks to give up their names in exchange for numerical designations, the first major objection to the scheme lay in the inadequate provision for note redemption. In view of the fact that national bank notes were redeemable only at the point of issue, it was pointed out, on the basis of past experience with other types of currency, that they would inevitably tend to depreciate when in circulation at a distance from that point. As a result, there would still be many gradations of value in the currency, and "to say that these notes constitute a uniform currency, because they are all issued on the deposit of Government bonds, and are numbered and have pictures alike on them, is as reasonable as to suppose that all dealers would be alike solvent and trustworthy, because they started with equal capital, and kept their signs all of one color and their coats of the same cut."[62] Even McCulloch agreed with this contention. "It is not expected," he admitted, "that the notes of the National Associations, scattered from Maine to California, will be of absolutely uniform value throughout the Union."[63]

Secondly, it was contended that the new bank notes would not meet the needs of business because of their extreme inelasticity. To the disciples of the Banking School this was a grave defect, since the quantity of notes issued was to be rigidly maintained at the maximum figure of $300,000,000, while "a sound paper currency is one uttered for the movement of goods or produce to market, and returns upon the issuer with the sale of these goods."[64] In this objection, it will be noted, there is implicit an abiding opposition to any currency secured by government bonds.

Thirdly, it was pointed out that "any law requiring the country banks . . . to hold fixed per-centages of specie would be contrary to the teachings of experience."[65] Such scattered reserves would not be available to meet any serious emergency and, when taken in connection with the prospect of large redeposited reserves in the correspondent banks of the cities mentioned in the act,[66] might be a menace rather than a safeguard for the banking system.

Finally, it was insisted that, in view of the decline in the volume of business, there was not enough financial activity to make the existing banks profitable. Any increase in the number of banks, or any enlargement of their aggregate resources, could not fail to have an inflationary effect upon the national economy.[67] On this point, once again McCulloch agreed. "The inauguration of a new system of banking, under such circumstances [of inflation], is peculiarly hazardous; and I have been, from the time of my appointment, more apprehensive that too many banks would be organized, than that the system would not be sufficiently attractive to induce capitalists to become connected with it."[68]

This inflationary threat was no intangible chimera invoked to terrify a nervous populace. It was an immediate reality. Despite the excellence of his intentions, Chase's financial policy had been about as unsound as anything that could have been imagined. To a certain extent, he was the victim of circumstances beyond his control, notably in regard to the legacy of fiscal inefficiency and monetary chaos which he had received at the hands of his predecessors in office, but it cannot be denied that his own methods of public finance did much to make matters worse. With the best intentions in the world, he had inadvertently driven the country from a specie standard to inconvertible paper that depreciated steadily, and piled up an enormous government debt. When Fessenden entered the Treasury in the summer of 1864 he had, as a contemporary writer phrases it, "to assume what may be called the *débris* of the splendid patrimony of the country, which, with *carte blanche,* was put into Mr. Chase's hands, but has, with his manipulation, been so wasted as to have the nation now . . . . almost in a state of bankruptcy."[69]

On July 11, 1862, and again in January, 1863, Congress had passed laws providing for substantial issues of Greenbacks, over and above the first "temporary" issue that had been made while the National Currency Act was being discussed. As a result, there were outstanding, in 1864, some $470,000,000 of government paper,[70] made up as follows:

PAPER MONEY INFLATION

Laws of	Type of Currency	Amount
July 1861 ⎱ Feb. 1862 ⎰	Treasury notes (later retired).	[$ 60,000,000]
Feb. 1862..................	Greenbacks................	150,000,000
July 11, 1862..............	"	150,000,000
Jan. 17, 1863..............	"	100,000,000
Mar. 3, 1863..............	"	50,000,000
Mar. 3, 1863..............	Fractional notes............	20,000,000
		$470,000,000

Moreover, although the Treasury had repaid its debt to the New York, Boston and Philadelphia banks early in 1862,[71] it had continued to finance its operations by steadily mounting sales of government obligations. "Among the different forms of public debt were 'certificates of indebtedness,' payable within one year from their date; 'temporary loans' payable at ten days' notice; 'compound interest notes,' principal and interest payable at maturity; and 'seven-thirty Treasury notes,' convertible at the holder's option into five-twenty bonds or payable in three years from date."* As a result of the extraordinary ability of Jay Cooke in negotiating the flotation of one government loan after another,[72] the total debt had grown from less than $90,000,000 at the beginning of the war to $1,740,000,000 by the summer of 1864. During the following year, it was raised to $2,682,000,000 by mounting deficits and, even after the war had ended, it continued to grow to the staggering total of almost $2,800,-000,000 by the summer of 1866.[73]

Even if this vast crop of government bonds had been sold to investors, and purchased by them out of savings, the operations of the Treasury would have exercised an inflationary effect through their influence on the velocity of circulation of money. But, as a matter of fact, the bonds were sold primarily to banks, encouraging a rapid expansion in the volume of both notes and bank deposits.†

* Hooper in *Congressional Globe*, February 5, 1869, p. 920. It should perhaps be pointed out that *"seven-thirties"* were notes paying 7.3 per cent interest, while *"five-twenties"* were bonds redeemable by the government in five years but not maturing until the end of twenty years.

† It is interesting to notice that contemporary thinkers fully appreciated the inflationary aspects of a policy that financed growing public deficits by the sale of bonds to the banks. Cf. *Hunt's*, LI, 30-35, especially p. 32.

If additional reserves were required to support the growing superstructure of banking liabilities, there were Greenbacks available in ample quantities and, far from checking the expansive process, the government itself encouraged, on occasions, an easy money policy in order to facilitate the marketing of its obligations.[74] It is not surprising, therefore, to find that, in New York City, the dollar-amount of bank clearings quadrupled during the period from 1860 to 1864.[75]

As always happens, there were evangelists who pointed out that these policies were the best conceivable. "Government loans," it was contended, "increase a nation's capital to the amount of the loans," while old-fashioned things like taxes were regarded as definitely harmful.[76] But to people who were still subject to the steadying influence of half-remembered traditions and older customs, the process was distinctly alarming. The price of the gold dollar, in terms of Greenbacks, rose steadily month by month, until it reached the dizzy height of two dollars and sixty cents on November 9, 1864. Moreover, the quotations fluctuated unexpectedly from day to day in a fashion that made reasonable business planning impossible.[77] Early in 1862, it had become necessary to establish a specialized Gold Exchange in New York, to facilitate the operations of the bullion brokers, and in 1865 the volume of transactions had become so large, and the public interest so intense, that an Evening Exchange was set up to enlarge the opportunity for speculations in gold.[78] This latter development, however, was officially frowned on, as conducive to gambling.

To the government, the rising price of gold was highly

unsatisfactory, and stern attempts were made to blame the speculators for it. When vituperation did not reduce the price sufficiently, the Treasury began to try its hand at controlling the gold market by manipulated purchases and sales of bullion at what appeared to be appropriate quotations, but the operations did not produce much stability. "Mr. Chase had only to show himself at the Sub-Treasury [in New York] and the price of the precious metals at once gave way," but it rose just as soon as he returned to Washington![79]

To an unbiased observer, the Gold Exchange was merely an unusually sensitive market that, in its major swings at any rate, indicated the economic effects of the government's inflationary policy. All the other signs, although sometimes more tardy in their revelation, pointed toward the same conclusion. Commodity prices climbed almost as rapidly as the gold quotations;[80] imports tended to increase and exports to diminish,[81] while the number of business failures throughout the country fell from 2,733, in 1860, to 495, in 1863, and 510, in 1864.[82] Not a single symptom of inflationary prosperity was lacking, since the money market itself operated in a high fever of excitement that precipitated successive panics and recoveries every year.[83]

To organize a sound national banking system in such circumstances, was a task that might well daunt even the bravest man, particularly in view of the manifest defects of the act of 1863. But McCulloch tackled his job vigorously and confidently. His experience as a practical banker enabled him to appraise accurately the reactions of other bankers to the suggested reforms and, since his

Bank of the State of Indiana had been one of the largest branch systems in the country, he was not unprepared for the administrative problems that he faced as Comptroller of the Currency. In the circular that he sent out to all national bankers early in 1864, suggesting the general principles that should govern the operation of the new banks, there is set forth an ideal to which every good banker would pay allegiance today.[84] After describing the appropriate relationships between the directors and officers, as well as between the latter and the general public, he goes on to discuss the all-important lending operations. Liquidity and diversification are stressed, and a generous attitude toward customers encouraged, while the whole gist of the argument is summed up in a concluding paragraph that is little short of remarkable when one remembers the circumstances in which it was written. "Pursue a straightforward, upright, legitimate banking business. Never be tempted by the prospect of large returns to do anything but what may be properly done under the National Currency Act. 'Splendid financiering' is not legitimate banking, and 'splendid financiers' in banking are generally humbugs or rascals."

In McCulloch, as in Chase, however, there was a burning desire to establish a *national* currency and a *national* banking system. While he was ready to accept valid criticisms, and eager to correct the situations that gave rise to them, the central aim of the whole plan was never for one moment forgotten. When, under the act of 1863, state banks possessing United States bonds to the amount of at least half their capital had been given the right to deposit those bonds with the Treasurer of the United States and receive national currency to eighty per cent of their market value,[85] the Comptroller expressed his readiness to obey the law but emphasized his desire to see it changed. "I have hoped, however," he wrote during the summer of 1863, "that very few banks would claim the advantages of it [i.e. Section 62]. The engrafting upon a national system of banking of a provision that, to some extent, *denationalizes* it, was, in my opinion, a great mistake. . . . The intention of the law was to provide a national circulation . . . which should be subject to Government supervision and control. Nothing would be more sure to destroy the symmetry of the system, nor be more likely to bring it into disrepute, than a distribution among the banking institutions of the States, 'good, bad and indifferent' of the national currency."[86]

Nor had he any doubts or hesitations regarding the envisaged object that he desired to attain. "There will not be, in my judgment, for any considerable time, two systems of corporate banking (one State and the other National) in the United States. . . . One or the other will occupy the field; and . . . it requires no spirit of prophecy to predict which of the two is destined to give way."[87] Although the contest between the state banks and the national system was bitter,[88] the necessities of American commerce and public finance required a sound monetary system. All the constructive criticisms that practical bankers wished to make were welcomed, and even invited,[89] but the vested interests of banks could not be allowed to block the path of progress.

To facilitate the attainment of these national aims, McCulloch suggested a comprehensive revision of the act that would improve it from the angle of the existing banking institutions. This recommendation was accepted, and Congress passed, early in June, 1864, a new National Bank Act which laid the foundations of future development much more effectively than its predecessor had done.[90] Besides providing for the clarification of many sections of the older act, thus simplifying the legislative framework of the national banking system, the law of 1864 made several important changes that were designed to meet the criticisms raised by eastern bankers during the preceding years.

First of all, the capital required of national banks was increased, to escape the danger of too many small institutions. The minimum was set at $100,000, although the Secretary of the Treasury might permit $50,000 banks in communities of less than six thousand people. In towns of more than fifty thousand people, however, a minimum capitalization of $250,000 was required and, in all cases, one-half of the capital had to be paid in before the bank could commence operations. To overcome the objections of existing banks to the numerical designations provided in the original act, the law was changed to allow a state bank to retain its old name when it took out a national charter, while the protection of the public money was improved by providing that national banks selected as public depositories should deposit appropriate security with the Treasury. In the grant of powers, the making of loans on real estate was specifically omitted from the revised act.

Of much greater importance than all these, were the changes designed to meet the objections to scattered reserves and inadequate redemption facilities for the notes. Seventeen cities, including New York and Chicago, were designated by name as, what we now call, "reserve cities" (although this name did not come into official use until a later period). All national banks in these cities were required to hold in their vaults, at all times, a reserve in lawful money equal to at least one-quarter of their aggregate liabilities for notes and deposits. Banks in other parts of the country, or "country banks" as they were later called, were required to maintain a minimum reserve of fifteen per cent of their aggregate liabilities and, of this, three-fifths might consist of demand deposits with banks in the designated reserve cities. By this means, the act was expected to achieve an appreciable concentration of reserve funds in the designated cities, and to make the aggregate banking reserves more effective.

Similar provisions were adopted regarding the redemption of national bank notes. While all national banks were still required to redeem their notes at the place of issue, and to receive at par the notes of all other national banks, an additional obligation was now imposed. Each national bank in the designated reserve cities was required to select a bank in New York City as its redemption agent, and to arrange for the redemption of its notes at that bank, while country banks were required to select a similar redemption agent from among the banks in the designated reserve cities. As a result, it was assumed that all the national bank notes issued in a given region would circulate freely at par, since all of them would be redeemable at the financial center of that region. If the redemption agent failed to perform this function satis-

factorily and promptly, it was liable to insolvency proceedings of a kind identical to those that would have followed the failure to redeem its own notes. In New York,
moreover, the notes of all the leading banks throughout
the country would presumably be payable at par, so that
it was no longer possible to suggest that the currency was
not uniform because the costs of redemption differed
from one note to another.

This improvement of the law did not, however, encourage any rapid expansion of the national banking
system. By the end of 1864, the number of banks had increased from the June figure of 469 to a total of 681, and
the aggregate capital had increased to almost $144,-
000,000.[91] Even this was regarded as a dangerously rapid
rate of increase by the editor of the *Merchants' Magazine*
and, since he saw no natural advantages in a national
charter, he felt called upon to explain the growth by the
desire for speculative profit. If state banks joined the national system it must be because "the advantages to stockholders in selling the gold on hand, dividing the surplus,
and beginning anew under a system which never con-
templates a return to specie payments, are apparently
very great."[92]

Not until March, 1865, did the total circulation of national bank notes rise above $100,000,000, so that the new
"uniform national currency" had but little effect on
monetary conditions during the war. In addition to the
large amounts of government paper money in the hands
of the people, there were still hundreds of state bank issues afloat and, when *Heath's Infallible Counterfeit Detector at Sight* was published, late in 1864, the reviewer

emphasized the fact that it would be "very useful to those . . . who would rather carry good, than bad money, in their pockets."[93] The efforts to establish a sound monetary system were still far short of the goal toward which they had been aimed.

Moreover, although Lee's surrender at Appomattox brought the period of active hostilities to a close, it did nothing to solve the fiscal and financial problems that the war had created. A sound and uniform curency was just as important for the proper handling of the economic and financial problems of reconstruction, but it was becoming increasingly apparent that the state banks of the country had no intention of abandoning their note issue privileges unless they were forced to do so. Even in 1863, the Washington correspondent of the *New York Times* had presciently realized that Congress must decide "whether the National currency shall take the field exclusively, or whether it will subject the country to the manifold evils growing out of competition between the latter and local currency, about the constitutionality or legality of which there is a decided and radical difference of opinion."[94]

Among those who desired a uniform national currency, and were convinced that the federal government possessed, under the Constitution, powers adequate to the attainment of that aim, there was fairly general agreement as to the method of procedure that should be adopted. As early as 1856, Secretary of the Treasury Guthrie had suggested that a tax on the notes of small and weak banks would eliminate many of the worst types of notes, and this idea became the slogan of all who were dissatisfied with monetary conditions.[95] Western opinion, if anything, was more enthusiastic over such taxation than that of any other part of the country. Senator Doolittle, of Wisconsin, suggested, early in the autumn of 1861, that small state bank notes be taxed out of existence,[96] and the Chicago banking house of Sturges and Sons supported the idea with enthusiasm.[97] Giving voice to the general sentiment, the *Chicago Tribune*, insisted that "a swingeing tax law which would at once compel [the state banks] to do business on the new basis, or to wind up, is the complement of the [national banking] plan,"[98] and Medill wrote to Chase urging him to adopt such a policy.[99]

Chase, however, needed no prompting. "I have," he replied to Medill, "recommended the tax you favor"[100] and, expressing himself in a stronger vein a few weeks earlier, he had pointed out to a correspondent that "we must have an *exclusive* national currency. The state bank currency must be driven out of existence." Indeed, more than one contemporary writer suggests that his resignation from the office of Secretary of the Treasury was due, in part at least, to his inability to persuade the administration to recommend the "swingeing tax" on state bank notes that he desired.[101]

It is not surprising, therefore, that this device was ultimately brought into use when other methods of persuasion had failed to establish a uniform national banking system throughout the country. Under Section 6 of the Internal Revenue Act passed in 1865, a tax of ten per cent was imposed "on the amount of notes of any State

Bank or State Banking Association" paid out by *any bank* after the first day of July, 1866.[102]

Such a tax was clearly prohibitive. No state bank could afford to issue any more notes and, since the tax was levied on any bank that paid out such notes across its counters, it was obvious that the existing circulation of state bank paper would have to be sent home for redemption at once. Banks that wished to issue notes, which meant all banks except a few in the larger cities, were compelled to take out national charters,[103] so that the new system grew by leaps and bounds.[104] By the end of June, 1865, as the figures in Table VIII clearly show, the number of national banks was twice as large as it had been in January, while the aggregate capital of the new institutions had increased even more rapidly. When the end of the year arrived, there were few state-chartered banks still in existence, and the number of national banks was as great as the number of all banks in the United States before the Civil War,[105] a development that is even more striking when we remember that in 1865 there

TABLE VIII

GROWTH OF THE NATIONAL BANKING SYSTEM

1863–1866

Date	No. of Banks Chartered	Capital ($ millions)	Circulation ($ millions)
Oct. 1, 1863	94	7.2	....
Jan. 1, 1864	137	14.5	....
Apr. 1, 1864	357	42.2	12.1
July 1, 1864	469	75.2	25.8
Oct. 1, 1864	524	89.3	51.4
Jan. 1, 1865	681	143.6	76.3
Apr. 1, 1865	973	225.2	111.6
July 1, 1865	1,378	341.0	147.0
Oct. 1, 1865	1,578	399.3	194.2
Jan. 1, 1866	1,626	407.5	240.1
Apr. 1, 1866	1,644	409.4	264.2

were, as yet, very few national banks in the southern states.

This sudden success of the attempt to abolish state bank notes was not entirely a matter for rejoicing from the viewpoint of the Comptroller of the Currency, since it enlarged the administrative problems with which he had to deal. Under the National Banking Acts of 1863 and 1864, the maximum issue of the new currency had been fixed at $300,000,000, and it was provided that this amount should be apportioned among the several states on the basis of their relative population and banking resources. As long as there were few national banks, and their issue of notes was unimportant, the apportionment presented none but theoretical problems,[106] but as the aggregate issue approached the maximum, these matters attained considerable practical significance. It was by no means easy to reduce the aggregate amount of the note circulation that had already been allotted to a particular state, as was discovered when the Comptroller attempted to make provision for the southern states and the territories.[107] New banks were sometimes unable to obtain the right to issue notes, unless they paid a substantial premium to older institutions to induce the latter to contract their outstanding circulation and consent to a reduction of their currency privileges. Even though the maximum amount was raised to $354,000,000, the problems of apportionment remained a fruitful source of friction for more than a decade, and the only satisfactory solution that could ultimately be found was the abolition of the legal maximum issue. That matter, however, belongs to a later page of history.

Equally acute problems were encountered in the effort to set up a satisfactory mechanism for the redemption of national bank notes. In June, 1864, the Comptroller had requested each national bank to designate its redemption agent under the terms of the newly enacted legislation,[108] and the request was promptly complied with. By the middle of the following year, the banks of New York, Boston and Philadelphia were attempting to work out a plan as prompt in its operation as the old Suffolk System had been in New England. "Under the arrangement the bills of all National Banks becoming parties thereto will be received at par by a redeeming bank in each of these cities, and forwarded by the bank receiving the same to their particular specified point of redemption, and from thence to the banks from which they were first issued."[109]

Unfortunately, the plan did not commend itself to many of the country banks, since it would have forced them to maintain adequate balances in one or other of the redemption centers.[110] Moreover, outside of New England, most bankers still felt that the presentation of bank notes for redemption should be discouraged rather than facilitated; they had no interest in a scheme that was deliberately intended to reduce to a minimum the quantity of notes actually in circulation. By October, the discussion of the plan had advanced no further, and it was suggested, as an alternative, that a Bank of Redemption should be incorporated at New York for the purpose of redeeming all national bank notes in a fashion similar to that in which the old Suffolk Bank of Boston had operated.[111] While this change of method would not meet the objection of country bankers to any plan for prompt redemption, it was hoped that, by reducing the cost of the service, it might mitigate their hostility. Nothing came of the idea, however, and for the time being, the eastern bankers could achieve no more than the clumsy and imperfect redemption mechanism laid down by the act itself.[112]

Obviously, the national banking system, at the end of 1865, was far from perfect, and there were many contemporary observers who recognized its defects. But the effort to develop a uniform bank-note currency had apparently succeeded. National bank notes circulated throughout the length and breadth of the country and, in 1866, when some bank-note forms were stolen from the Treasury building in Washington, and crudely filled out with signatures that bore no resemblance at all to those of any officials of the bank whose name they bore, it was found that nobody had refused to accept them.[113] Details regarding the individual bank had ceased to be important, since the notes circulated on the credit of the federal government by whom their ultimate payment was guaranteed.

Today, in the clear light of retrospect, the achievements of the monetary reformers may not seem to justify the satisfaction experienced by people like Chase and Medill at the end of 1865. Forty years afterward, the monetary system of the United States was again under indictment, while even more serious charges were hurled at it during the years following the World War. It is worth remembering, therefore, that the ideals of the reformers were missed, not because of any lack of zeal, but because of imperfect understanding of the problem. Like the currency reformers in England twenty years earlier, they had adopted a definition of money that was out of touch with the economic realities of the period. Although there were many contemporary indications of the growing monetary significance of bank deposits,[114] such deposits were ignored in the currency legislation, and this oversight was destined to prevent the attainment of the uniform monetary system that had been envisaged. For the moment, however, this defect was not apparent to either the bankers or the legislature.

As to the part played by the national banks in financing the Civil War, there is little to be said. This argument had been used as a means of obtaining support for the plan from powerful groups who showed little interest in currency reform but, despite the rather labored encomiums of Jay Cooke,[115] the contribution of the banks was insignificant. At the time of Lee's surrender, the bonds bought by all the national banks in the country amounted to less than four per cent of the aggregate amount of securities sold by the government during the war.[116]

REFERENCES FOR CHAPTER IX

[1] *Hunt's*, XLVI, 128.
[2] *National Intelligencer*, February 4, 1863; Davis: *The Origin of the National Banking System*, p. 13.
[3] See below p. 320.
[4] *History of Banking*, I, 461.
[5] See below pp. 298-300.
[6] *Hunt's*, LI, 2.
[7] Cf. *Hunt's*, XLVII, 157-174 and 224-294, for details of the increased taxation.
[8] Knox: *op. cit.*, p. 134.
[9] *Hunt's*, XLV, 330-331; Knox: *op. cit.*, p. 135.

[10] *Hunt's,* XLV, 331.

[11] *History of Banking,* I, 459.

[12] *Hunt's,* L, 10.

[13] *Ibid.,* XLVI, 102.

[14] John J. Knox, *Hunt's,* XLVIII, 32.

[15] Quoted by Davis: *op. cit.,* p. 31.

[16] *Idem,* p. 43.

[17] *Hunt's,* XLII, 684-697; XLIII, 574-583; XLVI, 128; LI, 30.

[18] *Ibid.,* XL, 19-37.

[19] *Idem,* 22.

[20] *Hunt's,* XLVI, 114; XLII, 575-585, where the idea of a 100 per cent specie reserve is advocated.

[21] *Bankers Magazine,* XI, 417 ff. and 589 ff.; *Historical Magazine,* IX, 253 ff.; Davis: *op. cit.,* pp. 9-10.

[22] *Hunt's,* XLVI, 113-128.

[23] Cf. Davis: *op. cit.,* pp. 45-48 for the text of Potter's Plan.

[24] *Bankers Magazine,* XX, 769.

[25] Knox: *op. cit.,* p. 238.

[26] Cf. Chase to C. A. Hecksher, Davis: *op. cit.,* p. 99.

[27] For the text of this bill see Davis: *op. cit.,* 113-153. It should be pointed out that considerable controversy has developed regarding the authorship of this bill, but in the light of the widespread public discussion it is only natural that ideas from many different minds should have been incorporated in it. All the claimants are probably entitled to some part of the honor of authorship. Cf. Davis: *op. cit.,* pp. 56-62.

[28] *Chicago Tribune,* February 13, 1863. The *New York Times* of February 16, 1863, gives a similar explanation.

[29] *Hunt's,* XLVI, 477-479.

[30] Knox: *op. cit.,* p. 133.

[31] Cf. Davis: *op. cit.,* pp. 67-68.

[32] *New York Journal of Commerce,* January 12, 1863.

[33] Davis: *op. cit.,* pp. 71, 75 and 78.

[34] *Idem,* p. 72.

[35] *Idem,* pp. 79-82.

[36] Knox: *op. cit.,* pp. 240-241.

[37] Cf. Davis: *op. cit.,* pp. 155-197 for text.

[38] *Section 20.*

[39] *Section 11.*

[40] Cf. Davis: *op. cit.,* pp. 83-85 and 199-202. Hepburn (*History of Currency in the U. S.,* revised edition, p. 308) appears to be in error in his treatment of this point.

[41] *Hunt's*, XLIX, 57-60.

[42] *Idem*, 139, where a complete list is given.

[43] Cf. Kane: *The Romance and Tragedy of Banking*, I, 19.

[44] *Hunt's*, L, 80.

[45] *Idem*, 220.

[46] *Ibid.*, LI, 136-137.

[47] *Idem*, 137.

[48] *Idem*, 88.

[49] Davis: *op. cit.*, p. 95.

[50] *Idem*, p. 96.

[51] *Hunt's*, L, 308-309.

[52] Cf. Knox: *op. cit.*, p. 241.

[53] *Chicago Tribune*, February 24 and March 21, 1863.

[54] Davis: *op. cit.*, pp. 50-51.

[55] *New York Times*, January 28 and 31 and February 2, 1863.

[56] *Hunt's*, XLVI, 120-123.

[57] *Ibid.*, XLIX, 389.

[58] *Ibid.*, L, 8 and 14.

[59] *Idem*, 308; Davis: *op. cit.*, 95-96.

[60] *Hunt's*, XLIX, 290-296 and 316.

[61] *Ibid.*, LI, 248; *Bankers Magazine*, XX, 771-772.

[62] *Hunt's*, L, 221; also pp. 12-13, 220 and 307.

[63] *Ibid.*, XLIX, 402.

[64] *Ibid.*, L, 220.

[65] *Ibid.*, XLVI, 113-118, particularly p. 115.

[66] Cf. *Bankers Magazine*, XVII, 838.

[67] *Cincinnati Gazette*, November 15, 1864; *Hunt's*, L, 310; LI, 136 and 454-455; Kane: *op. cit.*, I, 44.

[68] *Hunt's*, LII, 157.

[69] *Ibid.*, LI, 17-20 and 177.

[70] Cf. *Hunt's*, L, 128.

[71] *History of Banking*, I, 459.

[72] Cf. Oberholtzer: *op. cit.*, I, 105 ff.

[73] Cf. *Hunt's*, LII, 55; LIV, 78.

[74] Cf. *Ibid.*, LIII, 54 for an interesting example of this.

[75] *Hunt's*, LI, 377; see also *Chicago Tribune*, January 30, 1863.

[76] Cf. *Hunt's*, XLVII, 512-521.

[77] Cf. *Hunt's*, LIII, 119-125 for a complete tabulation of daily quotations throughout the war period.

[78] *Hunt's*, LIII, 232-233.

[79] *Ibid.*, LIII, 465; also L, 317-318 and 359-360; LI, 95-95; LII, 29.

[80] *Ibid.*, LI, 242, 244 *et seriatim*.

[81] *Idem,* 35; LII, 114.

[82] *Ibid.,* LII, 114.

[83] *Ibid.,* LI, 289 and 370; LII, 287; LIII, 233. For detailed statistics showing the influence of Treasury operations on the market, see *Hunt's,* L, 297; LIV, 95-98 and 135-137.

[84] Cf. Kane: *op. cit.,* pp. 29-31, for salient points of this circular.

[85] Section 62; Conant: *Modern Banks of Issue,* p. 411 ff.

[86] *Hunt's,* XLIX, 403.

[87] *Idem,* 402; *Bankers Magazine,* XVIII, 448.

[88] *Hunt's,* L, 219-220; LII, 212-213.

[89] *Ibid.,* LII, 309.

[90] *Ibid.,* LI, 65-86 and 87.

[91] *Ibid.,* LII, 452-453 and 153-158.

[92] *Idem,* 55; also LI, 296-297.

[93] *Ibid.,* LI, 334.

[94] *New York Times,* February 2, 1863.

[95] Cf. *Hunt's,* XLVI, 428; L, 15; LII, 31.

[96] Davis: *op. cit.,* p. 49.

[97] *Idem,* 63-64.

[98] *Chicago Tribune,* February 7, 1863. See also February 4, 1863.

[99] Davis: *op. cit.,* p. 65.

[100] *Idem,* 98.

[101] Cf. *Hunt's,* LI, 247.

[102] Cf. *Ibid.,* LII, 385-386.

[103] Cf. *Ibid.,* LIII, 141.

[104] *Idem,* 56-57, 146, 315 and 466; LIV, 315.

[105] *Ibid.,* LIV, 315.

[106] *Ibid.,* LIII, 57-58; LIV, 223-224, where official statistics of the distribution were given.

[107] *Ibid.,* 368-372 and 396-398.

[108] *Ibid.,* LI, 91.

[109] *Ibid.,* LIII, 56.

[110] *Idem,* 141-142.

[111] *Idem,* 311-312.

[112] *Idem,* 324-326.

[113] Knox: *op. cit.,* pp. 102-103.

[114] Cf. *Hunt's,* L, 11; LI, 31-33; LIV, 63.

[115] Cf. Davis: *op. cit.,* 105.

[116] Beckhart: *Annals,* January, 1922, p. 7.

CHAPTER X

NATIONAL BANKING COMES TO CHICAGO

1862–1868

CHICAGO, at the outbreak of the Civil War, had no incorporated commercial banks in operation, and the Merchants Savings, Loan and Trust Company, together with the newly opened agency of the Bank of Montreal, offered the only substantial sources of funds available for the accommodation of business. Even the second Bank of the State of Illinois, which had been an unconscionable time a-dying, was finally wound up in the autumn of 1862.[1]

There was, however, a galaxy of private banking houses, as the list given in Appendix III clearly indicates, and it might appear on first glance that a total of eighty-six banking offices was adequate to meet all the needs of a city embracing little more than one hundred thousand people. But any conclusion based on simple arithmetic must necessarily be misleading, since the firms included in the list differed from one another in every conceivable respect. In size, they ranged from large establishments, such as those of Burch, Scammon or Sturges, down to individual concerns with little or no capital; in the scale of their operations, some were limited by the fact that the firm was unknown a mile from its office while others had established connections all over the United States and even in foreign countries.² As to the nature of their activities, the absence of adequate records makes it impossible to establish precise classifications but, on the basis of newspaper articles and advertisements, a reasonably accurate picture of the services that they offered to business can be obtained.

Out of the eighty-six houses listed, thirty attempted to carry on a general banking business, being limited in their operations only by the extent of the resources under their control. Twenty confined themselves largely to the business of dealing in uncurrent notes and other forms of money brokerage, sometimes combining this activity with that of acting as an agent of potential borrowers in the negotiation of loans. Eight houses were concerned primarily with domestic (and occasionally foreign) exchange transactions, while seven were specializing as bill brokers and foreshadowing the later development of the commercial-paper houses in their efforts to sell to capitalists the promissory notes of business houses that wished to borrow amounts in excess of those obtainable from local sources. In addition, there were twenty-six houses that operated chiefly as real-estate brokers and financiers, obtaining their funds from eastern savings banks or individual capitalists and lending exclusively upon the security of real-estate mortgages.³

Each of these fields of financial activity has already been encountered in the earlier development of the Chicago money market, but it is necessary to call attention to a significant innovation. In 1861, three private banking houses* advertised themselves as stock brokers or

* Cyrus B. Cobb; Ketchum, Son & Co., and F. G. Saltonstall.

dealers in securities, and the tireless activity of Jay Cooke and his agents in the sale of government war bonds was destined to lead to a rapid expansion in the investment-banking business of Chicago.[4] Houses such as Boyd's, Dakin and Harris, Ruxton and Company, and even Scammon, all entered eagerly into the profitable business of selling government bonds but, within a very short space of time, Preston, Willard and Kean became the outstanding bond house in the city.[5] This position the firm was destined to hold until the end of the decade.

Chicago already possessed, in embryo, practically all the diverse types of financial institution that make up a modern money market, but the embryos were often small and unsatisfactory, while there was no coordination whatever among the several financial houses. Moreover, the private bankers, being legally forbidden to issue any form of circulating notes, could do nothing to fill the monetary vacuum resulting from the collapse of the free-banking system. As state bank-note issues expanded under the inflationary pressure of wartime fiscal policy, the issues of banks in other states poured into Illinois. "There is not less than twenty millions of this heterogeneous trash circulating in our State—hated and despised by everybody, but shoved on the community by Eastern bankers because they can shave it a half per cent,"[6] as commission, when it is presented for redemption. Even when Congress authorized the issue of fractional paper currency, to take the place of privately issued shinplasters, the distribution of it was so badly managed that Chicago banks could secure a supply only by appealing to their Senators in Washington,[7] while all of the Greenbacks that reached

Illinois were either hoarded, under the influence of Gresham's Law, or else shipped to the east in payment of debts due at seaboard cities. It is no wonder that the *Tribune* wrathfully described the currency in circulation as "poor, mean, unsafe, inconvenient and tormenting," and roundly demanded the elimination of the "notes of the shin-plaster shops called local banks."[8]

Nor is it surprising that Chicago, and all Illinois, should have been wildly enthusiastic about the legislation providing for the creation of national banks. Even though the votes of the Illinois delegation in the House of Representatives had been cast on the basis of party affiliations,[9] the bankers and businessmen unanimously reiterated the sentiments that had been expressed two years earlier.[10] Although the defects of the original National Currency Act were recognized as clearly in Chicago as they were in New York, every merchant felt that the most imperfect national banks would be an improvement on the existing situation. Despite their defects, such national banks would augment the available supply of capital funds, and issue a currency more nearly uniform than anything that Illinois had previously experienced.[11]

Out of the first twenty-six national banking charters granted by the Comptroller, two were awarded to Illinois institutions,[12] while, by the end of 1863, seven First National Banks were operating in various parts of the state. Of these the most important, by far, was the First National Bank of Chicago, which received one of the earliest group of charters issued from the Comptroller's office and, by opening its doors for business on July 1,

1863, achieved the distinction of being the second national bank in the country to commence operations.*

Although the firm of Aiken and Norton was neither among the oldest, nor the more important, of Chicago banking houses, it is amply evident that Edmund Aiken, the sole survivor of the original partnership, was one of the most farsighted financiers in Chicago during the early sixties. Even while the original National Currency Act was still being debated in Congress, Aiken was bringing into his offices, at the old Board of Trade building, a small group of merchants and capitalists who were eagerly interested in the idea of establishing a national bank in Chicago. By May 1, 1863, the aims of this group had so far crystallized that they were able to draw up the Articles of Association of the proposed bank and forward to the Comptroller an application for a charter.†

In that original application are set forth the names of the sponsoring group that Aiken had gathered round him, and these men undertook to subscribe the initial capital of $100,000. Like the earlier list of the sponsors of the Merchants Loan and Trust Company,[13] these names, recorded in the copperplate handwriting of the unknown scribe who kept the records of the group, include several of the financial leaders of the city. The list, which follows, is worth recording:

* Since the First National Bank of Davenport, which opened its doors on June 29, 1863, is no longer in existence, the First National Bank of Chicago can claim to have been in operation longer than any other national bank in the United States.

† Much of the material in this and subsequent chapters is taken from the Minute Books of the First National and other Chicago banks, from the Minute Books and Records of the Chicago Clearing House Association and from other unpublished records.

Edmund Aiken........................ 175 shares
Samuel M. Nickerson................. 100 shares
Byron Rice.......................... 50 shares
Samuel W. Allerton.................. 100 shares
Benjamin P. Hutchinson.............. 175 shares
John B. Sherman..................... 100 shares
Tracy J. Bronson.................... 100 shares
John C. Fargo....................... 50 shares
George N. Kennedy*.................. 50 shares
Samuel G. D. Howard................. 100 shares

On May 7, while still waiting for a reply from the Comptroller of the Currency regarding their application for a charter, the shareholders met for the purpose of completing the formal organization of the Bank. All the original shareholders, with the exception of Kennedy, were elected as directors and, in that capacity, they immediately elected Aiken to the Presidency of the Bank. Fargo, who was elected Vice-President at this meeting, sold his stock shortly afterward and was replaced by Nickerson, while Edward E. Braisted, an employee of the Merchants Savings, Loan and Trust Company, was persuaded to accept the office of Cashier. Parenthetically, it may be suggested that the salaries of the officers were by no means generous, even for that period, since Aiken received no more than $2,000 a year for his services as President, while Braisted's salary was initially fixed at $1,500.

By May 27, Aiken was able to inform the Comptroller that the requisite initial deposit of thirty per cent had been paid on the capital stock, and the letter was a modest understatement of the facts. Contrary to one of the most deep-seated traditions of western banking, the capital was fully paid in by June 1, a whole month before the

---

* Kennedy, who was a resident of Syracuse, N. Y., was the only subscriber outside of Chicago.

Bank was to commence operations. On June 22, the institution was authorized to begin business, receiving Charter Number 8 from the Comptroller's office, and on July 1 it opened its doors to the public in the offices previously occupied by Aiken and Norton.

Chicago welcomed the First National Bank with open arms.[14] Both the press and the mercantile community were enthusiastic about the project, and strong in their approval of the men under whose direction it had been launched. The *Tribune* congratulated the stockholders on their selection for the Presidency of a man "who so thoroughly understands the business of the city," while Aiken's reputation among bankers in other parts of the country was attested, shortly afterward, by his election as Vice-President of an "association of bankers" formed at New York in 1864.[15]

The testimony of figures offers additional proof of the popularity of the new Bank. Even before it opened for business, the directors decided to increase the capital to $250,000. On November 11, a further increase to $300,-000 was agreed upon, and three months later this figure was again raised to $400,000. In March, 1864, the capital was increased to $500,000, in May to $600,000 and in November to $750,000 while, at the annual meeting on January 2, 1865, the shareholders decided to raise the capital of the Bank to $1,000,000—the maximum allowed under the original charter.[16] Moreover, the record of dividend payments shows that the directors were in no way overoptimistic in their estimates of the amount of capital that the Bank could use with profit. On May 2, 1864, before the first full year of operation had been completed, a dividend of 16 per cent, free of federal taxes, was declared on all stock, while the three thousand shares comprising the first $300,000 of capital stock received an additional bonus of 5 per cent derived from profits on the bond account. In November, another dividend of 10 per cent was declared, and semiannual dividends of this amount were paid during 1865 and 1866. Not until 1867, when the growth of banking competition and the problems of postwar reconstruction had seriously diminished banking profits in all parts of the country, was it necessary to reduce the annual dividend to a mere 10 per cent, nor was a single dividend date passed until the summer of 1869, when substantial losses from bad debts made it advisable to use the available profits to augment the surplus of the Bank.

Three months after it opened its doors, the First National Bank had on its books $273,000 of deposits owing to customers: by the beginning of 1865, this figure had risen to $1,290,804 and, when 1868 drew to a close, the deposits were in excess of $2,600,000. Moreover, although the Bank had qualified as a United States depository by the end of 1863, the increase in its business was not due to the receipt of public moneys. In January, 1866, the government deposits stood at $198,000 and they never again reached that figure during the sixties. Bankers' deposits, on the other hand, rose from $282,000, in 1866, to more than $900,000 in 1869. Ten days after its doors were opened for business, the Bank had sent out to other financial institutions the letter reproduced facing p. 346, inviting them to designate it as their Chicago correspondent. The rapid increase in bankers' balances is an indication of the response. Even before the end of 1864, the First National Bank was carrying the accounts of forty-one national banks and six state or private institutions, while it, in turn, had opened accounts with five banking houses in New York, two in Boston and one in Philadelphia.

Aggregate loans and discounts, exclusive of bond investments, rose from less than $150,000 in October, 1863, to $2,159,000 in January, 1869, another demonstration of the fact that the new institution, from the moment of its foundation, was engaged primarily in commercial-banking operations of the kind that McCulloch was trying so hard to develop throughout the national banking system.

In regard to note issue, the peculiar conditions that existed in Chicago created an insatiable demand. The First National Bank, during the initial period of existence, could have circulated as many notes as it was willing, and able, to issue. The supply of Greenbacks was far from adequate to meet the city's demand for currency of wide acceptability and stable value.[17] Even before the Bank opened for business, the directors had purchased $100,000 of bonds and deposited them with the Treasurer of the United States as collateral security for note issue; in September, they decided, in view of the popular demand for currency, to purchase another $100,000 of bonds and double the amount of notes for which they had originally applied. Owing to the delays in printing and engraving, the notes did not reach Chicago until the early part of 1864, but the enthusiasm of the popular reception accorded to them contrasts markedly with the acid com-

First National Bank of Chicago
No 32 Lasalle St
Chicago July 15 / 63

Sir:—

This Bank organized under the Act of Congress entitled " An Act to provide a National Currency, secured by a pledge of United States stocks, and to provide for the circulation and redemption thereof, approved July 25th 1863 " — with a Capital of $ 250,000. and authority to increase it to $ 1,000,000., has deposited its bonds and is now open for the transaction of a general banking, exchange and collection business.

It will be a desirable correspondent for Banks and Bankers in the East and West in all branches of banking and collection business.

Bankers' accounts will be allowed interest on special agreement.

Prompt attention given to all business entrusted to its Care.

Signatures   E. Aiken Prest
              E. E. Braisted Cr

LETTER OF THE FIRST NATIONAL BANK OF
CHICAGO TO CORRESPONDENT BANKS, 1863

ments of the New York press.[18] "The National currency is beautiful in all respects, and as good as it is beautiful," cries the *Tribune,* unconsciously demonstrating the extent to which economic factors may influence even the aesthetic sense. "Our people, we presume, will, in a very few days each have one or more of these bills in their pockets. They will be good to put under one's pillow and go to sleep on. No danger of these bills being worthless till the whole nation becomes bankrupt."[19]

Encouraged by such warm approval, the directors of the First National immediately decided to increase their note issue to $400,000 and, when that figure was reached toward the end of 1864, a further increase to $600,000 was promptly agreed upon. By September, 1865, this amount was all in circulation, and there can be no doubt that the Bank would gladly have applied for another substantial increase in its authorized issue. But, when the capital was raised to $1,000,000 in January of that year, the Comptroller had pointed out that, in view of the maximum limit imposed on the total circulation of all bank notes, under the National Banking Act, the increased capital would not qualify the Bank for any expansion of its note circulation. Six hundred thousand dollars was to be the maximum figure. Indeed, a few years later, the question of reducing the authorized circulation of the First National by $100,000 was seriously suggested by the Comptroller as a part of the general problem of redistributing the national bank-note circulation among the states in a more satisfactory manner.[20]

In view of the phenomenal expansion of its business, the Bank soon outgrew the accommodation offered by the quarters of Aiken and Norton, so that it moved, at the beginning of 1864, to the offices previously occupied by Rutter, Endicott and Company.[21] By 1867, however, the directors began to consider the erection of a new building that would more adequately meet their needs and, in March, they purchased a plot of ground at the southwest corner of State and Washington streets. One-quarter of the price was paid in cash, the remainder being due in three equal annual installments, with interest at 7 per cent per annum. Apparently the purchase of land on this plan, first popularized by the Canal Commissioners, had become a standard practice in Chicago.

The building of these new premises may be said to mark the end of the pioneer stage of its existence, during which the First National had demonstrated to Chicago the soundness of the new banking system, particularly in view of the fact that the change was made under new management. In 1866, Braisted had resigned, in order to accept an appointment in the south, and his successor had stayed with the Bank only two years before surrendering his office to Lyman J. Gage, who was persuaded to leave the Merchants Loan and Trust Company in order to join the official family of the First National. A year earlier, in January, 1867, the Presidency of the institution had been rendered vacant by Aiken's death, and the whole community mourned the loss of an outstanding gentleman as much as the Bank sorrowed at the removal of an able and courageous leader.[22] Samuel M. Nickerson was elected by the directors to fill the empty room, and he, together with Gage, was destined to direct the for-

tunes of the institution during more than two decades of
rapid growth.

The First National, although it had been the pioneer,
did not enjoy for long the distinction of being the only
national bank in Chicago. When we remember the inadequate banking facilities of the city at the time when
the National Currency Act was passed, it is apparent that
there was ample scope for several incorporated banks,
and the success of the pioneer institution encouraged
others to follow its example. Moreover, if further evidence were needed of the prestige of the new banking
system, there was the fact that John Dunham, who had
been the President of the Merchants Loan and Trust
Company, accepted from McCulloch an appointment as
National Bank Examiner for the State of Illinois.[23]

Within a month of the opening of the First National
Bank, there were rumors that a group of merchants were
planning to establish another bank with a capital of $1,-
000,000, and the *Tribune* hoped that "the project will
prove a triumphant success. No city upon the continent
has more need of such a bank, or would furnish it a larger and more profitable business."[24] Progress was apparently slow, however, although the various groups of sponsors continued their preliminary discussions and the
newspapers continued to encourage them to greater and
prompter activity.[25] By December, readers of the *Tribune*
were impatient. "The banking capital here is entirely
inadequate to the wants of our business men," a correspondent insists. "The want of Bank facilities seriously
interferes with business here during the close of navigation, particularly with the pork packing business . . .

and unless we have more banking capital, it must affect that and other important branches of business."[26]

Before the end of the year, a Second, Third and Fourth National Bank had been projected,[27] and all these were open for business by the end of March, 1864. None of the new banks, however, started with the million dollars of paid-up capital which the newspapers had optimistically anticipated each time they heard rumors of a new institution. By the end of April, 1864, a Fifth National Bank had come into existence,[28] and three other national banks were operating in Chicago before the end of December. The aggregate banking capital of the city at the end of 1864 was twice as large as it had been at the beginning of the year, and three times as large as that in use at the beginning of 1862.

The process of expansion did not, however, stop with the end of 1864. In January of the following year came the Union National Bank and the Merchants National Bank,[29] followed in February by the City National Bank and the Commercial National Bank.[30] The Traders National Bank came into existence later in the spring. Of all these the Union National Bank, under the enterprising guidance of William F. Coolbaugh, was destined to be the most important. By the middle of 1866, it was already the leading bank in Chicago, with deposits in excess of those of the First National, and the fact that these deposits represented to an unusually large extent the balances of correspondent banks offers adequate testimony to the reputation of the Union National throughout the country. Moreover, the payment of dividends amounting

TABLE IX

EARLY GROWTH OF NATIONAL BANKS IN CHICAGO

1863–1865

Year Established	Name of Bank	Initial Paid in Capital	Private Banking House from Which It Originated	First President	First Cashier
1863	First National	$100,000	Aiken & Norton	Edmund Aiken	E. E. Braisted
1864	Second National	100,000	E. I. Tinkham & Co.	J. A. Ellis	E. I. Tinkham
	Third National	120,000	....	J. H. Bowen	Ira Holmes
	Fourth National	100,000	....	Benjamin Lombard	H. R. Symonds
	Fifth National	100,000	....	Josiah Lombard	Isaac Lombard
	Northwestern National	500,000	Solomon Sturges & Sons	Buckingham Sturges	George Sturges
	Mechanics National	250,000	J. Young Scammon	J. Y. Scammon	C. F. W. Junge
	Manufacturers National	225,000	....	W. H. Brown	D. J. Lake
1865	Merchants National	450,000	....	Chauncey Blair	H. B. Symonds
	Union National	500,000	W. F. Coolbaugh & Co.	William F. Coolbaugh	C. J. Connell
	City National	250,000	....	Asa D. Reed	J. P. Taylor
	Commercial National	200,000	....	P. R. Westfall	Charles Ennis
	Traders National	100,000	F. Granger Adams	J. O. Rutter	T. P. Tallman

to 25 per cent during its first year of operation indicates that the institution was exceptionally profitable.

Thirteen national banks, which are individually described in Table IX, were, therefore, operating in Chicago at the end of the Civil War. Their aggregate capital amounted to $5,000,000, and the deposits were approaching $30,000,000.[31] Moreover, it may not be out of place to mention the fact that the officers of these institutions were among the leading financiers of the city.

With the names of Tinkham, Scammon, Sturges and Adams we are already familiar, while J. K. Botsford (who was one of the first directors of the Merchants National) would carry us still further back, since he was among the Chicagoans who acted as witnesses to the Treaty made with the Potawatomis in 1833. Rutter, of the Traders National, had obtained his early banking training with George Smith, and Benjamin Lombard, of the Fourth, had already established his reputation as the President of the Union Insurance and Trust Company. Coolbaugh, Gage, Nickerson and Solomon Smith (the newly elected President of the Merchants Loan and Trust Company) were also men who had already acquired prestige among their fellows and were destined to enhance their reputation with the passing years.

Regarding the precise nature of the operations performed by the new national banks there is less evidence available but, in view of the fact that there appears to have been a good deal of consultation among them in order to secure uniformity of policy, it may not be unreasonable to generalize from the information that has come down to us.* Even at this early date, the banks appear to have adopted the practice of receiving special deposits at interest, blatantly suggesting that this practice "enables a person to have his money earning interest, and, at the same time, payable on demand."[32] Moreover, they also engaged in the practice of selling bonds and, strangely enough, revenue stamps, for the purpose of augmenting their earnings by the amount of commission received.[33]

Greater interest attaches to the manner in which the banks lent funds to the community, and here there is more information available. Real-estate loans were expressly omitted from the powers conferred by the National Banking Act of 1864,[34] but with this single exception, the banks were free to lend in any way they chose, so that a considerable diversity of lending operations developed at an early stage. Simplest of all were the transactions in bills of exchange, which accounted for about one-tenth of the total.† The dealer in grain, or other marketable produce, would forward shipments to the east and draw against the consignee a thirty- or sixty-day bill payable in New York. This bill would be readily discounted by the Chicago banks, usually at ten per cent, and in many cases it would be forwarded to New York and rediscounted there at six or seven per cent. This profitable type of business grew less attractive, however, as competition tended to reduce the lending rate in

* An interesting evidence of coordinated policy is the joint advertisement in the *Chicago Tribune* for February 19, 1864, advising the public that the banks will close on Washington's Birthday. More important examples are given below in regard to the discussion of the Clearing House.

† These proportions are based very largely upon the information contained in the early ledgers of the First National Bank of Chicago.

Chicago. By 1869, bills of exchange had fallen to little more than three per cent of the total portfolio, and commercial paper of the modern kind had tended to usurp their place. But bills of exchange and commercial paper, together, had risen to more than one-fifth of total loans and discounts by this time.

Approximately one-third of the portfolio in the summer of 1869 consisted of demand loans, secured by stocks and bonds as collateral, and the amount of government bonds among the collateral was of negligible importance. This figure represents the high point of security loans during the decade, the average amount being slightly more than a quarter of the total, but it is indicative of the fact that Chicago was not, at this period, far behind New York in the attention that it gave to the financing of security operations.

The remainder of the loans, averaging a little more than half of the total, consisted of "time accommodation loans" granted to local customers for the financing of business operations. Most of these appear to have been comparatively small, self-liquidating loans granted for short periods, if averages are any guide to the interpretation of the picture. During 1867, the First National Bank made 3,213 individual loans, aggregating $9,873,650; the average amount of the loan was, therefore, $3,073 and its average duration was forty days. The customary rate of interest, even in 1869, was still 10 per cent. Many of these loans appear to have been secured by warehouse receipts, and all the larger credits were passed upon either by the Board of Directors as a whole, or by a special committee appointed for that purpose.

TABLE X

STATEMENT OF CONDITION OF THE FIRST NATIONAL BANK OF CHICAGO

(In thousands of dollars)

1864–1869

	Jan. 1, 1864	Jan. 12, 1869
Liabilities		
Capital stock paid in	$300	$1,000
Surplus fund	...	200
Profit and loss	16	152
Notes in circulation	...	590
Due to individual depositors	145	3,289
Certified checks outstanding	...	61
Due to U. S. Treasurer	195	...
Due to banks and bankers	91	916
Bills payable	...	21
Total	$747	$6,229
Resources		
Loans and Discounts	242*	...
Commercial paper		583
Bills of exchange		112
Time accommodation loans		1,584
Demand loans on U. S. bonds		29
Demand loans on other securities		899
Overdue paper		68
Overdrafts	41	25
U. S. bonds to secure circulation	106	672
Other U. S. bonds	70	125
Other stocks, bonds and mortgages	...	23
Due from approved redemption agencies in N. Y.	41	871
Due from other national banks	14	35
Due from other banks and bankers	9	31
Banking house	...	286
Revenue stamps on hand	2	3
Exchanges for clearing-house and city checks	89†	228†
Specie and legal-tender notes	128	625
Miscellaneous	5	30
Total	$747	$6,229

* Ledger figures in 1864 do not permit a satisfactory subdivision of the Loans and Discounts.

† These figures include "notes of solvent banks" in 1864, and notes of other national banks in 1869.

The local success of the national banks, and the growing scope of their operations gave rise, however, to an agitation for the elimination of state bank notes that was more intense in Chicago than in any other part of the country. The first appearance of the national bank notes in the city, and the general recognition of their efficiency as a circulating currency, raised to fever heat the enthusiasm of the *Tribune* for a prohibitory tax that would eliminate "these rags of heterogeneous banks."[35] As a medium of exchange, state bank notes had proved utterly unsatisfactory and, in addition, it was apparent that the issue of national bank notes would exercise a strong inflationary effect if Greenbacks and state notes continued to circulate without any diminution in their aggregate quantity.

Nor was the press alone in its campaign for sound currency; the mercantile community was just as enthusiastic, and the bankers were inclined to go at least part of the way toward the elimination of unsound currency. Indeed, the bankers took the first step in this direction by agreeing that, after April 10, 1864, they would not accept any notes of the Union Plank Road Company of Michigan City.[36] But this process of deciding upon each issue separately was much too slow to satisfy the business community. Before the end of March, a meeting of wholesale grocers in Chicago had resolved "that the Mercantile Association be requested to take some action in relation to the miscellaneous currency now afloat"[37] and, on April 4, the members of the Board of Trade agreed that after April 15 they would accept in payment nothing but

"United States legal tender notes, and national bank notes, or their equivalent."[38]

When taking this important decision, which automatically excluded from business payments all of the state paper which did not circulate in Chicago at a parity with Greenbacks, the members of the Board of Trade had also passed a resolution calling upon the bankers of the city to aid them in their endeavor to purge the monetary system. But the bankers, many of whom held substantial amounts of state bank notes, had no wish for any such sweeping action, and no appetite for the losses it would inflict upon them. A meeting of bankers and businessmen was promptly called, but Solomon A. Smith, upholding the earlier traditions of the Merchants Loan and Trust Company, was the only one of the leading bankers who unequivocally supported the Board of Trade resolution. Coolbaugh "had not the slightest objection to it," but thought that no action should be taken until they had carefully considered the economic consequences of such a step, while Aiken felt that, in view of the inadequacy of the currency at the time, steps should be taken to make more state notes redeemable in Chicago rather than to throw them out of circulation. The meeting ended by requesting "the bankers of this city acting in concert, to name such time as they may think it expedient to establish Treasury notes as the basis of business," and to report their decision to the Board of Trade two days later.[39]

At the Board of Trade meeting on Monday, April 10, the report of the banking committee was presented. Aiken explained at length the excellence of national bank notes, and announced, amid much applause, that the national banks of Chicago had agreed to redeem at par all notes of any national bank that were presented to them in the ordinary course of business. There was not, however, any desire on the part of the bankers to exclude state currency, so that the merchants took matters into their own hands, and resolved "that on and after the fifteenth day of May next all our transactions shall be based on Treasury notes or their equivalent."[40] On the following day, the bankers supported the decision, in part at least, by issuing a circular stating that they would not pay out or receive the notes of any banks in Pennsylvania, New Jersey, Michigan, Maryland, Ohio or Indiana.[41]

At this stage the matter appeared to be settled. On April 14, the Board of Public Works announced that it would accept nothing but Greenbacks and national bank notes for water rents and other dues;[42] two weeks later, the merchants of Galesburg decided to anticipate the action of Chicago by adopting a similar resolution that was to take effect immediately.[43] But as the time for final action approached, the bankers of Chicago weakened. At a special meeting of the Board of Trade on April 22, Scammon (apparently speaking for the bankers as a group) proposed that all paper redeemable at par in Boston, New York or Chicago should be accepted, and that the date for enforcing the new rule should be postponed somewhat.[44] On neither point were the members of the Board of Trade willing to concede an inch; they reiterated their decision to throw out depreciated notes on May 15, and refused to widen the definition of acceptable currency. Boston and New York paper was at a discount in Chicago, so that the resolution was amended by striking out both towns, and defining acceptable currency as that redeemable at par in Chicago.

Thoroughly disgruntled, the bankers held a meeting of their own at the Sherman House, on May 7, with Scammon in the chair, and "there was much stormy discussion." Gage, who kept the records of the meeting, appears to have said little, but Scammon, Sturges and others severely criticized the attitude of the Board of Trade. It seemed for a while that the meeting might break up in vehement disorder. Coolbaugh rose to the occasion magnificently. He "addressed the meeting in an able manner, in which he showed the folly of the bankers attempting to stem the flood-tide of public opinion by refusing to make Legal Tender Notes the basis of all transactions. It was a matter, he said, which the bankers could not control, and if they stood in the way of the Board of Trade and the patriotic sentiments of the Northwest, they would speedily be swept out of existence."[45]

As a compromise resolution, to test the sense of the meeting, Coolbaugh then proposed "that on and after the ——— day of ———, 1864, we, the bankers of Chicago, will receive and pay out, as par funds, United States notes, National Bank notes, and such other notes as are redeemed in legal tender notes in the city of Chicago, only. Thereafter, for the present, solvent New England bank notes, and the notes of such other solvent banks as are redeemed at par in New York, shall be taken at one-quarter per cent discount; Ohio, Indiana, Iowa and New York State bank notes, and such Illinois banks as are not redeemed in Chicago at par, one-half per cent discount.

Nothing but United States notes, National Bank notes, and such other notes as are at par in Chicago, shall be paid on checks, or in the settlement of balances between banks and brokers."[46] This was a diplomatic gesture and, when the meeting unanimously endorsed it, the national banks were perfectly willing to fill in May 15 as the date on which it should go into effect. To this there was renewed objection by the private bankers: "some advocated the fifteenth of June, and it was subsequently resolved, as a compromise [sic], that it take effect on the first of July."

If the bankers hoped to beat a strategic retreat from the attack of the Board of Trade by means of this resolution, they were doomed to disappointment. The newspapers greeted the plan with elaborate and biting satire, and one hundred and thirteen leading merchants of Chicago indignantly published a manifesto in the following unequivocal terms: "We, the undersigned, members of the Board of Trade, agree, on and after the 15th inst., to base all transactions, either buying or selling, on Legal Tender Treasury Notes or their equivalent."[47] In the face of that ultimatum, the bankers capitulated. On the day on which the merchants' manifesto was published, there was inserted in the newspapers a statement, signed by officers of all the national banks and many of the private bankers of Chicago. "The undersigned banks and bankers of the city of Chicago hereby agree that on and after Monday, May 16, 1864, we will receive on deposit at par and pay out at par only Legal Tender notes, National Bank notes, and the notes of such other banks as redeem at par in the city of Chicago: It being understood that all checks dated prior to May 16th may be paid in the present currency, and all balances due between banks and bankers on Monday morning are to be settled on the same basis."[48]

In all monetary history there are few incidents more fascinating than this one. By the formal and spontaneous action of the business community, Chicago obtained a sound and uniform currency a full year before Congressional action attained a similar ideal for the country as a whole; this action was taken in the face of open hostility from a large number of the leading bankers. Few historical episodes refute more conclusively the theories that regard governments and banking system as the omnipotent dictators of monetary policy, and it is at least partially true that "the *Tribune* and the Chicago Board of Trade started the ball which, gaining strength as it rolled, finally crushed out the last remnant of illegitimate banking."[49] The city had reason to exult, since it anticipated by three years the tardy action of the state legislature in eliminating wildcat notes from circulation.[50]

This was not, however, the only significant gesture that Chicago made during those Civil War years in which it increased phenomenally in both size and importance. Although, to modern minds, there is something ironical about a patriotism that manifests itself in the spending of money to bribe other people to go and do the fighting, there can be no question that, judged by the standards of that age, the mercantile community was enthusiastically, almost fervently, patriotic in its devotion to the Union cause. At the outbreak of hostilities the Board of Trade devoutly resolved to purchase an American flag to hang in the trading room,[51] a gesture that evokes, in sad irony, the memories of civilian bellicosity in more recent days. "Hell hath no fury like a non-combatant." As the war progressed, large sums of money were raised to pay, and equip, Board of Trade Regiments, while the question of requiring all members of the Board to take an oath of fealty to the Union cause was seriously discussed.[52] When the *Chicago Times* ventured to criticize the wisdom and justice of the war, it was solemnly banned from the reading room by a full meeting of the Board, and its reporters were requested to stay away from the market rooms.[53]

Of the intensity of this patriotism, no wiser and no more foolish than that of other warring peoples in comparable circumstances, there can be no doubt. But, while it may be impious to relate such spiritual exaltation to mundane matters of business profits, it must be confessed that the war brought rich economic rewards to the faithful city. During the autumn of 1864, there was a financial flurry that forced several of the weaker financial institutions into bankruptcy and even caused embarrassment to the powerful Merchants Loan and Trust Company,[54] while the early postwar deflation during the winter of 1865-66 caused considerable unpleasantness.[55] But with these exceptions, the decade of the sixties was for Chicago a period of abundant and continuous prosperity.

As a result of the creation and expansion of national banks, the businessmen of the city were more adequately supplied with capital than at any previous period in its history, and the available supply of funds was still further augmented by the influx of frightened capital from the border states. Even more important was the fact that transportation facilities, upon which the whole economy of Chicago rested, were expanded rapidly and continuously as a result of the war. Although the transcontinental railroads may have been planned as political chains to bind the eastern and western sections of the nation together, they served as channels along which Chicago merchants could send out representatives to invade markets that were previously inaccessible.[56] Local railroad construction in southern Illinois opened up still more markets, and so acute was the realization of the importance of transportation that the fear of an extortionate railroad monopoly produced a revival of enthusiasm for the improvement of canals and navigable rivers.[57]

Moreover, while transportation was opening up new markets to Chicago, the demand for her products in older markets was expanding rapidly. War is always voracious, but to the demands of the Union armies for food there was added the increased purchases of European countries, which experienced particularly poor harvests in 1860, 1861 and 1862. In spite of various handicaps, not the least of which was the withdrawal of labor as a result of enlistment, Illinois strengthened her agricultural leadership of the northwestern states during the years from 1860 to 1870.[58] At the peak of the agricultural boom wheat was selling at three dollars and a half a bushel and flour at eighteen dollars a barrel.

Under such stimuli, the trade of Chicago flourished. In 1860, the aggregate commercial transactions of the city did not exceed $100,000,000 and the largest mercantile house reported only $600,000 of sales. By 1868, the volume of business had quadrupled, and seventy-eight houses reported sales in excess of $1,000,000. Nine houses showed more than $2,000,000 of transactions, four over $3,000,000 and the largest of all reported aggregate business amounting to $9,798,000.[59] Even when the fall in the value of money is taken into account, this growth is still amazing.

Most significant of all, however, was the steady expansion of the grain and produce business,[60] and the increasing importance of the Board of Trade. By the end of the war, the membership was more than three times as large as it had been at the peak of the boom in 1857, and the volume of transactions had increased even more sharply. The efficiency of the market had been increased to such an extent, by means of standardized grades, elevator inspection and telegraphic communications, that the influence of the operations in the Pit was felt throughout the United States and in foreign countries. Speculation was rampant and corners became more frequent, while the power of the Board is amply indicated by the fact that when, in 1867, the legislature defined short selling as an illegal gambling operation, the members calmly ignored the law and continued to sell short until it was repealed.[61]

The expansion in the importance of the grain trade was rivaled, however, by the equally rapid growth of the meat-packing industry,[62] which was already beginning to feed the peoples of many foreign countries as well as the residents of all sections of the United States. Even at this time, there were heard the early rumblings of protest against the packers' monopoly and when, in 1865, the legislature incorporated the Union Stock Yard and Transit Company with power to manage a cattle yard, a series of branch railroads, a bank and a hotel, there was a good deal of opposition.[63] Had the public realized that almost all the capital of this enterprise was subscribed by nine of the outstanding western railroads, the indignation might have been even greater. The lumber trade also, although destined to decline in the near future, expanded steadily during this period and contributed an important part to the commercial prosperity.[64]

All these activities, although expanded by the encouragement of war, had been a familiar part of the economic life of Chicago during the preceding decade, but the rapid industrialization that occurred during the sixties was an entirely new development. The industrial expansion that had swept over the United States during the fifties, through the increasing demands for foodstuffs and raw materials which it evoked, had exercised a revolutionary effect on Illinois. The state found itself in possession of much excellent land, a growing population and an inadequacy of capital funds, so that an expansion of its agricultural activities appeared to offer the greatest prospect of profit. But with the outbreak of the Civil War, and the expansion of banking resources during the sixties, the whole situation was changed. Illinois could no longer obtain with ease the manufactured goods that she needed and, having more capital than she required for agriculture, decided to engage in industrial activity. The possession of coal mines, and the proximity to good iron ore, encouraged the tendency and, early in 1863, the newspapers were advising the bankers to advance the necessary capital. "Let them invest their funds in manufacturing, in the development of our mines. . . . The West now needs manufactures more than anything else, for there is no use in sending our wool, hides and scores of other products to New England to be manufactured."[65]

Most of this industrial expansion was concentrated in Chicago and the surrounding area, where the number of factories tripled between the outbreak of war and the end of the decade. Everything, from whips and wash-boards to iron ingots and carriages, was produced in steadily increasing quantities, and the aggregate value of the industrial output increased tenfold. Taking the state as a whole, the number of manufacturing establish-ments grew from 4,268 to 12,597, and the workers em-ployed in them increased from 5,593, in 1860, to 82,979 ten years later.[66] "By the method of trial and failure the commonwealth that had in five decades risen from the wilderness ranked first among the states in its flour and gristmills and in its sirup and molasses factories, second in its manufactories of agricultural implements, and fourth in the number of establishments for the manufac-ture of carriages and wagons, of saddlery and harness, of tin, copper, and sheet iron, of cooperage, of furniture, and even of millinery." The foundation of the Pullman Palace Car Company and the growth of militant trade unionism were synchronous events in a decade of rapid change.

Although, as late as 1851, Chicagoans could find a re-minder of bygone days in the small band of Potawatomis encamped on the prairie a few miles away,[67] the city was rapidly developing into the great western metropolis of the United States. Many of the immigrants who were

moving toward the west were so entranced by its opportunities for employment that they decided to remain, and
others were drawn magnetically by the spreading rumors
of Chicago's reputation. Having barely reached a population of one hundred thousand at the time of Lincoln's
election, Chicago found herself with more than three
times that number of people when the fire broke out in
1871, and the efforts to accommodate so great an influx,
coupled with the demands of expanding industry, led
to dizzily mounting real-estate prices.[68] New construction,
expanding by leaps and bounds, was utterly unable to
keep pace with the demand for buildings.

Even in 1865, the *Tribune* had admitted bitterly that
the city still possessed too many vestigial traces of its
origin. "Everybody understands that we have the foulest
streets, the dirtiest river, the most inefficient police, the
most nauseous water, the most fogyish Board of Public
Works and Board of Health in the world, unless we look
for their equal in Turkey, China or Dahomey."[69] But
the leaven of business prosperity produced substantial
improvements. By 1859, three systems of horse-drawn
streetcar lines had been inaugurated; in 1864, a new system of waterworks was projected and, within three years,
the undertaking had been successfully completed; in
1871, the deepening of the Illinois and Michigan Canal
reversed the flow of the Chicago River and diminished
somewhat the sewer stench that had persistently hung
over the business district of the city.

Since these trends of economic activity and civic improvement continued steadily after the conclusion of the
war, there was an ever-increasing demand for financial

accommodation. The thirteen national banks in Chicago, supplemented by more than sixty others throughout the rest of the state,[70] were utterly inadequate to provide for the growing business needs of the state, so that further banking expansion was inevitable.

In Chicago, Nickerson appears to have led the movement. The Union Stock Yards Bank, which had been established by Solomon Sturges under the general corporate charter of 1865, was reorganized, in 1868, as a national bank without any note-issue privileges. Stickney, who had been connected with George Smith and Company for many years, was appointed Cashier of the reorganized institution and Nickerson, while continuing to serve as President of the First National Bank, accepted the Presidency.[71]

A year later, the National Bank of Commerce was established, with $200,000 capital,[72] followed afterward by the creation of the Corn Exchange National Bank with $250,000. Orson Smith, whose name was to be famous in the annals of Chicago banking, was appointed cashier of the latter institution.[73] In 1871, the Cook County National Bank, with a capital of $300,000, received a charter, while the well-known private banking house of Greenebaum Brothers decided to incorporate its business under the title of the German National Bank of Chicago.[74] Meanwhile, several of the older national banks, if one may apply the term "older" to institutions that had been in existence for less than a decade, had increased their capital, so that the eighteen institutions in this group were in a particularly strong position.

Such an increase in the number of financial institutions inevitably gave rise to a demand for some kind of cooperative organization. Even in the matter of clearing checks, the steady enlargement of the financial community had necessitated an informal meeting each day at the offices of the Northwestern National Bank, to facilitate the exchange of items, while it was obvious to everyone that a satisfactory solution of outstanding banking problems would only be achieved by frequent discussions among the bankers and joint action whenever those discussions reached a conclusion.

It was decided, therefore, to set up a Chicago Clearing House Association, on the model of similar organizations that already existed in Boston, New York and Philadelphia[75] and, on the evening of March 3, 1865, a group of seven men met at the Sherman House to discuss the project. It is significant that none but national banks were represented at the meeting.

Under the leadership of Scammon and Gage, the group decided to hold a slightly larger meeting, at the same place, a week later. Sixteen banks were represented on that occasion (ten national, three state and three private institutions) and, since all were unanimously in favor of the scheme, it was decided to proceed with the formal organization. Coolbaugh was elected President of the Association, and Josiah Lombard Vice-President, while a Clearing House Committee was selected with Braisted, Tinkerham, Holmes, De Koven and A. C. Badger as its members.[76]

Within a few days, rooms had been hired "at Mr. Scammon's building," and Gage was appointed as manager of the Clearing House. On April 6, the first clearings occurred.[77] But Gage was too valuable a man for the Merchants Loan and Trust Company to lose so easily, and they persuaded him to return to his old position as Cashier. Nothing could more clearly indicate the regard in which he was held than this decision of his old bank, unless it be the fact that the Clearing House Association, which reluctantly awarded a salary of $2,000 a year to his successor, had unanimously voted $3,000 when it was expected that Gage would act as manager.[78]

Of the nineteen banks that were members of the Clearing House at its inception, none but the First National is still in existence as a separate financial institution. At that time, however, the list comprised the outstanding banks of Chicago, and there was every intention of restricting membership in the Association to such institutions. As early as May, 1865, two applications for membership were refused, and none were acted upon favorably until the autumn of 1866, when four of the larger private banks and one state institution were admitted to membership.*

Although settlements between banks were originally made "in lawful money," arrangements were soon made for a more convenient procedure. By the end of May, 1865, the Association was issuing Clearing House Certificates, in denominations of one thousand dollars, to members who deposited government bonds or currency of an equal amount, and the majority of settlements were made in terms of certificates by the middle of June. Indeed, so worried was the Clearing House Committee

---

* An exception to this statement should be made in the case of the Chicago Agency of the Bank of Montreal, which became a member in May, 1865, but resigned in 1867 when the Agency was abolished.

about the valuable collateral deposited by the banks, that it asked the Association to relieve its members from personal responsibility and proposed a resolution that "the Committee shall procure a suitable iron or tin box, with the name of the Association printed upon it to contain securities deposited as collateral to Clearing House Certificates, said box to be well and securely locked and left as a special deposit with the United States Land and Trust Company in their vault and safe."

Apparently the first general problem attacked by the Association was that of the hours of bank operation. Under the stimulus of competition, there was a growing tendency to open banking offices earlier, and close them later, than had been customary during previous years— a tendency that became serious when the First National and the Union National, the two largest banks in the city, announced that "for the better accommodation of their customers" they would be open for business from nine until four."[79] On the eighth of June, after much discussion, the Clearing House adopted a rule that, "on and after July 1st, the banking hours of the different members of this association shall be from 10 a.m. to 3 p.m.," and there was no question about the intention to enforce the practice. When the Third National Bank was found to be operating for a longer period than the rule allowed, it was immediately suspended from membership in the Clearing House, and was not readmitted until August, 1866, when it agreed to adopt the common practice.

By that time, matters of greater importance were engaging the attention of the banks. In view of the proposed changes in the National Banking Act, the Chicago Clearing House passed a unanimous resolution opposing the suggested requirement that all national bank notes be redeemed in New York. Moreover, recognizing the futility of isolated action, on June 29, 1866, it was resolved "that this Association respectfully invite representatives of the National Banks of Ohio, Indiana, Michigan, Illinois, Iowa, Missouri, Kansas, Wisconsin, Minnesota and the Northwestern Territories to meet in convention in this city on the twelfth day of September next for consultation with reference to such measures as may be deemed proper for the protection of their interests." Out of that action, encouraged perhaps by the five hundred dollars appropriated for the entertainment of the delegates, was born the National Bankers' Association for the West, with Coolbaugh as its first president.[80]

To recite all activities that the Clearing House performed for the common good of its members would be tedious. Its enthusiasm for the prosecution of "James Buchanan Cross, a noted and skillful forger," and its arbitration of the tangled relations that developed among some of its members as the result of gold speculations are important only because they indicate the extent to which the Association was becoming the focus of all banking activity throughout the city. In a very real sense, the Chicago Clearing House had, by the end of the sixties, become the nucleus of the rapidly growing financial structure of the money market. Technically efficient, and dowered with the prestige of its distinguished membership, it contributed much to the soundness of banking operations, and as early as 1867 it had begun to insist that all members, even the private and unincorporated banks, should furnish periodical statements of financial condition as a demonstration of their solvency.* For the first time in the financial history of Chicago, there existed a community of interest among the bankers, and machinery through which those common interests could be protected and advanced.

Moreover, several opportunities presented themselves, before the Clearing House was five years old, to prove its worth in matters outside these specialized functions. Acute problems had to be solved within the national banking system as well as in regard to the competition between that system and the institutions chartered by the several states.

The failure of national banking associations had shown that unsound management could wreck a national bank just as easily as it had destroyed the earlier state institutions,[81] while the extent and bitterness of innumerable local controversies demonstrated the failure to find satisfactory solutions to the pressing problems of bank taxation and note redemption. By 1867, the discussion of the need for legislative action to settle these questions had become so widespread that John Thompson came out of retirement and confidentially offered his services to the national banks of the country as an expert lobbyist.[82]

Both of these problems were especially serious in Illinois. Although, during the early days of the national banking system Chicago opinion had strongly urged the need for note redemption at some central point, as a means of insuring par circulation for the issues of all na-

* Unfortunately, this resolution was rescinded in 1869, and not revived for several years.

tional banks,[83] a howl of indignation arose when it was suggested that New York should be the central point. The only result of such a plan, it was suggested, would be "to place all the money of the country in New York to be loaned to stock gamblers without any collateral," whereas "the National Banks of the Northwest ought to redeem in Chicago, for the immense trade of this city can probably employ in a legitimate way the deposits the banks would keep here."[84] Obviously it was special pleading, and the motivating interests are apparent in the arguments cited, but the feeling was no less intense for that reason. Although somewhat mollified by the arrangement that permitted country banks in the northwest to use Chicago as a redemption center, the people of the city were by no means convinced that the legal preeminence accorded to New York was either deserved or desirable. Nor did the fact that Chicago banks were already holding large balances, in their capacity of agent for country banks in the surrounding states, tend to diminish this feeling. They were determined to fight the financial hegemony of New York persistently and continuously. At times the dangers inherent in redeposited reserves were cited as an argument,[85] although it is hard for the impartial reader to see how these dangers would have been lessened if the funds of country bankers were deposited in Chicago.

While note redemption was a broad problem, which continued to excite controversy for half a century, taxation was local and pressing. Each of the national banks was confronted with it whenever a demand for state or local taxes was received and, although a few of them (including the First National Bank) paid the earlier assessments to avoid dispute, joint action was decided upon in the autumn of 1865. Operating through a committee of the newly established Clearing House Association, and aided by counsel, the banks decided that they were no more liable to state taxes "than the United States Mint or Post Office," in view of the fact that they were incorporated federal agencies. Moreover, as a supporting argument, it was insisted that the capital of the banks, being invested in United States bonds, was not taxable in any case.

Since Illinois laws provided for the taxation of banks on the basis of their capital, these arguments appeared unassailable, and the Clearing House Committee decided to fight the matter out in the courts (to which many national-bank stockholders had already resorted).[86] In this contention they were successful, so that the Governor immediately took steps to pass a law providing for the taxation of bank stock in the hands of its owners. During the regular session of the legislature, in 1867, the bill "was smothered in a mysterious manner," but it was finally enacted at a special session in July, and upheld by the courts in spite of the objections of the Clearing House members.[87]

Meanwhile another problem had arisen, which was destined to become more and more serious as the years passed. Although the advocates of the National Banking Act had intended to eliminate all state institutions from the commercial banking field by depriving them of the right to issue notes, the legislation of 1865 did not accomplish this purpose. For a year or two, there were no new state banks created, and many of the older institutions went into liquidation or joined the national system, but this feeling of impotence did not last. Even though they could not issue notes, state banks still had ample opportunities for profitable activity. The use of checks drawn against deposits was increasing rapidly, especially in urban communities, and there was nothing in the law to prevent state institutions from undertaking deposit banking. Savings banking and the newly developed trust business, moreover, offered profitable side lines that national banks could not undertake, and to some people there was a real advantage in the fact that state charters were often more loosely drawn, and less rigidly enforced, than those issued by the Comptroller of the Currency.

As a result of all these factors, the national banks in Chicago, like those in other parts of the country, were forced to meet serious and unexpected competition. Although the Bank of Montreal had decided to close its Chicago Agency in 1867,[88] more than a score of new banking institutions came into existence to take its place as the list of page 377 of state charters granted from 1861 to 1870 clearly shows. Even Building and Loan Associations were beginning to make their appearance as a supplement to the services offered by the older types of financial house.[89]

Such an increase of banking competition would have been unpleasant in any case, but the position of the older institutions was made more uncomfortable by the reckless willingness of the legislature to grant charters to anybody who was wealthy enough to obtain votes in the customary fashion. In 1866, "lobbyists and log-rolling forces were so active that just to meet their insistent demands would have consumed the forty-two days allotted by the constitution to the normal session. Batches of questionable private bills were forced through both houses without an adequate investigation of their contents; into one omnibus three hundred and twelve such items were bundled."[90] In the session of 1867, under similar conditions, the legislature granted charters to twenty-five banking institutions.[91] Some of these were commercial banks, others were authorized to do nothing but a savings-bank

TABLE XI

DEVELOPMENT OF STATE BANKING IN CHICAGO 1861–1870

Date of Charter	Name of Bank
1861	Merchants Association Savings Bank
	Merchants, Farmers and Mechanics Savings Bank
	Prairie State Loan and Trust Company
	Real Estate Loan and Trust Company
	State Savings Institution of the City of Chicago
1863	Marine Banking Company
1865	Producers Bank
	Treasury Bank
1867	Hibernia Banking Association Savings Bank
	Illinois Land and Loan Company
	International Mutual Trust Company
	Mutual Trust Society
	National Loan and Trust Company
1869	Central Bank of Chicago
	Chicago Banking Company
	Cook County Banking Association
	Exchange Banking Institution
	German Savings Bank
	Germania Bank
	National Banking Company
	Pacific Bank
	Scandinavian Bank
	Swedish Commercial Company Scandinavian Bank
	West Side Banking Association
1870	Commercial Loan Agency
	Fidelity Savings Bank and Safe Depository
	Merchants Savings Bank

business; some were exclusively trust companies, while a few combined fiduciary powers with other banking operations. The same process was repeated in 1869, when sixty-seven banks were created[92] and fifty-six insurance companies were added to the seventy-two which had been chartered at the preceding session.

Never in all its history had the State of Illinois had so many incorporated banks, and Chicago was in the forefront of the expansionist movement. Moreover, in the face of increasing competition, it is interesting to note that the practice of giving special services to customers was already making its appearance. The State Savings Institution advertised that it "receives deposits of FIVE CENTS and upwards from all classes of persons, includ-

TABLE XII

AVERAGE DEPOSITS DURING DECEMBER, 1867, OF THE MORE IMPORTANT PRIVATE BANKS AND STATE INSTITUTIONS OPERATING IN CHICAGO

J. M. Adsit................................... $	131,500
Boyd Brothers.................................	2,300
A. C. & O. F. Badger..........................	90,598
Cushman, Hardin & Brother.....................	146,212
C. Follansbee & Son...........................	115,999
Greenebaum & Foreman..........................	58,274
Henry Greenebaum.............................	350,273
Joseph M. Lyons & Co..........................	20,000
Lunt, Preston & Kean..........................	178,190
Merchants Association.........................	167,664
Marine Banking Company........................	267,909
Merchants Savings Loan & Trust Co.............	1,518,654
Meadowcroft Brothers..........................	99,953
Mayer, Leopold and Co.........................	59,847
Merchants, Farmers & Mechanics Savings Bank...	308,680
C. L. Niehoff & Co............................	12,822
Silverman, Lazarus & Co.......................	61,986
G. C. Smith & Brother.........................	276,840
Snydacker & Co................................	27,581
State Savings Institution.....................	1,785,273
Tyler, Ullman & Co............................	42,807
Treasury Bank.................................	118,024
Winslow & Christensen.........................	12,790

ing Minors and Married Women, and allows interest at the rate of six per cent,"[93] while one institution advertised its willingness to arrange transatlantic steamship accommodations.[94]

Finally, to complete the picture, it must be pointed out that the activities of the private bankers were not diminishing in importance. New houses were coming into existence almost as rapidly as old ones were removed from the list by incorporation under state or national charters, and the figures in the foregoing table indicate that their aggregate contribution to the resources of the Chicago money market was substantial.[95]

Amid all this expansion, however, one retrograde step must be recorded. The embryonic capital market, which had developed in Chicago during the war years, did not long survive the conclusion of hostilities. The interest of private bankers in the sale of bonds waned when the pressure of patriotic enthusiasm was removed and the Chicago Stock Exchange, which had come into existence, in 1865, amid great enthusiasm, died of inanition a few years afterward.[96]

REFERENCES FOR CHAPTER X

[1] *Bankers Magazine*, XVII, 476.
[2] *Chicago Tribune*, August 8, 1863; February 4, 1864.
[3] Cf. Andreas: *op. cit.*, II, 634, for a description of one such house.
[4] Cf. *Chicago Tribune*, July 1 and 24, 1863.
[5] *Chicago Tribune*, August 13, October 20, December 7, 1863; February 4 and 20, 1864; February 8, 1865.
[6] *Ibid.*, March 29, 1864. See also July 23, 1861; October 2, 1863.
[7] Cole: *op. cit.*, p. 363; Huston: *op. cit.*, I, 185 and 195.
[8] *Chicago Tribune*, March 24, 1863.
[9] *New York Times*, February 21, 1863.
[10] *Chicago Democrat*, June 27, 1861; Andreas: *op. cit.*, II, 337 and 348.

[11] *Chicago Tribune,* March 9, 1863; January 13, 1864; *Bankers' Magazine,* XVIII, 161-165.

[12] *Hunt's,* XLIX, 139.

[13] Cf. Harper and Ravell: *op. cit.,* pp. 31-37.

[14] *Chicago Tribune,* June 30, July 1 and 4, October 1, 1863.

[15] *Ibid.,* October 23, 1864.

[16] Cf. comments of *Chicago Tribune,* March 10, 1865; *Bankers Magazine,* XIX, 857.

[17] *Chicago Tribune,* November 24, 1863.

[18] See above pp. 316-318.

[19] *Chicago Tribune,* January 11, 1864.

[20] *Bankers Magazine,* XX, 948.

[21] *Chicago Tribune,* January 1, 1864.

[22] Cf. *Ibid.,* January 15, 1867; also *Resolutions Passed at a Special Meeting of the Chicago Clearing House Association,* January 15, 1867.

[23] Andreas: *op. cit.,* II, 627.

[24] *Chicago Tribune,* July 21, 1863; also June 25, 1863.

[25] Cf. *Ibid.,* September 23, October 14, 1863.

[26] *Ibid.,* December 8, 1863.

[27] *Ibid.,* December 8, 17 and 24, 1863; January 13, February 15 and 27, March 14 and 18, 1864.

[28] *Ibid.,* April 20, 1864; Andreas: *op. cit.,* II, 629.

[29] *Chicago Tribune,* January 8, 1865, supplemented by information obtained from the Minute Books and other records of the Union National Bank.

[30] *Chicago Tribune,* January 16, February 1 and 24, 1865.

[31] *Bankers Magazine,* XX, 187; *Hunt's,* LIII, 382; *Chicago Tribune,* April 5, 1865.

[32] *Chicago Tribune,* March 31, 1865.

[33] *Ibid.,* February 7, April 2 and 7, 1864; February 22, 1865.

[34] Cf. Kane: *op. cit.,* I, 85, for a discussion of this point.

[35] *Chicago Tribune,* December 11, 1863; January 13 and 25, February 5, March 29, April 14, 1864.

[36] *Ibid.,* March 30, 1864.

[37] *Ibid.,* March 31, 1864.

[38] *Ibid.,* April 6, 1864; Andreas: *op. cit.,* II, 354.

[39] *Chicago Tribune,* April 9, 1864.

[40] *Ibid.,* April 12 and 16, 1864; *Chicago Morning Post,* April 12, 1864; Andreas: *op. cit.,* II, 354.

[41] *Chicago Tribune,* April 13, 1864. An exception was made in the case of notes issued by the Bank of the State of Indiana and the Bank of the State of Ohio.

[42] *Ibid.,* April 14, 1864.

[43] Andreas: *op. cit.,* II, 624.

[44] *Chicago Tribune,* April 23, 1864.

[45] *Ibid.,* May 8, 1864.

[46] *Idem.*

[47] *Chicago Tribune,* May 12, 1864; Andreas: *op. cit.,* II, 355.

[48] *Chicago Tribune,* May 12 and 13, December 31, 1864.

[49] *Ibid.,* March 8, 1865.

[50] *Public Laws of Illinois,* 1867, pp. 48 and 49. Approved February 28 and March 7, 1867.

[51] Andreas: *op. cit.,* II, 336.

[52] *Idem,* 343-344.

[53] *Idem,* 347.

[54] *Idem,* 635; *Hunt's,* LI, 370; *Chicago Tribune,* September 30, October 5 and 14, 1864; *Chicago Times,* October 1, 3, 4, 8 and 14, 1864. Andreas says that the Merchants Loan and Trust Company closed its doors temporarily but the other sources, although indicating its embarrassment, do not record an actual closing.

[55] Cole: *op. cit.,* p. 384; *Hunt's,* LIII, 233; *Chicago Tribune,* March 17, 19, 24 and 29, 1865.

[56] Cole: *op. cit.,* pp. 360-361; Hoyt: *op. cit.,* p. 83; *Hunt's,* XLVII, 87-97.

[57] Andreas: *op. cit.,* II, 349 and 353; Cole: *op. cit.,* pp. 354-355, 357-359 and 384.

[58] Cole: *op. cit.,* pp. 373-374; Andreas: *op. cit.,* II, 336.

[59] *Bankers Magazine,* XXIII, 306; Hoyt, *op. cit.,* pp. 83-84.

[60] *Hunt's,* LIII, 182-195; Andreas: *op. cit.,* II, 350-365.

[61] Cf. Andreas: *op. cit.,* II, 359-361.

[62] *Hunt's,* LIII, 193-195; LIV, 376-384.

[63] Cole: *op. cit.,* p. 385.

[64] *Hunt's,* LIII, 195-196; LIV, 101-107; Masters: *Reciprocity Treaty of 1854,* p. 201.

[65] *Chicago Tribune,* June 27, 1863.

[66] Cole: *op. cit.,* pp. 364-368; Hoyt: *op. cit.,* pp. 84-85; *Hunt's,* LIII, 364-366.

[67] Cole: *op. cit.,* p. 436.

[68] Hoyt: *op. cit.,* pp. 78-79. See also *Chicago Tribune,* October 8, 1863, when the trend was already apparent.

[69] *Chicago Tribune,* July 4, 1864; January 10, August 28, 1867; Cole: *op. cit.,* p. 350.

[70] Cf. *Bankers Magazine,* XXI, 523 for details.

[71] *Chicago Tribune,* February 20, March 1, April 7, 1868; *Bankers Magazine,* XXIII, 102-103; Andreas: *op. cit.,* pp. 628 and 632.

[72] *Bankers Magazine,* XXIV, 148; XXV, 311; Andreas, *op. cit.,* II, 632.

[73] Andreas: *op. cit.,* II, 632; *Bankers Magazine,* XXV, 387.

[74] Andreas: *op. cit.,* II, 633; *Bankers Magazine,* XXV, 564.

[75] *History of Banking,* I, 418, 423 and 430.

[76] Cf. *Chicago Tribune,* March 13, 1865.

[77] Cf. *Ibid.,* April 7, 1865.

[78] Cf. *Ibid.,* April 9, 1865.

[79] *Ibid.,* April 25, 1865.

[80] Cf. Andreas: *op. cit.,* II, 630.

[81] Kane: *op. cit.,* I, 36, 38-43 and 43-45; *Hunt's,* LIV, 429-430.

[82] *Chicago Tribune,* February 2, 1867, which reproduces the confidential letter with ironic commentary.

[83] Cf. *Ibid.,* March 8, 1864.

[84] *Ibid.,* April 16 and 19, 1864; January 30, 1867; Kane: *op. cit.,* I, 56.

[85] *Chicago Tribune,* March 16, 1867.

[86] *Bankers Magazine,* XX, 590; XXII, 331-334 and 811; *Chicago Tribune,* January 13, 1867.

[87] *Chicago Tribune,* March 13, 1867; *Bankers Magazine,* XXIII, 837; Cole: *op. cit.,* p. 407.

[88] Andreas: *op. cit.,* II, 626.

[89] *Idem,* 632.

[90] Cole: *op. cit.,* p. 405. See also pp. 389-390 and 404-409.

[91] *Private Laws of Illinois,* 1867, I, 56-120.

[92] *Private Laws of Illinois,* 1869, I, 60-228. For typical charters of the several types of institution see *An Act to Incorporate the Chicago Banking Company,* pp. 93-94; *An Act to Incorporate the National Loan and Trust Company of Chicago,* pp. 104-105; *An Act to Incorporate the City Savings Bank, Private Laws of Illinois,* 1867, I, 92-94.

[93] *Chicago Tribune,* February 11, 1864.

[94] *Bankers Magazine,* XXII, 397.

[95] Returns of the United States Assessor, *Chicago Tribune,* January 19, 1868.

[96] Andreas: *op. cit.,* II, 325-326; *Bankers Magazine,* XXII, 186-187; Huston: *op. cit.,* I, 519-521.

CHAPTER XI

CONTROVERSY, PANIC AND CONFLAGRATION

1869–1871

DURING the few short years from 1869 to 1871, there was brewing in the United States the desperate monetary controversy that surged onward to its first climax in the battle between Bryan and McKinley twenty-five years later. That alone would give the period a fascination to anyone interested in the growth of monetary and credit institutions but, to enhance the color of the story, there are passages of melodrama as purple as any in the history of the nation. Against the fantastic background of reconstruction in the south, and political corruption in Washington, Gould and Fisk staged the drama of the Gold Panic, in 1869, and before the financial reverberations of that escapade had died away the stage was lit by the leaping flames of Chicago's conflagration.

To attribute all these events to financial causes would be absurd, since true historic narrative can seldom be written in the vein of a Greek tragedy that follows slow-moving fate from its primal causes to a final catastrophe that is inevitable. History is not as single-minded as the gods, since there are myriads of men who influence the march of events by the individual decisions that they make in the face of environmental problems. But the story of these fabulous years is one in which the monetary policies of the government, and the expansive activities of the banks, are generously woven into the fabric of the tapestry: without an appreciation of its financial elements the story is unintelligible.

At the end of the Civil War, the United States was faced with a currency problem almost as serious as that which had confronted Illinois in 1841 and again in 1860.* Specie had disappeared from circulation, and the paper currency was circulating at a discount of more than 30 per cent. Of the $900,000,000 of notes available for use as money, more than $200,000,000 consisted of interest-bearing legal tenders,† $185,000,000 was in the form of national bank notes, $65,000,000 in that of state bank notes still in circulation, and the remainder Greenbacks.[1]

To McCulloch, as Secretary of the Treasury, this situation was thoroughly unsatisfactory. In common with many thoughtful people, he was impressed with the potential dangers of the inflationary policy pursued by the government throughout the war, and enthusiastically agreed with the widely expressed desire for a rapid return to specie payments. Since gold was at a substantial premium, however, it was apparent that considerable contraction of the paper currency must precede any attempt to return to the gold standard at the old parity of the dollar, so that the Secretary used every penny of the Treasury surplus to retire Greenbacks. Even the *Chicago*

---

* Illinois had solved her own currency problem. The Auditor's Report for 1865 shows no more than $531 of the old state bank notes outstanding.
† Most of these were held as investments and did not circulate to any great extent.

Tribune, later a severe critic of McCulloch, was enthusiastic about this policy. The existing state of affairs, it asserted, "points plainly to the expediency of gradually funding the currency. . . . The moment the Government begins to receive more currency than it re-issues, the currency begins to fund itself by the laws of supply and demand. This will grow until we again resume a specie basis, which will probably be one of the earliest results of peace."[2]

In April, 1866, Congress officially recognized the wisdom of the policy. The Treasury was authorized to proceed with the funding of the currency, either by exchanging bonds for the outstanding Greenbacks, or by selling the bonds on the market and using the proceeds to retire the paper money. Only two restrictions were imposed upon the enthusiasm of McCulloch. In the first place, it was provided that the total bonded debt should not be enlarged by this policy, which meant that retirement of the currency depended upon surplus revenues. In the second, the maximum contraction of the Greenbacks was limited to $10,000,000 during the six months immediately following the passage of the act, and to $4,000,000 during each subsequent month.

Under this warrant, the Treasury slowly pursued its policies, looking to the ultimate return to a gold standard. By the end of 1866, $100,000,000 of the interest-bearing legal tenders had been retired and the Greenbacks in circulation had fallen by some $40,000,000. Meanwhile, McCulloch, applying banking principles to the monetary operations of the Treasury, had begun to accumulate a gold reserve for note redemption.

To many people, these methods appeared too slow. Although the premium on gold had fallen considerably below the high point reached at the beginning of 1865, a slow currency contraction did not hold out much hope that the gold standard would be restored in the early future. By 1867, impatience became vocal, and there were reiterated demands that the Treasury should retire the Greenbacks more rapidly, either by higher taxation or by means of a large bond issue.[3] As an alternative, it was suggested by those who disliked the national banking system, that contraction might be accelerated by wiping out the national bank notes,[4] while a few writers went closer to the heart of the problem and pointed out that contraction of the currency was impossible as long as bank deposits increased more rapidly than notes were withdrawn.[5]

But Pilgrim's road to Paradise was not more painful than the path that must be followed by a country that tries to return to its old metallic standard after a serious digression into the valley of paper-money inflation. The glittering vision of resumption is seldom as close as the optimists think it, and the continuous contraction of the currency, by which it must be attained, means a deliberate forcing down of all price levels. Business profits diminish and disappear; farm mortgages become intolerably burdensome, and the depression of business forces men into the inertia of unemployment.

By the beginning of 1867, there was a general outcry against the monetary policies of the government, and the loudest protests were heard from the west. "Mr. McCulloch's reckless contraction system is steadily pursuing the even tenor of its way, to the enforcement of specie resumption, and at the same time prostrating trade, tying up capital, paralyzing industry, and drying up the sources of revenue needed to defray the expenses of the Government. . . . The fact is, that Mr. McCulloch has become insane on his contraction theory, and nothing can remove the hallucination from him."[6] When the New York papers insisted that the country needed more contraction, and not less, the *Tribune* satirized them unmercifully and paid facetious tribute to Horace Greeley's inability to understand the meaning of statistics. When "Long John" Wentworth voted against the repeal of the contraction program in the House of Representatives, he was accused of working for the "hard times policy . . . in opposition to the known sentiments of ninety-nine per cent of his constituents."[7] McCulloch was called upon to resign if he would not abandon his policy.

In a sense, the attitude of Chicago, as reflected in the pages of its more conservative newspapers, was eminently sound. By this time, it had become apparent that the return to specie payments could not be achieved suddenly, and the prospect of long years of currency contraction was intolerable to a growing community. Chicago, like many another American community, had developed phenomenally because of the accelerating effects of spasmodic inflation, but an extended period of deliberate deflation would retard further progress and, if serious enough, produce stagnation. Why not keep the currency at the existing level, and allow the rapid economic growth of the country to absorb it? "The currency would, gradually but quickly enough, appreciate to par with gold. The rapid expansion of trade and commerce and the increase of population will soon absorb all of the existing 'inflation' and 'depreciation' of the currency. Just let it alone, and the country will grow into specie payments, in a short time, without any stringency or convulsion."[8] If this plan were not acceptable, devaluation was suggested as being infinitely less harmful than deflation.[9]

The adoption of a policy of "growing up to the currency" would have prevented any immediate depression of business from monetary causes, since commodity prices would have fallen only to the extent to which costs of production declined. But it was not fully realized that prices would still have fallen, and to the debt-burdened section of the people any decline in price levels was painful. Demands for further inflation began to be heard from many parts of the west, and the Democratic party, under western influence, began to accept the philosophy of currency expansion. Vitriolic condemnation of the "bloated bondholders" was heard in the political campaign of 1868, and Illinois, as a western state with "soft money" traditions, was strongly in favor of inflation.[10]

As always occurs during a period of inflationary enthusiasm, an infinite variety of monetary panaceas was recommended to the general public. Most of them can be grouped under two broad heads. In the first place, there was a widespread demand that the Treasury should pay off its bonds in Greenbacks, diminishing the burden of debt and augmenting the supply of money at the same time. Secondly, from all parts of the country, came resolutions demanding the retirement of national bank notes and the issue of Greenbacks in their place, a measure that was not inflationary in itself but might be regarded as a first step toward subsequent currency inflation.[11] During September, 1867, the citizens of Illinois, assembled at Ottawa, passed one of the earliest resolutions along these lines, and many other communities followed the example during the ensuing years. "We denounce the national banking system as one of the worst outgrowths of the bonded debt, which unnecessarily increases the burden of the people thirty millions of dollars annually" on account of the interest paid on the bonds deposited to secure circulation.

Chicago was in a quandary. While there had been emphatic disapproval of the earlier policies of deflation, the businessmen of the city had no desire for another inflationary debauch. Holding rather carefully to the middle of the road, the *Tribune* expressed its disapproval of the plan to replace national bank notes by Greenbacks in phrases that are more creditable to the sentiments than to the mathematical ability of the writer. "An issue of three hundred millions more irredeemable shinplasters would reduce the purchasing power of the existing currency by not less than two hundred and fifty millions, and the people would lose that much in the value of their money. . . . The value of national and all other corporate bonds would tumble down and widespread mischief and misery would be inflicted."[12] Moreover, incessant political controversies on the subject of money were tiresome, and bad for business, so that Chicago insisted, with increasing vehemence, that the whole subject be taken out of the realm of politics by funding all the Greenbacks into bonds and permitting free banking on a national scale. If more currency were needed the national banks could supply it, by purchasing bonds and depositing them as security with the Treasury, but there would be no expansion unless there was a demand for money adequate to absorb the additional notes.[13] Best of all, the decisions as to any increase or decrease in the currency would be decided by bankers, and not by politicians angling for votes.

The Republican party, which had gained the support of the eastern states during the decade since its radical origins in Illinois, stood firm against fiat-money inflation. At the request of the President, Congress passed resolutions reiterating the ultimate intention of the United States to pay its debts in full, and to return to a gold standard at the earliest possible moment. Meanwhile, in February, 1868, it was considered expedient to call a halt in the deflationary policy; no further contraction of the Greenbacks was to be permitted.

Two years later, a less equivocal decision was reached, largely as a result of the melodramatic series of incidents which are known as the Gold Panic of 1869. As always happens during a period of monetary uncertainty, speculation was rampant during the years immediately following the Civil War. But the speculation in gold, infinitely more important than the operations in any other field of economic activity, held the center of the stage.

Fundamentally, the gold market was the arena in which speculators made bets on the future of the currency, since changes in the value of the circulating paper were vastly more important in their influence on the price of gold than any of the factors that might influence the market in more normal times. If any man, or group of men, could influence the value of the Greenbacks, it was possible to make a fortune out of gold speculations,[14] and the value of Greenbacks was determined primarily by the quantity of them in circulation and by the current policies of the administration in Washington.

Gold had declined fairly steadily from 145, in September, 1868, to 130¼ in March, 1869, at which time heavy purchases by Jay Gould forced the price up to 140. Other brokers followed his example, and the price rose still further, almost reaching 145 by the end of May; from that point it slumped to 136 at the end of July.[15] Assuming that the price could be forced above this figure, Jay Gould, with the cooperation of Jim Fisk and Corbin, the brother-in-law of President Grant, decided to corner the market. In August the conspirators persuaded Grant that it would be unwise for the Treasury to sell gold during the autumn, on the ground that a low price for gold might hamper the export of agricultural products, and Grant wrote to Secretary Boutwell endorsing such a policy.

Feeling safe in the knowledge that no gold would be dumped on the market by the Treasury, Gould and his associates began buying heavily during the early days of September. The price of gold rose sharply, but not considerably, reaching 137⅝ on September 4. Even this increase attracted a considerable amount of public attention, however,[16] and gold began to flow to New York from all parts of the United States. Increased purchases were necessary, on a substantial scale, if the speculators were to succeed, and Jim Fisk appears to have taken charge of the buying operations. "The malignant influence which Catiline wielded over the reckless and abandoned youth of Rome, finds a fitting parallel in the power which Fisk carried into Wall Street, when, followed by the thugs of Erie and the debauchees of the Opera House, he swept into the gold-room and defied both the street and the treasury."[17]

But the speculators began to feel uncomfortable, in spite of the powers that Fisk was supposed to wield. Corbin again wrote to Grant, on September 17, urging him to prevent the Treasury from selling any gold, but this letter only served to arouse Grant's suspicions. He became worried about the activities of his brother-in-law and, adopting a strangely devious method of communication, asked his wife to suggest to Mrs. Corbin that Corbin should sever his connection with the speculators. When this letter reached New York, on September 22, Corbin at once informed Gould that he wished to withdraw from the ring, and a heated altercation followed. Gould understood the effects of the President's perturbation, however, in spite of his abuse of Corbin. While he still encouraged his accomplices to greater effort, and invited other brokers to join the syndicate, Gould quietly sold a large part of his own holdings of gold!

To finance the continued activities of the group it was necessary to find money. The Tenth National Bank of New York was, therefore, persuaded to certify checks to the amount of $25,000,000 on Thursday, September 23, and $14,000,000 on the following day. To make the whole thing more fantastic, the action on September 24 occurred at a time when there were three examiners in

the Bank who had been sent there for the specific purpose of preventing the certification of checks to an
amount in excess of the actual balance of the depositors!

But the melodrama was drawing rapidly to its inevitable conclusion. When Grant returned to Washington,
and saw Boutwell on the morning of Friday, September
24, it was agreed that the Treasury should sell gold at
once. The New York Sub-Treasury received this order at
12:05 midday, but a few minutes before that James
Brown, a New York banker, had walked into the Gold
Room and offered to sell "one million at 162; another million at 161, and five millions more at 160." It was an unbe-
lievable session. "Several hundred men were shouting at
the top of their voices . . . like a war party of Comanche
Indians. Three men were carried out fainting, and one
prominent operator became temporarily insane, and ran
about endeavoring to escape imaginary individuals who
were threatening to shoot him."[18] Within the space of
fifteen minutes, under the offers of gold from Brown and
the Treasury, the price fell from 166 to 133 and "half of
Wall Street was involved in ruin."

As far as Chicago was concerned, the direct repercussions of New York's "Black Friday" were not immediately serious. Undoubtedly there had been some interest
in gold speculation, but it had not played a large part in
the total operations of the money market. During the
midsummer stringency, which affected seaboard cities in
July, 1869, funds and currency were both plentiful in
Chicago,[19] although the unusual developments in New
York created some uneasiness among western bankers. In
September, when the gold speculation was at fever pitch,

the Chicago banks were able to accommodate all their regular customers without difficulty,[20] although the western demands for currency had reduced their deposits somewhat and tightened the market to a perceptible degree.[21] Even at the moment of frenzied panic, Chicago was an interested but unaffected onlooker.[22]

On the basis of this evidence, it seemed as though the Gold Panic was no more than a local paroxysm of the New York market, and it was certainly regarded as such by the rest of the country during those hectic September days. Yet, fundamentally, its effects went much deeper. In the first place, the financial failures that it caused involved substantial losses, and could not fail to disturb the tenor of operations in the New York market. In the second place, the September drama had driven home to all thinking people the fact that American business was sitting on top of a cauldron. A monetary system that could be manipulated by a group of fearless speculators, with the queerly naïve help of the administration, was not one that inspired the confidence requisite for the development of long-range business policies, so that there resulted from the gold speculation an unusual degree of financial nervousness, and an intense desire for more satisfactory monetary policies.

As a result, an elaborate compromise measure was enacted by Congress, in 1870, as a temporary solution to the currency problem. An increase of $54,000,000 in the maximum issue of national bank notes was authorized, bringing the aggregate up to $354,000,000, and provision was made for the reduction of bank-note issues in the northern and eastern sections of the country in order that banks in the south and west might be allowed to increase their circulation. As a partial offset to this expansion of the currency, provision was made for retiring $45,000,000 of the interest-bearing legal tenders, most of which were held by eastern banks as reserves. Such a measure was calculated to please all parties. "To the inflationists who contended that more notes were necessary, and who came mainly from the west and south, it gave an issue of $54,000,000 new bills and a redistribution of $25,000,000 of old currency. . . . And, what was more pleasant to them, it was done at the expense of the envied east, which had not only to give up $25,000,000 of their ill-gotten circulation, but likewise had to surrender $45,-000,000 of temporary loan certificates. On the other hand the conservative bankers of the east were willing enough to yield the $25,000,000 which they suspected would never be required of them, and the three per cent certificates that would, of course, without any inflation, be replaced by legal-tender notes."[23] In the general satisfaction resulting from the measure it was even possible to enact the much-discussed Funding Act providing for a reduction of interest on the outstanding government debt.[24]

Moreover, the settlement of the currency question, for the time being at any rate, facilitated further development of the Chicago money market. With the exception of a serious stringency in the autumn of 1869,[25] which arose from the dislocation caused by the Gold Panic in New York, banking expansion in Chicago continued steadily throughout this period. Whether we measure them by the volume of resources, or by the quality of service offered to their customers, the banks of the city were at last playing their full part in its financial growth, and the improved structure of the money market made it easier for Chicago to draw upon the fund of European capital that was steadily flowing into the United States prior to the outbreak of the Franco-Prussian War.[26]

During the early part of 1869, a banking house like George C. Smith and Company was able to advertise that, in addition to its facilities for drawing exchange drafts on several important foreign cities, it was the special agent and representative of the Bank of Montreal, Drexel and Company of Philadelphia, the Union Bank of London, the London and Westminster Bank, the City Bank of London, Brown Shipley and Company, and Drexel, Harjes and Company of Paris.[27] Nor was this an isolated case. The importation of foreign capital, particularly to finance western railroads, as well as the financing of Chicago's expanding foreign trade, had necessitated the development of an international network of financial relationships, and the leading Chicago bankers were already known in important European money markets. In 1871, Henry Greenebaum was nominated for the mayoralty of the city on the grounds that, because of his high standing with foreign bankers, "he could be the means of obtaining, or causing to be obtained, many millions of foreign capital to be loaned to the mechanics, manufacturers, and others of the laboring and productive classes!"[28]

Similarly, in regard to the undertaking of specialized types of financial activity, the Chicago money market had been improved beyond recognition. Real-estate financing was undertaken by savings banks and building and loan associations, to supplement the facilities offered by private bankers and state-chartered institutions; fiduciary business was growing in volume under the fostering care of the newly established trust companies, and investment banking of the modern kind was beginning to make its appearance. Reference has already been made to the diversity that developed in the lending operations of the national banks, which constituted the core of the market, and it is interesting to notice the rise of a new type of financial institution that stands, in the scale of evolution, midway between the older factor and the modern finance company. In 1871, the National Loan and Trust Company was able to advertise that it specialized in collection business, and offered to store and insure the goods on which it made advances.[29] Moreover, the legislation of 1869, which made it illegal to do business in Illinois under any name other than that of the proprietors, unless the business or banking house had been formally incorporated, did a good deal to clarify the local situation in Chicago.[30] For the first time, the general public was able to distinguish clearly between private banking houses and state-chartered institutions.

While it is not possible to obtain accurate statistics of the condition of all banks in Chicago, it is clear from the available evidence that the national banks constituted the largest and most important segment of the money market. For the whole of Illinois the aggregate resources of national banks amounted to nearly $72,000,000, but Chicago accounted for considerably more than half of this total as the figures in Table XIII[31] clearly indicate. Moreover, it is of interest to notice that, whereas the

TABLE XIII

CONDITION OF ALL NATIONAL BANKS IN CHICAGO ON JUNE 10, 1871

Resources

Loans and discounts	$19,586,735.44
Bonds for circulation	6,006,600.00
Bonds for deposits	....
U. S. bonds on hand	246,000.00
Other stocks and bonds	464,037.38
Due from redeeming agents	4,061,228.86
Due from national banks	1,072,755.74
Due from state banks	258,306.12
Real estate, etc.	729,323.81
Current expenses	340,047.54
Premiums paid	122,588.06
Cash items	66,080.53
Clearing-house exchanges	1,744,011.31
National bank notes	828,591.00
Specie	99,651.90
Legal-tender notes	5,347,219.48
Three per cent certificates	205,000.00
Total	$41,178,177.17

Liabilities

Capital stock	$ 6,950,000.00
Surplus fund	2,279,000.00
Individual profits	1,044,727.01
National bank circulation	5,311,289.00
State bank circulation	....
Dividends unpaid	460.00
Individual deposits	16,258,889.31
U. S. deposits	....
Deposits U. S. disbursing officers	....
Due to national banks	5,016,773.04
Due to state banks	4,072,926.32
Notes rediscounted	244,112.49
Bills payable	....
Total	$41,178,177.17

individual deposits in Chicago banks amounted to more than three times the notes in circulation, for the rest of Illinois bank notes amounted to more than seventy per cent of aggregate individual deposits. Outside of the large cities the bank note still constituted the most important medium of exchange supplied by the banks, and checks were infrequently used even at this late date.

But, despite the prestige with which the national banks had begun their existence and the manifest advantage they enjoyed in the monopoly of note issue, it is amply apparent that their popularity was declining rapidly toward the end of the sixties. Even within the framework of the national banking system there were outstanding grievances that had not been cured by the various amending acts, while the phenomenal expansion of state-chartered institutions indicates the extent to which bankers preferred the wider range of freedom that such charters offered. In New York, the tendency led to a wholesale reversion of national institutions to state charters,[32] but Illinois and other western states witnessed no such general movement. Instead of abandoning the national system, the western bankers decided to organize themselves for the purpose of improving it. A National Banking Association had been organized, with this thought in mind, as early as 1864, and Chicago bankers were among the staunchest members. Coolbaugh, for many years, was the dominating personality in the Executive Committee.[33]

In large part, the grievances of Chicago were those which she shared with other parts of the country and, to the man in the street, the most serious was undoubtedly the deterioration in the physical condition of the national bank notes. Out of some $315,000,000 of notes issued to national banks between 1863 and 1869, only $16,000,000 had been returned in exchange for new notes so that, as one contemporary writer points out, "the state of the currency is not too strongly described by the word *filthy*. There is a serious risk in counting any large number of small bills in the ordinary way of wetting the fingers at the lips; and the effluvium arising from a closed box of currency would justify the interference of the Board of Health."[34] This condition of affairs was primarily due to the unsatisfactory provisions of the act regarding redemption, since nobody had any particular reason to return the notes to the issuer, and Chicago (although its banks had selected their New York redemption agents as the law required) had its own special reasons for objecting to the redemption arrangements.[35]

TABLE XIV

New York Redemption Agents of Chicago National Banks July, 1871

Chicago Bank	New York Agent
First National Bank	Fourth National Bank
Second National Bank	Bank of North America
Third National Bank	Kountze Brothers
Fourth National Bank	Kountze Brothers
Fifth National Bank	National Bank of the State of N. Y.
Northwestern National Bank	Bank of New York
Union National Bank	Metropolitan National Bank
Merchants National Bank	Third National Bank
Mechanics National Bank	Metropolitan National Bank
Manufacturers National Bank	Kountze Brothers
Cook County National Bank	Kountze Brothers
City National Bank	Ninth National Bank
Commercial National Bank	Merchants Exchange National Bank
German National Bank	National Park Bank
Corn Exchange National Bank	Continental National Bank
Traders National Bank	Importers & Traders Bank
Union Stock Yards National Bank	Third National Bank
National Bank of Commerce	American Exchange National Bank

In the light of public dissatisfaction with the national currency, it was confidently expected that state banks would soon acquire, once again, the legal right to issue notes,[36] and the Illinois Constitutional Convention that met towards the end of 1869 seems to have been dominated by this idea.[37] The new Constitution explicitly forbade the creation of banks or banking institutions by special legislative charter, unless such charters were approved by a referendum, but provision was made for the passage of a general banking law, subject to the same conditions of popular approval. If such a general law was passed, the security for note issues was to consist entirely of obligations issued by the United States or the State of Illinois, both rated at ninety per cent of par value, and any institutions created were required to publish "full and accurate quarterly statements" of their affairs. All stockholders in banks were to be liable, in the event of liquidation, for an amount equal to the par value of their shares and, recalling past experiences painfully, the Constitution provided that "the suspension of specie payments by banking institutions, on their circulation, created by the laws of this State, shall never be permitted or sanctioned."

These banking provisions, which were obviously copied from those of the National Banking Act, represented a marked improvement over anything that had previously been written on the statute books of Illinois. The *Chicago Tribune,* which felt that the Constitution was endangered because it was "altogether too good to be acceptable to a large class of unscrupulous, sharp-witted and corrupt men,"[38] strongly urged the people to ratify it at the special election held for that purpose.[39] Because of this advocacy, or of the intrinsic merit of the document, the Constitution was overwhelmingly approved by the voters on July 2, 1870, but, since the federal prohibition of note issues by state banks remained in force, the immediate effects of its adoption were negligible. No general banking law was passed until 1887, and the national banks, despite popular criticism, still held the center of the stage.

In the autumn of 1871, however, the setting of that stage was suddenly and tragically altered. Despite the phenomenal development of Chicago during the years that had swept rapidly by, the city was still, structurally, a mushroom metropolis of cheaply constructed houses with artificially elaborate exteriors. Of the sixty thousand buildings in the city, forty thousand were constructed entirely of wood, and many others incorporated a substantial amount of that material. There were fifty-six miles of wood-block pavement and six hundred and fifty-one miles of wooden sidewalks. In defiance of all safety, wooden cottages and huts were built around manufacturing establishments, warehouses and gasworks, while the only pumping station in the city had been roofed with wood.

A reckless Olympian in search of material for a Gargantuan bonfire could not have desired anything more appropriate and, even if Mrs. O'Leary had possessed neither cow nor barn, Chicago stood in grave danger of a holocaust. After weeks of drought, the city was parched to tinder, and fires were a daily occurrence—some of them so serious that, as in the case of one on Saturday, October 7, wide areas were devastated and eastern newspapers appeared with headlines describing "The Great Fire of Chicago."[40] From any logical viewpoint, the fire that broke out in Mrs. O'Leary's barn shortly before nine o'clock on the evening of Sunday, October 8, was no more serious than any of those that had occurred during the previous week.* At its inception there was nothing alarm-

* As a matter of fact, the *New York Times* reporter, who had exaggerated Saturday's fire because of a lack of other news, appears to have been very skeptical about the importance of the conflagration on Sunday. Not until midnight was he willing to consider it as anything unusual. Cf. *New York Times*, October 8 and 9, 1871; also February 6, 1938.

ing about it. But owing to the exhaustion (and, perhaps, inefficiency) of the fire-fighting forces, there was considerable delay in dealing with the incident. That delay, coupled with a gale of wind, made possible a conflagration that swept across the whole of Chicago, leaping the river in a moment and reducing to a pile of ashes magnificent buildings that everyone had believed to be fireproof. For two hideous nights and a day, the flames leaped onwards until they subsided under the rains of Tuesday morning, but by that time they had ravaged more than two thousand acres in the heart of the city, destroyed seventeen thousand buildings, and rendered a hundred thousand people homeless.

The experiences of the people of Chicago during those days have been vividly recorded by contemporary pens,[41] but even the readiest pen must be supplemented by the imagination of the reader if we are to envisage the conditions that existed when law and order had disappeared, homeless families were separated, and everyone was trying frantically to save as much as possible from the onrush of the flames. "Wagons were rushing through the streets laden with stocks of goods, books, valuable papers, boxes of money and everything conceivable; scores of men were dragging trunks frantically along the sidewalks, knocking down women and children; fabulous sums of money were offered truckmen for conveyances. The scene was indescribable."[42]

In this raging devastation, the whole business district of the city was engulfed. Although the First National Bank building withstood the flames, its contents were gutted; there remained only a gaunt skeleton of walls and eyeless windows when the fire had passed. Every other bank, excepting the little Union Stock-Yards National and two smaller state institutions, had been completely destroyed, as had all the insurance companies and mercantile establishments. Even the records of business and financial houses were destroyed, in many cases, despite Herculean efforts to save them, and those that were retrieved from endangered buildings were not always safe. Flames often licked them up before they had reached a place of security, and those that gained temporary safety from the flames were sometimes stolen by thieves who mistook them for property of more general value.[43]

The protection of bank vaults, in such a conflagration, was but a doubtful safeguard. In the case of most of the large banks, the vaults were subsequently found to have preserved their contents intact, and a linen coat, with a box of matches in the pocket, which had been in the vault of the *Chicago Tribune* building, was not even singed when the safe was recovered from the ruins after the fire.[44] The records of the Merchants Loan and Trust Company, however, were utterly destroyed,[45] while, in the case of George C. Smith and Company, the safe and all the records it contained were so completely destroyed by the fire that not a vestige remained to mark the place where the safe had stood.[46] In the case of the Union Trust Company, although the Minute Books and other corporate records were lost, the information contained in the ledgers came through the fire satisfactorily. Despite the fact that many pages of the books were badly charred, the writing was found to be perfectly legible owing to the peculiar chemical properties of an unattractive purple ink which the Bank had adopted solely because of its friendliness to the inventor.*

Realizing the intensity of the fire, and fearing some such result as that which occurred in the above cases, heroic efforts were made by several bankers to remove their assets to a place of safety. Officers of the Merchants Loan and Trust Company fled through the crowded streets carrying bundles of notes and securities worth hundreds of thousands of dollars. Stephen W. Rawson, the President of the Union Trust Company, took his horse and buggy down to the bank and, removing most of the currency and securities from the vault, took them home and hid them in the oatbin of his barn. For two days he stood guard over the treasure, with an old horse pistol in his pocket.[47] Most melodramatic of all was the experience of Tinkham, of the Second National, who removed six hundred thousand dollars in currency from the bank vaults and, packing it in a trunk, hired a negro for a thousand dollars to carry it to the Milwaukee Railroad station. In the crowded streets, Tinkham lost sight of the negro, and was driven down to the edge of the lake by the rapid progress of the flames, but when he reached the station, hours later, the negro was patiently sitting on the trunk and waiting for his thousand dollars.[48] According to the *New York Times,* the cashier of another bank, engaged in similar endeavor, was less fortunate. Thieves waylaid him and seized all the money that he was trying to save.[49]

But the varying fortunes of the bankers were matched

* For many years after the fire this purple ink was used for all permanent records of the Union Trust, but the idea does not appear to have impressed many other banks.

by the differences of psychological reaction among their customers during those early moments of consternation. Lyman J. Gage, eager to know the extent of the loss that the First National Bank had suffered, hastened to examine the vaults when they had scarcely had time to cool, but he did not arrive any earlier than some of his customers. The incident, as described in his *Memoirs*,[50] deserves retelling.

"Filled with a sense of triumph that the bank would survive the great disaster," he writes, "I closed the vaults and took my way to the street. In the ruined hallway stood four men not known to each other but all recognized by me as heavy depositors, to all of whom were due large sums. I thought of the scripture declaration: 'Where the carcass lies, the eagles gather.'

"The first of the four was a foreign gentleman who as a private lender of money maintained a large balance. Approaching me, he inquired in an agitated half-whisper, 'Have you been in the Bank? Is the money safe?'

" 'Yes,' I answered.

" 'Well,' he continued, 'I have here my check for $30,-ooo. It is for nearly what the bank owes me. If you will hand me the money, I will give you $6,ooo for yourself.'

"I refused, saying, 'You will get your money when others can get theirs—not before.'

" 'You refuse my offer? It seems to me that $6,ooo is a good deal of money for a man to make at a time like this, is it not?'

" 'That may be, but if I should accept your proposition, I would not make the money. I know your kind. Within a week the bank will open for business. You will then learn that your claim was perfectly good, and I would be forced to give back the $6,000 bribe you now offer. Get out!' . . .

"The second man was a prosperous banker from Jacksonville, Illinois. He extended his hand in friendly greeting and delivered himself thusly: 'I don't want anything; I ran up last night to take a look at the ruins. We have a large credit due us on your books, near two hundred thousand dollars. We had accumulated it for a special object which this fire will cause us to postpone; therefore, we have no present use for the funds. It looks as if you were in bad shape here, and it will take time for you to straighten things up. Just treat us as well as you will other people; that's all we ask. Good-bye and good luck.' He was hearty and sincere and his words were fraught with encouragement.

"The third man I recognized as a gentleman-farmer from an adjoining county. He approached me and said, 'I am Mr. B———, County Treasurer of ——— County; and my bond with securities is up with the County. I have $25,000 of its money in your Bank. If I lose it, I am a ruined man. Last night I did not sleep, and now if you can, I wish you would tell me the worst, so that I may know where I stand.'

" 'Well, Mr. ———, will you believe me if I tell you?'

" 'Yes, yes, tell me—I will believe you!'

" 'Then here are the facts: the Bank has suffered a heavy loss, but it is still sound and can pay its debts. If you will come to our new office one week from today, we will then pay you the entire sum, if you then desire to withdraw it.'

"He did not speak for a moment. Turning partly away, he covered his face with his hands and wept convulsively, tears of joy no doubt.

"The fourth, and last, man was a Hebrew cattle man and packing house owner in the stock yards—a man of wealth and large affairs. Seeing him, I thought he was there with the supposed instincts of his race and would bring forward some proposition for his own advantage, which would prove embarrassing to me. I determined to test him out. He had kept in the background and had not heard my talk with the others. Coming forward then, he extended his hand with the question, 'How is it?'

"Throwing my hands upward into the air, I snapped my fingers. 'It's that way with the Bank,' I exclaimed. 'You are smart enough to see it, aren't you?'

" 'Yes,' he responded, 'anybody can see that, but I am not asking about the Bank, I am asking about you—how is it with *you*?' 'When it's that way with the Bank (repeating the previous gesture), it's that way with me.'

" 'Just what I thought,' he said, 'but don't be discouraged. If the Bank never starts again you can make more money for yourself in five years in my office at the yards than you can in twenty in the Bank. Have you any money in your pockets?'

" 'Yes,' I answered, 'between two and three dollars.'

" 'That's no money," he declared. 'Even your grocery-man might refuse to trust you now.' By this time he was highly excited and very voluble. He plunged his hand into his pocket and drew forth a large wad of bank notes —five hundred dollars or more I should guess. Dividing the roll into two parts, about equal, he pushed one of them toward me, without counting. 'Here take this, God knows you may need it, and I know you would not take from the Bank until all have the same opportunity. Take it!' he repeated, 'And if you need more, it's yours. I have plenty; $50,000 is now in transit from New York by express. Remember this, Morris (referring to himself) would divide with you his last dollar, if you should need it.'

"To his balance in the Bank, he made no voluntary reference. He would have been excusable for doing that, for it exceeded $165,000. As I looked at the man and listened to his hearty, generous words, my heart grew warm within me. I could no longer play the dejected part I had assumed. Declining to accept his offer of cash, I told him that all was well with the Bank. . . . There was no craft, nor guile, in the man's thoughts, words or purposes. He spoke as a man uplifted by the spirit which animated him."

Nothing, perhaps, of all that has come down to us from the fire, tells as much of the varying human reactions to it as that little record of half an hour in Gage's life. Cupidity and open-handed generosity, warm friendliness and blank despair, rubbed shoulders with one another. And the same conflicting emotions spread over the whole city during those hours in which every member of the community was stunned by the suddenness of disaster. Bross, with irrepressible optimism, might insist that a bigger and greater Chicago would rapidly rise upon the ruins of the old city;[51] far away, in London, or even in St. Louis, the thoughtful writer could suggest that Chicago would probably, in the long run, recover much of the economic importance that it had lost through the fire.[52] This philosophical state of mind was less easily acquired by men who stood watching the flames of Monday and the ruins of Tuesday. To one of these, on Monday night, the outlook was dark indeed. "Our capital is wiped out of existence. You never can get what money is stored up out of these vaults. There isn't one that can stand this furnace-heat. Whatever the fire consumes tonight is utterly consumed. All loss is total; for there will not be an insurance company left tomorrow. The trade of the city *must* go to St. Louis, to Cincinnati, and to New York."[53]

Other cities in the United States were not, however, immediately impressed by the opportunities for economic expansion that the destruction of Chicago might afford them. A body does not develop by the destruction of its organs, as the famous Roman parable long ago pointed out, and the city of Chicago was already an important organ in the economic structure of the world. The effects of the fire spread out like the stone-caused ripples on a pond, and every part of the country was immediately horrified at the appalling economic and human loss. An enormous quantity of capital had been wiped out, and the United States was developing so rapidly that capital was scarce.[54]

In New York, as soon as the full extent of the fire was realized, a feverish panic developed on the stock exchange. "Stocks which had been considered among the best on the list, fell from one to two per cent during the early transactions . . . and to a similar extent subsequently, so that at the close of the market in the afternoon they stood as much as nine or ten per cent below the prices in the morning, and bade fair to go still lower."[55] For this reaction there were many reasons. In the first place, it was apparent that any diminution in the volume of Chicago's trade would seriously affect the revenues of the railroads operating out of that city, which were among the most important in the country. Secondly, the rebuilding of the city would require large sums of capital so that the merchants and bankers of Chicago might be expected to sell a substantial portion of their security holdings to raise the money for reconstruction. But, most important of all, it was immediately recognized that unprecedented losses would be inflicted upon the insurance companies as a result of the fire. These companies, which had already come to occupy a significant place in the money market, would be compelled to call the loans that they had made on the street, and to sell large amounts of securities, in order to meet the claims made upon them.

These suspicions were well founded. As a result of several years of optimistic overexpansion, the insurance companies of the country were in no position to stand the strain. By November, fifty-nine companies in various parts of the country had gone into bankruptcy, including thirteen from Chicago and twenty from the State of New York, while the forty-three companies in New York that remained solvent were compelled to pay out one-quarter of their total assets to meet the claims upon them arising out of the Chicago fire.[56] Moreover, the seriousness of the situation was accentuated by the fact that the New York banks were in no position to meet the drain upon them resulting from the above factors and from the withdrawal of currency to the west that immediately ensued. While they held comparatively large gold reserves, these were of no avail to meet the demands of depositors since gold was at a premium and did not circulate.[57] Of Greenbacks they held very little, and the inadequacy of the amount was made worse by the fact that a group of stock speculators had "withdrawn and locked up" a large quantity of the paper currency in order to produce stringency in the money market.[58] Even before the fire, there had been runs upon some of the smaller uptown banks in New York.[59]

As a result, the financial crisis was not easily surmounted. Although, on October 10, a group of bankers deliberately forced security prices up to what were considered more reasonable levels,[60] the market broke again a few days later and, by October 18, the prices of many stocks had fallen to levels far below those reached on the first day of panic.[61] Not until Monday, October 23, two weeks after the fire, were the nerves of the money market sufficiently calmed to enable the banks to meet the situation with some degree of coolness, and to arrange for the orderly liquidation of the large blocks of securities that had to be turned into cash.[62]

In this panic, for the first time, Europe came to the aid of the American financial system by pouring funds into the country through the purchase of American securities at bargain prices. Had this not been true, the repercussions of the fire would have been even more serious for the economy of the country. "In 1836, or even in 1857, we were so isolated financially that a comparatively trifling blow was sufficient to crush the entire credit system. Now we are so intimately linked in our business relations with the whole commercial world that two cities like Chicago might be laid in ashes without necessitating a general commercial convulsion."[63]

Since London was called in to cushion the blow that had fallen upon New York, it was inevitable that the Chicago fire should produce a reaction in the London money market. This reaction was naturally less severe than the New York panic, because London was in a stronger position at the time. Moreover, the ripples that flow out from the center of disturbance tend to diminish in intensity with every increase in the distance that they travel. But, with all these qualifications, it was still true that English insurance companies had lost more than £1,-000,000 as a result of the fire,[64] that many English merchants had close business relations with Chicago houses, and that heavy American sales of securities on the London market were expected. A slight recession in security prices was inevitable; even consols fell heavily and a sharp rise in the rate of interest occurred.[65] At no time, however, was there a trace of panic in the market, so that the process of liquidation was smoothly and expeditiously performed.

In more than one sense, therefore, the burning of Chicago may be said to mark a turning point in its financial history. During less than four decades, it had grown from an outpost community on the edge of the wilderness to a financial metropolis that was knit by a thousand ties to the money markets of the Atlantic seaboard and to the financial centers of Europe. The funds for its relief that flowed in generously and spontaneously were but one small indication of the interest of other communities in its development,[66] and the humanitarian concern for Chicago's distress was closely related to the economic importance of the city's resurgence. During these short years, when comedy and melodrama are queerly striped with tragedy on the pages of financial history, we reach the end of an epoch; with the rebuilding of Chicago another epoch begins.

REFERENCES FOR CHAPTER XI

[1] Cf. Hepburn: *op. cit.*, pp. 205-207, for general description of conditions.

[2] *Chicago Tribune,* March 13, April 12, 1865.

[3] Cf. *Bankers Magazine,* XXII, 81-85 and 351-354.

[4] Cf. Amasa Walker, in *Bankers Magazine,* XX, 163.

[5] *Bankers Magazine,* XXII, 345-348.

[6] *Chicago Tribune,* January 27, 1867. See also January 18 and 20, February 4, 13 and 23, and March 15, 1867.

[7] *Ibid.,* February 23, 1867.

[8] *Ibid.,* February 24, 1867.

[9] *Ibid.,* February 1, 1867.

[10] Cf. Cole: *op. cit.,* pp. 411-412 and 436; Hepburn: *op. cit.,* pp. 210-211.

[11] Hepburn: *op. cit.,* pp. 209, 214 and 313; Kane: *op. cit.,* I, 53-56.

[12] *Chicago Tribune,* May 24, 1870.

[13] *Ibid.,* September 3, 9, 15 and 17, 1869.

[14] Cf. *Ibid.,* September 28, 1869.

[15] *The Report of the Gold Panic Investigation* (House Report 31, 41st Congress, 2 Session) presents a comprehensive picture of the whole campaign of the speculators, and has been freely drawn upon in the following paragraphs.

[16] Cf. *Chicago Tribune,* September 4, 7 and 8, 1869.

[17] *Report,* p. 7.

[18] *Chicago Tribune,* September 25, 1869.

[19] *Ibid.,* July 1 and 8, 1869.

[20] *Ibid.,* September 21, 1869.

[21] *Ibid.,* September 2 and 14, 1869.

[22] *Ibid.,* September 23, 24 and 25, 1869.

[23] Knox: *op. cit.,* p. 272. See also *Bankers Magazine,* XXIV, 641 and 671-674; *Chicago Tribune,* May 31, 1870; *Commercial and Financial Chronicle,* X, 69 and 165.

[24] *Chicago Tribune,* June 5 and 23, 1870; *Commercial and Financial Chronicle,* X, 165.

[25] *Chicago Tribune,* October 4 to 10, 1869.

[26] *Commercial and Financial Chronicle,* X, 262.

[27] *Bankers Magazine,* XXIV, 70-71.

[28] *Chicago Tribune,* October 23, 1871.

[29] *Bankers Magazine,* XXV, 564-565.

[30] Cf. *Ibid.,* XXV, 288-289.

[31] *Report of the Comptroller of the Currency,* December 4, 1871, pp. 628-629. See also *Bankers Magazine,* XXVI, 520-521; *Commercial and Financial Chronicle,* XIII, 73.

[32] Cf. *Bankers Magazine,* XXIV, 46-58.

[33] *Idem,* 854-855.

[34] *Idem,* 342.

[35] Cf. *Ibid.,* XXVI, 182-183; Kane: *op. cit.,* I, 56-57.

[36] *Chicago Tribune,* May 13, 1870.

[37] *Constitution of the State of Illinois,* approved and ratified in 1870, Article XI, Sections 5-7.

[38] *Chicago Tribune,* June 26, 1870.

[39] Cf. *Ibid.,* May 13, 1870.

[40] The literature of the Fire is so large that it can receive no more than a passing mention. Of those that have been consulted, Andreas: *op. cit.,* II, 701-780 is comprehensive but hard to read; *Reminiscences of Chicago during the Great Fire* (Chicago, 1915) is very readable but highly selective. Good comprehensive studies are offered by Colbert and Chamberlin: *Chicago and the Great Conflagration* (Philadelphia, 1871) and Sheahan and Upton: *The Great Conflagration; Chicago, Its Past, Present and Future.* All these have been drawn on in the following paragraphs.

[41] In addition to the above references, see *New York Times,* October 9, 1871; *Chicago Magazine of Fashion, Music and Home Reading,* II, 324-336.

[42] *Reminiscences of Chicago,* p. 6.

[43] Cf. *Chicago Tribune,* October 11, 1871, for instances.

[44] Andreas: *op. cit.,* II, 732.

[45] Harper and Ravell: *op. cit.,* p. 46.

[46] Andreas: *op. cit.,* II, 732.

[47] Harper and Ravell: *op. cit.,* pp. 50-51; Letter of Stephen W. Rawson, December 22, 1898.

[48] *Bankers Magazine,* XXVI, 390.

[49] *New York Times,* October 13, 1871.

[50] *Memoirs of Lyman J. Gage,* pp. 48-51.

[51] *New York Tribune,* October 14, 1871.

[52] London *Times,* editorial, October 11, 1871; *St. Louis Times,* October 13, 1871.

[53] *Reminiscences of Chicago,* pp. 10-11.

[54] *New York Herald,* October 10, 1871; *New York Tribune,* October 12, 1871; *Boston Traveller,* October 11, 1871; *Philadelphia Press,* October 11, 1871; *Philadelphia Inquirer,* October 11, 1871; *St. Louis Democrat,* October 12, 1871; London *Times,* October 11, 1871. An admirable account of the reaction of other cities may be found in Chapters XXIII and XXIV of Dreiser's *The Financier* which, although fiction, is based on careful study of contemporary sources.

[55] *New York Times,* October 10, 1871.

[56] *Commercial and Financial Chronicle,* XIII, 655-656; *Chicago Tribune,* November 2, 1871.

[57] Cf. Sprague: *Crises,* p. 7.

[58] *New York Times,* October 16, 1871.

[59] *Ibid.,* October 16, 1871.

[60] *Ibid.,* October 11 and 12, 1871.

[61] *Ibid.,* October 14, 16, 17, 18 and 19, 1871.

[62] *Ibid.,* October 21 and 23, 1871.

[63] *Chicago Times,* October 20, 1871.

[64] London *Times,* October 12, 1871.

[65] *Ibid.,* October 14 and 16, 1871.

[66] Cf. *Commercial and Financial Chronicle,* XIII, 487.

CHAPTER XII

CHICAGO RESURGENT

1871–1873

THE citizens of Chicago attacked the problems of reconstruction with an urgent enthusiasm that left little
time in which to listen to the croakings of the pessimists.
Before the ashes were cool, the Governor of Illinois was
indignantly opposing the federal plan to establish martial law in the ruined city, insisting that the state was
amply able to police its territory,[1] while the newspapers
were united in clamant optimism. "Whoever imagines
that Chicago is dead, needs but to spend a day among
her ruins; to witness the preparations even now begun
for rebuilding her fallen palaces; to hear the words of
unconquerable resolve, and to witness the deliberation
with which men set about executing great plans for the
future, to be disabused of a notion so supremely absurd."[2]

Although immediate assistance came from every corner
of the world, as mute testimony of the interest that had
been aroused by Chicago's ordeal,* men were eager to
stand on their own feet once again. Early on the morning
of Tuesday, October 10, an apple-woman set up her
stall at the corner of State and Randolph streets,[3] the

---

* The *Chicago Times*, on October 19, 1871, suggested facetiously that "no
well-regulated American newspaper is now considered complete without three
maps of the burned Chicago district per week."

417

pioneer of all the trade of the future, and a few hours afterward a real-estate dealer named Kerfoot was busily erecting a wooden shack on the site of his old offices at Washington and Clark streets.[4]

To most of the merchants, however, the resumption of business operations was much more urgent than the rebuilding of ruined stores and warehouses, since trade and commerce could not wait for the construction of new premises. Commerce spread rapidly into what had been the residential districts of the city, taking possession of dwelling houses and other premises that had escaped the fire.[5] Although the vast department store of Field, Leiter and Company was able to establish itself, with reasonable comfort, in the old carbarn of the South Side Railroad, at State Street and Twentieth, other firms were less fortunate. In many cases, half a dozen types of business were forced to crowd themselves under a single roof. "A shoe store is in the basement, with long strings of gaiters and slippers hanging where the hat-rack was; a bench for customers improvised from an inverted box where the sideboard stood; fertile boxes of shoes are in the kitchen and coal-hole. And over the front, five yards of outstretched cotton cloth bears the simple legend, 'Shoes.' Upstairs is a button factory, with pendulous and fascinating strings of buttons festooned across the aristocratic windows. The bedrooms higher up are lawyers', doctors' and insurers' offices, and into the dormer windows of the roof shoot a large quiver full of telegraphic wires."

To facilitate the resumption of normal activity, credit was granted liberally by wholesale and retail houses,

WILLIAM F. COOLBAUGH

while every consideration was extended to those debtors whose losses precluded immediate payment of old obligations.[6] The familiar clamor of advertising was resumed as soon as there were newspapers in which to advertise, and many of the announcements are characterized by dry humor that no misfortune could repress.[7] A watch manufacturer pointed out that his goods, having "passed through the great conflagration," were thoroughly adjusted to changes of temperature, while the purveyors of fire extinguishers reaped a rich harvest by sardonically pointing out that more people should have been equipped with them a week earlier.*

Business resumption, however, depended in very large measure upon the resumption of banking activity, and there was serious doubt as to the ability of the banks to begin operations immediately. While the *Tribune*, on Wednesday, October 11, insisted that "some of the banks will ultimately pay the whole of their deposits,"[8] the arguments advanced to support this contention indicate the writer's lack of conviction. Even though most of the financial institutions in the city had been in reasonably good shape before the fire, their premises had been completely destroyed and, until the safes were cool enough to be opened, nobody knew the extent of the loss.

Most of Wednesday was spent in the task of examining these safes, and obtaining temporary quarters, either at Burlington Hall, on State Street, or on West Randolph Street, near Jefferson, which were the two locations favored by most bankers. The Union Stock-Yards

* As testimony to the efficiency of this advertising, it may be pointed out that one of the banks expended six hundred dollars in the purchase of fire extinguishers the day after it moved into temporary quarters!

National Bank, which had not been touched by the fire, actually opened for business on that day, as did the Cook County National Bank and the Mechanics Savings Bank, which had succeeded in establishing themselves in new offices.[9] Moreover, the Bank of Montreal, realizing the opportunities for profitable operation, promptly decided to reopen its Chicago branch, and George Smith was reported to be sailing from Scotland to resume his financial activities in the northwest.[10]

Many bankers, however, were not ready for such precipitate action. Although most of them had found the contents of their safes unharmed,[11] there was a feeling of pessimism when they gathered on Wednesday afternoon at the residence of C. T. Wheeler, the Vice-President of the Union National Bank.[12] About eighty men were present at the meeting, and none of them appears to have thought that Coolbaugh was unnecessarily cautious when he suggested that the banks could not pay more than twenty-five to forty per cent of their deposits in the immediate future. All that could be done was to appoint a committee, under the chairmanship of Solomon A. Smith, to draft resolutions informing the public of what the banks were able to do.

But this committee, inspired apparently by Solomon A. Smith and C. B. Blair, seems to have acquired a new confidence during its discussions. On Thursday, in reporting back to the larger group, it suggested that all banks should reopen as rapidly as possible, accepting new deposits as trustees for their customers and undertaking to pay at once an amount equal to fifteen per cent of the deposit balances standing on their books at the time of the fire.[13] These suggestions were unanimously adopted by the bankers present at the meeting, and heartily endorsed by the *Tribune*, so that the savings bankers, gathered in another meeting, were encouraged to formulate similar plans for the immediate payment of twenty per cent of the amounts owing to customers.

Such confidence is contagious, and tends to spread rapidly. By Saturday, many bankers were inclined to feel that they had been too cautious, realizing that unnecessary reluctance to pay depositors might retard business recovery and injure their own prestige.[14] A few of them thought that it would be possible to pay "all checks of depositors for reasonable sums," and an even larger number felt that some date should be fixed, not more than sixty days in the future, at which all depositors would be paid in full if they so desired. Another meeting, this time of national banks exclusively, was, therefore, called on Sunday, at which the Comptroller of the Currency, who had hurried from Washington, was present. After a careful examination of resources and liabilities, it was discovered that all the institutions represented were in solvent condition, so that Blair immediately proposed to expunge the previous resolution limiting payments to fifteen per cent of the balances before the fire.[15] In its place, Coolbaugh proposed that all national banks should reopen, at their temporary offices, on the morning of Tuesday, October 17, paying all the legitimate demands of their depositors in full. The resolution was adopted unanimously.

This action on the part of the national banks may, without exaggeration, be regarded as the initial stimulus toward the resumption of normal business activity in Chicago. It offered to the community, much sooner than many people had expected, a renewal of the financial facilities which were even more vital to efficient reconstruction than they had been in quieter seasons. Most of the larger state banks immediately decided upon a similar policy and even the Merchants Loan and Trust Company, which had lost many of its ledgers and other records, decided to resume operations. The directors authorized the President and Cashier to use their judgment in determining the amount of the balance due to each customer.*

The First National Bank opened its doors "for business as usual" on the morning of Monday, October 16, at 449 Wabash Avenue.[16] That evening, the members of the Clearing House Association, which appears to have been moribund during the days of actual crisis, met at Standard Hall for the purpose of clearing the items that had accumulated "during and since the late great fire," and Solomon A. Smith, with the unanimous approval of the members, "moved that the clearing be made tonight". When that was done, Lyman J. Gage proposed that regular clearings should be resumed on the following day.

Twenty-one banks, including three that were not formal members of the Clearing House, were able to settle their claims on one another at that session. The remaining eight members did not participate because they "had

---

* It is interesting to notice that, although in most cases the claim of the depositor was the only evidence of the bank's obligation, the net loss of the bank on an aggregate of more than $2,000,000 deposits amounted to only $58,500—a quiet testimony to the honesty of most of the bank's customers. Cf. Harper & Ravell: *Fifty Years of Banking*, p. 46.

either sent their checks out of town for safety or were unable to open their vaults," but these obstacles were speedily overcome during the next few days.

On Tuesday morning, October 17, all the national banks, and most of the larger state institutions, were open for business at the addresses shown in the following announcement, and several of them actually encouraged full examination by responsible customers with a view to eliminating any lingering doubts, on the part of the public, in regard to their affairs. Thus, in the case of the First National Bank, "at the invitation of L. J. Gage . . . a dozen of its country bank customers examined its condition, and passed a set of complimentary resolutions

BANK DIRECTORY

SHOWING THE ADDRESSES OF THE LEADING CHICAGO BANKS ON
OCTOBER 17, 1871

City National Bank.........................Clinton and Washington streets
Commercial National Bank.................532 Wabash avenue
Cook County National Bank................223 Michigan avenue
Cushman, Hardin and Company...........57 Calumet avenue
Fifth National Bank........................449 Wabash avenue
First National Bank........................449 Wabash avenue
Fourth National Bank......................475 Wabash avenue
Hibernian Banking Association.............446 Wabash avenue
Illinois State National Bank................101½ West Randolph street
Lunt, Preston & Kean......................Halsted and Randolph streets
Manufacturers National Bank..............454 Wabash avenue
Merchants, Farmers and Mechanics
    Savings Bank.........................64 South Halsted street
Merchants Loan and Trust Company.......414 Wabash avenue
Merchants National Bank................ ⎰225 Michigan avenue
                                        ⎱281 Cottage Grove avenue
National Bank of Commerce...............543 Wabash avenue
Northwestern National Bank...............526 Wabash avenue
Third National Bank......................436 Wabash avenue
Traders National Bank....................447 Wabash avenue
Union National Bank.....................543 Wabash avenue

NOTE: It should be pointed out that these quarters were very temporary. Some of the banks changed their location several times before moving back to permanent offices.

expressing their conviction of its entire soundness, and commending it to the public."[17]

Within two weeks of the outbreak of the fire, every financial institution in the city was operating once again and, with the exceptions of slight runs on one or two of the smaller savings banks, there had been no evidence whatever of public distrust. Indeed, as often happens when courageous action has restored confidence to a frightened community, the banks actually found that the volume of new deposits exceeded the amount of current withdrawals.[18] Within a few days, the Chicago banks were in possession of more cash than they could use and, after the beginning of November, currency was moving toward New York for deposit in correspondent banks.

With the resumption of mercantile and financial activity, it was possible for the community to turn its attention to the task of rebuilding the city. Every increase in the volume of activity made the temporary quarters of the bankers and businessmen more uncomfortable, and and no new premises of an appropriate kind were available until offices and warehouses had been rebuilt. Except for the walls of the First National Bank and Tribune buildings, there were nothing but piles of debris along the streets that had composed the business district.*

As early as October 12, a mass meeting was held, with Scammon in the chair, to discuss the best method of undertaking the physical reconstruction of the city. While no formal action appears to have been taken in regard to methods, there was enthusiastic unanimity in the de-

* Parts of the Court House and Post Office also survived the fire, but these were of no use to businessmen in search of appropriate accommodation.

cision to rebuild without delay, and the *Chicago Evening Post* sang a paean of jubilation a few days later. "Chicago is rising to the music of energy and enterprise, as the towns of Troy to the strange song of Apollo. Instead of sitting down to lament, her people are building busily, and the snow is sure to whiten roofs and not ruins only."[19]

Despite unusually early frosts, which would normally have prevented all building operations, activity went on apace. "It is December," remarks one observer, "but an artificial summer is created to keep the work from freezing up; a bonfire is blazing before the mortar bed . . . and . . . smaller fires blaze briskly all around within the rising wall—a fire on every mortar board, which keeps the mortar plastic and the blood of the bricklayer uncongealed."[20] To any observer, unaware of the circumstances, the sight must have appeared fantastic, provided that he could find his way through the chaos to see what was going on. "Who can count the number of zigzags he is compelled to perpetrate, or the ascents and descents of sidewalk he must go through on Wabash avenue? What bold equestrian feels able to cope with the Thermopylaes of State street? . . . It is a repetition at every step of a Scylla of broken brick and a Charybdis of fragmentary stone or flying sand and lime, with the additional horror of tons of the finest dust closing the eyes in the wayfarer's passage through these dangerous openings."[21]

But the work progressed with phenomenal rapidity, despite serious inconvenience from labor troubles[22] and the shortage of materials. Even though the City Council permitted the erection of frame structures, until the folly of that leniency was demonstrated by a serious fire in

1874,[23] most of the buildings were of brick or stone. In many cases they represented a considerable improvement on the homes and offices that had preceded them, so that the temporary fall in the prices of real estate soon reversed itself. Land was a good thing to own in a growing city, and speculation in this field kept pace with the steady expansion in construction activity.[24]

All these developments naturally required substantial financing and, in the early stages of the reconstruction, the banks, being anxious about the liquidity of their position, were not eager to make loans.[25] Although some funds were made available through the discount of bills drawn to finance grain shipments, the aggregate amount of the loans and discounts of Chicago banks actually decreased by more than twenty per cent during the month following the outbreak of the fire. Such caution appears excessive, in view of the fact that total deposits grew steadily during the same period, but it must be remembered that these new deposits were purely temporary and resulted from the flow of relief funds and insurance money to the distressed city.

Even in the case of grain shipments, the reluctance of the banks to lend compelled the railroads to assume banking functions for a short period. Responsible shippers were authorized to draw on the railroad balances in Chicago as a means of obtaining immediate payment for their cargoes, reimbursing the company after the sale of the grain by depositing money in its New York account.[26]

As recovery progressed, however, the attitude of the banks became more liberal and, in the light of their strong cash position, the money market developed an extraordinary degree of ease during the winter of 1871 and the spring of the following year.[27] Moreover, under the spur of growing business activity, a considerable expansion of banking facilities occurred. Loans and discounts of all national banks in Chicago, which amounted to $19,586,735 in June, 1871, had expanded to $25,591,-000 two years later, although individual deposits during the same period had only increased from $16,259,000 to $18,716,000 and the note issue had grown by less than a million dollars.[28] For state and private banks, unfortunately, there are no comparable figures, but the scanty data available in the form of individual financial statements suggests that the expansion was even greater, proportionately, in the case of these institutions.[29]

In part, this development was due to the expansion of the older banks, several of which increased their capital during the period from 1871 to 1873. Indeed, in more than one respect these years witnessed a startling modernization of the financial institutions of Chicago, under the initial stimulus of the fire. In addition to expanding their capital investment, many banks abbreviated their names, abandoning the long titles that had been popular at the time of the Civil War and adopting shorter designations. The Union Insurance and Trust Company became the Union Trust Company, the National Loan and Trust Company became the Bank of Chicago, and the Merchants Savings, Loan and Trust Company decided that it would get along safely without the word "Savings" in its title. In a busy modern city, the old titles were too long. "There is neither profit nor pleasure in these long-drawn-out names. It is a bore to pronounce them, and a greater bore to write them. Life is too short and time too precious to waste in such useless labor of lips and pens."[30]

At the same time, the ledgers of the banks themselves indicate an internal modernization that was almost as great. Although it was still necessary to pay somebody to sprinkle the streets in summer, in order to lay the dust, the banks seem to have abandoned flypapers and given up the use of sawdust on the public portion of the floor when they moved into the new buildings. Even though the First National Bank began to provide lunches for its employees, with ample quantities of milk and lemonade, as early as 1873, the predominant tendency was for all banks to become more formal in their operations as they grew larger. The old family atmosphere, in which expenses of a dollar for blacking and seventy-five cents for a shoebrush were deemed important enough to be recorded in the General Ledger, was rapidly disappearing.

Moreover, during the same period, there was a rapid increase in the number of banking institutions operating in Chicago, as Table XV clearly indicates. Four new national banks were incorporated, and the office of the powerful Bank of Montreal had been reopened on November 15, 1871.[31] In addition, there were at least nineteen other banking institutions created to supplement the facilities offered by those already in existence, although most of these were too small to be admitted to the Clearing House Association.[32]

In one sense, however, the most interesting development of the period was the establishment of the Illinois Trust and Savings Bank in 1873, by means of the purchase of a charter previously granted to the Sterling

Bank, of Sterling, Illinois.[33] Although functionally similar to the older Merchants Loan and Trust Company, the Illinois Trust attracts attention because it foreshadowed the development of bank affiliates which was to characterize the American financial scene during the first quarter of the twentieth century. Under the laws establishing them, national banks at this time had no power to undertake fiduciary activities or to operate a savings department, and it requires no great feat of imagination to realize that this fact was an important motive in persuading William F. Coolbaugh (of the Union National Bank), George Sturges (of the Northwestern National) and John De Koven (of the Merchants National) to create an institution designed, "in addition to the savings business, to give special attention to the management of trust funds."

These banking developments did not, however, completely solve the financial problems connected with the rebuilding of the city. The national banks, which comprised the largest institutions, were legally prohibited from making real-estate loans, and could not afford to tie up any large proportion of their resources in unsecured loans for fixed capital purposes, while the state and private banks were not large enough to meet the tremendous demand for long-term capital funds.

In part, at least, this demand was met out of the thirty-eight million dollars initially received from insurance companies that had written policies on the property destroyed by the fire and, although the amount of the claims (which aggregated almost one hundred million dollars) forced many of the insurance companies into bankruptcy, additional sums were later collected through the agency of the policyholders protective committee which Coolbaugh directed.[34] Moreover, many life-insurance companies, with ample funds at their disposal, were encouraged to make substantial loans in the Chicago district in view of the fact that rates of interest on the best mortgage loans ruled from 8 to 10 per cent per annum throughout 1872.[35] For the rest, Chicago was able to tap the capital markets of Europe, partly because of the widespread interest that the fire had aroused and partly because the larger banks, led by the First National, were already developing close financial relations with European banking houses. When the import of foreign capital into America was resumed after the Franco-Prussian War, Chicago merchants and industrialists were in the market as eager borrowers.

Although Chicago, intent upon her own problems, had little time in which to study developments in other parts of the country, it is necessary to turn our attention to the flood tide of national prosperity in which the local business boom of the recovering city was rapidly caught up. By the middle of November, 1871, the United States had recovered from the shock that it received when the news of the Chicago fire flashed along the wires and filled the pages of the newspapers.[36] The wave of speculation and business expansion, which had begun in 1869, resumed its upward sweep, encouraged in large measure by the government's monetary policy, and as prosperity increased the previous enthusiasm for resumption of specie payments was considerably dampened.[37]

Underlying this expansion was the program of railroad construction developed in the late sixties and early seventies, which increased the mileage of American railways from 47,254, in 1869, to 71,565, in 1873.[38] During the years from 1866 to 1868, inclusive, the railroads had expanded their facilities at the rate of two thousand miles a year, but from 1869 to 1872 the average annual increase was six thousand miles and, in the single year of 1871, nearly eight thousand miles of new road had been constructed.

Many factors, other than the pervasive influence of monetary policy and bank expansion, contributed to this development. In order to open up the northwest, and improve the transportation system of the country, the federal government gave generous land grants to encourage the construction of new railroads—grants that were sometimes large enough to offer the prospect of fantastic wealth to railroad promoters.[39] Moreover, even without land grants, the profits of some of the larger railroads were increasing considerably as a result of consolidations and agreements to restrain competition in regard to rates and fares.[40] Most important of all, however, was the eagerness of European investors to supply the funds needed for railroad construction. Under the stimulus of the newly organized investment trusts, England developed an unreasoning enthusiasm for American railroad securities,[41] and purchased them at a rate which added hundreds of millions of dollars to the foreign indebtedness of the United States.

Illinois, despite the temporary setback occasioned by the Chicago fire, participated with enthusiasm in this railroad boom, and Chicago, by reason of her strategic geographical position, reaped most of the benefits. Between

1860 and 1868, railway mileage in the state had increased by no more than six hundred and fifty miles, but the rapid expansion from 1869 to 1873 added more than twenty-five hundred.[42] After the record construction of 1871, aggregating more than a thousand miles, the Railroad and Warehouse Commission of Illinois published a table showing that three-quarters of the land in the state was within five miles of a railroad and only five per cent was more than ten miles away. No other state in the union had as comprehensive a railway network.

But in Illinois, and particularly in Chicago, the increasing speculative activity in the grain market was almost as significant a characteristic of the boom as the railroad expansion. After the fire, the warehouses and elevators that had been destroyed were promptly replaced by larger and better structures and, to an increasing extent as the years passed, the ownership of these elevators passed into the hands of men who were already active in the grain trade as dealers or carriers.[43] Speculation on the Board of Trade increased by leaps and bounds, so that problems of financing became acute. While all the Chicago banks were interested in produce loans, the Corn Exchange National and the Union National appear to have handled most of the speculative financing at this time, but the combined facilities of these institutions could not satisfy the demand for funds. Much of the speculation was, therefore, financed by long-time loans from eastern or European capitalists,[44] leaving the local banks free to use their funds in the more agreeable task of financing grain shipments through the discount of the first-class bills of exchange to which the trade gave rise.

As occurs during every period of prosperity, the banks of the country attempted to use their resources to the fullest possible extent, since by so doing they were able to offer the maximum accommodations to their customers and reap for themselves the largest possible profit. In the early seventies, however, this tendency concealed a particularly dangerous situation.

Under the National Banking Act, as amended, country banks might keep three-fifths of their reserve on deposit with national banks in reserve cities, and banks in these reserve cities were allowed to deposit one-half of the required reserve, including that held against country-bank balances, with national banks in New York City. Since cash in a bank's vault earned no dividends for the institution, while deposit balances with banks in the reserve centers usually carried interest, there was a general tendency for country banks to carry as much of their reserves as possible with city correspondents, while the latter, in turn, made full use of the New York banks.

Such a scheme of redeposited reserves was not necessarily unsound. By centralizing them, it tended to reduce the aggregate size of the monetary reserves required to support the banking system. But its fundamental soundness was predicated on the assumption that the city banks, and particularly those in New York, would hold excess reserves (over and above their own requirements) sufficient to enable them to meet the demands of country banks in times of seasonal strain or crisis. This assumption was not warranted in 1872. The banks of the reserve cities, taken as a whole, held average reserves that were very little above the required twenty-five per cent of demand liabilities during the years from 1869 to 1872, while the average reserve ratio of the national banks in New York was never as high as thirty-one per cent.[45] Moreover, the concentration of reserves was even more serious than the above paragraphs would indicate. During this period, fifteen of the fifty New York City banks held practically all the bankers' deposits acquired by the city, and seven of them held between seventy and eighty per cent of the bankers' balances. Far from realizing the responsibility of their position, these seven key banks kept reserves that were no larger than those of other New York banks which were doing a business that was primarily commercial in character.

It followed from this condition of affairs that abnormal demands from banks in any part of the country would immediately create a serious stringency in the New York money market, and this is exactly what happened in the spring of 1872, when the agricultural demands for funds were augmented by speculative demands from the Chicago grain market.[46] No attention was paid to this danger signal, however, since the stringency was popularly attributed to the inelasticity of the bank-note currency. When matters eased, during the summer, the unpleasant experience was promptly forgotten.

Early in the autumn, the agricultural demand for money again tightened the money market, and rates of interest hardened perceptibly.[47] Nor was the general state of mind improved by the rather sensational failure, on September 19, of the First National Bank of Washington, D. C., an institution with which Jay Cooke had been closely associated.[48] To an unbiased observer, the financial and business situation could not appear anything but unhealthy, yet contemporary journals reveal little appreciation of this fact. Even when the reserves of the New York banks fell considerably below the legal requirements, the conservative *Commercial and Financial Chronicle* only suggested that the Comptroller of the Currency should close his eyes to the fact, and leave conditions to work themselves out.[49]

As a matter of fact, this is exactly what the Comptroller did, although the Secretary of the Treasury gave more immediate assistance by selling five million dollars of gold in the market and purchasing an equal amount of outstanding government bonds in exchange for legal-tender currency.[50] Once again, with the passing of the agricultural drain, the market grew temporarily easier.[51] Although a few New York banks attempted to increase their reserves by selling national bank notes to brokers in exchange for greenbacks, at one-quarter of one per cent discount,[52] no effort was made to correct the fundamental unsoundness of the banking system.

Since business was still expanding, although at a diminished rate of growth, it was natural that the seasonal demand for funds in the spring of 1873 should produce a financial stringency similar to that of the previous year.[53] If anything, conditions were even worse than they had been in 1872, and several business houses were forced into liquidation by the scarcity of funds and the high rates of interest, but no more attention was paid to this warning than to those that had preceded it. The New York banks merely waited for funds to flow back to the city from other parts of the country, in order that business activity and the stock-market boom might resume their upward course and, by the middle of the summer, it appeared, from superficial observation, that this passive policy was justified by pragmatic standards. The contraction of the spring had given place to a renewed expansion of bank credit, and security prices were rising once more.

By this time, however, prosperity was growing thin: repeated warnings had indicated the glaring weakness of the banking system, and careful analysts were beginning to recognize the unsoundness of the methods by which railroad construction had been financed during the preceding years. On September 8, this latter fact was dramatically evidenced by the failure of the New York Warehouse and Security Company,[54] which had been active in the financing of the Missouri, Kansas and Texas Railroad. Five days later the lesson was reenforced by the failure of Kenyon, Cox and Company, a banking house that numbered Daniel Drew among its partners.

Even at that stage, a large number of people still believed that a policy of inaction would ultimately correct the business and financial situation, but, on Thursday, September 18, they were startled from lethargy with appalling suddenness. The great house of Jay Cooke and Company, preeminent banker to the United States government during the Civil War and leading financier of the railroad boom, closed its doors.[55] As soon as the news was received on the Stock Exchange, the market was panic-stricken. Selling orders poured across counters, and along the telegraph wires that connected New York with all parts of the country; by the afternoon prices of all securities were "declining frightfully." That so great a banking house should fail seemed incredible: men could scarcely believe their ears and, "within an hour or two after the announcement, hundreds of people gathered about the concern, on the side-walks, and peered curiously into the windows, as if some wonderful transformation was about to be witnessed."

But there was no transformation. Jay Cooke and Company did not open the following morning, and the financial hurricane raged with a fury that had not been equaled for a quarter of a century.[56] Fisk and Hatch, which had been almost as active as Jay Cooke and Company in railroad financing, was compelled to close its doors, while Friday and Saturday witnessed the failure of more than twenty smaller banks and brokerage houses.

Since the reserve position of the New York banks in September, 1873, was no better than it had been twelve months earlier,[57] the impact of the panic upon them was severe. The seasonal flow of funds to agricultural districts was augmented by demands for currency on the part of people who were rapidly losing confidence in the entire financial system and, since reserve city banks reduced their holdings of vault currency very little, while country banks actually enlarged their stock of money during the panic, the full brunt of the drain fell upon the New York institutions.

On September 13, the reserves of New York banks as a group were already below the legal minimum requirement of twenty-five per cent, largely owing to the weak position of the seven banks that held the bulk of the bankers' balances, and the continuous withdrawal of currency to the interior increased the deficiency. Moreover, since the Treasury had throughout the summer held as little currency as possible, in its efforts to ease the condition of the money market,[58] it was unable to do very much to alleviate conditions when the crisis actually occurred. Although more than thirteen million dollars' worth of outstanding government bonds were purchased for cash, many of the sales were made by savings banks, and these institutions proceeded to lock up the currency by demanding full notice of withdrawal from their depositors.

When the stock-exchange panic aggravated the banking situation, by diminishing confidence still further and causing serious runs on some of the largest banks in the city,[59] conditions became intolerable. The Union Trust Company and the National Bank of the Commonwealth were compelled to close their doors early on Friday, September 19, while the National Trust Company and three smaller banking houses faced the same necessity before the close of business. So complete was the breakdown of the money market, so widespread the panic, that, on Saturday morning, the governors of the Stock Exchange had in their hands letters from more than sixty brokers and bankers who announced that they would be compelled to suspend business before the next session of the market.[60] To prevent such a catastrophe, the Stock Exchange was closed at eleven o'clock.

For the events leading up to this collapse, the New York banks were, in large measure, responsible. But when the crisis actually occurred, they responded magnificently.[61] In order to release all available currency to meet the demands of customers, it was decided on September 20, to issue Clearing House Loan Certificates, based upon good collateral, which could be used to settle clearing balances among the banks; in order that all banks might be in an equally strong position, the currency reserves of Clearing House members were pooled, so that each bank could draw upon the central fund. In effect, therefore, the New York banks as a group "were converted, to all intents and purposes, into a central bank, which, although without power to issue notes, was in other respects more powerful than a European central bank, because it included virtually all the banking power of the city."[62]

These decisions on the part of the Clearing House Association enabled the New York banks to meet the situation with confidence. Currency was paid out promptly and courageously, so that the local panic was quickly allayed, but continued shipments of paper money to other parts of the country produced a further diminution in aggregate reserves by September 24, and it was decided to issue more Clearing House Loan Certificates. Within a single week the reserve ratio had fallen from twenty-three to seventeen per cent, and every evidence suggested that the demands of correspondent banks would continue to draw currency away from the city. Since Clearing House Loan Certificates did not provide a single dollar of legal-tender currency to meet this drain, sterner measures were necessary. The banks, therefore, decided to exercise their discretion in the payment of checks, refusing to pay out large amounts unless there was good reason to believe that the demand was legitimate.

Most of the checks presented were still paid in full, including practically all those drawn by correspondent banks, but there was no longer any certainty that a man

TABLE XV

THE BANKING INSTITUTIONS OF CHICAGO

(January, 1873)

NATIONAL BANKS

Organi-zation	Name of Bank	President	Cashier	Capital and Surplus	Deposits
1864	Union National	W. F. Coolbaugh	G. A. Ives	$1,200,000	$4,312,823
1864	Third National	J. I. Pierce	L. V. Parsons	950,000	2,889,119
1863	First National	S. M. Nickerson	L. J. Gage	1,300,000	2,810,240
1864	Commercial National	H. F. Eames	M. D. Buchanan	650,000	1,563,275
1871	German National	H. Greenebaum	H. Schaffner	575,000	1,211,894
1871	Corn Exchange National	J. S. Rumsey	Orson Smith	550,000	1,028,774
1864	Merchants National	C. B. Blair	Jno. De Koven	720,000	992,408
1864	Mechanics National	J. Y. Scammon	P. R. Forrest	300,000	908,677
1864	Manufacturers National	I. Holmes	J. A. Holmes	550,000	885,820
1871	Cook County National	D. D. Spencer	C. G. Bulkley	505,000	880,000
1864	Fifth National	C. B. Sawyer	I. G. Lombard	600,000	767,990
1871	National Bank of Illinois	E. Schneider	W. M. Scudder	505,000	719,646
1864	Northwestern National	G. Sturges	Wm. C. Oakley	950,000	706,547
1865	City National	A. D. Reed	A. B. Miner	350,000	704,426
1864	Second National	J. A. Ellis	J. P. McGregor	150,000	647,256
1865	Traders National	J. O. Rutter	T. P. Tallman	225,000	612,344
1869	National Bank of Commerce	P. C. Maynard	E. Maynard	257,000	550,042
1864	Fourth National	H. R. Payson	G. Taylor	206,885	367,512
1869	Union Stock Yards National	W. F. Tucker	E. S. Stickney	129,000	316,881
1872	Home National	A. L. Chetlain	G. W. Fuller	181,000	123,666
1872	Central National	W. F. Endicott	J. McK. Sanger	200,000	60,000

TABLE XV—*Continued*

STATE-CHARTERED COMMERCIAL BANKS

Organization	Name of Bank	President	Cashier	Capital and Surplus	Deposits
1857	Merchants Loan and Trust Co.	S. A. Smith	C. Henrotin	$1,500,000	$1,600,000
1873	Hide and Leather Bank	C. F. Gray	T. L. Forrest	300,000	100,000
1871	International Bank	B. Lowenthal	F. A. Hoffman	200,000	250,000
1867	Hibernian Banking Association	J. V. Clarke	H. B. Dox	111,000	200,000
1872	Bank of Chicago	S. J. Walker	W. H. Park	. . . . . .	150,000
1870	Germania Bank	C. Knoblesdorff	W. J. Haller	100,000	245,000
1872	Franklin Bank	F. Jones	G. S. Eddy	100,000	211,627
1863	Marine Company of Chicago	J. Y. Scammon	S. S. Rogers	500,000	300,000

FOREIGN BRANCH BANKS

	Capital and Surplus	Deposits
Established 1871. Bank of Montreal (branch)	$10,000,000	$250,000

TABLE XV—*Continued*

SAVINGS BANKS

Organization	Name of Bank	President	Cashier	Capital and Surplus	Deposits
1863	State Savings Institution	J. C. Dore	C. D. Bickford	$210,000	$4,629,867
1869	German Savings Bank	H. Greenebaum	A. Wise	212,500	1,523,669
1861	Merchants, Farmers & Mechs	P. R. Westfall	S. Myers	100,000	1,330,000
1861	Prairie State Loan & Trust Co.	J. W. Scoville	C. B. Meyer	150,000	807,867
1869	Commercial Loan Company	T. Wheeler	F. Meyer	100,000	666,211
1867	Hibernian Banking Association	J. V. Clarke	H. B. Dox	111,000	500,000
1872	Union Trust Company	S. W. Rawson	W. B. Hoswell	125,000	566,000
1873	Cook County Savings Bank	M. D. Ogden	G. P. Hansen	100,000	300,000
1872	Fidelity Savings Bank	J. C. Haines	J. Gage	200,000	406,204
1872	Bank of Chicago	S. J. Walker	W. H. Park	115,000	180,000
1863	The Marine Company of Chicago	J. Y. Scammon	S. S. Rogers	500,000	366,338
1872	Franklin Bank	F. Jones	G. S. Eddy	100,000	182,988
1870	Chicago Savings Institution	B. W. Phillips	F. W. Junge	......	145,338
1872	Mechanics Savings Bank	J. R. Shipherd	O. C. Sabin	......	115,420
1872	Citizens Savings Bank	W. M. Mayo	E. F. Nexsen	......	......
1873	State Street Savings Bank	O. N. Shipman	J. B. Sabine	......	......
1869	Dime Savings Bank	....	W. K. Reed	......	......
1873	City Savings Bank	....	....	......	......

Savings deposits held by private bankers $300,000

TABLE XV—*Continued*

PRIVATE BANKERS

	Capital and Surplus	Deposits
Lunt, Preston & Kean	$140,000	$859,164
J. M. Adsit	120,000	200,000
Follansbee & Son	100,000	250,000
Other private bankers	....	300,000

could obtain currency when he needed it. Even in New York, currency rose to a premium,[63] while the domestic exchange market throughout the country was utterly disorganized.[64] The tendency to hoard currency and the difficulty experienced in meeting pay rolls offered additional evidence of the monetary collapse, and local substitutes for money were issued in many parts of the country to alleviate the distress. Nevertheless, in the face of an utter collapse of the financial system, the New York banks continued, as far as possible, to meet all the demands upon them, so that by the middle of October their currency reserve amounted to less than five per cent of their net deposit liabilities.[65]

But what of conditions in Chicago during this financial storm? In view of the additional business arising from the reconstruction after the fire, and of the influence of widespread speculation on the Board of Trade, the city had enjoyed a degree of prosperity as great, or greater, than that found in any other part of the country. Moreover, although Boston and Philadelphia still possessed much larger financial resources, the bankers of Chicago were rapidly assuming a position second only to that of New York as reserve agents for banks and bankers in other parts of the country.[66] The First National Bank, which is the only one of the three leading institutions whose ledgers have been preserved, was already holding the deposits of eighty national banks spread over fifteen states, to say nothing of a much larger number of accounts kept with it by state and private bankers. In the case of the Union National, the outstanding bankers' bank in Chicago at this time,[67] the number of such accounts must have been very much larger.

The Chicago banks, as a group, however, were no more conscious of their responsibilities than were the New York institutions. The growing importance of the city as a reserve center produced no increase in the average size of the cash reserves held by the national banks. Indeed, the reserve ratio in the summer of 1873 was somewhat lower than it had been in 1870, although the amount of deposits due to banks and bankers had risen from $7,500,000 to $11,250,000, an increase of exactly fifty per cent. Well might the *Chronicle* point out that the concentration of bank resources in Chicago was an embarrassing tendency. "If it spreads in any notable degree, it will materially complicate the future working of the money market."[68]

Moreover, banking expansion in Chicago, the extent of which is amply indicated by the figures in Table XV, had introduced elements of weakness into the structure of the money market. Many institutions were noticeably less liquid than they had been immediately before the fire, and some of the smaller ones were thoroughly unsound. In the case of the Scandinavian National Bank, for instance, which closed its doors during the early days of 1873, there was deliberate mismanagement on the part of the President,[69] who absconded to Europe, while the evidence regarding institutions like the Farmers Bank suggests that there had never been any adequate quantity of actual capital invested by the promoters and owners.[70]

It might be expected, in the light of these facts, that the repercussions of the New York panic would be particu-

larly serious, yet the initial impact was scarcely perceptible to the man in the street. The newspapers suggested that no local trouble was anticipated, and praised
the sound condition of the banks,[71] but the situation was
not as comfortable as journalistic optimism suggested.
Even at this stage of the panic, many Chicago banks had
started to call loans, in an attempt to strengthen their
position by credit contraction, and this fact, coupled with
the failure of Jay Cooke and Company, brought about a
slump in real-estate prices. A precipitous decline in grain
prices began on September 19, which carried wheat down
from one dollar and thirteen cents to ninety cents in four
days and, late in the afternoon of the first day, the banking firm of A. C. and O. F. Badger closed its doors.[72] On
September 20, the Franklin Bank was compelled to suspend because of its inability to meet a large debit balance
at the Clearing House,[73] but the newspapers attempted to
restore confidence by insisting that it had not had a very
good reputation since the fire.

Meanwhile, the contraction of credit continued, and
Chicago banks were drawing on their New York balances
to a much greater extent than was necessary to meet the
demands of their own correspondents. New York exchange was unsalable because none of the banks wished
to increase its balance in that city, and currency was
moving in large quantities from the Atlantic Coast to
Chicago by September 23.[74] But, in spite of the apparent
success of their efforts to throw the full burden of the
panic demands onto New York, the leading bankers of
Chicago were worried. The refusal to purchase New York
exchange in any large amounts was paralyzing the grain

trade; elevators and stockyards were being crowded to their utmost capacity,[75] and the railroads were compelled to refuse shipments from the primary markets owing to a lack of additional storage space.

On the evening of September 24, therefore, the President of the Clearing House Association called a meeting to discuss plans "for mutual protection," a phrase that significantly indicates a desire to strengthen the banks rather than a wish to restore normal business activity. After considerable discussion, it was found impossible to draft any constructive plan that would meet with the approval of a majority of the bankers present,[76] so that the only action taken was to follow the decision reached by New York bankers earlier in the day. By a unanimous vote of the members present, it was "resolved by the Chicago Clearing House Association that, until further action (and in view of the disturbed condition of affairs in New York and other cities and the difficulty of converting balances into currency) and upon advice of the Bank Examiner, its members be recommended and authorised to suspend Currency payments on any large demands made upon them either from Country Banks or over their counters."

Suspension of currency payments at the discretion of the banks was a serious step to take, particularly in view of the fact that it was not accompanied by any of the collateral measures that had been adopted by New York and other important cities. But the situation itself was growing serious, as the general public discovered two days later.

On Friday, September 26, five national banks closed

their doors in Chicago, and among them was the Union National, the greatest bank in the west. A few weeks earlier, its statement had shown aggregate deposits of $1,841,461 owing to national banks alone, and $1,325,573 due to state and private banks. Taken together these liabilities amounted to more than one-third of the bankers' balances in Chicago. The failure of such an institution naturally spread consternation throughout the surrounding territory, producing more intense panic than any other event during those hectic days of crisis, while in Chicago the impact of its suspension was accentuated by the closing of the Cook County National, the Second National, the Manufacturers National and the National Bank of Commerce.[77] Two days later, the Third National Bank, which was second in size to the Union National, was also forced to suspend in the face of a run,[78] and several of the smaller state and private banks failed to open their doors.

Such an avalanche of failures produced serious runs on all the other banks. At the First National Bank, crowds thronged the building on both Friday and Saturday but "Mr. L. J. Gage, the courteous Cashier, was serene, and dispatching business with an unruffled temper. . . . Every check was met promptly."* Nor was the run a matter of small consequence. The aggregate New York balances of the Bank, which had amounted to almost $500,000 on September 17, had already been reduced to $184,463 before the afternoon of Wednesday, Septem-

* *Chicago Tribune,* September 27 and 28, 1873. Gage's handling of the situation evoked universal admiration, and the eulogies in the press were as enthusiastic as the resolution of thanks passed by his Board of Directors after the panic.

ber 24. When the doors were closed on Saturday, after the two worst days of panic, the New York balances had fallen to $41,295. Cash on hand showed little reduction, however. On Wednesday, the total vault reserves stood at $682,349; when business ended on Saturday there was still $634,495 on hand.

These figures clearly indicate the extent to which the burden of the panic was shifted to New York, even by a strong bank, and the same story holds true of Chicago banks in general. Moreover, since, in the case of the First National Bank, aggregate deposits fell from $4,129,668 on September 17 to $2,755,316 at the close of business on September 27, it is apparent that a considerable liquidation of assets was necessary to meet the demands of frightened customers. Yet, even on the latter day, Gage still insisted that the Bank was prepared to meet all demands upon it by its customers, and pointed out that he regarded the temporary suspension by other Chicago banks as ill advised.[79]

But the First National was not alone in its attitude. The Merchants Loan and Trust Company, and the Bank of Montreal also paid the checks of all their customers in full, although these three appear to have been the only banks that did not take advantage of the Clearing House resolution.* Indeed, there arose a sharp controversy among Chicago bankers as to the wisdom of the policy that Gage upheld, and Coolbaugh was the leader of the opposition. Even the suspension of the Union National

* The strength of these institutions, and a few others, was attributed, in part, to the fact that they were chiefly owned by men who were also large depositors and, therefore, interested in protecting (rather than wrecking) the banks. *Chicago Tribune,* September 27, 1873.

was due, in part, to Coolbaugh's firm conviction that it would be suicidal for Chicago banks to continue to pay out currency when suspension had already occurred in all the other important cities. "To pay out currency until she was exhausted," he insisted, "might maintain for Chicago an enviable temporary supremacy, but it would be the gratification of an honorable pride at the expense of her immediate future safety, and place her eventually helplessly in the power of those who would not be slow to take advantage of her nakedness."[80]

Whether the contention was right or wrong, there can be no doubt that the suspension of banking activity was a revolutionary step to take. It was, for that reason, accompanied by an equally novel decision. In order to assure the public that the closing of the Union National was due to external monetary panic, and not to any inherent unsoundness, Coolbaugh and the other directors issued a public statement that deserves a high place in the annals of banking. Its wording was very simple. "We, the undersigned, resident directors of the Union National Bank, of Chicago, hereby declare to the Public that we will, and do hereby hold ourselves personally responsible as individuals, for the payment of all the deposits now held by said bank, or which may hereafter be made with it." At the meeting of the Clearing House Association held on the evening of the suspension, this statement was ordered to be spread upon the minutes.

This meeting at the Clearing House was called, in view of the unexpected development of the panic, to consider the issue of Clearing House Loan Certificates along lines similar to the plan adopted by the New York

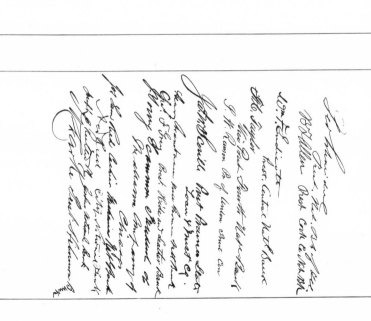

LETTER FROM CHICAGO BANKERS TO COOLBAUGH, 1873

bankers, but there was no unanimity among the members regarding the proposal. Although, after much debate, a resolution authorizing such certificates was defeated by eleven votes to eight, the participants in the discussion were not satisfied with the result. A motion to adjourn was defeated by twelve votes to six and, finally, as a compromise, the chairman was authorized to appoint a committee to consider the matter and report back to a special meeting of the Association on the following day.

At the adjourned meeting the same conflict of opinion was evident. Three members of the committee presented a majority report favoring the issue of certificates without any pooling of reserves, but the other two members presented a minority report which, while approving the general idea of such an issue, insisted that more careful consideration should be given to matters of detail. The minority report was adopted by the meeting and when Greenebaum, of the German National, tried to reverse this decision he received support from only four banks— the Fourth National, Mechanics National, Cook County National and Hibernian. The idea of Clearing House Loan Certificates was definitely unpopular.

On the morning of Monday, September 29, the six banks that had closed their doors on the previous Friday opened for business once more, and all of them, except the Union National, were able to sustain themselves in the face of the demands that were made by customers during the day.[81] The latter institution, however, was confronted by unusually heavy demands from its creditors, so that it was forced to close again in the afternoon. That evening a meeting of stockholders was hastily called, and it was decided to put the Bank into voluntary liquidation.

This action on the part of the stockholders, which appears to have been inspired by Coolbaugh's irritation at the public distrust of his Bank, was needlessly precipitate. During the early days of October, a distinct improvement was apparent in the Chicago money market, although several weeks were to pass before normal financial activity was restored.[82] By drawing down their New York balances the bankers of Chicago were bringing substantial quantities of currency into the city, and this inward movement was augmented by the arrival of dealers who were prepared to purchase grain for cash in order to facilitate the resumption of shipments. On September 29 alone, the currency brought in by the Express companies amounted to $2,000,000,[83] while for the week ending October 2 the shipments exceeded $16,000,000. In view of these facts, Coolbaugh began to regret his earlier action. The Union National was a solvent institution and, when several of the leading bankers of Chicago sent a joint letter* assuring him of their "undiminished good will," and expressing the hope that the Bank would resume operations, he immediately telegraphed the Comptroller of the Currency to learn whether the action taken by the stockholders' meeting could be rescinded. He was luckier than he had expected. In view of the fact that some of the stock had been voted by proxy at the shareholders' meeting, the Comptroller telegraphed that the

---

* This letter is reproduced facing p. 450. It is interesting in the light of the controversy between Gage and Coolbaugh to notice that the First National Bank is not represented among the signers.

decision to go into voluntary liquidation was illegal.*
Another meeting of stockholders, held on October 13,
voted to resume operations, and on the following day the
Union National Bank was once again open for business.[84]
Moreover, the directors of the Bank, to show that they still
had every confidence in Coolbaugh, passed a formal resolution to that effect and, a few weeks afterward, increased
his salary from $10,000 to $15,000 a year.

At this point, with the panic in the Chicago money
market allayed,[85] it is well to pause a moment in order to
take a comprehensive view of what had occurred. The
panic of 1873 was the first great financial debacle after
the creation of the national banking system; it was also
the first panic in which Chicago carried any considerable
responsibilities as a reserve center.

In view of the sharp contrast of policy between New
York and Chicago, and of the fact that all other large
cities followed the example of New York[86] in the matter
of Clearing House Loan Certificates, it was inevitable
that controversy should arise regarding the merits of the
policies followed by Chicago banks during the critical
period. From the account of the panic given in previous
pages it is clear that there was no unanimity of policy
among the leading institutions of the city, which is itself
an indictment, but it is also clear that Sprague is in error
when he states that suspension of cash payments in Chicago was complete.[87]

Taking the national banks of Chicago, as a group, we
find that loans were reduced from more than $25,000,000,
on September 12, to $19,000,000, on October 13, a con-

* See messages reproduced facing p. 454.

traction of more than twenty per cent. Moreover, between the same dates, the cash holdings of the banks actually increased from $5,700,000 to $6,300,000, while reserve balances in New York were reduced by seventy-five per cent. Such a credit contraction, reinforced by hoarding of currency on the part of most of the banks, could not fail to accentuate the crisis in the local market. Prices declined precipitously, and substitutes for currency were issued by private firms as well as by the City of Chicago.

Such a policy, while it undoubtedly strengthened the position of the banks that did not fail, is contrary to every canon of banking theory. In time of crisis, the holder of the banking reserves can alleviate the situation only if those reserves are paid away promptly and courageously, and such a policy must be reinforced by a liberal attitude in regard to the granting of loans even though the rate of interest is raised to a point where it will discourage those who do not seriously need the funds. When the community is confident that cash and capital funds are available in case of need there is no panic.

In neither of these regards had the banking institutions of Chicago lived up to the ideals of central banking practice that should govern the reserve agents of country banks, although a few institutions like the Merchants Loan and Trust Company and the First National Bank had made valiant efforts to prevent a complete suspension of currency payments. By contrast with the action taken so promptly by the New York Clearing House Association, the policies of Chicago appear weak and timorous, but New York had behind it a century of experience as a reserve center while Chicago had assumed that burden

less than a decade before the panic. Although economic improvements are never created overnight, it is not too much to say that out of those days of tribulation during the autumn of 1873 there was born in Chicago a new feeling of financial responsibility. The panic, in a sense, constituted the birth pains of the central reserve city that was soon to arise.

By November, in all parts of the country, the dramatic excitement of the panic had passed.[88] On the first of October, the New York Stock Exchange opened for trading once again and during the early days of the following year the Clearing House Loan Certificates issued in New York and other cities were all retired. On January 29, 1874, the Chicago Clearing House Association unanimously decided that the resolution by which banks had been authorized to refuse currency payments on large checks should be "rescinded, cancelled and annulled." A condition of quiescence and ease pervaded the money market.[89]

But the financial consequences of the crisis continued to affect the general economic situation. On June 29, 1874, occurred the resounding failure of the Freedman's Savings and Trust Company in Washington, with its thirty-four branches in various parts of the country.[90] Even before that time, there were troubles in Chicago, since the Marine Company was reported to be in serious difficulty toward the end of March.[91] Scammon, and one or two of his friends, had borrowed very heavily in order to finance real-estate speculations, and Scammon was compelled to transfer some $245,000 of his personal property to the Company in an attempt to save it.[92] The effort was fruitless. The institution failed early in 1875, leaving behind it a series of lawsuits that did not reflect very creditably upon Scammon's management.[93] Meanwhile, on January 20, 1875, the Cook County National Bank announced its suspension, as a result of a shrinkage of assets aggravated by the failure of an eastern insurance company, and in this case the repercussions once again threw an unfavorable light on banking practices during the boom.[94]

Nor were these indications of weakness ignored in contemporary discussions. Although the New York banks had been very restless under the arrangement involving the pooling of reserves,[95] feeling that the sound institutions were being unfairly taxed to pay for the sins of their weaker brethren, the report of the Clearing House Committee presented an admirably lucid analysis of the whole situation.[96] This report, which has been accurately described as "the ablest document that has appeared in the course of our banking history," drew attention to the inadequacy of bank reserves before the panic. Criticizing many aspects of correspondent relations among banks, it called attention specifically to the evils of paying interest on bankers' balances and to the dangers of receiving uncollected checks as cash deposits. On these matters there was little argument. Spurred on by the vivid memory of the panic, banks in both New York and Chicago made an effort to correct some of the defects that had caused that experience. Reserves were increased during the period of monetary ease, and many banks abandoned the practice of paying interest on demand deposits.*

* The directors of the First National Bank of Chicago agreed as early as October 17, 1873, "that the practice of paying interest to banks and bankers on daily balances be discontinued."

Moreover, the Chicago Clearing House Association, which had shown so little effective power of leadership during the years from 1871 to 1873, began to take a much stronger position. In December, 1873, in rejecting an application for membership, it was decided that a minimum paid-up capital of $250,000 should in future be required of all banks that wished to belong to the Association. In January of the following year, the Mechanics National Bank, in the light of its unsatisfactory financial condition, was asked to resign from the Clearing House and, when it protested against the decision, was expelled.

Economic conditions in general, however, had gone from bad to worse. Business was utterly stagnant, and agriculture was so severely depressed that the farmers were clamorous in their demands for relief. Railroad regulation was demanded, in order to insure low freight rates for agricultural produce, a movement in which Illinois was the pioneer,[97] and there was a growing tendency to criticize the monetary policies of the government. In Chicago, the real-estate market, which had been exuberantly prosperous during the years that separated the fire from the panic, had fallen into a state of utter listlessness,[98] and unemployment throughout the United States was so severe that thousands of workers were migrating back to their homes in Europe.[99] By the middle of 1876, the leading journals of the country were resignedly preaching about "the blessings of hard times"[100] and could see no prospect of immediate business improvement.

Chicago, at the economic crossroads of the nation, suffered acutely from these long years of depression. Foreign lending had stopped in 1873,[101] and business stagnation combined with falling real-estate prices had created embarrassing financial problems both for the business enterprises of the city and its political governors. From 1873 to 1875, the floating debt of the City of Chicago rose steadily and, when the courts held that certificates of indebtedness were being issued illegally, a chaotic fiscal situation ensued.[102] To meet the crisis, the First National Bank, the Third National Bank and the Merchants Loan and Trust Company made substantial loans to the City Comptroller, but even this action aroused criticism from those who felt that affairs had deteriorated to a point where no improvement was possible.[103] Depression and pessimism held undisputed sway throughout the land.

REFERENCES FOR CHAPTER XII

[1] *Chicago Tribune,* April 17, 1872; Bogart and Thompson: *op. cit.,* p. 67.

[2] *Chicago Times,* October 19, 1871.

[3] *Lakeside Reminiscences,* p. 127.

[4] Andreas: *op. cit.,* III, 61.

[5] Cf. *Lakeside Reminiscences,* pp. 129-132; *Chicago Tribune,* October 12, 13 and 14, 1871.

[6] *Chicago Tribune,* October 12 and 14, 1871.

[7] Cf. *Chicago Tribune,* October 12, 13 and 14, 1871, for several good examples.

[8] *Ibid.,* October 11, 1871.

[9] *Ibid.,* October 12 and 16, 1871.

[10] *Ibid.,* October 16, 1871.

[11] *Ibid.,* October 14 and 18, 1871.

[12] *Ibid.,* October 12, 1871.

[13] *Ibid.,* October 13, 1871.

[14] *Ibid.,* October 14, 1871; Harper and Ravell: *op. cit.,* pp. 46-47.

[15] *Chicago Tribune,* October 16 and 18, 1871.

[16] *Ibid.,* October 16, 1871.

[17] *Ibid.,* October 17 and 18, 1871.

[18] *Ibid.,* October 19, 1871; *Commercial and Financial Chronicle,* XIII, 631.

[19] *Chicago Evening Post,* October 19, 1871.

[20] *Lakeside Reminiscences,* p. 136.

[21] *Chicago Tribune,* May 12, 1872.

[22] Cf. *ibid.,* April 28, May 5, 1872.

[23] *Ibid.,* July 18, 20 and 22, October 9, 1874.

[24] *Chicago Times: The New Chicago; Chicago Tribune,* April 7, 20, 21 and 23, December 14, 1872.

[25] *Chicago Tribune,* October 21, November 7, 1871.

[26] *Ibid.,* October 20, 1871.

[27] *Ibid.,* November 14, 1871; April 7 and 25, 1872; Bogart and Thompson: *op. cit.,* p. 272.

[28] All figures for national banks are taken from the *Annual Reports of the Comptroller of the Currency,* unless otherwise stated.

[29] *Chicago Tribune,* December 16, 22 and 27, 1871; January 4, April 3, 1872; January 30, 1873.

[30] *Ibid.,* May 11, 1872.

[31] *Ibid.,* November 15, 1871.

[32] *Bankers Magazine,* XXVI, 74, 148, 634 and 979; XXVII, 72, 307, 395, 488, 673, 667, 752 and 912. All the new national banks were admitted to the Clearing House, while the Bank of Montreal (which had been one of the original members in 1865) was readmitted on January 7, 1873.

[33] *Bankers Magazine,* XXVIII, 229; *Commercial and Financial Chronicle,* CXXVII, 1481.

[34] *Chicago Tribune,* November 18, 1871; May 4, 1872; *Commercial and Financial Chronicle,* XIII, 493, 501 and 655-656; Bogart and Thompson: *op. cit.,* p. 271.

[35] *Commercial and Financial Chronicle,* XXVI, 151-152. Connecticut companies alone had lent $14,000,000 on Chicago real estate by the end of 1877.

[36] *Commercial and Financial Chronicle,* XIII, 589 and 653.

[37] *Ibid.,* XV, 344; XVI, 38, 342 and 783; Bogart and Thompson: *op. cit.,* p. 276.

[38] *Commercial and Financial Chronicle,* XV, 18; XVIII, 5-6; *Bankers Magazine,* XXX, 605.

[39] *Commercial and Financial Chronicle,* XIV, 219; *Report on the Affairs of the Union Pacific Railroad, 42nd Congress, 3 Session, H. R. Report 78.*

[40] C. A. and Mary Beard: *The Rise of American Civilization,* pp. 191-193; Bogart and Thompson: *op. cit.,* pp. 83 and 332.

[41] *Commercial and Financial Chronicle,* XV, 323; XVI, 614 and 709.

[42] *Bankers Magazine,* XXVIII, 782; *Commercial and Financial Chronicle,* XVI, 345.

[43] *Report of the United States Industrial Commission on the Distribution of Farm Products,* May 1900, Vol. VI; *Report of the Federal Commission on the Grain Trade,* September 1920 (especially Vol. II, Ch. III); H. M. Larson: *The Wheat Market and the Farmer in Minnesota, 1858-1900.*

[44] *Sixteenth Annual Report of the Chicago Board of Trade,* 1873; *Bankers Magazine,* XXVII, 307; *Chicago Tribune,* April 28, May 12 and 15, 1872.

[45] For an extended discussion of this point see O. M. W. Sprague: *History of Crises under the National Banking System,* Ch. I.

[46] *Commercial and Financial Chronicle,* XIV, 205, 445, 476 and 509; *Chicago Tribune,* May 15, 1872.

[47] *Commercial and Financial Chronicle,* XV, 309.

[48] Cf. Kane: *op. cit.,* I, 103 ff.

[49] *Commercial and Financial Chronicle,* XV, 374 and 405.

[50] Sprague: *op. cit.,* pp. 26-27.

[51] *Commercial and Financial Chronicle,* XV, 853; XVI, 7.

[52] *Idem,* 69.

[53] *Idem,* 373; Sprague: *op. cit.,* 29-30.

[54] *Commercial and Financial Chronicle,* XVII, 341; Cf. Sprague: *op. cit.,* pp. 35-36 for the preliminary phase of the panic of 1873.

[55] *New York Times,* September 19, 1873; for an account of the march of events from this point onwards, cf. Horace White: "The Financial Crisis in America," *Fortnightly Review,* 1876, pp. 810-829.

[56] *Commercial and Financial Chronicle,* XVII, 375; *New York Times,* September 20, 1873.

[57] *Commercial and Financial Chronicle,* XX, 300; Sprague: *op. cit.,* pp. 82-83.

[58] *Commercial and Financial Chronicle,* XVII, 141.

[59] *New York Times,* September 20, 1873.

[60] H. H. Porter: *A Short Autobiography,* p. 28.

[61] *New York Clearing House Report,* November 11, 1873 (reproduced in Sprague: *op. cit.,* pp. 91-103); *Commercial and Financial Chronicle,* XVII, 448; XVIII, 28.

[62] Sprague: *op. cit.,* p. 90.

[63] Cf. Sprague: *op. cit.,* p. 57, for the daily quotations during September and October.

[64] *Chicago Tribune,* September 20 and 25, 1873.

[65] Cf. Sprague: *op. cit.,* pp. 54-56.

[66] *Commercial and Financial Chronicle,* XVI, 205.

[67] *Chicago Tribune,* September 27, 1873. Unfortunately the ledgers of the Union National Bank of this period are no longer in existence.

[68] *Commercial and Financial Chronicle,* XVI, 205.

[69] *Bankers Magazine,* XXVII, 581.

[70] *Ibid.,* XXVIII, 68.

[71] *Chicago Tribune,* September 18 and 19, 1873.

[72] *Ibid.,* September 20, 1873.

[73] *Ibid.,* September 21, 1873.

[74] *Ibid.,* September 24, 1873.

[75] *Ibid.,* September 25, 1873.

[76] *Ibid.,* September 25 and 26, 1873.

[77] *Ibid.,* September 26 and 27, 1873.

[78] *Ibid.,* September 28, 1873.

[79] *Ibid.,* September 27, 1873.

[80] *Idem.*

[81] *Ibid.,* September 30, 1873.

[82] See below p. 455.

[83] *Chicago Tribune,* September 30, 1873.

[84] *Bankers Magazine,* XXVIII, 394.

[85] *Chicago Tribune,* September 28, 1873; February 13, 1874.

[86] Canon: *Clearing Houses,* pp. 91-97.

[87] Sprague: *op. cit.,* p. 63.

[88] *Bankers Magazine,* XXVIII, 394; *Commercial and Financial Chronicle,* XVII, 793.

[89] *Chicago Tribune,* January 27, 1874; *Commercial and Financial Chronicle,* XVIII, 129.

[90] Kane: *op. cit.,* I, 79-84.

[91] *Chicago Tribune,* April 1, 1874.

[92] *Ibid.,* April 8, May 5, 1874.

[93] *Ibid.,* June 10, 1877.

[94] *Ibid.,* January 20, 1875.

[95] *New York Times,* October 10 to 23, 1873; Sprague: *op. cit.,* pp. 121-123.

[96] This report is reproduced in Sprague: *op. cit.,* pp. 91-103.

[97] Bogart and Thompson: *op. cit.,* pp. 82-96.

[98] *Chicago Tribune,* April 15 and 28, 1874.

[99] *Commercial and Financial Chronicle,* XXI, 121.

[100] *Ibid.,* XXIII, 75.

[101] *Ibid.,* XVII, 582.

[102] *Ibid.,* XXI, 488; XX, 457 and 544; XXVI, 192.

[103] *Chicago Times,* October 17, 1876.

CHAPTER XIII

THE IMPACT OF RESUMPTION

1874–1879

THE excitement of prosperity during the late sixties and early seventies had diverted popular attention from the fact that the United States was still operating on a paper currency inherited from the Civil War. Under the impact of the immediate postwar recession, there had arisen vociferous demands for an immediate return to the gold standard, and the combined influence of business depression and deflationary policy had reduced the aggregate circulation of paper money from $913,000,000, in 1865, to $694,000,000 in the summer of 1869.[1] The value of the paper dollar in gold, which had been as low as thirty-eight cents in 1864, had doubled as a result of the currency contraction.

By 1870, however, the deflationary pressure had relaxed considerably. Currency in circulation expanded until it reached the figure of $781,000,000 in June, 1874; bank deposits increased even more rapidly. Wholesale prices moved upward sharply, and retail prices were arrested in their downward course, while wages (which had remained unduly low throughout the war) were raised substantially. Prosperity was rampant, and even though a few voices in the wilderness still urged the country to reestablish the gold standard at the earliest possible moment, the people as a whole had no stomach for further deflation. Why should they sacrifice the prospect of growing profits and a higher standard of living on the altar of devotion to an outmoded golden calf?

Such an attitude was not strange. From the beginning of monetary history, people have seldom wished to alter a monetary system that permitted them to attain prosperity, and it is probable that such an attitude will persist until the end of time. Monetary institutions are only means to an end, never ends in themselves, and a standard that facilitates profitable human activity must always appear satisfactory to those who reap the profits.

Economic circumstances changed, however, with the panic of 1873. As profits gave place to losses, and the accounts of business failures replaced the stories of accomplishment that had filled the newspapers, public attention turned once more to the monetary problems that had been temporarily forgotten. The inflationary expansion after 1869 had unquestionably intensified the severity of the subsequent panic, so that those who had preached resumption during the years of plenty were now able to add the whiplash of remembrance to their remarks. Moreover, under a paper standard, American business, after 1874, was suffering from one of the severest depressions in its history. A metallic standard could not be any worse, and it might be considerably better.

To point out that such arguments are born of expediency does nothing to clarify the discussion. Out of the depths of depression there arose a monetary controversy that was destined to split both of the great political parties, since neither of them was willing to take a definite stand on the questions raised.[2] Even though the arguments that filled the land were often unsound from the angle of economic theory, there was a real conflict of interest between the opposing groups that no amount of verbiage could distort or compromise. Each group of protagonists stood to reap a material advantage from the adoption of the policy that it recommended, and unless that fact is remembered the persistence of monetary controversy becomes incomprehensible. Since nobody appears to have suggested the permanent maintenance of the existing monetary system, with no change in policy, it was obvious that the United States had to choose between inflation and deflation. It was equally obvious that moderate inflation would ease the financial burdens of heavily mortgaged farmers, while the opposite policy would increase the real income of the rapidly growing rentier class. Each individual, and each class, was fighting for its own interests, and the monetary and banking system of the country was necessarily the battleground.

As soon as the excitement of panic was over, in 1873, demands for monetary expansion began to be heard, and even before they had gained volume the Treasury decided to reissue some three millions of Greenbacks for the purpose of relieving the financial strain.[3] In the light of subsequent events, it is hard to conceive anything more dangerous than this otherwise insignificant Treasury decision, since it gave a lever to the inflationist forces. If an additional issue of currency could be made to ease the strain of a financial crisis, why not authorize another increase to lighten the burdens of depression? Early in

1874, the members of the Illinois legislature, and other prominent citizens of the state,* were memorializing Congress, pointing out that "they, representing the vast agricultural and commercial interests of the West and South, believe the volume of currency not sufficient for the business of the country, and they also believe contraction is in the interest of Eastern capital to the detriment of Western and Southern industry."[4]

In this document the issue was squarely joined. By one method or another, the inflationary forces, which were largely concentrated in the west and south, wished to enlarge the currency; conservative forces mustered in the mercantile and industrial districts of the east wished to contract it in order to return to gold.[5] Rallying all their forces to defeat the bill before Congress, which was intended to increase the circulation of Greenbacks to $400,-000,000, the latter pointed out that any such action would inevitably undermine the confidence that was so necessary to business recovery and insisted that, if resumption of specie payments was achieved, the benefits conferred upon the nation by that act would vastly transcend any that might be gained from specious monetary panaceas. Even theology was not immune from the infection of monetary controversy, since the Senate chaplain opened the session for consideration of the bill by endeavoring "to inform the Almighty on the merits of inflation and contraction of the currency, and prayed the Divine aid in bringing the inflationists to a sense of the iniquity they were trying to accomplish."[6]

---

* The *Chicago Tribune*, which did not favor inflation at this time, acidly points out that, among the nineteen hundred citizens of Chicago who signed this petition, there was not a single "well-known resident of the city."

To many citizens of Chicago, the inflationary proposals were as bitterly distasteful as they were to any of the maligned "Eastern capitalists." The members of the Board of Trade united in protesting that the currency was already overexpanded,[7] while a special meeting of the Chicago Clearing House Association, in taking similar action, insisted that no legislation would be in the best interests of the country that did not look to "the establishment of specie payments at the earliest practicable moment, this being alone the basis not only for sound finances, but also demanded by the spirit of the Constitution."[8] The *Tribune*, itself, while opposing the bill, still retained its moderate position. While the addition of $44,000,000 to the currency of the country would not, it pointed out, be calamitous, such a policy would give rise to steadily increasing demands for further monetary expansion. "The first barrier having been thrown down, it will be easier to take the second step, and presently those who wanted only a little inflation will find that the power to say how little they shall have has gone out of their hands."[9]

But Chicago, and the northwestern states, were not as unanimous in sentiment as these statements might suggest. When the immediate danger of inflation was removed by Grant's veto of the bill, which had passed both houses of Congress, the newspapers of the territory were almost evenly divided in their comment. Five hundred and fourteen papers, of which less than three hundred were Republican praised the action of the President, while four hundred and eight, including two hundred and thirty Republican organs, criticized it vehemently.[10]

Only the banking fraternity appears to have maintained a united front.[11]

The bankers, and particularly the national bankers, were even more deeply interested in the controversy than other sections of the populace. In view of the fact that national banks had been established for the purpose of preventing an unregulated expansion of state issues, they were from the very outset objects of suspicion to the inflationists. Moreover, since they were, on an average, large financial institutions, they shared the odium attaching to all forms of wealth in the minds of those who thought that the deflationary policy was engineered by the rich for their own private advantage. As a result, there was a constant clamor for the abolition of the national banking system and the replacement of national bank notes by Greenbacks, against which all the verbiage of argument appeared ineffective.[12] To make matters worse, it was generally believed that, under Boutwell and Richardson, the Treasury was not entirely out of sympathy with this idea.[13]

To strengthen the position of the national banks, the deflationary forces in Congress succeeded in passing the Act of June 20, 1874. The reserves that had previously been required against notes were abolished, and such notes were no longer to be redeemed over the counters of banks in the larger cities that served as reserve agents for their correspondents. Instead, it was provided that all national bank notes should be redeemable at the United States Treasury, and that banks should deposit with the Treasurer for that purpose a redemption fund equal to five per cent of their outstanding note issue. Provision was also made for the replacement of mutilated or worn-out notes, and national banks that wished to retire a portion (or all) of their issue were authorized to do so by depositing an equal amount of legal-tender currency with the Treasury, receiving back again the bonds they had deposited as collateral. Moreover, to implement the Act of 1870, which had been completely ineffective, and to extend the facilities of national banks established in southern and western states, the act authorized the Comptroller to increase the issue of national bank notes in these areas by $55,000,000, withdrawing that amount of notes from banks in other parts of the country. Finally, to close the last loophole against the inflationists, it was provided that the amount of Greenbacks in circulation should never exceed $382,000,000. Even though McCulloch was not fully satisfied with the measure,[14] it represented a tremendous victory for what was, even then, called "the sound money group."

Return to the gold standard could not, however, be achieved solely by prohibiting an increase of government paper currency. A comprehensive program was necessary, one that should build up the necessary gold reserves, maintain the budget in balance, and provide for an elastic bank-note currency to serve the needs of the community after the Greenbacks had been retired.[15] The forces of resumption, therefore, decided to follow up the advantage they had gained in the spring by introducing a general bill that would definitely commit the nation to such a policy. Even the President, in his message to Congress, was persuaded to speak in its behalf[16] and General Garfield, at his platitudinous worst, strongly urged its passage.[17] After a bitter Congressional struggle, the measure was passed in January, 1875, and victory seemed assured for the deflationary bloc.[18]

Under the Resumption Act, as it came to be called, the United States was definitely pledged to return to the gold standard on January 1, 1879, and to that end the Secretary of the Treasury was required to accumulate a reserve for the redemption of the currency. Meanwhile, the act proposed to replace the fractional paper money by subsidiary silver coins and, in order to supply an adequate currency in larger denominations, removed the maximum limit of $300,000,000 to the aggregate issue of national bank notes. Henceforth national bank notes might be issued to an extent that was limited only by the aggregate capital of the banks and the quantity of government bonds available as collateral, but the aggregate circulation of Greenbacks was to be reduced by an amount equal to eighty per cent of any issue of national bank notes beyond the $300,000,000 originally stipulated. In the course of time, therefore, it was confidently expected that national bank notes would entirely replace the legal-tender paper to which the Civil War had given rise.

Strange as it may seem, some conservative organs were not very enthusiastic about the act. Pointing out that the door was opened to a phenomenal expansion of national bank notes, the *Chronicle* labeled the Resumption Act as a "disguised inflation bill." Bank notes would, under the terms of the measure, expand more rapidly than Greenbacks would contract,[19] and "sooner or later those forces which are now busy, though latent, will make their power felt in a speculative expansion of credit and a dangerous inflation of the currency." Even the *Tribune* could only give the measure its "qualified support," and felt that the proposed retirement of the Greenbacks would not actually be carried out.[20]

Chicago bankers, however, were more enthusiastic. Although Coolbaugh felt that supplemental legislation would be necessary to achieve the purposes of the act, Nickerson insisted that the fears of bank-note inflation were absurd.[21] For institutions like the First National Bank, he pointed out, the deposit business was preferable to note issue and, in view of the fact that government bonds were selling at a premium of fourteen per cent, it would be profitable to retire the existing notes and dispose of the bonds. Such action had not been possible before the Act of 1874. Only in the case of newly created national banks would there be a demand for additional circulation, and the retirement of notes by existing institutions was expected to more than offset any such demands.

As a matter of fact, Nickerson was right in his prophecy. Additional bank-note issues applied for under the act aggregated slightly more than $44,000,000, so that the amount of Greenbacks outstanding was reduced by only $35,318,984 before the retirement of any more was prohibited by the Act of May 31, 1878.[22] But, during the same period, the retirement of national bank notes under the older law amounted to $75,000,000,[23] so that the total amount of paper money in circulation declined from $781,000,000 in 1874, to $684,000,000 in the summer of 1878.[24] In Chicago alone, the aggregate note issues of the banks were reduced from $5,757,600 to the negligible amount of $543,900.

So rapid a currency contraction, supplemented by a reduction in aggregate deposits and by the prohibition of all kinds of scrip under the Act of February 8, 1875,[25] could not fail to exercise a depressing effect upon the general level of prices. While the causes of the business depression included many nonmonetary factors arising out of the haphazard expansion that had occurred during the previous boom, it was absurd to suggest that deflation was painless.[26] The long period of declining price levels that followed the Civil War, accentuating the severity of business depression, was due primarily to monetary forces, while to the distressed farmer and the unemployed worker the deflationary policy of the government appeared as a deliberate effort to aggravate his misery. In all parts of the country cries of protest arose, and the inflationists organized themselves to recapture the ground they had lost in 1874 and 1875.[27]

Even in the east, inflationism made itself felt and, in 1877, a convention of the Workingmen's Party was held at Harrisburg, Pennsylvania, which demanded in its platform the unconditional repeal of the Resumption Act, the abolition of the national banks, "and the issue of currency by the government based upon the wealth of the whole nation."[28] It was in the west, however, that the movement had its greatest strength, and the representatives of Illinois were in the forefront of the agitation. When the independent convention at Decatur, in February, 1874, demanded "a monetary system based upon the faith and resources of the nation," the *Chicago Trib-*

une alluded to the affair as a "gathering of sorehead, nondescript log-rollers,"[29] but the demands could not be evaded by abuse. In 1876, monetary extremists of all kinds rallied in a great convention, at Indianapolis, to fight for a similar program and, although little was achieved in the Congressional elections, Illinois found itself at the end of the year with a legislature in which the Greenback independents held the balance of power.[30]

By the end of 1877, the inflationist forces in Washington had also increased in strength and were able to force through the House of Representatives a bill for the repeal of the Resumption Act, while, even in the Senate, the measure was defeated by only a single vote. Nor was the movement any longer confined to radical visionaries and "rag-baby mountebanks." The growing severity of deflation was causing such acute distress throughout the country that many intelligent people began to feel that a change of monetary policy was necessary. In the columns of the *Bankers Magazine*, serious articles presented the advantages of a managed paper currency,[31] and the *Chicago Tribune* editorially castigated those who wished to accelerate the resumption of specie payments. "Had the East loaned gold to the West, and it was now proposed to substitute for gold a new and hitherto unknown and . . . depreciated legal-tender, the complaint might have some force; but the creditor, having unloaded his sixty-cent dollars on the West, can hardly object to being paid in the same kind of currency."[32] When, on April 1, 1878, the Banking and Currency Committee of the House of Representatives began Hearings on the desirability of repealing the Resumption Act, the Congressional dele-

gation from Illinois was almost unanimous in its enthusiasm for the idea.[33]

In spite, however, of this growing realization of the
hardships inflicted upon the community by deflation, the
Greenback party was unable to attain its goal. To many
people, fiat money was anathema. They regarded it as
something from which the country must purge itself, no
matter what sacrifices were involved in the process, in
order that a metallic standard could be restored. It was
this veneration of metallic money, rather than the
Spartan philosophy of eastern economists, that defeated
the Greenback party.

But, for that very reason, the silver agitation that began
in 1877 had a much better chance of success. Although,
from the angle of monetary theory, the coinage of silver
might be just as inflationary as any issue of fiat paper,
the popular reception of the two proposals was entirely
different. Silver had been one of the traditional monetary
metals of the United States since the time of the country's
foundation; it had served as money for thousands of years
before that time, and the man in the street could see no
good reason why it was "surreptitiously" excluded from
the Mints in 1873. There is nothing surprising, therefore,
in the fact that the Free Silver campaign came so near to
success on more than one occasion.

Perhaps no coinage act in the history of the world has
ever created as much public wrath as the rather arid bill
prepared by John Jay Knox in 1873. It represented no
more than a painstaking codification of existing laws,
clarifying doubtful points and eliminating those sections
of earlier laws that had become obsolete, and since no

silver had been brought to the Mint for free coinage since the Act of 1834, the legal right of free coinage must certainly have seemed obsolete. While it is undoubtedly true that the bill aroused little attention on its way through Congress, because of the uninteresting nature of the subject matter, there is no evidence whatever of secrecy or malign intent, and "the crime of 1873" (if such it be) lies in the apathy of legislators and voters, rather than in the Machiavellian schemes of unknown villains.

By 1876, however, the increased production and reduced price of silver made it profitable to offer that metal to the Mint for coinage, for the first time in many decades, and when the producers attempted to dispose of it in this way they discovered that the Mint would no longer accept it. To make matters worse, the countries of the Latin Monetary Union had also abandoned the free coinage of silver during 1874, so that the silver miner, with large supplies of metal on his hands, found the size of his market very much narrowed. Naturally he was annoyed, and his indignant protests were endorsed by all those groups in the country which objected to the policy of deflation.

On careful analysis, the silver agitation in the United States, which was destined to exercise a profound effect on politics for a quarter of a century, is shown to be much more complex than it is often made to appear.[34] While it is true that much of the support came from silver producers, and their Congressional representatives, who were interested in developing a better market for the metal, there were many others who participated in the agitation for totally different reasons. To some, silver was a link to the Orient that facilitated international trade;[35] to others, it was a monetary metal which must be used to offset the growing scarcity of gold.[36] A few enthusiasts looked upon the remonetization of silver as a means of facilitating the return to gold, since it would assuage the pangs of deflation,[37] while many regarded the idea as an inflationary device that would be just as effective as paper money in attaining the rising price levels that they desired. Moreover, the diversity of aims was no greater than the variety of methods proposed for attaining them. In addition to the large body of opinion that desired the free and unlimited coinage of silver at the old ratio,[38] there were others who wished to abandon gold entirely in order to establish a monometallic silver standard.[39] And, over and above all these, was the small group of devout believers in the inherent superiority of international bimetallism, who worked earnestly against hopeless odds to attain an international agreement which would restore silver permanently to its position of monetary importance alongside of gold.[40]

Once again Illinois was in the forefront of the battle although, in view of the diversity of opinions enrolled under the banner of silver, it was hard to develop a program as simple as that which had been adopted by the Greenback party. Indeed, one of the earliest results of the silver agitation was the passage by the Illinois legislature of an act designed to confer full and unlimited legal-tender powers upon the subsidiary silver coin issued by the government of the United States.[41] Although the bill could not possibly have had any economic significance, and was important only as an indication of public opinion in the state, the *Tribune* endorsed it heartily as "a step towards the general restoration of silver as a legal tender."[42] Moreover, when the Governor vetoed the measure, on the grounds that it was unconstitutional as well as undesirable, the newspaper was indignant. The veto was described as a malign attempt to serve the interests of eastern capitalists at the expense of those of the citizens of Illinois.[43]

In a sense, the attitude of the *Chicago Tribune,* which had consistently maintained a middle-of-the-road position in monetary matters, may be taken as indicative of the moderate section of public opinion. As is apparent from earlier chapters, the journal had consistently set its face against that form of inflationism which demanded a substantial expansion of the currency through the issue of paper money. Even during the early days of the silver controversy, it was inclined to adopt a neutral, or even hostile, position. But, by the middle of 1877, it was making a public recantation. Caring "more to be right, and to advocate what is true and just, than to adhere to an error or mistake in order to be consistently wrong . . . The *Tribune* . . . has been laboring to promote the restoration of the silver dollar, its free coinage, and its legalization to an unlimited amount as a legal tender."[44]

Inasmuch as this journalistic *credo* appears to have been widely followed by other newspapers, it is not surprising that the silver forces felt that the time was ripe for action when Congress met in the autumn of 1877. Beginning operations in the House, where inflationary sentiment was usually stronger, they were able to carry the Bland Bill, reestablishing the free coinage of silver without any limitations whatever, although the fact that ninety-two members refrained from voting shows the anxiety of many people to evade the question entirely. In spite of this abstention, the size of the majority was enough to provoke uneasiness in many minds.[45] When the measure came before the Senate, the anticipated opposition failed to develop, despite the earnest pleas of both the President and the Secretary of the Treasury. By an amendment, which the House agreed to in short order, the coinage of a specific amount of silver was substituted for the unlimited right of free coinage, and when the President attempted to kill the measure by veto it was repassed by thumping majorities on February 28, 1878.[46]

This Bland-Allison Act, which authorized the Secretary of the Treasury to purchase not less than two, nor more than four, million dollars' worth of silver each month and coin it into silver dollars, was clearly a compromise measure. It provided for the coinage of a small quantity of silver as a sop to the inflationists and the silver-mining interests, but authorized the issue of silver certificates in order to satisfy those who regarded the silver dollar as a clumsy medium of exchange. To placate the conservative elements, it placed a limit upon the amount of silver that might be coined, while it attempted to encourage the bimetallists by authorizing the President to call a conference of the leading powers "for the purpose of establishing, internationally, the use of bimetallic money, and securing fixity of relative value between these metals."

As a result, it satisfied nobody, although there were some who defended it as an initial step in the right direction.[47] "The victory is one of the people. It is a victory that was needed to remind the world that Wall street no longer controls and dictates national legislation. For the first time perhaps since the War there has been legislation on a question of finance which has not been inspired by and in the interests of those who live by gambling in money and public securities."[48] But for the deflationary group, the act represented a severe setback. For the first time since the passage of the Resumption Act, their policy had suffered a reverse, and there was "a general howl of rage through all the places of New England and New York."[49] Banking groups throughout the country expressed themselves openly in opposition to the measure,[50] and the Chicago Clearing House Association passed a resolution that declared the new silver certificates useless for the purpose of settling balances among the member banks.

But there was no abandonment of resumption, as the goal of monetary policy, on the part of those responsible for guiding the nation's destinies. Sherman, who had publicly insisted on a return to the gold standard as early as 1875,[51] was now the Secretary of the Treasury, and his enthusism for resumption was supported by that of President Hayes. Moreover, the bankers from all parts of the country remained firm in their allegiance to a metallic standard. In 1878, urged on by speeches from Lyman J. Gage and others, the American Bankers Association pledged its "aid and support to the Government in a return to the specie standard in the transaction of the financial affairs of our country."[52] To a growing number of persons it was becoming clear that the real need of the

western and southern states was capital rather than currency.[53] Even though the price declines engendered by
deflationary policies had affected farmers and laborers
adversely, the anguish of contraction was nearly over.
The paper dollar had appreciated to such an extent that
it was almost at par with gold, and a renewed wave of
inflation would only undo all that had been accomplished.
Such inflation, moreover, would dry up the stream of
capital funds, both from the east and from Europe, since
it would create in the mind of the lender an uncertainty
as to the value of the monetary unit in terms of which the
debt was to be repaid.

When all these arguments have been appraised, however, it still remains true that resumption of specie payments was achieved more by the action of economic forces
than as a result of political arguments. The painful experiences of the present generation, under postwar deflationary policies, are sufficient to convince any careful
student that no country could possibly triple the value of
its monetary unit in fourteen years by will power alone.
To attempt such a feat in a static economy would involve
such a degree of individual privation, and such destruction of business enterprise, that the country would be
utterly ruined.

To understand the events of those years, we must remember that the economy of the United States was not
static. In a very real sense, the country "grew up to its
supply of currency," so that business expansion rather
than currency contraction must earn the award of those
laurels of achievement which historians have often laid
upon the brows of political executives. To admit this is

not a derogation of the work that was done by successive administrations during those troublous years. By setting their faces firmly against the easy road of inflationism, they made it possible for the expanding activities of the country, and its growing population, to absorb the large currency issues that were left as a legacy of the Civil War, and so great a degree of consistency is no mean achievement. But it is easier to prevent expansion than it is to achieve contraction, and the evidence of all available statistics, if we remember the extent to which bank checks were coming into use as a medium of exchange, indicates that the total supply of money in the country was much greater in 1879 than it had been in 1865.

The business expansion that occurred between 1869 and 1873 carried the United States a long way toward resumption. A steady increase in the demand for money carried the value of the paper dollar from the low point of thirty-five cents, at the end of the war, to within fifteen per cent of parity at the time when the panic of 1873 broke loose. Only when the onset of depression halted the expansion of economic activity did this process of appreciation become painful to the man in the street, provoking the clamant inflationism that has been described in the preceding paragraphs.

But, by the autumn of 1877, there were signs that business conditions were improving somewhat.[54] Although banking and industrial operations still showed meager profits, there was a distinct spurt in mining, and many agricultural sections of the country were greatly stimulated by European demands. The following year showed even greater improvement.[55] Agricultural harvests were extraordinarily large at a time when Europe was close to famine, so that railroads and commercial organizations of all kinds profited from the phenomenal growth of exports. The banks of the country were in an unusually strong position and eager to finance these business operations and, from the beginning of 1878, there was heard once more "the ceaseless tread of a vast army of immigrants on the march to the free West."[56] Railroads and land offices reported that they were deluged with applicants for lands, and states, like Illinois, which had no more useful free land to offer, were able to share in the prosperity because of record crops of cereals.

It was this business spurt that carried the United States over the last hurdle toward resumption. Men who were making profits or earning wages had no time for monetary controversy, and by the end of the year it was reported that "a very conservative spirit prevails, and Mr. Sherman is left in control of the situation."[57] Meanwhile, to strengthen the position of the Treasury, a gold reserve of considerably more than one hundred million dollars had been accumulated and a series of funding operations had consolidated the public debt of the country on a four and a half per cent basis.[58] Even as the year drew to a close, there were still fears that Congress might do something to interfere with the resumption program, but on December 21, 1878, the *Chronicle* announced with "positive gratification" that the Banking and Currency Committee of the House had gone home for the holidays, so that no new legislation could be reported back before the end of the year.[59] The struggle was almost over.

With the dawning of 1879, the country was once again

on a gold standard. "The currency of the United States, by the triumph of natural causes, and by the still higher moral triumph of honest popular convictions and honest legislation, has been restored to the solid ground of the precious metals."[60] For the first time since the outbreak of the Civil War, there was but one monetary system in the United States. All forms of money were redeemable in gold at the Treasury, so that it was no longer necessary for merchants and bankers to keep separate gold accounts for specific transactions. On January 1, 1879, holders of United States bonds were willing to accept Greenbacks, instead of gold coin, in payment of the interest that was due, and so great was popular confidence in the ability of the government to maintain specie payments that, on the first day of business under the new policy, the Sub-Treasury at New York received four times as much gold as it paid out in exchange for paper! "By five o'clock," Sherman wrote, "the news was all over the land and the New York bankers were sipping their tea in absolute safety."[61]

In Chicago, to be sure, there was a little delay. Under the law, the Secretary of the Treasury was only compelled to redeem the Greenbacks in New York, so that they circulated at a discount of one-quarter of one per cent in Chicago. Moreover on January 2 the Chicago Sub-Treasury refused to pay gold coin on government checks.[62] This, however, was a purely temporary setback, due entirely to the technical difficulties of perfecting arrangements for redemption in all parts of a country as large as the United States. A few days afterward Chicago, too, was jubilant in the reality of an operating gold standard.

REFERENCES FOR CHAPTER XIII

[1] *Bankers Magazine,* XXXIII, 144.

[2] Cf. Beard: *Rise of American Civilization,* II, 312 ff.

[3] *Commercial and Financial Chronicle,* XVII, 479.

[4] *Bankers Magazine,* XXVIII, 748 and 831.

[5] *Commercial and Financial Chronicle,* XVIII, 233, 363, 709 and 750.

[6] *Chicago Tribune,* April 18, 1874.

[7] *Ibid.,* April 13, 1874.

[8] *Ibid.,* April 11, 1874.

[9] *Ibid.,* April 6, 1874.

[10] *Ibid.,* May 13, 1874; *Bankers Magazine,* XXVIII, 988.

[11] *Chicago Tribune,* April 24, 1874.

[12] *Commercial and Financial Chronicle,* XVIII, 441.

[13] Knox: *op. cit.,* p. 149.

[14] *Commercial and Financial Chronicle,* XIX, 74.

[15] Cf. *Ibid.,* XVII, 614; XIX, 153 and 233.

[16] *Ibid.,* XIX, 593.

[17] *Bankers Magazine,* XXX, 698 ff.

[18] *Commercial and Financial Chronicle,* XX, p. 39.

[19] *Ibid.,* XIX, 649; XX, 25, 172 and 509.

[20] *Chicago Tribune,* January 21, February 1, 1875.

[21] *Ibid.,* January 19, 1875.

[22] *Commercial and Financial Chronicle,* XXVI, 533; Knox: *op. cit.,* pp. 155-156.

[23] Knox: *op. cit.,* p. 156; *Commercial and Financial Chronicle,* XXI, 76; XXII, 602-603.

[24] *Bankers Magazine,* XXXIII, 144.

[25] Knox: *op. cit.,* p. 124.

[26] *Commercial and Financial Chronicle,* XX, 604.

[27] Cf. Beard: *op. cit.,* p. 320 ff.

[28] *Commercial and Financial Chronicle,* XXV, 246-247.

[29] *Chicago Tribune,* February 17, 1876; Bogart and Thompson: pp. 109-111.

[30] Knox: *op. cit.,* p. 141; Bogart and Thompson: *op. cit.,* p. 121.

[31] *Bankers Magazine,* XXX, 890.

[32] *Chicago Tribune,* June 15, 1877.

[33] Knox: *op. cit.,* pp. 141 and 143 ff.

[34] By far the best analysis is contained in Jeanette Nichols: *American Historical Review,* XLI, 25-53, and *Political Science Quarterly,* XLVIII, 565-588, while a briefer picture is offered by N. Carrothers: *Fractional Money.*

[35] *Bankers Magazine,* XXXI, 128.

[36] *Idem,* 1; *Chicago Tribune,* January 2 and 27, 1878.

[37] *Chicago Tribune,* May 21, 1877.

[38] *Ibid.,* June 27, 1877.

[39] *Bankers Magazine,* XXXI, 217-222.

[40] *Idem,* 530; XXXIII, 259; *Chicago Tribune,* May 12, 1877.

[41] *Chicago Tribune,* May 20, 1877.

[42] *Ibid.,* May 30, 1877.

[43] *Ibid.,* May 31, June 1, 1877.

[44] *Ibid.,* July 5, 1877.

[45] *Commercial and Financial Chronicle,* XXV, 468.

[46] *Ibid.,* XXVI, 1, 175 and 201.

[47] *Bankers Magazine,* XXXIII, 783.

[48] *Chicago Tribune,* March 1, 1878.

[49] Cf. *Commercial and Financial Chronicle,* XXVI, 1, 175 and 201.

[50] *Idem,* 25.

[51] *Ibid.,* XXI, 119; *Bankers Magazine,* XXX, 778.

[52] *Commercial and Financial Chronicle,* XXVII, 211.

[53] *Ibid.,* XXI, 73; XXII, 221 and 338.

[54] *Ibid.,* XXV, 321; XXVI, 3.

[55] *Ibid.,* XXVIII, 4-5; XXVI, 378.

[56] *Ibid.,* XXVI, 482.

[57] *Ibid.,* XXVII, 577.

[58] *Ibid.,* XXIV, 453; XXV, 49; XXVI, 3, 351 and 377.

[59] *Ibid.,* XXVIII, 637.

[60] *Bankers Magazine,* XXXIII, 489. See also *Commercial and Financial Chronicle,* XXVIII, 1; *Chicago Tribune,* January 4, 1879.

[61] Beard: *op. cit.,* 331.

[62] *Chicago Tribune,* January 3, 1879.

CHAPTER XIV

THE LEAN YEARS

1875–1886

THE years that separate the panic of 1873 from that of
1893, although streaked with the lurid colors of monetary
controversy, constitute a period of consolidation rather
than of dramatic efflorescence. Owing to the operation of
the factors discussed in the preceding chapters, augmented
by others that will become apparent as the discussion
proceeds, the general level of prices was falling steadily
throughout these two decades. Business was compelled to
seek profits by means of strict economy and increasing
efficiency, instead of surging upwards joyously on a wave
of monetary inflation as it had done during the years
before the Civil War.

Yet this period of falling price levels witnessed phenomenal economic progress in the United States. Within
the short space of a single generation, the country attained eminence among the great powers of the world,
and American industry forged ahead so rapidly that its
output soon exceeded that of both England and Germany.
It may not be out of place, moreover, to call attention
to a monetary aspect of the situation that may help to
explain the startling contrast, during these years, between surging industrial expansion, on the one hand, and

clamant inflationary demands from distressed farmers and impoverished laborers, on the other. In industry, the process of invention and mechanization enabled producers to reduce costs of production much more rapidly than prices were falling, so that profits were large enough to create substantial fortunes among the entrepreneurs. "The Robber Barons" were fighting for substantial prizes, and the fact that industry was but little in debt made the burden of falling prices negligible.

But the farmer was not able to reduce his costs of production as rapidly as the price of his output declined, and the fall of prices was itself accelerated by the opening up of new agricultural areas, in distant parts of the world. Improvements in transportation intensified farming competition. Moreover, farmers were heavily in debt and the reduction of their money incomes made mortgages increasingly troublesome.* Only through the adoption of policies of monetary inflation could the farmer see any prospect of immediate relief. Similarly, in the case of the laborer, mechanization of industry created the problem of what has since been called "technological unemployment," while the rapid expansion of the population enabled employers to depress wages considerably. The worker, therefore, unreasonably blaming the price level for his woes, was eager to support the inflationary program that the farmer suggested.

The complex forces that molded the modern American economy were already in full operation, and Chicago's position in the heart of the country exposed her to the

---

* Western farm lands owned by Connecticut life-insurance companies as a result of foreclosure tripled in amount during the four years following the panic of 1873. *Commercial and Financial Chronicle,* XXVII, 613.

full impact of all of them. It is not surprising that Chicago was to experience more inflationary enthusiasm than any other large city during the years when her industrialists were astounding the world with the efficiency of their methods and the extent to which economies could be attained by the development of by-products. Industrial prosperity and agricultural tribulation both played an important part in the city's life.

Before the wide sweep of economic expansion had been fully appreciated, the city was already strengthening its position. By the middle of the seventies, it had become the undisputed commercial center of the northwest and the upper Mississippi valley. Grain, meat and other agricultural products were supplied to the rest of the country, and to all the world besides, through the commercial facilities that Chicago offered,[1] and the city maintained a lively interest in the continuous improvement of the railroads and canals by which these goods were transported. Many of the manufactured articles required by the farmers were, in turn, produced by the expanding workshops and factories of the city and, by 1874, Chicago merchants were actively engaged in the business of importing from other parts of the world such commodities as coffee, sugar and spices, in order to divert to their own pockets the profits that had previously been reaped by middlemen in Boston and New York.[2]

Nor was the Chicago money market a laggard in this development. Despite the admirable handling of the panic by the New York Clearing House Association, the unsatisfactory showing of particular banks in that city during 1873 had roused serious doubts in other parts of the country as to the wisdom of carrying large reserves with any New York institution. At first, the tendency had been to split the accounts of a bank among two or more reserve agents in New York,[3] a practice that became simpler and more general when the reserve agents were relieved of the responsibility for redeeming the notes of correspondent banks. By 1876, however, a further change had occurred. More and more banks, particularly in the central and western sections of the country, began to withdraw their balances from New York and deposit them with Chicago institutions, so that the importance of the latter city as a reserve center increased rapidly.[4] Whereas, in 1873, the amounts due by Chicago national banks to all banks in other parts of the country had amounted to only $11,200,000, the figure had risen to $28,000,000 by 1886—an increase of more than one hundred and fifty per cent. During the same period, the reserves of other banks in New York, although still many times larger than the Chicago aggregates, had risen by only fifty per cent. Moreover, it must be remembered that even in 1886, banks in Chicago and all other reserve cities, unless they held the full amount in their own vaults, were legally compelled to carry their reserves in New York. It was only the country banks that could elect to transfer their accounts to Chicago.

Unfortunately, it is not possible to offer a detailed analysis of the extent to which the holding of bankers' balances in Chicago developed, since a large portion of the essential records have been destroyed or lost in the course of time. But, in the case of the First National Bank, which appears to have been responsible for about one-third of the total business at this period, there were more than four hundred correspondent accounts in 1880. Of these, one hundred and fifty-four represented national banks, while the balance of two hundred and eighty-eight was composed of state and private institutions, and a fairly accurate idea of the geographical extent of the business can be gained from the following table.

TABLE XVI

GEOGRAPHICAL DISTRIBUTION OF CORRESPONDENT BANKS
CARRYING BALANCES WITH THE FIRST NATIONAL
BANK OF CHICAGO IN JUNE, 1880

	National Banks	State and Private Banks
Illinois....................	39	79
Wisconsin................	25	38
Iowa.....................	20	90
Michigan................	19	13
Minnesota...............	13	11
Indiana..................	13	5
Kansas..................	3	10
Other...................	22	42
Total................	154	288

By the beginning of the eighties, as a result of this development, Chicago banks were assuming a growing responsibility for meeting the annual demands for currency to finance the harvesting of crops in these states. From the Minutes of the Clearing House Association, it is apparent that substantially more than one hundred million dollars was sent out, each year, to correspondent institutions and, of this amount, one-third was provided by the First National Bank. The Merchants Loan and Trust Company, the Commercial National Bank and the Union National Bank (which were the only other institutions in the city that did a substantial correspondent business) each provided about one-sixth of the total.

Moreover, in addition to developing closer relations with banks in other parts of the country, Chicago institutions were beginning to make themselves felt in the New York market. For many years they had depended on that market as a source of funds in time of need, customarily borrowing from their reserve agents by the rediscount or pledge of commercial paper,[5] but by the end of the seventies they had begun to reverse the process by lending surplus funds directly in the New York call-money market.[6] Even in the creation of the American Bankers Association, in 1875, Chicago bankers played an important part. Three of them were among the signers of the original call to the Saratoga convention and, at a subsequent meeting, De Koven, of the Merchants National, and Gage, of the First National, were elected to minor offices.[7]

During these years, both in Chicago and throughout the country, the preeminence of the national banks was being destroyed by the further growth of state and private institutions. When the national banks were given a monopoly of note issue during the Civil War, state and private banks had suddenly dwindled in importance. By 1866, the Comptroller of the Currency found less than three hundred of them in existence, with aggregate deposits of no more than $63,588.* But with the growing custom of making payments by bank checks, and the collateral developments in regard to trust and savings busi-

---

* These, figures for banks other than national, are notoriously unsatisfactory, but they do give an approximate idea of the developments in process.

ness, which national banks could not legally undertake, the number of state-chartered institutions expanded rapidly. By the end of the seventies the Comptroller was expressing alarm at this development since, even within the American Bankers Association, only 2,082 banks out of 6,152 members were national institutions.[8]

In Illinois, the statistics of state and private banks are even less satisfactory than those for the country as a whole, since nobody seems to have felt any responsibility for their collection. Of the Merchants Loan and Trust Company we know something, and considerable information is available regarding the Union Trust Company, but data is very sketchy regarding the other Chicago institutions. In Table XV, on pages 440-443, data is presented for a small group of state and private banks (the only ones for which such statistics can be found) and, in 1876, the Comptroller reported that there were forty-six state and private banks in Chicago with aggregate deposits of more than $16,000,000.[9] Both sets of data are woefully incomplete, however, because the available records show that nearly one hundred banks and bankers were then operating in the city. Unfortunately, these records seldom give precise information regarding capital or deposits.

This absence of statistical interest is not, however, surprising. The free banking system had broken down twenty years earlier, and no general banking law had been enacted to replace it since the adoption of the new Constitution in 1870. Moreover, banks could not, under that Constitution, be incorporated by special charter. It was apparent, therefore, that no new state banks could be created after the formal repeal of the Free Banking Acts, in 1874,[10] and most of the institutions still operating under state charters were labeled as savings banks. This name gives no indication of their functions. All of them did a commercial banking business that competed in every way with that of the national banks, while the latter found themselves handicapped in the struggle by the limitations imposed through administrative regulation and judicial decision.[11] Even though the state courts insisted on a particularly onerous interpretation of the double liability of state-bank stockholders,[12] the freedom of action of those institutions still appeared enviable to the national bankers.

Meanwhile, this growth in the importance and complexity of the Chicago money market was accompanied by an increasing air of metropolitan formality on the part of the banks themselves. Although the Union Trust Company also opened its offices from six to eight o'clock on Saturday evenings, all the banks now opened at ten and closed at three. Bank buildings, moreover, were taking on a modern splendor and exclusiveness. One of the banks, when leasing new offices, amazed the landlord by insisting that the basement below the banking floor should not be used as a saloon! The Union Trust Company, when it moved to the corner of Dearborn and Madison Streets, formally decided that funds should be spent to install plate-glass windows on the ground floor and lay stone sidewalks outside, while the new quarters of the First National Bank at Dearborn and Monroe Streets were reported by the National Bank Examiner to be superior to those of any other institution in the country. In 1883, the offices of this bank were lit by electricity, and the practice of providing luncheon for the staff and officers had led to the installation of kitchens and dining rooms that attracted high praise in the examination reports. Even in the matter of salaries, there was a gradual approach to the height and diversity of modern times. While Coolbaugh, as President of the Union National, and Gage, as Cashier of the First National, each received salaries of $15,000 a year, to which an annual bonus of $5,000 was often added, the Presidents of smaller banks received no more than $5,000 or even $3,000. For junior officers a salary of $2,000 to $2,500 appears to have been customary, while the income of employees ranged downward from that figure to as little as $600 for clerks. On the whole, a skilled laborer in most lines of industry, provided that he enjoyed reasonable continuity of employment, appears to have received better rates of pay than any bank employee below the rank of junior officer; but the permanence and prestige of bank employment, together with the possibilities of promotion, were already attracting to Chicago banks a type of man that earned high praise from examiners. Even at that period, there were serious discussions among bankers as to the best method of developing professional pride and outlook among bank employees, and the members of the Clearing House gave the matter serious attention during the course of a long evening session in 1883.

In the light of these developments, it is natural to find an increasing specialization of institutions, as well as a growing standardization of financial operations. Real-estate loans were handled exclusively by state and private institutions, although the savings banks played an increasingly important part in this type of business as their resources expanded. Savings accounts were received by the same group of institutions, and the small amount of fiduciary business that was given to corporate trustees appears to have been handled primarily by the Merchants Loan and Trust Company and the Illinois Trust and Savings Bank. Even less important were the operations in corporate and municipal securities, most of which were handled by the houses of N. W. Harris and Company and S. A. Kean and Company by the middle of the eighties.

In the case of the national banks, lending operations were confined largely to commercial loans and to loans against security collateral, the relative importance of each type of operation differing from one bank to another.*

Loans secured by stock-exchange collateral were not, however, comparable in their function to the extensions of credit under that heading that were made, on so large a scale, during the first quarter of the twentieth century. In modern times, the primary purpose of such loans is to finance speculation in securities, but during the nineteenth century they frequently represented an advance of funds to an entrepreneur to enable him to expand his business operations. As a result, security loans played a much more important role in the expansion of industry at that time than they do today, and the risks assumed by the lending banks were correspondingly greater. In some cases the stocks and bonds received as collateral were not listed on any recognized exchange, while the

---

* It may be interesting to note that the banks which were most notoriously interested in security loans (such as the Third National and the Cook County National) had a very short life. Even the Union National, which had strong leanings in this direction during the early seventies, encountered serious difficulties.

market for those that were listed was usually very thin. It is probable, therefore, that such loans were customarily granted on the basis of the character and general reputation of the borrower and a portion of the loans evidenced by unsecured promissory notes (which even at this time amounted to about twenty per cent of the total loans, discounts and investments of Chicago banks) may also be assumed to have been granted for similar purposes.

On the purely commercial side of banking operations, where the First National Bank was rapidly becoming the leader of the market,* substantial loans were made against all sorts of merchandise collateral. Grain, tea, provisions, wool, coffee and whisky appear to have been the commodities most favored, but the full list would run the gamut of all the articles produced by Chicago industries or sold by its merchants. Customarily, such loans were secured by warehouse receipts and evidenced by demand notes on which interest was collected on the first of each month, although in a growing number of cases the business was handled by the discount of promissory notes with a definite maturity date.

But it was in the financing of the export business generally, and particularly in the financing of grain and packing-house products, that the greatest strides had been made. Spurred on by the success of the Bank of Montreal and by the legislation permitting lenders from other states and countries to operate in Illinois,[13] the Canadian Bank of Commerce, the Merchants Bank of

* It should be noted that the First National, despite its emphasis on commercial banking, had outstanding during the seventies a volume of security loans that was seldom less than *one-third* of its total loans, discounts and investments, and sometimes exceeded forty per cent of that total.

Canada, and the Bank of British North America all opened branches or agencies in Chicago between 1875 and 1881. These institutions, moreover, were particularly interested in financing the grain trade, and took a substantial amount of this business away from the Chicago banks,[14] so that Canadian banking methods naturally influenced the practices developed by the First National, the Corn Exchange National and the Commercial National Banks, which were the most important local institutions in the field. In the export business, therefore, transactions were primarily financed by the discount of a documentary bill of exchange drawn upon the buyer, while dealings on the Board of Trade were financed, (even in the case of the national banks) by the extension of large overdraft facilities. As security, the recipient of such overdraft facilities was required to deposit warehouse receipts with the bank, a procedure that appears to have fully satisfied the national bank examiner, and interest was collected monthly as in the case of demand loans.

Largely as a result of its interest in this business, and of the vision of Gage and Nickerson, the First National Bank rapidly developed an extensive foreign-exchange department. Although the Union National did not engage in foreign-exchange operations until 1881, and the Merchants Loan and Trust Company until 1883, the First National had established important connections in Europe before the panic of 1873. By the middle of the seventies, its operations had outdistanced those of Preston, Kean and Company, its only important competitor, and during the early 'eighties the foreign-exchange depart-

ment was receiving annual praise from the national bank
examiner as one of the outstanding departments of its
kind in the United States. In 1878, accounts were maintained, with sixty-nine foreign correspondents, in pounds
sterling, francs, marks, lire, kroner, Austrian florins and
Dutch florins with an aggregate currency value of some
$650,000; by 1883, the number of accounts had grown
to more than eighty and the aggregate value of the balances in American currency exceeded $1,250,000. By this
time the Bank was actually discounting bills for the account of European merchants and bankers, and Chicago
was becoming an important part of the international
financial mechanism.

One further development in the functioning of the
Chicago money market deserves attention. Prior to 1870,
the interest-rate structure had been extremely rigid, and
loans were almost always granted at the standard rate of
10 per cent, the maximum allowed by Illinois law. This
tradition appears to have been somewhat weakened, even
before the panic of 1873,[15] since money was abundant at
8 per cent, in 1872, and during the previous year "on the
street money [was] quoted on short time from seven to
eight per cent and on call at from five to six per cent."[16]

During the years of depression after the panic, the
traditional rate of 10 per cent disappeared permanently
and the reenactment of usury laws in 1874 and 1875[17]
was of no significance to the commercial banks. By 1875,
call loans were being made at rates as low as 6 per cent,
and the *Tribune* reported that borrowers would not take
any 9 per cent money even in real-estate loans,[18] while

a few years later first-class mercantile paper could be discounted at from 5 to 6 per cent and loans secured by government bonds paid only 4 per cent. "Fair business paper" could be discounted at 8 per cent, which by this time had come to be recognized as the normal maximum, and, good real-estate loans were negotiated at rates as low as 5 per cent.[19] Moreover, this reduction of interest rates was accompanied by the development of greater elasticity, as a result of increasing competition among the banks and of the growing contacts of both banks and business houses with the New York money market. Henceforth, the cost of money in Chicago was to depend more and more upon the precise nature of the transaction, the type of credit instrument used and the general condition of the money market, an indication of modernization that is more significant than almost any of the others that have been discussed.

TABLE XVII

GROWTH OF THE CHICAGO CLEARING
HOUSE ASSOCIATION

Date	Number of Members	Annual Clearings in Millions of Dollars
1865	20	319
1866	25	453
1867	23	580
1868	25	723
1869	24	734
1870	26	810
1871	26	868
1872	29	993
1873	30	1,047
1874	26	1,101
1875	24	1,212
1876	22	1,110
1877	19	1,044
1878	18	967
1879	18	1,257
1880	18	1,725

The Clearing House Association, through all these years of development, steadily strengthened its position. In the face of a decline in membership resulting from bank failures, and of a reduction in the volume of clearings during the years of depression, the Association continuously extended its efforts to improve and strengthen the Chicago money market. Immediately after the panic of 1873, it was decided that no banks should in future be admitted to membership unless they had an unimpaired paid-up capital of $250,000. In order to tighten up the control exercised over institutions that were not members of the Association, it was agreed that member banks which cleared checks for such institutions should assume responsibility for the ultimate payment of cashier's checks and certificates of deposit issued by the non-members.

By 1876, a powerful group of members under the leadership of Gage, who had been elected to the Presidency of the Association, was eager to have the Clearing House appoint an official examiner, so that all member banks might be periodically examined under the auspices of the Clearing House. Such a proposal was too revolutionary for the times, but it was agreed that the Clearing House Committee might appoint one or more of its members to make an examination of any bank connected with the Clearing House whenever the Committee thought such action desirable. Moreover, it was resolved that "the Comptroller of the Currency be requested to instruct the National Bank Examiner to report to the Clearing House Committee when any National Bank of the city has, in his judgment, impaired its capital or is doing a hazardous business." These actions reflected a growing willingness on the part of the Association to assume responsibility for constructive action, and the Comptroller, in replying to the last resolution, expressed high appreciation.

There was, however, one serious problem that marred the harmonious progress, a problem that arose from causes beyond the control of Chicago bankers. Under federal laws, national banks were taxed on their capital and, since they were often taxed much more heavily than other financial institutions,* the protests became increasingly clamorous when business depression had seriously reduced the volume of bank earnings.[20] Not until 1877 did the Comptroller of the Currency take any step in the matter, and legislative relief was not obtained until an even later date, so that banks in many instances took matters into their own hands. By reducing the amount of their capitalization, they could effectively reduce the size of their tax bill. In 1877, the Bank of Commerce in New York voluntarily sacrificed its position as the largest bank in the country by returning one-half of the paid-in capital to its shareholders,[21] and several Chicago banks, having found protests ineffective,[22] did likewise. Within a few weeks, the Corn Exchange National, Northwestern National, Fifth National and Merchants National returned to their stockholders capital funds aggregating $2,400,000.[23] When other banks, for a variety of reasons, also reduced their capitalization, it became apparent that the process was distinctly unfavorable to the future de-

* While a Chicago national bank with $1,500,000 capital paid $24,000 in county taxes in 1876, the office of the Bank of Montreal paid only $1,800 and Preston, Kean and Company (the largest of the private bankers) paid $73.80! Cf. *Chicago Tribune*, May 12 and 13, 1877.

velopment of Chicago, as well as dangerous to the soundness of the national banking system.

Before any final solution of the problem could be
reached, however, there occurred in Chicago a series of
events which were destined to have enduring repercussions. As has already been suggested, the savings banks
that flourished in Chicago at this period were not in any
sense comparable to the mutual savings banks of the
east. While the latter were soundly managed by trustees,
who received no profit from the bank, in order to encourage thrift among the poorer classes of the population,
the savings banks of Chicago and other western cities were
in many cases highly speculative institutions, run by
men who wished to avoid those restrictions of the national
banking system which would have prevented them from
financing themselves to the extent they thought necessary. Loans and discounts of all kinds were generously
made, and if there was any degree of specialization it
was the concentration of savings-bank resources upon the
financing of highly speculative suburban real-estate developments. Moreover, since depositors received 5, or
even 6 per cent, upon their savings, it is apparent that the
managers were compelled to assume a large degree of risk
in order to earn rates of interest high enough to show
a profit for the institution.[24]

Perhaps the best commentary on the extent to which
such savings banks served their promoters, rather than
the thrifty public who patronized them in ignorance, is
furnished by the extensive financial and political war
that was waged at Springfield when the older institutions
tried to prevent Henry Greenebaum from obtaining, for

the German Savings Bank, a charter that would enable him to encroach on their lucrative preserves.[25]

Since real-estate prices had fallen seriously after the panic of 1873, institutions that had lent heavily to finance land developments were in an uncomfortable position. Early in May, 1877, the Bank of Chicago was compelled to suspend operations as a result of the shrinkage in value of its assets,[26] and the opening of June witnessed the failure of Bowen Brothers, a prominent real-estate firm that had borrowed large sums from many of the Chicago banks.[27] By the middle of July, a series of bank runs and failures had occurred in St. Louis, and substantial quantities of currency were being drained away from Chicago by correspondent institutions.[28]

These were the harbingers of the storm, but nobody paid serious attention to the situation, even though it was known in financial circles that the condition of the savings banks of Chicago was far from sound. On August 29, the storm broke. After weeks of a steady but undramatic drain upon its resources, the State Savings Institution of Chicago closed its doors and suspended payment. When a receiver was appointed, it was discovered that D. D. Spencer, the President, had used the Bank entirely for the financing of his own projects; most of the assets consisted of unsecured promissory notes bearing his signature, and he had absconded to Europe with whatever cash remained in the Bank the evening before it closed.[29] Although a grand jury found indictments against Spencer and other officers for embezzlements exceeding $700,000, nothing came of the matter. The customers of the Bank bore the loss and, ten years afterward, Andreas was able

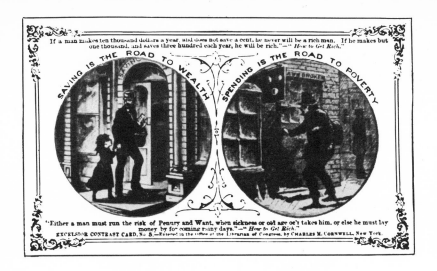

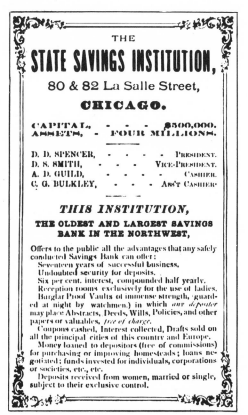

ADVERTISEMENT OF THE STATE SAVINGS INSTITUTION, 1875

to report that Spencer was still living comfortably in Germany.[30]

Such a catastrophe, involving thousands of persons from every section of the city, naturally led to runs on most of the other banks and, on September 19, the Merchants, Farmers and Mechanics Savings Bank was likewise compelled to suspend operations.[31] Once again, the same tragic story was repeated. Sidney Myers, the actual manager of the Bank, had made large loans to himself and, when the run started, had pledged practically all the good assets of the institution as security for a loan that would enable him to meet the demands of depositors. When the Bank closed, the total amount of cash in the vaults was sixty-two dollars and, since the indictment of Myers for embezzlement added nothing to the property in the hands of the receiver, the depositors of the institution had to be content with a dividend of ten cents on the dollar.

The "Beehive" (as Myers' institution was familiarly called) and the State Savings Institution had been the largest savings banks in the city, so that public confidence in the remainder rapidly faded away. On September 24, the Fidelity Savings Bank was forced to apply for the appointment of a receiver,[32] and the Chicago Savings Institution and Trust Company decided upon a similar step one month later.[33] In both cases, the records showed the same story of unwise loans and a steady shrinkage of assets during the years of depression, so that no great hopes of recovery were held out to depositors. In these cases, however, unwisdom does not appear to have been aggravated by downright dishonesty.

With each failure there arose a feeling that the strain was over, but the autumn of 1877 held still further shocks in store. As a result of serious rumors regarding its condition, the Clearing House Committee decided to examine the Third National Bank. That examination revealed so serious an impairment of capital that the Clearing House Association unanimously resolved, on November 21, to suspend the Bank from membership. As soon as they received the news, the directors of the Third National decided to close the doors of the Bank and took steps to put it into liquidation.[34] They attributed their difficulties to the general decline of asset values and the heavy withdrawals of public deposits made by the County Treasurer just before the failure. Even at this stage the *Tribune* insisted that the event was nothing more than "the collapse of an institution under a pressure that has been on it for several years."

Two days later, however, the Central National Bank closed its doors, largely owing to the unexpected calling of a large loan by the Third National during its final agonies.[35] This Bank, which had never been particularly strong, weakened its position still more by taking over the assets of the Commercial Loan and Trust Company, in 1875, and a portion of the business of the National Bank of Commerce in 1876. In the face of diminished asset values and the steady withdrawal of funds, its ultimate failure was inevitable, but the actual crisis appears to have been precipitated by the sudden departure of W. F. Endicott, the Cashier, who took most of the available cash with him.[36]

Finally, as the panic moved onwards to its climax, the

wave of failure engulfed the group of institutions operated by Henry Greenebaum, all of which appear to have
been unnecessarily tied up with his own personal fortunes. On December 5, the German National Bank, of
which he was President, asked its depositors to be patient and give the Bank time to liquidate its assets,[37] but
in view of the general uneasiness and of the fact that
"it was an open secret that the banking interests of the
city would be greatly subserved by the voluntary retirement of the institution,"[38] there can have been little hope
that the request would be granted.

On the following day, the stockholders of the Bank
decided to put it into liquidation,[39] but the mischief had
been done. A run developed on the affiliated German
Savings Bank and, when the officers insisted that all customers would be required to give thirty days' notice, several of them immediately applied to the courts for the
appointment of a receiver. Meanwhile, on December 6,
the New York affiliate, trading under the name of Greenebaum Brothers and Company, was compelled to make an
assignment for the benefit of its creditors,[40] and after
holding out for another twelve days, the parent firm of
Henry Greenebaum and Company closed its doors.[41]
Every link in the Greenebaum chain had broken, and
all that remained was a weighty indictment against the
founder, incorporating more than twenty different
charges of embezzlement.[42] Moreover the German-Amer-
ican Savings Bank, which had no connection with Greenebaum, appears to have suffered from the fact that its
name was too much like that of the failing institutions.

It was compelled to close its doors in the face of a run on December 11.[43]

With the end of the year, this strangest of panics subsided. Of tragedy there had been plenty, but it had to be sought in the homes of those whose small savings had been wiped out overnight. It did not stalk the streets as it had in the hectic days of 1857 and 1873. Of excitement there was practically none. The failures had not come at the top of a boom, to strike pessimistic terror into the heart of the speculator. Rather they represented the death rattle of institutions that, like King Charles, had been an unconscionable time a-dying. Men were not shocked: they were cynically and sadly disillusioned. Never before had there occurred so widespread a revelation of frauds, forgeries and failures, yet nobody clamored his indignation. Even the press was apathetic.[44]

Yet, during those dark November days, there was played out the last tragic act of a great drama, an act utterly independent of the wave of failures and yet so closely knit to the process of financial disintegration that it could not otherwise have occurred. On the night of November 14 William F. Coolbaugh walked out into the park and, at the foot of the Douglas monument, shot himself.[45]

Coolbaugh had been the greatest banker of the northwest, and the Union National Bank under his able guidance had attained an eminence that no other bank in Chicago could approach. As recently as the summer of 1872, the Union National had on its books loans and discounts twice as large as those of the First National, its nearest competitor, while the amount of bankers' balances that it held was even greater in proportion. Coolbaugh had made his first great mistake in his conflict with Gage, on the subject of banking policy in the panic. In the light of retrospect it could well be argued that his point of view had been sound, and that Gage was taking an undue risk when he insisted on keeping his bank open and paying the demands of depositors in full. But Gage had won his battle with fate. The First National had been able to face the drain without closing its doors, and during those days when Gage was meeting customers with imperturbable sangfroid, Coolbaugh was sitting at home and his Bank was in a state of informal voluntary liquidation.

During those two autumnal weeks, in 1873, Coolbaugh had abdicated his position. At the beginning of 1876, the First National Bank became the largest in Chicago, in terms of deposits, and by June, 1877, its business had grown to a point where it was twice as large as that of the Union National, whose assets and liabilities were both steadily shrinking. Within three years, the First National was to become the fourth largest bank in the whole country, and while its business was forging ahead the Union National was writing on its books each month an operating loss of almost $40,000. It was this loss of prestige, aggravated by failing health and a fear of paralysis, that drove Coolbaugh to the tragic climax of his great career.

Nothing that occurred during all those days of panic produced as great a public reaction as the news of the suicide. Newspapers were filled with interviews and stories of his life. The directors of his Bank held a special meeting as soon as they heard the news, and wrote upon the Minute Books a testimony to their deep sense of loss. Within an hour of that meeting, the members of the Clearing House met to record their high appreciation of one who had been a leader in the creation of the Association, and its President during the dangerous formative years. All the banks in Chicago closed during the funeral service.

But it was upon the Union National Bank, which he had fostered with deep affection, that the penalty of Coolbaugh's death fell most heavily. Within a few weeks the volume of deposit liabilities was cut in half, as both merchants and correspondent banks hastened to withdraw their balances. The National Bank Examiner, who had been inspecting the Bank at the time when the tragedy occurred, insisted that it was "not only a solvent bank, but [in] a condition of unusually large cash means,"[46] but frightened depositors only hastened to take advantage of that fortunate fact. Early in December, the directors of the Bank invited three of the largest stockholders to make a thorough examination of its assets and liabilities, and when their report was received it was published by the Board with a declaration of their firm intention to continue the Bank in operation. Gradually the drain dwindled, and finally stopped, but it had come very near to wrecking the institution. Under the Presidency of C. T. Wheeler, who was promoted from the Vice-Presidency to succeed Coolbaugh, there began the uphill task of rebuilding the Bank, but ably as that work was done, the Union National Bank was never able to retrieve its primacy.

Meanwhile, the finances of the city government had become almost as chaotic as those of the failed banking institutions. With expenditures greatly exceeding its income from taxation, and its borrowing powers exhausted, it was compelled, in the spring of 1878, to issue city scrip.[47] Since the paper paid no interest, and could not possibly be redeemed by the city before the summer of 1879, the scrip was exceedingly unpopular. City employees refused to accept it on the ground that nobody else would take it in payment, and a temporary solution of the fiscal problem was not attained until several prominent citizens, with the cooperation of the larger banks, formed a syndicate to take over the scrip at ninety-two cents on the dollar.[48] From a financial viewpoint, the years from 1876 to 1878 do not provide one of the bright pages in the annals of Chicago.

Yet the experiences of those years were destined to produce much good. While savings banks, as such, never recovered the full confidence of the population after the panic was over, an immediate and insistent demand was made for some type of institution that should adequately care for the small accumulations of the poorer classes. It was an uphill battle, however. Not until many years later did it produce the Postal Savings System, at which it initially aimed,[49] and the passage of specific savings-bank legislation in Illinois.

Meanwhile there was a tendency in Chicago and the surrounding districts to make use of building and loan associations, which offered facilities for encouraging both thrift and home ownership. While some associations had been formed under the general corporation law of 1871,[50] it was not until the passage of a special law, in 1879,[51] that any rapid growth occurred. From that point onwards, expansion was continuous. By 1880, the associations were numerous enough to hold a convention in Chicago, at which the Building and Loan League was born, and three years later there were nearly six hundred of them, with aggregate assets of more than seventy million dollars, operating in the State of Illinois.[52]

As often happens, however, the legislature was much more prompt in providing regulations and penalties than it was in the development of a constructive program. At the session of 1879, it was inspired to pass an act providing that any banker or bank officer who accepted a deposit when he knew his bank to be insolvent should thereby become guilty of embezzlement, and be liable to a fine equal to twice the amount embezzled, in addition to the usual prison sentence. To avoid any argument as to whether the insolvency of the bank was known, it was further provided that suspension of the institution within thirty days of receiving a deposit should be *prima facie* evidence of intent to defraud.[53] Any deliberate intention to misuse the funds of depositors was, by the same act, changed from embezzlement to larceny, with appropriate increases in the penalties imposed.

Moreover, it was declared unlawful for a savings bank to make loans to its own officers, and the same rule was extended to cover trust funds in the care of the institution, while the receivers of savings banks in liquidation were required to file elaborate reports on their stewardship whenever called upon to do so by the depositors.[54] Even the courts began to take a more serious view of the

responsibility of bank officers and directors, insisting that
the latter were required by their position to know what
was going on in the institution with which they were
connected.[55]

The continuing change in the interest-rate structure of
the market was, however, a more important force in the
process of regaining financial strength. With the panic of
1877, 6 per cent interest on savings disappeared just as
completely as the 10 per cent rate on loans had vanished
a few years before. At the beginning of 1878, institutions
like the Union Trust Company were paying only 4 per
cent on deposits left with them for more than sixty days,
and the First National Bank had reduced the rate of interest on special deposits to 2 per cent. While it may be
argued that these rates were still generous, and that the
interest paid on deposits was high enough to endanger
the banking system on many subsequent occasions, the
Chicago market had definitely adjusted itself to a lower
level. In 1879, the usury law itself was amended to prohibit any rate of interest exceeding 8 per cent.[56]

Most significant of all the repercussions of the panic
was the strengthening of the position of the national
banks. With the exception of the Central National and
the Third National, these had all come through the
troublous years of depression with flying colors. Even the
Union National was making rapid progress in rehabilitation during the years of business prosperity that began
in 1879.

After long years of agitation, in which the Chicago
Clearing House Association and similar bodies from other
parts of the country had cooperated with the American

Bankers Association, the laws governing national bank taxation were amended in 1883. Large capitalization was no longer a handicap, and from 1879 to 1887 the aggregate capital and surplus of Chicago national banks grew from less than six million dollars to more than twenty. In part this was due to the creation of several new institutions,* but most of the increase came from the steady expansion of older banks, which were increasing their resources to keep pace with the growing volume of business. By 1880, Chicago had definitely attained second place among the cities of America in terms of aggregate bank deposits: only New York could demand priority.

But, in 1882, there arose another problem of vital importance to some of the older national banks. When they had been created during the hectic days of the Civil War, their charters had been granted for twenty years or less, and between January 1, 1882, and February 25, 1883, the corporate existence of some four hundred national banks was due to expire.[57] Among these was numbered the First National Bank of Chicago, which at that time was larger than any other two banks in the city put together, and was responsible for approximately one-eighth of all the business transacted at the clearing house.

At the suggestion of the Comptroller of the Currency, a bill was introduced into Congress, in December, 1881, to provide for the extension of national bank charters at his discretion. Owing to legislative delays, however, the

---

* The institutions established during these years were the Atlas National Bank, American Exchange National, Drovers National, Chicago National, Continental National, Hide and Leather National and the National Bank of America (as successor to the Fifth National). The Corn Exchange National and the Traders National gave up their charters to become state institutions. See Appendix VIII for details.

law was not enacted until July 12, 1882, a date too late to be of any assistance to more than fifty banks, whose charters had already come to an end.

Since its charter expired with the end of May, 1882, the directors of the First National of Chicago began to be alarmed at Congressional procrastination several weeks before that date arrived. Gage hurried to Washington, but the Comptroller could do nothing, and held out little hope that legislation would be passed soon enough to solve the problem. All that he could suggest was that the Bank be put into voluntary liquidation by its stockholders, and a new national bank chartered to take over the assets and liabilities of the old institution.[58] No time was wasted after Gage's return. On April 25, the stockholders decided that the Bank should be put into voluntary liquidation four days later, and that all its assets and liabilities should be taken over by the successor corporation on the basis of an elaborately determined schedule of values. By the end of the month, all the details of the transfer had been attended to, and a new charter (Number 2670) obtained from the Comptroller of the Currency. On Monday, May 1, the new First National Bank opened for business in the same offices in which its predecessor had closed the preceding Saturday. There were the same officers and employees, as well as the same books, and although the Clearing House Association went through the summary formality of admitting the successor corporation as a new member, its membership inherited all the rights and privileges of the old one. Seldom has a corporate reorganization been as smoothly accomplished.

Yet this moment of reincorporation seems to crystallize

the prestige that the First National Bank had attained. Far and away the largest financial institution in Chicago, it was also the fourth largest bank in the whole country. To its reputation among the bankers of the nation Gage's election to the Presidency of the American Bankers Association in 1883, and again in 1884, offers ample testimony. Even the national bank examiners were impressed, for a letter accompanying the report of 1879 calls attention to "the unprecedented success of the institution and its able management, its efficient corps of subordinates and the precautions shown in the safeguards adopted throughout all of the various, complex and voluminous details. . . . No bank in New York, or elsewhere, can show so clean a record."

To facilitate further expansion, the capital of the Bank was raised to $3,000,000 a few weeks after the reorganization and, even before that, new ground was broken in Chicago banking practice by the incorporation of a subsidiary company to take over and operate the bank building. All the stock of this National Safe Deposit Company was owned by the Bank. In 1883, for the first time, all employees of the institution were required to file bonds.

All this discussion of incorporation and corporate rights appears to have affected the Clearing House Association which, at the beginning of 1882, decided to abandon its old legal form of a partnership and apply for a charter from the state. But the change of legal form made no difference whatever to its persistent efforts to increase the efficiency and soundness of the Chicago money market. In the new by-laws it was specifically provided that all banks applying for membership should be examined by the Clearing House Committee, and $200,000 was specified as the minimum capitalization that would render an applicant eligible. Moreover, every member was again required to furnish a sworn statement of its condition five times each year, in the form required by the Comptroller for national banks.

Nor were these regulations allowed to fall into desuetude. In 1881, an examination of the International Bank caused the Clearing House Committee to demand a bond of $500,000 to guarantee its clearing debts until such time as its condition should improve. Shortly afterward, when reports of condition were received which disagreed with figures that the Bank had filed with the Collector of Internal Revenue, the International Bank hastily resigned from the Association in order to avoid expulsion.

Significant strides were also being made in the direction of standardizing the charges imposed for banking services. Early in 1884, it was recommended that all Chicago banks should charge customers for checkbooks at a rate of not less than forty cents for every hundred checks but, long before this, a similar effort had begun in the much more important field of domestic exchange. A committee under the chairmanship of Gage had been appointed, in 1874, to consider the question of uniform exchange rates and, after long discussion and much diplomacy, the banks adopted standard quotations at the beginning of 1879. Each month the schedule was considered anew by the Clearing House Committee, which also took action on any complaints that members were infringing the agreement. Moreover, to insure standard quotations throughout the market, it was resolved that "members of this Association will not be allowed to clear for Banks or Bankers who are not members unless such non-members agree to the rules regulating Exchange."

Even in the field of investment banking, constructive developments were afoot during these same years. To supplement the operations of the many individuals who did a bond and brokerage business, the substantial house of N. W. Harris and Company was organized early in the eighties. In 1882, Kean took over the investment operations of Preston, Kean and Company, and founded the house of S. A. Kean and Company. The harmonium from the back of his office went with him, so that the staff of the investment house might have the same inspiration of daily religious services that he had provided in the offices of Preston, Kean and Company.[59]

Once more the Chicago Stock Exchange was galvanized into an appearance of life, and this time, despite some relapses into coma, it succeeded in maintaining a continuous existence. In 1882, a "new and comprehensive" exchange was organized, which went into operation at 115 Dearborn Street.[60] For the first time in its history an approved list of securities was adopted and, with the active cooperation of several New York brokerage houses, trading was commenced on May 15 of that year. The financial facilities of Chicago appeared complete and flourishing.

Business activity throughout the United States was, however, in a precarious position at the time of these developments. The wave of prosperity that followed the abundant harvests of 1878 to 1880, coupled with the psychological confidence engendered in the money market by the resumption of specie payments, had enabled the

Treasury to carry through another refunding operation in 1879.[61] The rate of interest on the public debt was reduced to a nominal 4 per cent, and the yield was actually below that figure, while the fact that many of the bonds were purchased in Europe tended to augment the supplies of capital funds awaiting investment in the United States.

A period of great monetary ease prevailed,[62] and it was natural that speculation should rear its head.[63] Throughout the railroad industry there were new programs of expansion, although there was more manipulation of securities than construction of roadbed. On the stock exchange securities rose by feverish spurts, and the Chicago Board of Trade witnessed a series of short-lived, yet very disturbing, corners.[64] For a while there was so much interest in securities in Chicago, particularly in mining stocks, that the Chicago Mining Board was established to supplement the facilities of the regular exchange, and the anticipated increase in the demand for funds led several of the remaining state banks to raise the rate of interest that was offered on savings deposits from 4 to 4½ per cent. "A review of the business for 1880 in Chicago shows unparalleled prosperity."[65]

But this boom was an anemic affair compared to the joyous effervescence of prosperity in the years before 1873. It rested almost entirely upon the record harvests of American farms at a time when Europe was eager to purchase foodstuffs at any price, and industry was in no position to take advantage of the opportunity offered by that coincidence. By 1882, business activity subsided quietly into the lethargy from which it had been awakened four years earlier. There were no startling failures, no melo-dramatic days of crisis; the relapse was scarcely more evi-dent to the man in the street than the first stirrings of activity had been four years before. To many an indus-trialist and worker, it was but the continuation of the long depression that had begun in 1873.[66] Mercantile failures resumed the upward climb that had scarcely been interrupted by the events of 1878 to 1881, and by 1883 they were higher than they had ever been.

Chicago greeted the relapse sullenly, but without ex-citement. Financially, her condition had been greatly improved by the purge of 1877, and continuous efforts to correct the remaining defects had made it even stronger during the passing years. When the Union National Bank renewed its charter, it was examined thoroughly by the Clearing House Committee and found to be in excellent condition. When the Traders National Bank was em-barrassed by the filing of several suits against its President, the Committee persuaded the directors to make its posi-tion impregnable by writing off illiquid loans and in-creasing the amount of its capital by new investment. Most serious of all were the persistent rumors regarding the condition of Preston, Kean and Company, the largest private banking house in the city. At the beginning of 1882, these rumors had appeared serious enough to war-rant a Clearing House examination, as a result of which the partners had put large amounts of additional capital into the bank, but in the following year matters were aggravated by an absconding employee who made off with considerably more than $50,000. Even though there was no doubt that the firm could pay all depositors in full, despite the loss, it was apparent that a larger capital was highly desirable for so great a volume of business. In the spring of 1884, therefore, the partners decided to create the Metropolitan National Bank, and transfer to it all the assets and liabilities connected with the commercial banking operations of the old firm. That such a step was necessary is clearly evident from the critical tone of the Comptroller's letter on May 28, immediately after the first examination of the new bank, but the step taken by Preston, Kean and Company had removed the last important point of danger in the Chicago money market.

In New York, the picture was much less pleasant. Despite the good intentions of the New York Clearing House during the panic of 1873, and the insistence of President Grant on banking reform a few weeks later,[67] no serious attempt had been made to correct those aspects of banking policy that had aggravated the crisis.[68] Indeed, it seems probable that conditions had become increasingly unsound during the intervening years.

In 1884, therefore, New York suffered a financial purge even more serious than that which Chicago had undergone seven years earlier. From the beginning of the year the money market had been dull and the stock exchange weak, so that the unfortunate suggestion of the Treasury that temporary embarrassment might force it to pay in silver[69] almost precipitated a panic in March. Large gold exports occurred and substantial amounts of coin were withdrawn by interior banks before confidence was restored.

On May 6, the failure of the Marine National Bank[70] gave new cause for alarm, which was augmented two days later by the suspension of Grant and Ward, a brokerage house of which ex-President Grant was the most prominent (although least active) partner.[71] Against aggregate debts of more than $16,000,000, the firm had only $700,-000 of resources at the time of its suspension, and even the sober *New York Times* was indignant at "all the rascalities" which ultimately led to the conviction and imprisonment of Grant's two partners.

As a result of these developments, and the exposure of fraud and corruption arising out of them, a new withdrawal of currency began on May 10, which reduced the reserves of the New York banks by twenty per cent in the short space of two weeks. But worse was to follow. On May 13, the public learned that John Eno, the President of the Second National Bank, had taken $2,000,000 from that institution to finance his security speculations,[72] and immediate suspension was only prevented by the action of the culprit's father in making good the loss. A day later the firm of Hatch and Foote was unable to meet its engagements, and the Metropolitan National Bank of New York closed its doors in the face of a run.[73]

At that point there were all the makings of a first-class panic, yet somehow the situation never got out of control. On the afternoon of the fourteenth, the New York Clearing House Association had decided to issue loan certificates similar to those provided in 1873, but in this case there was no attempt to pool reserves.[74] Out of the eighty-two member banks in the Association, only a score actually took out certificates but, since those were the weakest institutions in the city, there is no question of the importance of this action in relieving the acute

situation. As soon as it obtained this assistance, the Metro
politan National Bank reopened; the panic was over.

Upon Chicago, these events had no effect whatever.[75]
No failures occurred, nor were the banks subjected to embarrassment, while rates of interest never rose above 8
per cent at any time during the panic.[76] So strong, indeed, was the position of most of the banks in the city that
it was reported that many of them "would not object to
seeing their cash resources run down a little." In its enthusiasm at the contrast between conditions in the two
centers, the *Tribune* preached an editorial sermon on the
fact that "what Wall Street needs is a revival of religion."[77]

Yet, in a sense, Chicago was to suffer severely from the
aftermath of New York's purge. Although her banks were
sounder than they had ever been, and had strengthened
themselves still more by several increases in capital during the early months of 1885, the panic had dimmed the
last flickering ember of business prosperity. Feeble flur-
ries in the stock market only evidenced the extent of the
growing economic lethargy,[78] because in every part of the
country industrialists and merchants were curtailing their
operations. So surely did business dwindle on the Chicago
Stock Exchange that the associate members from New
York united in a petition for its liquidation, while the
declining profits earned on the grain business caused all
of the Canadian banks, except the Bank of Montreal, to
close their Chicago offices in 1886.

Once more depression stalked the land. Although Gage
pointed out to the American Bankers Association the
"plausible character of the sophisticated arguments of the

fiatists," and found an enthusiastic audience for his remarks,[79] the hungry unemployed who stood outside Hav-
erley's Minstrel Theatre on that evening did not applaud.
Once more, there were eager demands for a policy of
monetary inflation that would relieve the appalling misery of the thousands who had been deprived of farms or
jobs by the steady fall in the general level of prices.

Moreover, out of these years of trial there emerged the
concept of militant trade unionism, a novel development
in the broad panorama of American life. In 1877, there
had been a great railroad strike in Chicago, with riots that
disorganized the city for several days, and after 1884 the
city was to find itself in the very center of the bitter struggle between workers and employers.

Out of that struggle neither side emerged with clean
hands. Both employers and employed were guilty of acts
of senseless savagery that have left a dark blot on many a
page of history, and even the public as a body was guilty
of more than one act of unreasoning and willful ven-
geance. Though the fledgling trade unions were utterly
defeated in 1877, and again in the stockyards strike of
1880, the movement was pushed onwards by forces too
deep-seated for its leaders to be stayed by ridicule or
crushed by insult. The cry of communism scared nobody
but those who were already afraid of organized labor, nor
was the growth of organization stemmed when the
Tribune reiterated its heavy sarcasm. "If the chief end of
man is to become a lazy lout, a shiftless vagabond, a pesti-
lent petrifaction, a brawling, long-haired idiot, a public
nuisance, and an enemy of his race, let him turn Com-

munist."[80] The words have a strangely modern sound, but they do not solve problems.

When, in the autumn of 1884, the Federation of Trades designated May 1, 1886, as the day on which they expected to win their struggle for an eight-hour day, the answer of the manufacturers was the creation of their own organizations, backed by all the civil power of the community. It is no wonder, then, that events marched savagely, yet inexorably, onwards to the May Day meeting, in 1886, which will always be remembered in Chicago as the Haymarket Massacre.[81] The bomb that exploded on that evening did more than spread casualties among the police. It revealed to the world an almost hysterical tension of both sides of the dispute and, in revealing, relieved it. It killed, too, the immediate hopes of efficient trade unionism, which may, in the light of subsequent years, have been too high a price to pay for relief.

Other historians have discussed the savagery of the embittered city toward the "anarchists," and the story need not be told again.[82] But it is pleasant to recall that, even in this crisis, the urbanity of Lyman J. Gage was still to aid in healing the wounds of the community.* When Governor Oglesby felt inclined to pardon the anarchists, Gage was asked to ascertain the sentiments of the business leaders of Chicago and, in a secret meeting at the First National Bank, he worked hard to persuade those leaders to adopt an attitude of mercy and wisdom. The effort failed, largely owing to the intransigeance of Marshall Field, but

* In fairness, it should also be pointed out that E. S. Dreyer, another Chicago banker who served as foreman of the jury that convicted the anarchists, subsequently became the leader of the movement that demanded a pardon for those who were imprisoned. Cf. Barnard: *Eagle Forgotten*, p. 214.

Gage was not vanquished. If he could not save the lives of those who were condemned, he might at least do something to allay the popular hysteria and, at his suggestion, a small group of outstanding citizens created the Economic Club, in order to develop "a better comprehension of the ideas and motives which actuate men in their relations to each other in the social state."[83] There were "lawyers, ministers of the Gospel, business men, trade unionists, single-taxers, one prominent Socialist, one philosophical Anarchist, and perhaps other radicals" in the group and, despite popular opposition, Gage nurtured it until it grew into the great Open Forums of the Civic Federation of Chicago. When these forums began, there were many people so terrified at the danger of allowing radicals to talk in public that they wanted a force of plain-clothes policemen in the hall, but Gage rejected all such counsels of timidity. It is pleasant to reflect that his own benign and bearded presence in the chair may have done something to soften the acrimony of dispute, and pave the road to social progress.

REFERENCES FOR CHAPTER XIV

[1] *Chicago Tribune,* May 24, 1877.
[2] *Ibid.,* May 5, 1874.
[3] *Commercial and Financial Chronicle,* XVIII, 281.
[4] *Ibid.,* XXIII, 73 and 411.
[5] *Chicago Tribune,* May 5, 1877.
[6] *Journal of Business,* X, 331.
[7] *Commercial and Financial Chronicle,* XX, 440; *Bankers Magazine,* XXXIV.
[8] Knox: *op. cit.,* p. 128; *Commercial and Financial Chronicle,* XXV, 99.
[9] *Annual Report of the Comptroller of Currency,* 1876, p. cxxiv.
[10] *Revised Statutes of Illinois,* 1874, pp. 1018, 1019, 1027 and 1031.
[11] Cf. *Chicago Tribune,* May 5 and 8, 1877.

[12] *Ibid.*, June 10, 1877.

[13] *Laws of Illinois*, 1875, p. 65; Cf. *Commercial and Financial Chronicle*, XXVII, 15, for judicial decision upholding the act.

[14] *Chicago Tribune*, November 15, 1877.

[15] Cf. D. M. Dailey: A Review of Money Rates in Chicago, *Journal of Business*, X, 322-345, for an excellent analysis of the changing interest-rate structure during this period.

[16] *Chicago Weekly Journal*, September 13, 1871.

[17] *Laws of Illinois*, 1874, p. 294; 1875, p. 85.

[18] *Chicago Tribune*, January 26, July 8, 1875.

[19] Dailey: *op. cit.*, p. 331; *Chicago Tribune*, January 6, 1878.

[20] *Commercial and Financial Chronicle*, XXII, 601; XXIII, 608; XXIV, 25; XXV, 171.

[21] *Ibid.*, XXIV, 599.

[22] *Chicago Tribune*, May 10 and 13, 1877.

[23] *Ibid.*, May 13, 1877.

[24] Cf. *Commercial and Financial Chronicle*, XXV, 221; XXVI, 77-78.

[25] *Chicago Tribune*, December 8, 1877.

[26] *Ibid.*, May 8, 1877.

[27] *Ibid.*, June 5, 1877.

[28] *Ibid.*, July 15, 17 and 18, 1877.

[29] *Commercial and Financial Chronicle*, XXV, 221; *Bankers Magazine*, XXXII, 324.

[30] Andreas: *op. cit.*, III, 437.

[31] *Bankers Magazine*, XXXII, 324.

[32] *Idem.*

[33] *Chicago Tribune*, October 30, 1877; *Bankers Magazine*, XXXII, p. 486.

[34] *Chicago Tribune*, November 22 and 23, 1877; *Bankers Magazine*, XXXII, 486.

[35] *Chicago Tribune*, November 24, 1877; *Bankers Magazine*, XXXII, 486.

[36] *Bankers Magazine*, XXXII, 567.

[37] *Chicago Tribune*, December 6, 1877.

[38] *Ibid.*, December 7, 1877.

[39] *Ibid.*, December 7, 1877; *Bankers Magazine*, XXXII, 566.

[40] *Chicago Tribune*, December 7, 1877.

[41] *Ibid.*, December 18, 1877.

[42] *Bankers Magazine*, XXXIV, 494.

[43] *Chicago Tribune*, December 12, 1877.

[44] *Commercial and Financial Chronicle*, XXVI, 3.

[45] *Chicago Tribune*, November 15, 1877.

[46] *Ibid.,* November 15, 1877.

[47] *Commercial and Financial Chronicle,* XXVI, 436.

[48] *Idem,* 495 and 522.

[49] *Chicago Tribune,* November 8, 1877.

[50] Bodfish: *History of Building and Loan Associations in the United States,* p. 372.

[51] *Laws of Illinois,* 1879, pp. 83-87.

[52] Bodfish: *op. cit.,* p. 375.

[53] *Laws of Illinois,* 1879, pp. 113-114.

[54] *Laws of Illinois,* 1879, p. 236.

[55] *Bankers Magazine,* XXXVIII, 149.

[56] *Laws of Illinois,* 1879, p. 184.

[57] Knox: *op. cit.,* pp. 171-173; Kane: *op. cit.,* I, 244.

[58] Knox: *op. cit.,* pp. 172-174; Kane: *op. cit.,* I, 111.

[59] Huston: *op. cit.,* I, 538.

[60] Cf. *Ibid.,* I, 538 ff. for details.

[61] *Commercial and Financial Chronicle,* XXVIII, 79, 105, 131, 269 and 385.

[62] *Ibid.,* XXVI, 251; XXIX, 313; *Bankers Magazine,* XXXIV, 249.

[63] *Commercial and Financial Chronicle,* XXIX, 314; *Chicago Tribune,* June 10, 1881.

[64] Bogart and Thompson: *op. cit.,* pp. 294-295.

[65] *Bankers Magazine,* XXXV, 633.

[66] *Commercial and Financial Chronicle,* XXXVIII, 3-7.

[67] Hepburn: *op. cit.,* pp. 316-317.

[68] Sprague: *op. cit.,* pp. 353-359; Knox: *op. cit.,* pp. 181-185.

[69] *Commercial and Financial Chronicle,* XXXVIII, 239.

[70] *Ibid.,* XXXVIII, 549; *Chicago Tribune,* May 7, 1884.

[71] *New York Times,* May 10, 1884; *Chicago Tribune,* May 10, 1884.

[72] *New York Times,* May 14, 1884.

[73] *Commercial and Financial Chronicle,* XXXVIII, 581; *Chicago Tribune,* May 15, 1884.

[74] *New York Times,* May 15, 1884; Sprague: *op. cit.,* pp. 118-119.

[75] *Chicago Tribune,* May 5 to 28, 1884.

[76] *Commercial and Financial Chronicle,* XLII, 355; Dailey: *op. cit.,* p. 333.

[77] *Chicago Tribune,* May 16, 1884.

[78] *Commercial and Financial Chronicle,* XXXIX, 193, 219 and 243.

[79] *Chicago Tribune,* September 24, 1885; *Bankers' Magazine,* XL, 276; XLI, 200.

[80] *Chicago Tribune,* March 24, 1879; August 22, 1877.

[81] *Ibid.*, May 5 to 12, 1886.

[82] *Ibid.*, June 29, August 20 and 21, 1886; Barnard: *Eagle Forgotten*, pp. 75-124; Bogart and Thompson: *op. cit.*, pp. 170-173; Brown: "Haymarket After Fifty Years," *Christian Century*, LIII, 659-662.

[83] Lyman J. Gage: *Memoirs*, pp. 69-72; Barnard: *op. cit.*, p. 111.

CHAPTER XV

METROPOLIS

1887–1893

BANKING reform, during the Civil War period, had been approached largely from the angle of improving the monetary system of the country. While other aspects of the problem were not entirely ignored, the primary aim of Chase and McCulloch had been the establishment of a uniform currency that should circulate from Maine to California, and the National Banking Acts were heralded because they established such a currency. It was inevitable, therefore, that the monetary controversies which excited the country from 1863 to 1896 should involve much discussion of the banking system, and this interest was strongly reinforced by the expanding financial needs of American business. Banking law and banking policy, despite an inherent tendency toward conservatism which always characterizes the financial system, could not escape the influence of the industrial revolution.

By 1887, the Comptroller of the Currency reported that he had received more than forty different plans designed to improve the banking system,[1] and he added yet another by suggesting an elaborate scheme of his own for the revision of the National Banking Act.[2] Two years later, in the summer of 1890, Sherman was to offer a

similar suggestion in the Senate, on his own behalf.[3] Despite the prevalence of reforming enthusiasm, however,
none of these proposals reached the statute books, and the
only significant banking legislation that came from Washington was the Act of March 3, 1887, which provided that
cities of satisfactory size might be designated reserve cities,
or even central reserve cities, if three-quarters of the national banks in such a city should request the Comptroller of the Currency to do so.[4] Such a provision, while
it was important to Chicago, could not be regarded as
reforming the banking system in any significant fashion.

But, if the federal mountain had labored to produce so
small a mouse, the travails of the state legislatures had
given birth to a variety of laws of tremendous significance.
State banking institutions had discovered by this time
that they could operate profitably, despite the federal
prohibition of note issue, and there was a widespread
demand for laws that would facilitate their creation.
Moreover, the citizenry and the mercantile community
demanded, with equal vehemence, that the state authorities should take steps to supervise and regulate the operations of the banks they had created. On both counts,
therefore, the years from 1885 to 1891 witnessed the enactment of a large body of state banking law, the first
widespread development of that kind since the passage of
the National Banking Acts.[5]

Illinois participated in this movement with enthusiasm. Ever since the revision of the Constitution, in 1870,
there had been continuous agitation for the passage of a
general banking act and, in 1874, a bill had been introduced into the legislature providing for the creation of

state banks similar in all respects to the national institutions, save for the fact that they were endowed with generous fiduciary powers. This proposal had been killed by the vigorous opposition of the Chicago savings banks and trust companies,[6] which were anxious to prevent additional competition within their sphere of operations. Strange as it may seem, that opposition, together with the apathy of the legislature, was able to prevent any action from being taken on this subject for nearly two decades after the adoption of the Constitution.

By the session of 1887, however, the power of Chicago state bankers had waned considerably, while the demands for banking legislation had increased in volume, so that a comprehensive banking law was written on the statute books of Illinois.[7] Save for the omission of any authority to issue notes, this act was very similar to the National Banking Act in its description of the powers of the new institutions, and of the general conditions under which they were supposed to operate. Even the provision regarding double liability of stockholders was carried over into the state act. The State Auditor, under powers comparable to those of the Comptroller of the Currency, was given the right to grant charters, and to supervise the banks as long as they were in existence. Four times a year, he might require statements of condition from them, and once a year, at least, he was required to examine each bank in detail. There were, however, significant differences from the national banking system. In the first place, the Illinois legislation did not prescribe any specific cash reserves for the institutions that were to be set up, leaving that question wholly to the judgment of the individual

LYMAN J. GAGE
Reproduced by courtesy of The First National Bank of Chicago

banker. Secondly, state banks were implicitly authorized to lend on real estate and, thirdly, the minimum capitalization of $25,000 was only half that required of the smallest institution that could be created under the federal laws.

In November, 1888, the law was ratified by a majority of the voters at the election, in the manner required by the state Constitution, and went into effect immediately. But difficulties soon arose. Owing to clerical inefficiency, the act provided that banks could be organized with a capital of $50,000 in towns of "not to exceed ten thousand inhabitants," but made no provision for banks in larger cities. Both the Attorney-General and the Supreme Court held that no bank could be chartered in Chicago under the terms of the law,[8] despite the heavy sarcasm of the *Tribune* in insisting that the meaning of the legislature was perfectly clear.

An amendment was, therefore, passed in 1889,[9] under which banks could be established in all cities, with increases in the required minimum capital in accordance with the size of the population. But the amendment did more than that. It specifically reiterated the power to lend on real estate as security, and conferred on all state banks the power to receive and execute trusts, so that the competitive position of the new institutions was distinctly favorable. National banks could do neither of these things.

The legislature was not, however, satisfied to pass one banking act. Having taken the bit into its teeth, and received an enthusiastic endorsement from the electorate, it decided to enact a comprehensive program of financial legislation. In 1887, a law was passed to provide for the regulation of trust-company operations,[10] stating specifically that corporations might undertake all those fiduciary activities that were permissible for a natural person. Trust companies, however, might not receive deposits in excess of ten times the amount of their capital and surplus and, for the further protection of the general public, each company was required to deposit with the Auditor of Public Accounts the sum of $200,000 in United States bonds, Illinois securities, or mortgages on property within the state. This fund was specifically held for the benefit of creditors in case the institution should fail. Annual examinations by the Auditor, comparable to those of state banks, were also authorized, and every trust company was required to furnish that official with a statement of its condition at the end of each year. Two years later, in view of the steady growth of fiduciary institutions, the required deposit was raised to $500,000 in the case of companies managing trust funds that exceeded two million dollars in aggregate value.[11]

In the light of Chicago's experiences in 1877, it was natural that legislative regulation of savings banks should also receive considerable attention. During the session of 1887 a law was passed providing, in elaborate detail, for the creation of mutual savings banks similar to those that flourished in New England,[12] but very little came of the attempt. Although the law was admirably drafted, and actually led to the incorporation of two savings banks in Chicago, early in 1888, it fell foul of the state Constitution. No provision had been made for submitting the bill to the electorate, apparently on the grounds that mutual

savings banks were not banks because they were prohibited from doing a general banking business, and the
Supreme Court declared the measure invalid in 1889.[13]
Since that time, it may be pointed out parenthetically,
no specific legislation regarding savings banks has been
enacted in Illinois, largely because savings deposits were
rapidly becoming a recognized adjunct of the commercial
banking business. But, despite this fact, the excellence of
the savings bank law arouses a feeling of regret that it
should have become inoperative on legalistic grounds.

To round out the program, several other laws were
passed. Building and loan associations, which were rapidly increasing in number and importance, were subjected to annual examination by the Auditor and, at the
same time, several minor changes were made in the earlier
laws governing their lending operations.[14] Moreover, associations that were chartered by other states were authorized to do business in Illinois, provided that they
deposited with the Auditor a fund of not less than $100,-
000 to satisfy the claims of residents of the state in the
event of liquidation.[15] As a further contribution to the
growing complexity of the money market, surety companies were authorized to grant bonds in the same way
that natural persons had always done,[16] while bucket
shops (an evidence of the speculative tendencies of Chicagoans!) were sternly prohibited.[17]

Never before had Illinois developed so comprehensive
a body of laws dealing with financial institutions and,
since the more important measures had run the gantlet
of a referendum, it is apparent that the people of the
state were vastly more interested in banking develop-

ment than they had been on any previous occasion. Much water had rolled under the bridges since those earlier days when the *Tribune* had been screaming its indictment of the rag barons, and the population of Egypt had regarded all bankers as miscreants.

Nor was the new enthusiasm for banking confined to Illinois. Throughout the whole west and south there was a feverish spell of legislative activity, followed by an equally intensive development of state banking institutions, so that between 1875 and 1890 the number of those institutions quadrupled.[18] Eastern capital was spilling over from railroading and agricultural development to facilitate the growth and multiplication of financial institutions throughout the western states and territories, and even the older sections of the country witnessed a rapid increase in the number of trust companies. By 1890, such institutions were legalized, by the federal government, within the borders of the District of Columbia.[19]

National banks, although they could not keep pace with the expansion in the number and aggregate resources of state institutions, also increased in absolute importance during these years. Under the amendment of July 12, 1882, the government-bond holdings of national banks had been considerably reduced in those cases where the bank did not wish to issue notes and, since the high price of United States securities had previously deterred many from accepting a national charter, the effect was immediate.[20] Between 1882 and 1890, the number of national banks in the country increased from 2,187 to 3,573, while the aggregate capital rose from

$600,300,000 to $872,800,000. Total deposits, however, increased by only one-third.

It is apparent, therefore, that, even within the national system, there was a growing tendency toward the creation of a large number of small banks.[21] Every new community wished to have one or more financial institutions within its borders and, since the national system still enjoyed a high prestige, the Comptroller was asked to grant charters in all those cases where the community could afford the minimum capitalization required under federal laws. Where that requirement was beyond the resources of the people, it was usually possible to charter a state institution with smaller capitalization, so that, for the first time in American history, the whole country was covered with individual banks of all sizes and conditions, which had absolutely no legal relationship to one another. Independent community banking, with its new-found horror of branches, was rapidly becoming the dominant characteristic of the American financial system.

Compensatory influences were, however, at work beneath the surface. Neither waves of community pride nor oratorical insistence on community independence could persuade a realist to ignore the fact that a financial system composed of thousands of unrelated banks must inevitably be weak and inefficient. Few communities are financially strong enough to take care of themselves at all times, and the ideal of unit banking provided no channel by which the weaker sections of the country could draw upon the resources of the financial centers during periods of stress.

By means of correspondent relationships, based upon

the practice of redepositing reserves, the bankers of the country set out to weld this multiplicity of individual units into a workable system.[22] Deposits in reserve cities, originally carried because they were more profitable than the holding of an equal quantity of vault cash, were enlarged because of the services that city banks could offer to their customers. By this means, a species of clearing system developed throughout the country which, though inefficient and costly, facilitated the flow of funds from one section to another.

Moreover, to supplement the machinery provided by correspondent agreements, there grew up a number of commercial-paper brokers, with connections in several parts of the country. Such brokers or dealers, who usually combined the commercial-paper business with other types of financial operations, had already developed the practice of purchasing promissory notes from the borrower and selling them, without endorsement, to eastern buyers (although many of them were still willing to handle paper as brokers, and receive a commission from the lender). By this means, larger borrowers could, if their credit standing was high, obtain access to distant money markets when funds were not easily obtainable from local banks, and the extent to which this service was made use of is clearly apparent from the fact that a Chicago house like Herman Schaffner and Company handled about $35,000,000 of commercial paper each year for its customers.[23] As the operations of these brokers extended over wider areas, and the legal and customary status of promissory notes became more definitely crystallized, there developed a kind of national money market to which all important borrowers had access when funds were scarce or expensive at the local bank.

New York, by virtue of its position and historical development, was necessarily the focus of this embryonic financial system. It was in New York that much of the commercial paper from other parts of the country was sold, and all banks of any size, no matter where they might be situated, tended to carry at least one correspondent account with a New York institution. As a result, the concentration of funds in New York proceeded just as rapidly as the multiplication of small banks in other parts of the country, so that the conflict between centralization and independence, which has characterized every financial crisis since 1873, had already made its appearance. On the one side, the growing importance of state institutions appeared to favor increasing decentralization, while the importance of foreign capital, which was imported chiefly through New York institutions, tended to augment the hegemony of that city.[24] Although Chicago banks, such as the First National, might do a very large foreign-exchange business in financing the export and import of commodities, the New York houses, for many years to come, constituted the most important channel for the sale of American securities to European capitalists.

Underlying these tendencies toward unit banking and the financial hegemony of New York, there was, however, another revolution in banking processes that was destined to exercise even more influence upon the structure of the American financial system. The bank note, around which the national banking system had been built, was rapidly declining in importance. For many years, checks drawn against bank deposits had been steadily replacing bank notes as a medium of payments, especially in urban communities, but during the eighties the banks themselves began to question the advantages of note issue. Owing to the high price of government bonds, the profits of issue were negligible or nonexistent and when the required bondholdings of national banks were reduced by Act of Congress, in 1882, there was a steady tendency toward voluntary retirement of circulation. This process was accelerated when fiscal surpluses caused a rapid retirement of the national debt, so that, between 1883 and 1890, the aggregate bank-note circulation declined from $362,000,000 to $197,000,000.

To some extent, this contraction in the supply of circulating currency was offset by the equally steady expansion in the supply of silver dollars and silver certificates issued under the Bland-Allison Act,[25] which increased from $133,000,000 to $349,000,000 during the same period, but this apparent counterbalancing was largely coincidental. In view of the tremendous increase in the physical volume of American production, the growth in the population and the rising level of incomes, it is obvious that a sharper fall in price levels would have occurred if the total supply of money had remained constant.

In reality, the total supply of money expanded rapidly, without any clear perception of that fact on the part of the community at large. While political and economic factions argued violently about silver and fiat paper, the average man was disregarding both types of money and making his payments by means of checks drawn against bank deposits, chiefly because checks were safer and more convenient. This was not a new process. At the time of the Civil War, checks had been widely used in wholesale transactions throughout the east; by the seventies, their use had been pretty general in all large cities throughout the country. But, by the end of the eighties, almost all transactions, save for a diminishing volume of cash retail trade, were conducted by means of checks.[26] Even in the smaller communities, this tendency was apparent, and the *Commercial and Financial Chronicle*, in 1887, estimated that checks were doing the work of at least three billion dollars of circulation. In comparison with a figure of that magnitude, the discussions regarding bank notes and silver certificates fade into insignificance.

Such a change of custom regarding payments had unexpected results. Under the national banking system, the monetary results of banking policy had been limited, so far as notes were concerned, by elaborate governmental regulation and restriction; but the volume of bank deposits grew with every increase in the loans and discounts of the banks, as long as reserves were ample and the business demand for funds was strong. Given these two conditions, which were both satisfied in ample measure during the quarter-century following 1890, there was nothing in state or federal legislation to prevent a phenomenal deposit inflation on the part of the banking system, and it is to this unexpected repercussion of increasing check payments that we owe both the Federal Reserve Act of 1913 and the Banking Act of 1935.

Those events, however, are ahead of our story. In the

eighties and early nineties the leading American banks were liquid to a degree that now seems incredible, so that the volume of loans was limited by the rate at which the supply of eligible paper increased. In 1888, for instance, more than ninety per cent of the resources of the First National Bank of Chicago were composed of cash items and loans and discounts, according to the report of the National Bank Examiner. Of the loans and discounts, the following figures indicate that some forty per cent were due either on demand or within thirty days, while less than twenty per cent ran more than ninety days before maturity. Even though the concept of eligible paper included promissory notes which, unlike the older bills of exchange, did not always indicate a prior production of wealth,[27] the standards of banking liquidity prevented too rapid an inflationary development.

TABLE XVIII

LOANS AND DISCOUNTS OF THE FIRST NATIONAL BANK OF CHICAGO

May 12, 1888

	Number of Items	Aggregate Face Value
Due on demand.............	273	$ 3,462,925
Past due...................	98	168,966
Not ticklerized.............	82	205,679
Due in May, 1888..........	1,752	2,238,941
Due in June, 1888..........	2,354	3,302,062
Due in July, 1888..........	1,670	3,056,934
Due in August, 1888........	582	1,118,989
Due in September, 1888......	106	318,200
Due in October, 1888.......	35	121,802
Due in November, 1888.....	19	77,981
Due in December, 1888.....	7	9,950
Long time.................	25	114,791
Foreign...................	4	52,756
Total.................	7,007	$14,249,976

In one sense, however, it is not entirely true to suggest that there was no supervision of commercial banking policy. Under the Legal Tender Acts and the silver legislation, the Treasury had acquired a large measure of control over the supply of currency in circulation; under the operations of the Independent Treasury, with the government holding a substantial portion of its money in its own vaults, it was possible for the Secretary of the Treasury to influence banking policy by his power to increase or decrease the aggregate bank reserves available at any given moment of time. This supervision, however, was not always wise or well timed, and the *Chronicle*, in 1888, had good cause to complain that "our money market is a complex affair. Trade influences are subordinated wholly to the tax-gathering and Government accumulating machinery; that again is modified by the currency making arrangements . . . while the movements of these wheels within wheels are all . . . equalized and regulated by bond purchases and depository bank expedients. A very odd condition of affairs for such a practical, ingenious people, jealous of its rights and proud of its privileges!"[28]

Archaic and illogical though the system was, it had not created serious problems prior to the panic of 1873, partly as a result of its modification during the Civil War to allow the Secretary of the Treasury to make use of depository banks in certain circumstances. When the fiscal revenue exceeded the expenditure of the government, the hoarding of currency in the sub-treasuries invariably produced a temporary stringency that disturbed the money market but, in the nature of things, the period of unpleasantness was short. Since the annual expenditure was always equal to, or even in excess of, the federal income during the early postwar period, the money flowed back into the channels of finance and trade after a short incarceration, and the banking system adapted itself to the seasonal influences of governmental financing.

But, during the eighties, the public revenue grew much faster than the expenditures of the government, as a result of higher tariffs and an expanding volume of trade. Year by year, the fiscal surplus grew larger and, since the Republican party was opposed to any reduction of tariffs or any enlargement of the sphere of governmental operations, it seemed that, in the long run, the whole currency supply of the nation would disappear behind the impregnable doors of the sub-treasury vaults. An inescapable dilemma was presented by the interaction of political traditions and economic events, which aroused popular indignation as early as 1887.[29]

Secretary Fairchild, in order to ease the strain, resorted to greater use of depository banks.[30] By increasing the number of banks authorized to receive government deposits, and raising the maximum balance that each might hold from $500,000 to $1,000,000, he was able to rid the Treasury of some of its incubus. By increasing the appraised value of United States bonds, deposited as collateral, from ninety to one hundred and ten* he encouraged a larger number of banks to qualify as federal depositories.

Temporarily, the expedient succeeded. During the autumn of 1887, Treasury funds were pumped into the

---

* The deposited collateral was composed chiefly of four per cents, which were selling at one hundred and twenty-five and one-half in the market.

banking system on a lavish scale, so that the usual seasonal drain was scarcely perceptible, but the banks themselves became alarmed at the policy during the following spring. If the government should at any time withdraw its balances to meet an emergency, the depository institutions might be crippled, and the fear of such action caused the banks to confine their operations very largely to demand loans.[31] To escape from such a situation, intolerable to bankers and businessmen alike, many institutions refused to accept any more deposits from the government, and a few of the more restive ones insisted on returning all that they had previously received.[32] Escape from the dilemma was not to be achieved by that road.

Hastening to adopt another expedient, in the hope that it might prove more palatable, the Secretary persuaded Congress to adopt a resolution proclaiming the continuing validity of the Act of 1881, under which fiscal surpluses might be used for the purchase of outstanding government bonds.[33] Armed with this authority, he announced that, on and after Monday, April 23, 1888, the Treasury would purchase at "a fair price" all United States bonds offered to it,[34] and the response of the financial community was instantaneous. By the end of June, some $26,000,000 of government bonds had been purchased at a cost of $32,207,125,[35] and further purchases were made on the same scale during following months. But it was a hard battle. Surplus revenues accumulated so fast that the sums in the Treasury were not greatly diminished by the policy, and the balances with depository banks remained practically constant.[36] Well might the *Chronicle* point out that it would "be a day of rejoicing when the Treasury is put out of the business of making or regulating the money market."

Yet the problem was more complex than that fervent wish implied. That Treasury policies were often harmful is not open to question, nor is there any doubt that they were usually motivated by political rather than economic considerations. But, in the amorphous condition of the American money market, where the clearing houses represented the only other agencies to which a bank could turn in times of distress, the Treasury performed a function of vital importance. By a careful timing of its policies, it was able to pour funds into the money market during the recurrent autumnal stringencies[37] and, in view of the customary low level of bank reserves, there was no other financial institution that could have eased the situation to a comparable degree. By 1891, the *Bankers Magazine* records the complaints of "the croakers" that the Government was at fault in not having a surplus "to pour into the stream of circulation when it begins to run low."[38]

The comment was due, in part, to the fact that business expansion had already reached a point where it perceptibly influenced the money market. By the end of 1886, a distinct revival was already apparent, and prosperity cumulated during the years from 1887 to 1889.[39] As a result of the extraordinarily easy money market, due in part to bond purchases by the Treasury, there was an ample supply of funds available at low rates of interest for all types of business operations. Failures diminished in number and importance, security prices zigzagged upwards and the physical volume of production increased by more than ten per cent between 1886 and 1890.

But it was in the south and west that prosperity was most intense. Throughout the period, there was a steady drain of both capital and currency away from the eastern centers to finance the surging enterprise of the newer sections of the country, and to provide a medium of exchange for their growing population.[40] Despite the uncertainty injected into the transportation picture by Congressional debates on the Inter-State Commerce Act, and the even more unpleasant activities of state railroad commissions in promulgating rate reductions,[41] the years from 1886 to 1890 witnessed another outburst of railroad construction. During 1887 alone, some twelve thousand miles of track were laid in various parts of the country, at a cost of more than two hundred and fifty million dollars,[42] and for the five-year period the new construction amounted to more than thirty thousand miles. All the western roads running out of Chicago were in the very forefront of this boom, which survived the labor troubles of 1888, and did not collapse until overbuilding and rate reductions had seriously reduced railroad earnings in the following year.[43]

Moreover, ample supplies of funds, coupled with good crops and improving railroad facilities, bred a veritable fever of land speculation in many of the western states. Wherever the railroads went, the wave of speculation followed the tide of immigration and settlement, while the necessary financial facilities were provided, in large measure, by the land-improvement companies that grew up in hundreds of communities to serve as channels by which eastern capital might be sucked in. In 1887, the stock of the Topeka Land and Development Company was so warmly received in Boston that four-fifths of it was taken upon the day of issue,[44] and other eastern centers were no less eager to participate in enterprises that were regarded as a royal road to fortune.

Illinois, by this time a settled community with a highly developed and diversified economy, did not participate directly in the speculative activities of the pioneering territories. But the years of prosperity accentuated her industrial development, and brought to Chicago a volume of business operations that increased steadily with the growing wealth of the western states that looked to the city as a market and source of supply. Chicago was abundantly prosperous, and becoming increasingly urbanized by the development of streetcar lines. In 1886, Yerkes had acquired the North Chicago Railway and in the following year the West Chicago Railway also came under his control.

Moreover, Chicago was the arena of a speculative battle, quite early in the period, that attracted attention from all over the world and had serious repercussions in many parts of the United States. Harper, a prominent operator on the Board of Trade, decided at the end of 1886 to corner the wheat market, and carried on his campaign for months in the face of repeated bear raids and steadily growing visible supplies of grain. Adding to his own fortune the entire resources of the Fidelity National Bank of Cincinnati, and borrowing heavily from banks in all parts of the country, he had invested more than three million dollars in the scheme by the following sum-

mer. He and his associates, at that time, held more than
seventy-five million bushels of wheat.

On June 14, 1887, the great corner collapsed with a
resounding crash. Nothing like it had ever been known
in Chicago. June wheat broke from ninety-two cents to
seventy-two cents, and July wheat from eighty-three and
a quarter cents to seventy-four cents. Harper, in addition
to the loss of his fortune, was indicted and sentenced to
prison, and in his failure he carried down the Fidelity
National Bank and more than a dozen brokerage houses.[45]
Yet the Chicago banks, as a group, had so little to do with
the manipulation that they were unaffected by the crash,
and the market as a whole soon recovered its buoyancy.
Even on the Board of Trade itself, the "Harper Corner"
was forgotten during the years of speculative prosperity
that followed it.

But the breach between agriculture and industry,
which had been so apparent during the controversies
over resumption, had not been healed. While it was true
that abnormally large crops sometimes brought momen-
tary wealth to the farmer, he did not share during these
years of falling prices any of that substantial prosperity
which encouraged the expansion and integration of
American industry. Mortgages grew steadily more burdensome with every decline in the general level of prices,
particularly in those areas where the virginal fertility of
the soil had been mined during a long chain of preceding
years, and once again the farmer and the distressed laborer combined their voices in ardent pleas for renewed
monetary inflation. Even before the ink on the Bland-
Allison Act was dry, there were demands that its infla-

tionary force should be augmented by repealing the prohibition of state bank notes,[46] and the clamor for some
form of monetary expansion grew steadily louder.

But, after the panic of 1884, the emphasis of the "currency reformers" was placed primarily on silver. While
many persons seriously desired the restoration of international bimetallism, "believing that the world will never
experience a full return of prosperity as long as silver remains demonetized,"[47] the majority were attached to silver only because they regarded it as the easiest way in
which to attain their inflationary goal. Paper money was
out of fashion, but a good deal of Congressional enthusiasm had been mustered for the Bland-Allison Act in 1878,
so that monetization of silver on a more extensive scale
appeared to be within the realm of political possibility.
Moreover, the price of silver had fallen substantially during the eighties, and the sincere enthusiasm of inflationary cranks was strongly supported by all the forces at the
command of the silver-mining interests, who were deeply
interested in any plan that would increase their profits
by raising the price of the white metal and enlarging the
market in which it might be sold. Few lobbies in the history of the United States have been as continuously per-
nicious, or as blatantly greedy, as that operated by the
silver-mining group during the half-century or more that
followed the demonetization of that metal. Well might
the *New York Times* insist, when legislation was introduced in 1890, that "it is, of course, a purely political
bill. There is no finance in it and no statesmanship. It is
a foal by cowardice, out of greed. . . . The prime motive . . . is to furnish a market at speculative prices for

the product of a small number of silver mines belonging to wealthy men, who demand this favor as the price of their adherence to the Republican Party."[48]

The favor was granted. The west, against its own political convictions, had given its votes to enact the McKinley tariff, and eastern support of the silver bill was the price demanded for that service. Moreover, speculative cupidity, which expected a rise in commodity prices as a result, lent ready support to the measure.[49] On July 14, 1890, the Sherman Act became law and the government of the United States was committed to the purchase and coinage of four and a half million ounces of silver every month. To finance the plan, an issue of Treasury notes, which were later to be replaced by silver certificates resulting from the new coinage, was authorized. Even stranger than its enactment, however, is the enthusiasm with which that legislative action was received in unexpected quarters. While the *Chronicle*, and most eastern journals, deplored the continuous tinkering with the currency,[50] the *Bankers Magazine* was distinctly optimistic. In words that have a peculiarly modern ring, it insisted that "the new silver law is a great experiment, and is worth trying. We are a great people, and have done more within the last thirty years in the way of working out new economic problems than any other Government in the world. . . . Experimentation is always in order, and this last experiment is fully justified."[51] Even in the nineteenth century one does not often find such sublime faith in the social virtues of selfishness!

The United States, however, was not the only country to feel the feverish stimulus of speculation during those exuberant years. Although no other nation resorted to policies of monetary tinkering comparable to the silver legislation of this country, there was throughout much of Europe a growth in bank deposits sufficient to nourish a boom comparable in all respects to that which excited America. Speculation was rampant over the western world. While railroads held the center of the American stage, France was absorbed in the construction of the great Panama Canal, and English capitalists were fired with the prospect of the fortunes to be reaped from investments in Africa and South America. Argentine cedulas were more discussed in the London market than any domestic security, and a thousand investors were familiar with the economic prospects of tropical Africa for every one that understood the condition of affairs among the shepherds of Cumberland.

Such speculation cannot feed upon itself. Human optimism will build a vast fabric of dreams upon the smallest of foundations, but some foundation there must be, some evidence of fruitfulness to encourage further investment. Early in 1890, the fruits were either invisible or bitter. Although the *Chronicle* bravely insisted that business was still prosperous,[52] the forced reiteration of its arguments betrayed its own infection with the general skepticism. Railroad earnings had fallen badly, as a result of overexpansion and the initial enthusiasm of regulatory bodies, France was aghast at the utter failure of de Lesseps' grand enterprise, and the financial collapse of Argentina was bringing the whole fabric of international investment down upon the head of the London money market. The morning after the debauch was not pleasant and, because of its growing attachment to the world money market, America could not escape the repercussions.

The money market was in no condition to stand this strain. London was overexpanded and, to make good its unexpected Argentine losses, it called upon New York. American securities were dumped upon the New York market by British houses and, owing to a substantial rise of interest rates in London, short-term funds began to move eastward across the Atlantic.[53] Gold flowed in considerable amounts from New York to London during June and July. But New York was too enfeebled to serve as a buffer for very long. Security sales by English houses, acting upon a market that was already shaky, forced prices down rapidly, and the gold exports reduced still further the inadequate reserves of the New York banks. Moreover, to make matters worse, currency was moving toward the west in considerable volume.

Although, on January 21, 1890, the Secretary of the Treasury had given notice that no more government bonds would be purchased, because of the diminished amount of money on hand,[54] this policy was reversed to alleviate the growing stringency. On April 19, a circular was issued, offering to buy additional securities, and more than $17,000,000 was paid out of the Treasury as a result.[55] By the beginning of August, however, the influence of this injection was no longer perceptible and conditions were rapidly growing worse.

On July 31, the Bank of England raised its rate to 5 per cent, and gold was again drained away from New York[56] in a volume that was augmented by the fears regarding the dollar which the Sherman Act had engendered.[57] New York banks, which had held surplus reserves of almost $9,000,000 at the beginning of the month, showed a deficit of $655,725 by August 16 and, despite renewed bond purchases by the Treasury after the eighteenth, the deficit had increased to $2,512,975 by August 23.[58] Interest rates on call loans rose to 25 per cent per annum during the second week of the month, and soared to the dizzy height of 186 per cent on the twenty-first.

Currency was still moving westward in August but, during the early part of September, the Treasury operations had produced a little ease in the money market. The panic appeared to be over; New York rejoiced in the fact that it had been met without a single failure, and with very little commotion. But the improvement in conditions depended solely upon the ability of the Treasury to pump money into the market faster than it was drawn out in response to European and western demands. During September, almost $60,000,000 was provided by the government, and the financial community clamored for even more assistance.[59] Unfortunately, the Treasury was not a bottomless well. In eight weeks it had provided enough currency to take care of all western shipments and enable the New York banks to raise their reserves above the legal requirement, but the end of its operations was in sight. On October 1, the money in the Treasury was $60,000,000 less than it had been a year before, and $120,000,000 less than its holdings on the same date in 1888.

By the middle of October, it was apparent that the financial uncertainty had not been removed by the fiscal operations that had concealed it temporarily. Once again the reserves of the New York banks fell below the legal minimum, and the stock market slid rapidly downwards, so that the following weeks witnessed a steady but unobtrusive financial deterioration.[60] In the light of their own sad situation, the stocks of American railroads led the rout,[61] but it was clearly apparent that renewed selling by English houses was one of the primary factors in the situation. London was far from through with its difficulties.

After making no change at their customary Thursday meeting, the directors of the Bank of England unexpectedly raised bank rate to 6 per cent on the morning of Friday, November 8, and consternation gripped both London and New York. Within a few days, the Bank of England was compelled to borrow three million pounds in gold from the Bank of France, and New York was shivering on the verge of panic.[62] On November 11, therefore, the New York Clearing House Association decided, for the third time in its history, to resort to the issue of loan certificates in order to aid those member banks that were in acute distress.*

Actually there were but few Clearing House Loan Certificates issued, but the effect of the action, by removing all fears of bank failure through inadequate reserves, improved the situation tremendously. Despite the closing of the North River Bank, the panic subsided. Call-money rates jumped, once again, to 186 per cent per annum, as a result of the embarrassment of Barings,[63]

---

* Particularly the Bank of North America, the Merchants and Traders Bank and the North River Bank. Cf. *Commercial and Financial Chronicle*, LI, 655-656.

in London, but conditions had improved considerably by the end of November. Nor can there be any doubt that the prevention of more serious panic was entirely due to the deliberate actions of the Bank of England, in the London market, and the Clearing House Association in New York. Once again the need for concerted action in moments of emergency had been demonstrated and, to emphasize the lesson, the directors of the National Bank of Commerce, at the suggestion of J. P. Morgan, passed a resolution congratulating the Clearing House Committee.[64]

Chicago, through all these hectic days, pursued the even tenor of her way without serious disturbance, an emphatic testimony to the fact that her destinies, at this period, were more closely linked to the western states than to the financial world of New York and London. Western business continued to enjoy a substantial measure of prosperity throughout the whole of 1890,[65] and Chicago reaped the benefit of it. Although Chicago banks were connected with London and other European centers by virtue of their foreign-exchange departments these departments were engaged in financing trade rather than speculation. The volume of foreign operations was almost identical with that of 1889, and the decrease in English business was offset by a comparable increase in French and German drafts, so that there was little reaction from the crisis that was shaking the international money market. In correspondent balances there was a slight shrinkage, but the strength of the Chicago banks rendered that development unimportant and, in many cases, the loss was amply recouped by drawing down the balances that they held in New York. Moreover, it should be pointed out that the reduction of bankers' balances in the central reserve cities was due almost entirely to the timidity of country bankers. There was little public hoarding. In all, the reserves of New York, Chicago and St. Louis were reduced by $7,100,000, while the aggregate reserves of country banks *increased* by $6,700,000.

Even in regard to business operations, Chicago suffered little in 1890. In the middle of the year, interest rates were below 6 per cent on commercial loans, and at the worst period of the crisis they did not rise much above 7 per cent. For normal business operations there were ample funds, and "the complete independence of the Chicago commercial world from the speculative whirlpool in Wall street was never more perfectly illustrated."[66] On the local stock exchange, the prices of railroad securities naturally followed the New York quotations downwards, and there was a sharp decline in Chicago street-railway securities, but no panic developed. Only on the produce market was there a temporary stagnation of business, resulting from difficulties regarding the negotiation of sterling bills in mid-November, but the inconvenience lasted less than a week before the dealers were able to resume operations and make up for lost time.[67]

It was natural, therefore, that Chicago should lead the vanguard of business recovery in 1891, with all the western country following closely in its train.[68] Nor did the Atlantic seaboard lag very far behind. Early in February, the last of the Clearing House Loan Certificates were retired, and banking and business operations were expand-

ing *pari passu*. But it was an anemic and feverish prosperity that ensued, spasmodic in time and unevenly
distributed between industries and geographic areas.

Fundamentally, the expansion was speculative rather
than constructive. In so far as there was a railroad boom,
it was marked by security manipulation and watered re-
capitalizations, rather than by the laying of new track
or the physical improvement of existing facilities. Agricultural prosperity, where it existed, depended more
upon the manipulation of prices than upon increased
crops, and it is typical of the period that there should
have been a succession of attempted corners on the Board
of Trade which culminated in the notorious wheat corner organized by Cudahy, and other leading Chicago
operators, in the spring of 1893. It is also typical that
Cudahy should have been financed by New York banks,
rather than Chicago institutions,[69] since the latter were
much less interested in speculative operations. Perhaps,
too, there is something significant in the fact that these
years witnessed the first examples of modern bank-ban-
ditry in the depredations of the notorious Dalton Gang,
which culminated in the sensational holdup of both the
banks in Coffeeville, Kansas.[70] Even a modern gang would
find it hard to improve on the brazen technique of that
affair.

To suggest that Chicago was immune from the speculative spirit of the age would be absurd. Moreover, it
would be contrary to all the traditions of the city. But
it is nevertheless true that, during these years, Chicago
achieved a considerable measure of constructive improvement that could not have been equaled by any other im-

portant city in the United States. Eastern capitalists, under the leadership of Yerkes, were expanding the street-railway system rapidly, and European investors were again focusing their attention on the city despite the insistence of the *Tribune* that the new securities "most successfully floated abroad recently are those of the 'scaly' kind."[71] Real estate improved steadily, and building activity spread steadily outwards from the center of the town to the suburbs that were rapidly rising on land that had been desolate prairie a year or two before.[72] "The Stickney region, Harvey, Cicero, the Tolleston region and the immediate neighbourhood of Jackson and Washington parks" developed with phenomenal rapidity.

Nor was the banking system immune from these influences. During 1891, as an evidence of the general unsoundness, there occurred throughout the United States more bank failures than in any previous year since the creation of the national banking system,[73] and nothing is more indicative of Chicago's relative strength than her comparative immunity from casualties. Among the incorporated banks, the Park National Bank and the Security Loan and Savings Bank, neither of which were important institutions, were the only failures.

Among the private bankers, however, the failure of S. A. Kean and Company caused considerable discomfort.[74] Since the commercial banking business of the original house of Preston, Kean and Company had been transferred to the Metropolitan National Bank seven years earlier, the immediate effects of the suspension were not widely felt, but the psychological reaction was important. S. A. Kean and Company was the largest private banking house in Chicago, and one of the oldest, so that public opinion suddenly became skeptical about the others and demanded the publication of more information regarding their condition. Many of them complied with the demand and, feeling that further steps were necessary to protect their position, some of the leading houses applied for state charters. Thus Haugan and Lindgren, one of the soundest private banks, asked the national bank examiner to investigate its condition and report to the general public, which he did. Almost immediately afterward, the firm was incorporated as the State Bank of Chicago, in order to preserve the good will that Sturges' favorable report had created.

These developments, however, were scarcely more than a ripple on the steady tide of banking progress which characterized the years from 1887 to 1892. Although many people had regarded the Act of 1887 as unattractive, in that the banks of any community which elected to become a central reserve city would thereafter be compelled to hold all the required reserves in their own vaults,[75] Chicago did not listen to the arguments. Before the ink was dry upon the act, the directors of the First National Bank of Chicago had resolved to take steps to petition the Comptroller of the Currency to raise the status of the city. Other banks followed rapidly, so that the necessary three-quarters of the national banks were soon united in the application, and Chicago became a central reserve city in which all banks throughout the country, except those situated in New York and St. Louis, might legally deposit a portion of their required reserves.

Bankers from every section of the United States showed

their approval of Chicago's action by choosing one of the banks in the city as their reserve agent, and the tendency was especially marked throughout the western states. Aggregate bankers' balances in the national banks of Chicago, which had amounted to $28,000,000 in 1886, increased steadily until they reached a total of more than $61,000,000 in the summer of 1892—an increase of one hundred and twenty per cent in six years. More than a thousand banks maintained balances with the First National by the end of this period, and even the Metropolitan National Bank, a comparatively small institution, had the accounts of sixty national banks and one hundred and seventy-five state institutions. For their correspondents, the Chicago banks were willing to make collections in Chicago, Milwaukee, St. Paul, Minneapolis, St. Louis, Kansas City, Detroit, Cleveland, Toledo, Indianapolis and Cincinnati, as well as additional centers in the case of some of the larger banks, "remitting for same on the day of payment less seventy-five cents per thousand." As an alternative, such items might be credited to the account of the correspondent bank on the day of receipt, and the balance remitted each Saturday, in which case the amount charged was only fifty cents per thousand. In the case of out-of-town banks that designated a Chicago institution as their reserve agent, items on all these points were credited at par, and interest (usually at 2 or $2\frac{1}{2}$ per cent) was allowed on all balances in excess of a specified minimum.

Since many of the Chicago banks had established connections with financial centers throughout the world, as a result of the development of the specialized foreign-exchange departments, already referred to, they were also able to offer to correspondent banks the benefit of this organization. Moreover, all of them undertook to furnish New York, or other eastern, exchange at par, in order that western bankers should suffer no loss on eastern remittances by choosing a Chicago bank as correspondent.

Under the stimulus of this new position as a central reserve city, the financial business of Chicago expanded rapidly. Existing national banks, in view of the profits derived from their operations,* tended to enlarge both their capital and the number of their employees, and several new national banks were incorporated during the period.† Between 1886 and 1892, the aggregate capital and surplus of these institutions increased from $16,-000,000 to $32,000,000, while total resources expanded in similar proportion from $91,000,000 to $178,000,000.

Moreover, the state banks during these years were rapidly attaining a more significant position.‡ In 1887, there had been, in the whole state of Illinois, only forty-eight state institutions, with aggregate capital of less than $2,000,000 and resources of about $7,000,000;[76] by the spring of 1892, there were twenty-one such banks in Chicago alone, with nearly $85,000,000 of resources and

* The Metropolitan National earned a *net* profit of 321⁄2 per cent in 1889, and in several other cases the showing was nearly as good.

† Bankers National Bank, First National Bank of Englewood, Fort Dearborn National Bank, Globe National Bank, Lincoln National Bank, Oakland National Bank, Prairie State National Bank, and United States National Bank. See Appendix VIII for details.

‡ Among the more important state banks established in Chicago were the American Trust and Savings Bank, Bank of Blue Island, Calumet State Bank, Chemical Trust and Savings Bank, Chicago Trust and Savings Bank, Citizens Bank of Evanston, Farmers Trust Company, Globe Savings Bank, Merchants Exchange Bank, North American Loan and Trust Company, and Northern Trust Company. See Appendix VIII for details.

$18,000,000 of capital and surplus.[77] If both state and national institutions are combined, it is apparent that the aggregate resources of the Chicago money market had tripled during six years.

Nor was there any lack of effective leadership. The Clearing House Committee, composed throughout this period of Lyman J. Gage, J. J. P. Odell, Orson Smith, Isaac G. Lombard and C. J. Blair, did magnificent work in prescribing the standards of banking operation and demanding a rigid adherence to those standards on the part of all members of the Clearing House Association. By prescribing the form of the report that members were required to make four times a year, they encouraged better accounting records and insured the production of comparable statements that revealed the true position of the banks. By careful examination of these statements, and a threat of expulsion from the Association in the case of banks that made a poor showing, they were able, in many cases, to correct incipient weakness before it became dangerous.

Having no legal competence, the Committee could not do very much to influence the management of banks that were not members but, in the case of state banks that applied for membership, it rejected all but such as agreed to hold cash reserves comparable to those required by the National Banking Act. Moreover, by employing the national bank examiner to conduct the preliminary examinations of both state and national applicants, it insured a thorough and uniform analysis in all cases.

Concurrently with this commercial banking growth, Chicago experienced a resurgence of investment-banking activity in which the commercial banks played the leading role. Ever since 1847, there had been a few brokers and dealers in mortgages and securities and for many years there had been an embryonic stock exchange, but these facilities had lacked the coordination and large volume of resources necessary to successful financing on any scale. Not until the period we are now discussing was any serious attempt made to remedy these twin defects but, under the spur of speculative enthusiasm, rapid progress was made between 1887 and 1893.

As far as the organization of the market was concerned, the Chicago Stock Exchange was so near to coma, in the spring of 1887, that the Western Union Telegraph Company removed all its instruments from the floor of the Exchange. The few members in attendance had to rely upon newspapers, or private sources of information, for New York quotations and, since this information was neither prompt nor uniform, the market was far from close. Most of the dealings in securities occurred in the offices of the numerous private banking houses, which combined all sorts of functions under one roof, and the price at which the transaction was closed depended in large part upon the shrewdness of the customer and the efficiency of the broker. By the end of May the annual dues of the Exchange were lowered to twenty-five dollars in order to attract new members.

In 1888, however, business prosperity and cheap money combined to stimulate the security business,[78] largely as a result of the growing interest in local street railways and gas companies. During the three following years, improvement continued steadily, so that telegraph instruments once again appeared on the floor of the Exchange in May, 1890, and at the end of the year the *Tribune* rejoiced in the fact that "the Chicago Stock Exchange made greater progress in 1890 toward becoming an institution of prime importance in the financial situation of Chicago and the West than it had made in all the previous years of its existence."[79] From that point, the development of an organized securities market continued without interruption. While the improvement was not continuous, the investment-banking mechanism never again collapsed into the chaos apparent during 1886 and 1887.

This improved organization of the market was, however, closely related to the growth in the resources available for security operations, since adequate resources are obviously essential to continuous trading. Few of the private banking houses had owned any considerable amount of capital, and Preston, Kean and Company, which was one of the largest among them, had been seriously embarrassed by the inadequacy of its resources for many years before the failure of its successor company. Only the firm of N. W. Harris and Company appeared to possess enough capital to finance independent operations.

Toward the end of the eighties, however, a few of the large commercial banks in Chicago began to interest themselves in the market for investment securities, partly on account of the small demand for commercial loans and partly with a view to making supplementary profits out of trading operations. In this field the First National Bank of Chicago was among the pioneers. Operating through the Foreign Exchange Department, which was subsequently renamed the Foreign Exchange and Bond Department as an indication of its growing security operations, the Bank began to deal actively in bonds during the middle eighties. By 1891, it had reached the stage where it was able to take over, and distribute, an entire issue of $1,276,000 Chicago City four per cents, and during that year it sold more than seven million dollars' worth of bonds at an aggregate profit of eighty thousand dollars. That was no mean achievement in a declining market, and it is not surprising to find that, when conditions improved, in 1892, a net income of more than twice that amount was earned from the sale of eleven millions of securities. By that time, the First National had developed an important position as an originating house, taking many of its issues directly from the borrower. Moreover, in the case of large issues, elaborate syndicate operations had been worked out with several of the largest eastern houses which covered both underwriting and distribution. As far as sales were concerned, the Chicago market was invariably reserved for the Bank.*

Under the leadership of the First National, ably seconded by the Harris organization, the capital market of Chicago expanded rapidly. By 1892, it had developed to a point where, ignoring New York entirely, the Sanitary District of Chicago was able to sell an issue of $2,000,000 of bonds with principal and interest *payable in Chicago,* the first time that such a thing had ever been attempted!

---

* Among the issues so handled, during 1892, were the $5,000,000 loan issued by Chicago for the World's Fair, the $1,560,000 Chicago Gold Loan, the $1,400,000 Cook County Funding Loan, the $4,100,000 Refunding Loan of the West Division Railway Company and the $1,800,000 5 per cent Loan of the Cass Avenue and Fair Grounds Street Railway Company of St. Louis.

These investment operations undoubtedly contributed to the growth of the First National Bank, which was probably the largest institution of its kind in the United States at the end of 1892.* They contributed also to the growing complexity of the money market, which was rapidly assuming the metropolitan air that characterizes it today. But in spite of the brilliant leadership of her outstanding bankers, the eminence of her institutions and the steady augmentation of her resources, it is necessary to remember that Chicago was still in a very real sense tributary to New York. While her loyal protagonists did all that was in their power to suggest that the difference between the two centers was not so great as it seemed,[80] the eastern city controlled ten times the resources of her western sister. As a result of her phenomenal growth, Chicago could exult in the fact that "not only the Northwest, but the Southwest, looks to this city for the extra funds necessary to meet the normal demands of business. This may be set dòwn as an inevitable result of the fact that Chicago is the commercial capital of the west, from Texas to Montana."[81] But Chicago herself still looked to New York for assistance. When Chicago became a central reserve city, the New York balances of Chicago banks were not reduced by a single penny, despite the fact that such balances could no longer be counted as part of the legally required reserve.[82] At this stage of its development, the Chicago money market assumed significance because, for large sections of the country, it augmented considerably

* *Bankers Magazine*, XLVII, 229. At this time the First National also adopted a new practice by constructing a warehouse on the west side to serve as storage space for books and other records that had to be moved out of the bank building because of the increase in operating personnel. Cf. *Bankers Magazine*, XLVII, 228.

the services that New York could offer, and provided an efficient intermediary link between the small country banker and the eastern metropolis. There was, as yet, no serious indication of a weakening of New York's hegemony.

Nevertheless, Chicago was growing rapidly, and her substantial progress, at a time when other parts of the country were exhausting themselves in a fever of speculation, demands attention. In part, it was due to the rapid economic development of the west, to which attention has already been drawn, but Chicago also contributed something by her own efforts on behalf of the World's Columbian Exposition. In 1892, there occurred the four-hundredth anniversay of Columbus' arrival on the western shores of the Atlantic and, seven years before that anniversary, it was decided that the celebrations should include a great world's fair in Chicago. In July, 1889, Mayor Cregier appointed a committee of leading citizens to carry out the project, and a month later the "World's Exposition of 1892" was incorporated under the laws of Illinois, with a capital of five million dollars. Lyman J. Gage, of the First National Bank, was unanimously selected to head the enterprise.[83]

Unfortunately, it is easier to dream than to achieve. Up to this point, the project was pleasant to contemplate, and involved little hard work, but troubles were only beginning in 1889. Senator Cullom, of Illinois, introduced a bill into Congress to provide for a "World's Columbian Exposition of Arts and Industries," in order to give official approval to the scheme, and several other cities immediately awoke to the fact that such a fair might be very profitable for business. New York, St. Louis and Washington all entered the lists to compete with Chicago, and a Congressional Committee was appointed to decide upon the merits of the several claims. After much debate, Chicago won the prize, although New York, in a desperate effort not to be beaten, had promised to provide ten million dollars for construction in addition to an appropriate site. Chicago was compelled to match the offer.

Then followed the long and trying period of fulfilling all the promises that had been made, a story that would seem too fantastic for credibility if there were not so many other fantasies that have become realities in the history of Chicago. Calls were made upon the subscribers to the World's Exposition corporation, in June, 1890, for 20 per cent of the amount of their subscription and, to encourage promptness, engraved certificates were offered as a premium to all who paid the full amount of their subscription at once. Moreover, on June 12, the stockholders voted to increase the capital of the corporation from five to ten millions, and to seek out new subscribers. The title was also changed to "World's Columbian Exposition."[84]

In view, however, of the difficulties that had been encountered in raising the original subscription of five million dollars, few people expected to meet with success in a second effort. As a matter of fact, the total subscriptions never exceeded six millions, and the actual cash receipts from subscribers were $5,614,425. An effort was, therefore, made to have the city subscribe five million dollars on its own account which, although the authorities were willing, necessitated the passage of an amendment to the

state Constitution for the purpose of enlarging the borrowing powers of the City of Chicago. By November,
1890, the amendment had been approved, and the bonds
were sold early in 1892. Meanwhile, the remainder of the
capital of the corporation had been demanded from the
subscribers, so that by the summer of 1892 the Committee
in charge of the project had received a total of eleven million dollars.

Unfortunately the budget of expenses exceeded seventeen millions, and the Committee indignantly opposed
the suggestion that they should limit the scale of their
operations to the funds that were actually available. Gage,
in addressing the directors of the corporation, insisted
that expenses could not be reduced. "Neither the people
of our city, of our State, of our country, or of the world
would be, or ought to be, satisfied with any exhibition
that will not worthily exemplify the progress of the world
in art, science, and industry, and which will not typify
the highest achievements in architecture, in art, and in
all things which illustrate the utilization by man of the
resources and powers of nature."[85]

Nor were the citizens any less enthusiastic about the
development of an exposition that should go down in
history as one of the wonders of the world. The splendid
white city that was rising under the fostering care of
the architects evoked continuous wonder from every spectator, and the suggestions that poured into the Committee demanded even greater extravagances. "A building
fifty stories high," was desired by one enthusiast, while
others insisted on "a temple which shall be constructed
on the plan of Solomon's; an amphitheater to hold a hun-

dred thousand people; a building a thousand feet high in the form of an eagle; a rotating colosseum; a building resting upon the animals mentioned in Revelation, six stories high, each containing representatives of animals in metals, and so constructed that they shall be able to make their characteristic noises in grand chorus; a structure in the form of a mausoleum wherein all the Presidents and their wives shall be buried; a building with forty-two towers, each representing one of the States . . . and the most extraordinary theater ever conceived, to consist of a park and opera-house combined, with gardens on the roof, and so constructed that parties may drive into their boxes."[86]

In all this there was no suggestion of economy, yet it is hard to be extravagant without funds. The Board of Directors, therefore, appealed to Congress for a grant of five million dollars, on the ground that the fair was a national celebration. Congress appeared agreeable, but matters dawdled on through the summer of 1892 without any favorable action. Not until the beginning of August was anything accomplished, and even then Congress only authorized the coinage and payment to the Committee of $2,500,000 in Columbian Exposition souvenir half-dollars, with a portrait of Columbus on one side and a Spanish caravel on the other.

By selling these coins at a dollar apiece, the Exposition treasury was temporarily replenished, but the process of coinage was slow and the public demand none too large. More immediate aid was necessary and, in the autumn of 1892, it was decided to sell five million dollars' worth of World's Columbian Exposition 6 per cent debenture bonds. Initially, the market for the bonds was good. Many were taken by wealthy citizens, and an aggregate amount of $2,300,000 was taken up by the banks of the city, each of which purchased bonds to the extent of 5 per cent of its capital and surplus. In all $3,600,000 were disposed of before the end of the year.

Suddenly, in March, 1893, a new blow fell. Congress ordered the Secretary of the Treasury to withhold the remainder of the souvenir half-dollars, amounting to $570,000, until the Board of Directors had given surety for their ability to pay the costs of judging the exhibits and providing the prizes that were to be awarded, an expense that the Board had expected the Federal Government to bear.[87] Chicago was indignant, insisting that the original appropriation had been made for the specific purpose of contributing to construction costs. Such a trick as that attempted by Congress could not, the directors insisted, "have been attempted between individuals in the great business world without speedy redress through legal process." But Congress did not change its position, and the best that Chicago could get was a compromise under which the $570,000 in dispute should be specifically allocated to the expenses of judges and awards.

Further financing was necessary. The State of Wisconsin appropriated one hundred thousand dollars in April, but this was a mere drop in the bucket.[88] The railroads running out of Chicago were, therefore, persuaded to purchase more than a million dollars' worth of the unsold bonds,[89] in addition to the $530,000 of stock which they had purchased in 1890. Finally, in order to raise the money necessary to pay the final expenses of construction and opening, a million dollars' worth of the souvenir coins were deposited with the banks of the city as collateral for a loan of equal amount. Since the coins were legal tender, and could form a part of the banks' reserves, no interest was charged on the loan.[90]

October 20, 1892, the anniversary so carefully fixed by Chicago historians,* had passed long before the Fair was ready to open. But on May 1, 1893, the great work of the organizers was finished. On that day, "amid a profound silence, which was far more impressive than would have been the blare of trumpets or the roar of cannon, the Columbian Exposition was opened . . . by a touch from the finger of Grover Cleveland, President of the United States."[91] Chicago had triumphed over all obstacles. Exhibits from every corner of the world were collected in the buildings of the Exposition, and among the crowds of visitors that thronged the metropolis were citizens of all nations and people of every race. For a golden moment, Chicago was the center of the world.

---

* *Chicago Tribune,* October 21, 1892. New York authorities fixed their celebration for October 11, and gave the *Tribune* an opportunity to explain sarcastically to "ignorant easterners" the precise significance of the change from Julian to Gregorian calendars!

REFERENCES FOR CHAPTER XV

[1] *Chicago Tribune,* January 2, 1888.
[2] Kane: *op. cit.,* I, 146; *Commercial and Financial Chronicle,* XLVI, 56-57.
[3] *Commercial and Financial Chronicle,* LI, 62.
[4] Knox: *op. cit.,* pp. 285-286; *Commercial and Financial Chronicle,* XLIV, 382.
[5] *Bankers Magazine,* XLV, 833.
[6] Bogart and Thompson: *op. cit.,* p. 290.
[7] *Laws of Illinois,* 1887, pp. 89-94.
[8] *Chicago Tribune,* January 1, 3, 4 and 18, 1899; April 6, 1889.

[9] *Laws of Illinois,* 1889, pp. 58-60.

[10] *Laws of Illinois,* 1887, pp. 144-147.

[11] *Laws of Illinois,* 1889, pp. 99-100.

[12] *Laws of Illinois,* 1887, pp. 77-88.

[13] *Chicago Tribune,* March 20, 1889.

[14] *Ibid.,* February 10, 1889; *Laws of Illinois,* 1887, pp. 131-132; 1889, p. 98; 1891, pp. 88-89 and 90; 1893, pp. 83-86.

[15] *Laws of Illinois,* 1893, pp. 86-87.

[16] *Laws of Illinois,* 1887, p. 143.

[17] *Laws of Illinois,* 1887, pp. 96-97.

[18] *Bankers Magazine,* XLVI, 89.

[19] Kane: *op. cit.,* I, 418.

[20] *Commercial and Financial Chronicle,* XLV, 718.

[21] Cf. *Annual Report of the Comptroller of the Currency,* 1885; Knox: *op. cit.,* p. 188.

[22] Cf. Watkins: *Bankers' Balances,* Chs. I and II, for a general discussion of this development.

[23] *Chicago Tribune,* November 7, 1890; June 4, 1893; *Bankers Magazine,* XLVI, 89; XLVII, 691-694.

[24] *Commercial and Financial Chronicle,* XLIV, 136; XLVI, 662 and 665.

[25] *Idem,* 16; L, 574-575; *Bankers Magazine,* XLV, 96.

[26] *Commercial and Financial Chronicle,* XLV, 69.

[27] Cf. James: "The Background of Monetary Management," *Bulletin of the Robert Morris Associates* (1935) for a more detailed discussion of this point.

[28] *Commercial and Financial Chronicle,* XLVI, 718. Cf. Kinley: *op. cit.,* for an extended discussion.

[29] *Commercial and Financial Chronicle,* XLV, 38, 659.

[30] *Idem,* 488.

[31] *Ibid.,* XLVI, 492.

[32] *Idem,* 430-431.

[33] *Idem,* 492.

[34] *Idem,* 500.

[35] *Idem,* 813.

[36] *Ibid.,* XLVII, 2-3; XLVI, 144.

[37] *Ibid.,* XLVII, 271 and 393; L, 82; *Bankers Magazine,* XLV, 260.

[38] *Bankers Magazine,* XLVI, 6.

[39] *Commercial and Financial Chronicle,* XLIV, 38; L, 10-13.

[40] *Ibid.,* XLIV, 286 and 412; *Chicago Tribune,* January 14, 1888.

[41] *Commercial and Financial Chronicle,* XLV, 418.

[42] *Ibid.,* XLVI, 8.

[43] *Ibid.,* XLVII, 395.

[44] *Ibid.,* XLIV, 666.

[45] Kane: *op. cit.,* I, 141-144; *Commercial and Financial Chronicle,* XLIV, 792.

[46] *Commercial and Financial Chronicle,* XXIX, 643.

[47] *Ibid.,* XLVI, 463.

[48] *New York Times,* June 9, 1890.

[49] *Commercial and Financial Chronicle,* L, 572 and 604-605.

[50] *Idem,* 642; *New York Times,* May 10, 1890.

[51] *Bankers Magazine,* XLV, 257.

[52] *Commercial and Financial Chronicle,* L, 3-4, 293 and 433.

[53] *Ibid.,* LI, 32, 63 and 96. See also Sprague: *op. cit.,* Ch. III.

[54] *Commercial and Financial Chronicle,* L, 186.

[55] Cf. *Report of the Secretary of the Treasury,* 1890, pp. xxviii-xxxii, for details of this, and subsequent, operations.

[56] *Commercial and Financial Chronicle,* LI, 124.

[57] *Idem,* 222.

[58] *Idem,* 182, 220 and 258; LII, 15-17.

[59] *Ibid.,* LI, 358, 360, 434 and 474.

[60] *Idem,* 494, 510 and 548.

[61] *Chicago Tribune,* November 8 and 10, 1890.

[62] *Commercial and Financial Chronicle,* LI, 624 and 654; LII, 16.

[63] London *Times,* November 15 to 18, 1890; *Commercial and Financial Chronicle,* LI, 692-693.

[64] *Bankers Magazine,* XLV, 417.

[65] *Commercial and Financial Chronicle,* LI, 692.

[66] *Chicago Tribune,* November 12, 1890. See also November 7 to 19; Dailey: *op. cit.,* p. 334.

[67] *Bankers Magazine,* XLV, 412.

[68] *Commercial and Financial Chronicle,* LI, 730 and 762; *Bankers Magazine,* XLV, 484.

[69] *Bankers Magazine,* XLVII, 732 and 805.

[70] *Chicago Tribune,* October 6, 1892.

[71] *Ibid.,* February 28, 1889.

[72] *Ibid.,* January 1, 1891; January 1, 1892.

[73] Kane: *op. cit.,* I, 155; *Bankers Magazine,* XLV, 929-932.

[74] *Bankers Magazine,* XLV, 583; *Chicago Tribune,* January 3, 1891.

[75] *Commercial and Financial Chronicle,* XLIV, 410.

[76] Knox: *op. cit.,* p. 729.

[77] Chicago *Economist,* VII, p. 193.

[78] *Chicago Tribune,* January 1, 1889.

[79] *Ibid.,* January 1, 1891.

[80] *Chicago Tribune,* January 8, 1888; November 12, 1890.

[81] *Ibid.*, January 8, 1888.

[82] *Commercial and Financial Chronicle,* XLVII, 338.

[83] *New York Times,* May 22, 1890; Huston: *op. cit.,* pp. 264-269; Gage: *Memoirs,* pp. 74-76.

[84] These, and subsequent, financial details are derived from the *Report of the President to the Board of Directors of the World's Columbian Exposition,* Chicago, 1892-1893, pp. 51-78.

[85] *Report of the President,* p. 61.

[86] *Chicago Tribune,* June 15, 1890.

[87] *Ibid.,* April 4, 1893; *Report of the President,* pp. 75-76.

[88] *Chicago Tribune,* April 8, 1893.

[89] *Ibid.,* April 16, 1893.

[90] *Report of the President,* pp. 77-78.

[91] *Chicago Tribune,* May 2, 1893.

CHAPTER XVI

CURRENCY FAMINE—AND FEAST

1893–1894

CHICAGO itself, in 1893, fascinated the visitors from other parts of the world almost as much as the marvels of the World's Fair that they had come so far to see.[1] Paul Bourget, from the top of the Auditorium Tower, "a chaotic cyclopean structure which connects a colossal hotel with a colossal theatre," gives us a vivid picture of the scene that spread beneath his gaze. "Far as the eye can reach Chicago stretches away, its flat roofs and its smoke—innumerable columns of whitey-grey smoke. They rise straight upwards, then stoop to heap themselves into vaporing capitals, and at last meet together in a dome above the endless avenues.

"It needs but a few minutes for the eye to become accustomed to the strange scene. Then you discern differences of height among these levels. Those of only six or seven stories seem to be the merest cottages, those of two stories are not to be distinguished from the pavement, while the buildings of fourteen, fifteen, twenty stories, uprise like the islands of the Cyclades as seen from the mountains of Negroponte. A mighty murmur uprises from below like that of no other city. There is an incessant tinkle of locomotive bells, that seem to be sounding in advance the knell of those they are about to crush. They are everywhere, crossing the streets, following the lake shore, passing over the river which rolls its leaden waters under soot-coloured bridges, meeting and crossing each other's tracks, pursuing and overtaking one another. Now you distinguish an elevated road, and there, beside the railways on the level street, you see other trains on the avenues, three or four cars long but without locomotive. It is the cable system. And there are steamers, lowering their yards and coming to anchor in the harbour."

During the two short decades since the fire, the city had grown steadily, pushing its towers higher into the sky and stretching out into the prairie its tentaclelike suburbs. Enterprise and speculation had worked a miracle; enterprise and speculation, like warm fructifying spirits, filled the towering buildings whose cavernous offices contained thousands of human beings, and traveled out along the highways where factories and stores stood side by side with dwellings. Even advertising had sounded a clarion call that is still recognizable. "Louis XIV was crowned King of France at the age of five years"; the hoardings shouted, "X———'s pepsin had been crowned with success as a remedy for indigestion before it had been publicly known a single year."

But Chicago, and every other city in the United States, was standing nervously on the threshold of panic at the very moment when Cleveland touched the electric button that opened the World's Fair. The surgent speculation that had carried the nation along since 1890 was already wavering. That fact could not be driven from the thoughts of businessmen by all the marvels of the White City with its domes like those of Ravenna, its colonnades that vied with Rome and its lagoons so redolent of Venice. At the beginning of 1893, business was decidedly dull[2] and, although the stock market experienced feverish spasms of activity during the spring, investors were apathetic.[3] Business in general was characterized by a lethargy that contrasted strangely with the operations of earlier years, and many railroads, strained by past expansive efforts, were on the verge of bankruptcy. Before the end of February, the Philadelphia and Reading Railroad, reputed to be among the strongest in the country, passed into the hands of receivers.

This shivering uncertainty of business was not entirely due to the aftermath of speculation. Speculation itself had been encouraged by the inflationary monetary policy imposed on the government under the terms of the Sherman Act and, although the coinage of silver had not realized the pleasant dreams of those who anticipated rising prices, it had created a haunting specter that paralyzed business initiative. International bimetallism was not attainable, as the Monetary Conference at Brussels had clearly demonstrated to all except those who were fanatically devoted to the silver cause, and in January there were recurrent rumors that the British government might close the Indian mints to the free coinage of silver.[4] To a man like Gage, who represented the business sentiment of the country, there was "but one thing for the government to do. . . . [It] should at once stop its single-handed contest at maintaining the silver market of the world," and repeal the silver-purchase provisions of the hated legislation.[5]

But there was little prospect of repealing the Sherman Act, despite reiterated journalistic demands,[6] and the situation of the Treasury was rapidly growing critical. The budgetary surplus of more than a hundred million dollars, which had cushioned the financial system against the shock of panic in 1890, had dwindled to nothing during the intervening years. Moreover, the purchase of silver at the rate of four-and-a-half million ounces a month, coupled with the steady withdrawal of gold by those who distrusted the financial strength of the government, had created a situation in which the ultimate gold reserves behind the paper currency were perilously small. At the beginning of 1893, there was only $108,000,000 of gold in the Treasury, as contrasted with $218,000,000 five years earlier, and the banks of New York, Chicago and Denver were so worried by the situation that they voluntarily offered the government a portion of their gold reserves in exchange for paper money.[7]

Such action, in itself, is evidence of the fear that gripped the financial community, a fear that the United States might be forced to abandon the gold standard because of its inability to pay gold when the holder of paper money presented it for redemption. And, in April, this lurking, unspoken fear was suddenly crystallized. The Secretary of the Treasury announced that, when the gold reserves in his vaults fell to the legal minimum of one hundred million dollars, he would be compelled to redeem Treasury notes in silver.[8] At once, the whole financial community was filled with a dread unequaled since the panic

of 1873. Although President Cleveland publicly over-
ruled the statement of his Secretary, insisting that all
forms of currency would be equally redeemable in gold
as long as the Treasury could acquire a single ounce of
that metal,[9] public alarm was not allayed. Americans
continued to hoard gold, quietly and unobtrusively, and
foreigners who held American securities proceeded to dispose of them as rapidly as possible. "Credit was suddenly
paralyzed in every section" of the country, and gold flowed
steadily eastward from New York.[10]

Moreover, to intensify the unpleasantness of the situation, London was drawing gold from all parts of the
world to strengthen its own position. Once again, distant speculations had weakened the London money market, this time as a result of Australian finances, which had
collapsed with a resounding crash. From the beginning
of April to the middle of June, Australian bank failures
followed one another with deadening monotony, and the
Bank of England was twice compelled to raise the rediscount rate in order to protect its own position.[11]

The New York banks, upon whom the burden of gold
exports fell, were fortunately in a somewhat stronger position than usual. But the margin of safety was perilously
small in view of the fact that the business atmosphere
was so charged that a single spark would cause financial
conflagration.

At the beginning of May, the failure of the National
Cordage Company provided the spark.[12] The concern itself was of no great importance, and its financial position
had been recognized as unsound for several months, but
the failure precipitated a catastrophic decline of security

prices. Wall Street was virtually in a panic and a wave of suspensions and bankruptcies swept across the country. The house of cards had collapsed.[13]

Chicago, riotously speculative in its enthusiasm for the World's Fair, was ripe for panic. During 1892, the volume of building activity had been approximately 50 per cent greater than during the busy year of 1890, and much of the money necessary to finance this enterprise had come from Chicago banks and local capitalists. Since the Fair was expected to attract millions of people to the city, and to encourage each visitor to spend his money liberally, extravagant investment was encouraged by the prospect of generous reward. Even the older and larger banks had been persuaded to advance money to the optimists, although the caution born of experience had set reasonable limits to the aggregate amount of their loans, while several of the newer institutions had plunged recklessly into the wave of speculation with blithe enthusiasm.

During the early months of 1893, there was an appreciable weakening of the real-estate market; some of the smaller financial houses that had been particularly interested in this type of business closed their doors. Moreover, when panic hit the New York stock market in May, security prices in Chicago declined in sympathy.[14] None of these developments appeared unusually serious, however, and, by May 6, the *Economist* was able to scan the horizon and report to its readers that "the whole financial sky has cleared somewhat."[15]

The prophecy was too optimistic. On the evening of Monday, May 8, the Chemical National Bank suspended so suddenly that its Cashier was taken by surprise.[16] The failure did not, however, surprise Gage, by this time President of the First National Bank, nor any other conservative banker of the city, since the institution had been looked upon with strong disfavor ever since its creation in December, 1891. Despite the imputation of strength conveyed by its million-dollar capitalization, the Chemical National had been incompetently managed from the start, and its primary purpose appears to have been the financing of those who owned and managed it. "Of the fifteen directors of the association ten were either themselves directly liable to the Bank upon their personal notes, were endorsers for others or were interested in corporations which owed the institution an amount aggregating at least $225,000. Seventy-one of the shareholders, owning forty-seven hundred and seventy-two shares of the capital stock, owed the Bank nearly $700,000, some of which indebtedness apparently was for original stock subscriptions."[17] So few first-class assets were held by the institution that the Clearing House Committee, although called upon for aid, advised unanimously and emphatically against the granting of any loan.[18]

Normally speaking, the failure of so unsound an institution would have strengthened, rather than weakened, the money market, but the spring of 1893 was not normal. Public fear was accentuated markedly, and the Capital National Bank, of Indianapolis, paid the penalty of too close an association with the Chemical by following it into the hands of a receiver.[19] Moreover, the whole situation was rendered more serious by the fact that, when Congress had authorized the operation of a branch bank in the Fair Grounds,[20] the Chemical National had promptly paid twenty-thousand dollars for the exclusive concession. During the early days of May, a large business had been done at this branch, chiefly with foreign exhibitors and concessionaires, so that the deposits at the moment of failure amounted to more than a hundred thousand dollars.

Despite the catholicity of their taste, the managers of the Fair insisted that they did "not desire an exhibition of a failed national bank among the interesting collection on the Midway Pleasaunce," so that a committee of wealthy Chicagoans was hastily formed to guarantee the deposits. Meanwhile, the Northern Trust Company agreed to take over the branch and operate it during the remainder of the Fair.[21]

Before these arrangements had been completed, however, the Columbia National Bank had closed its doors,[22] imposing a similar action on the United States Loan and Trust Company, with which it was affiliated. Once more the Clearing House Committee, although called on for assistance, refused to advance any money to the enfeebled institution. Lyman J. Gage and John R. Walsh, the examiners for the Committee, found that the assets of the Bank consisted largely of country-bank stocks, about the value of which it was impossible to obtain accurate information, and perhaps they remembered that, in June, 1891, the Columbia National Bank had been refused admission to the Clearing House Association on the grounds "that the stock of the Bank was largely paid for by giving to the Bank the notes of the stockholders." Even the Comptroller of the Currency had been expecting the failure for several months.

In spite of these premonitions, the failure of the Columbia National Bank was epochal. Not only was it the largest among the many banks that suspended during 1893; it was itself a fantastic institution.[23] Zimri Dwiggins, the presiding genius of Dwiggins, Starbuck and Company, had created the United States National Bank in 1887 and, since it achieved little success at first, reorganized it as the Columbia National Bank, in 1891. In 1892, he acquired control of the United States Loan and Trust Company, an Indiana corporation previously engaged in the granting of farm-mortgage loans, and reorganized it through the distribution of its assets to the original stockholders. Around that trinity of financial institutions the Dwiggins chain of banks was built up. The Chicago agency of the Trust Company, the offices of Dwiggins, Starbuck and Company, and the Columbia National Bank were, in effect, one and the same thing, and Dwiggins was the inspiration of their triune activity. He was the executive head of both banks, and appears to have controlled the affairs of each without consulting the directorate of either. As President of the Bank he made contracts with himself as President of the Trust Company, and *vice versa,* and did not seem to think it necessary to leave any written evidence of his dealings between the two corporations. In the partnership, Starbuck was no more than a tool of his abler colleague.

The scheme of operations was simple. Since a large part of the capital of the Columbia National was represented by stockholders' notes, while the original capital of the Trust Company had been returned to its stockholders during the reorganization of 1892, it was necessary, in some fashion or other, to obtain the funds that were needed to finance Dwiggins' ambitious dreams. The Trust Company undertook the task, selling to the public half a million dollars' worth of income bonds. According to Dwiggins' plan, this money was to be invested in the stock of selected country banks, of which either Dwiggins or Starbuck assumed the Presidency, and whenever the holdings of such securities amounted to $250,000 it was planned to issue 5 per cent collateral-trust gold bonds against the bank stocks as security. In that way, the war chest would be perpetually replenished for further operations and, since the country-bank stocks were expected to pay dividends of 10 or 12 per cent, the operation would be highly profitable to the promoters. Ultimately it was expected that the holders of the Trust Company income bonds would be repaid out of earnings so that Dwiggins and his partner would remain as sole owners of the chain.

Since bank dividends averaged higher than 5 per cent at this period, the scheme had some chance of success if it had been soberly operated, but such a method was too slow for Dwiggins. To accelerate matters, in his capacity as President of the Trust Company he exchanged the income bonds for country-bank stock at par, since that was easier than selling the bonds on the market. Then, to persuade the country bankers of his large resources, he would deposit with them, at low rates of interest, an amount of money equal to the value of the stock purchased. But, since this practice demanded more funds than were actually available, Dwiggins was compelled to resort to even more frenzied finance. As President of the Trust Company, he held the stock of the country bank and a certificate of deposit for the amount that he had deposited with it. Therefore, as President of the Columbia National Bank, he would purchase from himself, as President of the Trust Company, the certificate of deposit at face value, being careful to endorse the instrument without recourse. By this means additional funds were acquired from the Bank to repeat the operation.

Even this did not exhaust the fertility of Dwiggins' imagination. As President of the Trust Company he would offer to lend the country bank, at 6 per cent, a substantial sum of money, on condition that it appointed the Columbia National Bank as its reserve agent, and deposited the entire amount of the loan with that institution. As President of the Bank, he offered to pay correspondents 4 per cent interest on reserve balances, so that the country bank saw in the scheme an opportunity to build up its reserves very cheaply. Meanwhile, between the two institutions, Dwiggins earned 2 per cent on the loan without any advance of funds.

Baldly stated, the whole scheme appears fantastic. But, for a little while, it worked. With an actual investment of some two or three hundred thousand dollars in the three institutions, Dwiggins succeeded in disposing of $250,000 of income bonds and acquiring an equal amount of bank stock. He had unloaded upon the Columbia National Bank more than $241,000 of the collateral trust bonds and not less than $250,000 of certificates of deposit in country banks, while the Trust Company, in which Dwiggins appears to have been primarily interested, had somehow obtained $231,000 of the best assets of the Bank. Twelve small banks in Illinois and Indiana had been acquired, and were managed by one or other of the partners as President, while thirty others had designated the Columbia National Bank as their Chicago correspondent and reserve agent. To give a façade of respectability to the whole scheme, the Illinois Trust and Savings Bank had been appointed as trustee for the issues of collateral-trust bonds.

When the Columbia National passed into the hands of the bank examiner, the whole structure collapsed and most of the country banks that were involved promptly closed their doors. It was "an ugly blow to confidence" throughout the whole western territory but, strangely enough, did not exercise as serious an effect upon Chicago as might have been expected. Neither the Chemical National nor the Columbia National had any large business in the city itself, and although the Evanston National Bank followed the Chemical National into liquidation, the remaining banks were in a comparatively strong position.[24]

But, despite diurnal eulogies of local banking soundness in the Chicago press, the failures could not be entirely ignored. Local stocks had fallen sharply when the Columbia National closed its doors, and the real-estate market subsided into complete stagnation. In the bond department of the First National there was complaint that the sale of any securities was almost impossible, and where sales were made the bonds were parted with "at slaughter prices." Even the Clearing House Committee* was disturbed over the situation and, on May 22, held a

* I. G. Lombard, L. J. Gage, C. J. Blair, Orson Smith and J. J. P. Odell continued to serve as the Committee until the end of 1895, without any change.

long meeting to discuss the propriety of preparing forms of Clearing House Certificates "for use in case the Association should at any time deem it prudent to issue them." Such a discussion was portentous, in view of the fact that Chicago had never issued such certificates during previous panics, and it is significant that no action was taken because "the opinions were not unanimous."

For three weeks after the failure of the Columbia National there were no exciting events in the city, and people, finding relief in the Fair from the general atmosphere of economic stagnation, began to think that the panic had passed. On Saturday, June 3, however, the well-known financial house of Herman Schaffner and Company broke under the strain. Owing to the diminished volume of the commercial-paper business, the firm had lent funds to finance speculators in street-railway stocks and, when the bottom dropped out of the market for such securities, Schaffner hired a boat and rowed out into the Lake to meet his death.[25] He did not return, and the firm passed into the hands of a receiver.*

When Monday dawned, the fears of the population, growing steadily over the week end, had crystallized into something approaching a panic.[26] Long lines of frightened depositors waited outside the doors of every savings bank in the city. At the Illinois Trust and Savings Bank, thirty-five thousand depositors presented themselves at

* It deserves to be recorded, however, that immediately after the failure of Herman Schaffner and Company, A. G. Becker, an employee of the firm and a relation by marriage of its owner, set up in business for the purpose of repaying the obligations of the bankrupt concern. Although the task required many years to accomplish, Becker persisted in his endeavor, and perhaps there is an unusual degree of poetic justice in the fact that, in the process, the firm of A. G. Becker and Company grew to be one of the largest commercial-paper houses in the country.

the counter during the day, and the perspiring tellers kept paying out money until three o'clock in the morning. At the Hibernian Banking Association the run was less severe, but the details of the story are much the same, while the Union Trust Company and the Prairie State Savings and Trust Company had similar experiences. Only at the Globe Savings Bank and the Dime Savings Bank was any effort made to enforce the rule that depositors must give notice of withdrawal, although it was agreed after the run had finished that such action would be taken by all banks in future.[27] Most amusing of all was the attitude of Lazarus Silverman. When the run on his bank started, "he stood beside the teller and helped him build a fortification of greenbacks and yellow coin on the paying counter in view of those who stood in line waiting to draw their savings."[28] It was good psychology.

The commercial banks, moreover, shared some of the discomfort of the savings institutions. City depositors and country bankers both took steps to draw down their balances, and the Chicago banks themselves hastened to shift as much of the burden as possible by drawing currency from New York.[29] Only in the case of the American Exchange National Bank did the drain prove serious, however, and in that case the Clearing House banks promptly came to the rescue by advancing $475,000 to the distressed institution.

As a matter of fact, this June panic was largely confined to the poorer classes and the smaller enterprises: important bankers and leading businessmen appear to have kept their heads. When the run on the Illinois Trust and Savings Bank occurred, Marshall Field and P. D.

Armour announced that full payment would be made to all depositors of the Bank who presented their passbooks at Field's Store or Armour's offices.[30] The James H. Walker Company announced that it would accept certificates of deposit, or certified checks, of all Chicago savings banks in payment for goods purchased,[31] and John Cudahy advertised that such certificates of deposit were always acceptable "for their full face value, including interest, in payment for any one of the elegant new seven and eight room houses now complete and ready for occupancy in John Cudahy's Addition to Morton Park."[32] Fundamentally Chicago savings banks were sound and, in several cases, wealthy men actually deposited during the days of panic amounts in excess of the sums that were being withdrawn by the throngs of nervous people who remembered 1877, or had heard the legends regarding it.

Even the small depositor recovered confidence after he had discovered that all demands were being met promptly, and the panic subsided rapidly. By the end of June, a substantial improvement was evident in regard to public psychology, which reflected itself in a lessened stringency at the banks, and on July 28 the American Exchange National Bank was able to repay to the clearing banks the last installment of the loan that it had received during the run.

For this improvement, many factors were responsible. In the first place, there was renewed hope that the silver policy of the government would be abandoned. At the beginning of June, the President made it known that he intended to call a special session of Congress for the express purpose of repealing the Sherman Act, and the stock market immediately gained appreciable strength.[33] In Chicago, however, there were important local factors that augmented the effect of this announcement. First and foremost among these was the Columbian Exposition which, despite the widespread economic crisis, was attracting millions of visitors from every part of the United States and many foreign countries. Such visitors brought money with them and, in the face of horrified protests by W. T. Stead and other conventional onlookers, Chicago tried hard to make them spend it freely. Optimists expected that the Fair would bring at least a hundred million dollars to the businessmen of the city[34] and, although there were occasional complaints from other quarters, the railroads and hotels reaped a rich harvest during the summer months.[35]

While there are no precise records of the amount of money spent by American visitors, the evidence regarding the expenditure of foreigners, who must necessarily have constituted a small minority of the total crowd, is impressive. The Bank of Nova Scotia, the Crédit Lyonnais and the Comptoir National d'Escompte all opened offices in Chicago to take advantage of the foreign-exchange business created by the Fair, and the number of letters of credit drawn by European houses upon the older Chicago banks was twenty times as great as it had been during the previous year.[36] In the case of the First National Bank alone, $638,000 was paid out under foreign letters of credit, an average amount of $256 being drawn by each visitor to the Fair.

Moreover, to supplement the flow of currency attracted in this manner, substantial amounts were received from the grain trade. Partly to encourage the movement of grain, which would result in payments to Chicago houses from other centers, and partly to strengthen their own position, the Chicago banks reduced materially the aggregate amount of the loans granted to customers for the carrying of grain.[37] The results of this policy began to show themselves early in July. So convinced was Chicago of its financial soundness by that time, that gold was actually sent to New York, and the Clearing House Association spent two long and peaceful meetings discussing the desirability of closing at noon on Saturdays during the winter.

New York was not so fortunate. Hundreds of banks, and more than three thousand business enterprises, had failed in various parts of the United States during the first six months of the year, creating a nervous demand for currency that fell primarily upon the New York banks. In addition to drawing down their balances with New York correspondents, country bankers presented large quantities of paper for rediscount,[38] and the resultant shipments of currency amounted to $12,847,000 during the first week of June.[39] Much of this moved to Chicago and the west. Moreover a 4 per cent bank rate in London was still drawing gold across the Atlantic so that, despite the most cautious lending policies, New York bank reserves were falling perilously close to the legally required minimum.[40]

In these circumstances, on June 15, the New York Clearing House Association again decided to issue Clearing House Loan Certificates.[41] On previous occasions, such a step had always been taken when local banks were in imminent danger of collapse, but this was not true in 1893. No bank was in difficulties, and none of them made any immediate application for certificates, but it was felt that measures should be taken to strengthen the banking system in case the twofold drain upon New York's reserves continued. "In times of distress the New York banks are always called upon to bear the brunt of the financial battles, and their action this week [in authorizing certificates] is a notice that they are prepared, should the occasion require, to stand together not only for their own protection but for the protection of the interests of the banks and the mercantile and financial community in other parts of the country."[42]

The action was statesmanlike, although some contemporary critics considered it hasty, and the Philadelphia and Boston Clearing Houses promptly followed suit. Moreover, there were collateral factors that tended to diminish the financial tension. Although currency still continued to move toward the interior, compelling several New York banks to take out Clearing House Certificates around the end of June, a sharp decline in the sterling exchange rate reversed the flow of gold.[43] London was recovering from the Australian crisis and British capitalists, who had regarded all American industries as unsound in the spring, were beginning to realize that bargains might be picked up on the New York stock exchange.[44] By the middle of July, New York, although still envious of Chicago's comfort, was beginning once again to breathe freely.

But, by the irony of fate, it was on Chicago that the bolt descended out of a summer sky. On July 17, the

Missouri National Bank, one of the most important institutions in the west, closed its doors. Six smaller banks in Kansas immediately followed it into the hands of receivers.[45] A day later, the three largest national banks in Denver were forced to close, as the result of a serious run during which "the depositors thronged the streets and bank offices urgently demanding their money," and by the end of the week the casualties in that city amounted to a total of six national banks and five state or private institutions.[46] Other serious failures followed in quick succession among the banks of Louisville and Indianapolis while, saddest of all, the Wisconsin Marine and Fire Insurance Bank, inheritor of the glorious mantle of George Smith, went into the hands of a receiver. It was "an institution which everyone thought was rock-rooted and solid as the eternal hills."[47]

Chicago could not hope to escape the impact of this wave of failures. Many of the fallen institutions were correspondents of banks in the city, all of them had operated in the territory where Chicago banks had active business connections, and the Wisconsin Marine and Fire Insurance Bank had been a legendary example of financial soundness throughout the northwest for more than half a century. In a world that seemed to be falling to pieces around them, the country bankers hastened to draw their money out of Chicago banks.[48]

By drawing down their own balances at New York, and refusing to purchase New York exchange, which was almost unsalable by the end of July, the Chicago banks met the storm successfully. Old loans were called, and new loans were granted so sparingly that one group of western capitalists was unable to borrow one hundred thousand dollars even when it offered collateral worth twice that sum, together with the signatures of two men each reported to be worth several millions.[49] One banker complained, rather bitterly, that the Chicago banks "are being constantly placed in the position of having to stand in the gap between some country bank and a failure, and they are getting thoroughly tired of that role, for it is not only unpleasant but takes a good deal of money."[50]

That complaint was probably born of irritated weariness, for the strain was great. A country banker who visited the First National Bank on the worst day of the panic has given us an unforgettable picture of James B. Forgan, its new Vice-President, during those trying hours.[51] "He certainly looked as if he had just forgotten to sleep or to visit his barber. I could read the situation in his appearance and manner. When I appeared in his office he was interviewing a banker from Waterloo, Iowa, who made the absurd demand on Forgan that he agree to advance him twenty-five thousand dollars *if the panic conditions became worse.*

" 'Why, my dear man,' says Forgan, 'if it grows much worse we may ask you for twenty-five thousand or more. How do ye like that?' But the man was persistent and unreasonable, accompanying his demand with the statement that he had kept a deposit at the First National Bank for ten years of not less than ten thousand dollars and had never borrowed a cent during that time.

"Forgan's patience at last gave way. He rose to his full six feet one, and pointed a finger at his questioner. 'I thank ye for your confidence in the past and your patronage but when ye ask me to guarantee ye a cool seat in Heaven when Hell breaks loose ye are unreasonable, and that's my last word to ye!' "

No bank in Chicago collapsed under the strain of those July days, although aggregate deposits had declined $23,000,000, or more than twenty per cent since the beginning of May, in the case of national banks alone. Compared with conditions a year earlier the shrinkage exceeded twenty-seven per cent. But the pressure upon the business community was terrific. In less than two months, the national banks contracted loans by more than $16,000,000, and by the end of September the contraction had grown to $24,000,000. While all national banks in the United States reduced their loans by less than fifteen per cent, in Chicago the reduction exceeded twenty-six per cent,[52] so that the collapse of local business was more violent than that experienced by any other large city in the country.[53]

It is not, therefore, surprising that business protested, but astounding that the protest was so mild. Although there had been earlier murmurs of complaint, it was not until July 26 that the President of the Clearing House received a letter signed by Marshall Field, Philip D. Armour, R. R. Cable and other leading merchants.[54] That the strength of the Chicago banks deserved praise was admitted, but the signers of the letter insisted "that, in maintaining your strong position there is danger that you may overtax the ability of your debtors in forcing your claims against them; or, if not so, the interests of the business community may be prejudiced by the withholding of such timely and justifiable aid as legitimate

business and industry may require." To obviate that
danger, the issue of Clearing House Loan Certificates
was suggested, and attention was called to the fact that
both the bankers and the business community, in New
York, had reaped substantial benefits from such a policy.

This letter was read to a full meeting of the Clearing
House Association on July 27, and Gage promptly proposed that Odell should present a report that appears to
have been drawn up by the two of them before the meeting. By the terms of this report, the Clearing House Committee was authorized to issue Clearing House Loan Certificates, against appropriate collateral, and to establish
such rules and regulations as were necessary in regard to
the issue. Immediately, a violent discussion ensued. A
proposal to refer the matter back to a special committee
was defeated. Preston, seconded by Hammond, then proposed the adoption of the report, and Blair, seconded by
Lombard, promptly proposed an amendment by which
no certificates could be issued until the directorates of all
the member banks had formally approved the plan. After much discussion, Blair's amendment was defeated
and Preston's motion carried, the vote being nine to fourteen in each case. The Chicago Clearing House Association, for the first time in its history, had authorized the
issue of Clearing House Certificates, and New York was
jubilant![55]

In the light of the bitter controversy attending this
decision, it is interesting to pause a moment in order to
recognize the nature of the dispute. Of the financial ability of Chicago's leading bankers there was no question,
and the soundness of her banks had not been impugned

by as much as a rumor. Moreover, it is sound commercial banking practice to strive for liquidity when danger threatens. But, once again, it must be remembered that Chicago banks were not strictly commercial institutions. Banks in a reserve city assumed central banking functions by virtue of their position, and again it must be reiterated that the fundamental principle of central banking is to lend freely at high rates of interest during moments of crisis. The arguments regarding Clearing House Certificates were not waged by good bankers against bad ones; they were not disputes between strong and weak institutions. The controversy lay between those who insisted on adherence to sound commercial banking principles, on the one side, and those whose vision encompassed the broader responsibilities of central banking, on the other.

Recognition of the precise nature of this dispute is important. In authorizing the issue of Clearing House Certificates, the Association had placed the responsibility upon the shoulders of the Clearing House Committee, composed of five of the ablest bankers in the city. The failure to issue certificates was not due to the fact that Chicago banks were too strong to need them, nor was it due to the fact that no bank applied for them; it resulted from the opinions of the Committee members. From the minutes of the Committee itself, and the current discussion in the press, it is apparent that Lyman J. Gage and J. J. P. Odell were in favor of such an issue, while C. J. Blair, Orson Smith and Isaac G. Lombard, the Chairman of the Committee, were strongly opposed to it.[56] Because the majority frowned upon the whole idea, the applications of member banks for such certificates were denied, and alternative measures were taken to meet the troublesome situations that arose.

Nor was there any lack of problems to try the mettle of the banking community. On the day when the Clearing House Association was debating Odell's report, the Union National Bank reported to the Committee that it was in sore straits. Deposits had been withdrawn so rapidly that its cash was entirely exhausted, and it was unable to rediscount paper or raise loans because of the stringency of the money market. Unless immediate assistance was furnished, the Bank would be compelled to close its doors once again. Since a thorough examination of the Bank, made by Lombard and Bank Examiner Sturges during the midnight hours, revealed that the institution was fundamentally sound, the clearing-house banks advanced an aggregate amount of $951,000 distributed among themselves by an assessment equal to seven dollars per thousand on the total deposits of each.

Once again a dangerous situation had been corrected, but the Clearing House Committee must have felt that it was assuming the task of Sisyphus. The nervousness of country bankers was increasing, and the withdrawals of currency continued steadily.[57] On August 1, the Cudahy wheat corner collapsed, owing to the refusal of the banks to grant further loans or even continue those previously made.[58] The market went to pieces, despite the efforts of Armour and Company to support it, and eight of the largest operators on the Board of Trade went down into bankruptcy with Cudahy.

That same afternoon, Lazarus Silverman went to New

York with a bundle of securities in his valise, to try and borrow enough currency for the continued operation of his bank. But the New York bankers were no more eager than Chicago institutions had been to come to his aid. The securities had no market quotations and many of them were "entirely unknown to anybody but those immediately connected with the properties." Moreover, while there was never the least hint of personal dishonesty, it was obvious from a cursory examination that Silverman's slipshod methods of bookkeeping made it impossible to obtain a true picture of the firm's condition. To expect a loan was, perhaps, unreasonable, but the failure of his mission necessitated the suspension of his bank the following afternoon.[59]

Moreover, to increase the financial uncertainty and excitement, the inflationists chose this particular moment to hold a great Silver Convention, in Chicago.[60] At a moment when bankers were almost unanimous in the fervent hope that the Sherman Act would be promptly repealed, crowds of enthusiasts assembled to denounce Secretary Carlisle and anathematize Cleveland as "the Hessian intrenched at Buzzard's Bay." On the silver question, they insisted vociferously, no compromise was possible; every effort should be made to attain the goal of free coinage at the old ratio of sixteen to one.

No wonder the financial community shivered; it required little to precipitate failures in so tense an atmosphere. On August 6, the Clearing House Committee assembled hurriedly in a small room at the Auditorium Hotel, "believing that the meeting of the Committee would be least noticed there," and heard that the Ameri-

can Trust and Savings Bank was in trouble. A loan of
$650,000 by the other banks was agreed upon as the only
safe policy in the circumstances, but it was apparent to
all the members that the "general financial situation . . .
looked dark and disappointing when looked at in the
most favourable light." Nor did the ensuing days provide any cause for optimism. On August 7, the Bank of
Commerce needed assistance and, as the Committee was
adjourning, just before midnight, a telephone message
from a conference of several bankers, then being held in
a private residence, announced that two other banks*
were in deep water. In a mood of despondency, Blair
penned a footnote to the minutes he had just written:
"It looks as if nothing can save a general panic amongst
the banks of this city."

Nor was the despair unreasoning. By this time, New
York itself was beginning to crack under the strain, ag-
gravating the difficulty of Chicago's position. The wave
of bank failures had produced a nervous withdrawal of
correspondent balances from New York comparable to
that experienced by Chicago bankers, and the renewed
silver agitation, coupled with British action in closing
the Indian mints to the free coinage of that metal, had
disturbed the composure of the whole financial community. Moreover, on July 25, the Erie Railroad had gone
into receivership, and security prices had slumped to an
even lower point than that touched in the spring panic.[61]
Call-loan rates went as high as seventy-four per cent.

Despite the fact that European investors were purchasing substantial quantities of American securities at

* Metropolitan National Bank and National Bank of Illinois.

the bargain prices ruling on the New York Stock Exchange, and that British funds were attracted to the short-term money market by the high rates of interest, conditions in New York were deteriorating rapidly.[62] Although the steadily increasing issue of Clearing House Certificates had equalized the strain among the banks, it could not prevent the diminution of their aggregate reserves. By the middle of July, New York bank reserves, which had fallen by $30,000,000 in six weeks, were already $5,-000,000 below the legal minimum: by the end of the month the deficiency exceeded $14,000,000.[63] Every conceivable kind of currency was used to meet the demands of out-of-town banks, one draft for $25,000 being paid by the shipment of silver dollars at the expense of the New York bank.[64]

Suddenly, the whole money market collapsed under the strain. While there was no concerted action among the bankers, the institutions that they controlled, one after another, ceased to pay out currency in any large amounts. On Monday, July 31, the Chicago banks found their own troubles aggravated by the fact that New York correspondents were unable to forward the currency demanded of them.[65] By the middle of the week brokers were paying a premium of one per cent for currency in any form,[66] and the premium in New York rose as high as five per cent during the following week.[67] Thus "developed the feature that will forever characterize the stringency of 1893. . . . Almost between morning and night the scramble for currency had begun and culminated all over the country, and the preposterous bulk of our circulating medium had been swallowed up as effectually as, in a scarcely less brief period, gold and silver had disappeared before the premium on specie a generation before. Currency was hoarded until it became so scarce that it had to be bought as merchandise at a premium of one to three per cent in checks payable through the Clearing House; and to enable their families to meet petty bills at the summer resorts the merchants and professional men of the cities were forced to purchase and send by express packages of bills or coin."[68] In some communities, of which Minneapolis and St. Paul were outstanding examples, the Clearing House issued circulating scrip in small denominations and, in many others, cashiers' checks for round sums were accepted as a general medium of exchange.[69]

The domestic-exchange market, as a result of these developments, was utterly disorganized by the beginning of August.[70] Because of the numerous bank failures in all parts of the country, and the equally widespread expectation of further failures, many banks refused to give immediate credit on checks drawn on distant points. At best, they accepted such items for collection only. But when it became apparent that banks, even while continuing to operate, might not be able to supply currency if called upon to do so, there appeared to be little advantage in forwarding the items for collection. Why build up balances in a distant community when every penny of the bank's resources was needed at home?

In Chicago, this problem was particularly acute. Toward the end of July, New York exchange was selling at a discount of two dollars per thousand,[71] although the cost of shipping currency did not exceed seventy-five cents, which offered clear evidence of the threatened currency famine. In August, when the New York banks had already suspended currency payments, Chicago institutions became increasingly reluctant to tie up their money in New York drafts. Exchange dropped to a discount of fifteen dollars per thousand by August 6,[72] and, three days later, although the quoted rate gave a discount of from twenty-five to thirty dollars, New York drafts were practically unsalable at any price.[73]

Such a situation was intolerable. The stockyards were paralyzed and the grain trade stagnant, because shippers could not afford to sell their New York drafts at such prices even if it had been possible to find a buyer.[74] Moreover, since Chicago banks were still paying out currency in substantial amounts, country bankers developed the habit of sending New York drafts directly to that city for collection, in order to build up a legal reserve at that point, while they drew down their Chicago balances for the purpose of providing themselves with the currency that was so urgently needed. If Chicago was to preserve its reputation for maintaining currency payments, something had to be done in a hurry.

The solution of the problem was dramatic. On August 1, the First National Bank of Chicago instructed its London correspondent to ship half a million dollars in gold at once, by the fastest available steamer, and additional orders of a similar kind followed in quick succession. If New York had fallen, Chicago would call upon London for aid in the maintenance of specie payments and, in the light of his reiterated convictions, it is not surprising that Gage should have been responsible for the decisive step.

Although the crisis was still acute, and the currency famine becoming daily more serious, Chicago recovered hope. The days of financial agony were numbered by the time required for a steamer to cross the Atlantic, since all the leading banks of the city had hastened to follow the example of the First National.[75] By the end of the week, more than three million dollars was on its way, so that both bankers and businessmen squared their shoulders in the face of immediate trials, and waited expectantly.

During those days of waiting, there must also have come to many people in Chicago, and elsewhere, a deeper realization of the significance of the gesture. Chicago had become a great money market, depending customarily on New York but fully able to step out into a position of leadership in moments of crisis. Able bankers and efficient machinery, the two essential ingredients of greatness, were both present in ample measure. Foreign balances existed that could be drawn upon, and the reputation of Chicago banks was high enough to permit the sale of finance bills in London. Moreover, there were bankers shrewd enough and cool-headed enough to realize that the purchase of grain bills at a substantial discount, although it tied up funds for a couple of weeks and drew down still further the diminishing currency reserves, might be sound and profitable if those bills were sent to London and gold imported in return. Even more profitable was the purchase of New York exchange for currency, and the use of the proceeds in New York to purchase cables on London, an operation that tended to improve matters in regard to both the domestic-exchange market and the currency situation. Those early August

days witnessed the rise of Chicago bankers to the position
of statesmanship leadership that they had been unwilling
to assume a few weeks earlier.

On Friday, August 11, the golden flood first reached
the city. "Everyone in financial circles was hurrahing,"
and the newspapers were jubilant. "Half a million in
yellow gold will arrive in Chicago this morning. A quarter of a million more will come early next week and a few
days later the brawny employés of the express companies
will roll packages containing an equal amount more on
trucks which will head for the First National Bank, where
the preceding $750,000 will have gone."[76] Even Gage, as
he watched the gold arriving, appears to have been excited. This, he told the reporter, "will influence the situation. More money will be put in circulation, and, as
money attracts money . . . the currency that has been
hidden away will come out."[77]

With each succeeding day, the volume of gold in the
city increased, and Chicagoans watched the news of steamship arrivals at New York with unwonted interest. In
addition to substantial operations by the Chicago office
of the Bank of Montreal, for which no statistics were published, the aggregate engagements of gold for import
amounted to almost eight million dollars by the end of
the second week in August,[78] the total being divided
in the following proportions:

Illinois Trust and Savings Bank	$2,500,000
Bank of Nova Scotia	1,920,000
First National Bank	1,350,000
Crédit Lyonnais	1,200,000
Comptoir d'Escompte	225,000
P. D. Armour & Co.	500,000
Aldis, Aldis & Northcote	250,000
	$7,945,000

By August 17, it was reported that "the stream [of gold] has been so steady that now Chicago is healthier, financially, than any other city in the country,"[79] and the steady decline in aggregate bank deposits had been reversed. So confident did Chicago bankers feel regarding the results of their gold policy that they were willing to sell small parcels of the precious metal, at a good premium, to banks in New York and Philadelphia.[80]

Chicago, in fact, had more gold than it wanted. "Gold can be had for the asking, but no one asks for the yellow metal. The paying teller [at the First National Bank] said yesterday that . . . the sight of a $5,000 bag was enough to drive away any request for gold."[81] As Gage remarked acidly, there was not much sign of a currency famine when the public was so particular that it refused gold coin. Moreover, since currency was no longer at a premium in Chicago, the domestic-exchange market improved rapidly. By August 19, the banks were buying substantial amounts of New York drafts, while the discount had fallen to ten dollars per thousand,[82] and the improvement continued until quotations reached a premium of twenty-five cents on September 6.[83] The crisis was over in Chicago.

New York did not recover quite so rapidly. On August 26, a premium of one per cent on currency was still reported, and not until September 2 were coin and notes freely obtainable at par by all who wanted them.[84] In this case also, substantial aid was received from gold imports, while an important influence was exerted by the diminution of western demands for currency, and by the steps taken to increase the circulation of national bank notes.[85] By the second week in September, when both England and France took steps to stop the westbound flow of gold across the Atlantic,[86] the currency famine was a thing of the past, and the domestic-exchange market was functioning normally in all parts of the United States. Bank reserves in New York had again reached the legal minimum, and Clearing House Certificates were being rapidly retired.

Cleveland's determined efforts to bring about the speedy abandonment of the silver-purchase policy undoubtedly contributed to this solution of the monetary problem.[87] When Congress met on August 7, the President presented a simple but emphatic message, in which he insisted on the immediate repeal of the Sherman Act and pointed out the serious results that it had already produced. Despite the existence of a strong silver sentiment in the House, where William Jennings Bryan (a young Congressman from Nebraska) made a brilliant speech in favor of bimetallism,[88] the administration majority was able to act with reasonable promptness. On August 28, the vote was taken in favor of repeal,[89] and the conservative newspapers of the country were jubilant. "This vote has inspired hope in every financial centre of the country."

In the Senate, however, matters moved less expeditiously. Despite the urgent insistence of the business community that the dangerous legislation should be repealed as rapidly as possible, the Senate filibustered its way through more than eleven weeks of wasted time, providing an example of the interplay of politics and personalities that has seldom been equaled in American history.[90]

Business shivered in fear. At the beginning of September, an air of optimism had been apparent, and the *Chronicle* reported improvement in many fields of activity.[91] The depression, it was insisted, would be of very short duration and banks were already lending generously, although at fairly high rates of interest.[92] But all eyes were focused on Washington and, as the Senate debates grew longer, pessimism spread over the country. That serious depression would have occurred in any case is certain, but it is obvious that the nervousness of business tended to increase the severity of immediate liquidation. To the merchant and the banker, only two alternatives were possible. "If the Senate decides in favor of an honest and rational currency system, we shall have revival and progress; if it falls down before the silver idol, we shall suffer blight, and very probably panic again. The situation is simplicity itself."[93] Each passing day seemed to increase the danger of the latter course, since filibusters usually end in inaction, and the *Chronicle* pointed out to the recalcitrant minority that "few members of the Senate realize the anxiety and earnestness with which the public every morning and night turn to the published accounts of its doings."[94]

At long last, on October 30, the Senate voted for repeal, and the financial community breathed a heartfelt sigh of relief.[95] But by that time the buoyancy had gone out of business, and the whole nation was stagnant in depression. During the months of panic four hundred and fifteen banks of all kinds had closed their doors, more than one hundred and fifty of them being national institutions,[96] while the business failures were numbered in thousands. Moreover, it was apparent that the financial institutions which were still in operation would have to bear substantial losses.

Chicago, despite the failures that have been mentioned, was more fortunate than many communities. Only four banks had failed in the whole State of Illinois, none of them outstanding institutions, and all the state institutions had survived the strain. So strong were the Chicago banks, in fact, that by the middle of October their aggregate cash reserves amounted to forty-five per cent of deposit liabilities, and good borrowers were so eagerly welcomed in the bank parlors of the city that call money was going begging at 5 per cent.[97] Few commercial borrowers paid the quoted rate of 6 per cent on good paper if they had time to haggle. But borrowers were few and far between, so that bankers spent most of their time going over their assets and writing off bad debts. More than a million dollars' worth of paper was written off by the First National Bank early in 1894 and, by the summer of 1895, further losses made it advisable for the directors to reduce the surplus by a million dollars in order to write off all remaining assets that were of doubtful value. The Metropolitan National Bank seriously considered the advisability of cutting its capital in half, for similar reasons, and every other bank in the city was confronted with an equally unpleasant situation. As early as February, 1894, earnings had declined to a point where it became necessary, by joint action, to reduce the rate of interest on correspondent balances to 1½ per cent per annum.*

Depression spread over the whole country, and throughout Illinois and other western states it was particularly severe. Farmers suffered more than any other class in the community, since agricultural prices had been falling steadily under the pressure of monetary policy and improving ocean transportation. The impact of depression merely aggravated the tendency and made mortgages even more burdensome than they had previously seemed. But the working classes, in general, were almost as badly off, since bank failures and credit contraction had affected all types of western business operations with particular severity. Business failures and suspensions had created widespread unemployment and, even in those concerns which were still operating, wage reductions had been widely imposed.

Once again, therefore, the depression gave rise to a strangely modern series of labor troubles, most of which centered around Chicago. On May 11, 1894, the employees of the Pullman Company walked out on strike, nominally over a matter of the dismissal of certain workers and the unwillingness of the Company to arbitrate.[98] For weeks the strike dragged on ineffectually until, on the twenty-second of June, the railroad unions, under the leadership of Debs, decided upon a boycott of Pullman cars which rapidly developed into a general railroad strike.[99] It was an amusing situation, from the viewpoint

* The conflict between the desire for profits and a growing sense of the dignity of banking must have been particularly acute when, in May, 1894, the directors of the First National Bank discussed the renewal of the highly profitable lease to the saloon that occupied quarters on the ground floor of its building. After long discussion, the renewal was refused.

of an Olympian, since most of the railroad managers de-
tested Pullman as heartily as the strikers did, and felt
doubly aggrieved that they should have to fight his battles
for him.[100]

Despite the anathemas hurled at "Dictator Debs,"
and the serious inconvenience caused to Chicago by the
general breakdown of railroad transportation, the strike
dragged on until the middle of July. From early legal
skirmishes in the courts, the dispute was carried, through
riots, to a point where the federal government felt compelled to move troops into Chicago and establish a state
of martial law. Even then, the battle did not cease until
blood had been shed on both sides, and the strikers were
finally compelled to yield to superior force.

Like the earlier developments preceding the Haymarket Massacre, the strikes of 1894 accomplished nothing in the direction of better labor relations, but the bitterness of the dispute is indicative of the severity of the
depression. Moreover, operating in a vicious circle, the
strikes intensified the depression by discouraging initiative in the Chicago area, and disorganizing the economic
life of the city. By the end of the summer, business had
touched deep bottom, and there seemed small hope of
any immediate improvement. "Hard times are with us;
the country is distracted; very few things are marketable
at a price above the cost of production; tens of thousands
are out of employment; the jails, penitentiaries, work-
houses and insane asylums are full; the gold reserve at
Washington is sinking; the government is running at a
loss with a deficit in every department; a huge debt hangs
like an appalling cloud over the country; taxes have as-

sumed the importance of a mortgage, and fifty per cent of the public revenues are likely to go delinquent; hungered and half-starved men are banding into armies and marching toward Washington; the cry of distress is heard on every hand; business is paralyzed."[101]

REFERENCES FOR CHAPTER XVI

[1] Paul Bourget: *Outre-Mer, Impressions of America,* pp. 114-138; Quaife: *The Development of Chicago,* pp. 235-252.

[2] *Chicago Tribune,* January 21, 1893.

[3] *Ibid.,* April 7, 10 and 24, 1893; *Bankers Magazine,* XLVII, 646.

[4] *Chicago Tribune,* January 7, 1893.

[5] *Ibid.,* January 1, 1893.

[6] *Ibid.,* January 9, 12 and 16, 1893.

[7] *Ibid.,* February 11, May 2, June 4, 1893; *Bankers Magazine,* LVII, 662.

[8] *Chicago Tribune,* April 19, 20 and 21, 1893.

[9] *Ibid.,* April 23 and 24, 1893.

[10] *Ibid.,* June 9, 1893, also April 14, 17 and 22, 1893; Sprague: *op. cit.,* p. 158.

[11] *Commercial and Financial Chronicle,* LVI, 728, 771 and 910; Chicago *Economist,* IX, 761.

[12] *Commercial and Financial Chronicle,* LVI, 743; Chicago *Economist,* IX, 625.

[13] For a general account of the panic, cf. W. J. Lauck: *The Causes of the Panic of 1893;* A. D. Noyes: The Banks and the Panic of 1893; *Political Science Quarterly,* IX, 12 ff.; Sprague: *op. cit.,* Ch. IV.

[14] *Chicago Tribune,* May 1 to 6, 1893.

[15] Chicago *Economist,* IX, 627.

[16] *Chicago Tribune,* May 9 and 10, 1893.

[17] Kane: *op. cit.,* I, 204.

[18] *Chicago Tribune,* May 9, 1893.

[19] Chicago *Economist,* IX, 657.

[20] *Bankers Magazine,* XLVI, 735.

[21] *Chicago Tribune,* May 9 and 10, 1893; Kane: *op. cit.,* I, 204-205.

[22] *Chicago Tribune,* May 12, 1893.

[23] Kane: *op. cit.,* I, 200-204; *Chicago Tribune,* May 12, 1893.

[24] *Chicago Tribune,* May 15 and 19, 1893; Chicago *Economist,* IX, 658; X, 158.

[25] *Chicago Tribune,* June 4 and 6, 1893.

[26] *Ibid.*, June 6 and 7, 1893.

[27] Chicago *Economist*, IX, 795.

[28] *Chicago Tribune*, June 6, 1893.

[29] *Ibid.*, June 7, 1893.

[30] Huston: *op. cit.*, I, 252.

[31] *Chicago Tribune*, June 6, 1893.

[32] *Ibid.*, June 8, 1893.

[33] *Commercial and Financial Chronicle*, LVI, 946; LVII, 42, 78 and 92.

[34] *Chicago Tribune*, June 5, 1893.

[35] *Commercial and Financial Chronicle*, LVII, 51.

[36] Chicago *Economist*, X, 9.

[37] *Ibid.*, IX, 859.

[38] Sprague: *op. cit.*, p. 420.

[39] *Commercial and Financial Chronicle*, LVI, 946.

[40] *Idem*, 959.

[41] *Idem*, 990; Chicago *Economist*, IX, 827.

[42] *Commercial and Financial Chronicle*, LVI, 990.

[43] *Idem*, 1034; LVII, 48.

[44] *Chicago Tribune*, June 10, 1893, quoting the London *Financial Times*.

[45] *Chicago Tribune*, July 18, 1893.

[46] *Ibid.*, July 19, 1893; Chicago *Economist*, X, 71.

[47] *Chicago Tribune*, July 26, 1893.

[48] Chicago *Economist*, X, 105; *Chicago Tribune*, July 18, 1893.

[49] *Chicago Tribune*, July 19, 1893.

[50] *Ibid.*, July 20, 1893.

[51] Huston, *op. cit.*, I, 255-256. The date given by Huston is October 16; but the incident must obviously have occurred in July, since there was no such drain in October.

[52] *Chicago Tribune*, July 24, 1893; *Annual Report of the Comptroller of the Currency*, 1893, I, 209.

[53] Sprague: *op. cit.*, p. 421.

[54] Cf. *Chicago Tribune*, July 28, 1893.

[55] *Ibid.*, July 30, 1893; Chicago *Economist*, X, 72.

[56] Cf. Chicago *Economist*, IX, 834; X, 108.

[57] *Chicago Tribune*, August 2, 1893.

[58] *Ibid.*, August 2 and 3, 1893.

[59] *Ibid.*, August 4, 1893; Chicago *Economist*, X, 158.

[60] *Chicago Tribune*, August 2 and 3, 1893.

[61] *Commercial and Financial Chronicle*, LVII, 162 and 176.

[62] *Ibid.*, LVII, 171, 206 and 244; Chicago *Economist*, X, 129.

[63] Chicago *Economist*, X, 39; Sprague: *op. cit.*, p. 181.

[64] *Chicago Tribune*, July 30, 1893.

[65] *Ibid.*, July 31, 1893.

[66] *Ibid.*, August 4, 1893.

[67] *Commercial and Financial Chronicle*, LVII, 232. Cf. Sprague: *op. cit.*, p. 187 for daily rates of premium on New York during August.

[68] J. de Witt Warner, quoted by Sprague: *op. cit.*, p. 199.

[69] *Commercial and Financial Chronicle*, LVII, 272; Chicago *Economist*, X, 185.

[70] Cf. Sprague: *op. cit.*, pp. 204-205, for the statistics of domestic exchange quotations in several important cities.

[71] Chicago *Economist*, X, 47.

[72] *Chicago Tribune*, August 7, 1893.

[73] *Ibid.*, August 10, 1893.

[74] *Ibid.*, August 1 and 10, 1893.

[75] *Ibid.*, August 1 to 5, 1893; Chicago *Economist*, X, 133 and 135.

[76] *Chicago Tribune*, August 11 and 12, 1893.

[77] *Ibid.*, August 11, 1893.

[78] Chicago *Economist*, X, 192; *Chicago Tribune*, August 20, 1893.

[79] *Chicago Tribune*, August 18, 1893.

[80] *Ibid.*, August 18 and 20, 1893.

[81] *Ibid.*, August 18, 1893.

[82] *Ibid.*, August 20, 1893.

[83] Chicago *Economist*, X, 269.

[84] *Idem*, 213 and 239.

[85] *Commercial and Financial Chronicle*, XVII, 171 and 196.

[86] *Ibid.*, LVII, 329 and 411.

[87] *Idem*, 394-395; Chicago *Economist*, X, 475.

[88] Bryan: *The First Battle*, pp. 77-114.

[89] *Commercial and Financial Chronicle*, LVII, 234 and 366.

[90] Nichols: *American Historical Review*, XLI, 25-53; Chicago *Economist*, X, 369, 397 and 423; *Commercial and Financial Chronicle*, LVII, 656.

[91] *Commercial and Financial Chronicle*, LVII, 356; Chicago *Economist*, X, 239.

[92] Chicago *Economist*, 291; *Chicago Tribune*, August 29, September 7, 1893.

[93] Chicago *Economist*, X, 369.

[94] *Commercial and Financial Chronicle*, LVII, 656.

[95] *Chicago Tribune*, October 31, 1893; *New York Times*, October 31, 1893.

[96] Kane: *op. cit.*, I, 194-196; *Annual Report of the Comptroller of the Currency*, 1893, I, 10-12 and 75-78.

[97] *Chicago Tribune,* October 11, 12, 16 and 19, 1893.
[98] *Chicago Tribune,* May 12 and 16, 1894.
[99] *Ibid.,* June 23, 27, 28 and 29, 1894.
[100] *Ibid.,* July 2, 1894; Barnard: *op. cit.,* pp. 280-317.
[101] Harvey: *Coin's Financial School,* p. 3.

CHAPTER XVII

THE CROSS OF GOLD

1894–1900

CONSERVATIVE enthusiasm over the termination of the railroad strikes was natural, but enthusiasm did not restore prosperity. Chicago was engulfed in a depression that was not of its own making, but for three exciting years the city was to serve as the battleground of opposing economic philosophies. Never before had it been so clearly demonstrated that Chicago stood on the boundary that divided the older eastern states from the exuberant west.

In 1894, depression stalked the United States, and throughout the western world conditions were little better. Commodity price levels had fallen steadily since the conclusion of the Franco-Prussian War, in all the important countries of Europe, while, in America, the decline had begun five years earlier as a result of the deflationary policy adopted to bring the Greenbacks to parity with gold. On both sides of the Atlantic, the unemployed workers waited despondently outside the factory gates, while farmers and businessmen were all too often face to face with bankruptcy.

Such universal depression could arise only from a universal cause. It could not be explained in terms of particular administrations in Washington, nor cured by one-sided tariff manipulations on the part of each suffering country. What could be more natural, therefore, than to attribute the world-wide price declines to the equally world-wide demonetization of silver during the early seventies? For countless centuries silver had been a monetary metal, but in a few short years it had been displaced from its position of eminence. Germany had adopted the gold standard in 1871, the United States had abrogated the right of free coinage for silver in the famous "Crime of 1873," and the mints of the Latin Monetary Union were closed to the white metal in the following year. Price levels had started to fall, in all these countries, at approximately the same time as silver was demonetized.

To the economic historian, armed with a knowledge of recent developments in the field of monetary theory, it may seem illogical to place upon silver the entire blame for the fall in prices. Admittedly, the western world had adopted the gold standard at a time when gold production was no longer increasing, so that the resultant increase in monetary demand was bound to raise the value of the metal. But the increase in value was accelerated by several other factors, among which the growth in population and the rapid improvements in industrial technique demand an important place.

Elaborate analyses, however, are never as convincing, to the multitude, as simple arguments. Moreover, to a generation that accepted the quantity theory of money in its most mechanistic form, elaborate analysis did not disprove the simple argument that silver demonetization had reduced the supply of money below the appropriate level. While bank deposits and notes, along with other forms of "credit money," might facilitate the business transactions of the community, the quantity of standard metallic money, in its relationship to the demand for money was looked upon as the causal factor that determined the general level of prices. On this basic approach to monetary problems there was almost complete unanimity among American thinkers, during the closing years of the nineteenth century. Men who advocated the use of silver agreed, on this point of theory, with those who emphasized the desirability of a monometallic gold standard, even though the two groups might fight bitterly over collateral issues of practice.

It is not surprising, therefore, that many men should have insisted that, since silver had been standard money before 1873, the Coinage Act of that year had prevented such an increase in the quantity of money as would have kept prices from falling. The deduction was simple and, in the light of all the circumstances, accurate. Moreover, the United States has always had an affection for the white metal, due in part, no doubt, to the encouragement of those American interests which have long been among the greatest silver producers of the world. To this affection the policies of the Bland-Allison and Sherman Acts bear ample testimony and, although the silver-purchase policies had been abandoned under the pressure exerted by panic in 1893, there were many who felt that the Sherman Act should be replaced by legislation that involved an even more extensive monetization of silver.

THE PEN MORE POWERFUL THAN THE SWORD.

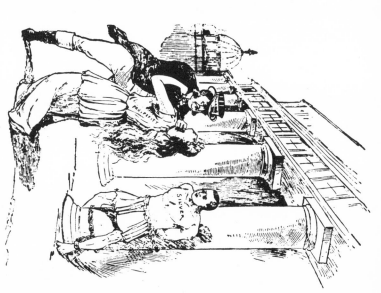

A brutal assault is made by a ruffian upon "Prosperity," a beautiful woman, in the sight of a prisoner, who trys to break his chains that he may go to her rescue.

ARGUMENTS FOR THE FREE COINAGE OF SILVER

Reproduced from COIN'S FINANCIAL SCHOOL

In 1892, both the Republican and Democratic platforms had endorsed the monetary use of silver, while the
Populist Party had definitely espoused free coinage of
both metals at a ratio of sixteen to one[1]—a ratio that was
destined to become famous in succeeding years. In the
same year, a conference of experts had met, by American
invitation, at Brussels for the purpose of exploring the
possibilities of international bimetallic agreement.

To this project England turned a deaf ear, even
though Balfour and other political leaders were aware
of the theoretical advantages of a bimetallic standard.
Indeed, in 1893, the British Empire poured cold water
on the hopes of the silver enthusiasts by closing the mints
of India to the free coinage of the white metal. But with
England adamant, the other European powers were not
willing to sign any agreement with the United States.
England was at the peak of her imperial prestige. Under
the gold standard, she had increased her wealth beyond
the dreams of avarice, and attained a position of envied
eminence. Other European powers were content to follow her prescription.

To many Americans, and particularly to those who
were actively interested in international trade and world
finance, the monetization of silver was tolerable only if
it were carried out by all of the leading nations. England's economic success had given the gold standard an
aura of sanctity, and they could not conceive of an American monetary standard so different from that of England that foreign-exchange rates would be continually
fluctuating. International trade, the dominant economic

characteristic of the late nineteenth century, was thought to require an international monetary standard.

At this point, the silverites parted company with their more conservative brethren. If the monetization of silver is a good thing, they insisted, why should American policy wait upon the whims of England? If the adoption of a bimetallic, or even of a silver, standard would end the decline in price levels, and restore prosperity to the United States, why hesitate because of the resultant instability of foreign-exchange rates? A hundred men were affected by the price of bread for every one that studied the sterling quotations, and the domestic trade of the country was vastly more important than its international dealings. The United States should control its own monetary destiny, they insisted, and that argument, heretical though it sounded during the eighteen-nineties, has a familiar ring to all those who have studied the monetary history of the world from 1920 to 1938.

Such a conflict of opinion could not be resolved by polite phrases or verbal compromises. It went to the heart of monetary policy. Moreover, it was a problem that did not fit conveniently into the political traditions of either of the older parties. Logically, the Republicans, as apostles of economic nationalism, might have been expected to favor independent American action while the Democrats defended the virtues of an international monetary system, but in this battle economic factors were more important than political shibboleths. All the motive power inherent in human selfishness was brought into play, splitting both parties from top to bottom. The debt-ridden farmer and the unemployed worker wanted

a monetary system that would raise prices and bring prosperity, and they were willing to fight for it no matter
whether their traditional affiliations were Democratic or
Republican. The man whose income was fixed in dollars was equally oblivious to the call of party, and clung
tenaciously to a monetary standard that would not allow
the value of those dollars to diminish in terms of goods
and services. That both beliefs were, in part, erroneous
makes no difference. It is the prevalence of a belief,
rather than its accuracy, that is significant, and in this
battle each side held to its guns with a persistence that
was not to be shaken. In such circumstances a bitter
struggle was inevitable, and to us of the twentieth century the conflict has an interest that transcends its melodrama. Economic problems, for the first time, were to
be solved on a national scale by the divine right of the
voter.

Having repealed the Sherman Act, and initiated an
international bimetallic conference, the gold-standard
group could comfortably assume the defensive, and protect their interests by doing nothing. But the advocates
of independent American silver legislation were not so
comfortably situated. Every step of the road had to be
contested, and they began, early in 1894, by introducing
a bill into Congress to provide for the coinage of the
seigniorage silver then in the Treasury.* Since the total
amount of metal involved did not exceed sixty million
dollars, the measure appeared innocuous, and many legis-

---

* Under the Sherman Act, silver dollars had been coined only to an amount
that equaled the price paid for the silver bullion. Since the metal was purchased at prices well below $1.29 an ounce, the difference (or seigniorage)
accumulated in the Treasury vaults in uncoined form. Cf. *Bankers Magazine*,
XLVIII, 415; Hepburn: *op. cit.*, pp. 356-357.

lators supported it in order to curry favor with voters who were indignant at the repeal of the Sherman Act a few months earlier.[2] In an unexpectedly short time, it passed both the House of Representatives and the Senate.

Although compromise was certainly not an outstanding characteristic of Cleveland, there was a general impression that he would sign the measure. A howl of protest, therefore, arose from the opponents of silver legislation, headed by the New York bankers. If the President had any doubts as to business sentiment they were promptly dispelled by these protests which, as the *Bankers Magazine* joyously states, "left the whole discredited lot of politicians at Washington, deserted and without constituents, among the business men, of either party, in any quarter."[3] The bill was vetoed.

This experience was enough to convince the silver forces that nothing could be accomplished without a long campaign of what was, even then, miscalled public education. They set about the task with enthusiasm and determination.[4] In addition to the American Bimetallic League, which had been created in 1892, a National Bimetallic Union came into existence three years later. Offices were established in Chicago, as the most suitable center for a nationwide campaign, and a weekly periodical known as *The Bimetallist* was published. Early in 1896, these two organizations were united with the National Silver Committee, a political group, to form the American Bimetallic Union, and the campaign was conducted with even greater fervor as a result of the union of forces.

The opponents of silver, for some time, regarded these

"educational efforts" with disdain. In view of the repeal of the Sherman Act, and the effective veto of the Seigniorage Bill, they assumed that the vast body of public opinion was on their side and that propaganda was unnecessary. By 1896, however, the outlook appeared distinctly less favorable. Men and money were hastily enlisted in the formation of the National Sound Money League, in which many bankers from New York and Chicago were interested, and offices were established in Chicago.[5] Taking a leaf from their opponent's book, the League issued a weekly periodical, under the title of *Sound Money,* and laid down a barrage of antisilver propaganda that was as elaborate and well-financed as that of the American Bimetallic Union. Each group insisted that it was nonpartisan: each admitted its academic impartiality and its love of truth. Such protestations were acceptable only to those who were already convinced. In the cold light of history, it must be admitted that both organizations were efficient, and extravagantly financed, dispensers of effective propaganda, with most of the financial advantage on the side of sound money.

Any comprehensive survey of the ammunition that was used in this battle of ideas and interests would require a volume to itself, but it is impossible to refrain from a brief reference to the most colorful aspect of the whole controversy. On the side of the silver forces, there were issued not only sober statements of monetary history and theory, but elaborate novels like Harvey's *Tale of Two Nations* in which the wicked plots of the rich were dramatically revealed. The demonetization of silver was elevated to a place where it became the climax of a great and skillfully planned drama of seduction.

But the most effective of all the silver publications was undoubtedly *Coin's Financial School*, published by W. H. Harvey in 1894. With a long experience of law and banking, the author combined an extremely facile pen, and there are few more effective examples of propaganda in all recorded history than this little book of one hundred and fifty pages. The whole thing purports to be the record of a series of lectures given by the youthful Coin to the leading citizens of Chicago, presenting in simple and colorful fashion the underlying facts of the monetary situation. Since almost all the Chicago newspapers were violently opposed to the silver program, Coin flays them sardonically, implying that they had neither the ability nor the courage to answer his arguments. The editor of the *Chicago Tribune* has no argument but vituperation; the editor of the Chicago *Economist* no knowledge of political economy except that which he gains from reading newspapers in the pay of the opposition forces.

Moreover, fully realizing the value of effective illustration, Coin reduces many of his arguments to the compass of a cartoon.* Silver is represented in the guise of a virginal maiden who is brutally and bloodily decapitated by Sherman. More pungently still, the maiden Prosperity is shown to be attacked by a ruffianly England, while athletic American Silver is trying to burst his fetters in order to rescue her—a telling argument against those who insisted that American monetary reform must wait upon England's willingness to abandon the gold standard. In

---

* Even Horace White admits the excellence of the illustrations in *Coin's Financial School*. "But what a gloomy fate would be ours," he adds sardonically, "if the destiny of the Republic lay in the hands of any skillful designer of comic almanacks." Cf. White: *Coin's Financial Fool*, p. 110.

the light of the cartoon, it does not require a great flight of emotional imagery to insist that "a war with England would be the most popular ever waged on the face of the earth. If it is true that she can dictate the money of the world, and thereby create world-wide misery, it would be the most just war ever waged by man."[6] Forty years afterward, when the United States had attained a position of opulent eminence, comparable to that enjoyed by England at the close of the nineteenth century, Owen D. Young suggested that "America is too rich to be loved." But seldom, if ever, have discussions of monetary problems risen to the heat of Coin's emotional belligerency.

The outstanding characteristic of the book was, however, its personalities. With no concern for the laws of libel, Coin introduces into his imaginary audience the outstanding Chicagoans who were numbered among his opponents. Lyman J. Gage, he tells us, is "at the 'top of the heap.' His word is law on the subject of finance."[7] But when Gage gets up during the lecture to ask a question, the young Coin is able to answer all his arguments so effectively that the questioner admits complete defeat. John R. Walsh, of the Chicago National Bank, is even more effectively silenced, and even Professor Laughlin is unable to find anything wrong with the arguments of the young monetary expert. Never had such a galaxy of talent been so effectively silenced and, even though there are occasional bursts of enthusiasm when the advocates of the gold standard are called "Imps of hell unchained, banqueting in selfish glee upon the heart's blood of the world,"[8] the argument is usually simple and perfectly lucid. Here was a book about money that the average man could understand, delightfully written and incorporating, in imagination, all the great men with whom the reader would like to argue. It is not surprising that three hundred thousand copies were sold in less than a year.

The opposition literature is less enchanting, but pleasant enough reading if one has a fine taste in vituperation and abuse.[9] In the first place, the writers were very serious about the whole matter, and very annoyed. Coin, who had taken the field first, had obviously irritated his opponents, many of whom were less facile than he was, and they resented the fact. Moreover, although Coin's facts were sometimes awry and his illustrations inapplicable, there could be no denial of the fact that his arguments were simple.

For the conservative group, a simple argument was impossible. Since they were pledged to bimetallism as a desirable monetary standard, as long as it was adopted by several great powers, they could not deny the virtues of silver as a monetary metal. While it may be true that something good for the whole world is not good for the United States alone, it is not easy to write a simple argument that will bring that fact home to a western farmer or a Chicago laborer, so that emphasis was placed upon abuse and fear. In *Coin's Financial Fool*, which is probably the ablest rejoinder to Harvey's book, Horace White abusively describes Coin as the Artful Dodger, continually pilfering and deceiving, while Uncle Sam stands by in the role of Oliver Twist. Solemn letters are reproduced from the persons named in Coin's discussion, insisting that they could not have been present because no such

Turn Your Spy-Glass, Mr. L. J. Gage, and Look Through the Other End. You will See that the Two Points are Larger than they Now Appear to You.

ARGUMENTS FOR SOUND MONEY

Reproduced from Coin's Financial Fool

PROFESSOR LAUGHLIN AT THE BOOK STALL

discussions actually took place—a piece of evidence that must have appeared unconsciously funny to all but the most ignorant members of the reading public. Moreover, having bitterly criticized the cartoons in Harvey's book, White takes care to use equally good ones in *Coin's Financial Fool*. Gage, it is suggested pictorially, would be less easily floored by the Machiavellian Coin if he had sense enough to use his wits, and Laughlin is shown to be deep in thought while his reputation is being stolen by the Artful Dodger. The cartoons are scarcely flattering to the people they set out to defend.

Flattery, however, has little place in a struggle as bitter as this one had become. Men believed that they were fighting for their very existence and, as often happens, the conflict grew more complex as it increased in bitterness. Owing to the bimetallic aims of the conservative group, it was not a simple fight between those who supported a gold standard and those who wished to monetize silver. Neither was it a clear-cut battle of deflationists versus those who wished to augment the supply of money.

Even the conservative group was growing tired of the steadily declining price level, while it was even more concerned about the recurrent currency shortages that arose in periods of seasonal or cyclical strain.[10] Partly from the desire to offset the "specious arguments" of the silver forces, and partly because of a fundamental realization that important improvements could be made in the American financial system, the whole question of banking reform was injected into the monetary controversy.

We must not, however, be misled by the high-sounding implications of the words "banking reform." The financial community was too well satisfied with itself to desire any thoroughgoing change in the banking structure, so that most of the discussion was concerned with the single problem of note issue.[11] All that was desired was a change in legislation that would increase the profits derived from bank notes, and render possible the issue of some sort of emergency currency during periods of monetary stringency.

In 1888, the Comptroller of the Currency had proposed an elaborate plan under which national banks might form currency unions, and thus acquire the right to issue notes against the deposit of good commercial paper as collateral,[12] but most of the early proposals were less far-reaching. The traditions of a bond-secured currency had become so deeply ingrained in American financial practice and imagination, prior to the panic of 1893, that suggestions for reform did not often soar above the idea of convertible bonds as a mechanism for giving elasticity to the currency.[13] Nevertheless, there were a few people who felt that satisfactory reform of the bank-note circulation could be attained only by providing for an "asset-currency," one issued against the general assets of the bank in a manner comparable to contemporary Canadian practice. Editorially, the *Bankers Magazine* espoused the idea in 1891[14] and Gage, soon after the appointment of James B. Forgan as Vice-President of the First National Bank, became an early enthusiast. Perhaps it is not without significance in this regard that Forgan had gained his early banking experience in Scotland and Canada.[15]

At its Baltimore Convention, in October, 1894, the

American Bankers Association actually suggested a comprehensive plan of reform that has come to be known as the "Baltimore Plan."[16] Under the supervision of the federal government, the plan proposed to allow a bank to issue notes against general assets to an amount equaling one-half of its capital and surplus, subject to a tax of one-half of one per cent. In addition, banks might issue additional notes, to an amount that might not exceed one-quarter of their capital and surplus, on payment of a tax which was heavy enough to discourage additional note issue in any but emergency periods. A guarantee fund, equal to five per cent of the total note issue, was to be deposited with the Treasury by the banks, out of which the notes of failed banks would be redeemed and, lest this might not convince the public of the soundness of the currency, all bank notes were to be unconditionally guaranteed by the federal government.

In Canada, a similar scheme had worked well, and Forgan championed it so ably in the United States that Cleveland became interested.[17] But Canada was not a good precedent. In the United States, the number of banks was vastly greater and, judged by Canadian standards, many of them were small and irresponsible institutions. To make the Baltimore Plan applicable, a large number of banking amalgamations would have been necessary,[18] and that could not occur overnight. It is not surprising, therefore, that some reformers were anxious to cut the Gordian knot by repealing the prohibitive tax on state bank issues.[19] By that means, a considerable expansion of the paper currency would quickly be attained.

To the advocates of silver, these banking proposals

constituted a dilemma. Since they desired an expansion
in the total quantity of standard metallic money, and
regarded excessive issues of credit money as unsound,
bank notes did nothing to solve their problem. But, since
bank notes might, for the time being at any rate, expand
the total supply of money and raise the price level, they
were willing to support those who wished to authorize
the free issue of currency by state banks. On the Baltimore Plan, however, they were adamant, regarding it
as a red herring introduced for the purpose of obfuscating
the monetary issue.[20] While such a method of operation
might increase the profits of national banks, and moderate the recurrent currency stringencies, it could do
nothing to meet the problem of a continuing dearth of
standard money such as existed, according to the contentions of the silver party, in the United States.

But bank-note issue was not the only complicating factor in the monetary battle. The experience of the country from 1884 to 1893 had shown that the Treasury was,
in a very real sense, the heart of the financial system and,
during the silver controversy, the problems of the Treasury attracted almost as much attention as the fate of the
white metal. The two were, in fact, inseparable, and each
reacted on the other in a way that exacerbated the arguments of the opposing forces. From 1894 to 1896, "the
Treasury disturbed the money market, not, however, in
the usual way by pouring in its surplus revenue, but by
drawing on the reserves of the banks at a time when the
banks themselves sorely needed them."[21]

To appreciate the situation clearly, it must be remembered that the moneys in the Treasury served two distinct

purposes. In the first place, they represented the funds
out of which current governmental expenditure had to
be paid: in the second they constituted the reserve out
of which gold was drawn for the redemption of such
government paper money as was presented by the holder
for that purpose. All the funds entering the Treasury
went into the common pool, which was drawn upon, without differentiation, for both purposes.

Emphasis upon this apparently unimportant detail of
Treasury operations is important because, during this
period of monetary controversy, the reserves were continually reduced to the danger point from the joint operation of both fiscal and monetary causes. While there can
be no doubt that some people, alarmed at the prospect
of silver legislation, drew gold from the Treasury in order
to hoard it, the extent of this drain has been grossly exaggerated by partisans of the gold standard. The solvency
of the government, and the maintenance of the gold
standard itself, was in greater danger from recurrent fiscal
deficits than it was from monetary fears. Of the $293,-
388,601 received from the sale of bonds during Cleveland's administration, $204,678,893 was used to pay cur-
rent governmental expenses: less than $90,000,000 can
be attributed to the withdrawal of gold by frightened
owners of paper money.[22]

The summary, however, anticipates the conclusion of
the story, and it is necessary to retrace our steps in order
to follow the march of events.[23] At the beginning of 1894,
there was less than $84,000,000 of available cash in the
Treasury, of which only $66,000,000 consisted of gold,
so that Secretary Carlisle decided to issue $50,000,000 of

bonds, under the Act of 1875, for the purpose of building up the reserve. To escape the odium that might attach to such a banking operation, at a time when bankers were being violently attacked by a large section of the populace, he tried to sell the bonds directly to the general public. In that attempt, he encountered little success. New York bankers were essential to the operation, which was easily carried through when their cooperation had been invoked, but the banking participation in the transaction did not increase the popularity of the administration. Indeed, when the public learned that some of the bankers had redeemed Greenbacks at the Treasury in order to get the gold with which to pay for the bonds, there arose a veritable howl of protest! Seldom, in modern times, have the advocates of conservative monetary policies provided their opponents with better arguments.

In spite of popular criticism, Carlisle was compelled to sell another $50,000,000 of bonds in November and, since the reserves of the New York banks were not able to stand the strain, institutions in other parts of the country were invited to join the syndicate.* All the gold received from the earlier issue, as well as that supplied by New York banks in exchange for Greenbacks,[24] had been withdrawn or paid out in the space of ten months. The reserve was down to $55,000,000.

As a result of the unbalanced budget and the monetary agitation, the second loan was no more beneficial than the first. Within ten weeks, the gold had left the Treasury and the reserve had fallen to $42,000,000. Sterner meas-

---

* The First National Bank of Chicago took $1,000,000 of the issue, and other Chicago institutions also participated.

ures were necessary and, in February, 1895, Cleveland signed the famous contract with the Morgan-Rothschild syndicate.

With the possible exception of the repeal of the Sherman Act, nothing did more than this contract to destroy Cleveland's reputation with the advocates of silver, yet it was not a very outrageous document.[25] If the terms were severe, they were not more severe than the occasion demanded, since the fiscal position of the United States was far from satisfactory. Moreover, the financial situation in Europe was such that the bankers might find considerable difficulty in fulfilling the obligations they assumed. In essence, the contract provided that the syndicate should supply to the Treasury three hundred thousand ounces of gold per month, most of which would have to be sent from Europe, taking in exchange 4 per cent government bonds. If the United States would issue bonds containing a gold clause, a reasonable enough request in the light of political conditions in the country at the time, the bankers agreed to reduce the coupon rate from four per cent to three per cent.

Cleveland, with a very natural desire to reduce the expenditure of the government, promptly asked Congress for the power to issue gold bonds, but the request aroused a storm of opposition. With enthusiastic unanimity, the silver forces denounced the contract, insisting that the administration had sold the welfare of the American people to a selfish crowd of international financiers, and forfeited the liberty so dearly won in 1776. It was a magnificent demonstration of emotion and, since the adoption of a gold clause in government bonds was regarded as a further step toward a gold standard, the silverites denounced the impudence of bankers who dared to offer a beggarly sixteen million dollars (the difference between four per cent and three per cent on the issue) in payment for the right to dictate American monetary policies. Cleveland's request was flatly denied, and the bonds were issued, without a gold clause, at the higher coupon rate.

If the contentions of the silver men were right, the banking syndicate must have been deeply chagrined at its failure to dictate American policy. History gives no evidence of that disappointment, and the economist would not expect to find such evidence, in view of the fact that the financial operation was a very profitable one to the participating bankers. From the Minute Books of the First National Bank of Chicago, which was a member of the syndicate, it appears that the bonds (which Morgan had taken from the Treasury at 104½) were awarded to those underwriters who supplied gold at 105¼. Those who paid in currency received the bonds at 112½. Since the public took over the bonds, in the course of a few days, at 118, the profit was exceptionally large for those participants who, like the First National of Chicago, were able to pay in gold from the metallic reserves on hand. Most of the purchasers, however, paid in currency and, to facilitate the necessary imports of gold, all the large foreign-exchange houses of the United States were mobilized under the skillful management of J. P. Morgan. Aided by a moderate business revival in the spring of 1895, and by renewed British interest in American securities,[26] the operation went smoothly forward. By June the gold reserve in the Treasury had risen to $107,500,000.

In the long run, however, the whole scheme was nothing but an expensive folly. No advantage was taken of the breathing spell to improve the fiscal position of the government, no solution was found to the monetary problems of the country. As a result, there was no decrease in the rate at which gold was withdrawn from the Treasury and, when business slumped again in June,[27] the process was accelerated. Although the syndicate furnished, in exchange for other forms of money, some $16,000,000 more gold than the contract called for, the effort was as fruitless as the labors of Sisyphus.[28] At the end of the year, the Treasury reserve had fallen to $50,000,000, and Carlisle was forced to sell another $100,000,000 of bonds to American bankers. Throughout two long years, the policies of the Treasury had aroused a furore of indignation among all the advocates of silver, and achieved nothing that was of comfort to those who favored conservative monetary policies. At the end of the period, the gold standard was no more assured than it had been in January, 1894; if anything, its prospects were even less hopeful.

As the national conventions of the several political parties approached, during the summer of 1896, it was obvious to everyone that the monetary issue, aggravated by discussions of bank reform and Treasury policy, would hold the center of the stage. Even the tariff was temporarily forgotten.

On the sixteenth of June, the Republican National Convention, meeting at St. Louis, witnessed the first political skirmish of the battle. Controlled almost entirely by eastern influences that were in favor of an international monetary standard, it was natural that the platform should tend toward conservatism. In spite of a stirring appeal by Senator Teller,[29] of Colorado, the Convention agreed by a large majority that "the Republican party is unreservedly for sound money. . . . We are unalterably opposed to every measure calculated to debase our currency or impair the credit of our country. We are, therefore, opposed to the free coinage of silver except by international agreement." Conservatism had triumphed, and Herman H. Kohlsaat of the Chicago *Times-Herald*, who had been among the leaders in the struggle, was filled with joy.

But, in the years that had gone before, the Republican party had been as firmly wedded to silver as its Democratic opponents, so that it was not easy to find a candidate whose record demonstrated his enthusiasm for the newly espoused cause. Under the shrewd management of Marcus Aurelius Hanna, William McKinley was persuaded to accept both the gold standard and the nomination,[30] but during his long political career he had defended silver more often than he had attacked it. As recently as 1891, McKinley had viciously attacked Cleveland for his dastardly efforts to "dishonor silver" and enhance the value of gold, so that his sudden access of missionary zeal for sound money must have been a novel experience.

To the Silver Republicans, headed by Teller, both the platform and the candidate were objectionable. Party alignments and political traditions could not outweigh the fundamental cleavage of ideas on the monetary question, and the minority seceded from the Convention in order to go over to the Democratic party in a body a few days later.[31]

Many of the older leaders of the Democratic party were just as conservative as their Republican opponents. Cleveland and his supporters had demonstrated that fact beyond the shadow of a doubt. But, before the Democratic National Convention met in Chicago, on the last day of June, elaborate preparations for its capture had been worked out by the silver group.[32] As early as February, 1895, conferences had been held in Washington to plan such a campaign and, during the closing days of the Fifty-Third Congress, a group of Silver Democrats had issued a clarion call to all their colleagues, insisting that the Democratic party should adopt a silver platform. Both Lane and Fithian of Illinois signed the manifesto, as did Congressman Bryan, of Nebraska, while Governor Altgeld was strongly in favor of the proposal,[33] not only because of his belief in silver but because of the bitter antagonism that he felt towards Cleveland as a result of the federal government's high-handed action at the time of the Pullman strike. Nor did the reformers rest on their oars. In June, 1895, a conference was held at Memphis, at which a National Silver Committee was appointed to carry out the plans by which control of Democratic party machinery was to be acquired, and this Committee called a larger conference in Washington during August to perfect its campaign.

During the hot Chicago days, in July, 1896, these preparations bore fruit.[34] Silver enthusiasts were present in large numbers, filling the lobbies of the Palmer House with noise and enthusiasm until "the temperature was somewhere in the vicinity of 150°."[35] It is a mistake, however, to think of that Convention as a simple struggle over the monetisation of silver. Altgeld, who dominated the scene, was fighting his personal battle with Cleveland and the platform that he wrote enshrines the liberal philosophy that the Governor had consistently espoused. In that document there are set forth almost all of the principles that have motivated the Democratic party during the twentieth century, and many that the Republican party has adopted, but it is doubtful whether any of the delegates, except Altgeld himself, realised their revolutionary significance. To most Democrats, silver was the central issue, and the silver men secured their first victory in the appointment of one of their number as Chairman of the Convention. But the silver plank in the platform was less easy to put over than the chairmanship and, for days, the matter was fought out in the Committee on Resolutions.[36] At last, the Committee presented two alternative planks to the Convention, transferring the discussion to the floor of the Colosseum.

To record all the wavering progress of that debate would be tiresome, but it is impossible to omit its dramatic climax. William Jennings Bryan, the thirty-six-year-old Congressman from Nebraska, whom the *Tribune* referred to as "the Boy Orator of the Platte," ascended the rostrum to deliver the closing speech for the silver forces. In an electric atmosphere, he held his audience spellbound, as he thundered denunciations of those who opposed him.[37] "With a zeal approaching the zeal which inspired the crusaders who followed Peter the Hermit, our Silver Democrats went forth from victory unto victory until they are now assembled, not to discuss, not to debate, but to enter up the judgment already rendered by the plain people of this country. . . . If they ask us why it is that we say more on the money question than we say upon the tariff question, I reply that, if protection has slain its thousands, the gold standard has slain its tens of thousands. If they ask us why we do not embody in our platform all the things that we believe in, we reply that when we have restored the money of the Constitution all other necessary reforms will be possible; but that until this is done there is no other reform that can be accomplished.

"There are two ideas of government. There are those who believe that, if you will only legislate to make the well-to-do prosperous, their prosperity will leak through to those below. The Democratic idea, however, has been that if you legislate to make the masses prosperous, their prosperity will find its way up through every class which rests upon them. . . . Having behind us the producing masses of this nation and the world, supported by the commercial interests, the laboring interests, and the toilers everywhere, we will answer their demand for a gold standard by saying to them: You shall not press down upon the brow of labour this crown of thorns, you shall not crucify mankind upon a cross of gold."

It was a magnificent and decisive oration, although the *Tribune* described it as nothing but "empty vaporings and strings of glittering phrases." The whole convention was stampeded and, "When Bryan had finished his speech a throng rushed to the platform to offer congratulations and his hand was nearly paralyzed, so fervent were the greetings of his admirers."[38] Seldom has Chicago, or any other American city, witnessed such a demonstration.

In short order, the platform proposed by Altgeld and the silver group was adopted in its entirety. "We are," the party insisted, "unalterably opposed to monometallism which has locked fast the prosperity of an industrial people in the paralysis of hard times. Gold monometallism is a British policy, and its adoption has brought other nations into financial servitude to London. It is not only un-American, but anti-American, and it can be fastened on the United States only by the stifling of that spirit and love of liberty which proclaimed our political independence in 1776 and won it in the war of the Revolution. We demand the free and unlimited coinage of both silver and gold at the present legal ratio of 16 to 1 without waiting for the aid or consent of any other nation."[39] Issue was squarely joined between the two great political parties. Moreover, the Democratic Convention was so much impressed by Bryan that they nominated him as the standard-bearer of the party. As soon as his great speech came to an end, the Texas delegation led a procession of state banners to his seat among the Nebraska members, and on the following day he was officially nominated, by a landslide, during the fifth ballot.[40]

For the opponents of silver there was no alternative but secession. Including in their number such prominent Chicagoans as John R. Walsh and Cyrus H. McCormick, these "Honest Money Democrats," as they styled themselves, held an independent convention at Indianapolis on September 2. A platform similar to that of the Republican party was adopted, and Senator John M. Palmer, of Illinois, was nominated as the Presidential candidate.[41] Cleveland and Carlisle, who had been repudiated by the vast majority of their own party, sent enthusiastic greetings to the rump.

Complex as the political picture had now become, there were still two other parties to be considered. Fortunately for the historian, both of them decided to throw in their lot with the Democrats since, despite a divergence of opinion on other matters, there was agreement on those monetary proposals which were the central theme of the campaign. On July 22, the National Silver Party and the Populist Party held their conventions in St. Louis.[42] Each of them nominated Bryan as its Presidential candidate and each included in its platform an unqualified demand for the free monetization of both gold and silver at a ratio of sixteen to one.*

But if the political picture was complex, with four independent parties in the field and two secessionist organizations, the issue was simple as far as the average voter was concerned. To him the choice lay between national silver inflation and international gold deflation. Never had he been given an opportunity to vote on anything as closely connected with his own economic welfare, and popular excitement throughout the country was at fever heat throughout the campaign.[43] It mattered little, in practice, that no responsible supporter of McKinley was

---

* At the Populist Convention, this action was taken only after considerable debate, since many members (in spite of their enthusiasm for silver) were reluctant to march under the banner of a party they had previously abandoned.

willing to deny his hope for international bimetallism, or that England and Germany were both becoming increasingly interested in the remonetization of silver as a means of accelerating business revival.[44] These difficult points of monetary theory, which were perhaps of greater importance than all the political manifestoes, were too abstruse to serve as campaign ammunition. Fundamentally, the battle was between those who expected that free coinage of silver would make them prosperous and those who feared that it would impair their fortunes.

Business, in the face of such a conflict, was almost paralyzed,[45] although there were feverish bursts of energy that were encouraged by every change in the campaign outlook. When a Republican victory seemed probable, signs of revival would appear on the commercial horizon; when, as more often happened, the financial community became panic-stricken at the Democratic prospects, the security markets declined precipitously and gold was hoarded or exported in large amounts.

In such circumstances, it could scarcely be expected that the campaign would be conducted with forbearance or politeness, particularly in view of the exchange of compliments that had occurred during the "educational" preliminaries. Even the log-cabin campaigns on the western frontier had not released so much invective as this struggle was to bring forth on public platforms and in the press.

The newspapers, which were usually in the McKinley camp,[46] tried to spread terror among their adversaries by insisting that free coinage of silver would destroy the savings of the thrifty and precipitate such a crisis in business that millions would be thrown out of work.[47] To supplement the argument they resorted liberally to invective. Bryan himself was said to be the spineless tool of the wealthy silver trust,[48] rather than the champion of the masses, while the editor of the *New York Tribune* found the inspiration of the Bryan faction in "the basest passions of the least worthy members of the community. . . . Its nominal head was worthy of the cause. Nominal because the wretched rattle-pated boy, posing in vapid vanity and mouthing resounding rottenness, was not the real leader of that league of hell. He was only a puppet in the blood-imbued hands of Altgeld, the anarchist, and Debs, the revolutionist, and other desperadoes of that stripe. But he was a willing puppet, Bryan was—willing and eager. None of his masters was more apt than he at lies and forgeries and blasphemies and all the nameless iniquities of that campaign against the Ten Commandments."[49]

But, if the newspapers contained fewer epithets descriptive of McKinley's cohorts, it was not because the Democrats lacked either imagination or vocabulary. On the public platform the Republicans were described as "English toadies and the pampered minions of corporate rapacity," and audiences were enthusiastically told that "the time has come to determine whether this nation is ruled by an Almighty Dollar or by an Almighty God."[50] The *Chicago Tribune* was shocked at such blasphemy![51]

In Chicago, the bitterness of the campaign was particularly evident because there, more than in any other large city, the forces were evenly divided. Both the Bimetallic Union and the Sound Money League were deluging the city with information and propaganda, speakers from both camps were frequently on hand, and almost all the political and business leaders of Chicago were active participants in the struggle. Moreover, Governor Altgeld was the acknowledged leader of the Democratic campaign, playing a part that was fully as important as that of Bryan, so that the Republicans sent their heaviest batteries of oratory to Illinois.

The banking community of Chicago, with the single outstanding exception of Hammond, of the National Bank of Illinois, was enrolled on the side of McKinley.[52] Even before the Democratic Convention, Walsh had tried to influence Altgeld in favor of "sound money" by making substantial loans to the Governor, whose business affairs were in bad shape. When Altgeld refused to modify his attitude at the request of the banker, the loan was immediately called and, had it not been for the financial aid that was promptly rendered by the National Bank of Illinois, Walsh might have succeeded in eliminating the Governor from the campaign. In October, the associated banks of the city raised a large fund among themselves "for the publication and dissemination of financial literature through the West bearing upon the important issues to be settled by the people on November third." When a great demonstration of the "Sound Money Forces" was planned for the twenty-fifth anniversary of the fire, the Clearing House Association decided to suspend operations for the day in order that its members might participate. As a result, while the opposition silver parade mustered only 12,569 individuals, according to the *Tribune*, there marched under the banner of sound money a total of 68,307, including J. Ogden Armour, Samuel W. Allerton, John Cudahy, M. J. Foreman and Harry Gordon Selfridge.[53] In the Colosseum, that night, twenty-five thousand people gathered to hear Chauncey M. Depew expound the monetary principles of the Republican platform.

The trade unionists, on the contrary, were just as strongly for Bryan. When he came to address their convention, on Labor Day, they staged one of the most impressive demonstrations of the whole campaign, and on each of his other visits to Chicago the Democratic candidate received an equally enthusiastic reception at their hands.[54]

The Chicago situation was, however, aggravated by events that had little or no relation to the political controversy. During the early part of the summer, the firm of W. H. and J. H. Moore, on behalf of a group of Chicago capitalists, had been carrying on an extensive speculation in the securities of the Diamond Match Company and the New York Biscuit Company. On the night of Monday, August 3, the partnership failed unexpectedly, partly as a result of short selling by members of the pool who had grown timorous, and the Chicago Stock Exchange was promptly closed to prevent a sudden flood of selling orders.[55]

Critical though the situation was, the leading bankers derided the idea of a financial panic. Both Gage and John J. Mitchell insisted that the collapse of the Moore brothers, and the closing of the Stock Exchange, were the best possible things that could have happened in the light of all the circumstances, but, in spite of this optimism, it was not easy to clean up the mess. For three months the Exchange remained closed, and although, on August 8, the Northern Trust Company was appointed trustee for the committee responsible for settling the large number of uncompleted transactions in Diamond Match and Biscuit securities, it was not until September 24 that a satisfactory plan of settlement was developed.[56] Since the participants in the speculative pool were among the leading bankers and businessmen of the city, the negotiations were conducted with the utmost secrecy but the final settlement required them to put up some two hundred thousand dollars for the indemnification of brokers whose contracts had not been fulfilled at the time when the Moore brothers failed.[57] Moreover, the situation was further complicated by the fact that Yerkes' interests had been carrying on a speculative maneuver in the stocks of the West Chicago and North Chicago traction companies. Contracts involving twenty-two thousand shares of stock had to be settled in some fashion before the Exchange could be opened and trading resumed on a normal basis.[58]

At last, on November 3, the nation went to the polls and, on the morrow, it was discovered that McKinley had won. Against the 6,511,073 votes cast for Bryan, the Republican candidate had received 7,107,822. It was not a large majority, and the size of Bryan's following indicated the extent of the silver sentiment, but any majority at all was large enough to delight the victors. Moreover Illinois, by a popular majority of 150,000, had cast its twenty-four electoral votes for McKinley and driven Altgeld from office, so that conservative people in Chicago were jubilant. "Yesterday's vote was a McKinley, honest money, and good government landslide. . . . The sun, as it rises this morning, shines upon a land from which all apprehensions of disaster and disorder have been banished. The good old days when there was work for all, and when that work was paid for in good money, are to return. Exit Bryan. Enter prosperity."[59]

On November 5, the Chicago Stock Exchange opened its doors once again and trading was resumed with enthusiasm.[60] Hoarding of gold, which had been carried on extensively in several parts of the country, ceased to be attractive, and the yellow metal flowed in a steady stream back to the vaults of the banks.

Moreover, a few weeks after the election, Chicago had an additional cause for jubilation. Lyman J. Gage, by this time so eminent a figure in the city that his name was synonymous with both soundness and success,[61] was invited by the President-elect to accept the office of Secretary of the Treasury, while Charles G. Dawes, another Chicago banker, was appointed Comptroller of the Currency.

The interview between Gage and McKinley was interesting.[62] Gage, who had fought for the gold standard persistently and strongly favored a low tariff, was not wholly convinced that McKinley was a worthy leader. "You," he pointed out to the President, "have the reputation of being a high protective-tariff advocate. Again, I am afraid that while the platform on which you were elected carries the gold plank, your convictions are less firm than mine as to the necessity of maintaining, at any sacrifice, our present money standard." To these objections McKinley returned an "indulgent smile" and a suggestion that his private convictions were not always identical with his public pronouncements. Gage, either because he was convinced or because he wished to strengthen the President's resolve, accepted the office.

When the appointment was announced, a chorus of jubilation went up from all parts of the country. That Chicago should approve the choice was natural, but New York was no less enthusiastic. "In selecting Mr. Gage of Chicago for Secretary of the Treasury the President gave to the public the strongest possible assurance that he was heartily in accord with the best thought of the country with respect to currency reform. Mr. Gage stands as the representative of plain dealing and a radical cure. Make-shifts and subterfuges, the tools of small politicians, are unknown in his practice and foreign to his character."[63]

Yet, in a sense, the pleasantest part of Gage's term of office must have been the few weeks before he returned the Presidency of the First National Bank to Samuel M. Nickerson and took the train to Washington. During that brief period he enjoyed the pleasures, without the cares, of office, since Chicago made every effort to do him honor.[64] When, on the first of February, he presented his letter of resignation to the directors of the First National Bank, they engrossed upon the Minute Book their "testimony to the universal respect and affection felt for him by all his associates," and expressed their "appreciation of the tact, ability and probity which he has so faithfully used to develop the strength of this institution" during a period of almost thirty years.

On the day before his departure from the city, the Bankers Club, which he had founded, gave a testimonial banquet, at which all the financial leaders of the city united in such eulogy that Gage looked at the tablecloth in embarrassment during most of the session.[65] It is probable, however, that he enjoyed most keenly the crowd of clerks, from all departments of the Bank, which surged unexpectedly into his office on the last morning to present a bronze and onyx inkstand which they had bought. "Mr. Gage was taken completely by surprise, and for a moment was so affected he could not speak."[66]

In Washington, conditions must have seemed less congenial. Although the Republicans had been elected on a platform in which the monetary and banking planks were outstanding, they had little desire for precipitate action on either matter.[67] McKinley, in his inaugural address, suggested the desirability of a national monetary commission to study the subject, but the suggestion was not acted upon by Congress. In point of fact, the Republican leaders were too much impressed by the strength of Bryan's vote to do anything about the gold standard. They hoped that, in the light of McKinley's past record on the currency question, it might be possible to win over some of the silver advocates by a policy of inaction. Nor were they any more enthusiastic about bank reform than Bryan had been.[68] Reform of any kind was not in the blood of the new political oligarchy; "we do not want," they insisted, "any of their rubber currency . . . the National Banking Act which carried us safely through the Civil War is good enough."[69]

With Machiavellian cunning, Speaker Reed united in the Banking and Currency Committee of the House as many incongruous elements as possible.[70] Since many of the members possessed great ability, the committee was continuously active in the discussion of reform measures, which created a good impression in the minds of the community. Since the views of the several members were always in conflict, there was no danger of unanimity and no possibility of legislation.

Gage retained his courage in the face of these odds. He realized that, among all the members of the administration, he was the one upon whom the business community depended for currency and banking reform,[71] and the consciousness of that responsibility strengthened his own resolve to persevere in what looked like a hopeless task.

Before the regular session of Congress, he had prepared a complete plan that was well worthy of adoption,[72] and this was submitted to the legislators in December. In the first place, he advocated the complete separation of the fiscal operation of the Treasury from its monetary functions, and the provision of adequate reserves to guarantee the successful performance of the latter. In the second place, to strengthen the banking system, he proposed that national banks might be established in small communities with a capital of twenty-five thousand dollars, instead of the fifty-thousand minimum prescribed by existing laws, and that national bank notes should be issued in an amount equal to one hundred, rather than ninety, per cent of the par value of government bonds deposited as collateral. These simple amendments to the existing law did not, however, go far enough to satisfy him. To give elasticity to the circulation, he suggested that when a bank had issued national bank notes, in the above fashion, to an amount equaling one-half of its capital and surplus, it should be authorized to issue half as much again against

the security of its general assets, without any specific deposit of collateral, along the lines proposed in the Baltimore Plan. In this way, he hoped to facilitate the transi-
tion from a traditional bond-secured currency, which he
disliked, to a bank-note currency that should be issued,
in its entirety, against the general assets of the banking
system.

To modern students, who have seen banking reform go
to lengths that Gage would have deemed incredible, there
is nothing exciting in these suggestions. But to the Congress of 1897 they appeared revolutionary. Although extended hearings were held before the House Committee,[73]
no action was taken in the matter.

Gage was not alone, however, in his fight for a better
monetary and banking system. If the politicians were apathetic, the businessmen were thoroughly aroused as a result of the election campaign. Within a fortnight of the
election that placed McKinley in office, a group of businessmen in Indianapolis had begun to think of a convention of the leading bankers and businessmen of the country, for the purpose of deciding upon a course of action.[74]
Early in December, a preliminary conference was held to
arrange the details of the meeting and, on January 12,
1897, there gathered at Indianapolis the representatives
of twenty-six states and the District of Columbia. More
than one hundred cities were represented by their leading
citizens, and Chicago was in the vanguard of the movement.[75] Both Herman H. Kohlsaat and J. J. Mitchell did
yeoman service on the Executive Committee.

As to the aims of the assembly, the preamble to the
resolutions that were adopted is very definite. "This con-

vention declares that it has become absolutely necessary that a consistent, straightforward, and deliberately-
planned monetary system shall be inaugurated, the fundamental basis of which should be: First, that the present
gold standard should be maintained; Second, that steps
should be taken to insure the ultimate retirement of all
classes of United States notes by a gradual and steady
process, and so as to avoid injurious contraction of the
currency, or disturbance of the business interests of the
country, and that until such retirement provision should
be made for a separation of the revenue and note-issue
departments of the Treasury; Third, that a banking system be provided which should furnish credit facilities
to every portion of the country and a safe and elastic circulation, and especially with a view of securing such a
distribution of the loanable capital of the country as
will tend to equalise the rates of interest in all parts
thereof."[76]

These aims, which are almost identical with those expressed by Gage in his report, represent the best thought
of the business and financial community at the period.
But it must be admitted, in frankness, that very little was
accomplished. When Congress failed to act on McKinley's
suggestion that a national monetary commission be appointed, the Executive Committee of the Indianapolis
Convention appointed a commission of its own.[77] Meeting
in Washington during the autumn, the Indianapolis
Monetary Commission drew up an elaborate report, and
prepared a bill that was introduced into the House of
Representatives, but the bill met the same fate as all
other monetary measures presented to the Fifty-fifth

Congress. Neither the enthusiasm of businessmen nor the financial support of national banks[78] could overcome the political obstacles that were raised and, when the Convention assembled again, in January, 1898, it could only resolve to publish Laughlin's elaborate report and begin a campaign of public education.[79]

In the light of all these factors, we may well ask how it happened that the gold standard did finally triumph in the United States. Both here, and in Europe, there was a growing feeling that falling price levels were due, in large measure, to the earlier demonetization of silver, and there could be no doubt that falling prices accentuated the severity of the recurrent business depressions. Nothing could have been politically wiser than the initial caution of McKinley's administration in matters of monetary legislation, since there can be little doubt that four more years of deflation would have carried Bryan triumphantly into office, in 1900, on a free-silver platform. Indeed, there is good reason to think that the election of 1896 might have been much less favorable to the Republicans had it not been for the poor harvests in Europe, which raised the price of American foodstuffs at a time when the farmer was almost convinced that he could never sell his products at a profit while the United States operated under a gold standard.[80] Moreover, the gold that was received in exchange for the export of wheat was largely responsible for the improvement in the position of both the Treasury and the banking system during the latter part of 1896 and the early part of 1897.[81] Once more in human history, economic factors shaped the course of political events.

Gage, in his *Memoirs*, suggests that his speech to the Commercial Clubs at Cincinnati was the turning point of the depression, and the reading of contemporary journals indicates clearly the tremendous effect that it had upon the business and financial community.[82] In the sense that his message of optimism touched the spring of business initiative, and set the wheels in motion once more, the contention is right, but there were deeper causes at work. Far away, on the Witwatersrand, two young chemists had discovered that the use of a cyanide process would enable gold to be extracted in incredibly large quantities from the limitless supplies of South African ore. Beginning in 1896, the gold production of the world began to increase and rapidly climbed to record heights. As the yellow metal trickled into the monetary circulation of gold-standard countries, the decline of price levels ceased. Almost at the very moment when Bryan was trying to convince the American public that a gold standard involved deflation and depression, the South African discoveries had created a situation in which gold inflation was to make that standard more popular than it had ever been before. Bryan was not vanquished by the political acumen of the Republicans, nor by the superior wisdom of the business world; he went down to defeat because science and industry had rendered obsolete the policies for which he fought.

By the middle of 1897, the United States began to share in the prosperity that was already spreading over Europe, and the western states were benefited more rapidly than any other part of the country as a result of the continuing European demand for foodstuffs.[83] In April, 1898, when the United States declared war on Spain, the prosperity of the country was intensified beyond all expectations.[84] Since the naval and military power of Spain was inconsiderable, the inevitable tragedies of warfare were minimized, and the country was able to rejoice in the phenomenal increase in the demand for all kinds of goods that arose out of the government's activity. Never had business been so active and, what was perhaps of greater importance, the activity continued unabated until the end of the century. Once more, the Treasury was confronted with the problem of distributing surplus funds among the depository banks, instead of fearfully watching the diminution of its own reserves.[85]

Despite his concern with problems of war finance during these busy years, Gage did not lose sight of the need for currency and banking reform,[86] and the financial community, in those intervals when it was not absorbed by the problems of prosperity, continued to support him in his efforts and eulogize the work that he was doing.[87] Moreover, with the approach of another Presidential election, the leaders of the Republican party remembered the pledges of the last campaign, and realized that currency legislation might prove a useful argument with the voter when they asked once more for his support. By 1899 abundant prosperity had silenced all criticisms of the gold standard, save those that were voiced by the small group of fanatical believers in bimetallism, and the war had united the country behind McKinley in a fervor of patriotic enthusiasm. If legislation were enacted, there was little fear that it would cost the Republicans any votes, while the fact that they had actually lived up to their campaign pledges might increase their popularity. By that queer species of logic that passes current in politics, it would be argued that the Republicans had given the country a gold standard and the gold standard had brought prosperity.

Prosperity, however, had moderated the desire for thoroughgoing reform. Gage's plan for an asset currency was "as dead as Julius Caesar,"[88] and there was little probability that anything more serious than a minor reform of details would be attempted.[89] Taking the matter out of the hands of the appropriate legislative committees, the party leaders held a conference at Atlantic City[90] and shaped the bill which, after it had been properly marshaled through Congress, received the President's signature on March 14, 1900, as the Gold Standard Act.

The financial press of the country greeted the act with shouts of victorious jubilation, trying to recapture some of the old enthusiasm of the Free Silver campaign. But a careful reading of the document raises emotions of sadness rather than joy. All the years of controversy had produced nothing but a measure that showed obvious signs of political shaping and contained few of the reforms about which there had been fairly general agreement a few years earlier. To be sure, a reserve of one hundred and fifty million dollars was set up in the Treasury for the redemption of paper money, but no separation of Treasury departments was attempted. Provision was made for national banks in small communities with a capital as low as twenty-five thousand dollars and notes were to be issued to an amount equal to the par value of the bonds deposited, but nothing was done about the decentralization of the banking system and the inelasticity of the currency. Most significant of all, the act declared that the gold dollar should be the monetary standard of the United States, but made no provision that would enable the Secretary of the Treasury to keep other forms of money at a parity with the standard. Apart from its influence on the political campaign, the Gold Standard Act had but small significance, and the influence that it exercised upon the banking system was, if anything, retrogressive.

REFERENCES FOR CHAPTER XVII

[1] Cf. Bryan: *The First Battle,* pp. 24, 25 and 190-210.

[2] Bryan: *op. cit.,* p. 128.

[3] *Bankers Magazine,* XLVIII, 727.

[4] Bryan: *op. cit.,* pp. 153-163.

[5] Hepburn: *op. cit.,* pp. 362-363.

[6] *Coin's Financial School,* p. 132.

[7] *Ibid.,* p. 25.

[8] *Ibid.,* p. 103.

[9] *Bankers Magazine,* L, 755-768; *Quarterly Journal of Economics,* X, 187-202; where an extended review of the opposition literature is given.

[10] *Bankers Magazine,* XLV, 481 and 494; XLVI, 169-171.

[11] Cf. Willis: *Federal Reserve System,* pp. 5-39.

[12] Kane: *op. cit.,* I, 135. This idea anticipates several features of the Aldrich-Vreeland Act of 1908.

[13] *Bankers Magazine,* XLV, 494.

[14] *Idem,* 481.

[15] Forgan: *Reminiscences of a Busy Life,* pp. 49-97.

[16] *Bankers Magazine,* XLIX, 322-325; Hepburn: *op. cit.,* 357-358.

[17] Forgan: *op. cit.,* p. 207.

[18] *Bankers Magazine,* XLIX, 325.

[19] Hepburn: *op. cit.,* pp. 345-348.

[20] Cf. *Coin's Financial School.*

[21] Kinley: *The Independent Treasury of the United States,* p. 254.

[22] Hepburn: *op. cit.,* p. 366.

[23] Cf. Kinley: *op. cit.,* pp. 250-254; Hepburn: *op. cit.,* pp. 354-359.

[24] *Chicago Tribune,* June 24, 1894.

[25] Cf. Bryan: *op. cit.,* pp. 134-135 for the text; also Kinley: *op. cit.,* p. 252.

[26] *Commercial and Financial Chronicle,* LX, 421, 498, 694, 783 and 863.

[27] *Idem,* 959 and 1092.

[28] Hepburn: *op. cit.,* p. 359.

[29] Bryan: *op. cit.,* pp. 170-176.

[30] Cf. Beard: *Rise of American Civilization,* II, 337.

[31] Cf. Bryan: *op. cit.,* pp. 170-176 and 178-187.

[32] *Ibid.,* pp. 154-167.

[33] *Ibid.,* p. 195; Barnard: *op. cit.,* pp. 349-354. The Illinois State Democratic Convention, in the early days of June, 1896, was strongly in favor of silver.

[34] Bryan: *op. cit.,* p. 188 ff.; Barnard: *op. cit.,* pp. 359-373.

[35] *Chicago Tribune,* July 3, 1896.

[36] *Ibid.,* July 3 and 7, 1896.

[37] *Ibid.,* July 10, 1896; Bryan: *op. cit.,* pp. 199-206, for the text of the speech.

[38] *Chicago Tribune,* July 10 and 11, 1896.

[39] Bryan: *op. cit.,* pp. 406-407.

[40] *Chicago Tribune,* July 10 and 11, 1896; Bryan: *op. cit.,* pp. 213-218.

[41] Bryan: *op. cit.,* pp. 386-391.

[42] *Ibid.,* pp. 238-279.

[43] Hepburn: *op. cit.,* p. 362.

[44] *Ibid.,* p. 361; Bryan: *op. cit.,* p. 483.

[45] *Commercial and Financial Chronicle,* LXIII, 588 and 688.

[46] The *Chicago Freie Presse* was one of the few reputable newspapers that consistently favored the remonetization of silver.

[47] *Chicago Tribune,* August 10 and 20, 1896; *Commercial and Financial Chronicle,* LXIII, 171-173 and 623-625.

[48] *Chicago Tribune,* August 8 and 10, 1896.

[49] Quoted in Beard: *op. cit.,* II, 340. Other sprightly examples of the compliments of the campaign may be found in *Commercial and Financial Chronicle,* LXIII, 48 and 50-51, or in the files of the *Chicago Tribune,* during August and September of 1896.

[50] Bryan: *op. cit.,* p. 257.

[51] *Chicago Tribune,* August 8, 1896.

[52] *Ibid.,* December 23, 1896; Barnard: *op. cit.,* pp. 354-355 and 374-389.

[53] *Chicago Tribune,* October 10, 1896. It must be remembered, however, that the *Tribune* was not impartial in this controversy.

[54] Bryan: *op. cit.,* pp. 303, 375-383 and 580-591.

[55] *Chicago Tribune,* August 5, 1896.

[56] *Ibid.,* August 9 and September 25, 1896.

[57] *Ibid.,* August 20, 23 and 29, September 17 and 22, 1896.

[58] *Ibid.,* September 26, 1896.

[59] *Ibid.,* November 4, 1896.

[60] *Ibid.,* November 5 and 6, 1896.

[61] Cf. advertisement in *Chicago Tribune,* July 26, 1898.

[62] Gage: *Memoirs,* pp. 89-92.

[63] *Commercial and Financial Chronicle,* LXIV, 440.

[64] Gage: *op. cit.,* pp. 92-103.

[65] *Chicago Tribune,* February 14, 1897; *Chicago Inter-Ocean,* February 14, 1897.

[66] *Chicago Tribune,* February 14, 1897.

[67] *Ibid.,* March 6, 1897; *Bankers Magazine,* LVI, 190-191; Hepburn: *op. cit.,* p. 371.

[68] Bryan: *op. cit.,* pp. 419-421 and 429.

[69] Willis: *op. cit.,* p. 25.

[70] *Ibid.,* pp. 12-13.

[71] *Bankers Magazine,* LVIII, 408.

[72] *Annual Report of the Secretary of the Treasury,* 1897, pp. lxxiv-lxxx.

[73] *Hearings before the Banking and Currency Committee of the House of Representatives on H. R. 5181,* December, 1897.

[74] All the facts regarding the Indianapolis movement are to be found in the admirable document written by J. Laurence Laughlin and published, in 1898, as *The Report of the Monetary Commission of the Indianapolis Convention.* For the history of the movement see pp. 3-18.

[75] *Commercial and Financial Chronicle,* LXIV, 100-101; *Chicago Tribune,* March 22, 1897.

[76] *Report of the Monetary Commission, etc.,* p. 8.

[77] Cf. *Commercial and Financial Chronicle,* LXV, 803.

[78] Willis: *op. cit.,* p. 10.

[79] *Bankers Magazine,* LVI, 190-191.

[80] *Chicago Tribune,* September 15, 17, 19, 22 and 24, 1896.

[81] *Ibid.,* August 27, 31; September 14, 20, 21 and 28, 1896; Chicago *Economist,* XVII, 7.

[82] Gage: *op. cit.,* pp. 123-125; *Commercial and Financial Chronicle,* LXIV, 1064 and 1067.

[83] *Chicago Tribune,* July 25, 1898; see also *Commercial and Financial Chronicle,* LXIV, 1202; LXV, 390; Chicago *Economist,* XVIII, 255, 283 and 285-286.

[84] Chicago *Economist,* XIX, 519, 605, 663 and 719; XXII, 95; *Chicago Tribune,* July 23 and 26, 1898, January 27, 1900.

[85] Gage: *op. cit.,* pp. 128-129.

[86] Cf. interview with Gage, *Bankers Magazine,* LIX, 779.

[87] *Commercial and Financial Chronicle,* LXXIII, 1183.

[88] *Chicago Tribune,* September 21, 1899.

[89] *Bankers Magazine,* LIX, 840; *Chicago Tribune,* September 18, 1893.

[90] Willis: *op. cit.,* p. 14.

APPENDIX I

TABLE SHOWING THE INDEBTEDNESS OF THE STATE OF ILLINOIS AS OF DECEMBER 31, 1842

State Stock Given to Banks

Bonds sold to the Bank of the State of Illinois, on account of bank stock..............	$1,765,000	
Bonds sold to Bank of Illinois at Shawnee-town, on account of bank stock.........	900,000	
		$2,665,000.00

Internal Improvement Stocks

Bonds sold to Irwin & Beers on account of Internal Improvements...............	1,000,000	
Bonds sold to Nicholas Biddle............	1,000,000	
Bonds sold to Hall & Hudson............	100,000	
Bonds sold to Boorman & Johnson........	100,000	
Bonds sold to Lieutenant Levy...........	4,000	
Bonds sold to January & Dunlap.........	300,000	
Bonds sold to M. B. Sherwood...........	50,000	
Bonds sold to John Delafield............	283,000	
Bonds sold to A. H. Bangs..............	50,000	
Bonds sold to Erie County Bank..........	100,000	
Bonds sold to Bank of Commerce.........	100,000	
Bonds sold to Commercial Bank of Buffalo..	100,000	
Bonds sold to Nevins & Townsand, by Dr. Barrett.........................	180,000	
Bonds sold to E. Riggs, by Dr. Barrett.....	50,000	
Bolds sold to Bank of United States, by Dr. Barrett.........................	100,000	
Bonds sold to M. Sherwood, by Dr. Barrett..	100,000	
Bonds hypothecated to State Bank of Illinois, by Dr. Barrett.......................	100,000	
Bonds sold to M. Kennedy and others, by J. D. Whiteside......................	120,000	
Bonds left with McAllister & Stebbins, by them sold..........................	71,000	
		3,908,000.00
Bonds sold to J. Wright & Co., of London...	£69,225	
Bonds delivered to Thompson & Forman..	11,780	
Bonds pledged to Thompson & Forman....	41,625	
	£122,630 =	544,122.00
Bonds sold to State Bank by J. D. Whiteside..............		100,000.00
		$7,217,122.00

Deduct 7 bonds of $1,000 each received from Commercial
Bank of Buffalo.................................... $ 7,000.00

Balance....................................... $7,210,122.00

Internal Improvement scrip, and scrip issued
by Board of Auditors.................. $896,669.94

Cash obtained by Fund Commissioner upon
724 bonds of $1,000 each, hypothecated
to Mc Allister & Stebbins, yet outstanding,
as per statement of Fund Commissioner,
with interest at the rate of 7 per cent per
annum on this sum..................   172,405.00

Sold to contractors on Northern Cross Railroad, 94 bonds of $1,000 each, 84 of which
were hypothecated to Fund Commissioner, by the contractors, for the sum of
$42,000, Illinois State Bank paper, leaving
balance of $10,000...................   10,000.00   1,079,074.94

Total debt on account of Bank and Internal Improvement
Bonds and scrip.................................. $8,289,196.94

Illinois and Michigan Canal Stock

Bonds sold by government.............. $1,000,000.00

Amount sold by Governor Reynolds to Presi-
dent of the United States Bank.........   1,000,000.00

Amount sold by Governor Reynolds and
Gen. Rawlings to John Delafield........   300,000.00

Amount sold by Gen. Thornton on Canal..   100,000.00

Amount sold by Gen. Thornton in London..   1,000,000.00

Amount advanced by Wright & Co. on contract with Judge Young and Governor
Reynolds, £30,000, by terms of contract
equal to............................   145,188.00

Amount bonds paid to contractors in 1841
and 1842..........................   197,000.00   3,742,188.00

Amount outstanding scrip..............   341,972.71

Amount of certificates of indebtedness is-
sued by Commissioners................   254,747.00   596,719.71

Total Canal debt.............................. $ 4,338,907.71

Other Debt

Bonds outstanding on account of State House $116,000.00

Amount due School, College, and Seminary
funds.............................   808,085.00

Amount due State Bank for warrants paid...   294,190.00 $1,218,275.00

Amount due to U. S. Treasury on account of
   surplus revenue (Not included in totals). . $477,919.44

Recapitulation

Total Bank stock	$ 2,665,000.00
Total Internal Improvement debt	5,624,196.94
Total Canal debt	4,338,907.71
Total State House	116,000.00
Total School, College, and Seminary funds	808,085.00
Total due State Bank for warrants	294,190.00
Total debt upon which interest accrues	$13,846,379.65

Note: The information contained in this table is derived from *Hunt's*, XXVII, 661–664.

APPENDIX II

The Banking Facilities of Chicago in 1856

Name of Bank	Officers or Partners	Length of Time Bank Has Been in Operation	Type of Business, as Stated by Advertisements
I. INCORPORATED FREE BANKS			
Bank of America, 41 Clark St.	George Smith, President E. W. Willard, Cashier	4 years	Note issue
Chicago Bank, Corner of Lake and Clark Sts.	Thomas Burch, President I. H. Burch, Cashier	4 years	Sight exchange on England for sale; note issue
Marine Bank, 154 Lake St.	J. Y. Scammon, President Benj. F. Carver, Cashier	20 years	Note issue
II. PRIVATE BANKS			
Banking & Exchange Office of F. Granger Adams, 44 Clark St.		4 years	Exchange on N. Y. Interest on current deposits. Premiums for gold, eastern bank notes, etc. Illegal currency taken for collection. Gold and silver, land warrants sold
J. M. Adsit's Banking & Exchange Office, 39 Clark St.		10 years	Deposits received. Drafts on N. Y., Boston and St. Paul, Minn. Time notes, acceptances and drafts discounted. Gold, silver and uncurrent money bought and sold. Illinois and Michigan Canal scrip bought. Collections
Banking & Loan Office of E. Aiken, 47 Clark St.			Business paper discounted and negotiated. Money loaned on city and country security. Time loans negotiated
I. Anderson, 24 Dearborn St.			Commission, real-estate and money broker
Bank of Commerce, N. W. Corner of Lake and Clark Sts.	Davisson, McCalla & Co., Proprietors	2 years	Deposits received. Paper discounted for depositors. Uncurrent money received from depositors. Collections made throughout U. S. and Canada. Exchange for sale. Loans negotiated on bonds, stocks, mortgages, etc. Facilities for purchase of state and other stocks and land warrants. Bankers
I. C. Barbor, 42 Clark St.		2 years	

Name of Bank	Officers or Partners	Length of Time Bank Has Been in Operation	Type of Business, as Stated by Advertisements
J. W. Bell, 16½ N. Clark St.		5 months	Exchange broker
F. H. Benson & Co., 46 Clark St.	F. H. Benson A. T. Sherman	5 years	Bankers and real-estate brokers
Blackburn & Co., 243 Lake St. (upstairs)			Money brokers
Brewster, Hoyt & Co., 24 Clark St.	H. P. Brewster Charlew J. Hoyt C. H. Stilwell	9 months	Bankers
Joseph E. Brown, 16 Custom House Bldg., 16 LaSalle St.			Real-estate and loan brokerage. Particular attention to sale of real-estate, negotiation of loans, collection of rents, payment of taxes
I. H. Burch & Co., 123–125 Lake St.	Isaac H. Burch Samuel Howe	12 years	Bankers
Nicholas D. Clapp, 111 Lake St.			Money broker
Jonas C. Clark, 83 Dearborn St.		18 years	Real-estate broker
Cotes, Dyrenfurth & Co., 135 Randolph St.	John H. Cotes		Foreign and domestic exchange bought and sold. Collections
John Denniston, 111 Lake St.		8 years	Money broker
Charles Dole & Co., 46 N. Water St.	Charles Dole James H. Dole Samuel Shackford	2 years	Brokers and commission merchants
B. F. Downing & Co., 100 Randolph St.	Benj. F. Downing John H. Kedzie	2 years	Real-estate and money brokers. Time loans negotiated on real-estate securities. Short-date notes discounted. Collection of notes, drafts, accounts, etc. Lands for sale in city and country
D'Wolf & McClay, 98 Randolph St.	Wm. F. D'Wolf James G. McClay		Real-estate and loan brokers
Daniel Elston & Co., Wells St. near Randolph	Daniel T. Elston Wm. H. Davis Orrin J. Rose Otho Klemm Edward Martin	2 years	Bankers
Evans, Whipple & French, 48 Randolph St.	Albert S. Evans T. Herbert Whipple Rolla French	4 months	Money brokers
Exchange Bank, 34 Clark St.	H. A. Tucker, President Hamilton B. Dox, Cashier	4 years	Bankers and dealers in exchange. Collections made in all cities of U. S. A.
Greenebaum Brothers, 45 Clark St.	Henry Greenebaum Elias Greenebaum	1½ years	Foreign-exchange and passage office. Deposits on current accounts. Discount short business paper; buy and sell eastern exchange and gold coin. Collections on Chicago and the N. W. Negotiation of good business paper, promissory notes, etc. Investing of money for nonresidents. Interested in Chicago's European trade. Shipments of grain, pork, etc. can be consigned to firm's agents

Name of Bank	Officers or Partners	Length of Time Bank Has Been in Operation	Type of Business, as Stated by Advertisements
			abroad. Liberal advances on cargoes consigned as above
Gurley & Farlin	See Metropolitan Bank		
W. G. Hathaway, 137 Randolph St.		6 months	Real-estate broker
Hoffman & Gelpcke, 58 LaSalle St.	Francis A. Hoffman Otto Gelpcke	2 years	Deposits received. Exchanges and letters of credit on principal cities of U. S. and Europe. Time loans negotiated on private bonds and mortgages. Western state, county, city or railroad loans negotiated abroad
E. H. Huntington & Co., 34 Clark St.		2 years	Bankers
N. P. Iglehart & Co., 56 LaSalle St.			Dealers in lands, lots and stocks. Money received on deposit for investment
James & Springer, 13 Metropolitan Block	J. L. James Geo. A. Springer	3 years	Real-estate brokers
Jones & Patrick, 42 Clark St.	Wm. Jones M. S. Patrick	10 years	Real-estate brokers
S. H. Kerfoot & Co., 48 Clark St.		4 years	Real-estate brokers
T. B. King 139 Randolph St.		1 year	Real-estate broker
Lull & Mayer, 104 and 106 Randolph	Oliver R. W. Lull Leopold Mayer	8 months	Loan exchange and passage office
McLenehan & Co., 69 S. Water St.			Brokers and commission
C. A. Marshall & Co., 16 Dearborn St.	Chas. A. Marshall Chas. B. Wells	15 years	Real-estate brokers, etc.
Metropolitan Bank, 48 LaSalle St.	Joel Gurley D. H. Farlin		Exchange on all principal cities of U. S. and Canada. Uncurrent money received
Miner's Exchange, Sherman St. near Van Buren	E. H. Miner	4 years	
Morford Brothers, 32 Clark St.	R. H. Morford	1 year	Bankers and exchange brokers. Dealers in land warrants
A. C. Oertel, 9 Clark St.		3 months	Real estate and collecting agent. Loan, foreign-exchange and passage office
Officer & Brother, 154 Lake St.	R. W. Officer S. P. Officer	1 year	Bankers
D. D. Palmer, Corner of Clark and 12th Sts.		3 months	Eastern exchange
Ernst Prussing, 50 Clark St. 215 Monroe St.		5 years	Real-estate broker and land agent
Charles G. E. Prussing, 40 Clark St.		11 years	Banker
Benj. F. Quimby & Co., 98 Randolph St.	Benj. F. Quimby Joseph H. Low		Dealers in negotiable securities
Daniel Richards, 29 W. Randolph St.			Banker and exchange broker
J. B. F. Russell & Co., 73 Randolph St.			Real-estate brokers
Lazarus Silverman, 40 Clark St.		3 years	Money broker. Deposits received
George Smith & Co., 41 Clark St.	George Smith Elisha W. Willard	18 years	Foreign and domestic exchange. Collections made in

Name of Bank	Officers or Partners	Length of Time Bank Has Been in Operation	Type of Business, as Stated by Advertisements
			all the principal cities of the U. S.
Smith, Waller & Co., 3 Masonic Temple	E. Randolph Smith C. S. Waller J. T. Doyle		Real-estate brokers
G. W. Snow, 47 Clark St.		20 years	Money broker
Staples & Sim, 144 Randolph St.	John N. Staples Thos. Sim	6 months	Real-estate brokers
State Bank, 55 Clark St.	William B. Rogers*		
Stave & Co., 108 Randolph St.	Lewis Stave Chas. Klem	4 years	Real-estate brokers
Strong & Wiley, 141 Randolph St.	D. C. Strong C. V. Wiley	6 months	Bankers and dealers in exchange. Uncurrent money, gold and silver coin, land warrants, etc. bought and sold. Loans on real estate negotiated. Collections in all parts of U. S. and Canada
R. K. Swift, Brother & Johnston, N. W. Corner of Randolph and LaSalle Sts.	R. K. Swift Lyman P. Swift J. S. Johnston	3 years	Deposits received, payable on demand or at specified date, with interest. Draws directly on N. Y., Boston, Philadelphia, etc. Drafts available in every city of U. S. and Canada. Remittances by telegraph. Collections made and remitted. Receives orders to buy and sell state, city, county and railroad bonds. Negotiates commercial paper. Invests money for capitalists. Issues drafts and letters of credit on principal bankers in Great Britain, etc.
Freeman Thomas, 137 Randolph St.		8 months	Real-estate broker
A. G. Throop, 48 Clark St.		6 years	Real-estate broker
Edward I. Tinkham & Co., 34 Clark St.		2 years	Bankers and dealers in exchange
H. A. Tucker & Co.	See Exchange Bank		
Wadsworth & Hitz, 66 Clark St.	Strong Wadsworth Louis J. Hitz		Bankers
Wheeler, Bunker & Co., 65 Clark St.	George H. Wheeler New York; Edward H. Bunker, Chicago	9 months	Bankers
G. C. Whitney & Son, 36 Clark St.	G. C. Whitney C. H. Whitney	1½ years	Bankers
P. Woodward & Co., 37 Clark St.		1½ years	Bankers and attorneys
G. W. Yerby, Superior St. near Market and Franklin		4 months	Real-estate broker

*According to the *City Directory*, George Smith and Co. also had an interest in the State Bank.

Note: This tabulation has been derived from information contained in the *Report of the Bank Commissioners for 1858*, *The Chicago City Directory for 1857*, *The Mercantile List* and the *Chicago Democrat*.

APPENDIX III

The Banking Facilities of Chicago in 1861

Name of Bank	Officers or Partners	Type of Business
I. PRIVATE BANKERS		
F. Granger Adams, 44 Clark St.		Banker
J. M. Adsit, 39 Clark St.		Banker
Aiken & Norton, Corner of Lake and Clark Sts.	E. Aiken J. D. Norton Jonathan Burr	Bankers and dealers in exchange. Collections made in all the principal cities in the U. S.
Isaac Anderson, 3 Larmons Block		Money and real-estate broker
Andrews & Otis, 48 Clark St.	Ebenezer Andrews Jonathan E. Otis	Money brokers
A. C. Badger & Co., Randolph St., S. E. Corner of Dearborn		Bankers
Thomas S. Baker, 38 and 40 LaSalle St.		Real-estate broker
Ira C. Barbor, 42 Clark St.		Money broker
Belden & Young, 2½ Clark St.	Charles W. Belden Caryl Young	Bankers
Boone & Larmon, 9 Larmons Block	Robert G. Boone Edward Larmon	Real-estate brokers
J. E. Brown, 8 Hilliard's Block		Money broker
F. W. Buckingham, 25 LaSalle St.		Bill and note broker
I. H. Burch & Co., Lake St., N. W. Corner of LaSalle	Isaac H. Burch John R. Valentine	Bankers
Banking House of B. F. Carver & Co., Marine Bank Bldg.	Benjamin F. Carver Coddington Billings Courtlandt G. Babcock	
Chambers, Lee & Co., 121 Lake St.	Bennett G. Chambers Oliver H. Lee	Bill and note brokers. Money to loan on Chicago city property or on good farms in state
Nicholas D. Clapp, 11 Marine Bank Bldg.		Banker
Edward C. Cleaver, 55 Clark St.		Money and real-estate broker

Name of Bank	Officers or Partners	Type of Business
Cleghorn, Leckie & Co., 13 LaSalle St.	John D. Cleghorn Archibald C. Leckie George H. Sellars	Exchange
Cyrus B. Cobb, 9 Telegraph Bldg.		Stock broker
E. H. Cummings, 42 Clark St.		Real-estate broker
Franklin H. Cutting, 2 Walker's Bldg.		Money broker
Davenport, Ullman & Co., Lake St., S. W. Corner of Clark	Gideon W. Davenport James J. Ullman	Bankers and dealers in exchange
John Denniston, 20 Telegraph Bldg.		Real-estate broker
B. F. Downing, 85 Clark St.		Bankers, money brokers, bill and note brokers, real-estate brokers
Edgecombe & Sibley, 212 Randolph St.	James L. Edgecombe Henry J. Sibley	Money brokers
N. Eisendrath, 1 Metropolitan Bldg.		Banker, bill and note broker
J. William Eschenborg, 38 and 40 LaSalle St.		Bill and note broker. Money broker
John C. Fuller, 102 Washington St.		Real-estate broker
Greenebaum Bros., Lake St., N. E. Corner LaSalle	Henry Greenebaum Elias Greenebaum Gerhard Foreman	Bankers
Greenleaf & Spink, Lake St., N. E. Corner of LaSalle	E. B. Greenleaf Alfred Spink	Bankers and dealers in exchange, gold and uncurrent money
Leopold Guthman, 103 Clark St.		Banker
E. Hale Hall, 8 Clark St.		Banker
Hoffman & Gelpcke, 44 and 46 LaSalle St.	Francis A. Hoffman Otto Gelpcke Alexander Silber	Bankers
Jones & Culbertson, 15 Wells St.	Daniel A. Jones Chas. M. Culbertson	New York exchange
Jones & Patrick, 42 Clark St.	William Jones Amos Patrick	Money brokers
S. A. Kean, 57 Clark St.		Money broker
Kedzie, Alexander & Co., 52 Clark St.	John H. Kedzie Lazelle E. Alexander	Bankers
Louis B. Kelley & Co., 108 Randolph St.	Louis B. Kelley Jonas S. Mechling	Real-estate brokers
Sam'l H. Kerfoot & Co., 1 Masonic Temple		Real-estate brokers
Ketchum Son & Co., 131 Randolph St.		Illinois and Wisconsin currency bought. Ex-

Name of Bank	*Officers or Partners*	*Type of Business*
		change for sale on N. Y., Boston and Philadelphia. Advances made on stocks and bonds for sale in the N. Y. market
John B. King, 60 LaSalle St.		Money broker
James Larmon, 8 Larmons Block		Real-estate broker
Philip Larmon, 8 Larmons Block		Real-estate broker
J. Lewis Lee, 32 Clark St.		Bill and note broker. Money to loan on city property in Cook and adjoining counties
Loeb & Rahm, 7 Metropolitan Block	Adolph Loeb Albert Rahm	Bill and note brokers
James A. Marshall, 3 McCormick's Bldg.		Real-estate broker
James M. Marshall, 8 Larmons Block		Real-estate broker
Thos. E. Marshall, 8 Larmons Block		Real-estate broker
Leopold Mayer, 103 Clark St.		Banker
Richard Meadowcroft, 22 Clark St.		Money broker
Robert Meadowcroft, 22 Clark St.		Money broker
B. B. Morris, 38 Clark St.		Banker
Thomas Morton & Co., Clark and Randolph Sts.		Dealers in exchange, gold, bank notes. Pays "highest rates in gold on N. Y. exchange" for discredited bills of Illinois, Wisconsin, Missouri, etc. Also checks, drafts and certificates of Merchants Savings Loan & Trust Co., Chicago Marine & Fire Insurance Co., Marine Bk.; B. F. Carver & Co.; F. G. Adams; H. A. Tucker & Co.
George W. Newcomb, 80 Dearborn St.		Loan broker
Albert C. Oertez, 75 Dearborn St.		Banker and dealer in foreign and domestic exchange. European

Name of Bank	Officers or Partners	Type of Business
		forwarding and commission
L. D. Olmstead & Co. Lake St., N. W. Corner LaSalle	Lucius D. Olmstead Lyman Baird	Loan agents and loan brokers
L. B. Otis & Co., 47 Clark St.	Lucius B. Otis James Otis	Loan brokers
C. C. Parks & Co., 156 Lake St.	Calvin C. Parks Julius Wadsworth	Bankers
Samuel W. Pease 51 Clark St.		Real-estate broker
H. J. Perrin & Co., 95 Lake and 34 Dearborn	Horace J. Perrin Joseph Sibley Darius Perrin	Bankers
Ernst Prussing, N. E. Corner of Clark and Washington Sts.		Dealer in foreign exchange, money and real-estate broker. Money to loan on real-estate securities in Cook and adjoining counties. Particular attention to collection of time loans and real-estate securities.
Benj. F. Quimby & Co., 140 S. Water St.		Exchange on N. Y.
Rees & Slocum, 88 Dearborn St.	James H. Rees David P. Slocum	Real-estate brokers
W. H. Rice & Co., 63 Clark St.	Wm. H. Rice Wm. F. Merriman	Bankers
William B. Rogers, 36 Dearborn St.		Money broker
F. G. Saltonstall, 24 Clark St.		Stock broker
J. Young Scammon, Marine Bank Bldg.		General banking business
Lazarus Silverman, 50 LaSalle St.		Banker
Leon Straus, 3 Larmons Block		Loan broker
Samuel Strauss, 11 Metropolitan Blk.		Real-estate broker
Solomon Sturges & Sons 15 and 17 Wells St.	Solomon Sturges Albert Sturges Buckingham Sturges	Bankers
Charles S. Taylor, 8 Meth. Ch. Blk.		Money broker
B. W. Thomas, 60 Wells St.		Real-estate broker
E. I. Tinkham & Co., 6 Loomis Blk.	Edward I. Tinkham John C. Ambler	Bankers

Name of Bank	Officers or Partners	Type of Business
H. A. Tucker & Co., Lake St., S. W. Corner Clark	Hiram A. Tucker Wm. Ruxton Lewis C. Ellsworth	Bankers
S. Wadsworth & Co., 34 Clark St.	Strong Wadsworth	Exchange broker
Walker & Honore, 2 Masonic Temple	Samuel J. Walker Henry H. Honore	Real-estate brokers
Dudley P. Warner, 102 Washington St.		Real-estate broker
Henry Wendt, 112 and 114 Dearborn St.		Bill, note and real-estate broker
White Bros. Randolph St., N. W. Corner of LaSalle	Frederick White Wm. G. White	Bankers
Wiley Bros. & Co., 157 Randolph St.	Christopher V. Wiley Benjamin B. Wiley	Bankers
E. K. Willard & Co., 33 Clark St.	Edward K. Willard	Buys checks on Chicago Marine & Fire Insurance Co., B. F. Carver & Co., F. G. Adams, H. A. Tucker & Co., Merchants Savings Loan & Trust Co. Sells exchange on N. Y.
Willard & Kean, 57 S. Clark St.	S. A. Kean F. Willard	Bankers and dealers in exchange, coin, bank notes and land warrants
Wing & Mitchell, 1 Aikens Bldg.	Abraham R. Wing Francis M. Mitchell	Money brokers
Wright & Tyrrell 5 Metropolitan Block	Robert C. Wright John A. Tyrrell	Bill and note brokers
William Young, 48 Clark St.		Real-estate broker

II. SAVINGS BANKS

Name of Bank	Officers or Partners	Type of Business
Hoffman & Gelpcke, 44–46 LaSalle St.	Francis A. Hoffman Otto Gelpcke Alexander Silber Rudolph Schloesser	Bankers
Illinois Savings Institution in the City of Chicago, 104–106 Washington St.	John C. Haines, President N. B. Kidder, Cashier John H. Kinzie, George W. Dole, Erastus S. Williams, Wm. B. Ogden, Conrad L. Diehl, O. R. W. Lull, G. S. Hubbard, John S. Reed, John C. Haines,	Receives deposits in gold and silver and bills of specie-paying banks. Allows interest at rate of 6 per cent per annum

Name of Bank	*Officers or Partners*	*Type of Business*
	Alexander C. Coventry,	
	George Schneider,	
	Jared Gage,	
	Nathan B. Kidder,	
	Trustees	

III. TRUST COMPANIES

Name of Bank	*Officers or Partners*	*Type of Business*
Merchants Savings Loan & Trust Co., 95 Lake St.	Hon. John H. Dunham, President	
	H. H. Magie, Vice-President	
	D. R. Holt, Cashier	
	W. L. Newberry,	
	Jonathan Burr,	
	Henry Farnham,	
	J. H. Dunham,	
	S. A. Smith,	
	John H. Foster,	
	H. H. Magie,	
	D. R. Holt,	
	Wm. E. Doggett,	
	F. B. Cooley,	
	A. H. Burnley,	
	C. H. McCormick,	
	T. D. Gilbert,	
	Trustees	
The Union Insurance & Trust Co., Exchange Bk. Bldg., S. W. Corner of Clark and Lake Sts.	Benj. Lombard, President	
	Van H. Higgins, Vice-President	
	B. F. Johnson, Secretary	
	Francis A. Hoffman, Treasurer	
Western World Insurance & Trust Co., 144 S. Water St.	Lucien J. Bisbee, Secretary	

Note: This tabulation has been compiled from information contained in *The Chicago City Directory*, *1861–62*, and the *Bankers Magazine*, XV.